*Tell Them
I'm On My Way*

Tell Them
I'm On My Way

ARNOLD GOODMAN

CHAPMANS

Chapmans Publishers
A division of the Orion Publishing Group Ltd
Orion House
5 Upper St Martin's Lane
London WC2H 9EA

British Library Cataloguing
in Publication Data

Goodman, Arnold
Tell Them I'm on My Way
I. Title
941.082092

ISBN 1-85592-636-9

First published by Chapmans 1993

Photoset in Monophoto Ehrhardt by
Selwood Systems, Midsomer Norton

Printed and bound in Great Britain by
Butler & Tanner Ltd, Frome and London

To a lifelong and stalwart friend
Professor L. C. B. Gower

Acknowledgements

My very real gratitude is due to several people, but in particular to my invaluable and devoted secretary of nearly thirty years, Carolyn Miller, but for whose painstaking work this book would never have seen the light of day. I owe her a very real debt. Also, Charles Osborne for reading and commenting on the typescript, and my publishers, led by Ian Chapman, who displayed immense patience and proffered a great deal of valuable advice, very little of which have I rejected. This book remains as much a tribute to them as to its author.

Contents

Illustrations

Preface

No one has a life of unalloyed delight, but I can claim to have had more satisfaction and a better opportunity for doing the things I wanted to do than most people. I have therefore been inordinately fortunate. I hope that this will be the principal feeling that will emerge in these pages.

It would be an impossibility to describe in detail and at length the activities in which I have been involved. It would also be undue complacency to believe that every such description would be of interest. I have had a variety of lives and a multiplicity of interests. My principal professional activity has been as a lawyer and almost my exclusive source of income, but I have had a toe in the academic camp. I have had a wide range of public activities, largely but by no means wholly devoted to the arts. I have been concerned in a number of industries – although never with an eye to, or unhappily, any prospect of, personal profit. I have been engaged in many intricate and difficult negotiations, sometimes with a degree of success.

In the course of a long and active life I have met a great number of people; some of them will fall for comment in this book. However, I entertain hostility to virtually nobody. This, I think, is a serious defect of character and I cannot remember any piece of malice that rolls across my tongue which I am avid to utter. I have met a number of good people; a vast, endless parade of commonplace people, and almost no one whom I would describe as evil. Those who might come into that category have the powerful defence of mental instability. I have met brilliant people, and they are very much the exception; witty people, even more the exception; but above all I have met kindly people, and there are sufficient of them to every thousand of the population to justify the human race.

I

An Orthodox Child

I WAS BORN on 21 August 1913 into a lower-middle-class area of North London and lived in a house which I discovered the other day to have been converted into a total slum. Hence anyone going in quest of a shrine for me – if anyone is so ill-advised – will have to rebuild the house and start again. It was a respectable area. My parents were both remarkable people. My father was an austere, scholarly man who rarely expressed any emotion. If you were to ask me what his tastes were, except that he loved reading and hated socialising, I would have difficulty in telling you.

Certainly my father had a passion for what I might call more conventional music. At the age of six or seven I was dragged to the Royal Albert Hall to hear Melba, Galli-Curci, Tetrazzini... Sometimes I feel that I have invented these recollections, and when a great name of the past has come to mind I shall shortly claim to have seen a performance of Richard Burbage. But I do not think that the names I have mentioned are a figment of my imagination. I can well remember Tetrazzini, a very massive lady, belting it out, although I was at an age when I could not participate in any kind of musical criticism. I remember Galli-Curci as a much svelter figure, singing away like mad. Then I can remember Clara Butt and Carrie Tubb, two enormous ladies, both British, who were the popular heroines of the time.

A visit to the Royal Albert Hall was always a delight. My father was a kindly man and he would take my brother and myself to tea afterwards, usually at the Trocadero – the up-market Lyons establishment of the day, beloved by the middle classes – where one ate an enormous tea at the then vast expense – which he could ill afford – of 3s 6d each. That tea consisted of tea, of course, in ample quantities, delicious egg-and-cress sandwiches, chocolate éclairs, scones and raspberry or strawberry jam. Stuffed and regaled with this tea, we would return home where our mother had prepared an ample supper which we consumed with equal appetite. Not surprisingly, I developed a very considerable quantity of *embonpoint*. The result is that throughout my entire life I have been an immensely massive figure, although now unhappily reduced. My shape occasioned a certain amount of ridicule at school, but it was short-lived because on the whole I got on well with my school mates. They came to recognise that, although I was probably the largest boy in the school, I was nevertheless an amiable character, and I never had any real problem with them.

My mother was a remarkable woman – a belief that was not restricted by any means to her own family. My grandfather (her father), who had come from Lithuania around 1890, was also a remarkable man. I know very little about my grandmother except that she died very early. My grandfather established himself in the East End of London, where most of the *émigré* Jewish community were originally established, and set up a small business as a South African shipper. This sounds a great deal more pretentious than it was. He had no ships, in fact I doubt if he had ever been inside a ship, but what he did was to confirm the orders from South African customers in the textile trade to British manufacturers and undertake the responsibility of paying for them if the customer did not pay. This, of course, involved business on a limited scale, since the manufacturers to whom he confirmed the orders had to be sure that he had sufficient resources to pay for the goods in the event of default by the principal customer. He had an unsullied reputation and was regarded, I understand, as a saintly figure. He became the local savant and adviser. Everyone in need of guidance used to seek him out. There is an engaging story about a man who came to see him to ask him to explain a document which he did not understand. My grandfather said to him, 'This is an invitation for you to attend a meeting of creditors.' 'Oh,' said the man, 'but I never go to meetings!'

I recollect him only very vaguely, since he died when I was about seven or eight, as a kindly old man with a grey beard. But I do remember being taken to see him in his little shop in the Commercial Road, where he lived with his family above the shop, and being popped by him inside a packing case to my mixed delight and terror. I sometimes reflect on the size of the packing case that would be required now to incarcerate me in similar fashion. But I recollect what a lovable old man he was and how he endeared himself to a child who would retain this memory firmly and indelibly.

He was a practising Jew but not particularly orthodox. This brushed off on to my mother, who remained throughout her life a most devoted member of the Jewish community, an immense worker for Jewish causes and a passionate Zionist, but she was never particularly concerned with the formalities of religion. Although she kept a kosher household in the sense that she would not cook pork or bacon, and no other portion of the wretched pig ever featured on the menu, she would put butter on the table when she felt that this was an inducement to keep my brother and myself eating meals at home. As those acquainted with the Jewish tradition will know, butter cannot be eaten with meat. She also was careful to serve any coffee or tea after the meal with a jug of milk adjoining, which we could take if we wished but which she certainly did not press upon us.

She was, moreover, an intensely moral woman. I do not imagine that she had the faintest idea of those subjects which are the constant conversation in today's atmosphere. I would lay a very large bet that she had never heard of a homosexual. And probably like Queen Victoria, who denied the existence of lesbianism, she would have denied it with equal emphasis. I doubt also that she was concerned with modern ideas of contraception. She would have been astonished at the activities of Mrs Gillick. My father, who was, I think, the least lascivious of men, contrived somehow to have two children. Since I have not the slightest doubt about my mother's virtue, he was undoubtedly the father of them, but I am completely convinced that, having done his duty in that direction, the sexual relationship between my parents ceased completely. However, this did not have the anticipated effect, which today is widely professed, of souring people in their disposition. Both seemed to be perfectly contented and happy without resorting to extramarital comforts. I know also that during the whole of my childhood I never heard the subject of sex remotely discussed.

My father's political opinions were limited to support for a few selected individuals. I never heard him express a political preference either for an extended franchise or for any form of taxation, or indeed on any particular topic at all. I did hear him express admiration for certain individuals. Lloyd George was his great hero and idol. It is difficult to believe today the hatred that existed for Lloyd George when he was at the height of his power. He was probably more loathed than any politician ever. I would suspect that beside him Mr Scargill would have been viewed as a figure enjoying general affection. The hatred for Lloyd George derived from the fact that he delivered the first really successful onslaught on property with a capital P. His 1911 budget aroused the most important constitutional crisis in British history. It was when the House of Lords refused to pass his budget that King George V – relatively inexperienced in kinghood since he had succeeded to a deceased brother who was destined for the role – had the appalling problem of deciding whether he would accede to Asquith's request to make a sufficient number of new peers to swamp the Tory vote in the House of Lords so as to be sure of passing the budget.

In the end, although I am not a constitutional expert, history tells us that the King actually agreed to make the necessary elevations. I have seen in Roy Jenkins's biography of Mr Asquith a list of the proposed new peers, which I must confess is a most stimulating document. I cannot remember whether it contained Bernard Shaw, but it certainly contained Bertrand Russell and a number of other immensely liberal figures. In the event, confronted with the possibility of being swamped by precisely the kind of people they abominated, the Tory peers succumbed. Lord Halsbury, the Leader of the Lords and of the 'last ditchers' (as the substantial majority opposed to the change were called), agreed to pass the necessary legislation so as to ensure the survival of the Upper House. I am quite sure that my late father in his wildest dreams did not imagine that any member of his family would enter the portals where the 1911 battle was being fought out.

To anyone who did not have the good fortune to meet her, it is impossible to exaggerate my mother's quite remarkable qualities. My father was an unsuccessful businessman. Like my grandfather – although quite separately from him – he carried on the business of a South African shipper. This, as I have explained, meant simply that he purchased goods on behalf of South African wholesalers or retailers, arranged for them to be shipped, provided credit (to the very limited extent to which the banks would accept his guarantee) and was rewarded with a modest commission. He was largely concerned with the textile industry. Heaven only knows how he selected them. He had absolutely no knowledge of fashion, no knowledge of women's clothing, and an abhorrence of anything connected with it. It must have been purgatorial for the poor man to be engaged in a trade, day after day, where these were the essential concerns and necessary attributes for success. It is not surprising that he was not successful. He teetered on the edge of bankruptcy but never in fact went over the edge. And it was entirely due to the determination of my mother that we were able to enjoy a reasonably comfortable living. Somehow, by some means, she was never short of a pound. She was what would be called a wonderful manager. If ever one needed anything, she would explain very carefully why the cheaper article had to be bought but always had the money for the requisite article even if it was not of luxury quality.

She was a determined patron of British goods. This is something of an irony today. I well remember when we moved from our humble home to a more respectable area. Very early in life we migrated to Hampstead – which was then the Mecca of the London Jews. She would take me by the hand – I was about to say my tiny hand, but it was never tiny – and lead me down the Finchley Road to a large establishment called John Barnes. She would then enter the shop and enquire for something. I remember her asking for a kettle. A kettle was produced, a very handsome one. She turned it over and almost spat, saying angrily, 'This is foreign!' and brusquely handing it back at the salesman. It is, as I said, extremely ironic because today one's reaction would be equally violent if one discovered it was British made!

Another quality of my mother was that without having been a Girl Guide she was always 'prepared'. I recollect coming back from school – and the school I then went to was very close to our home – accompanied by a small army of youths. My mother did not bat an eyelid. In no time at all a spotless white cloth was spread on our large dining-room table and within five minutes everyone was sitting down to an ample tea. This was such a commonplace that it never entered my mind for years afterwards that it was in fact an incredible performance having regard to our limited finance and that except on rare occasions we did not have a domestic servant. Later on she began to enlist a maid and I well remember having an affectionate relationship with one particularly elderly maid who looked after me with constant attention.

My mother was not, alas, a cordon bleu but nevertheless a very effective cook. I doubt very much whether in her whole life she ever made a sauce. But she did cook meat, sausages, eggs, and produced all the basic requirements for survival. And I may say that I tucked into them with extreme gusto without being conscious that the delicacies produced by French chefs were noticeably absent. Probably I would have lost a pound or two if the food had been more delicately prepared, but as it was I was more than reasonably satisfied, and my schoolfellows were delighted with it.

But perhaps what provoked most surprise about my mother was her ability to engage in so many pursuits. Beyond her high talents as a housewife, she was a competent pianist, had an agreeable voice, and was the best hostess I have met in any social sphere. It was almost a fault that everyone who arrived felt welcome. She would have been horrified by extending a reception that embarrassed anyone.

She had been a schoolmistress in the East End of London and amazingly had acquired a sufficient knowledge of Hebrew to teach it to, among others, the late Lady Gaitskell. I preserve as a cherished possession a tiny white metal medal awarded to my mother and inscribed 'To Bertha Mauerberger, aged seven, the most punctual attender at the school'. It is characteristic that during her lifetime she never showed this to me, but after she died I found it in the box in which she kept her few jewels.

Her domestic activities would have occupied the full seven days and more of almost any present-day woman, so that it was nothing short of a miracle that she could engage as she did in numerous outside activities. There were constant meetings of a variety of societies (some Jewish, some Zionist, some secular) in our small and unpretentious home, and it never entered the head of any one of their members that my mother should be other than the chairman. In justice, such a thought would never have entered her head. It may explain why I have gravitated to almost every unpaid chairmanship in England at one time or another – a characteristic inherited from my mother. The fact that she was chairman did not derive either from arrogance or conceit. It was the natural feeling that if things were to be done, she had to lead the flock. It is a cliché to claim that a person is loved by everyone, but I never met anyone who disliked my mother. Her kindness enveloped everybody, so much so that it occasioned no surprise, and often involved her in an enormous number of works about which she was uncomplaining.

One episode concerned my great-uncle, who had come from Lithuania with my grandfather but had received a superior education, and was employed in some tutoring capacity by the Rothschild household. He was a man of some learning, I gather, though I never met him. He had the misfortune to fall madly in love with a Rothschild daughter who – according to the wholly biased report from my family – reciprocated his feelings. He also had the unwisdom to suppose that he would be an acceptable suitor. Without a moment's hesitation and no show of trepidation, he presented himself to the then Lord Rothschild demanding the hand of the young woman. The approach was received with incredulity and horror. In any event, his suit was rejected, according to him, in very contemptuous terms. No one can believe that my great-uncle's later behaviour was not, to put it generously, eccentric in the extreme. Failing to recognise that his suit could not be expected to arouse great enthusiasm, he responded to its rejection by challenging Lord Rothschild to a duel. His expectation was that as a gentleman Lord Rothschild would have no alternative but to meet him at 6 a.m. in Hyde Park with swords or pistols. Very sensibly Lord Rothschild took a different line, that he had no wish to become involved in an encounter with a frustrated suitor.

My grandfather and my great-uncle both viewed his reaction with profound contempt, but what Lord Rothschild did was to call the police. My great-uncle was arrested and accused of threatening behaviour, or a threat to murder, or some equally disagreeable charge. The upshot was that my great-uncle departed for a mental institution, whether voluntarily or under duress I do not know. Such was his indignation at this treatment that, although apparently offered the opportunity of leaving on various occasions, he declined to do so and remained immured for the rest of his days. He was a man of great piety and would not eat any food unless it was kosher food. Throughout the whole of his incarceration my mother visited him regularly, taking him large parcels of kosher food.

The most interesting part was that when he was in the asylum, my great-uncle wrote a book which my grandfather, determined to establish his sanity, caused to be published at his own expense. Alas, the only copy I had has disappeared. It was called *A Voice from an Asylum*. My grandfather had it beautifully produced, with a half-leather binding, but he must have been very naive if he believed that the production of the book would establish beyond any question the balanced judgement of his dear brother. I read the book and recollect feeling that, when it came to my great-uncle's sanity, he would have been better advised not to have published it. This piece of family history was a source of some embarrassment at the time, and I am sure my mother would never forgive me for having recounted it in these memoirs, but it is irresistible to do so.

My mother's attitude to her two sons was very simple: it was one of total admiration. She found it difficult to believe that two more remarkable creatures could ever have been conceived. This was, of course, at times embarrassing, because whenever she encountered anyone who was not acquainted with us and therefore had not had the opportunity of detecting our remarkable intelligence and virtue, she proceeded to describe it in great detail! When we moved to Hampstead, I recollect meeting Isaiah Berlin, whose family lived on the other side of the street from us. I think that my mother and his mother held a sort of debating contest from time to time as to the relative qualities and standing of their particular infants. I would hesitate to suggest, and in fact would never believe, that either my brother or myself were in the same intellectual class as Isaiah, but this is not a proposition that would have been acceptable to my mother.

It was difficult to say that either of us was her favourite, but my elder brother, who from early childhood was an invalid, obviously attracted more of her attention and her concern. He exercised a much greater influence on her. In many ways he behaved more like a husband than a son. As soon as he attained an age when he could develop the tastes which distinguished him so remarkably from a great many other people, namely the most passionate affection for every form of art, he would take her off to concerts, to theatrical performances, to the opera: in fact he acted as a sort of post-graduate education officer for my mother, who had not been involved in any education since her schoolteaching days.

No one, I think, exercised a greater influence on me than my brother. He introduced me to the world of literature, to the world of music, drama, ballet and painting. He himself was barely educated, in the sense that although we had both gone to the same school, he barely attended the classes. Any sort of regimentation was abhorrent to him, and he would absent himself to sit in the park adjoining our school for hours on end reading, when he was supposed to have been in class; but the headmaster, who was a kindly man named Jenkin Thomas, sympathised with the situation and made no efforts to compel his attendance. He left school quite early, never having bothered to matriculate. His education, therefore, was full of holes. He had a considerable literary gift and spent his time writing plays, and also composed imaginary programmes for theatres, concerts, ballets and opera houses, together with detailed casting. He would have made a great impresario if he had ever had an inclination to earn any money. He was a totally unmaterialistic person, hence we were at pains to ensure that any small possessions that might be available to the family should pass over to him.

I myself started my schooling at a small kindergarten conducted by a lady called Miss Ada Christopherson. She was an angular spinster, equipped with a formidable knitting-needle with which she would rap us over the knuckles. I am not sure what she taught, but she certainly taught, or professed to teach, the piano. My mother, anxious that we should be educated to the highest possible degree and become masters of every art and culture, paid the extra fees for music instruction, as a result of which I had the purgatorial experience of receiving two lessons a week from Miss Christopherson. It is, therefore, not surprising that when I was offered the choice of a musical instrument I immediately elected to play the violin, which she did not teach.

My musical instruction continued for several years. Although it was clear from the faces of any listeners that the experience was not the most agreeable, I found the tones that I produced irresistible! I would sway gently in the wind while playing to myself, failing to observe the horror and astonishment among bystanders. It was only when I attained the age of seventeen that I began to realise that I was not destined to be a rival to Yehudi Menuhin, or any of the other great violinists. I attributed this to the fact that my instrument was inadequate. I therefore approached my father with the request that he buy me a Stradivarius. He was as capable of buying me a Stradivarius as he was of acquiring a gold-mine, but in any event he pointed out gently that my attainments on the instrument did not justify an expensive investment and that if I began to show greater skill he would consider the possibility of an improved violin. As we had reached this deadlock, I decided that I would forgo my musical education on the violin – much to the delight of the neighbours – and from that moment onwards I never touched the instrument.

The important achievement of my very limited musical education was to instil a lifelong affection for music which, although uninformed, has given me immense delight. A more sensitive man would frequently be shamed by his musical ignorance when in discussion with the people who really know, but that sense is swamped by my profound gratitude for the pleasure and delight that music has given to me. I owe this to my brother very largely and perhaps above all to my mother's constant urgings that we should acquire a genuine cultural appreciation. To books, to the theatre, to music, to opera, to ballet and to the drama I owe a debt beyond discharge and had I been deprived of my enjoyment from these activities I would have had an impaired and much more arid life.

I was never a religious person, in the sense of finding it possible to conform to all the requirements of any orthodox religion. But that is not to say that I lacked a spiritual belief. I must avoid the pretence that I had a real and pervading spirituality; but all my life I have held a firm belief that a creation as complicated as this one – this is a very simplistic belief based on no very profound philosophy – could not have come into existence unless there was a guiding spirit and a guiding force. In short, a man who has spiritual faith is, I think, a rational being in so far as he believes that there is *something* that is responsible for the universe. The man who renounces this belief is, in my view, irrational. Agnosticism, therefore, can be maintained, but atheism is to me perverse. While I have no certainty about anything, I have a certainty that there is and must be something that is responsible for our being. When one looks at the complexity of the human body, the structure of a plant or of an insect or of a fish, it is difficult to believe that it all came about by accident. I shall spare my readers further jejune observations about these eternal considerations. Readers will probably find them inadequate as a declaration of faith, but that indeed is the true position. My faith is an inadequate one: I do not go in quest of it to bolster me in times of need or trouble, but I still have the belief that 'there is something there'.

In spiritual exercises of a formal character I am, I am afraid, remiss. My father used to take us – my brother and myself – occasionally to a local synagogue. This we certainly did on the Day of Atonement. My father, whose deeper attitude to these things I never investigated, regarded it as adequate to worship on the high days such as the Day of Atonement and the Jewish New Year. Thereafter he satisfied himself with scholarly practices which were not related to religion. In fact it is my belief that he was highly agnostic in this matter and the books that he read – although his principal reading was in classical Hebrew – were not religious works. But on the Day of Atonement, for instance, we would trek off to the local synagogue and spend the entire day there. My brother and I would come out occasionally but we were oathed on our honour not to eat anything. And this is one of the few cases I remember when I restrained my self-indulgence and ate an enormous meal at the end of the evening after we returned home. My father remained in the synagogue, since although he was not a profound believer he was an expert in the ritual and one of the few people who understood the Hebrew that he was speaking.

I was never a distinguished student at school. My English master was the only master who was really satisfied with my work. I had a love of words and enjoyed writing essays enormously; but when it came to anything mathematical or scientific I positively loathed it and have retained this loathing throughout my life. Moreover, I was quite useless with my hands. In the so-called 'Arts' class, no one's work was worse, more thumb-marked, less resembling the object that we were supposed to be depicting than mine. And I was expelled from the singing class, which was a great humiliation. The singing master I always suspected to be anti-Semitic! I could find no other reasoned explanation why my light baritone, which gave me great personal delight, should be the subject of this expulsion.

However, I had the pleasure, during our singing class, of wandering through our roofless fives court and banging the ball against the wall while the others were engaged in singing the school ditty. It went under the title of 'The Elephant's Battery' and was a robust song with something like 'Aya Aya Aya hoot and buffalo!' I would have difficulty in reproducing the tune today, but the advantage it gave me was that I became a very adept fives player and was able to defeat anyone, almost, of my own age, notwithstanding that my bulk would have been regarded as a disadvantage.

My principal interests have always been, I suppose, artistic, although strangely enough, considering my bulk and relative incompetence, I have always been profoundly interested in sporting matters. At school I could never play soccer since it was believed by those in charge that my very size made it imperative that I should be a goalkeeper. This was based on the belief that I was so large that nothing could pass me. It had the fallacy that complementary to my largeness was a slowness of mobility that enabled any ball to get past me before I could get a leg or an arm to it. But I enjoyed playing soccer and greatly enjoyed doing so when my own team was so superior that the play continued almost indefinitely at the other end of the field.

Cricket was my passion. I loved it dearly. Every Wednesday afternoon my mother would prepare an immaculately laundered pair of flannel trousers, a white shirt, a pullover, a blazer of a modest character bearing the school emblem of a camel, representing the Company of Grocers which had formed the school, and off I would go to play cricket. I learnt the technique largely from practising in the tiny back garden that we had in our home. A small boy, so much smaller than myself that I could order him about, would bowl to me indefinitely and in return I would give him an over or two while he batted. In consequence I became quite a proficient defensive bat, but in view of the size of the garden it was an impossibility and indeed a great danger to do anything by way of hitting out because the ball would go over the wall into the garden of a particularly truculent and ill-tempered neighbour. He took the view that once a ball had landed in his garden it had ceased to belong to its original owner, and all the dictates of English law had no meaning for him at all: nor was I as yet in a position to pronounce them as I should today. However, what normally happened was that every so often we lofted a ball – it was usually a cork not a leather ball – into his garden. If he was there we fled. If he was not there, the smaller boy climbed over the wall to retrieve it, occasionally to the sounds of rage and indignation on the occasions when he spotted us from his window. We would stop playing for ten minutes, then begin again.

I cannot think of a better way of learning to become a defensive batsman, and I cannot think of a worse way of learning to become a scoring batsman. My left foot was constantly forward; I kept my eyes firmly on the ball; I could stay at that wicket for years whoever was bowling; but I could not score a run. In the result I think I achieved the school record of scoring seven throughout an entire house innings, retiring unbeaten when the tenth wicket fell. As a bowler I was a disaster. I recollect playing for my firm when I was an articled clerk and losing the match for them in a single over, when every one of my six balls was dispatched to the boundary. But I enjoyed cricket enormously and found it very useful when I was in the army, since as the only officer who played I captained the team and went all over the Southern Command playing various games on various grounds. Most of the grounds were pretty primitive, but there was a splendid ground at Sherborne School, another splendid one at Aldershot, and I think I derived as much pleasure from playing cricket during the war as almost any other activity.

In addition I acquired, for me, a degree of competence at tennis. I served with considerable efficiency and I had a good deal of tuition at one time from a tennis professional. He was an immensely patient man and would play balls at me which I would hit in all directions, largely out of the court, untiringly for hours on end at the modest rate of 3s 6d an hour. In fact I was a much better tennis player comparatively than I was a cricket player. I got a colour for University College, London, in playing tennis and I played in the Downing College team at Cambridge. I also succeeded in winning – or to put it more accurately – being associated with the winning of the Southern Command's mixed doubles tournament. I was then passionately in love with my partner who was a very attractive ATS officer, whose name I shall not divulge for fear of embarrassing her, although she must by now be a great-grandmother. It remains a hazy but rosy recollection.

That apart, I played a little golf, and I also enjoyed playing squash and played a great deal in the army with a reasonable degree of competence. After the War I used to play squash regularly at the West London Squash Club with a group of film buffs: Sidney Gilliatt, Frank Launder, the Boulting brothers, all came along on a Saturday afternoon and played. They ruined the healthy effect of the sport by eating an immense amount of fresh bread and strawberry jam, together with eleven or twelve cups of tea.

It was during my school years when, thanks to my indulgent, if indigent, parents, I developed certain tastes and interests that have remained throughout my life. First and foremost I developed an interest in words – an interest which has been projected into a great many of my activities. Although I have never had the literary patience to develop into a skilled writer, I have always enjoyed writing, first with a pen and pad, and later, when laziness overtook, by dint of dictation.

My earliest experience as a writer, which should of course have launched me to a sensational success, was to win a *New Statesman* literary competition, at the age of sixteen, or perhaps seventeen. The competition was for the most convincing letter written by a guest who has accepted an invitation to dinner from a simple, ordinary human being, but who subsequently receives an invitation from a much loftier person. To enable him to attend the more attractive meal, the guest explains to his humbler friend that illness has overtaken him. The letter was the explanation he gives when his treachery is later discovered.

I cannot recollect precisely what I said, but I wrote a letter of touching honesty, commenting on the sad state of our society which made it necessary for honourable people to resort to subterfuges to preserve their social and professional positions, and since in my circles the *New Statesman* was then required reading, I obtained a certain acclaim.

Owing to my loathing for scientific subjects it was a miracle that I ever matriculated. I was given special coaching in mathematics by a very pretty young woman. I was then at an age when I was conscious of these things, since my attention was distracted rather more by her appearance than the equations she was laboriously explaining. However, at the end of the day I passed the matriculation at the first attempt. I got a distinction in English and a distinction in history, but alas I got the lowest marks the school had ever scored in geography. Happily, history was the alternative subject, so it did not matter very much, but it greatly pained the nice geography master who really believed that I was one of his prize pupils. When he discovered that I was a prize ass in the subject his disappointment was very marked.

After matriculation I remained at my original school for a term or two, opting as might have been expected for the arts sixth rather than the science sixth. On the recommendation of my history master I then moved to another school in the superior district of Hampstead in which we now lived. This was a mistake, since I did not go there until I was sixteen years of age and so was already a senior boy. I went straight into the sixth form, knowing not a living soul. Those things that I most enjoyed at my old school, such as cricket, fives and rifle-shooting, were not available to me. What emerged was that I had engaged in these activities because my enthusiasm had masked my want of skill. It had carried me into some sort of team, but it did not give me an entry into these activities where I was completely unknown. As it was, I decided to leave school early and embark on my university career.

When I was fifteen I said to my father that I would like to go to Paris. He was not a man who immediately thought that I had developed some sexual urge to visit that promiscuous city, but knew that I wanted to go out of genuine interest in travel and people. He debated with himself and decided that the most he could afford was a £5 note. 'Can you,' he said, 'manage the trip on a five-pound note?' 'Not half!' I said. 'Not the slightest doubt.' And indeed it was completely true. I cannot remember what the fare was, but I went third class by train, via Calais, and enjoyed every minute of it, taking with me a delicious packed lunch manufactured by my mother that exceeded in succulence anything that anyone else had brought, and which I was obliged to share with seven other travellers.

On arrival I went to a hotel off the Rue de Rivoli, but very much off the Rue de Rivoli. It had been suggested to my father, was immaculately clean, and although the meals were sparse, they were of excellent quality and quite enough to sustain me. I paid a little over two pounds for my week's stay. The total cost of the excursion was, I well remember, £4 19s, since I had a shilling left after paying my bus fare from Victoria to our home in Hampstead.

My week in Paris was an absolute delight. I had never been there before, and naturally I saw all the conventional things and a few of the unconventional things and no worse for that. I scaled – or perhaps scale is the wrong word since the lift had the burden of the ascent – the Eiffel Tower; I wandered through Notre Dame; was shown into the little chapels, and saw all the jewels on view. I went to the Louvre and spent many hours in sheer delight. And I also made two visits to the theatre –

I could not afford the opera. It was the first time I had been abroad and the only extravagance to which I treated myself was coffee and a cake each morning. This took quite a part of £5.

But it was on a later visit that I had one special joy. I had been – and remain – in love with Danielle Darrieux ever since the day I first saw her in *Mayerling*. My indulgence in morning coffee and patisserie paid a rich reward on this later trip. I was sitting quietly with a cup of chocolate in Rumpelmayer's – it will be seen that by then my social sights had been raised – when a vision entered the restaurant, none other than Danielle. The rum baba in my mouth remained unchewed for several minutes while my eyes followed her around the room. I do not think I have ever set eyes on a more beautiful woman. Many, many years later I noticed in the press that she was to appear on the London stage. I decided that – although her photographs showed little or no change – I did not want my illusions to be shattered. So after anxious thought I did not go to the performance. I cannot remember any film that made a greater impression on me than *Mayerling*, entirely on account of Miss Darrieux, and if by any extraordinary chance she should read these memoirs it will provide the one and only opportunity of testifying to my passion.

This visit was a total success. It was followed rapidly by a second trip when I was seventeen. This time I wished to see Rome. I was beginning the study of Roman law as part of my legal studies and becoming increasingly fascinated with it. Again I conferred with my ever-compliant father about the finances of the trip, and this time he said that the most he could spare was £10. Ungratefully, I objected that this was insufficient for a four-week stay, whereupon with unexpected resistance he rejoined that two weeks would have to suffice. Reluctantly I agreed with him, but I was to have an exceptional piece of good fortune.

I stayed at a very nice clean *pensione* – the Pensione Boos – where I had what was called a *demi-pensione*, with breakfast and a choice of luncheon or an evening meal. Here again the charge was in British currency something around £2 a week. I travelled each day from the *pensione* either on foot or by bus to one or other of the marvellous sights that opened up a new world for me. It was then that I discovered a fatal affection for Italian *gelati*. It is only in later years, driven by stark medical necessity, that I have abstained, although providentially Italy is the only place where irresistible ice-cream is manufactured. It presents no difficulty to resist the delights of Walls, Lyons and other British manufacturers, hard as they may try.

It was while I was absorbing the Roman atmosphere that I had my sensational piece of good fortune. I was wandering through the Colosseum clutching my *Nagel* when a gentleman, who at that time seemed to me to be antique (I should now regard him as relatively youthful), approached me and asked me whether I spoke English. I pointed to my guidebook. He was obviously anxious to strike up an acquaintance.

It turned out that he was a retired American judge who had come to Italy on the melancholy mission of finding a final home for his wife's ashes. He was quite alone and clearly longing for someone to talk to. Our acquaintance developed rapidly. He plainly regarded me as a fortunate discovery. I regarded him as a godsend since he was a source of income and support to me. Although I am not by nature a cadger, at that age one has less compunction in accepting support from a relative stranger. He made it easy by refusing to allow me to pay for anything and my token resistance was not, I fear, as creditable as it should have been.

Thereafter daily we went to see the sights together. Each afternoon I returned to my excellent *pensione* for lunch, normally pasta and fruit, and afterwards I would join him again. At 5 p.m. we would go together to the English tea-room at the foot of the Spanish Steps, and there we would go through the same little pantomime. He would ask me every day whether this was 'real genuine British tea'. Strangely, he had never been to England. I assured him that it was real English tea. He would then ask whether the scones were genuine British scones. I told him that no better scones could be found in Britain outside of Scotland; that more delicious scones you could not find having searched from one end of the land to the other, as I devoured three, liberally spread with Italian jam. He was delighted to learn that his faith in the tea-room was justified since he took almost all his meals there.

He was an exceptionally nice man and a most agreeable companion. His one fault was the thoroughness of his determination to acquaint himself with every cultural aspect of that great city. This could be painful. One day on his daily telephone call to make the arrangements, he said to me, 'Tonight we are going to the Pirandello Theatre.' I was a precociously educated youth and had heard of Pirandello, but, needless to say, had never seen a play. I was able to tell my friend that he was a great Sicilian playwright whose reputation was second to none. 'The play we are going to see,' he said, 'is *Six Characters in Search of an Author.*' I pointed out to him gently that as the play was in Italian and neither of us spoke a word of that language it might not be a total delight, but this certainly did not deter him. As I had predicted, the play lost interest very rapidly. It is, as my readers will know, a complicated play and somewhere midway through I ventured to suggest that we had tasted of it sufficiently and might even leave with honour. It was the only time I saw him look angry. 'Leave in the middle of a play!' he said. 'It would be most discourteous.'

Thereafter I sat through to the tortured end without daring to repeat the suggestion.

This chance encounter made my trip a sensational success. My friend enjoyed talking law to me, although he was well aware of the callow state of my legal development. He was to my satisfaction a liberal-minded man, informed me that he invariably voted Democrat, and came from Illinois. He must have been a splendid judge. There are few men on whose fairness and integrity I would have relied more.

The visit to Italy was followed by frequent visits to other foreign parts. My brother had spent a year at Tours where the purest French is supposed to be spoken. I was sent there when I left school. I discovered subsequently that however pure the language spoken by the people of Touraine, it would have taken me a considerable period to acquire sufficient proficiency for my accent to make the slightest difference. However, I had a slight emotional mishap. I met and was much attracted by a Spanish girl – a fellow student at the Institut Étranger. This charming creature spoke very little French but quite good English. I could speak no Spanish and very little French. Hence our conversation was conducted entirely in English. We cycled together along the banks of the Loire; picnicked together, and indeed I spent all my free time with her playing truant from the Institut. Alas, I lost touch with her when I returned to England – encouraged to do so by my mother who was unsympathetic to my affectionate feelings. She had not regarded the Tours excursion as designed for romantic purposes.

Thereafter I visited a great number of places abroad. I went on two or three cruises which I enjoyed enormously – to Morocco, the Canary Islands, to Portugal and elsewhere. I cannot describe myself as well-travelled. I have never been to the Far East except for one brief visit to Hong Kong on the way back from Australia. I have never been to India. My frequent visits to the United States have been restricted to New York and the Eastern States except for a solitary visit to San Francisco. I have never been to South America.

I have only once been to Germany. This was prior to the Hitler regime but when the Nazis were coming into power. I have felt a strong disinclination ever to return. This I know now to be completely irrational. The present-day Germans have sought to make every human recompense that is possible, but the prospect of visiting Germany still fills me, not so much with distaste, as with a sense of wrongdoing. I have an instinctive feeling that I should not be prepared to come to terms with a nation that perpetrated such horrors on my own race. That this is unjust and unreasonable I recognise, but it has certainly influenced a decision to stay away. Needless to say I have, since the war, encountered a great many

virtuous and civilised Germans, which serves only to endorse the unreasonableness of my instincts.

Spain I declined to visit. When the Civil War broke out my sympathy
was wholly with the Republicans, although my common sense resisted
any appeal towards communism. It was only my firm belief that my
mother would have locked me up and kept me in chains at the first move
to enlist that enabled me to justify my failure to do so. I have to admit
that I am not of a heroic disposition and was greatly supported in my
disinclination towards heroics by the knowledge that my mother would
have moved heaven and earth to stop me.

My impulse to go was not a melodramatic one. It was a genuine feeling
that one ought to be there and it was heavily diluted by a simple cowardice
that convinced me in my heart that the best way of prolonging life was
not to visit Spain as a member of the Republican army. But when I saw
so many of the people I knew, most of them much older, depart to serve,
and when I heard of the fate of so many of them, to this day I feel a
considerable shame that – however futile my services might have been –
I failed to demonstrate my support for a cause which, had it been
successful, might well have averted the Second World War.

From an early age, we were a family possessing a dog. Living as we
did, in the early days, in a virtual slum area, the ownership of a dog was
an anomaly, and the possession of our dog, which was a Pomeranian
called Fluff, was a special anomaly. He was the apple of everyone's eye
and I well remember the terrible day when I returned from school to be
told that Fluff was unconscious. I studied the poor creature and arrived
at the conclusion that he was rather more than unconscious, that in fact
he had ceased to have any contact with this world and had moved to
higher planes. In any event my brother and I wrapped him in a rug and
raced him to the vet who confirmed that Fluff had, alas, departed this
life at an age which we believed to be twenty-two, although dog experts
maintain that this is unlikely.

Fluff was not succeeded for some little while, but he was finally
succeeded by a dachshund known as Figgy, short for Figaro. On *his* death
he was succeeded by a Pekinese known as Pucci, short for Puccini. It will
be observed that we were moving into a more intellectual class in
designating names for our dogs. Figgy involved us in one of the most
dramatic episodes in the life of my brother and myself. My mother had
to travel to South Africa to rescue one of my father's business enterprises,
and it was with great reluctance that she was persuaded to leave Figgy
behind. Although he could have been taken out of the country and would
have been admitted to South Africa, he could not have been brought back
again without a period of quarantine, and we were confident that Figgy –

who was jet black – would not have been happy in South Africa where, I have no doubt, he would have been a violent opponent of apartheid. Instead he was ultimately, and with great trepidation, entrusted to my brother and myself who at that time were living in the house in North-West London with our parents.

All went well until about three weeks before my mother was due to return. Sleeping soundly one night I heard a ferocious banging on the door. It turned out to be my brother in a state of great excitement. 'Figgy,' he said, 'is ill.' 'Ill?' I said. 'He seemed very well this evening and had a large meal earlier.' 'No, he is ill and he is very ill.' I put on a dressing-gown and rushed downstairs to see that poor Figgy was flat on his back, gently wagging his legs to indicate obvious pain and suffering. I tried to soothe him, to administer a little water or milk, but it was clear that Figgy was in a serious condition. So we wrapped the dog in a rug and put him in a motor car, while I went to telephone the vet. As it was four o'clock in the morning, he was initially not too cordial, but after a few minutes of explanation – he was a kindly man – he said, 'Well, bring him round.' So we drove Figgy to the vet, who lived two or three streets away. The vet examined him carefully, uttering the words that stick in my memory. 'This is a sick dog!' I did not say that we had arrived at the same conclusion without the benefit of a long professional training. 'What shall we do?' we asked. 'I fear that he will need an operation,' he replied, 'and this is not something on which I can claim to be an expert. My friend Mr Buggings, round the corner, knows better, but you can hardly wake him at this hour.' 'Can't we?' I said. 'Where is the telephone?' So we phoned Mr Buggings, who was far less amiable than the original vet, and burst into a flow of bad language of which I took not the slightest notice. 'We are coming to see you, Mr Buggings. We will be there with Figgy in ten minutes,' I announced.

Arriving there, we met a snarling Mr Buggings, but he did not have the heart to turn away poor Figgy. 'This dog,' he said, 'appears to me to have a stone. It is on the whole unprofitable to operate in these circumstances.' The words struck terror into our hearts. The notion of meeting our mother at the quayside at Southampton to inform her that Figgy was the late Figgy was a prospect that neither of us relished. We enquired where we could take Figgy for a final opinion. 'The only place I can recommend,' he said, 'is the Royal Veterinary College in Camden Town.' This, we discovered on telephoning, opened at 8.30 a.m. So we took Figgy home, tended him as best we could, gave ourselves cups of tea, and at eight o'clock in the morning we were on our way to the Royal Veterinary College. The vet on duty there examined Figgy to confirm the diagnosis that he had a stone, and the opinion that an operation was a very hazardous venture in these cases. It would be probably kinder, he opined, to put Figgy away quietly and send him off to the land where dachshunds could enjoy immunity from gall-bladders.

We enquired who was the specialist in the matter. He said it was one Professor Smith. 'Could he see Figgy?' we asked. 'Alas,' he said, 'he is on leave!' 'Where?' we demanded. 'Well, he has taken a week off for Wimbledon.' 'What is his telephone number?' Within minutes I was on the phone with the nice Professor Smith to explain the position, and he heroically undertook to come to the College that very afternoon if we would have Figgy in attendance. We took Figgy along, he had a look at him, said indeed he had a stone, that he could operate, that the chances were no better than 50/50, but that he was prepared to 'have a bash'. So we left Figgy in the care of Professor Smith and departed full of anxieties and worries.

The next morning he telephoned and said that the operation had taken place and was as successful as could be expected. What we had not realised was that the Royal Veterinary College were being driven nearly mad by my mother's friends who had, through the grapevine, learnt of the lamentable state in which Figgy found himself, and were ringing individually to the hospital for the latest bulletin. The resentment and indignation of the staff at the Royal College can be imagined, as they were prevented from giving any attention to any other dog, be it a St Bernard or a mastiff. Anyway, after a few days it became clear that Figgy had a chance of recovery. And after a few days more I telephoned to enquire whether I could pay him a visit, intending to take some flowers or chocolates. For some reason I had in my mind that a dog hospital was somewhere where each of the dogs would be tucked inside a bed with his nose emerging over a spotless counterpane, with a water jug by his side, and any other necessary conveniences to enable him to lead a full dog's life.

However, on arrival at the Royal Veterinary hospital at six o'clock in the evening, I found it locked up. I rang the bell and was told that there were no medical staff in attendance. But there was a caretaker. He displayed a great reluctance to let me in and informed me that he did not know where Figgy was. I said that if he would allow me anywhere where there were dogs I would identify Figgy instantly. Finally, after a little corruption, he admitted me, and I went into the ward to find, alas, that far from being ensconced in a comfortable bed, Figgy was enclosed with a number of other sickly-looking dogs in a cage. Poor Figgy was in a far corner of the cage looking terrible: he was matted, dirty and bleary-eyed. He opened one eye, caught a glimpse of me and trotted painfully to the bars, pushing his nose through for me to stroke, and it was clear to me that my visit was the first happy thing that had happened to him in the hospital. I stayed a while, fondling his nose, endeavouring to explain that it would not be long before he came home – though I am not sure my message reached him – and finally decided to leave. Here a grave miscalculation was made. Figgy viewed my departure with obvious dissatisfaction and let out a moan of distress and grief. Whereupon every other dog in the establishment joined him in sympathy and the noise could be heard from the bottom of Camden Town to the top of Hampstead Heath. The caretaker was in a state of terror. 'This will lose me my job! Do please stop it.' So I fled from the hospital, followed by the noise, in which I could detect the sad voice of the complaining Figgy.

A week later we brought Figgy home. He was still limping but obviously was going to survive the operation. We bathed him, powdered him, combed him, and generally pampered him for my mother's return the next day. And to our great delight when she returned, when we picked her up at Southampton, we were able to tell her that Figgy had undergone an operation but happily was fully recovered. Her anxiety was not relieved until she set eyes on him, when Figgy greeted her with a positive delirium of joy. His glare at us clearly indicated that had my mother been there these terrible things would not have happened. Figgy lived in fact two or three years longer. He finally died of a heart attack during an air raid. Providentially, I was on leave at the time and he died in my arms. I like to believe that my presence was some comfort to him.

My mother in her later days purchased a white Pekinese which, although she loved him dearly, was anything but angelic. Some will recall a story by the American humorist James Thurber, 'The Dog Who Bit Everyone'. This description could be easily applied to her last dog. He bit absolutely everybody except my mother, my brother and myself. It had the fortunate consequence of deterring visitors for miles around.

When my mother died in 1959 this animal was still living, bequeathed to my brother and myself, and we looked after him for another five years before he finally died. He had acquired a great reputation in the district for heroism. While still in the care of my mother, he was taken every day for a short walk down Platt's Lane, Hampstead. She was unsteady on her feet, and on one occasion she passed the house of a well-known variety artist who owned a Great Dane. The Great Dane bounded out of the house, intending probably no harm except to express kindness and affection, but he knocked my mother over. The Pekinese immediately jumped on to my prostrate mother, showed his teeth and drove the Great Dane away. Since the difference in size was in a ratio of fifty to one, he was immediately acclaimed as the Victoria Cross winner among the dogs of the area. Whenever my mother took him for a walk thereafter, neighbours who saw them rushed out with bits of cake, chocolate or biscuits and it was surprising that he did not die from a surfeit of attention.

2

Apprentice Lawyer

I DECIDED – AND it was my own decision – that I would leave my new school early. I had not enjoyed it very much; I had not settled in and had not been readily assimilated. A family discussion ensued about my future: a discussion to which I listened respectfully but took not the slightest heed of. Within a traditional middle-class Jewish family of fairly recent immigrant origin, the choice of a profession was regarded as limited by specialist considerations. The favourite choice was medicine. This was favoured because of the respect attaching to its practitioners and – although an unexpressed consideration – because it was a portable profession. The well-entrenched English Jewry of many generations back would not have given this a moment's consideration. They regard themselves as firmly established Britons.

My grandparents' and indeed my parents' generations were not so sure. By the time I had reached an adult age I was firmly convinced that the Jews were as secure and safe in this country as anywhere in the world and my own career has provided a demonstration. But there were still uneasy recollections of countries of origin which indulged in pogroms which expelled Jews from particular areas. I do not believe that when I grew up any Jewish family would have contemplated the possibility of the Hitler barbarities, but nevertheless insecurity weighed with them, even though in their remote thoughts. Hence the affection for a medical career.

In my case this choice was impossible. I loathed anything scientific and the only piece of science I have ever absorbed is to remember the chemical formula for water. I am not even sure I have got that right. Today, if I were choosing a profession, I would have been tempted to be a psychiatrist – one medical profession that did not require a scientific background – but that temptation would have been qualified because of the necessity to obtain a medical degree. Psychoanalysis would hold no temptations for me. Although unfairly or unjustly, I still regard it as something of a conjuring trick. Anyway, my choice of a profession derived from inclination rather than preconceptions. I had and continue to have a love of and an interest in words and in speech. I have always enjoyed composition and putting sentences together either on the page or in the mouth. Quite naturally I gravitated towards law. The family council decreed that my education needed to be an inexpensive one. I had at that stage acquired no scholarships, but there was a firm determination on the part of both my parents that I should go to a university. Jews with any rabbinical tradition have a love of learning above everything in the world. This had been imbued in me from a very early age. I shared the wish for a university education.

As the family resources were insufficient for the older universities, I decided – encouraged by my parents – to effect entry into University College, London. For some reason I first sought an arts course in history, French and Latin, but before actually making my decision I opted for a course in economics. I was admitted and had one term of economics listening to the cultured and agreeable tones of Hugh Gaitskell, who was then a lecturer at University College. Only later in life was I to know him well and become one of his advisers, but I regret to say that at the end of the first term of my study under his tuition I reached what for me was a momentous decision: it was that one or other of us must be wrong. I had not by then acquired either the self-confidence or the conceit to opt in my own favour but the uncertainty engendered was enough to make me change subjects. I owe it to Hugh Gaitskell that I entered into the study of the law and although he would have been surprised to learn that he had played any part in this momentous decision, I am grateful to him.

For the purpose of obtaining entry to the Law Faculty, I met and became friendly with a remarkable Roman lawyer – one of the two great Roman lawyers of his day in this country – Professor Herbert Felix Jolowitz. Jolowitz was born in England of wealthy German–Jewish parents. He studied at Cambridge and when I met him he was the Professor of Roman Law in the University of London. Roman law is one of the two great legal systems on which the law of almost every civilised country is based – the other being common law which operates in England. It was and for many years remained my principal interest in the law, and I owe my critical approach to common law to being acquainted with an alternative system which I rate much higher. Uncritical admiration for the common system of law derives mainly from people who know no other. Under Jolowitz I enlisted in the London LL B course and studied Roman law, contract law, equity, private international law and a variety of other subjects.

The Faculty at University College was a very distinguished one, but more important the collective Faculty in the three major London colleges – University College, King's College and the London School of Economics – I think outshone any other Law Faculty in the country. I was taught Roman law by Jolowitz – second only to my later tutor at Cambridge, Professor W. W. Buckland. I was taught real property law by Professor Hughes Parry – an acknowledged expert and the editor of a standard volume of conveyancing statutes. I was taught constitutional law by Professor Ivor Jennings, whose work on the Cabinet is a classic. There was, in fact, no subject I was taught except by an acknowledged expert of great standing.

At the School of Economics I indulged myself by an occasional attendance – probably illegal – in the lecture hall where Professor Harold Laski was delivering his lectures on politics and the social sciences. It was difficult not to be impressed by him. Many unkind things have been said about this remarkable man. He is accused of name-dropping, of unfounded pretensions and of unfounded claims, but to hear him deliver a lecture extemporised, without a single note, in perfectly rounded sentences, without any hesitation or falter was a revelation. He was, of course, a pillar of the Labour Party and his rather brutal rebuff by Clement Attlee was recorded by his enemies with satisfaction.

I admired him hugely and continue to do so. It is enough for me that in the published correspondence it emerges that he had won the admiration and friendship of the great American, Oliver Wendell Holmes. His career ended sadly through a misguided faith in the English legal system. At some stage during the election campaign of 1945 he was assailed by a Tory speaker making two allegations. The first, although in my view not the more serious, was that he had in his speeches and writings throughout a lifetime advocated resort to force if the Left wished to secure power. The second allegation was that at the beginning of the Second World War he had escaped to America to avoid military service. Both allegations were without justification and he was advised to sue for libel. Unfortunately for Laski, he failed to realise that his explanation of the first issue was too subtle and too sophisticated for a 'special' jury, that is, a form of jury, since abolished, based upon a property qualification, which would naturally be predisposed because of a class prejudice to judge him on his reputation rather than on a close analysis of his words.

To his ill fortune, when the conflicting forces confronted each other, Laski found himself faced with the most effective advocate that my professional lifetime has produced, the late Sir Patrick Hastings. On many occasions I went into court to hear this master of advocacy and to admire a technique which did not have a vestige of fairness about it. He was a former Attorney-General, surprisingly Labour, and responsible for bringing down the government which he served. But his authority and standing in the courts were such that he was allowed almost total licence. Laski was no mean adversary and the encounter was in fact much closer than has been represented. Nevertheless, at the end of the day Hastings's hectoring and arrogant technique, assisted by a judge who – as Laski pointed out – failed to make any part of Laski's case in the summing-up, was fatal. Laski never recovered from this reverse. The matter was the more unfortunate because of an unhappy error by Laski's own second counsel, Sir Valentine Holme KC. In dealing with the second allegation, to which the defendant could have had no answer because it was clearly established that Laski had offered himself for National Service on several occasions and been rejected because of his medical condition, Sir Valentine fell into a trap set for him by the judge. While his leader, Mr Slade KC, was temporarily out of court, Holme raised some question about the second libel when the judge asked him in seeming innocence whether having regard to the gravity of the first libel he thought it necessary to pursue the question of the second libel. Valentine Holme, a very experienced practitioner, but a man who regarded it as wise to defer to judicial suggestions, agreed that it was unnecessary to prolong the case and withdrew Laski's complaint about the National Service defamation. In the light of the subsequent decision, this was a tragic error. I recommend to those who would like to know more about this event to read the verbatim account of the trial published triumphantly by the *Daily Express* (the winners) who had been defending a report of the offending speech. However, it was years before the beginning of the Second World War when I first met Laski and his reputation in progressive circles was of the highest.

I remained at University College for several years and enjoyed it hugely. There I made some friendships that have endured the whole of my life: two in particular. The first was, of course, with 'Jim' Gower, now Professor L. C. B. Gower, who later became the Vice-Chancellor of Southampton University. He attained greater eminence in recent years by being appointed by the government in 1981 to conduct a one-man investigation into investor protection which shook the City to its foundations, earning him immense unpopularity with anyone who wants to defraud the public and the approval of a great number of people who think his views, although open to criticism in certain details, are generally wise and indeed profound. It must be unique for a single man to exercise as much influence on the commercial and financial world as Professor

Gower has in his report. Jim Gower is a man with whom I have maintained a friendship for fifty years. He combines with one of the most acute legal minds in the country a simplicity of outlook and a generosity of spirit of which I do not know the equal. It would embarrass him if I were to say more – in fact what I have already said will embarrass him – but there are times, I think, when a man needs to be embarrassed by his friends.

Another close friend whom I also met at UCL was Dennis (later Lord) Lloyd. He shared with Jim Gower the distinction of being the most brilliant legal scholar of his day. He was deprived of immediate success by his unfortunate inability to conceal his true feelings about anything. He continued to say what he felt and if he disliked something nothing on earth would produce false praise for it. This wholly virtuous characteristic robbed him of easy popularity, a fact demonstrated when after exceptional academic success his college – Caius College, Cambridge – failed to elect him as a Fellow or indeed to retain him after he had secured the most distinguished first of his year. His death this year was to me the loss of a very dear friend – a loss which was shared by a devoted wife of many years' standing.

During the time that I was enrolled as a student at University College, I was, of course, articled to a firm of solicitors, having decided after discussions with my parents that on the whole the wise choice was to become a solicitor. I contrived to combine the two occupations without any serious difficulty. I would attend lectures at UCL being by that time possessed of an ancient and totally unreliable motor car, returning to Gray's Inn for the remaining portions of the day.

Having decided to enlist as a solicitor, enquiries had to be made about suitable firms. I paid a visit to one particular firm where I was interviewed by a plump and prosperous-looking gentleman who was smoking a large cigar. 'No,' he said to me, 'there is no money in this profession.' Even at an early age I was a little given to sardonic rejoinders, but I restrained the one on the tip of my tongue and merely looked fixedly at him and said that it was obvious to me that the practitioners were living in a state of penury. I decided that this firm was not the firm for me; but providentially my mother had as a friend a Mrs Lowe, who had a family connection with the old-established firm of Rubinstein Nash. It was to Harold Rubinstein that she gave my mother an introduction. He was a very distinguished solicitor but in rather unusual circumstances, since he possessed virtually no academic background in the law and unhesitatingly disclaimed legal knowledge on almost every subject. Nevertheless, he was well liked and much trusted by a large and varied clientele. He was better known to the world as a dramatist who wrote plays which were rarely or never produced.

I went to visit Harold Rubinstein and took a liking to him at once. He was a mild-looking man, immensely courteous, immensely gentle, but with vehement opinions, as I found afterwards. He was a lover of liberty, and I would think in his political views a Liberal, but a passionate opponent of communism and anything to do with systems of government which were antagonistic to human liberty. I met him and both his brothers with whom he was in partnership: Stanley Rubinstein, the senior partner, whose main interest – as I remember – was in music and who was the secretary or president of a number of musical organisations, and his brother Ronald, who was by far the ablest lawyer of the three and who, alas, died prematurely, but not before he had contributed a remarkable lay-law book entitled *John Citizen and the Law*, which is still in print, and a more recent edition of which has been brought out by his daughter, who also later became a partner in the firm.

Discussions took place between my mother and Harold Rubinstein – my father was too self-conscious to attend any such meetings – and arrangements were made that for the sum of £300 I would become articled to the firm for the period of five years, and at the end of that period would be set free to go on my own. I arrived shortly thereafter at their offices at Raymond Buildings, Gray's Inn: a brick-built, late nineteenth-century building, with stone stairs leading up to the first floor, and a single toilet for the articled clerks on the floor above, while the rest of the unfortunate staff had to descend to the basement to meet the needs of nature. The offices were exceptionally uncomfortable in almost every direction. The articled clerks shared a single small room up a narrow flight of stairs, which alas I could no longer traverse today, where we spent the day quite often playing ping-pong on a desk, throwing darts, and generally finding something to occupy ourselves with. From time to time, however, we were given jobs and, flatteringly or otherwise, Harold Rubinstein decided that I could be useful to him and after a while proceeded to heap work on me in considerable quantity. Before very long he developed sufficient confidence in me to allow me to interview clients, which was the special privilege he reserved for the articled clerk in whom he had the greatest confidence.

The first client I interviewed was a lady novelist, if not of world eminence then certainly of great eminence among the less literary section of the population. Her name was Ruby M. Ayres, and she was *the* great romance writer of her generation. When I read one of her books I realised that they were, of course, unspeakable piffle; but they were innocuous piffle, had no vicious element of any kind, and simply retailed the story of how a young woman fell in love with the vision of a hero far beyond her social reach, and how slowly hand over hand up the rope-ladder of social eminence she clambered to attain a position where at last he could declare his love for her. This appeared to me to be the formula: a formula she adopted with enormous success. I believe that to this day she has sold more copies of her books than any other living writer in the English language. She was presented to me as a frail, helpless but kindly old lady, towards whom gallantry demanded that every assistance should be given. In consequence of this important assignment, the other articled clerks vacated our shambles of a room, after tidying it a little, and up the stairs came this old lady and sat down opposite me: white-haired, fragile and clearly in need of protection. 'Mr Goodman,' she said, 'I am very pleased to have your help and efficiency. I do not understand the first thing about anything to do with my affairs. Have a look at this Dutch royalty statement. If you add up the third column, you will find that it is four pfennigs light.'

It did not take long for me to realise that Miss Ayres needed very little assistance from me and that I was likely to be less vigilant about the pfennigs than she was. However, we parted on the best of terms, with the assurance that we would meet again. I think she had the sense to realise that whoever she might need to assist her in her search for pfennigs, I was not the right person, as I never saw her again.

While I was an articled clerk I was given the conduct of a case considered too trivial for any admitted lawyer to deal with. Our client was a spinster lady and the owner of a cherished bull mastiff. She came to see me accompanied by this animal which had the appearance of an inmate of Belsen. The animal had its bones sticking out and appeared to be in an advanced stage of malnutrition. Its owner was in a state of deep distress. She produced a photograph or two to show the dog in a previous incarnation and as plump and well an animal as anyone could hope for. 'Look,' she said, 'what they have done to him!'

Apparently she had been compelled to take a trip to Australia and she was not able to take the dog for the good reason that restrictions would have made it impossible to bring him in again without a six-month period of quarantine. She had therefore entrusted the dog to a well-recommended kennel. Again she said, 'Look what they have done to him!' The poor dog, it was clear, had been starved. He looked at me almost with pleading eyes and I could see that he was strongly associated with his owner's demand for justice.

I thereupon recommended that a claim for damages, based on breach of contract since the dog could not himself be a plaintiff in an action for tort, should be instituted to teach them a lesson. Unhappily, in my inexperience I relied upon the photographs of the dog before his penal servitude. I did not take any photographs of the dog in his starved condition. On the day when the case was to come to court, the lady again attended with the dog. 'But where,' I asked, 'is the plaintiff dog?' She looked at me strangely. 'This is the dog,' she said. Obviously she had been engaged in industriously stuffing him with carbohydrates. Our counsel made desperate efforts to persuade the judge that the vivid descriptions of the dog's condition justified success and I myself was put into the witness-box to give my own description of his former appearance. The judge took the view that a controlled diet would not even now be a bad thing and we retired ignominiously, although the good lady bore me no resentment.

In the course of five years at Rubinstein's I had an intriguing time. The practice was one that attracted all the literary and dramatic talent in the country, and a large portion of the musical talent and not a few painters, although there was less emphasis on that side of the artistic scene than on the literary side. I had the greatest satisfaction, as articled clerk, in interviewing authors and advising them on matters of copyright, of libel, and on matters of passing off, so that I could not help but become well-versed in these fields even before I was admitted as a solicitor.

Eventually the time came for me to take my finals and it became necessary for me to have a period off to prepare for them. To do this I searched around for some peaceful spot, and looking through the *New Statesman* one day found an advertisement for a quiet home in West Sussex which offered accommodation to a single person anxious to engage in a sedentary and studious occupation. I followed this up with a letter, and it turned out to be one of the most fortunate encounters of my life. I discovered that the advertiser was a distinguished publisher, George Milsted, a partner at one of the well-known publishing houses, Duckworth. He had a modern house, by no means attractive, but built in a most beautiful position – the last house in Ditchling between the village and the Downs. Calling there, I felt an immediate sympathy with George and Milly Milsted, his Scottish wife, who lived on their own and were very happy to have someone to share the house with them. So there I repaired for three months, quietly working during the day, and occasionally motoring them out in my old motor car to Brighton or the Plumpton races or wherever else it was they wanted to go.

The period of study at the Milsteds was well rewarded. I took the solicitors' finals which was – but no longer is – strangely divided into two parts. There was a 'pass examination', which you needed to qualify as a solicitor, and if you wanted you could leave it at that. But if you sought greater glories there was an 'honours examination' which was optional and which enabled you to obtain one of three classes of honours. I obtained first-class honours and the Daniel Reardon Prize, awarded to the candidate who obtained the second place in the entire examination. As a result of this, when I returned to Rubinstein's the original premiss that I should not remain with them was no longer valid, since they were attracted by the idea of employing a junior person who had obtained high academic distinction. Added to it I had previously taken a Master of Law degree at University College where, again, I had not done discreditably; but I decided that, as I was still only just past twenty, I would like to pursue my studies in two particular areas, namely Roman law and Roman–Dutch law.

I decided to go to Cambridge and was accepted by Downing College where I stayed for two years. I never really regarded myself as a totally integrated Cambridge product because I had gone there late, but I enjoyed those years enormously, largely because of the opportunities it gave me to study under Professor Buckland and to a lesser extent under a very amiable Roman–Dutch lawyer named Oliver. Buckland was indeed the greatest Roman lawyer of his generation. His textbook is still acknowledged as the leading work on the subject in this country. He produced a shorter version, a manual, of Roman law, and the effect of having studied under Buckland, and particularly of having been individually taught by him, has been a matter of pride for many years and has certainly enhanced a rather insubstantial claim to real scholarship.

One most attractive feature of this unassuming man was an easily recognisable liberalism – the foremost liberal mind I have ever met. A splendid example of this was demonstrated one afternoon when I went to pay my solitary call on him – which I did twice a week – where over a cup of tea he would delightfully illuminate the whole Roman law scene.

On this particular day I found him standing outside his house in Hills Road, obviously impatient for my arrival, wearing unusually his red academic gown and clearly prepared to set off somewhere. 'Ah,' he said, 'I am glad you have come. I am afraid I have to leave you for half an hour; there is a meeting at Caius and I must go to it.' So not incurious but sufficiently polite not to ask directly, I looked expectantly at him. 'They are about to elect a new Professor of International Law,' he went on. 'There is an obvious candidate who outshines every other candidate, but I am sorry to have to tell you that because he is Jewish there is a group determined not to elect him, and I am determined to see that he is elected.' The man in question was Herschel Lauterpacht. I said to Professor Buckland, 'What will happen if they do not elect him?' He looked at me and said quietly, 'I shall resign.' And I said to myself, 'They *will* elect him!'

I sat in his study for half an hour sipping a cup of tea, reading some book or other on Roman law, when he returned looking triumphant.

Lauterpacht had been elected with very little opposition. And he not only became one of the most distinguished international lawyers in the world, but he was subsequently knighted, became a King's Counsel and was appointed to be the British Judge at the International Court at the Hague, a career not without irony since one of the objections to him at Cambridge was that he had fought in the Austrian Army against the British. However, the episode did emphasise the determination and extraordinary breadth of mind of my tutor.

On my first arrival at Cambridge I had a feeling that there was something important missing. It only dawned upon me after my first week or so that what was missing was the entire female sex. Cambridge, of course, in those days did not admit women to the men's colleges and there was a carefully maintained apartheid whereby the girls were segregated at Newnham and Girton: the latter being a considerable distance from civilisation and involving an exhausting bicycle ride which could be justified only by a very ardent passion. However, there are aspects of a man's life about which privacy should be maintained. It is enough to say that, although a keen interest was aroused, I formed no effective attachments during my student career and it was not until my army days that any serious affection developed. Of this I have no more to say, except that I owe a debt of gratitude to a small number of women who over the years have given me their affection and often more than their affection.

Throughout my two years I lived out of college in rooms in Glisson Road, maintained by a husband and wife who had been in aristocratic service and knew how to do things. It was, in fact, the first time that I encountered gracious living. The wife of the house had been the cook and a very splendid cook she was. My dinner parties, for which 3s 6d per head was charged, were sought after by my small circle of Cambridge acquaintances. A welcome feature was the wine provided – I had not then attained the grace of being teetotal – which I secured from the college buttery. Port was 3s a bottle, and good dry sherry 3s 6d a bottle. A claret involved the mad extravagance of as much as 5s a bottle and a white burgundy, from my recollection, slightly less. Having the excellent cuisine of my Cambridge lodgings, there was small attraction to eat in Hall. I was not on particularly close terms with most of the diners and the food, to use a kindly word, was repellent – on the few occasions when I dined in Hall there was invariably served a concoction called hare soup. I lack the descriptive powers to describe this disagreeable item.

My two years at Cambridge were uneventful. Downing in my day was a small and unimportant college but has since developed into one of real prestige. Several years ago they made me an Honorary Fellow, but I did not return there until very recently for a Fellows' dinner, to discover how much grander it had become. Downing then did not have among its Fellowship any household names familiar to me and it was only later that I discovered the eminence that attached to one of its English Fellows, F. R. Leavis. I had the distinction of saying good morning to him almost every day for two years and the equal distinction of receiving no reply on any occasion. I like to think it was preoccupation rather than a deliberate snub.

I have regretfully to say, as a shocking example to the young, that at no time during any of my university careers was I a desperately hard worker. I enjoyed so many other things – cinema, theatre, music, opera, so far as my limited resources permitted, and an infinity of books – that the time for academic study was, alas, severely limited and severely rationed by me not to interfere with my more self-indulgent activities. I had a built-in warning signal which sounded off when an examination was so imminent as to threaten collision. I would then work literally day and night, reading *en route* to the examination, sometimes in a London Tube, some of the several thousand pages of reading material into which I had dipped.

At Cambridge a great deal of my time was spent in the cinema. Opposite my lodgings in Glisson Road was a 'fleapit' and quite often in the afternoons I would slip in at a cost of 1s 9d. There was a great variety of programmes, but if the film was dull I would be happily occupied meditating on some academic problem, generally to resolve it by the time I had emerged, making the price of the seat a veritable bargain. My working methods made it little short of a miracle that I achieved considerable academic success, but I would strongly urge all students to omit this page of my autobiography since it could easily spell disaster.

In my last year, the Cambridge Arts Theatre – now firmly established and one of the many cultural contributions of Lord Keynes – was opened. It was widely, and I have no doubt accurately, believed that Keynes's major motivation was to provide a stage for his ballet-dancer wife, Lydia Lopokova, who had not up to then been recognised as an actress and, alas, is still so unrecognised. The first production at the Arts Theatre was Ibsen's *The Master Builder*. The well-informed reader will remember that in the final scene Rebecca, the heroine and hero-worshipper of the eponymous builder, stands on the stage watching this character climbing up his tower. Miss Lopokova described his ascent to the audience in a quite remarkable accent. We were told that 'He is climbing oop and oop and oop,' and then, without the slightest change of expression or any show of emotion, she remarked laconically that 'He has fallen doon.' The audience, respectful of Keynes and his lady wife, showed no signs of mirth, but I had great difficulty in restraining myself. It is one of my most vivid theatrical memories.

When I left Cambridge I had acquired two degrees, principally in Roman law and Roman–Dutch law. I have to admit there was little competition, which explains why I had managed to secure a couple of firsts. Even so, I had still to look around for more permanent employment. Rubinstein Nash invited me to rejoin them in the role of managing clerk, with a broad hint that in due course – 'due' being undefined – I might be offered a partnership. But the role they had in mind was a conveyancer, i.e. a draftsman of deeds and documents relating to houses, flats and other cognate interests. This particular activity has since become the subject of embittered controversy.

It was not due to any prophetic vision about this aspect that I was deterred from accepting the offer. Except for those who find conveyancing a refuge from the more subjective aspects of legal practice and the necessity to advise people to take difficult and even dangerous decisions (which is the quintessence of legal skill), conveyancing is regarded with little allure by lawyers anxious for more colourful activities. The controversy at the moment is due to a belief that the sale of a house or the transfer of a flat should not require Socratic wisdom or immense erudition. In fact so complicated is land law – even after its purported simplification by statute in 1925 – that it does require an immense amount of totally otiose learning, and it should not. The unjustified belief is that this situation is manufactured by solicitors anxious to line their pockets with large fees. This is grossly unfair. It is, alas, the case that most solicitors lack either the ingenuity or the imagination to devise so profitable a situation. Like so many other aspects of British law, land law has developed without independent guidance or control into a hideous labyrinth requiring the expenditure of an enormous amount of time and effort to unravel. There is therefore something to be said on both sides of the controversy: that the law is unnecessarily complicated and should be enormously simplified, but that it is only very partially the fault of lawyers that it is so.

Unattracted as I was by the notion of becoming – and God forbid remaining – a conveyancer and nothing else, I negotiated with Rubinstein's about the prospect of being employed in other directions. I was, of course, particularly attracted by the notion of engaging in their acknowledged speciality, which was the law relating to artists and especially writers. But they were fully manned in these respects and somewhat reluctantly I decided to look elsewhere. I had not long to wait. On the floor above reposed an amiable eccentric, with whom I had been friendly throughout my period of articles, namely Ernest (known as Roy) Royalton Kisch. He came of a long-established English–Jewish family, originating in Hungary. His appearance was an impressive blend of the Arab and the Etonian. He had a spare and elegant frame and was always immaculately dressed – although, as I later discovered, with minimal expenditure – and his strong aquiline features and particularly alert and gleaming eyes savoured of the Bedouin, but in voice and gesture he was impeccably public school. He had himself been educated at St Paul's and Clare College, Cambridge. He was a devoted alumnus of both these institutions and had supported them generously from his not inconsiderable wealth. He was a pillar of Jewish elitist society, supporting every anglicised institution to which the Jewish 'upper classes' could belong. Thus he strongly supported the Liberal Jewish Synagogue in St John's Wood, of which I later became a somewhat unemphatic supporter.

He had served in the army in the First World War, attaining the rank of Major – a title by which he was often described – and had won a Military Cross. He was, I believe, the commandant of the Jewish Lads Brigade and some of his most loyal clients were former 'Lads' from that organisation who remembered with great affection his role as their commander. His wife was a not inconsiderable heiress and an extremely sweet and pleasant woman who never uttered a word of contradiction of anything he said, at least not in public.

His brother, Maitland Kisch, was the principal architect of his relatively small practice. He had founded, appropriately, the first of the property companies – a company called Town Investments – and the major part of the practice, ironically as I discovered, was the conveyancing work that came from it. However, most of that Roy Kisch liked to do himself, and I was therefore left to do the other odds and ends which were not particularly considerable until, through my own exertions, the practice began to expand in a variety of directions.

I had been offered £350 a year as a starting salary at Rubinstein's, which was then the rate for the job. To attract me into his employ, and Kisch was a man who set great store by the fact that I had rather spectacular qualifications in terms of results, he improved their offer by £50 and I started work at £400 a year, on which it was quite possible, as I lived at home, to spread myself. Kisch's office was, as I have said, in Gray's Inn. Not least of the attractions was the close proximity of an excellent Italian restaurant in Holborn called Manzoni's. There, for 1s 6d per day, it was possible to have a substantial luncheon, normally escalope of veal *napolitano*, implying a substantial addition of spaghetti. When some sauté potatoes and Brussels sprouts were added to the loaded dish, even my appetite was satisfied. For an additional 4d some kind of suet roll would be supplied, heavily soaked in golden syrup, and if I went wild and added 2d to the bill, a cup of very good coffee lent a proper final touch to the feast. On this lunch I regaled myself almost daily. It was not surprising that my girth increased in a geometric progression. The only variation was on a Friday when I would indulge in even greater extravagance and repair to the Holborn Restaurant at the corner of Holborn and Kingsway, now alas long gone. Their bill for the standard meal was 2s 6d which consisted of a tray of hors-d'œuvres of some six items, followed by roast beef, Yorkshire pudding and vegetables, and also including a sweet pudding of some sort. But coffee, alas, involved the payment of an additional 6d, and as it was the end of the week it was a rare occasion when I could afford this indulgence.

Life with Kisch was agreeable. The staff consisted in total of the two of us, a secretary for each of us, an articled clerk and an office boy. In consequence a great many tasks which would now be regarded as ignominious by a qualified solicitor fell to my lot, such as filing, press copying, answering the telephone when the office boy was out – and he contrived to be out for the greater part of the day – and above all, most pleasant, chatting away with the two ladies when there was nothing to do. I remained there for several years, that is from 1935 until the outbreak of the Second World War. I had for Kisch a great affection, despite one peculiarity which was a contradiction in his character. He was in some respects an immensely generous man. He gave very large donations to charities of all kinds and particularly to Jewish charities, but in his personal life he displayed a thrift that would have required a combination of a Scotsman, an Arab and a Jew to do it justice. It was, however, not too unamiable a thriftiness in view of his generosity in other directions.

An interesting association in my early years in practice was with Harold Abrahams, who when I knew him was practising as a junior barrister but whose claim to fame was, of course, as an Olympic champion who had won the 100 metres in 1924. Harold Abrahams was Jewish. Strangely, and it is strange as between two Jews, I never heard him mention the word and for that reason I felt some private restraint about seeking to discuss Jewry or Jewish affairs. I knew little about his family, or how deeply entrenched they were in Englishness, but it is always a matter of regret to any committed Jew, and I am certainly that, to find another Jew of eminence who is unwilling or uncomfortable to acknowledge his racial origins. But Abrahams was a nice man and I find it difficult to reconcile what I know about him with the picture painted in what has become one of the few recent successes of the British film industry, *Chariots of Fire*. The image depicted in the film was of a man so consumed by ambition that he offended against the canons of reticence and good taste that prevailed among his athletic colleagues. The outstanding solecism was that Abrahams is alleged to have hired a professional coach, presumably using his superior financial position to procure this advantage. I had no reason to believe that he was remotely rich – in fact everything I knew about him argued the contrary – and I would certainly have disbelieved that he would go against any convention. Abrahams was an immensely conventional man and he would have been particularly concerned to avoid any show of ostentation. He was a dull and untalented barrister, but, as a great friend of my senior partner and because I liked him personally, I employed him in the few cases for which his talents were adequate.

My most charming recollection of Abrahams was when, following a case at the Old Bailey, he invited me to have a cup of tea with him at a nearby Lyons tea shop, where the famous 'nippies' were serving the customers. We sat at a table and ordered two cups of tea, price 2d each, and two buns, price $1\frac{1}{2}$d each. Abrahams was clearly bursting to tell me something. 'Mr Goodman,' he said – we were on formal terms – 'I would like you to know that a tremendous change has taken place in my life.' He paused. 'I was married yesterday.' He stopped for a moment and concluded, 'I cannot tell you how blissful it is.' Since he had at that time been married for twenty-four hours or less, it struck me, even from my limited experience of matrimonial matters, as a rather speedy assessment. But I was touched and congratulated him warmly. It did in fact create a more confidential relationship between us in later dealings which I continued to have with him until he retired from the Bar, having had little or no success, to become a most distinguished athletics broadcaster and newspaper correspondent.

It was through Roy Kisch that I had my first encounter with an important politician – Edward Heath, whom I met when he was a sixth-form schoolboy at Broadstairs. The reason that brought Kisch – and incidentally myself – to Broadstairs, was the principal passion, indeed obsession, of his life, which was rose-growing. His prime ambition was to become the President of the National Rose Society (now the Royal National Rose Society): an ambition which I believe he achieved some years after my own association with him came to a formal end, although we remained on terms of friendship throughout his life.

For the purpose of growing his roses he had acquired a small plot of land at Broadstairs. His economical disposition made it impossible for him – although he could have afforded a fleet – to own a motor car and even less to employ a driver. From my very earliest days as an articled clerk I had run a motor car of some kind, usually of an antique variety, the first one of which cost £50. The availability of this luxurious transport was an irresistible attraction to Kisch, in consequence of which he would invite me to come and stay with him at Broadstairs for weekends, while he was engaged in pruning his roses or doing whatever else one does to roses. Since I knew nothing about roses, and would have committed mayhem to them had I been let loose with a pruning instrument, the task assigned to me was to locate the cockroaches in the rhododendrons, and I would spend mornings going along the rows of these plants finding the cockroaches and disposing of them in the most humane manner possible, which was simply to throw them away while they were still living.

In connection with the occupation of his plot of land, Kisch had indulged in the mad extravagance of building a small cottage, and in order to build the cottage he had contracted the services of a local builder, one William Heath – the father of the future prime minister. As a result of that association Kisch met Ted Heath and was immensely impressed by him from the outset. In fact from the start and over the years he would say, 'That boy will one day be prime minister.' Although he was clearly a very intelligent boy and intensely interested in politics, I never shared Kisch's belief about his future.

However, young Ted Heath was a frequent visitor to Kisch's little cottage and occasionally would come and sup with us on a Sunday evening. It was then that I first came to know him and maintain a link, perhaps best described as a friendly association, with him over the years. He has always been amiable, always seemed pleased to see me and to reap satisfaction from recollections of the early days. The quality that impressed me most about him was that seemingly he never forgot a friend – complemented, some critics may say, by too firm a recollection of his adversaries. Kisch had been kind to him in his early days, and many years later, when I had long ceased my own association with Kisch but would visit him for tea on a Saturday or Sunday afternoon, Ted Heath was a frequent visitor in circumstances which I thought entirely creditable since at that time Kisch could not have been of any further assistance to him. At that time Heath retained a shyness which has, I think, endured even into his days of glory, but I sensed, and have always had proof of, a genuine kindliness and a willingness to assist people that I believe are readily recognised by his political colleagues.

During my period with Kisch before the war, most of my work consisted of personal advice to various respectable businessmen – friends of Kisch – but very few who came through any connection of mine. The only spectacular case in which I was involved – which became a leading case and is to be found in all textbooks – was Reed v. the Croydon Corporation in 1938, a test case against the Corporation to determine their responsibility or otherwise for a typhoid epidemic.

The outbreak was very serious and a government commission was set up with a KC, Mr Harold Murphy, to investigate the reasons for it. He published a report which disclosed reasons which turned out, in the course of further investigations when I became involved, to be some way removed from the facts.

A great many people succumbed to the epidemic in Croydon. There were few if any deaths, but a number of people were seriously ill. We were consulted by a friend of Roy Kisch, one Mr Arthur Reed, the secretary of a successful company, whose daughter had caught typhoid and had been seriously ill, with grave fears for her life. Happily in the end she did live, but she was one of the considerable number of people who sought damages from the Croydon Corporation because of their responsibility for the outbreak. Needless to say, this young lady acted through her father. She was the only victim we represented, but when I had read the report of the Inspector, and had read some other comments and conclusions on the matter, I decided that the responsibility was inescapable. It was a bold decision, but enabled me to issue the first writ against the Corporation. As a result, when a test case came to be selected, it was inevitable that it should issue from the first writ. I, then a young and inexperienced lawyer, had the responsibility of running this important case on behalf of a great number of people.

The cause of the outbreak was the culmination of a tragic set of circumstances. When the matter had been thoroughly investigated by the various experts I called in, who were geologists, pathologists and the like, the facts that emerged were extremely discreditable to the Corporation. Within the course of a few days the Medical Officer of Health had gone on leave and his deputy had not appreciated that there should have been daily analysis of the water that was being supplied from the Addington Well to the main reservoir. In consequence it was some weeks before it was discovered that the bacillus *E. coli*, which was, as it were, the pilot fish advertising the presence of the typhoid bacillus, existed in the water. In the same week the Chief Engineer was on leave, and his deputy, with innocent inexperience, had decided that it was necessary to repair certain piping. It was not, however, appreciated that repairing the piping would involve using an alternative system that bypassed the chlorinating plant, so the infected water was being fed to the public unchlorinated and untreated.

At that precise moment a further risk to the safety of the water supply was the need to effect repairs to an adit (a channel) in the Addington Well. For that purpose it was necessary for workmen to be lowered down the well to the entrance to the adit and thereafter to proceed some hundreds of yards along the channel to the point where the repairs were needed. A team of Council employees was used to carry out the work but they were never given a medical examination and it was never suggested that any enquiry had been made from them about previous illnesses. As it happened an enquiry would indeed have been worthless, however honest their response. The particular workman responsible for the infection was what is known as a parasitic carrier. That is to say, he had in fact had a typhoid infection but had never been conscious of it. In consequence a dangerous carrier was unbeknown to anyone admitted into the water supply in circumstances where he was working at such a distance from the surface that it was almost inevitable that when he felt the urge of nature he would relieve himself on the spot and without coming up. This danger would have been neutralised by the chlorination process had it been in operation. The combination of these unfortunate circumstances resulted in an epidemic that caused some hundreds of illnesses – many very severe.

The problem that confronted me was that all the clients came from middle-class backgrounds and that no single one could possibly afford the risk of litigation against the Council. Arrangements were made for modest contributions from each of them. I was satisfied that the outcome of the litigation must be a judgement in their favour, but it was necessary at least to ensure the disbursements, including counsels' fees. I was able to procure the services of Mr Wallington KC who later became a much disliked divorce judge. His appointment to the Divorce Bench was a mistake. There had previously been Catholic divorce judges who had not allowed their religious beliefs to interfere with the efficient and speedy discharge of their duties, but Wallington was an exception. He profoundly disapproved of divorce and regarded it as his duty to make it as difficult as possible for petitioners to succeed in dissolving their marriage contrary to their religious vows. However, he was the best choice I could obtain for the money.

His junior support was of a spectacularly successful nature. The senior junior was a brilliant Wykehamist named Sylvester Gates who left the law early to become a distinguished banker. Supporting him as his junior was one of my oldest friends, Dennis Lloyd. It was a pleasure to me to give him his very first brief in this important case. It was for him a landmark in his career. He was called upon by Wallington to prepare a note from which Wallington made his opening address, and it was clear that but for that note Wallington would have had a very imperfect knowledge of the case. Lloyd was able to absorb all the complicated facts and reduced them to a concise and comprehensive form which served Wallington well. His presentation, based on Lloyd's note and reinforced by the legal learning of Gates, brought the case to a successful conclusion.

A happy feature of that for Lloyd was that Wallington presented him with a 'red' bag. Junior counsel normally carry their papers and law reports in blue brocade bags, and senior counsel – QCs – in red brocade bags; but if a junior has rendered special service to a QC he can be given a red bag as a mark of distinction. That Lloyd should have obtained this in his very first case was probably without precedent and I was happy to have been responsible for it by giving him the brief.

It was in the Croydon case that I first encountered Sir Walter Monckton, KC, one of the great advocates of his day. He was a man who created an outstanding impression from his very first appearance. The public came to know him in later years as the trusted and special adviser of the Duke of Windsor; he negotiated the Duke's abdication terms and I believe that the Duke remained close to him until Monckton's death. In the Croydon case he made the very best of an immensely difficult task; so much so that there were times during the case when I had a real fear that he would persuade the judge to a wrong result. Happily the judge, Mr Justice Stable, himself engaged in his very first piece of litigation as a judge, arrived at the correct conclusion and gave a judgement against which the Council wisely decided not to appeal.

There was one controversial aspect where I still believe the judge erred. My client – the parent of a girl who had contracted typhoid – very wisely moved the rest of his family out of the infected area and took accommodation in the Langham Hotel, now rebuilt. The judge ruled that this was an unnecessary precaution and would not allow him the expenses involved. I believe that today, with a greater knowledge of the ferocity of such epidemics, a judge might well arrive at a different conclusion.

The preliminaries to the case had some interesting aspects. When it was clear that the plaintiffs would lack sufficient resources to conduct the case without financial risk, I made an application which in its impertinence must have been both novel and without precedent. I asked if I might meet the Croydon Corporation and invite them to finance my client in his daughter's case against them. I was treated with great courtesy and invited to a meeting of the committee concerned. They listened attentively to my request, which was based on the argument that it was imperative that the issue should be determined and that it might only be possible to determine it if funds were made available. I had the satisfaction at least of causing them to debate the matter for a good half-hour before they decided – and I can make no complaint – that it was not really their function to finance attacks on them.

For some years after I qualified, I used to progress to the Commercial Road in London where Jim Gower, Dennis Lloyd and I had set up a sort of legal clinic, where we saw impecunious clients free of charge. The three of us would sit from 6.30 p.m. every Tuesday evening, often till past midnight, when twenty or thirty people would come through seeking advice. This was before the Legal Aid scheme came into existence, and we encountered every kind of oddity and a great number of human tragedies.

The major tragedy one met was old people afraid of losing their accommodation. Old ladies would come in, who were living in garrets or attics, and beg to be reassured that they could not be turned out. Owing to the operation of the Rent Restriction Act – one of the most benevolent pieces of legislation ever passed and most hated by landlords – it was nearly always the case that they could not be evicted; but the extent to which they required reassurance was touching. They needed to be told with absolute certainty that they could stay in their garrets, to which they could hardly totter up the stairs, and that they could continue to live there so long as they were able to maintain themselves. Very often, as is well known, they were found dead in those garrets, having managed to maintain themselves there to the end against all the odds.

Most of the cases we had to deal with were cases of landlord and tenant, of people who had differences with their landlords. The next bulk of the cases was matrimonial, and here one noticed a strange infection developing. People would come along and say, 'I want a divorce.' And one of us would ask, 'Well, why do you want a divorce?' 'Well, because I'm tired of him' or 'I'm tired of her.' 'Oughtn't you to go on trying?' we would suggest. Then they would say, 'But Mr X was here last week and you advised him that he could get a divorce. Why can't I have one?' Whereupon you tried to explain to them that common sense decreed that if they found one wife or one husband unsatisfactory, they would not find the alternative much better. However, whether or not they succeeded in persuading us to help them obtain a divorce really depended on their persistence, not upon the hostility they displayed to their spouse.

We discovered after a while that there was one very real difficulty, which was that some expenditure was necessary to get a divorce in the days before Legal Aid; the average charge for a solicitor – provided it was an undefended divorce – was then £50 or £60, which was of course a fortune to a great many people. Jim Gower and I conferred one day and said: why don't we recommend that they try to get a divorce by an appearance in person? And we decided to experiment. A case came along who seemed reasonably articulate. We helped him to fill in the forms, he took them to the High Court, paid the fees, and in due course the case came into the list.

I was not present at the hearing, but Jim Gower went along to see what would happen. And he told me that what did happen was as one might have expected. When the case was called, the petitioner, having heard his name, screwed up enough courage to rise and repeat the formula that we had taught him: 'My Lord, I am a petitioner appearing in person.' He stuttered these words and was unable to say a word more. The judge was none other than the self-same Wallington to whom I have alluded in my Croydon typhoid case. He was not unkindly, as he almost immediately demonstrated, but his manner was a grave and formidable one, not specially designed to encourage a nervous litigant making his first forensic appearance.

He said to him, 'Mr X, if you are a petitioner in person, would you be so kind as to outline the circumstances in which you wish to divorce?' This was completely beyond him. He stood there mouth open for five or ten minutes, until ultimately the judge, unable to assist him, turned to the busiest junior of the day, who was sitting in front of him with a stack of briefs all healthily marked 15 guineas – the fee a counsel then charged – and said, 'Mr So-and-So, would you be kind enough to assist this petitioner?' Mr So-and-So showed every reluctance. He began to see the end of his busy practice if every petitioner in person was encouraged. Nevertheless he had no choice. So he took the petitioner outside, heard all the facts from him, came in, dealt with the case on his behalf in five minutes, and our client appeared triumphant and glowing with victory. This was again an illustration of a quirk of human behaviour: a desire for getting something when there are no grounds for it, for the simple reason that other people are getting it.

We maintained our legal aid practice – if I may call it that – for three or four years. We would travel down on the Tuesday, we would interview our clients, and then we would go to a small Jewish sandwich bar across the road and eat the most delicious fresh salt-beef sandwiches with pickled cucumber. We took a secretary with us and we used to dictate letters by the score and provided a service for nothing that is now costing the nation millions of pounds. But things have changed, since today everyone regards it as their right to have such service, whereas we retained the discretion to turn away any unworthy claimant whom we did not think ought to receive assistance or who we felt quite sure could pay for it.

In another case, long before the immigration problem existed in this country, it emerged that some coloured people had purchased a house and were slowly terrorising the tenants into leaving, so that they could let it off to their friends at much higher rent. In this particular case, the landlords concerned (and I want to make it clear that the worst landlords I have met have not been coloured but pure Europeans) had not only broken down the door but had also beaten up the tenant and done some violence to his wife. I was asked what I thought they should do; whether it was sensible to obtain a Police Court summons. I decided that the best way to hurt these people and also to safeguard the tenant was to harm their pockets. So I issued some County Court proceedings and we appeared before a Judge Hargreave, who had the special quality of being stone deaf. This was a great advantage because he had a hearing machine in front of him which he could switch off at will. This he switched off whenever counsel came to make his closing address. He read the case, obviously took a view, and said to me, 'I see that you are only paying fees that will enable me to give £50 damages, Mr Goodman. Would it not be wise – I am not prejudging the case – to double that?' I saw which way the wind was blowing and promptly reached into my pocket and paid the additional fees enabling £100 damages to be awarded.

We then called the policeman who had gone to the scene when the original incident took place. He gave the evidence, the tenants gave their evidence, and the landlord appeared, very cleanly and scrupulously dressed, obviously trying to give the appearance of total innocence and looking as if butter would not melt in his mouth. Happily, he had a countenance so instinctively villainous that no one would have been deceived by any form of get-up he might have used. In the event the judge, as I anticipated, awarded £100 damages and I returned with the articled clerk who had accompanied me. The articled clerk looked round and said, 'We are being chased by black men!' 'Oh,' I said, 'we must fight to the death!' But the purpose of their approach was not by any means hostile. 'Don't mind us,' they said, 'but would you appear for us in a case we have tomorrow?' I excused myself gently and went on my way.

It was about this period in my life that I first became conscious of a conflict between those activities which one enjoyed, either for themselves or because of a sense of virtue, and other activities which one needed to do to keep alive, i.e. to earn money from them. In the course of a long professional life there are certain matters that are bound to stand out in one's recollection. They are by no means the most important – viewed from the outside – or indeed the most profitable. In my case I find the things I remember best are those from which I derived no profit at all or may indeed have suffered a financial detriment. This is an eccentricity in my character that has frequently caused comment and unhappiness among my partners. It is also difficult to make people believe that it can be a sincere expression of my intentions, but *tant pis*. If something interests me I find it irresistible to do it and I consider the financial implications afterwards – sometimes with deep regrets and a few tears.

One such episode is the story of Margaret Passer – alas a victim of the Nazis – who died, I have reason to believe, from want of care and nourishment in German-occupied Prague. It is not a particularly important story, although a tragic one.

Some two years before the outbreak of the Second World War, I spent a weekend with my friends George and Milly Milsted, who had an exceptionally attractive Czech guest: a young woman in her early thirties, recently divorced and childless, and – as I then believed – miserable on that account. It turned out to be otherwise. She had an expression of sadness and indeed gloom which I later discovered arose from a deep and irremovable sense of impending disaster – in the result, fully justified. I struck up quite a close friendship with her and occasionally we would take trips together, sometimes with and sometimes without the Milsteds, to various parts of Sussex.

On the first few occasions that I met her she remained friendly but aloof, but suddenly when we were walking together over the Downs one evening something seemed to be released and she burst out with her real concerns. She started by telling me how immensely devoted she was to George Milsted – as indeed everyone who knew him must have been. She saw in him the very antithesis of everything she disliked in pre-war Europe: simple, candid, honourable, fair-minded; he revived for her a quality of humanity in which she had ceased to believe. It was on this occasion that she told me she was half Jewish – her mother. Her reason for this revelation was to enable her to express criticism of the bellicose views I had been expounding at dinner about the British and French attitude towards Hitler and the fact that he had been allowed to go so far without effective intervention. She thought that such an attitude coming from someone Jewish was unwise. 'It is not right,' she said, 'for anyone Jewish to speak like this, because if there is a war it will be blamed on the Jews.' I scouted this with some indignation. 'I am afraid it is a risk that right-minded people must take. Anyone who believes that a war has been precipitated by the Jews would be deranged or unbelievably biased, but it would be monstrous timidity if Jews at least did not express their bitter hatred of Hitler and the hope for his early death.'

It is difficult now to sense the resentment that anyone Jewish had in the immediate pre-war period about Hitler and his enormities. There are maniacs or villains who today deny the fact of the Holocaust, in the face of the incontrovertible evidence that appeared in photographs, films and television of the heaped skeletons and corpses. We had seen none of this prior to the war. The concentration camps had not yet been liberated, but the spectacle of respectable Jewish citizens being compelled to wash windows on their knees in the Unter den Linden in Berlin and the other sickening humiliations imposed on Jews of the utmost distinction, including Einstein and Freud and hundreds of others, first struck a note of incredulity and then a note of passionate horror.

Lacking any heroic qualities I demurred, as I have said earlier, from joining the Republican side in the Spanish Civil War. I did not hesitate for one moment, notwithstanding a healthy and commendable streak of cowardice, to enlist shortly before the outbreak of war in the battle against Hitler and his evil regime.

My slight impatience with Margaret was a passing matter. She told me of her great apprehension: of her future in Czechoslovakia in view of her Jewish blood. It was an apprehension, alas, all too fully confirmed by what I learnt much later of subsequent events. Her purpose in talking to me was to ask whether I would keep and safeguard a small collection of jewellery that she had brought with her on this trip and which to leave safely in England was her motive in coming. I told her that I thought this would be a heavy responsibility and that she would be better advised to open an account in some Joint Stock Bank and leave the jewellery in whatever branch she selected. But for some reason – due, I think, to an inbred suspicion of institutions that I have noticed among citizens of anti-Semitic societies – she preferred to leave her jewellery with someone she trusted. At the age of twenty-four I found it flattering that she should select me for the role. Shortly before she left to return to Czechoslovakia, she handed the jewellery to me. I knew nothing whatever of jewellery but they appeared to be handsome pieces. I listed them and gave her a receipt and then deposited them in my own bank.

For the short period before war broke out I received an occasional, but always very discreetly worded, letter assuring me of her good health and enquiring about mine. I replied – deliberately making no reference to the jewellery. The last letter was some months before the outbreak of the war. Hitler had entered Prague in 1939 and from that moment onwards I received no further letters. When war broke out, I disappeared into the army and for the next six years had no time to give much thought to the jewellery, although I frequently thought about its owner.

On my return to practice I wrote to Czechoslovakia on two occasions. One of my letters was returned and I had no reply to the other. I then enquired of the Czech Embassy. At first the enquiries were fruitless but later a message came through that Margaret Passer was dead. I found out only afterwards that it was, as I have said, due to neglect and privation.

Subsequently I received a letter from someone claiming to be her successor in Czech law and in consequence entitled to any property she might have left. She had not mentioned his name to me and I requested that he should produce some credentials. Almost at that moment a second letter arrived from a lawyer in America stating that he represented her cousin, and it was my recollection that she had expressed the wish that this cousin should receive the jewellery if anything happened to her. I had a very difficult task in deciding to whom to hand it over. The

American lawyer visited London, satisfied me of his bona fides and that of his client and I restored the property to him on his producing a letter of authority from the cousin, together with photographs and certain other documents of identity.

This story remains in my memory, not because of any virtue in my participation, not because I displayed any particular skill, not even because I had indeed exercised appropriate caution in seeking out the beneficiary. I was confident that I was handing the jewellery over to the right person; no complaints have been received from anyone else, and I have never heard another word in the matter. But it is a recollection that I cherish because I had formed a regard and affection for the poor lady and was able in a small way to bring her some comfort at the time of her deepest anxieties. I retain a vivid memory of a very good woman.

3

War Without Violence

IN JULY OF 1939 I enlisted in the Territorial Army. It was clear, as it had been clear for a considerable period, that a war with Germany was inevitable. The Goodmans are not fighting stock; we had no military tradition, and there is no record of any ancestor who ever raised a weapon against another human being. I was much influenced in this decision by my senior partner, Roy Kisch, who had served with distinction in the First World War and who had retained associations with Territorial and other military units. He took the view that it was ignominious for a young man – and particularly one who was Jewish – not to seek to participate in the battle at the earliest opportunity. He conveyed the impression that the outcome of the war largely depended on my decision to enlist.

I was, in fact, not slow to follow his advice, although I rather doubted whether my own contribution to the war would prove conclusive. But anyone Jewish had such a burning resentment towards Hitler and the Nazis, vigorously supported in my case by a hatred of Fascism, that it would have been poor form indeed had I lost any time in offering my feeble services.

Devoid personally of any association with the army, navy or air force, or even with the Boy Scouts, I set off to find some suitable organisation which could make use of me. I had no special heroic visions. I saw myself rather in the role of the wives of the early settlers in America, who stood by their husbands at the stockades reloading the guns as the Indians attacked. This appeared to be an ideal role for me, if only I could find some Indians. In any event, I conferred with Jim Gower. He took the same view as I did: that something needed to be done but perhaps not too much. Jim Gower and I had been friends since we were both sixteen. We had very similar political and social views. I could best describe it as a sort of conventional unorthodoxy. We did not like to make exhibitions

47

of ourselves by rebellious declarations, but in our hearts and minds we were instinctive rebels against a great many entrenched beliefs. We have, I hope, both remained so throughout what has now become our long lives. I have not detected any significant change in Jim Gower's character in the many years I have known him. I trust he would say the same of me.

We decided to make a joint approach to any military unit that might be willing to take us, in the unspoken belief that it would be a foolish unit that rejected such riches. Devoid of any training, however, we were wise enough to recognise that it would require a high degree of perception on the part of any military commander to understand the potential that was in us; certainly as a pair Jim Gower and I approached the coming Armageddon in a light-hearted and possibly even a frivolous manner.

Before we set off on our quest we were joined by a third musketeer in the person of Dennis Lloyd – equally bereft of military training. Dennis was of more serious material. He had never regarded life as much of a joke. Of the three of us he probably had the best mind, but he had been held back, I think, by an innate caution and some pessimism – a belief that things would not necessarily go right. He, too, strongly shared our view that heroics would be in the worst of taste. Nevertheless, all three of us had a sincere and determined desire to serve.

Our enquiries produced depressing information. Wherever we asked it was clear that nobody wanted any volunteers for National Service. All the established military, naval or air-force units were full; everyone was 'rushing to the colours'. We had almost resigned ourselves to the humiliating recognition that we were useless as warriors or even as camp-followers when word reached Gower that a new army unit was being formed at Enfield in North London, under the command of Britain's most distinguished and flamboyant archaeologist, one Mortimer Wheeler, later Sir Mortimer Wheeler, weighed down with military, civic and educational honours.

The three of us trekked off to Enfield and joined a line of middle-class youths, whom we identified as schoolteachers or bank and insurance employees, all the nicest elements of the middle classes: well educated, well disciplined, without pretension or riches, and destined to become absolutely first-class soldiers. All of them, like ourselves, were seeking to find something to join in their determination not to be late for the great clash.

We joined the queue and after a short wait I found myself facing Mortimer Wheeler and the man whom I later discovered was to become the Adjutant, both in civilian clothes. The interview was very short. Mortimer Wheeler struck me as a grotesque figure. I cannot really do

him justice, and anyone who wants a fair assessment of him should read
Jacquetta Hawkes's biography, which is one of profound admiration
tempered with some criticism. My feeling towards him, based on associations in the army of quite a lengthy period, was the reverse. It was
nothing but critical, and I realise that since he did me no harm my
judgement was anything but fair. But he seemed to me a posturing,
preening, burlesque of a soldier, attired in the smartest of riding breeches,
although there was not a horse within miles, wearing shining riding-boots
which he forced his unfortunate batman – why he had a batman I never
discovered – to polish. On the whole he was not a figure I admired, but
he was certainly a brilliant archaeologist. As people who remember *Animal,
Vegetable or Mineral* will know, he also had an extraordinary knowledge
that distinguished him from every other poor wretch who was unwise
enough to feature with him on the programme and which enabled him to
identify any object that appeared. Where others would say that some
unidentifiable lump was a primitive Indian weapon, he would immediately
discern that it was a Hittite hot-water bottle. The programme became a
public favourite, as indeed he did.

The formalities connected with our enlistment were brief and uncomplicated. We filled in some forms indicating that we were loyal British
subjects and, slightly more sinister, indicating to whom communications
should be addressed when we fell in battle. I do not think we took any
form of oath and, subject only to a medical examination, we were
more than three-quarters of the way to becoming soldiers. The medical
examination was perfunctory. It consisted of the shortest interrogation.
We were asked if we were fit and well, to which all three of us replied
emphatically that indeed we were. My later experiences with the young
doctor concerned confirmed a firm belief that it was wise to ask us how
we were since he was unlikely to have any other means of finding out.
So along with some three hundred others, we became members of the
48th Light Anti-Aircraft Battery, one of three batteries constituting the
42nd Light Anti-Aircraft Regiment.

At that time, and for some while afterwards, we had not the least idea
of what we were intended to do. A clue, of course, was to be found in
our title. It was unlikely that we would use tanks in a battle with enemy
aircraft. Obviously we were intended to use some sort of artillery, but we
discovered that we possessed little more than some antique Lewis guns
(a light machine-gun). Later, as time progressed, we were issued with a
couple of twin Vickers guns firing a belt of two-pounder shells. These
were much more scientific and elaborate than any others we had, since
they were coupled with a 'predictor' which was used to sight the target
plane before firing the gun. However, it was recognised early on that the

likelihood of my becoming a proficient gunner was slender, and I ended up deputed to more pacific but no less useful duties.

My experience in the unit confirmed my first impression: that it would have been difficult to meet a nicer, more co-operative, more generous collection of men than those who had enlisted at Enfield. Almost without exception, they had as little military training as the three of us. Like myself, most of them had been at schools where there were no OTCs, or they had failed or declined to qualify for 'Cert A', which was the requirement for an immediate commission. I had the slightest edge on them – very short-lived – that my own school had had what was called a battalion where we paraded once a week during summer months and practised stumbling military movements with wooden weapons. Additionally, my school had a rifle range where I had become a proficient shot with a .22, so that woe betide any German who might approach within fifty yards of me when equipped with such a weapon – which I never was. However, with the wooden rifles I had learnt the conventional military positions. I could slope arms, present arms, shoulder arms, order arms and generally manipulate the light wooden rifle with the skill of a juggler. I found to my distress, however, that my obsolete talents in this direction could not be put into effect with a full-weight army rifle, but I at least had some of the rudiments which the others lacked.

After enlisting it was an anticlimax to be told that we could return home until summoned. We had a vague notion that we should have been rushed to the coast to repel an immediate German invasion. We were not, in fact, sent for until a few days after 3 September 1939 – the day war broke out. On arrival we were directed to a drill hall where we were to sleep, spending the rest of the day in various places receiving military training that was not particularly taxing and turned out, of course, to be totally useless for the rest of the war. The drill hall lacked everything except a floor. Each member of the unit was issued with a palliasse on which to sleep, with blankets and a pillow. Fortunately – and it was a mark of the quality of my colleagues that they had no resentment or jealousy – I had, urged by my loving mother, brought with me a collapsible camp-bed, some specially soft blankets and a mattress to go with them. Hence at no time and at no place between September 1939 and November 1945, when I was released from the army, did I sleep in any discomfort. On the first night, and for the fortnight or so while we were in the drill hall, I set up my bed, oblivious of the difficulty that my colleagues were having on their palliasses. I did feel a slight compunction about Jim Gower and Dennis Lloyd, but there was nothing I could do for them except to offer them my army blankets – an offer which was contemptuously rejected.

When we awoke on the first morning, there was one very disconcerting discovery: that my assessment of every member of the battery as a responsible middle-class youth was wrong in one particular case. Sadly, Mortimer Wheeler had contrived to enlist a thorn in our flesh. Formerly a private in a regular army regiment but, as we later discovered, dishonourably discharged, Gunner Particle, as I shall call him, was the most debauched and depraved human being that I had encountered up to then: I had not yet moved among the wealthier classes. This young man was of limited intellect but very great cunning. We found on awakening that he had cleaned out the entire battery of everyone's personal possessions. My watch had gone, my wallet had gone, my change had gone, my cigarette case had gone, my fountain pen had gone, but a similar discovery was made by everyone else in the drill hall. Cries of rage filled the air and an immediate suspicion was directed at this villain. His cunning had served him well. There was no sign of any of the missing possessions and no one could remember even the most stealthy approach during the night. He remained under suspicion, affecting an outraged innocence that any accusation should be levelled against such a worthy soul.

He stayed with us for many months and the story of his exploits in that time would make a chapter in themselves. He continued to steal anything he could and he invented the most preposterous excuses for borrowing money. He had obviously singled me out as a soft touch. On the second day of the war, wearing his pitiful expression, which we came to know well, he approached me with a story that on that very day he was going to get married. Unfortunately he lacked the fare to get to the church and was loath to disappoint his bride. I was intrigued. I pointed out to him severely that a man who did not have the fare to the church could not be regarded as a very suitable husband. It seemed to me, as I said to him, extremely improvident to contemplate a lifelong association with such meagre resources, but he assured me he was deeply in love with the young woman, adding for a makeweight that she was pregnant. I found the appeal irresistible and gave him a ten-shilling note. When the next day I asked for a report of the wedding, it was clear that this was not a welcome enquiry. From time to time he repeated his approaches on different pretexts. On one occasion he appeared carrying a flower pot in which remained a wisp of a carnation, in order to borrow half-a-crown from me to attend his grandmother's funeral. I provided him with diminishing sums, finally down to a single shilling, and then declined any further bounty.

Eventually it seemed entirely appropriate, in view of the antisocial nature of Particle's behaviour, to make use of a newly promulgated Army Council Instruction whereby a command psychiatrist could, in cases of such utterly useless personnel, recommend their discharge from the army. We ascertained where the nearest psychiatrist was located and wrote him a lengthy letter reporting on Particle's behaviour. Particle, mounted on a bicycle, was supplied with the letter carefully sealed and we sent him off with the high hope that relief from Particle was nigh. He returned on the bicycle later, suspiciously triumphant and bearing a letter from the command psychiatrist. When we opened it the letter read something to this effect: 'I can find nothing wrong with this man that has not been induced by the exceptionally cruel and unsympathetic treatment he has received from his unit. As an instance, I understand that when he announced the recent bereavement of two relatives the news was greeted with laughter and ridicule. I am not prepared to recommend this man for discharge.' My faith in psychiatry was largely shaped from that moment and has only been partially reinstated in recent years by acquaintance with some remarkable psychiatrists. But we were left with Particle.

In the end – after a further few weeks of constant trouble – I found a solution. Across the road was a gunpowder factory. I remarked to Particle when he came to see me on one of his usual borrowing quests, 'Particle, have you ever considered more remunerative employment?' He looked puzzled. 'Across the road, Particle,' I said, 'there is a gunpowder factory. How much are you paid?' He told me his pay was a few shillings a week, but, as he pointed out, he was under stoppages of pay for various crimes that would have prevented him from receiving anything for several hundreds of years. 'You do know,' I said, 'that at the gunpowder factory they are paid a minimum of £4 a week for quite short hours.' He looked at me and I looked fixedly at him. No further words were spoken. The next day Lance-Bombardier Particle had disappeared, absent without leave; in due course, after a sufficient interval, deserted. He had taken employment in the gunpowder factory. We saw him almost daily, strolling nonchalantly in civilian clothes on the other side of the road. He knew that he was immune from arrest so far as we were concerned. The idea of retrieving him was our greatest horror. I have no doubt that he went on to become an industrial tycoon, but wherever he may be, if he is still anywhere, I wish him well. He was certainly one of the most interesting encounters of my army career.

It was at the beginning of the war that I totally forswore alcohol. So far as drink was concerned, I had been brought up in a relatively conventional Jewish atmosphere, but an Anglicised Jewish atmosphere where drink was very much at a discount. I never encountered the habit or observed people overindulging in it until I was well into my adolescence.

In my own home to be served a drink was a rarity. No one hankered after it and no one asked for it. My mother, a housewife of astonishing skill, notwithstanding that she had minimal time for that pursuit, used to make an enormous vat of cherry brandy once a year. At least it was her notion of what cherry brandy was; it was no one else's notion. A huge number of cherries were cooked in a vast pan, and when they were cold and congealing a quantity of pure spirit was added to them. At the end of the day an undrinkable mixture, with a tang of cherries and the burning sensation of the spirit, would evolve.

I avoided drinking this potion if it was humanly possible. But every so often, in deference to my dear mother, I would take a sip or two. Oddly enough my father delighted in it. Whether it enabled him to gratify an unrequited lust for alcohol which had been denied to him throughout his married life, I never knew. Certainly on the rare occasion when I saw him eating out of the house there was no alcohol, but this was because the meals that he took were in an elevated sort of teashop, Slater's or Heal's, which in those days had chains around London.

Anyway, nothing much happened during the first year of the war and in consequence an enormous amount of drinking went on in the unit at night. Although I got no particular enjoyment from alcohol, there was a social need to join in. In the result I found myself waking up in the morning with severe headaches. One morning I woke up in a particularly sorry and woebegone condition and took a firm resolve that while I was not keen on being killed by Hitler in the course of my military activities (if so lofty a name can be given to my army posturing), I was even more reluctant to be killed by the brewers. Accordingly that evening I announced that I had become teetotal. This caused astonishment, although not profound astonishment, as remarks had already been made about the relative conservatism of my intake. However, it was accepted in good part by my colleagues. I continued to provide my round when the time came, but I sipped tonic water while it lasted and then went over to tomato juice or whatever was available. Tonic water vanished quite early in the war, the reason being that it contained a quantity of quinine, which was required for medicinal purposes. It was not until quite late – in the 1950s – that tonic water appeared again on the market, a piece of information I am happy to provide quite gratuitously.

The battery started its military activities under something of a cloud, although it was guilt by association. A sister battery had the distinction of shooting the first plane brought down over England. Unhappily it was British. Although it was not our fault, and we always stoutly maintained that such idiocy could only have been perpetrated by another battery, nevertheless we were included in the condemnations that required the entire regiment to have further and intensive training in aircraft identification. We spent hours learning to tell the difference – using models –

between a Heinkel and a Spitfire and between a Messerschmitt and a Hurricane. In a very short space of time the battery became expert not only in identification but also in handling the different types of gun with which we were issued. I should have been surprised if any battery in the country showed greater proficiency than our own.

It was, of course, a discouragement that our guns had no range that was remotely relevant for the subsequent Blitz, in which we were fully engaged. The maximum range of our Bofors guns was 3,000 feet. It was extremely rare for any attacking planes over London to come below 10,000 feet except on the isolated occasions when they indulged in dive-bombing – something which the Germans, no doubt advised of the exceptional skills of the 48th Light Anti-Aircraft Battery, carefully avoided. However, this does not affect my belief that the battery would have had a very respectable score of enemy planes if the craven German pilots had not been wise enough to remain at a safe distance.

When it became clear to those in charge, namely Major Wheeler, that my contribution, although considerable in bulk, would be most valuable on account of brain rather than brawn, I was transferred to the battery office where I found a state of total confusion. A multitude of army forms were being filled in by a regular regimental sergeant-major who had been attached to the battery to instruct us in army administration. He knew precisely nothing about anything but had a genius for pretending otherwise. If asked, for instance, how one procured greatcoats, he would reply: 'Submit army form 212f to divisional headquarters at Warrington.' When the army form had been obtained with great difficulty it was found to be a return for soldiers infected by diphtheria during the Crimean War. In a very short time further reference to this gentleman mercifully ceased and, promoted from gunner to lance-bombardier, I found myself in complete charge of the battery office. This was particularly useful at my home since my mother was unable to distinguish between a bombardier and a brigadier. Then again within days I was made a full bombardier (the artillery equivalent of a corporal) and in no time after that I was made a sergeant. It must have been one of the most rapid promotions in army history – like Napoleon but at a slightly lower level. I remained frozen at sergeant level for at least three weeks, when I was the beneficiary of another's misfortune.

The battery quartermaster-sergeant was a veteran of the First World War. Unhappily he was discovered to be purloining petrol for use in his own car. Everyone who had a car, including myself, was similarly engaged, but he was the one culprit to be caught. As Wheeler loved army formality, he could not resist the opportunity of a full-scale court martial to deal with this atrocious crime. The poor wretch was put under open arrest and was to be seen wandering forlornly around the yard. At the court martial he was found guilty, but the decision was not to shoot him. He was reduced to the rank of sergeant and posted to another battery, thereby creating a vacancy for battery quartermaster-sergeant to which I was immediately promoted. This had the satisfactory outcome that my pay, upon which at that time I was almost totally dependent, was substantially increased and I was able to lead the life of Riley.

The post of quartermaster-sergeant carried with it a considerable extension of duty and in consequence an immense increase in influence. Anybody who wanted anything material sought my help: from the man who had lost his steel helmet or respirator, to the man who needed an invalid diet or the use of a motor car or the use of some army transport, or indeed almost anything else. A more taxing responsibility was to arrange for the reception of the weapons and their safeguarding. It is impossible to assemble 350 men without having a small number totally irresponsible and one or two irresponsible to a point of lunacy. Thus on one occasion, when a Bofors belt was being loaded with two-pounder shells, I discovered the bombardier in charge making use of a small sledge-hammer to hit the shells on their heads so as to force them into the belt. That a disaster did not ensue was a miracle.

A special duty that inevitably fell on my shoulders was to make any arrangements that needed to be made for the Jewish personnel in the battery. They were not an overwhelming number. Apart from my dear friend Dennis Lloyd – a loyal but wholly unreligious Jew – there were only three. One of them, a short and unamiable second lieutenant, was strangely equivocal about being Jewish to the extent of having described himself in his enlistment papers as a Unitarian. This was, of course, a philosophical truth since the Jewish faith prescribes a single undivided deity, but when I queried the description with him, he justified it on the ground that, if captured by the Germans, it would have been unfortunate for them to have known that he was Jewish. This made sense except for his appearance, which would alas have left little doubt in their minds.

However, the remaining pair posed an occasional problem. One was a Sergeant Lazarus, of good, solid, middle-class Jewish stock, who in later years became a distinguished chartered surveyor and a leading member of his profession. The other was a Gunner Cohen who came, I think, from humbler origins, although with the Jewish community your social position is usually where you can contrive to place yourself.

My first doctrinal encounter was with Lazarus. He buttonholed me one morning to reproach me, as a Jew in charge of the battery's rations, with having provided nothing but bacon, or a substantial bacon element, in every breakfast. This had been a cause of satisfaction to me – to be able to claim that day after day the battery sat down to bacon and eggs, which I considered a masterpiece of provident provisioning. 'I have,' he complained, 'been breakfastless since I came to the battery.' I was moved and drove down to the NAAFI to enquire whether there was any breakfast food that did not involve the hated pig. 'We have,' said the manager, 'a nice line in kippers.' I was elated. Placing a continuing order for them, I returned to the battery with a large boxful to report this success to Lazarus, who gratifyingly expressed a great liking for kippers. All was well for some months until I encountered Lazarus in the courtyard of the elementary school, which was our headquarters, with a long face and an immediate grumble. 'I have,' he said, 'had nothing but kippers for breakfast for the last several months and I now hate the sight of them.' I rejoined at once. 'You are,' I said, 'an ungrateful wretch. I can do no more for you except to recommend porridge and toast!'

Gunner Cohen presented no dietetic problem – although I believe he was more pious than Lazarus. However, one day when the battery had left London and we were temporarily stationed in a field at Earls Barton, a few miles from Northampton, the gunner approached me. 'Q,' he said, 'what are you going to do for me tomorrow?' The reply presented no difficulty. 'I am going to do for you tomorrow exactly what I did for you today – nothing.' However, this did not satisfy him. 'Don't you know,' he said, 'that tomorrow is the Day of Atonement? I must in some way observe it.' It seemed clear to me that something needed to be done to provide him with facilities.

I travelled into Northampton and down the main street, looking on each side of the road for a dress shop. Shortly I alighted on one, called Molyneux Ltd. Under that caption in small letters it said: J. Rosenbloom, proprietor. Inside the shop I enquired if I might see the proprietor and an amiable-looking middle-aged man emerged. 'Might I venture to ask whether – as I believe – you and I are co-religionists?' I said. He immediately assented. I then explained the dilemma in that we had a Jewish private soldier who needed to be looked after for the Day of Atonement and we had no means of doing it. His response was warm and generous. 'I will come and collect him this evening, before the Kol Nidrei. He can join us at the pre-fast supper and come with us to the synagogue. We will keep him overnight; he can spend the day in the synagogue, break his fast with us afterwards and I will return him to you late in the evening.' To all of this I immediately assented, subject to obtaining the approval of our commanding officer, which I had not the slightest doubt would be forthcoming. The plan worked admirably, with a slight hiccup that Cohen was not in fact returned to us for a couple of extra days! I recently gave a lecture on 'The Advantages of Being Jewish', but whatever the shortcomings of that great race – and I prefer to leave others to dilate on them – the spirit of comradeship and mutual help is unequalled in any other community.

Before very long Major Wheeler, who like myself was set for rapid promotion but at a different level, was posted away to command the entire regiment. His successor was a colourful character, but colourful in a totally different way. He was a Major McWhatt: a regular officer from the Indian Army and on that score not in the least beloved by Wheeler who had a built-in resentment of regular officers, by the side of whom he obviously regarded his territorial status as inferior. McWhatt's career was short and chequered. He made himself well-liked in the battery: he was a genial character, not averse to alcohol and with an eye for the ladies which occasioned his absence on most evenings in some receptive home in Waltham Abbey.

I liked him very much and approved of the fact that he interfered very little with the running of the battery, except for the occasional odd eccentricity. For instance, in relation to Gunner Particle who at that stage still continued unchecked, McWhatt decided that the appropriate course was to give him some authority and responsibility. Particle had always claimed that he was trained as a cook. 'I shall put him in charge of the cookhouse,' declared McWhatt. This was near imbecility, and we protested that Sergeant Birch was already there and doing a very good job. 'Ah,' he said, 'but he is the sergeant cook! I will put Particle in charge of the orderlies.' So Particle was dispatched to the cookhouse. A few hours later, interested in what might be happening, I visited the cookhouse to find a strange scene. Twelve or fourteen orderlies were gathered together in a small group in a corner of the room muttering and casting murderous looks at Particle. Particle, all alone, was standing in front of an army cooking tub, cutting loaves of bread into slices and dropping them one by one into the boiling water in the tub. I approached Particle and asked him what he was doing. 'I am making a bread pudding,' he said. My knowledge of cookery is limited but it was clear to me that no bread pudding could ever eventuate from this process.

The uncomplicated Major McWhatt possessed one singular talent. I am told others possess it but I had never previously encountered it. He was capable of drinking a pint of beer from a glass while standing on his head, defying all the laws of gravity. He would demonstrate this talent when in sufficiently relaxed mood, i.e. when sufficiently lubricated by the same liquid. On one occasion during the first year of the war, a sergeant who had been employed in the film industry suggested to McWhatt that it would be a nice thing to have a film showing for the battery on a Sunday evening and that he could make the arrangements with the Regal

Cinema at Waltham Abbey. McWhatt agreed enthusiastically. The sergeant concerned made the arrangements and procured the loan of some popular Hollywood film.

The film showing was a great success and when it was over McWhatt invited those people who had been concerned with the arrangements to take tea in the Officers' Mess. The tea went merrily and when after a while stronger drink was substituted for tea McWhatt decided that this was an appropriate audience before whom to display his solitary talent. He stood on his head and consumed his pint of beer to loud applause. Unhappily, the wife of the organising sergeant, who was also present, decided that she would seek to emulate McWhatt's feat. She too stood on her head, although she was not successful in drinking the beer. Unfortunately, from the point of view of modesty, she was not suitably attired for this exercise. We had at that time in the battery a young and rather bumptious second lieutenant who decided, when the lady was most vulnerable, to permit himself a familiarity. This outraged her sergeant husband who proceeded to knock the young officer down. At this moment the battery captain, who was no friend of McWhatt's, decided to summon Colonel Wheeler from regimental headquarters to observe the scene of carnage. Wheeler arrived in a magically short space of time, as though he had been poised waiting for an opportunity. He observed the hideous scene and immediately placed McWhatt under open arrest, taking him back in his car to regimental headquarters, a house called Monkton.

We all dispersed to our various quarters but in the morning Jim Gower and I communed and decided, as we both had good cause to like McWhatt, that something ought to be done. I still possessed and ran a small Ford Prefect motor car. In this we drove up to Monkton and saw a forlorn Major McWhatt pacing about in the garden. We approached him to convey our sympathy, to which he replied in a mood of deep dejection that this was his ruin. He was convinced that Wheeler would have him court-martialled and cashiered. We sought to comfort him and I remember asking him whether as a regular soldier he did not have some powerful friend to whom he could appeal. The idea did not commend itself to him, but he did concede that he was a friend of the Major-General commanding the First Anti-Aircraft Division, to which the 42nd Light Anti-Aircraft Regiment belonged. Where, we asked, was it stationed. He told us that it was stationed in Knightsbridge.

Ignoring the spectacular impropriety of what we were doing, Jim Gower and I drove off to Knightsbridge and requested an interview with the General. This presented no difficulty as the General was coming out of the building as we were going in and, somewhat surprised to see two strange soldiers, asked what we wanted. We informed him that we had come to tell him unofficially that Major McWhatt, an officer in whom we believed he might be interested, was in considerable trouble and needed assistance. We added the innocent observation that his misfortune had been brought about by Colonel Wheeler. It was clear that the name provoked an immediate reaction. The effect on the General was absolutely electric. He strode from the building and leapt into his car and we heard him directing the driver to proceed immediately to Waltham Abbey.

We followed in my tiny Prefect but had no hope of keeping up with the General's car. However, pulling up a short distance from the entrance of Monkton, we had a most satisfying sight: Colonel Wheeler standing rigidly to attention by the entrance; Major McWhatt, bearing a suitcase, emerging from the entrance, accompanied by the General; the two climbing into the General's car and the car speeding off into the future. It was the last occasion we ever set eyes on McWhatt, although I had the satisfaction of reading in Army Orders some weeks later that he had been posted to another regiment on promotion to Lieutenant-Colonel.

After several months in Enfield the news came that the ambitious Wheeler was anxious to convert the battery into a mobile battery, designed to move from place to place. The members of the battery lacked nothing in patriotism but they were rational human beings. It seemed to them that a good place to remain and defend was their home area, where they could regularly visit their wives and families, and call in occasionally to have a square meal if they were hungry. At the same time they were deployed around buildings they knew, in the defence of which they had a very real interest. However, our mobile role did not arise until after the initial London Blitz, in which indeed we participated fully in the sense of being there, but futilely there since the opportunity to fire at an enemy plane was indeed rare. The Blitz has been fully, dramatically and accurately described by better pens than mine. The loss of life, the destruction of buildings, the general carnage would have been intolerable but for the prevailing courage and determination of the population of London. There was hardly a night for weeks that was not disturbed by the shriek of the siren announcing the imminent arrival of enemy planes. Nearly always the gunfire and the action would be in some area of London remote from us, so that one was not always conscious that anything was in fact happening; but quite often the enemy approached and frequently approached too close for comfort. Determined efforts were made to bomb the targets we were protecting. So far as I can recollect, no bomb fell square on them, but a great many fell around them. The most exhausting part of the whole activity was the loss of sleep. We were standing-to night after night for weeks on end and during the day the normal requirements of battery life needed to be fulfilled: the rations had to be procured;

ammunition replenished and the whole elaborate task of army administration continued with. It was an exhausting period, in its own way an
exhilarating one, but for a young man who had led a thoroughly pampered
life, in the sense of total protection from any kind of discomfort by a
determined mother, it was almost a welcome release.

What was heart-warming was that however intense the bombing at any
one time, it was impossible to discern any drop in morale. In fact at no
time during the war, however disastrously it appeared to be progressing,
did I ever perceive the slightest sign that anyone anywhere in the battery,
and later in other units in which I served, contemplated the possibility of
defeat. This unshakeable conviction was due to two factors: one, of course,
was Winston Churchill who exercised an influence, indeed a mesmerism,
over the entire country that was probably unique in British history. Oliver
Cromwell, who had comparable qualities, influenced only one section of
a divided country. Winston influenced and exalted an entire population
wherever it might have been. The second factor was a more subjective
one: it was the absolute detestation of the horrors and enormities that the
Germans had perpetrated. It was these two factors which combined to
make the country invincible, or at least sufficiently invincible to remain
on our feet until massive help arrived from the Russians and later the
Americans.

Shortly after the cessation of the first London Blitz, we finally became
a mobile battery. Packing up took place on a large scale and the Enfield
recruits, who constituted most of the battery, took fond farewells from
their wives, which were not too tearful because of the confident belief
that we would be back before long. The hideous truth was happily not
appreciated: that it would be only a relatively short period before the
battery was dispatched to a remote foreign area from which the majority
were never to return. But our travels about England were pleasant and
cheerful and we had an interesting Cook's Tour – Birmingham, Manchester, Wolverhampton, Carlisle. We had no military band to ride in
front of the train of forty or fifty vehicles pulling the guns and containing
the troops, supplies and ammunition. I still continued to exercise the
privilege of driving my own little Ford Prefect, which by that time had
got itself camouflaged on the officious direction of a transport officer. He
found it difficult – quite reasonably – to accept that a civilian vehicle
should be included in the convoy and could only allay his conscience by
making it look as army-like as could be contrived.

Our most spectacular adventure – apart from encountering a German
Blitz at many of our destinations – arose from the spirited temperament
of Colonel Wheeler. Our route to Carlisle – with the usual cavalcade of
vehicles and my Ford Prefect bringing up the rear – should of course

have been on the main roads, but Wheeler decided otherwise. It appeared to him to be more consistent with military valour to take a less secure route.

We were proceeding towards Penrith when I observed to my astonishment that the leading vehicles had turned left and were bumping along a steep mountain track. When five vehicles had gone thus far the entire procession stopped and remained stationary. Curiosity overcame me and I walked along the convoy to the track, which was just about the width of one vehicle and led up to a terrifying drop on the right-hand side. I edged my way along it until I found Wheeler – descended from his ancient Lancia which had been leading the company – engaged in an unseemly altercation with the driver of the leading lorry, an irreverent cockney who was refusing to go any further as the higher it went the narrower the track became.

'I am giving you an order to proceed,' said Wheeler angrily. 'I am sorry, Sir,' said the driver, 'but I am not going an inch further.' 'Why not?' barked Wheeler. 'Because I enlisted to fight Hitler, not to fall off mountains,' was the not unreasonable logic of the reply. At this point Wheeler emitted a snort, leapt into his car and drove up the hill, vanishing from sight and abandoning the entire battery to its fate. Others took charge and slowly the five vehicles that had made the partial ascent were manhandled back onto the road. It took several hours, in consequence of which we arrived at our destination, a camp in Carlisle, in the early hours of the morning.

My last days with the 48th Battery were sad and were indeed the harbingers of great tragedy. I was summoned by the officer then commanding, Alan Steele, to be told that some orders had come through for the battery to proceed overseas. He did not divulge the destination to anyone and I do not know whether he himself knew at that stage; but he was kind enough to ask me whether I wanted to accompany the battery since at that time a commission was imminent. I did not hesitate to declare my very fervent wish to go with the rest of them. Whereupon he told me that I would need medical clearance and he would arrange for me to see the MO. In the event I was sent off to a civilian doctor in Manchester.

He was a small, sharp-faced, alert Jewish doctor, who examined me carefully and then pronounced. 'I cannot pass you,' he said, 'for the major reason that you have asthma.' No doctor had ever identified asthma. I had never suffered any symptoms and I can only conclude that as I was then a very heavy smoker – a practice long since abandoned – he had heard wheezes in my chest, which he suspected to be asthma. I protested to him that my medical record would disprove his diagnosis, but he said,

'Additionally, you are very fat.' This was an assertion I could hardly challenge, although many months of army life had produced a much-reduced version of Goodman from the original enlistee. 'You would,' he said, 'be an encumbrance if your battery had to retreat.' I assured him that in the retreat he could rely on me to be in the forefront. But humour was not his strong suit and he flatly refused the reclassification that I sought. There is very little doubt that I owe my life to this man's erroneous diagnosis.

Some weeks later I saw the battery off at Manchester Station at midnight. I found the occasion a very moving one. Almost everyone in the battery was a friend and I had a disagreeable feeling that I was in some way betraying them by staying behind; a feeling I am happy to say that no one echoed since the reason was well known. I shook hands with Steele and the other officers, made a special farewell to the people with whom I was most intimate, and saw the train steam out. I was not then to know, or indeed for many months to learn, that the battery had sailed straight to Java, had landed only days or possibly even hours before the Japanese invasion, had engaged the enemy in an infantry role for which they had had no training, firing their Bofors guns over open sights, and were captured to a man. Of the entire battery of more than 300, I believe that less than sixty of the other ranks returned and only four or five of the officers, including, I am happy to say, Alan Steele, who died recently after a career as a literary printer of some distinction.

Shortly after their departure, my posting to an Officer Cadet Training Unit came through. I spent eight weeks in a training course of supreme uselessness, starting with a lecture by a regimental sergeant-major on mess etiquette – in the middle of the world's greatest war. I was particularly attentive to his instructions about the number of visiting cards we needed to leave when posted to a new garrison town and upon whom, from the commanding general onwards, they should be left. Not one of the officer cadets had any visiting cards and the notion of our perambulating about a garrison town scattering cards like confetti was one of the more comical moments of my army career.

I was sufficiently successful at the OCTU to be commissioned a second lieutenant in the Royal Army Ordnance Corps and was immediately posted to Southern Command headquarters. This was regarded as a plum posting. The reason, I discovered, was that my dear friend Jim Gower, who had received a direct commission by some freak of fortune, was already at Southern Command headquarters and had exercised an unwonted skill in wire-pulling to secure that I joined him.

My lengthy stay at Southern Command headquarters – where I remained for the rest of the war – was free from any real excitement.

The Ordnance Corps was certainly not the elite of the British army but we were saved from the contempt of the fighting units by the fact that they needed us desperately and were always in quest of our goodwill, since we had control of the multitude of stores, equipment and weapons of every kind.

The ordnance section of the command was located in a charming house – previously the home of the GOC Southern Command – called, incongruously, Government House. There we lived in considerable comfort. I established friendly relations with my fellow officers in the command, the bulk of whom were stationed at Wilton House, the splendid home of the Pembrokes. My fellow ordnance officers were unexciting, except for my friend Gower and a colourful George Duckham of Duckham Oil, who was eccentric to a degree that was positively charming. His method of washing his underclothes was to climb into a bath wearing them, and while there soaping them vigorously at every point he could reach and allowing them to dry on him when he emerged.

History to some extent repeated itself, since Gower and I had once again to save our commanding officer, one Brigadier Bacon, from disaster. The Brigadier was one of the so-called 'hungry forty': forty ordnance officers who had acquired senior rank and were eligible for the ultimate promotion – the major-general in command of the entire Ordnance Corps. There was, of course, only one such, so that thirty-nine of them were in hungry competition. Brigadier Bacon's principal pastime was to study the Army List to see how many of the other thirty-nine had passed on, met disaster or retired from the service. I think by the time I met him he was rated nine or ten. However, the current major-general, one Major-General Richards, was believed, and I think rightly believed, cordially to dislike Bacon and sought to achieve his downfall. On one occasion, he very nearly did.

I was the duty officer one evening at Command headquarters – I had now been promoted to captain, or possibly even major – when the telephone rang from an ordnance depot at Bridgwater, administered by us, saying that one of our junior officers was paying a visit of inspection; having been told that the depot was cumbered up with broken chairs and tables, he had immediately directed them to be destroyed in a bonfire. At that time there was a maniacal concern with salvage. The ultimate crime was to throw anything away, be it a matchbox, a piece of iron fencing or what you will. That good, serviceable timber should be destroyed by fire would have been regarded as a crime against the Holy Ghost.

I immediately countermanded the order, but too late. Word about the *auto-da-fé* had reached the town and indignant protests were already being made. I directed that the officer concerned should return at once and reported the situation to the Brigadier the next morning. That disaster had struck was shortly demonstrated by the arrival of a dispatch-rider from Major-General Richards at the War Office in London demanding an explanation for what he described as 'outrageous waste'. The message added that he had commanded a Colonel Finch – later to become a good friend and client – to conduct an immediate investigation on the spot and that the Colonel was on his way by train.

Bacon was reduced to a human jelly. 'I am,' he moaned to Gower and myself, 'a ruined man. Richards will have me. Undoubtedly there will be a court martial.' Jim and I conferred and proffered some advice. Major-General Richards, we pointed out, was a departmental officer and he had ordered an investigation by another departmental officer in Southern Command where his writ certainly did not run. We recommended that Bacon should communicate with the Major-General in charge of administration in the Command to report this situation. His morale, however, had been so shattered that he could not summon the resolution to do this. Whereupon I telephoned through to the Major-General, deferentially informed him that I was speaking on behalf of Brigadier Bacon, and advised him that Major-General Richards had sent a departmental ordnance officer into his Command to conduct an investigation. The response was most gratifying: a series of indignant barks. 'Major Goodman,' he said, 'I am giving you an order. You will ensure that this colonel is intercepted and ordered by me to return to London at once.' I had the satisfaction of contacting the railway traffic officer at Exeter to convey this message on the platform to Colonel Finch. The interception was successful.

I continued with my innocuous and passive activities until my release from the army in November 1945 with a farewell party at Salisbury. Shortly before my departure for London, however, I was pursued by a gallant doctor in the RAMC who was about to be court-martialled for amorous overtures to a WAAF to whom he had sent slightly demented messages and slightly obscene drawings depicting various degrees of corporal punishment. I undertook to defend this gentleman at his court martial, but it was postponed for some weeks – so that I was no longer in the army – and I continued his defence as a civilian lawyer. The story did little credit to the army. The poor wretch was sent off to a military psychiatric unit at Dumfries; received insulin treatment, which was an early version of electric-shock therapy, and when he was adjudged recovered was then put on trial at Aldershot. The only happy element was the outcome of the court martial.

At Aldershot I noticed sitting on a bench a slightly forlorn figure in WAAF uniform. Wholly improperly, I approached her and she admitted that she was the principal prosecution witness. I then asked her whether the doctor concerned had really behaved badly, to which she replied, 'He was a perfect gentleman, except for those letters.'

'Did you like him?'

'I liked him very much.'

'Do you still like him?'

'Indeed I do.'

'Would you like to give evidence for him?'

She readily assented. Thereupon, almost before the proceedings started – and courts martial have very little knowledge of proper legal procedures – I was able to interpose her as a witness, when she testified to the fact that Dr X had always behaved perfectly, had never made any kind of physical gesture or approach, and that the last thing in the world she wanted was to do him any injury. In the outcome I recommended Dr X to plead guilty and a very minor penalty was exacted, which was of no importance since he was returning to civilian practice and it did not involve – as he had feared – the possible forfeiture of the DSO that he had won gallantly at Arnhem.

My army adventures might give the impression that I was not conscious of the historic nature of the events that were unfolding around me. When I thought about them, or was reminded of them, I was indeed conscious, but the fact remains that the individual ant has very little notion of the grandeur of the antheap. I returned to civilian life never having heard a single shot fired in anger except for one adventure in quest of lifebelts that is probably still covered by the Official Secrets Act. My friend Jim Gower had been posted to the 21st Army Group, conducting an invasion some months before the end of the war, but despite the most strenuous efforts Bacon would not release me for overseas service for the simple reason, alas, that I was too useful to him. However, a war uneventful in martial terms was nevertheless replete with fascinating incidents and an opportunity for learning more about the human race than at any time before or later in my life.

4

Starting Again

WHEN I LEFT the army I had to set about repairing an interrupted career, but as always I was imbued with the same quiet confidence that earning a living would not be a particularly formidable task. Associated with an unshakeable and at times nearly suicidal lack of interest in amassing money, my anxieties on the material front were nil. My former partner – Roy Kisch – invited me to rejoin him and although, in retrospect, it might have been more advantageous to have looked elsewhere, I liked him very much and it was the line of least resistance.

Kisch and I reformed our partnership, this time in another tiny set of rooms at the same address, 6 Raymond Buildings, Gray's Inn. The office was up two steep flights of stone stairs and it comprised one general office, just large enough to hold our staff of six, plus one articled clerk, with a modest-sized room for Kisch – the senior partner – and a cubicle for me. There was a tiny hall and a loo confronting the entrance, which was a continuous source of embarrassment as one inevitably emerged as a prominent client was coming through the door. However, we settled in snugly and I was happy there for nearly four years.

So far as the financial aspects were concerned, I was fortunate to have some academic activities which added a mite to my professional income, which at the outset might have sustained one meal a day, i.e. a meal adequate for my not inconsiderable frame. Our practice was, of course, much depleted by the time we resumed it in early 1946. The arrangement was that again I was to become a salaried partner: my name would appear on the notepaper but I would receive a fixed income of £600 a year with no participation whatever in the profits. This was rather more than the going rate at the time and was in fact very generous, particularly since my senior partner guaranteed the sum to me whatever the partnership results.

But I needed and was gratified to secure an examinership for the Law Society's Final Examination, where I was appointed an examiner in a mixed bag of topics constituting one of the eight papers to be taken by the candidates. There were three examinations a year and the payment was at the rate of four shillings a paper. At each examination there were approximately 500 candidates, so that I was receiving a very welcome addition of about £300 a year. One particular candidate earned my undying affection. At each examination he would hand in a completely blank paper. I noticed his name three times a year during the several years I was examining. He was worth twelve shillings a year to me – unearned – and if he ever reads this book I would like him to know how grateful I am to him. There have been various explanations proffered, the least likely that he entertained some sort of affection for me. The most likely was that he was being maintained by trustees so long as he remained a Chekhovian student.

This was not the only source of additional funds which I procured while I was still struggling to achieve an adequate professional income. Almost immediately after the war I was invited by Cambridge University to accept a special lectureship in Roman–Dutch law, one of the two subjects in which I had specialised. The incumbent lecturer – Dr Oliver – had retired full of years and honours and there was some difficulty in finding a substitute for this highly specialised subject, which then had relevance only in South Africa and Ceylon.

I accepted the appointment, but on the basis that I could fit it in without much interference with my professional life. This was agreed and I was committed to give two lectures a week in the Cambridge Law Schools. It was a welcome invitation since I had always enjoyed keeping a toe in the academic world and indeed did so until it developed into an entire foot on my becoming the Master of University College, Oxford.

The additional income from Cambridge was especially welcome. I am too indolent to go in quest of my income tax returns, but it was certainly not less than an additional £7 a week, from which, however, had to be deducted travelling expenses. To dovetail this activity into my solicitor's life had the unhappy consequence that I was probably the most hated lecturer in the whole of academia. I left London on a train just before 8 a.m., arriving at Cambridge at 9 a.m. A taxi would race me to the Law Schools where I was due to deliver my lecture at five minutes past nine – the prescribed time for Cambridge lectures. The same taxi delivered me back to the station just after 10 a.m. so that I was back in London well before noon to perform my duties of the day. The loss of time was minimal; but the unfortunate students, anxious to learn what little I had to teach them – and so far as Roman–Dutch law was concerned, this is not false modesty – had to get out of their beds much earlier than they would have wished. What was even more hateful to them was that my second lecture of the week (the first was on a Wednesday) was on a Saturday morning – a day which was normally dedicated to indolence or dissipation. It is a mystery to me that I escaped assassination.

The staff at Kisch's was a splendidly amiable one: Margaret Haines, a first-class secretary who worked for everybody; Miss Brinkworth, a benevolent and kindly elderly spinster who long-sufferingly worked for Kisch – whose eccentricities were neutralised to a large extent by a genuine good nature; and within a short while Margaret Smith, who had worked for me as an ATS secretary in Southern Command and whose secretarial and temperamental qualities were beyond praise. Her principal value – as I now realise – was her failure to gratify my vanity in any way. I have always regarded myself somewhat complacently as being rather funny and it was healthy to observe the steely indifference with which Miss Smith received my anecdotal humour. It was a constant battle between us. My vain hope was that one day her slightly contemptuous expression and curl of the lip might break into the faintest smile at one of my better jokes. This never happened. It was immensely salutary for me: sycophants laugh immediately the joke is signalled and long before it is delivered. Miss Smith was a magnificent secretary and served me loyally and indeed affectionately. The affection was especially manifested when I was taken ill and needed a gall-bladder operation which kept me in hospital for many weeks. I had certainly become affectionately disposed towards my nurse – inevitable, I believe. Miss Smith, sensing danger, descended upon the hospital, supervised the packing of my bags and evacuated me to my home, all without a word being spoken.

We were joined a little later by a former sergeant from Southern Command, Frank Usher. At Southern Command headquarters I had formed a close link with Usher because we both played cricket whenever the opportunity arose. The difference was that Usher was an absolutely first-class cricketer, who had had a trial as a medium-pace bowler for Middlesex, whereas my principal asset as a cricketer was a personal bulk that made it impossible for the bowler to see the wicket when I was batting. In the result I had a value as an opening bat that was enhanced by the fact that – being usually the senior rank playing – appeals for lbw. were unlikely to be successful.

Usher rendered me one great service. When, about four years after rejoining Kisch, I joined a larger firm, I naturally took with me the staff I had enlisted from the army; but a difficulty was that the new firm already had an experienced woman cashier and an assistant. This lady was naturally immensely jealous and apprehensive about the arrival of a

possible rival and would not permit Usher to have any involvement in
the cash office. My new partners suggested that he might look for
employment elsewhere, but this was not a notion that commended itself
to me. In the result, Usher would sit in my office, a very large and
handsome room overlooking Gray's Inn Gardens, with absolutely nothing
to do except to make an occasional errand to replenish our stocks of
cigarettes. I was, up to the crucial date, an immensely heavy smoker. I
placed a regular order for 1,000 cigarettes a month with Sobranie – my
first clients – and this quantity was invariably exhausted by the twenty-
fourth of the month. I reformed in rather special circumstances, not
induced by considerations of either economy or health.

Sitting in my room, Usher remarked to me one day, 'I shall have to
give up smoking. I know that you dare not ask for any increase of salary
for me' – a totally true statement since my partners were irritated by his
very presence – 'so I must economise and I intend to give up smoking.'
I reflected for a moment and then said, perhaps rashly, 'Mr Usher' –
which was how I always addressed him – 'if you give up smoking, I will
give up smoking also. It will be good for me and it would be thoroughly
unfair that you should have to sit here all day long watching me smoking.'
The mutual decision was reached. We smoked our heads off until the end
of the week and from the following Monday until this present day I have
never smoked a cigarette or a cigar or a pipe. In fact it would take very
little to send me back to my old bad ways. Hence I am profoundly
indebted to Usher, although the sad fact was that he himself lasted until
only the Tuesday and tragically continued to smoke from then onwards
until his early death, which I am sure was contributed to by his smoking
habit.

Not long after my return to the practice, Kisch invited my assistance
in an artistic problem. Although an educated man, he had no real interest
in the arts other than in literature. Somewhere on his travels he had
encountered two strange Bohemian young brothers. Their names were
Mendel and Gustav Metzger. Their story was an unusual one, even for
members of the army of Jewish refugees from Hitler's Germany. Both
had somehow contrived to arrive in England, the elder Mendel aged
sixteen, the younger Gustav aged about fourteen. They had arrived alone
and knowing no one; a kindly Jewish lady provided them with a minute
weekly stipend and on this they contrived to live in a room in the East
End of London, differing from other rooms by possessing only three
walls. The fourth wall – blown out during the Blitz – was replaced by a
stout tarpaulin. They ate largely by purchasing overripe fruit, cutting
away the defective portions and making meals of the rest.

They were of remarkable and even distinguished appearance: the elder brother had saintly, almost Christ-like, features, with long locks and a beard which was never shaved. The younger was clean-shaven and less handsome. He was in every sense the junior member of the team. How Kisch had discovered them I never found out, but they were represented to me as aspirant artists. It was on that score that he approached me since, somewhat optimistically, he regarded me as an authority on all artistic matters.

In no time at all I had taken them over and was espousing their cause. The urgent need was to provide them with some money and I myself had little to give. They enrolled in the John Cass Art School in the City of London and with Kisch's assistance I went in search of some form of grant or scholarship. Kisch was himself a member of the Council of a Jewish organisation called the Education Aid Society, to which we made an immediate application. The Society's chairman was Sir Robert Waley-Cohen, the father of a subsequent Lord Mayor. He was, I suspect, a man of strict Conservative views and he had no time for the two strange youths who must have represented everything he disliked most: they had no settled income, no settled home, no desire to do any regular work and wished to become artists. 'They ought to be in the army!' he snorted when we presented ourselves to him for investigation. I replied tartly that I could think of no army that would utilise the services of these two wispy youths and we departed from the scene.

However, Kisch was not that easily defeated. He asked me what I thought was the route to Sir Robert's heart. It seemed to me that, although Sir Robert knew little about art, he would certainly know and be impressed by celebrity names. I recommended to Kisch that we should endeavour to get some eminent artist – the name a household word – who could recommend them to the Society. He asked for suggestions and my first proposal was Jacob Epstein. Neither Kisch nor I knew Epstein, but I did know a daughter of Ambrose McEvoy, whose husband had been in the army with me. McEvoy had been a great friend of Epstein. I telephoned the daughter, who kindly agreed to speak to Epstein and later telephoned to say that he would be only too pleased to see me.

I arrived at Epstein's large house in Hyde Park Gate with a folder of drawings by the two brothers – all, I must confess, in my view absolutely horrible. Epstein was in the kitchen sitting at a vast deal table. I placed the folder before the great man, but as his fingers closed I asked if I might make one observation. 'I would not wish it to influence you,' I said hypocritically, 'but on your decision will rest whether these young men eat or not.' Epstein gave me a fixed look and said nothing. He opened up the folder and thumbed through the various drawings, muttering audibly to himself, 'Not bad. Some talent here I see.' In the end, when I left the room with the folder, I had with me a letter from Epstein testifying to his belief that these young men had some talent which should be encouraged.

But his service was not to go totally unfeed. Just before I went through the door he said rather hesitantly, 'There is something you might do for me.' Needless to say, my gratitude would have produced almost any exertion. He opened a drawer in the deal table and pulled from it a handful of income tax assessments. 'What shall I do with these?' he said. I sat there for the greater part of an hour writing appeals.

The letter from Epstein served its purpose and a grumbling Sir Robert Waley-Cohen was obliged to concede a grant. It was an annual grant and each year for three or four years I found a different authority to recommend the young men. The year after Epstein it was Frank Dobson, the sculptor, and the year after that it was Eric Newton, the art critic of the *Sunday Times*. Getting his opinion involved greater complications. He needed to see some of their painting and for that purpose we went together to their three-walled studio. The Metzgers, alas, did little to help themselves. Of Gustav Metzger he enquired the meaning of a very strange configuration on the wall. 'It is a suicide,' said Gustav simply. Eric Newton was not happy to leave it there. 'Is it,' he said, 'your notion of the physical qualities of a suicide, or is it some sort of abstraction?' Gustav curled his lips and replied, 'Either you understand or you do not understand.' Thus rebuffed, Eric turned to Mendel and asked him whether he had been influenced by any British artist, to which Mendel replied without hesitation, 'I hope not.' Notwithstanding these discouraging exchanges, the genial Mr Newton provided the necessary letter, but I think that was the last year of an application.

I am happy to be able to record the later progress of the Metzgers. Mendel took to normality: married, and with a small daughter – now a talented professional violinist – went off to Strasbourg to become an authority on Hebraic literature. Gustav vanished from my life when I had the temerity to suggest that he might seek to recover the income tax element on a small covenant that I had entered into on his behalf. He obviously was not prepared to have any associations with government, even such beneficial associations as the return of income tax. I think he regarded the making of this suggestion as putting me beyond the pale and that was the last I saw of him for many years; but I received a report recently from Lucian Freud that he was alive and well and is still a power in the auto-destructive artistic world – a community who have the wholly welcome notion that their works of art should be destroyed immediately after completion. In respect of those that I have seen, I would not dissent.

Another colourful character who came into my life soon after I returned to practice was Dr Joseph Dallos. Dr Dallos enjoyed – in his own world – an international repute. I have never been able exactly to assess the reality of this claim but he is credibly believed to be the person mainly responsible for the introduction of the contact lens. He was a Hungarian and had developed this important process in Hungary before coming to England some years before the Second World War. That his reputation was already an established one was demonstrated by some documentation I saw relating to his application to become a British subject. It was supported by the great names in ophthalmology, led by Duke Elder and others of comparable standing. The five-year resident qualification was waived in Dallos's case and he became a naturalised British subject in record time. He was a mercurial, volatile, highly emotional and immensely intelligent man, and he had a more than fair ration of Hungarian charm.

These qualities showed themselves on his first visit to me, introduced by a Hungarian publisher-friend of his. He came into my office, a thin, eager man, with a sharp intelligent face covered with gloom. 'I do not know,' he said, 'why I have bothered you for this appointment.' I could not provide him with an answer. 'I have no need to consult you,' he said, 'since I intend when I leave here to commit suicide.' I carefully avoided any kind of reaction but looked at him steadily and said, 'Dr Dallos, if that is your intention you have been very improvident. You should certainly have disposed of yourself before you incurred my fee!' His response, after a slightly surprised interval, was to burst out laughing and the threat of suicide disappeared.

He told me that he had recently divorced his wife and was in a state of great dejection because of financial problems, and we discussed his future, which clearly required careful planning. He left me and I heard no more until about a fortnight later when he again came to see me. 'I am leaving for Hungary tomorrow,' he said. 'I am about to remarry.' I enquired about the detail and he told me that he was proposing to marry a cousin. I asked the age of this lady. He told me that she was twenty-one. I did a rapid calculation and pointed out that she must have been seven when he last saw her in Hungary. He agreed this was so but defended his choice by saying, 'I have great confidence in my family.'

The next thing I knew of him was a telephone call from Austria some two weeks later. He had been in Hungary and had smuggled his bride across the border where they had either come under fire or been at risk of fire from the patrolling guards. He was now installed in Vienna with one special difficulty: with characteristic impulsiveness he had set off on this adventure with no more than the currency allowance of £20. 'I am without any money. Can you please wire me £50?' In those days I lacked the banking connections I might have had today. I told him that the exchange control was a very rigorous one but I would do my best. I telephoned the Bank of England and by good fortune contrived to speak to a senior official. 'Do you,' I asked, 'have any romance in your soul?' The official replied, 'Not very much.' I retailed the circumstances to him and he promptly replied, 'Very well, have £50.'

Four or five days later Dallos arrived in my office accompanied by an attractive young woman, who had obviously been in tears. 'I want you,' he said, 'to tell this young lady that she must marry me. After the trouble and expense to which I have been put, it is intolerable that she now says that she does not want to marry me or has doubts about it.' I pointed out to him that I could speak no Hungarian but if he would undertake to translate faithfully I would tell her what I thought. He gave me the undertaking and I told her in the simplest language that I thought she had absolutely no obligation to marry him; that if she did not want to marry him, he had a duty to see that she was speedily returned to Hungary if that was what she wanted. Dallos heard this with displeasure but without protest. I then took it upon myself to go further. 'I am the worst person in the world to advise you, Dr Dallos, as I am an unregenerate bachelor. I have no doubt that you have this young lady shacked up in your tiny Hampstead flat. I suggest that you install her in a comfortable hotel; take her out shopping and to see the sights; introduce her to a few people, and see what happens.' They left my office, but a few days later I was telephoned by Dr Dallos who told me that they were to be married at the Marloes Road Register Office.

The marriage turned out a total success. The bride was a firm character and was precisely what was needed to guide Dallos away from his temperamental impulses. She developed in the most unexpected way. She first qualified as a pharmacist and later as a medical practitioner. When Dallos died, she had for some years been in charge of the largest casualty department in any British hospital. From his point of view he could not have made a better choice and when I saw them on various occasions it was clear that she was absolutely devoted to him.

It was at about this time that I received a telephone call – not entirely a welcome call – from my uncle. My mother's younger brother was the financial success of the family. Maurice Mauerberger became one of the most important industrialists of his day in South Africa. His fortune was made virtuously in the sense that it was not associated with diamonds or gold or any kind of gambling, but had a solid industrial background in the manufacture of textiles; in the acquisition and development of a canning industry, and in a number of other industrial activities including, later in life, an involvement in the reclamation of the foreshore of Cape Town. Out of all these activities he made a vast and honourable fortune.

However, in so doing he did not endear himself to mankind.

For a number of reasons – largely from disagreeable quirks of temperament – he made more enemies than anyone I know, and he particularly enjoyed estranging those close to him. His wife Helen had been introduced to him by my mother. She was the daughter of one of my mother's oldest friends. From his point of view the marriage was a successful one. She remained a docile and obedient wife – devoid of any domestic talents and expressing, so far as I can remember, no opinions on anything.

Apart from a desire to alienate mankind – and if ever there was a Miller of Dee my uncle was such a one – nothing would have distressed him more than to know that he had won universal affection, and apart from his dutiful children I never heard an approbatory remark made about him anywhere. He was mean to the point of mania and loathed the idea of anyone benefiting from his wealth, but his one saving grace was the creation of a great charitable trust in his name which posthumously redeems many of his lifetime qualities.

He had left England at the age of fourteen, totally uneducated. He had an immensely quick mind and his mental arithmetic would have been worthy of Einstein when it came to divining the economics of any business transaction, though he had a profound contempt for education and made absolutely sure that none of his five children went to a university. I recollect in conversation with him, when he was staying at a luxury London hotel, his query about why I needed to pay a visit to Rome. 'You can,' he said, 'see it all in postcards. Why take the trouble and expense of going there?' It was, I believe, Whistler who, when asked to explain one of his paintings to a counsel engaged in his cross-examination, told him that it would be as futile as trying to explain a Beethoven symphony to a deaf man. An even greater futility would have been to try to explain to my uncle anything relating to the splendours of human thought.

He was, I must confess with pain, a horrible man. In consequence of his horribleness, my father, who was sensitive and scholarly, loathed him and was very reluctant to admit him to the house. My mother, whose universal love of mankind could extend even to this pestiferous brother, insisted on seeing him when he came to London, and in justice to him he had a sufficient sense of family solidarity to bestow on her a minute income, for which he exacted a very full price.

Because of my father's distaste for him I had rarely met him in my early years. Hence it was with great surprise that I received the telephone call from Maurice Mauerberger in my office. He introduced himself brusquely and explained his purpose. He wanted me to come to South Africa immediately. He had heard from various quarters that I was reasonably well-regarded in London legal circles. 'I need legal advice and there is no lawyer in South Africa I can trust,' he said. This was a characteristically vicious assertion, since he had a pathological suspicion of everyone around him, and in view of the company he kept, very largely justified. 'I am afraid it is an impossibility,' I replied. 'I am heavily involved in practice and my much older partner would be very unwilling to let me go.' 'Tell him I will make it worthwhile,' he said: words I ruefully remember. 'It is not a matter of money,' I went on, as it turned out foolishly. 'But come you must,' he said. 'You have never been to South Africa and you will enjoy a visit.' Indeed I had never been to South Africa, loved travel, particularly enjoying sea travel, and was tempted. 'I will talk to my partner and send you a cable,' I said. 'Make sure you come,' were his parting words.

I travelled out by plane, with a firm promise – the only one fulfilled – that I would return by sea. The plane was a flying boat. I had only flown once before in my life and it was a fascinating experience, although not uneventful. It took some four days, stopping at various points, and while over Lake Victoria the pilot announced that one engine had failed. The plane came low and, whether it was a figment of my imagination or a reality, I was sure that I could see the snapping teeth of crocodiles in the water. However, we completed the journey, arriving in Johannesburg where I was greeted at the airport by uncle and conveyed to the eighth floor of the Carlton Hotel, the significance being that it was the only floor air-conditioned and uncle liked comfort – for himself.

He proceeded to tell me the family tale. His son and heir, and hitherto his pride and joy, Joseph Mauerberger, had been contentedly married to an attractive Egyptian Jewess. However, he had of recent weeks encountered a young Englishwoman, of good middle-class stock, who had emigrated to South Africa for unexplained reasons and who was currently serving on the cosmetic counter at Stuttaford's, the leading Cape Town department store. Joseph had taken a shine to her and, it was reported by my uncle, spent a great part of his time – which should have been occupied in important business affairs – leaning on the cosmetic counter at that store, admiring this young lady's beauty. The point had been reached when Joseph had decided to divorce his Egyptian wife and to offer marriage to the young Englishwoman: a proposition which appeared to me to be unexceptionable, or at least which did not arouse my horror to the same extent that it had in uncle. I gleaned that his objections were twofold: first that the young woman was, not unexpectedly, a Christian, and second, perhaps more important, that he regarded her as an adventuress – so far as I could see without a shadow of justification. But Joseph's passion was unchangeable and, despite uncle's pleas, he remained firm of purpose.

This was too much for uncle and a *casus belli* occurred one morning when he summoned his son into his office to demand once again that he come to his senses. Joseph continued to refuse, whereupon uncle produced a form of transfer of the entire shareholding in his various companies that he had bestowed on his son and compelled Joseph by one means or another – the means were subsequently investigated in litigation – to sign the shares back to him. Joseph left the room and within seconds, such was the love for uncle, almost every attorney in Cape Town had volunteered to assist Joseph to get the shares back again. Battle was joined and it was at this point that uncle had decided that he needed my help.

I heard the whole story with increasing disapproval and, following the pattern of cautious family lawyers in England, remarked to uncle, while sitting in his rooms at the Carlton, that it was evident that the matter must be settled. Uncle reacted like a man-eating tiger asked to give up steak and emitted a bellow of animal rage. 'Settle!' he said. 'I will see him at the bottom of the Bay!' It was clear to me that any further settlement proposals were for the time being unwise.

The next day I had the fascinating experience – one of the few agreeable experiences of my visit – of motoring a thousand-odd miles from Johannesburg to Cape Town and of realising for the first time the immense emptiness of this vast country. The journey was not improved by the fact that uncle – who, I had just discovered, had only one eye, the other one being of glass – insisted on driving his Pontiac, with a native driver in the back seat, sent out from time to time to collect sandwiches and mineral water for our meals.

In Cape Town we made for uncle's house in Wynberg, a prosperous white suburb. It was a large house in substantial grounds, with a separate building to house the black servants, and within seconds I realised for the first time the character of South Africa's problem. It was in simple terms that it was a slave state, with profoundly dissatisfied slaves.

It is impossible to imagine an establishment of greater wealth and greater discomfort than my uncle's house. My aunt took no part in the domestic arrangements, taking innumerable hours to dress and make up. In consequence, during my three weeks' stay, there were four or five changes of native cook. The first applicant who came for the job was automatically engaged, providing an interesting range of meals. One that lives in my memory was the first dinner cooked by the native boy who had arrived that morning. He was told to start the meal with corn on the cob. His method of cooking it was to scrape off all the corn and serve it in hot water in soup plates. There were guests to dinner who apparently expressed no astonishment, but even they found it impossible to eat the main dish which was meat burnt to a frazzle. Uncle was the owner of a canning factory and had provided the house with a large supply of tinned sardines and these finished the meal. It was one of uncle's more remarkable qualities that he suffered from no social embarrassment.

I made one further misguided effort to settle the matter. I was asked by a cousin of mine – the son of another aunt – to have dinner one evening with Joseph and the young woman in question. Uncle gave his blessing to what would otherwise have been an act of treachery, expressing the hope that even at that stage Joseph might wish to recant. Before leaving, however, I enquired of uncle whether – although I had no knowledge of the lady – it might be possible to offer her some financial inducement to return to England. When I met her it was clear that such an inducement would have been firmly rejected, but the point did not arise since uncle's reaction to the suggestion was not dissimilar to my first mooting of a possible settlement. I fled from the house with his roars echoing in my ears.

I formed a favourable view of the young woman, who was attractive and intelligent, although for the life of me I could not understand why anyone would want to marry into uncle's family and have him as a father-in-law. I concluded my visit by making various legal recommendations – in consultation with South African counsel – for the conduct of the law suit. It seemed to me, knowing my uncle, that time would heal the situation – as indeed it did. I recommended a course of action that would have taken at least five years and during that time both sides could come to their senses.

Having done what I could *chez* Mauerberger, I prepared to return home. On my final day uncle asked me to come into his study where he was sitting at his desk with a large cheque-book, which gave rise to interesting expectations. 'I must,' he said, 'pay you a fee.' I went through the characteristic motions of a slight demur – unwisdom in the extreme. Before I had even faintly demurred, uncle said, 'Well, if you do not want a fee, that is all right,' and closed the cheque-book. In the end I returned to England with a second-hand Remington typewriter, without a lid, and with a dinner-jacket manufactured for me by a local tailor, to enable me to travel respectably on a Union Castle boat, still maintaining the conventions of Empire.

Travel abroad on some professional matter was for the most part a delight to me at this time, since it took many years before I was in a position to finance such trips from my own earnings. My first visit to the United States also came soon after I resumed my practice with Kisch. I had had dealings with the States on legal matters but it had never previously been necessary for me to visit there. The opportunity came out of a very surprising and indeed melodramatic situation.

Out of the blue, since I had had no previous contact with the clients, I was visited one day by various relatives of an Italian Jew, who had died in Egypt after establishing an extremely prosperous textile business in that country. The relatives who came to see me were his son, his daughter and his son-in-law (the husband of another daughter). The deceased had lived in Egypt for many years as an expatriate but had always maintained his Italian nationality and allegiance. I had never met him because his need for my services arose after his death. As it turned out, he would have been well advised to consult me during his lifetime. The story read like a novelette and at first I found it difficult to credit. It was only later, when I had the opportunity of meeting and talking to the principal villain, that I believed totally the allegations made by his relatives.

The old gentleman had been happily married for many years. After the death of his wife, in need of companionship he had married a much younger and very attractive Italian girl, also living in Egypt. It was at a time when Jews in Egypt were not only unpopular but subject to considerable discrimination and indeed very apprehensive about their future position. This was because of the bitter relationship then existing between Israel and Egypt. Concerned for the future of his family, the deceased made some arrangements to safeguard their position. He dispatched his young wife to the United States with the plan that she would remain there long enough for him to channel his fortune to her in the New World and that when sufficient wealth had been safeguarded he would join her for a new life. The arrangement worked to the extent that great sums of money were exported – by what means I was never told – and the lady came into the possession of this substantial fortune, on the footing that it would be held for the family.

When the time was ripe for him to leave Egypt and rejoin his wife and his money, he applied for ratification of a US visa which had been obtained some months earlier. When he visited the American Consulate for this purpose he was informed to his horror and disbelief that the visa had been cancelled a few weeks earlier without any notification to him. He had no idea what had caused the cancellation and perhaps happily for him gleaned no idea during the short remainder of his life. The effect on him was so devastating that he had a heart attack and died within a couple of days.

When the family investigated the position, they found that the picture of the virtuous wife exiled in order to safeguard the family fortune differed lamentably from the reality. The young lady concerned had found an American lover; had invested the money on his advice in a block of flats and other property in her own name, and had contrived by some arrangement with her lover to secure the cancellation of the visa. The family's resentment could be well understood. It was in a quest for justice that they visited me in my tiny office in Raymond Buildings.

I communicated with the New York lawyers I knew best: the firm of Greenbaum, Wolff & Ernst, now unhappily no longer in existence. The leading member of the firm, Maurice Ernst, was a famous public figure who had been a friend of Franklin Roosevelt and was a prolific writer on social and legal topics, although most of his writings were not specially readable. The only criticism I make of this splendid man was his persistence in sending me a volume of his writings as soon as it appeared, when I was under an obligation to write something about them, which involved reading them. However, this apart, there was not a ripple in a friendship which lasted well over forty years.

It was Maurice Ernst who suggested that I should go to the States to deal with the delinquent lady. I travelled with the son-in-law: a most intelligent and likeable man. We were met at the airport by Maurice and one of his young partners, Richard Ader, who passed us on to Herbert Wolfe, a senior partner in the firm, with occasional resort to the third senior partner who, slightly unexpectedly, retained the military rank of General: General Greenbaum. He was a magnificent character, a member of the Council of Princeton University, who lived at Princeton and devoted a good deal of time to university affairs.

A council of war was held and a hostile letter written to the lady demanding redress. I might have expected that she would seek the advice of an immensely fashionable lawyer, Louis Nizer, whose subsequent account of his legal life – *My Life in Court* – became a best-seller. A meeting was suggested – I think from our end. Mr Nizer was a peacock among legal prima donnas. He was also a highly successful strategist. Whether from design or accident, he clearly thought it could do me no harm to be left cooling my heels for a while. The message came through that Mr Nizer was 'trying' a case in Chicago, meaning in American terminology that he was conducting it.

It was late one Friday evening, several days later, before I could obtain an audience with this august gentleman. Greenbaum, Ader and I visited Mr Nizer's splendid office – and the splendour was not exaggerated. He was himself a small man of rather swarthy appearance, with well-pomaded hair. For some reason his desk was on a small plinth, with an arrangement of lights which ensured that he was the central figure at the meeting. We were introduced with cordiality and I proceeded to outline the nature of our claim and our complaint. I occupied a few moments. He then indulged in a burst of oratory that went on for several minutes while he explained to me how outrageous the claim was in relation to this innocent and virtuous lady. When he had gone on rather longer than I could tolerate,

I raised my hand and he stopped in mid-stream. The breaking point was when he described the lady as a 'recently bereaved widow'. This was too much for me. 'Mr Nizer,' I said, 'it is perfectly true that I am probably the largest lawyer practising in London and it is fair to regard me as big enough to make two. But it has never yet been suggested that I am big enough to make twelve.' The point struck home and he changed his tack.

He said that the most convincing thing was for us to see the lady, who by a remarkable coincidence was in attendance in an outer office. With the concurrence of my American colleagues, I agreed. The sequel might have been a scene from *East Lynne*. Supported on the arm of Nizer's secretary, an elegant and graceful figure came through the door, wearing deep black, with accompanying veiling over her face. When she removed the veil there was indeed quite an attractive appearance, although I must confess, knowing the background, I was looking at her through a red haze. 'I was anxious that you should meet this lady, Mr Goodman, in order that you should know with whom you are dealing,' Nizer remarked. My reply, I am afraid, was not appropriate for a British gentleman. 'I am very glad to have this opportunity, Mr Nizer, since it is rarely that one can tell an individual who is a moral monster that she is that to her face. I have rarely encountered greater villainy, although admittedly in a short career.' To my great delight the lady fainted. Mr Nizer raised his hands in horror and she was removed from the room. 'Mr Goodman,' he said, 'you are pushing this too far.' 'There is no distance to which I won't push it,' was my reply, and we then had a slightly more constructive conversation. He would not advise any settlement unless we withdrew our allegations. This we flatly refused to do and the negotiations broke off.

The whole story was a long one. It involved a further meeting in Geneva and discussions that went on for a considerable while. The solution was found by Herbert Wolfe. It related to a taxation complication which might well have bankrupted the entire estate and it made sense for the warring parties to come to terms before everything was lost. At this point the matter was finally settled, although the lady concerned had very little time in which to enjoy her ill-gotten gains. She died within two or three years of my American adventure.

Everybody is interested in health. It is, therefore, perhaps justifiable to include in an autobiographical account of one's life some reference to it, and who has preserved it or who has sought to destroy it.

I was, so far as I can recollect, a healthy child. I may or may not have had measles, mumps or scarlet fever, but if I did I have no recollection of them. My first recollection of any serious ailment is when I was at

Cambridge, when I contracted German measles. I remember receiving a little note from my tutor, sympathising that I had fallen a victim to what he pompously described as 'the Teutonic version of measles'. This was on the whole a satisfactory experience. I was immured in an isolation hospital with about twenty other undergraduates who, after two or three days of fever, were in full health and full spirits and tore the place apart. My devoted mother came to see me three or four times in the course of my illness, demonstrating the superiority of Jewish maternity over any other kind – no other undergraduate had any visit from any kind of relative at all.

From then onwards things proceeded tranquilly until I contracted a severe attack of rheumatism when I was in the army. As I was then being ministered to by an elderly family doctor who had looked after us for years, and who was the sweetest, kindest, gentlest and most ignorant of men, I continued to suffer the torments of the damned, until I went to visit my dentist, who informed me that I had an infected tooth which was probably the cause of the rheumatism. He consulted with my doctor, removed the tooth, the rheumatism disappeared, and I was able to return to duty. This was especially satisfactory as my commanding officer, Major McWhatt, who viewed army doctors with the same degree of confidence as I did, had strongly recommended that I should return home indefinitely and come back only when I was better. What he did not know was that the most incompetent of army doctors was, compared with my own medical practitioner, a medical genius and the Pasteur of the day.

My next episode of ill health was at one and the same time more serious and more entertaining. It was in 1955, when I was staying at Brighton with my old friend Frank Coven. In the course of the night I developed an agonising pain in the stomach. I did not have the least idea what this was and attempted to dose it with Eno's Fruit Salts, and other palliatives that I had used over the years and which had served me well, but nothing reduced the pain.

I bore it until the early hours of the morning when I could restrain no longer from waking up my host, who telephoned the doctor. The doctor arrived and provided the same degree of utility as most doctors. He looked at me, prodded me in the painful parts, and said, 'I do not know what is wrong with you, but it is clear that you are in pain.' This was an unassailable proposition about which I was not disposed to argue. He recommended that in the morning I should seek admission to the Royal Brighton Hospital.

In the morning I telephoned my own devoted practitioner – by now he was well over seventy – to tell him that I was on the way to the Royal Brighton Hospital. 'I absolutely forbid it,' he said. 'You must come back and be looked after by me.' Whereupon a car was commissioned, which took me to my mother's home where I was put to bed. The pain by that time had ceased, but only as I discovered later because the jogging of the journey had dislodged the obstruction that caused the pain and gave an illusory effect that I was cured. Needless to say, my practitioner was delighted and concluded that in some way this cure was attributable to his wise guidance. It was quite clear, he told me, that I had suffered a bout of colic. 'Dr M,' I said, 'nobody has had colic since Nelson's day.' He pooh-poohed the suggestion and informed me that the right thing was to stay in bed for a few days and I would be as good as new.

He had hardly left the room before the pain resumed in even fiercer form. I telephoned him and dragged him back again. 'Ah,' he said, 'there *is* something wrong with you! The trouble is that I am now elderly' – a fact of which I was also well aware – 'and I find it difficult to get up in the middle of the night. I propose, therefore, to leave you with this tube of pills which are morphia, and if you are in great pain, put one under your tongue and suck it.' I discovered afterwards that this was advice so lethal that no competent practitioner would have entertained it for one second, but I accepted the tube of morphia tablets and used them several times during several nights. They certainly were effective in the sense that they took the pain away.

After this had gone on for some weeks, I telephoned again to my devoted practitioner and said that really we had to do something about this. 'I feel that – and I hope you will not take this as a reflection on your skills – I ought to see a specialist,' I said. 'Certainly,' he replied, 'I know the very man.' I was a little apprehensive about his choice and enquired whom he had in mind. 'Ah!' he said. 'A man of such eminence that no one can have any doubt about his ability. I am referring to Sir Adolf Abrahams.'

Adolf Abrahams was one of three remarkable brothers, one of whom – Harold Abrahams – I knew well and have already described; the other brother, Sir Sydney Abrahams, was a distinguished colonial administrator. Sir Adolf had been the chief physician of the Westminster Hospital. I should emphasise *had been*. When we went to see him in his rooms – I believe in Harley Street – I observed a gentleman of great antiquity, sitting at the end of an enormous desk with a huge register in front of him. He looked like a plucked hen; he was very tiny – I reckon about 5 ft 4 in – and he looked at me with some scepticism and considerable disapproval. Obviously on account of his own athletic prowess he took strong objection to my weight, which indicated a life of total indulgence and very little athletic prowess.

He wrote down in his immense register almost all the particulars that anyone can think of: my age, nationality, date of birth, fingerprint, my mother's age, my father's age, my grandfather's age, and went on for ages recording all this. He appeared to me to be better engaged as a policeman than a doctor. But finally he picked up a small wooden hammer with which he proceeded to conduct a medical examination, tapping me in various spots and enquiring whether as a result of these fierce taps I felt any discomfort.

At the conclusion of his 'examination', he pronounced judgement: 'You are,' he said with senatorial emphasis, 'very fat.' I could not disagree with this conclusion, although I was tempted to say that I was not proposing to pay him a pocketful of guineas in order for him to inform me of something that was patently obvious from the most perfunctory glance in a mirror. 'Being fat,' he said, 'an operation would be singularly difficult and dangerous.' This, of course, was hardly reassuring if I needed any operation. 'I therefore do not recommend that you do anything,' he said. 'You have got an inflamed appendix, but if you leave it long enough it will, undoubtedly, abate and the discomfort will disappear.' My own elementary knowledge of medicine was that if you left an inflamed appendix long enough it would burst and kill you. But I was in no mood to argue with him; my desire was to get out of his presence at the earliest possible moment.

As we left the room I noticed my devoted doctor looking very pleased. 'I told you that nothing needed to be done,' he said. 'Dr M,' I replied, 'we are now going to find another specialist.' He looked disappointed at this conclusion. 'If you think so, I will find another.' 'Oh no you won't! I will,' I said. I had then a very great friend who was a distinguished psychiatrist, Alexander Kennedy, of whom I will say quite a bit later. I telephoned Kennedy and asked him if he could recommend a good specialist in London for a man who had a most excruciating stomach pain. 'There is,' he said, 'an up-and-coming man called Ronald Bodley Scott, and I strongly recommend you to consult him.'

I telephoned Dr M and asked him to make an appointment with Dr Bodley Scott as soon as possible. 'Never heard of him,' he said. 'Don't worry about that, just make the appointment,' was my peremptory direction. That he had never heard of him was in fact an indication of his knowledge of the medical profession, since Bodley Scott was the Queen's physician and was later knighted. However, we trundled off to see him; he examined me for about five minutes and announced that I had a gall-bladder in urgent need of removal and he recommended that the operation should take place at the earliest moment. As we left him I noticed that on this occasion Dr M looked disappointed – we had been recommended to take some action that might relieve me of my agony.

I returned home and he said that he would make arrangements to find a suitable surgeon. Again I said, this time more weakly, 'No you won't. I will.' And once again I telephoned Alexander Kennedy for a recommendation. He suggested a man called Hedley Atkins. I rang up, once again, Dr M to ask him to arrange for Hedley Atkins to remove my gallbladder. Here again Dr M said he had never heard of him; not surprising as Atkins later became the President of the Royal College of Surgeons and was knighted. It was perfectly clear that a man had only not to be known by Dr M to attain the greatest eminence in his profession.

The very next day Dr M telephoned me with some triumph. 'You cannot be operated on for a month,' he announced, 'because Mr Hedley Atkins is in Cape Town and will not be returning until then. But I have arranged,' he said with great pleasure, 'that he will perform the operation the day after he returns.' If he was satisfied with that, so was I. But then there was a sensational development. Dr M came in to see me the next day and I saw a change in his expression to one of great alarm. I had not realised it but I had turned completely yellow, since my bile duct (as I later learnt) was by then completely blocked. 'We must have the operation done without a minute's delay,' he averred. 'I will go in quest of a surgeon.' Again I said, even more weakly, 'You won't, I will!' And I rang him up later to say that I wanted to be operated on by Mr Victor Riddell, who was the senior surgeon at St George's Hospital, and well spoken of. Obviously for the first time Dr M was impressed with the urgency of the situation, since Victor Riddell was down at Hampstead and in my bedroom in my mother's house within three-quarters of an hour. He took one look at me and said, 'You will be operated on this evening at the London Clinic.' As it turned out, the operation could not be done until the next day.

I cannot speak too highly of Victor Riddell for the care that he bestowed on me. He performed the operation with obvious skill; the delays involved had the effect of converting it, so I was told, from an operation with very low mortality, about 1 per cent, to an operation with a considerable mortality, of several per cent. However, fortunately no one told me this at the time, and I was duly operated on, seemingly successfully, except that I remained in the Clinic for six weeks, and during that period there was a recurrence of the pain due to the fact that a single gallstone had remained blocked in the duct and had to work its way out. The devotion shown by Victor Riddell to the case was displayed perhaps most conspicuously when on the morning I told the nurse I was in pain, Mr Riddell, who lived in the country, was by my side within the hour. He gave me some injection to send me to sleep and when I woke up the next morning he was by my bedside again, obviously having arranged to arrive in time for my awakening.

These events were disagreeable at the time but they passed off reasonably happily, and were considerably mitigated by the extremely pretty nurse that I had in the London Clinic. I have already described how Miss Smith, my secretary at the time, carried out a one-woman rescue operation to remove me from the hospital and, as she thought, from temptation. There is a legend that in order to be henpecked it is necessary to be married. But this is not so – no man is as henpecked as he is by his secretary.

5

Books, Music and More

I WAS PERFECTLY content in my partnership with Kisch, and would probably have remained there for the rest of my life, unadventurously dealing with a modest practice and enjoying myself hugely at concerts, the opera (when I could afford it), a great number of theatres and cinemas, and socialising with agreeable companions. But a tragedy elsewhere changed the course of my life.

Rubinstein Nash, the firm where I had been articled, suffered a grave loss in the death of Ronald Rubinstein – the most effective lawyer in the partnership and one of the most effective lawyers in London. He had run Rubinstein's very considerable litigation practice, particularly in libel and other publishing-related matters since they were accepted as the leading literary lawyers in the country. I had declined their offer of employment as a conveyancer after completing my articles with Harold Rubinstein, but following Ronald's death, the two surviving partners visited me and asked if I would rejoin them to replace Ronald and to run their litigation. It opened up a prospect of wider and more interesting activities, and after discussions with Kisch we reached a cordial arrangement. It was that I would – except for a few personal clients – take over the practice of E. Royalton Kisch & Co., leaving with Kisch the conduct of his own family affairs and a few personal or family clients. I then merged my newly acquired practice with Rubinstein's and became in terms of seniority the third partner. I was provided with a splendid room and joined a firm with which I had had the most pleasant associations during my years of articles.

At Rubinstein's there appeared an endless succession of the most famous literary and artistic names in the country. I advised J. B. Priestley, Graham Greene and Evelyn Waugh – the last in a brief and rather torrid encounter, when it was clear that the view he took of me was about as favourable as the view I had taken of him. He arrived in my office with a large ear-trumpet, to seek my advice about an action for libel against a woman journalist who had tried unavailingly to visit him for an interview. Something she had written later about this had offended him enormously. Having heard the story, I advised him that I thought it was probably libellous but for the life of me I could not see why a man of his distinction should bother about it. He looked at me with studied contempt as a man of no spirit and left the office, complete with ear-trumpet.

I never met him again but have derived very great pleasure from his earlier novels. They do not need my worthless commendation as works that are likely to survive. I found *Brideshead Revisited* incense-soaked and the 'Sword of Honour' trilogy – greatly acclaimed – insufferably snobbish; but these are personal views, shared by no one. Later I formed a strange and unexpectedly friendly relationship with his son Auberon, with whom I made common cause over Biafra and a mutual admiration of Ann Fleming. In many people Auberon provokes positive apoplexy, but not in me, and although I represent most of the views he cordially dislikes, they have not affected a friendly relationship.

I advised J. B. Priestley on a couple of occasions. He consulted me about an American film called *We Are Not Married*, which bore a suspicious resemblance in plot and characterisation to his famous play *When We Are Married*. The theme was identical: that of three or four couples, of total and smug respectability, married on the same day by the same clergyman, who discover to their horror on the twentieth anniversary of their wedding that the clergyman had not been ordained.

We instituted proceedings for breach of copyright and passing off and the action was settled. I recollect with pleasure taking Priestley to the Law Courts to apply for an injunction on a day of the legal vacation, when it was the convention for any counsel of standing supposedly to be away, and the court was full of very young, spotlessly white-wigged barristers. In his broad Yorkshire accent Priestley whispered to me, 'Who are these baby barristers?' I explained the convention to him and he was greatly amused. The action was satisfactorily settled: the film company recognising the frailty of their legal position.

Contact with Graham Greene was established when he telephoned me one day to ask, 'Can you hear it, Mr Goodman?' Regretfully, although then not yet even partially deaf, I could hear nothing. 'Listen more closely,' he said, and I could then hear a faint tap. 'That intolerable noise is driving me mad and preventing me from working. You must come round and hear it.' When I arrived at his flat in St James's Street – above or next door to where Overton's, the fish restaurant, has now been successfully established for many years – there was indeed an amount of building work being done to put the restaurant into shape. I explained to

Mr Greene that the courts expected a high degree of tolerance from adjoining owners if necessary building work was being done, since otherwise all building would be brought to a halt. The explanation did not satisfy him, but in the end I persuaded him not to apply for an injunction.

I discovered – and this was a nice evidence of loyalty – that Greene's friendly regard for the famous Prunier restaurant, on the other side of the road, may have been an additional inducement to create difficulties for the upstart rivals who were about to compete. In any event, Overton's is still there and Prunier's, alas, has long vanished, to be replaced – horror of horrors – by a Japanese restaurant. To me this was a personal loss as I loved Prunier's and nothing on earth would induce me to eat Japanese food.

One much later meeting with Graham Greene was in September 1975, on the day that a bomb had gone off at the Hilton Hotel. I was myself, later that day, attending a wedding reception at the In and Out Club in Piccadilly. As I had some short period of time to occupy before I went to the reception, I strolled over to the Ritz for some tea. There I saw Greene and he greeted me on the footing that I was well known to his brother, Hugh Carleton Greene, as indeed I had become through the Open University. What amused me was his obvious satisfaction at the explosion which, in a way, struck me as surprisingly callous. But his reason was entirely rational, 'That will teach those Americans to support the IRA,' he said. I must say that there was strong logic in this. I never saw him again, but no one who met him could have failed to recognise that he was an exceptional human being. He was not an easy man to get to know, or to converse with unless one became a much closer friend than I ever did, but there radiated from him a sense of high intelligence and an obvious demonstration of the qualities that have made his novels some of the most remarkable of recent times.

But apart from literary wrangles, there was the occasional other case of special interest. One such was an action for libel brought against a young, struggling doctor by an Irish doctor – in contrast, elderly, rich and immensely successful. The young doctor was an idealist who had become involved in a bitter quarrel with the older man because he believed that the claims made by him – that he had discovered a treatment for tuberculosis – were without substance and dishonest. At a public meeting, the young man asserted his belief and described the other doctor as a quack. The outcome was a libel action.

Despite the most strenuous exertions by our King's Counsel – an extremely nice but, alas, not very subtle performer who was quite unable to deal with a very cunning adversary – the judge decided in favour of the Irishman and awarded £1,000 damages against the young doctor. This was shattering for him since he had no money, would probably have gone bankrupt, and might at that time on that account have been struck off the medical register. At the conclusion of the case I thought quickly and, before the parties had departed from the court, I asked the solicitor on the other side if – of course in his presence – I could talk to the plaintiff. I had a feeling that the Irish qualities of warm-heartedness and generosity might be turned to account once he realised he had been totally vindicated from the accusation.

We retired to one of the consulting rooms in the Law Courts, where I spoke as feelingly as I could to the successful litigant. 'This young man is just about to leave for Central Africa, where he has enlisted as a medical adviser in an immensely deprived area. He does this for the same reason that he attacked you – a genuine but perhaps misguided concern about people's needs. This case – a grave error of judgement – may well ruin him. I understand that you are a wealthy man, that £1,000 can mean little to you, but I have a feeling that you might respond to a plea, and it is that plea that I now make to you not to ruin a virtuous young man at the outset of his career.'

The solicitor, clearly annoyed at my wholly unorthodox approach, sought to intervene, but his client brushed him aside. 'Tell me more about your young man,' he said. 'Has he got a wife and children? What other means has he got?' I told him that he was recently married, had no children, was entirely without means and that he and his wife were sailing for Africa within a few days. He reflected and then said that he would like to have half an hour to think about it. He returned to say that he would waive any claim for damages but that his costs would need to be paid. I could not have hoped for any more or as much, and I promptly agreed. The costs were procured by a whip-round among medical colleagues and the young doctor departed, I hope a chastened man, reflecting that virtue was not necessarily the key to success in a court of law.

A case at this time which produced unexpected humorous features was brought to us by Victor Gollancz, one of the few imaginative publishers that I have met, whose firm was an immensely valuable client. Gollancz was the brother-in-law of Harold Rubinstein – my master in the law. I had been articled to him. Rubinstein was a quiet and gentle man who made no claim to being a great lawyer. He regarded with amusement my own interest in the niceties of the subject, but the absence of deep legal knowledge did not interfere with his becoming a most trusted and valuable adviser to an immense number of people.

Harold Rubinstein was a distinguished literary dramatist, although only one of his many published plays had a West End production. The greater part of his output was one-act plays, frequently presented by amateur dramatic societies. Many of them had a historical, biographic content: plays about Shakespeare and Dr Johnson. He could have made no money out of his writing, but it obviously gave him great delight. He wrote a number of plays based on a correspondence he had unearthed written by his own grandfather in Hebrew to another relative, and I was able to serve him by procuring a translation of these letters from my father, who much preferred scholarship to any of his unwelcome business activities.

Harold doubled his professional life with the secretaryship of the British League of Dramatists. It was characteristic that regardless of the very wide disparity of rewards, he devoted most afternoons of the week to these activities. His work as a dramatist was, I think, something of a penance to Victor Gollancz. They were devoted friends, and it is clear that Gollancz regarded it as a bounden duty to publish the plays which could, I am sure, have had only the smallest of sales. I understand that each time a package arrived with a new manuscript, Gollancz shed a figurative tear.

I have not met another solicitor who aroused such affection among his clients as did Harold. He is, and remains, much missed. Despite his mild disposition, he was a man of the firmest principles. Although in almost everything a libertarian, he was a passionate anti-communist. We had many an interesting debate about this. I have no particular affection for communism but it seems to me purblind to ignore the fact that the system kept a vast country in relative social tranquillity for seventy years. The argument presented is that the entire population was terrorised by police and army; but it has, I feel, to be too simplistic. Both the police and the army are members of the population and children of other members of the population. It is too facile a belief to carry total conviction; but this book is not the place to discuss political theories, so I will spare the reader any further excursion into my beliefs on these topics.

Anyway, I must return to Victor Gollancz and the farcical case in which he involved me. He asked me on the telephone, 'Who does your criminal work?' I replied that we did not do any criminal work, which rightly or wrongly is regarded by lawyers as of inferior social quality. 'Somebody must,' he said, 'because Bill has been arrested.' It then emerged that Gollancz was referring to a recent employee. It is enough for the purpose of this account to describe Gollancz – as indeed he was – as a 'do-gooder' of quite exceptional dimensions, and as a man who was certainly on the side of the angels, even though many of the angels might have preferred to have him on the other side.

One of his occupations was to pay a weekly prison visit where he encountered Bill – then in Pentonville for one of a series of many burglaries of lead from church roofs, which was his speciality. When he emerged Gollancz, keen on regeneration, gave him a job in his packing house, packing the books. It turned out on investigation that Bill's attendance at work was somewhat erratic. It seemed that he came only on pay-day and then stayed long enough only to collect his pay and to depart back to a Church Army hostel where he resided.

On the evening of Gollancz's telephone call, Bill had been arrested. The police asserted that he had been seen on the roof – roofs were clearly a fascination – of a grocery warehouse in The Cut in the Waterloo Road, and that they had observed him throwing some large objects down to an accomplice on the ground. The objects were sides of bacon, abandoned when the two villains ran away as the police arrived. Bill strenuously denied to Victor Gollancz that he had been one of them and claimed that it was a case of mistaken identity. Gollancz appeared at the office shortly after the call and demanded that we should immediately go to Wormwood Scrubs, where Bill was being detained, to organise his defence. He had absolutely no doubt about his innocence. His conviction arose from a certainty that Bill would not tell him a lie.

It was a cold day and I was then an even larger man than I am now. Victor Gollancz was a substantial figure and the two of us were wrapped in heavy winter overcoats. We obtained a taxi and sat together on the back seat, fitting into which was something of a problem. On the way down Victor was industriously engaged in persuading me that it was unarguable that Bill was an innocent and misjudged man. On arrival at the prison there was an immediate hiccup. The governor, when consulted, demurred at allowing visits other than on the prescribed day. Finally, intimidated by Victor Gollancz, he agreed that we could see Bill, although with a trace of malice he told us that we could not see him in the visiting-room reserved for visits by lawyers since Victor was not one. So we saw Bill in a stall: the prisoner being on one side of a glass barrier through which we spoke, and Victor and I pressed into a space intended for one normal-sized occupant.

Before Bill was produced, Victor gave me a final admonition. 'If you have any doubt about his innocence,' he said, 'look at him when he smiles. You will see that it is the smile of virtue.' This is a remark that remains in my mind. At no time during our interview did Bill smile and without the benefit of the smile he presented a classic 'Lambrosian' case – that villainy can be best identified from the configuration of the villain. I asked Bill to give us his account of the episode. It was simple. He had been strolling along the Waterloo Road with his friend when he needed to urinate. He decided that the empty patch of ground where the bacon was alleged to have landed was suitable. I asked him first why he had not proceeded for another fifty yards or so where there was a public convenience, and secondly why, if he had done nothing wrong, he had run away. Neither explanation was convincing but nothing that he said would have disillusioned Victor, who instructed me to throw myself into the case with all the vigour I could command. I did so and enjoyed it hugely.

The police were truly confounded. I had ascertained that Bill had some fourteen previous convictions for the lead-stealing antics and on each previous occasion he had 'gone quiet'. On this occasion he was surrounded by solicitors, QCs, scientific witnesses and the best resources that forensic evidence could supply. This was a complete novelty to the police and it no doubt caused them to look at Bill with new eyes.

Bill was wearing the clothes that he had worn on the fateful night. I arranged to have them analysed and they revealed no trace of bacon fat, although probably traces of a good many other fatty stuffs. A meteorologist provided evidence as to what the light would have been at that time on that day. George Wigg (an acquaintance from my army days, always willing to involve himself in any situation in opposition to authority) went to the exact spot from where the police claimed to have seen the bacon-throwing, and one of my witnesses, who had been allowed entry on to the roof, walked about within sight of Wigg's night-glasses. I retained for Bill an eminent criminal counsel, who later did his best for the wretched Stephen Ward, and a highly competent criminal junior.

Nevertheless, at Bill's trial – which I did not attend – the jury were unable to reach a verdict. This, I discovered, was by a margin of eleven to one: the majority anxious to convict and one valiant objector insisting on Bill's innocence. This was, of course, before Roy Jenkins introduced the possibility of a majority verdict – which was just as well for Bill.

The consequence of the disagreement was that there had to be a second trial, and Victor Gollancz, wincing a little, nevertheless undertook to finance that, as he had the first trial. On the occasion of the second trial I went down to court at a moment when I judged the evidence would have ended. I arrived for the judge's last observations before charging the jury to reach a verdict. I sadly concluded that those observations were not designed to be very helpful to Bill's cause. They amounted to a virtual invitation to find Bill and his colleague guilty. I noticed that the jury consisted of nine men and three women, arranged in three rows of four, each row containing one of the women. One of the ladies – rather elegant, well-dressed and attractively auburn-haired – was obviously of a superior social class to the other two.

When the jury retired, I remained in the court, alone except for one spectator – a prosperous-looking gentleman holding his bowler hat and umbrella. He approached me – to make conversation – and enquired if I could guess how long the jury would be out. I told him that I had no idea but they were not out very long in these particular courts. I then asked him of his interest in the case and he told me that a member of the jury was his wife. 'Is she,' I hazarded, 'the auburn-haired lady?' 'She is indeed,' he said. I then asked him what he thought she would do. 'Ah!' he said emphatically. 'She will not convict.' I enquired why he had this certainty. 'Because,' he said, 'she made me drive her down to The Cut late yesterday evening so she could determine for herself whether the police could see what they claimed to have seen, and she arrived firmly at a negative conclusion.' 'But she will surely be persuaded by the others,' I said. He remarked, somewhat ruefully I thought, 'You do not know my wife.'

When the jury returned there was a significant rearrangement. The three ladies sat together in the front row; the nine men were scattered elsewhere. All the men looked profoundly discontented and the foreman furious. The three ladies looked like the proverbial cat who had swallowed a canary. They had plainly achieved something. When asked by the judge whether they had arrived at a verdict, the foreman remarked with some anger, 'We have not, My Lord.' The judge admonished them to try again, pointing out how unfair it was to the accused and to everyone else concerned, but the foreman responded very firmly: 'There is no prospect of arriving at a verdict and it would be a waste of time.' 'Then I must accept it,' said the judge, 'and I must discharge the jury.' What the jury did not realise was that a hung jury in those circumstances meant the acquittal of the accused since the practice is not to put defendants up for a third time.

Gollancz left the court triumphant, leading a grateful but mystified Bill back to his labours. Gollancz's biographer tells us that he wrote me a note expressing gratitude and that, notwithstanding a bill of £300 for the two trials, he would nevertheless have incurred the same expenses again in similar circumstances: as noble an assertion as any I have heard. Bill's subsequent career, again according to Gollancz's biographer, was satisfactory. He was never again accused of a crime, but whether he became a distinguished publisher is a matter of greater doubt.

It was while I was at Rubinstein's that I first encountered one of the greatest advocates that I have met in the course of a long legal career – and I have met historic names such as Patrick Hastings, Norman Birkett, Walter Monckton, Andrew Clark, Stafford Cripps and others. D. N. Pritt is long forgotten by the present generation, but he was a remarkable man and in his day enjoyed rare distinction, for the reason that, although encountering a good deal of hostility because of his extreme left-wing views, he was nevertheless regarded as such a master of law and advocacy that a great many people reluctantly swallowed his views for the benefit of advice that was regarded as of unique quality.

He was educated at Winchester and Oxford – strangely enough either place capable of producing dedicated left-wingers. It is only necessary to instance Michael Foot and Roy Jenkins (Oxonians), and Richard Crossman – both a Wykehamist and an Oxonian. I retained Pritt without any reserve. If a man can win cases, his political views, so far as I am concerned, are irrelevant, unless they are so odious as to create an irresistible revulsion, and of these there have been very few.

It is not exceptionally difficult to find good lawyers, although they represent a modest minority in both ranks of the profession. It is much more difficult to find good advocates, although quite a number of practising advocates esteem themselves far beyond their real quality. A disconcerting experience for a visitor to the Law Courts would be to wander from court to court to hear the bumbling inadequacy of the presentation of most cases, and I have often found it agony to sit behind an acclaimed advocate listening to a thoroughly inadequate presentation. For the sake of professional reputations and concern for my own purse, I will not provide instances, though if any reader engages me in a quiet talk out of earshot of anyone else, discretion might no longer prevail.

Pritt achieved the balance between law and forensic oratory in a fashion as good as, and often better than, anyone else I have known. He had a relatively quiet oratorical style, a keen sense of humour – except when his political views were impugned – and to me he demonstrated a welcome geniality and simplicity that were distant from the pomposities of many of his contemporaries.

An irritating feature of Pritt, but absolutely built-in, was his inability to resist any opportunity to parade the virtue of his political views. Several times when I took a client to see him – usually a successful businessman of respectable Tory inclination – he would affront him by expressing socialist opinions that were, at least to the client, in no way endearing. Indeed I retaliated on one occasion and earned his displeasure for quite a week or two. When we had settled in for a consultation in his chambers, he opened the batting by pointing to a plate – not particularly handsome – attached to the wall. 'Stalin gave me that,' he said proudly. The client reacted as if Pritt had announced that it was a gift from Beelzebub. However, not discouraged by the absence of a favourable response, he went on to discuss the virtues of the Russian legal system. 'It is,' he said, 'the subject of uninformed hostility, and is as fair or fairer than anything you can find anywhere else.' My eyebrows rose, my client spluttered, but

Pritt continued gaily on. 'Then you cannot know,' he said, addressing the client, 'that under the English legal system in a criminal trial, in most circumstances the prosecution has the last word. In Russia,' he said preeningly, 'the defence always has the last word.' This was too much for me and I interjected mildly, 'And it normally is his last word.' Pritt gave me an embarrassed glare and I noticed that for some months he was in difficulties about accepting the briefs from Rubinstein Nash, but the breach was rapidly repaired when on one or two occasions he enlisted my services in libel actions on his own behalf. In both he made it clear to me that all he required was a retraction.

One case was against the *Daily Telegraph* for what he took to be an insinuation, arising out of his defence of Jomo Kenyatta in Kenya, that he was in some way supporting the Mau Mau rebellion. This was an imputation that rightly he was not prepared to tolerate. I cannot imagine Pritt countenancing murderous activities. Kenyatta was then viewed with great hostility by all the white settlers, but later became a British Empire idol because he did more than anyone to ensure the safety of the relatively few whites in the country. However, it was not long before the newspaper recognised the error of its ways and an apologetic statement was made in open court, together with the payment of his costs.

Among other personalities whom I first encountered at Rubenstein's it would, I think, be a serious omission not to include Gilbert Harding. This man enjoyed an enormous fame, as anyone does who is associated either with broadcasting or with television. His fame largely depended on his brusque manner and upon an appearance that somehow commended itself to the public. He was certainly not a beautiful man, but had a large moustache and an exceptionally aggressive, indeed bullying manner, particularly when interviewing. He was in fact an extremely kind man, and this was demonstrated when he was reduced to tears in what is now a memorable interview with John Freeman. John Freeman pressed him on some family circumstances and mentioned his deceased mother.

My own association with Harding arose in a rather characteristic way. He consulted me in 1953 because he was being sued for libel. The circumstances were, I think, unique. He had been engaged – he took a fee for appearing at dinners – to make a speech at a Rotarian dinner at some suburban hostelry. On arrival he became somewhat aggrieved that he could not use the lavatory without inserting a penny. Older readers will remember that this was a routine in a number of places and, so far as I know, still remains the practice at various railway stations.

Anyway, this incensed him. When he rose to make his speech, he prefaced it by saying he could not understand why he had accepted an invitation to address a third-rate audience, at a third-rate establishment, where he was served a fourth-grade meal. This annoyed the owners of the hostelry very considerably, particularly as they naturally depended for custom on organisations such as the Rotarians. My understanding was that it was a worthy establishment that gave good value for money. Gilbert Harding was very apprehensive of the libel suit and its likely effect on his pocket. However, I negotiated with the landlords and succeeded in extricating him from it without any costs, having finally persuaded him to sign, if not a grovelling, then a respectable apology. Harding was a nice man with no special talents, except the ones that make a television performer, namely, unjustifiable self-confidence and a not very literate fluency, accompanied by a wide if superficial knowledge of contemporary matters, particularly the identity of other television performers.

My stint as a partner at Rubinstein Nash was overall a pleasant one. I liked all my partners, notwithstanding occasional but unimportant differences of view. Stanley Rubinstein, the senior partner, was the doyen of musical lawyers, advising nearly all the prominent British musicians, and especially Sir Henry Wood, the founder of the Promenade Concerts, for the preservation of which at a time of crisis I have some responsibility. I enjoyed meeting the clientele at Rubinstein's and there is no doubt whatsoever that those associations were an immensely formative influence on my later career.

Towards the end of my fourth year at Rubinstein's, however, I was brought to a realisation that the tiny staff who had come with me were not particularly happy. I was visited by Margaret Smith and Frank Usher, who represented to me – in the mildest fashion – that we would all be happier if we started a new firm. The idea appealed to me and at the end of 1954 the firm of Goodman Derrick & Company was formed and has been in existence ever since.

I had met Derrick at Southern Command headquarters where, as a lieutenant, he worked under me, then and forever a major. He came to see me one day to seek advice about his career when demobilised. He had taken a law degree at Oxford – not I should imagine a very good one – and had then somewhat unusually enrolled in the Royal Academy of Music to study the organ. It was clear that he would never be a gifted lawyer but he was an extremely reliable and conscientious man. He also, and modesty was a very firm quality, assessed his musical talents as being forever amateur. I suggested to him, therefore, that it might be sensible for him to become a solicitor. There are important parts of the work of a solicitor that do not require special imagination or even eloquence, and foremost in these activities is conveyancing which, although requiring a substantial detailed knowledge, can usually be done in one's own time and certainly does not require any exhibitionist qualities. I recommended to Derrick that he should become this type of solicitor and he could then, if he chose the right location, spend his lunchtimes playing the organ at the City churches and at his own church on Sundays and other special occasions. He seemed to me entirely cast for this type of life. He had some private means and would not have been wholly dependent on his legal earnings, although as it worked out this was not an aspect that need have bothered him.

He liked my suggestion and as a result of it, when he was released from the army about a year after I had returned to civil life, he came to be articled at Rubinstein's and remained with me first as an articled clerk and later as a junior partner, although sadly he died very prematurely at the age of forty-nine. The advice I gave him, I hope, was good advice. He quite enjoyed legal work, although responsibility worried him, and he was certainly able to cultivate his music and did enjoy playing the organ in his spare hours all over the City and at his own church on Sundays. He had a most contented home life with a devoted wife, much concerned for his comfort and welfare, and an affectionate daughter who later sought to become a solicitor until marriage terminated a promising career.

My parting from Rubinstein's was a friendly one. No problems arose – as they often do on dissolutions of partnership – about whose client was whose. In fact the only mild disagreement that we had was over the question of whether Rubinstein Nash or Goodman Derrick took over the Screen Writers' Association – a body more interesting than profitable to a lawyer. We continued to act for them for some years since several of the members were close friends, but with the ageing and departure of that membership our association ceased.

The unexpected success of our new partnership was Derrick. He was much liked by the clients, although a number of them must have detected that he was not the greatest lawyer since Justinian. He was the most gentle and least controversial of characters. The advice he gave to people was always specific and designed to conciliate and assuage problems. He was in partnership with me for over fifteen years until his untimely death. His name remains in the firm and I hope will so remain while the firm exists.

To establish a new firm, it was necessary to locate and acquire some premises. My friend Dennis Lloyd, gaining experience and reputation as a junior counsel, suggested that we should try to move into the Inner Temple – the Inn to which he belonged. Even in those days I enjoyed a certain amount of goodwill with leading members of the Bar and we contrived to rent some offices at Hare Court. It was a gimcrack set of offices, up two flights of rickety stairs, the principal feature of which was a floor which leaned at a considerable angle from left to right. The office had an old-world charm which compensated for rather inadequate plumbing and a structure which involved a climb to a second floor of attic rooms which housed three or four of the new organisation.

The firm consisted of me, having the most prestigious room in which it was certainly possible to swing a cat, or at least a kitten; of an outer office on the most precarious part of the sloping floor which housed Miss Smith, Mr Usher and another secretary – the best that could be obtained for a minimal salary; and a small office boy named Sid, who was exactly what office boys are represented to be ever since Dickens – perky, friendly, slightly cheeky, but in his case immensely reliable and hard-working. From time to time I still meet him – and even now he is not an antique – having had a worthwhile career in a non-commissioned rank in the Royal Navy and later with another firm of solicitors. In addition to this team, there was another articled clerk and progressively from then onwards additional recruits, some of whom are still with the firm as partners.

A year or two after the formation of the firm we retained as our junior counsel one John Montgomerie. He replaced Dennis Lloyd who had decided – except for rare appearances – to adopt an academic career in the eminent position of Quain Professor of Jurisprudence at the University of London. John Montgomerie was probably the only lawyer I knew who could compare both in erudition and in modesty and lack of pretension with Dennis Lloyd. He was a man of few words in the sense that I know no one more sparing of them in human intercourse. His conversational exchanges came near to resembling a series of nods or positive grunts. He hated pretence and reduced every issue to its bare bones in as merciless and intellectual a fashion as anyone I know. Those who over any period sought his advice revered it. His was a disposition which did not easily attract clients, since it required personal qualities of a highly perceptive character to realise Monty's virtues and the value of his advice. But leaving the acquisition of clients to others, no one could be relied upon to preserve their clientele more certainly than he did.

What came to me after a while was that his splendid intellectual and moral qualities were by themselves inadequate – in a highly fallible world composed entirely of a solicitor clientele – to assemble a large, or even a sufficient, practice at the Bar. One day in conference with him in his chambers, I ventured to ask him directly whether he ever aspired to take silk. He replied with characteristic honesty that he did not think that his qualities as advocate would attract a large enough clientele to justify what for him would have been an exceptionally high professional risk. I ventured further to ask him whether he did not think that he would be better off as a solicitor, and if he took that view whether he would like to join Goodman Derrick as a partner. He asked if I would give him a little time, but characteristically his decision was firm and immediate. He telephoned me within the hour and said just one word: 'Yes'.

At that time, to change from the Bar to being a solicitor required the applicant to pass the Law Society's Final and I believe the one section of the Intermediate Examination involving trusts and book-keeping. It was almost ridiculous to require Monty to take these examinations. He was the editor of several important sections of Halsbury's *Laws of England* and the author of some of the prescribed books for the Intermediate Examination and the Final Examination. As I expected, he passed the test on his head, or more accurately on account of his head.

Other interesting recruits have followed during the several years that the firm has flourished – or at least relatively flourished. A few people joined us and left, but by and large our recruits have remained faithful to and I believe take pride in a firm which – although by no means the most prosperous – has a reputation and a standing considerably in excess of its size or financial success. This reputation has of recent years been much enhanced by the recruitment of a large number of publicly known clients, including several members of the royal family.

In the early days of Goodman Derrick – through the recommendation of an old friend, Frank Coven – I began to attract a clientele in the television world, at the moment when commercial television was being established under the 1954 Television Act. It was not a specially commendable world. The groups formed in pursuit of licences had both a comic and an excessively worldly flavour. Their concern was not, alas, to educate the public; they did not care very much about the way in which the public was entertained; but they published what were called 'Applications' which made the most highfalutin boasts and were salted with all kinds of highbrow pretensions towards increasing the educational level of the community. This had no truth in most of the applicants, had some partial truth in some of the applicants, and a good deal of truth – and I say this without any bias although I remained their adviser for many years – in the case of Sidney Bernstein's companies. He had a totally different approach to the matter and really did believe that he had a public duty and a public responsibility, which the evidence of the years has more than amply demonstrated.

My first introduction to the world of television came through a remarkable man named Stuart McClean. He became the managing director of Associated Newspapers: not an easy job, since at that time Esmond Rothermere was the chairman. Rothermere was a man of great physical attraction, of a good deal of charm, but a man completely unable to make up his mind, and to work under him must have been a refined torture. I got to know him well and we became quite friendly. Periodically, I went to lunch at Associated Newspapers' headquarters where he practised a regality that prior to that had only been associated with the aristocracy in pre-revolutionary France. The guests for lunch were shown into an elegant, small dining-room by a butler, and Rothermere would make a state entry. The food was always impeccable, but alas that could not be said about the conversation, which was always rather stilted. However, I liked him and I had a feeling that he did not disapprove of me.

McClean was a very different kettle of fish. He was a down-to-earth Irishman of exceptional ability, with a clear understanding of humanity, who would not allow his newspapers to descend to present-day vulgarities. In those days the *Daily Mail* was a popular Tory newspaper, conscious to a respectable degree of the decencies, and this I attribute largely first to the fact that Rothermere himself would not have approved of the scurrility and obscenity of present-day papers, and also because McClean himself would not have been associated with them.

McClean had a profound interest in the Daily Mail Ideal Home Exhibition. This had been suspended because of the war and started again after the war at the Olympia Exhibition Hall, where it was one of the most popular recurrent features of London life. Every kind of industry took stalls and there were other entertainments which brought in an enormous crowd and which enabled Associated Newspapers to make a substantial profit each year.

Inside the Hall was a separate display of gardens, laid out by the leading gardening companies. To obtain access to that portion of the exhibition, an additional 1s 6d, according to my recollection, was charged to the public. McClean was incensed because that 1s 6d had to bear a full Entertainment Tax. He consulted me as to whether anything could be done about this. It was in fact the first job I did for Associated Newspapers, or indeed for any newspaper.

I cogitated, looked at the regulations, and came up with what I thought a possible solution. I went to McClean and said, 'You know if the display has any live entertainment you will be taxed at a much lower rate?' 'What do you suggest?' he asked. 'I suggest that you put on a three-piece orchestra,' I replied. This he promptly did and the scheme worked, and one of the most intriguing spectacles was to see this tiny orchestra, completely inaudible, in a corner of a garden, scraping away at a violin and a cello and whatever the third instrument would have been.

From that moment onwards I can truthfully say I did not look back. When Associated Newspapers applied for a television licence and received it in conjunction with Rediffusion – taking, I think, a half-interest each – I was frequently employed in matters to do with Associated Rediffusion.

It was in connection with that company that Rothermere made his greatest mistake.

The early days of commercial television did not turn out to be the bonanza expected and those who thought they had struck Klondike gold when they were given licences were initially bitterly disappointed. Although I had no close acquaintance with the negotiations, my understanding was that Associated Rediffusion were required to find an additional large sum of money to keep the ship afloat. Rothermere decided that this was not a profitable speculation and sold out his interests to Rediffusion for a very modest sum. Within an exceptionally short period of time the entire situation had been reversed and the television companies were making great sums of money. Rothermere's decision must have cost his paper millions.

A happy result of working for Associated Rediffusion were television connections that spread widely and which were of major professional value. The first of these, and the most important from my point of view, was the syndicate aspiring to get a licence for Wales, which was led by Lord Derby. I was actively engaged in the formation of this syndicate which had as its business and public relations genius a man named Mark Chapman-Walker: an engaging character, although perhaps a bit too Tory for my taste. He was, as I recollect, an adviser to the Conservative Party, but we never discussed politics and remained close friends until near the end of his life when he took off to the Channel Isles. He combined an extraordinary sense of public relations with a high degree of rather agreeable *gravitas*. He was immensely efficient at organising syndicates and bringing together disparate groups in quest of an economic advantage, but his motivation was totally obvious and free from malice. He was a great intriguer but he intrigued only to secure a benefit for his side and never in order to inflict damage. It was largely on account of his efforts that in 1956 the licence was obtained by his syndicate and Television for Wales and the West (TWW) came into being. I became and remained their lawyer for many years and I enlisted into the company a number of interesting characters, prominent among them my friend Jack Hylton.

TWW's failure to secure the renewal of its licence in 1967 was, therefore, a serious loss to our practice. Unhappily for TWW, Lord Derby, who was the most active and industrious chairman of any television company, lacked the worldliness to realise that he should remain on the good side of Lord Hill, who was the chairman of the Independent Broadcasting Authority from 1963 to 1967. Lord Hill was affronted because Lord Derby clearly regarded him as a plebeian, as indeed he regarded everybody who was not a certified patrician. I formed a close and friendly relationship with Lord Derby and spent many a weekend at his home, but I constantly recognised that I did not belong to this world and was not accredited as a suitable member of it. I am not sure what the qualification would be: until a few years ago probably membership of White's Club. But whatever it might have been, I enjoyed the relationship with him and he reposed immense, and indeed excessive, confidence in my judgement. I attended every board meeting at TWW and became their closest adviser.

I am sure, alas, that Lord Derby's coldness towards Lord Hill contributed very largely to a totally unjust decision when the television licence was wrested away from TWW by a new syndicate under Lord Harlech. Lord Harlech was a delightful man but the prospectus written for his syndicate would not, I am afraid, have withstood a test by a lie detector. For instance, one of its claims was that Mr Richard Burton would appear regularly in productions for the company. I have not studied the programme lists but I would be startled if this promise was ever fulfilled. Be that as it may, TWW lost its licence and Lord Derby was deeply wounded. We made every kind of protesting noise, but Lord Hill was too wise an old bird to succumb to any sort of pressure.

It is a reflection of the skill with which the affairs of TWW were handled that even after the loss of its licence and the cessation of its television activities, the market value of its shares was not affected but maintained by the investments which had been skilfully established in other business activities. These included the purchase of a group of theatres (managed for TWW by Sir Donald Albery) and particularly the purchase of Dollond & Aitchison, then owning an important chain of ophthalmic opticians and now one of the largest optical chains in Europe, if not in the world. I am pleased to say they are still loyal clients. All these subsidiary activities were sold off at a good price and the shareholders could have no complaint, notwithstanding the loss of the television licence.

An interesting subsidiary activity from the television companies was the formation in the late 1950s of a company called Musical Facilities Ltd, formed at my instigation and which provided all the popular and classical music that Associated Rediffusion required. It was a company for which I recruited an exceptionally talented personnel.

First and foremost we enlisted Sir John Barbirolli as musical director, and he was in charge of all classical music upon which Associated Rediffusion might embark. This was largely composed of a series of concerts by the Hallé Orchestra of which he was, of course, then the musical director and the resident conductor. The Hallé had wisely decided not to contract with Granada (the local Manchester company) since it took the view that to have its programmes relayed in Manchester would mean that the concert-going public would be discouraged from attending the live performances: hence its contract with Associated Rediffusion.

The managing director of Musical Facilities was an interesting character, one Kenneth Crickmore, who, until his tragic early death, was Barbirolli's manager. As well as being Barbirolli's manager, he was manager of the Hallé and, in Figaro-like fashion, knew every trick of the trade.

The adviser on popular music was Steve Race, who has now become particularly prominent through the television screen for a musical quiz programme, as well as a large number of other programmes. I did not get very close to him, but he was a pleasant man who, unlike Barbirolli, gave very little trouble.

Barbirolli gave endless trouble. Whenever it was proposed to hold a concert that would be televised, he raised every kind of objection if it was proposed to employ a distinguished soloist. It later emerged that Barbirolli had a keen dislike of soloists. He much preferred a concert where he presided over the orchestra and there was no one else to draw away any attention or kudos. This was a strange quirk in a man of so securely established a reputation. I found him immensely likeable, without any kind of side, except in this one particular, where his behaviour could be reprehensible.

I particularly remember telephoning him one day to suggest that a concert should be held in which Yehudi Menuhin would perform. 'No!' he said. 'I will not appear with that man – he was a supporter of the Nazis!' This was as fanciful a piece of imagination as it was possible to devise. Yehudi was a firmly self-declared Jew and a man of great humanity and the idea that he had supported the Nazis was the most appalling scandal; but I formed the conclusion that to keep his concerts sanitised against any individual performer other than himself, Barbirolli would have invented almost any disparagement.

One could not fail to like him as a man. He was entertaining, intelligent, and an interesting conversationalist, with whom it was a joy to talk about music and musicians. One feature of his character, attributable, I am sure, to an upbringing in the most straitened circumstances, was his exceptional thriftiness – to use a neutral word. Crickmore would tell endless stories about his parsimony. For instance, when Barbirolli came to London he would, according to Crickmore, invariably stay at his mother's house in Lewisham. This should have been regarded as a demonstration of touching filial loyalty, but the unkind Crickmore presented it as a means of saving the price of a hotel room.

Another story he told was of Barbirolli's routine of entertaining members of the Hallé Orchestra, which to his credit he enjoyed doing. Crickmore assured me that no one could have discharged this function at lower cost. He himself cooked enormous quantities of spaghetti, which the orchestra

washed down with the cheapest plonk that could be procured. Crickmore's
pièce de résistance was the story of the purchase of a quantity of Algerian
wine from the local grocer at a few shillings a bottle. When the first bottle
was opened it was tasted by Barbirolli and Crickmore, both of whom
made gestures of great disgust. 'It is corked!' said Barbirolli, and Crickmore
totally agreed. He called at the grocer and asked if he would supply
another case in exchange for the defective wine, with a request that he
should collect the original case. However, when some time later Crickmore
called at the flat, he was surprised to see that the condemned wine was
still sitting there. 'How come?' he said to Barbirolli. 'Did they not deliver
another case?' 'They have indeed,' he said, 'but having tasted it again I
am sure those musicians won't notice.' And he had procured two cases
for the price of one!

Despite his parsimony and vanity – thoroughly justifiable as a sign that
he rated himself highly – Barbirolli was a warm and interesting character,
but he was not well-liked by all of the orchestra. He was a severe
disciplinarian, concerned above everything else to attain the highest
musical standards, and he did in fact contrive to make it one of the best
symphony orchestras in the country. In this he was aided by his altogether
charming wife, Evelyn Rothwell, a most talented oboist, who appeared to
view him with humorous affection and certainly exercised a moderating
influence on his more flamboyant moments. When he died in 1970 she
organised a fund in his name to assist young conductors, and for a time
I was a trustee of the fund and endeavoured to lend it some aid.

Barbirolli was undoubtedly one of the more important British – I
unhesitatingly call him that despite his Italian origins – musicians of his
generation. He attained eminence through one of the many extraordinary
twists of fate that have enabled great men to reach the heights from a
surface level. The story is that he was associated with an American
orchestra which retained the services of Toscanini, one of the world's
most eminent conductors. Toscanini withdrew from certain commitments
at short notice and it was decided to invite Barbirolli – who had already
established a local reputation – to substitute for him. His performance
was triumphant and loudly acclaimed: he never looked back. It was a
privilege to be associated with him.

But to return to the world of television. As a consequence of my
association with TWW, an even more fruitful relationship was established.
TWW was a regional company which had to participate in a scheme
established by the Independent Broadcasting Authority known as the
'Networking Scheme'. This meant that out of the eleven or twelve
licensed companies only four would in fact make programme material on
any scale, and this material would be networked 'through the entire

television network or circuit'. In the result the whole of England – divided up into four groups – would see one of the four programmes, and the programme companies not involved in the network would enter into a separate contract with one of the networking companies to supply its product and to obtain the product of the other three networking companies through the company it had selected.

One of the leading networking companies was Granada, which had as its chairman a most remarkable man in the person of Sidney (later Lord) Bernstein. Bernstein was a practical visionary. He was a shrewd businessman, but his sights were not restricted to making profits. He saw television as a means of producing a better human race. It is a view, alas, shared by few and has certainly not been realised by the result to date. But Granada can claim to have set a standard which has exceeded in quality that of any other television company, and certainly that of the BBC.

My association with Granada came in 1957 when TWW decided to elect, from the four networking companies, Granada to be its parent company and to take all its programmes, other than the modest quantity it manufactured for itself, from its parent. I was instructed to negotiate the agreement and to draft it. I had an enjoyable two or three days with Granada's company secretary, Joe Worton. He was a shrewd but benevolent figure who played an important role in keeping Granada's feet firmly on the ground when occasionally one or other of the people concerned was likely to take off for the stratosphere. Following the completion of the negotiations, Sidney Bernstein asked to see me and enquired whether I would be prepared to take Granada's legal work. I accepted with alacrity and they have remained firm and exceptionally interesting clients ever since.

Among other things, my association with Granada has demonstrated that the function of a solicitor cannot, alas, be restricted to a familiarity with the rule against perpetuities or other pieces of legal erudition. It requires a knowledge of the world and its occupants in excess of that required by practitioners in other fields. One difficulty early on was the hostility, amounting almost to a vendetta, between the *Daily Express* and Sidney Bernstein. It became of real importance in October 1958 when the *Express* discovered that a much-publicised parlour game, *21 Quiz*, had been conducted (without the knowledge of the company) by a producer – especially employed for the purpose – who had sought to cut corners by telling a few of the contestants the nature of some or all of the questions they would be asked. The *Daily Express* obviously intended to go to town with this discovery and when Sidney Bernstein approached me for advice he was convinced that the *Express* would reveal the story in an early issue.

What did I advise? I advised that to anticipate the publicity it might be as well for Granada to set up a separate investigation, chaired by a prominent lawyer, which would make it clear that by so doing the company had nothing to hide. He agreed with this proposal and I was sent off in quest of a suitable lawyer.

This gambit by Granada served well. The lawyer selected, Sir Lionel Heald, a former Attorney-General, presided with skill and discretion and arrived at the satisfactory conclusion that, although the misbehaviour of the employee was undeniable, it was also clearly undeniable that the Granada board knew nothing of the matter. Sidney Bernstein was understandably relieved at the finding and it assisted to establish my reputation with the company, where I went on to maintain a number of successful actions.

A prominent one, which I found especially interesting, was an action brought by a dubious revivalist group called The Process in 1972. The group was American but somewhat strangely its leader was a young Englishman. The Process had developed into a cult in certain States in the American South, where it enjoyed a considerable following. It had also – as was demonstrated by the ease with which it sustained the burden of the case – assembled a substantial treasury: no doubt, as is conventional in such groups, by contributions from its misguided members. The publishing wing of Granada had brought out a book which described the group and attributed heavy responsibility for the Manson murders to its teachings. The group, offended by this, brought a libel action against Granada in England; as Granada's loyal lawyers we were, of course, retained for the defence.

The case for The Process continued its slow and weary way until, a short while before it was due to be heard in the High Court, I received a telephone call from Sidney Bernstein to ask me to call at Granada's headquarters in Golden Square. When I saw him early one morning on my way to work – he had already been at work for some hours – he told me that he was exercised by advice he had received from one of our junior partners that it would be sensible to settle the case. Sensible it would certainly have been on the basis that it is lunacy to continue with any piece of litigation that can be reasonably settled. He asked me to look at the papers and I promised to do so that day.

I returned the next day to advise him that I did not agree at all with the advice he had received. My partner's advice was based on the practical view that the libel action would undoubtedly cost a great deal of money and that there was certainly some risk of failure, but I ventured that the risk was not only slight but in my view non-existent. I was strongly influenced towards this by reading a 'parish' magazine of The Process, which contained the recommendation to young people that the best way to make love was in a recently dug grave. I confidently, although perhaps recklessly, advised Sidney Bernstein that this fact alone would make it extremely unlikely that any British jury would make a substantial award of libel damages.

We were both fortunate and unfortunate in that the judge who decided the case was the highly coloured and highly flavoured Melford Stevenson – now deceased. He was a good judge in the sense that he would come down on the right side, but he was a Colonel Blimp of a judge who delighted in expressing the most reactionary views with obvious sincerity. However, he was the right judge to deal with The Process, the very idea of which would be bound to arouse extensive hostility – as indeed it did. When the young leader appeared in the witness-box wearing a clerical coat of the finest material and a gold cross on a chain, Melford Stevenson made him immediately uncomfortable by demanding to know what it was he had around his neck. 'It is, My Lord,' said the young man, 'a crucifix.' 'Oh no it is not!' said Melford Stevenson, immediately evincing the most welcome hostility. 'It is a cross.' Since I am not a Christian, I have had to enquire about the distinction, which is, I am told, that a crucifix is a cross with a Christ figure, while a cross without the figure is a cross.

In any event, Melford Stevenson proceeded in that strain from beginning to end. He could not conceal his dislike for The Process and in fact endangered our position because of his inability to dissemble it. I was horrified by his summing-up in which he did not put a single sentence of the plaintiff's case to the jury. The jury were out for a very short time and returned a unanimous verdict for Granada.

My misgivings were not long in being realised. The Process appealed and when the case came before a Court of Appeal presided over by Lord Denning, it was clear that the appellate judges were worried by Melford Stevenson's summing-up and the notable absence of any reference to the plaintiff's case, however feeble it might have been. However, Lord Denning can be relied upon where his own prejudices do not obtrude and the matter can be dealt with on common-sense principles. He obviously took the view that, however directed, a jury would have found against these plaintiffs and on that basis dismissed the appeal.

There was an occasion in the case when I made a fatal mistake – I think excusable. After my interview with Sidney Bernstein it became clear that we had to produce some evidence of the association between The Process and Manson. Accordingly, I telephoned the New York offices of the internationally famous detective agency Pinkerton to ask if they could dig up some evidence of the association. I had not realised the efficiency and enthusiasm of American detectives – contrasting happily with the virtual uselessness of the same profession in this country. I was telephoned a few days before the case, to be told that a Pinkerton officer had arranged to see Manson in jail the following day. 'For heaven's sake,' I urged, 'do no such thing! If Manson should tell you – as indeed he might, and whether it would be true or false we would have no means of establishing – that The Process had nothing to do with influencing him, this could certainly be fatal to our defence.' Pinkerton were clearly unhappy at having been denied the opportunity of exercising this imaginative initiative, but loyally conformed with our requirements and did indeed produce some relevant evidence that was very useful.

The plaintiffs were, of course, ordered to pay all the costs, which were not insubstantial, but showed no signs of indigence since we received a cheque within a few days of rendering the account.

The full history of Granada's contribution to television at large, and especially to commercial television, still needs to be written, and undoubtedly will be written, but in the meantime I am anxious to pay my own tribute to a company which has given me and my firm undivided support for well over thirty years. I have greatly enjoyed the association. Although maintaining the friendliest, and indeed a close, relationship, especially with Denis Forman and with the Bernsteins, it has never been one of intimacy. But that has not diminished my respect for their outstanding achievements in the media world, and our relationship has undoubtedly been coloured by a similarity of viewpoint on social and most political matters.

Sidney Bernstein was elevated to the peerage in 1969 by Harold Wilson and became and remained a loyal member of the Labour opposition in the House of Lords, and on many controversial issues (but by no means all) when physically able to be present, I have found myself going into the same lobby. He had my own objections to capital punishment; shared my own views about tyranny and injustice; did not relish the notion of flogging small boys, and generally was on the side of the angels, although, as I have remarked about the late Victor Gollancz, there have been occasions when the angels might have wished him on the other side.

I have already described two Granada cases, but from the juristic point of view it is unlikely that any case exceeds in interest and importance Granada's dispute with the British Steel Corporation – a matter very much publicised and involving considerations of high public concern.

The case will be found described *in extenso* in the Law Reports. It was tried at three levels – at first instance by a judge alone, the second an appeal to the Court of Appeal, and finally the House of Lords – and proceeded at the sedate pace associated with the law for many months. Goodman Derrick & Co. were concerned for Granada at every stage and

I was myself more conspicuously engaged than had been the case for some while, since my younger partners Jeffery Maunsell, Robin Perrot and Patrick Swaffer – all of them specialists in entertainment and media matters – normally dealt with the considerable volume of Granada and other television work that had occupied us for many years and provided rather more than the hors-d'œuvre for our lunch and dinner meals.

The case arose from a television broadcast of one of Granada's *World in Action* programmes: a series of programmes that had never studiously avoided controversy. This one was entitled *Steel* and was seen by the public on 4 February 1980. In the course of that programme Granada made known to the public certain information that the British Steel Corporation considered confidential. The timing was particularly sensitive since it was during the steel strike, when the activities of the Corporation were under scrutiny and of much public interest. It was clear that the information had emerged from documents circulated on a very limited scale to the board of BSC and inescapable that their disclosure had not been authorised.

A brief summary of the matter is that in the last week of January 1980 – when the steel strike was in its sixth week and exciting considerable political concern – a Granada researcher on *World in Action* received from a source, whose identity he gave the most solemn promise not to reveal, a number of undoubtedly confidential internal British Steel Corporation documents. The documents were not solicited, nor was any remuneration or benefit of any kind asked for or offered. The researcher informed Granada that it was his understanding that the source was a BSC employee, provoked by a deep concern for the steel industry and a feeling that the public was not being presented with a fair picture of the reasons for the dispute.

Not unnaturally, Granada's professional instinct was to reveal the documents. A judgement was formed that the documents did indeed throw a new light on BSC's attitude in the pay dispute and morally justified some scepticism about the government's declared policy of non-intervention in the Corporation's affairs. Particularly, some documents provided details of new, and record, output levels in some steel plants such as Cleveland, Teesside and South Wales. This contradicted public statements by the Corporation blaming the industry's ills on low productivity.

The documents gave in some detail instances of major errors in management planning that would be difficult to reconcile with the Corporation's vehement assertions that the trade unions were primarily to blame for the industry's difficulties. In particular, a document embarrassingly quoted an important official of the Corporation who, referring to an error of a mere £200 million, observed, 'You couldn't sell this record to a group of bankers in the City. I think it's a pity in a way that the Corporation can't go bust and that we can't all lose our jobs.'

Other documents detailed the involvement of Sir Keith Joseph, then the Secretary of State for Industry, and a particularly awkward memorandum was one written by the chief executive of BSC, warning of the possibility of strike action if the government insisted on imposing strict cash limits. The decision to use the documents was made by the editors of *World in Action* and by Granada's head of current affairs. They decided that the documents indeed raised questions of great public interest and that the duty to disclose overrode any question of confidentiality and the admittedly questionable way in which the documents were obtained.

The extenuations for Granada's actions thereafter were insufficiently highlighted in the much-publicised proceedings. It was careful to advise the Steel Corporation that it possessed such documents and furnished a list of those that it thought might be used in the programme. Thereafter it invited the late Sir Charles Villiers, the chairman of British Steel, and incidentally an old friend of mine, to participate in the programme and to be questioned on the documents. Sir Charles, with characteristic fairness and no doubt contrary to much advice that he received from more cautious people, creditably accepted the invitation. I too would have recommended that they found a more Machiavellian character to deal with the antagonistic television commentators.

On arrival at the studios on the afternoon of 4 February 1980, Sir Charles was shown a full script of the programme, including the selected extracts from the BSC documents – clearly so described. Neither Sir Charles nor any of the BSC officials with him made any protest at that stage about Granada having the documents or their intended use, or any complaints about the means by which they had been acquired. In fact, again with characteristic forthrightness, Sir Charles told the *Daily Mail* at a press conference after the programme that 'It was not a totally unfair programme. We got a pretty fair hearing. I did not learn anything I did not already know' – it would indeed have been a surprise had that been so – 'and no new information has been revealed. Most of the programme was accurate, but there are one or two things which were screwed up. I had a good time watching it, but I shall not be making any statement about it.'

Alas, Sir Charles's immensely relaxed attitude was not reproduced by the Corporation or maintained for longer than that afternoon. The day after the programme, BSC instructed their lawyers who protested to Granada in the strongest terms and issued a writ demanding the return of the documents (subsequently amended to an order that Granada should disclose the name of their informant). Granada could not return the documents without jeopardising the pledge of secrecy given on its behalf by its researcher, whom it supported conscientiously and without question throughout the proceedings, since certain numbers and codes on some of the documents would probably have revealed to whom at the BSC they had originally been issued, and although it was highly likely that that individual was not the culprit, the quest for the culprit would have been greatly facilitated.

Granada's dilemma was obvious. It made several efforts to accommodate BSC's request for the return of the documents, while maintaining its pledge. There was an assortment of proposals: that Granada would destroy the documents and any copies in controlled conditions monitored by BSC; that it would hand back the documents which did not identify the source and destroy the rest under monitored conditions; finally that it would place the documents in a bank vault, to be returned to the Corporation some years thereafter – the term to be agreed.

But BSC, predictably, were not interested so much in the destination of the documents as in identifying the culprit. All the proposals for an honourable compromise were firmly rejected and finally Granada, having been advised by us of the risk involved and deciding to accept it, removed all identifying marks from the documents and returned them after so doing, except for one or two which had been destroyed by accident during the making of the programme.

The court at first instance directed Granada – under threat of ruinous penalty – to disclose the name of the BSC informant. From Granada's point of view, the appalling dilemma in which it found itself was that no one in authority knew the name of the culprit; nor, despite the most intensive efforts, was Granada able to find out. It knew the name of its journalist employee who had received the documents and co-operated with the BSC delinquent, but the journalist was a man of principle, albeit of strangely selective principle. He had given his word to his informant that he would preserve his confidence and he flatly and continuously declined to break that promise.

In this matter Granada, as I would have expected, behaved immaculately. It did not think it proper to bring any undue pressure on its own employee to divulge the identity of the individual being sought. Its persistent enquiries could not make the discovery. The most it would do in relation to its journalist was to urge him to seek a release from his bond. Whether he did this or not I do not know, but certainly the name never emerged.

Granada's only course to avert financial disaster was to procure a ruling from a court that the non-disclosure was nevertheless excusable on some

ground of privilege. A firm decision was made not to divulge, the difficulty
arising from its own obdurate employee. I attended numerous meetings
when discussions took place, and what was memorable was Granada's
determination throughout the proceedings – however irritated it might
have been – to stand by its employee and to accept the consequences.

Whether there was any other practical possibility I rather doubt. The
employee was a man of very strong political views and it would certainly
have been necessary to resort to the torture chambers in the Tower of
London to extract the information from him. My own inclination was
one of great irritation, since I could see little or no reason for protecting
the betrayer and the morality of seeking to protect him seemed to me to
be dubious.

The case was first conducted for the defendants by Mr Alexander
Irvine QC – now Lord Irvine and a leading member of the Opposition
front bench in the Lords. To the distinguished legal team was later added
Mr Patrick Neill QC (now Sir Patrick Neill), the doyen – if not in age,
certainly in eminence – of learned counsel, then already established as
the Warden of All Souls College, Oxford. Almost all solicitors of any
prominence will claim at some stage to have 'made' the career of a
successful barrister. In relation to Pat Neill, Goodman Derrick & Co. can
certainly make the claim with some justification. When John Montgomerie
retired from the junior Bar (we having already lost the services of Dennis
Lloyd), I enquired around in order to make an appropriate selection for
a junior common lawyer. My inclination has always been towards counsel
who, in addition to professional aptitude, have high academic qualifications. I was told of a young man still not securely established, who
was a Fellow of All Souls and regarded by informed opinion as very
bright. I had a word with his senior clerk – the functionary who controls
the destiny of every barrister – and was told that he was available to take
heavy work. Our practice consisted of a modest number of very heavy
cases and we proceeded to brief him to our total satisfaction, and I believe
to his.

Pat Neill has a most engaging and pleasantly open personality, con-
cealing one of the most astute legal minds of our generation. He has since
combined with his academic duties a number of other vocations, some of
which he has recently discarded. He was the chairman of the Press
Council; the chairman of the Take Over Panel, and in his spare time
became an Appeal Judge in the Channel Islands. Our sadness when he
departed to become Warden of All Souls was mitigated by the fact that
he had been considerate enough to leave behind him a distinguished
brother of comparable attainments – Sir Brian Neill, now a Lord of
Appeal in Ordinary. When Sir Brian retired we were fortunately able to

employ Leonard Hoffmann (now Mr Justice Hoffmann), who, although a chancery counsel, had such a diverse and widespread knowledge of the law that he was constantly employed as a common lawyer as well as a chancery lawyer. It was an irony that in the Granada – British Steel case, Leonard Hoffmann was retained by the plaintiffs before we were able to appropriate him. There is very little doubt that the total success of the plaintiffs was in large part attributable to his skill in argument.

Lord Denning, in his judgement in the Court of Appeal, was highly critical – in my view excessively – of the behaviour of Granada towards Sir Charles and failed to give Granada any credit for the mitigating factors I have already mentioned. 'The interviewer acted like a cross-examiner as he kept interrupting Sir Charles. His conduct spoke for itself. It was deplorable.' It may well have been deplorable from Lord Denning's viewpoint, which was formed in another age entirely, but, right or wrong, the quality of television enquiry and the reporters conducting the enquiry has to be unsparing in cross-examination. Probably in this case they may well have gone too far, but it is very difficult not to go too far without failing to go far enough.

The whole question of investigative journalism is an arguable one. Whether private individuals should arrogate to themselves the function of a police force is something about which I have long had doubts. It is difficult to justify on the single ground of the selectivity of such enquiries, restricted to the few cases brought to the notice of the television company or newspaper, as opposed to the function of the police who are required to investigate any matter where there is a prima-facie reason for suspicion.

There is no doubt that the conflict between accuser and accused is what provides the public with its interesting spectacle. It is the modern equivalent of a gladiatorial conflict or, in more recent terms and more appropriately, a cock-fight. Nothing delights the spectators more than at the end of the encounter to see the mangled corpse of the victim, and it is even more pleasurable if the survivor also shows palpable signs of damage.

It was clear and not disputed that a large part of the *World in Action* programme, and especially the 'cross-examination' of Sir Charles, derived from confidential documents. When Granada returned the documents, after the Corporation had issued a writ, it admittedly had cut off the serial numbers. Lord Denning took a justifiably censorious view: 'The documents were beyond question the property of the British Steel Corporation. To destroy them or any part of them was as bad as the destruction of a witness.' Lord Denning then engaged in a conjecture, which turned out in the event to have a slightly comic aspect: 'The unnamed employee is a man probably in the uppermost levels of the British Steel Corporation.'

The case raised, of course, a crucial question on which, despite the erudite and ingenious arguments put forward, Granada could never hope to succeed unless the courts were prepared to break new ground, based on public interest. Lord Denning expressed the law – a view by no means universally shared – as being that newspapers should not in general be compelled to disclose sources, either by means of discovery before a trial or by cross-examination at a trial, or by subpoena. In his view the justification for the law so holding was that unless sources could be protected they would dry up. This may well be the case in relation to disreputable sources and one may doubt whether such an eventuality would necessarily be a bad thing. Loyalty is a quality of immeasurable value. I would need a lot of persuading that it is not more valuable than extending protection to what can brutally be described as treachery to relatives, friends and employers. This is a matter that will be discussed until the millennium, but in the present case Lord Denning, somewhat inconsistently, took the view that there was no privilege which would entitle Granada to refuse to disclose the name of the person who had revealed the secrets.

So, despite the distinction, the erudition and the ingenuity of the various counsel engaged, at the end of the day the position remained unaffected: that Granada was required to disclose the name of the 'mole' under pain of condign penalties, which if expressed in terms of a daily fine could have been financially damaging to the point of ruin. It is to Granada's great credit that at no time did it waver in its determination to fight the issue on grounds of public policy, or to fail to give support to all the executives who had been concerned in the matter, not least to the unfortunate journalist whose bosom contained the confidence which he was not prepared to divulge.

The law on the subject – despite determined and virtuous efforts to obfuscate it – was distressingly clear. A Norwich Pharmacal order, named after the case where such an order was first utilised, was resorted to by British Steel to require Granada to divulge the information it sought. The courts have a wide discretion to refuse to order the disclosure of information, but only if such disclosure would be contrary to some legitimate public or private interest. The existing authorities could only be interpreted to defeat any claim that such an interest existed in the British Steel case. At the time of this case an overriding public interest, which would have been required to protect Granada, had been limited to cases involving the security of the State; the proper functioning of central government; the detection of crime – including child maltreatment (established in a case affecting the NSPCC); and, somewhat surprisingly, gambling malpractices. There was no existing case in which the confidentiality of journalists' sources had been recognised as an overriding public interest and there was indeed a previous case affecting Vincent Mulholland, a *Daily Mail* journalist, who had been sent to jail because of his determination not to reveal his sources.

It was against this known state of the law that Granada faced the intimidating financial consequences, or even the custodial consequences, of a failure to disclose information which was not in its possession and for which it had been unavailingly in pursuit. But providentially things changed. Soon after the House of Lords had pronounced the last legal word, leaving poor Granada capsized in a turbulent sea, a change took place in the chairmanship of the British Steel Corporation, which transformed the situation: my friend, Sir Charles Villiers, retired. To his credit, notwithstanding his rough treatment by *World in Action*, he had unavailingly endeavoured to restrain the enthusiasm of his board for vengeance. Not unnaturally the board felt a sense of outrage at what had happened and could not have been expected to accept without question the assertion that Granada did not know the name of the culprit.

Sir Charles was replaced by Sir Ian MacGregor, whose entry into the British business scene had been the subject of some controversy since it involved a most unusual basis of remuneration: large by any token, and a large portion of which was to be paid to his previous American employers. It is my own opinion that Sir Ian realised that to conduct a war to the bitter end, against a popular television company defending the public's right to know, was not, from the point of view of sensible public relations, either wise or in the best interests of the Steel Corporation.

Through the good offices of Mr Mark Littman QC – a director of both Granada and the British Steel Corporation – whose assistance I sought in the matter, I was invited to communicate with the Steel Corporation's legal adviser and had a memorable Saturday lunch with him. It was clear that he had instructions to seek to terminate the matter if this could be achieved with due honour. We had a leisurely lunch, from which I could perceive hopeful signs, and when we returned to my flat in Portland Place we were in a position to summon Sir Denis Forman – then the chairman of Granada – who had been waiting on tenterhooks to hear the result of the lunch meeting. Food played a large factor in the matter. The heavy lunch had certainly reduced the belligerence of both parties and I was at pains to supply a good tea over which the ultimate discussions took place.

The Steel Corporation agreed to drop the pursuit. Granada undertook to pay the costs and gave an undertaking to make no further use of the purloined documents. No further arrangement was necessary, as from everybody's point of view the documents had more than served their purpose. I do not know and have not enquired whether the persistent rumour, that at the time the Steel Corporation already knew the identity of the culprit, was true.

Notwithstanding its very serious aspects, the case ultimately had a comic side when, a while after the settlement, and for the reported motive that the individual was incensed at the prospect that he was to be removed from the public eye, a man appeared on television to proclaim his guilt. Far from the lofty position attributed to him by Lord Denning, he had been engaged in the catering department in the Steel Corporation's main office. How he could have come into possession of the documents was obviously a mystery. But the mystery was compounded by the firm assertion of Granada that he was not the man concerned; that he had made the admission for the purpose of attracting publicity and interest in himself, and that the real culprit was some other person who, since his name was never revealed, was operating at an equally unascertained level.

But the case had one effect. It had stirred up a demand for some change in relation to the position of newspapers. The Contempt of Court Act 1981 was passed, which for the first time provided newspapers with a statutory protection for the confidentiality of their sources. But on examination, as is often the case, one needs to look very closely at governmental kindnesses of this character. In order to receive protection, the disclosure of the information must be contrary neither to the interests of justice, nor national security, nor the prevention of disorder or crime. In the case under review, the Act may well not have protected Granada because of the provision that protected information must not have been obtained illegally. The debate continues.

6

Meeting People

THERE IS PROBABLY no career that gives one a more rounded view of the human race than that of a solicitor. A barrister concentrates on particular legal problems, and examines them meticulously from a single point of view: the possibility of persuading the court that a particular viewpoint is right. A solicitor interviews people from almost every point of view, and hears all their peculiarities and oddities in an attempt to provide them with objective advice that, on the whole, will guide them accurately in the decisions they have to reach.

It is probably wrong for a solicitor to introduce his personal morality into his work, but it is an impossibility not to do so. In the course of my career, I have encountered such a wide variety of human situations, such a conflict of opinion and decision, that I have had every reason to determine, on a common-denominator basis, the quality of humanity. There remains with me the recollection of a hundred episodes. I cannot recount a hundred episodes and the reader would get exhausted long before I would. But I shall try to give a picture of the worst and the best human beings that I have met.

One of the most interesting personalities I encountered at the end of my period at Rubinstein Nash, and as a client at the beginning of my career as a partner in Goodman Derrick, was the late Leslie Hore-Belisha, who had been Minister of War and later became a peer. Leslie Hore-Belisha was Jewish. His father, Jacob Belisha, died early and his mother married a Mr Hore, a stockbroker. In order to satisfy his mother, or for some reason best known to himself, Leslie Belisha decided to adopt the hyphenated name of Hore-Belisha.

He practised at the Bar for a while and became a financier. He was involved in certain transactions – my experience of him was that he was a man of total integrity – which gave rise to criticisms in the City, and for a long time he was under a cloud as a person of not too scrupulous dealings. This I always regarded as massive unfairness. In any event, he entered politics as a Liberal, won a Liberal seat, and then when the National Liberal Party was formed became a National Liberal and achieved a high degree of parliamentary success. His first important office was Minister of Transport in 1934, and his name became traditionally and conspicuously associated with the 'Belisha beacon', which he introduced as a device for making it safer to cross the roads. I believe they achieved a considerable saving in lives and he achieved a high degree of notoriety.

Shortly before the Second World War broke out, Neville Chamberlain appointed him to be the Minister of War. It was a weird appointment. Although he had served in the First World War, it was in a very modest capacity, and he had no significant military experience. He came my way through a former partner in Rubinstein Nash, with whom he had been at Clifton and who had brought him to the firm as a client. There I did all his work. When I formed Goodman Derrick, Hore-Belisha was one of the first clients faithfully to follow me. He was a strange man. He had great charm which was 90 per cent unforced, 10 per cent slightly synthetic. I do not believe he was a man who had many friends. He married very late in life. The marriage, I think, was not a success, since when he died the lady was abroad in the Virgin Islands and did not return for the funeral. She simply sent me some instructions, as I was acting in the administration of the estate.

Hore-Belisha was a man of considerable speed of mind and wit, but he also had more than a touch of neurosis. For weeks on end, although he was Jewish, he would retire to a Roman Catholic retreat to ruminate about the world's problems and emerge invigorated and ready for fresh battles. It is difficult to imagine an appointment where he would have aroused more instinctive hostility among Establishment figures than to have made him the Minister of War, where he had to deal with generals, admirals, air vice-marshals and everyone else, who regarded him – and in fact Lord Ironside so described him – as 'a jumped-up little Jew boy', complaining bitterly that he was seen wearing suede shoes. No greater enormity apparently could have existed in the mind of Lord Ironside. An even greater offence, which was not disclosed, was that Hore-Belisha expressed and continued to express grave doubts about the Maginot line, and after a tour of France reported to the Cabinet that in his opinion there would be no difficulty whatever in Herr Hitler's troops turning this line without having to encounter the major impact of its defences. This, alas, turned out to be all too true. But because of the pressures from the generals and others, Hore-Belisha resigned from office in January 1940, and in fact was out of the government for the greater part of the war.

When the Labour Party decided that they would bring the wartime coalition government to an end, there was a short period in 1945 when Winston Churchill proceeded to form a 'caretaker' government until an election could take place. Hore-Belisha became Minister of National Insurance and for a few months was very happy, restored to a position of office and activity. At the election he fought as a National Liberal, but it made very little difference whether he fought as a Liberal or Conservative, or any kind of ally of Winston Churchill, since they were all over-whelmingly defeated. Churchill, from what Hore-Belisha told me, held him in high regard and was anxious to secure a position for him when he returned to power after the first Labour government fell; but it was found that for some reason – and I could never find out why – no constituency would adopt him. The explanations given were various. One was that at the time he did not have a wife. The second was that they dug up the City murmurs about his previous behaviour, and the third was that he just did not make the sort of impression that was required by a county gentleman wishing to represent a county seat.

At any rate, he ate his heart out for some time, completely unoccupied. I saw quite a lot of him, since one of his methods of filling his time was to evolve a necessity for completely superfluous legal documents, largely concerned with the boundary of his home, which was a delightful house in Wimbledon, tucked away by Wimbledon Common and quite invisible from the road, called Old Warren Farm.

I remember calling upon him one day in 1953 when he was in a state of great anxiety. He became very easily worried. The notion that he might have created an opportunity for public criticism of any kind was to him totally unacceptable. 'Mr Goodman,' he said, 'I have recently obtained a planning consent for an outbuilding which I described to the planning authorities as a piggery. Do you think I should continue so to describe it or come clean as to its actual use as a library?' He had been extremely alarmed when he had heard that the planning authorities intended to inspect the building, and he asked me whether I thought there would be any difficulty in persuading them that it might be a piggery.

I wandered with him towards the building, which had been nicely constructed, looked inside and remarked rather dryly: 'The only point I would make, Mr Hore-Belisha, is that pigs rarely walk upstairs!' It is perfectly true that my knowledge of pigs is so profound that I could assert this submission with the confidence of other, better acquainted, pig fanciers; but in any event he was greatly concerned, and I suggested that the simple thing to do was to write to the local council and come clean by stating that his revised intention was to use it as a library. The letter was written, no enquiries were made, and he was greatly relieved.

My most poignant recollection of Hore-Belisha is that of burying him. I acted for his estate, and his executor was, I think, a devoted secretary called Miss Sloane, to whom he left a substantial portion of his property. His wife did not return for the funeral, as I have said, but some while later. In any event, he died in 1957 in Paris, while making a speech at a dinner, and his body was brought back to England. I examined the will to see what the burial instructions were. On the face of it they appeared to present little or no problem, but examined more closely they presented a problem that Socrates would have had some difficulty in solving. He directed that he should be buried alongside his mother, in the Liberal Jewish Cemetery in Willesden, with Sephardic rights. The Sephardics are the branch that claim to be the aristocrats of the Jewish community. They come originally from Spain and the Middle East, and look down with contempt on their brethren who come principally from Eastern Europe in much greater number. I discovered that it was as if someone had asked that he should be buried at St Peter's, with a Methodist service!

The difficulties that arose are beyond description. The Liberal Jews were, if I may say so, splendid. They said they would do whatever I wanted them to do to facilitate the burial, since they recognised that it was neither human nor sanitary for the body to remain unburied for an unreasonable length of time. However, the Sephardics took a very different view. They were not prepared, at least at the outset, to allow any burial to take place except in a Sephardic cemetery. Finally a compromise – if it can be so called: it was a total capitulation – was reached. They agreed that Hore-Belisha could be buried alongside his mother but imposed the most humiliating conditions, though not so intended. Everybody connected with the Liberal Jewish organisation had to evacuate the cemetery – even the grave-diggers had to come from a Sephardic territory. I do not recall that they required devils to be exorcised from the small chapel, but the fact remains that a community of Sephardic rabbis arrived to take over and the service was of a length that I found somewhat disconcerting. Nevertheless, Hore-Belisha got buried.

A slight hiccup occurred as I was on my way from the Inner Temple, where my office was, to the Jewish synagogue in Golders Green, when I suddenly remembered that it was required of a Jewish service that there should be a quorum of at least ten people, and those ten people had, of course, to be practising Jews. I reviewed the number coming: the two secretaries, myself, and, so far as I could think, nobody else. Thereupon I stood at the bottom of Little Temple Lane, accosting every barrister who passed and who looked Jewish. I am delighted to say, to the credit of my colleagues, that except in cases where they were engaged in court that afternoon, I did not get a single refusal. Finally, I piled up two taxi-loads of Jewish barristers who proceeded to satisfy this particular requirement. I was chagrined to learn later, from a greater theological expert, that the requirement did not necessarily arise at a funeral. But I believe that it is better to be safe than sorry, and Hore-Belisha was dispatched with the correct complement of Jewish worshippers, which I am sure is something he would greatly appreciate in the afterworld.

A man whom many people might consider to be evil was a long-term client – a man who had an immense amount of intelligence and ingenuity but a positive hatred of his fellow man. He was Jewish and he had built up a very large business entirely from his own initiative. The business required a high degree of technical knowledge, which was rather strange to find in an industrialist who had had no technical training. His hatred of mankind extended to all members of his family, even his virtuous old lady of a wife. None of them was a match for him, and he occupied himself (when he had nothing else to do) with torturing his family by his behaviour.

He used to come and see me pretty regularly and his principal object in coming was to alter his will. But before coming to see me he would announce to his family what his intentions were, so that those who had regarded themselves as handsome beneficiaries last week now knew that they were to be disinherited and left penniless. He had a particular dislike for the son-in-law who had married his favourite daughter. I think an element of sexual jealousy entered into the matter, as from time to time one does encounter. The son-in-law was a hard-working and entirely innocuous person, who had done good work for him in the business, but this was no safeguard against the vagaries of the old man's behaviour.

I recollect one occasion when this client, whom I shall refer to as 'Mr X', arrived in my office with his son-in-law to tell me that he wished to reward his son-in-law for his good work. 'What would be,' he asked me, 'a fair proportion of my shares to give him?' I told him that generosity needed to be spontaneous and that it was not for me to suggest the extent of his magnanimity; he should make up his own mind. 'What would be enough, do you think?' he asked. 'Do you think it would be enough if I give him half of my shareholding, or would it be too much?' All this was in the presence of the son-in-law.

'You have only to look at your son-in-law's face at this moment,' I said, 'to see with what delight this prospect is being greeted.' Whereupon my client said, 'Could you draw up a document giving him half my shares?' As the old man left, the son-in-law stayed behind for a moment and, grasping me by the lapel, said, 'Please do it quickly, Mr Goodman, please do it quickly!' I did not make a reply of any kind as I had not bothered to make any notes, for I knew perfectly well what was going to happen.

The very next day, before 8 a.m., the telephone rang in my flat and Mr X said to me, 'Mr Goodman, do you think he was grateful?' I said, 'He was beside himself with gratitude. He was absolutely slobbering gratitude!'

'Oh! Are you advising me to do this? Is this a wise thing to do?'

'Mr X,' I said. 'It is not for me to advise a man to engage in generous action; this is your own spontaneous magnanimity, inspired – if I may say so – by your generosity of character.'

'Oh!' he said. 'So you are not advising me to do it?'

'I am not advising you to do it,' I insisted. 'I am telling you that if you wanted to do it, it would be a fine and noble gesture.'

'But are you advising me to do it?' he said, pressing hard.

I knew what he was after, but I fenced as best I could. 'I am not advising you *not* to do it,' I said.

'But you are not advising me to do it?'

'Well, it is an impossibility for me to advise a man to give away his property; it must come from your heart. If you wish to do it – and it will be a fine, noble, generous act – I shall be happy to carry out your instructions, which if I may say I was on the verge of doing when you left last evening.'

He said no more. But later that day his son-in-law rang me up to say, 'I gather you advised my father-in-law not to give me the shares.'

'You ought to know me better than that,' I replied, 'and you ought to know him better than that. I cannot tell you what advice I gave him because that would be improper, as he is not here in your presence, but I can tell you that I did not advise him *not* to give you the shares.'

'Did you advise him to give me the shares?' he asked.

'It is not for me,' I said patiently, 'to advise a man to be generous. I can only advise people as to the legal position. But I do assure you that I made it clear to him that if he did give you the shares, there would be unlimited gratitude on your part.'

'Yes,' he said rather sadly, 'I can see what happened. He was determined not to give me the shares and wanted a pretext.'

The end of the story was a horrible one. The son-in-law, having suffered from this man for years, attempted suicide. Happily he was saved, and sent his psychiatrist to see me, to advise on the best relationship he should have with his father-in-law. My advice to the psychiatrist was very simple. 'You are a doctor,' I said, 'and you will know whether this is sensible or not, but if I were you I would advise the son-in-law to put the furthest possible distance between himself and his father-in-law and have no further business relationship with him. He is an able man and he can find employment, or build up a business, unassisted and without being subjected to the humiliations and the sadistic torments his father-in-law is inflicting on him.' The son-in-law took the advice and subsequently built up a substantial business in another country and prospered. But that was by no means the worst of Mr X's behaviour.

One Saturday afternoon, I was in my flat in Ashley Gardens when the bell rang, and to my astonishment there was Mr X. 'What can I do for you, Mr X?' I said. 'Obviously it must be a case of emergency for you to appear on a Saturday afternoon.'

'Oh!' he said. 'I am urgently requiring to sell some jewellery.'

This, I must say, was a surprise to me. Mr X was an exceptionally wealthy man. He could not have any need to sell some jewellery on a Saturday afternoon for any normal reason. He produced some jewellery – quite nice pieces, though I had no idea of their value – and said to me, 'I must sell these at once.'

I knew they must belong to his unfortunate wife. So I thought for a while and said, 'Mr X, I tell you what I will do. I myself could use some jewellery and I will buy it. How much do you want?' He named a price and I gave him a cheque there and then.

'Why,' he said, 'do you want jewellery?'

'If I may say so, Mr X, that is an indelicate question.' And we left it at that, as I was not prepared to divulge to him my motivation, but I certainly left him with the idea that I had a lady in mind on whom I wished to bestow these handsome pieces.

I waited for what I knew would inevitably happen. Mr X had overlooked one certainty: that even a worm turns. Late on Sunday evening he telephoned me again. 'I must have the jewellery at once,' he said desperately.

'Good heavens!' I replied. 'How unfortunate! I disposed of it only this afternoon!' I was determined that on the whole he deserved a lesson.

'But you must get it back again,' he pleaded.

'How can I get it back, Mr X? You don't need a great flight of imagination to understand that I disposed of it in what I might call romantic circumstances. There is no means by which I can recover it.'

'You *must* get it back!'

He telephoned me four or five times every day for the whole of the following week, until ultimately I decided he had suffered enough. 'I have now,' I said to him, 'by dint of providing other jewellery, managed to persuade the lady to return the pieces without any rancour.'

'Oh!' he said, 'I will give you a handsome profit on it.'

'I need no profit on it,' I replied, 'but may I recommend to you that you do not try this performance again, or I am sure you will find that the most unexpected people can develop claws.' So I returned the jewellery to him, he gave me the cheque which he had not cashed, and that was the end of that episode.

Throughout his life he continued to behave in the same fashion. On a Sunday morning I would occasionally go to visit him, and it was always for the purpose of receiving instructions about alterations to his will. As he had become stone deaf, he needed to use a slate on which I would write replies to anything he told me vocally. On one occasion he said, 'I wish to disinherit all my relatives.'

'And what do you want to do with your property?' I wrote on the slate.

'I don't mind what I do with it. Give it to charity.'

So I wrote, 'No, I would not be prepared to do that; it would be a great injustice to your family.'

'What then are you prepared to do?'

I thought for a while and, as he was an enormously wealthy man, I wrote, 'I would be prepared to make a will leaving half your estate to your family and the other half to charity.'

In the result he made such a will, and in a way I benefited from it since he left the direction that his executors (of whom I was one) should choose the charities to which the money went, and that if there was any disagreement I should have the final say. Consequently a number of charities in which I was involved benefited considerably, as I never had a moment's disagreement with my co-executor, who was an amiable man, and who shared my view as to what was a worthy recipient.

I do not know of anyone who showed quite such meanness, such determination to hurt people, as this particular client. But I have met a number of disagreeable characters. A problem that confronts every solicitor, but only rarely members of the Bar, is whether or not to act for a client whose behaviour may be ungenerous or unkind. This dilemma arose perhaps once in every year. It had the most relevance when taking instructions about a client's will. It is not a solicitor's business to recommend how a testator should bestow his estate. Occasionally the client will ask for guidance and it becomes very important not to allow any preconceptions arising from friendship or hospitality to influence the decision. But very occasionally the client's approach to the matter may seem to be so reprehensible that implementing his decisions is distasteful to a point which justifies a refusal to do any such thing.

In one case the testator had married late in life and the marriage had borne the fruit of a single male child. I recollect a visit from the testator, who instructed me to make a will excluding this one child on the ground that he did not believe it was his. The testator was small, very ugly and had ginger hair. When he brought the child into the room – at my request – I observed that the child was small, very ugly and had ginger hair. If any person of perception had seen the father and the child together, it would have been perverse for them to believe that my client was not the father. I pointed this out, perhaps rather more forcibly than was discreet, and advised him that if he intended to disinherit the child, on what I thought was a totally specious ground, I would not be a party to it.

He was a man over whom I had exercised some influence. Shaken by my determined attitude, he instructed me to make a will which left his wife a life interest and to leave half the remainder to the red-headed midget. I think he recognised the justice of my disapproval. But shortly afterwards I heard – perhaps not surprisingly – that his wife had left him, taking the wretched child with her. The man concerned has since died and I do not know what final will he left, but I earnestly hope that the child was not disinherited.

Other cases where one can decline to act are the fairly obvious ones where the problem does not come within the area of one's usual practice. This for me is principally the case in relation to the criminal law. For instance, I turned Jeremy Thorpe over to Sir David Napley when it became clear that his problems would take him into a criminal court. In fact I would have had no connection with that case at all had my name not been dragged in gratuitously with a weird and rapidly discounted suggestion that I had given certain advice of a character in which impropriety and idiocy vied with each other. Not unnaturally I found the immense but momentary publicity given to the matter thoroughly unpleasant, and for once and foolishly did not comfort myself with the reflection that no sane person would believe it – as indeed turned out to be the case.

I derived the greatest comfort from the reaction of William Rees-Mogg, since immediately the allegation was publicised I telephoned him to say that I was writing a short letter to *The Times* but that I had to warn him it might be considered a contempt of court since the proceedings were still in progress. His reply was creditably emphatic that he would be happy to publish the letter and was not deterred by the academic possibility that it infringed some legal rule. He added the words that if anything would secure the acquittal of Jeremy Thorpe it was the ventilation of an allegation of this sort by the prosecution.

I had no further connection with the case but was gratified that Jeremy Thorpe was acquitted. It was unworthily pusillanimous that law officers and prosecutors were willing to rely on the tainted and corrupt evidence available to them – which it was clear no jury would accept – because of a fear that it might be said they had failed to prosecute on account of the public prominence of the individual concerned. Public prominence should not place you at any advantage over the rest of mankind, but it is a craven society where it is allowed to place you at a disadvantage.

The charge against Jeremy Thorpe, and the publicity associated with it, did irreparable damage to both his political and private career. I always found him an entertaining character, but I have an uneasy feeling that the flippancy or affected flippancy with which he confronted situations argued a frivolity of approach that had much to do with the dilemmas in which he found himself. This belief did not affect a personal friendship with him which happily remains to this day.

In the mid-1950s I was involved in a number of French legal matters and was a frequent visitor to France. During my stays in Paris I saw a lot of the late Gael Mayo and got an idea of the fascination and remarkably varied talents of this immensely beautiful woman – a beauty which, despite serious illness, remained to the last. I recommend her auto-biography, published under the characteristic title of *The Mad Mosaic*. She wrote several novels, all of them interesting and imaginative. In addition to writing, she painted, and on my own walls I have several of her paintings, which are of a high amateur standard, and certainly full of colour and imagination.

Gael also composed music and one day she brought to me the recording she had made of a light cabaret song which she called 'Poor Charlie, Don't Be Sad'. Charlie was based on an authentic character, an American lawyer who practised in Paris, and for whom she must have had more than affection at some point. I still possess this recording. In fact it is associated with a remarkable episode that to this day has never been explained to me. My sitting-room in London is on the third floor, and one day Gael arrived to play me the recording of 'Poor Charlie, Don't Be Sad'. We were sitting, together with her young daughter, sipping tea, when all of a sudden a window was flung open and there came through it an immense fireman, wearing one of the typical brass helmets, enormous thigh-boots, and carrying an axe. He gave no explanation for his presence, walked through the sitting-room, went out through the front door, and disappeared.

I cannot suggest that he was a phantom, nor had the tea made me drunk, and I was happily confirmed in what I had seen by the two other persons present. It remains one of the unexplained mysteries of all time, since there was no suggestion of a fire anywhere and he was on his own. What he was doing, where he came from and where he went, heaven alone knows. But I always associate this episode with my first – and alas last – hearing of 'Poor Charlie', which was not a record one was encouraged to play as often as Beethoven's Fifth Symphony.

I also at this time began a friendship with a French lawyer named Jacques Rosselli (now deceased), who practised in London and ultimately took silk. From time to time he introduced French clients to me. He belonged to the category of social lawyers who got along with a minimal knowledge of law and a remarkable gift for reassuring their anxious clients. It would be unfair to designate him as a playboy. He was whatever is midway between a playboy and a serious adviser.

He was a French *avocat*, which meant that in the ordinary way he operated from his flat in Paris, a large and comfortable establishment just off the Champs-Elysées; from a small flat in Lincoln's Inn; and (when he later became a member of the British Bar) a set of chambers in Lincoln's Inn largely devoted to company work. He eventually acquired the unique distinction of being not only a French *avocat* and a British barrister but also a British QC. He advised the French Embassy and his international clientele was large and various, principally of café society. If anyone in France was in need of shrewd British advice, and above all of access to influential British circles, it was wise to call on Rosselli.

He was a happily married man with a very Gallic eye for the ladies. He had in his youth been a featherweight or lightweight amateur boxing champion and a distinguished rugby player. He enjoyed and capitalised on the prestigious position of being the Secretary of the International Rugby Federation. Although my own interest in rugby, or indeed in any game where the ball is propelled even briefly by the foot, is minimal, I visited Paris on several occasions as his guest for international rugby matches, principally England and France, and I recollect the extraordinarily orderly procession of an immense crowd, both in vehicles and on foot, to the Stade de Colombes to witness the game. There is a happy contrast – and I am not unique in noticing – between the behaviour of rugby and soccer crowds. *En route* to Twickenham there is nothing but good-natured middle-class manners. *En route* to any soccer match there is mayhem beyond belief. I have from time to time been consulted about how to deal with this problem, which appears to be as insoluble as the problems of Ulster or the Middle East and almost as grave. I have yet to come up with any solution that does not involve the restoration of capital punishment, and even that I would think of dubious value with an alcohol-maddened crowd of hobbledehoys.

But returning to Rosselli, I consulted him on a number of the problems of my clients relating to France, particularly in connection with the acquisition of residences in the South of France – much sought after by the monied British bourgeoisie. In later years – although I never developed any aptness at this myself – Rosselli acquired a finesse in dealing with applications to the Bank of England to enable purchases to be made that ensured him of a continuing and immensely prosperous clientele. He died, alas, in 1974 and I was his executor in winding up his modest English estate.

Anyway, one day in 1963 he arrived in my office unannounced in a state of great excitement. His client was a Madame Dupré, the widow of the owner of one of the largest racing stables in France. She had entered a horse named Relko for the Derby and the animal had to her astonishment – and certainly to the astonishment of most of the punters – won very easily. This, of course, was a matter for congratulation, but congratulation was short-lived for, soon after the result was announced, Relko was disqualified on the ground that he had been drugged in order to win the race. With hindsight I now realise that to drug a horse to win a race is normally an impossibility; horses can be drugged to lose races, but a drug that will arouse a sufficient degree of additional speed and skill in a horse is, I think, a discovery still to be made. Nevertheless, at that moment of time the Jockey Club was obsessed with the notion of widespread drugging and that the winning horses, especially, were somehow being tampered with.

The Relko situation would have been, in the ordinary way, the uneventful one of the owner, the trainer, the jockey, or whoever else was concerned, appearing before the court martial of the Jockey Club; accepting without demur a decision that was undoubtedly adverse to them; and slinking away with their heads down, to disappear for ever from the racing world under the shadow of lasting ignominy. In the case of Relko, however, the owners were of a very different calibre: they were French – the Jockey Club meant nothing to them. What did mean something to them was that their hero horse, Relko, was being submitted to the ignominious accusation of having been drugged, and they refused to accept this decision.

I was consulted and undertook to represent this noble animal in order to clear his character of these appalling allegations. The first requirement, of course, was to discover why he had been accused of being drugged. The story was not a very convincing one: it was alleged that a foreign substance, which was some sort of drug, had been found in Relko's urine. What sort of drug was not clear, and whether it was a drug which could have urged Relko to greater speed was also uncertain. I sought to obtain the best scientific advice possible. It was discovered that the advice tendered to the Jockey Club came from a lady vet. Now, I am not anti-feminist and do not believe that a lady vet is any worse than a man vet, but what was perfectly clear was that this lady had got it into her head that there was a prevalence of horse drugging and that this drugging somehow contrived to give them a speed, resource and stamina they would lack without it.

The matter was put under appeal and a full hearing of the Jockey Club was ordered. I remember with amusement the day when, after lunch, I attended at Weatherby's, where the first hearing was to take place. There was an enormous collection of television cameras, reporters, policemen and others supervising the entry to the gate and enquiring of those entering who they were. As one after another went in, they identified themselves as the trainer, the stable-boy, the owner, until ultimately I was asked what I was and I replied that I was the jockey. In the moment of astonishment that overtook them, I entered without further ado.

The presiding official was none other than the Duke of Norfolk, who displayed a total impartiality throughout the proceedings by remaining fast asleep! However, there were others there. There arrived from France a vast contingent of indignant French, determined – if the worst came to the worst – to achieve their results by violence. The proceedings were further complicated by another, slightly chauvinistic factor: the French spoke some English but many spoke very little English. The English spoke no French. I had telephoned earlier in the day to Major Weatherby to suggest that it might be wise and desirable to employ the services of a competent interpreter. But he rather loftily declared that he could speak French and that it was unnecessary to have anyone else. The test of this occurred when the result was announced. Madame Dupré, who had come over from France, heard the announcement, which was to the effect that the case was adjourned until a later date. This, however, when translated to her, she took to mean that the horse was to be destroyed, and promptly fainted. When we brought her round, they reassured her that Relko was surviving and not even under sentence of death at that moment, but still labouring under the disgrace of a drug charge.

When we investigated the matter further, we enlisted the assistance of two very powerful authorities: one was the leading expert in Scotland Yard's forensic laboratories, and the other was a professor of pharmacology at the Equine Research Station in Newmarket. Both of these gentlemen declared that the horse was not drugged in any sense, except that its urine contained a foreign substance which was frequently found in grass. It is not unknown that horses eat grass.

The evidence of Relko's innocence was overwhelmingly established but unfortunately very grudgingly admitted. At the end of the day no apology was forthcoming from the Jockey Club, and the only thing that happened was that there was slipped into the Racing Calendar on 3 October 1963 – without any indication to us – a simple announcement of the Derby result, which was that Relko had won, and that the Stewards of the Jockey Club found no evidence which would justify a disqualification.

In the meantime, the bookmakers, who had been much more alert to the likelihood of events, had already paid out on Relko, so no money was involved. Madame Dupré was immensely grateful and we had a celebration at a London restaurant, at which everyone toasted everyone else, and even the Jockey Club was the subject of good wishes, although I think with some slight qualifications.

While in Paris a short while later, I was able to visit Madame Dupré. She lived in a handsome house in the Avenue George V off the Bois, where she had the most magnificent collection of Boudin paintings that I believe I have ever seen. She was not from my point of view a wholly delightful person. Beneath the veneer of synthetic charm there lurked to my mind a somewhat grasping disposition. Apart from the stud, she had also inherited two hotels in Paris, the George V and the Plaza Athénée, which enabled her to live in suitable style. I only discovered the more thrifty side of her nature when the question arose of paying my fees. For some, to me totally unaccountable, reason she was proceeding on the basis that my exertions on her behalf were inspired by affection rather than the continuing need that has beset me throughout my life.

Over the years, as my practice developed, I found myself advising a considerable number of people connected with the entertainment world. The one for whom I had the most to do was the late Jack Hylton, a very interesting character who played a large role in my early professional career. Jack Hylton gained fame early in life as one of the leading British bandleaders, before becoming an impresario. He was a Lancastrian who had a forte for enjoying life through what one might call rather venial debauchery. He was not a man who had an ounce of evil in him, but he had a passionate desire to enjoy himself and a determined realisation that the full degree of enjoyment could only be obtained by a full degree of self-indulgence. He was much given to womanising and had the most complicated domestic life.

For a period I doubt if there was a morning each year when he did not telephone to enquire, in his Lancastrian tone, what was on, and he became particularly incensed if he thought I was engaged in some transaction on behalf of other clients in which I did not involve him, so it became necessary to exercise reticence in order not to make him annoyed.

In his later years Jack Hylton's eccentricity took a strange turn and his love life intruded into his professional life, to an extent which, alas, was damaging. When commercial television was introduced into this country in 1954, the four initial companies were ABC, Granada, ATV and

Associated Rediffusion. ATV, with Lew Grade and Val Parnell and others, had almost a monopoly of light entertainment. I was consulted by Associated Rediffusion, the most pukka of the companies, then being conducted by a former naval officer called Captain Brownrigg. I was always on very good terms with him, and he asked me whether I had any suggestions as to how they could get access to light entertainment talent. I told him that there was only one man left available who had not been captured and that was Jack Hylton, who had access to a great number of comedians.

In the result, the most astonishing contract was entered into. Jack was commissioned to do half an hour a week and an hour a fortnight of absolutely anything that he chose to put on. The first year or two he supplied them with very good value. He produced Arthur Askey, Tommy Trinder, Tommy Handley and a whole collection of other outstanding comedians, and his programmes were immensely popular. But then, alas, he fell madly in love with an Italian cabaret singer and from that moment onwards he put her in every performance, week after week, for half an hour, or an hour, to a point where Brownrigg said to me one day, 'If we are going to renew this contract there must be some change in Jack Hylton's procedures, since we cannot go on having this young lady appearing constantly in every programme.'

I spoke to Jack severely and he pledged better behaviour, and for several months afterwards he did continue to produce artists of the original quality that had made his contract worthwhile. But then he relapsed and lost his contract. Fortunately, before losing it, Associated Rediffusion generously allowed him to become a founder-member of a newly established television company, namely TWW, in which he took a small interest and out of which he made a substantial fortune.

Having lost his television contract, one might have thought that he would have regarded his obligations to the Italian singer as fulfilled. But the Italian singer did not take that view and she exercised a high degree of pressure, indeed coercion, on poor Jack. As a result, he sent for me one day and told me that he was going to put her into a film. 'Jack,' I said, 'you are out of your mind! A film would cost you a quarter of a million pounds. Equipped with this talent it would be a disaster and you would lose every penny of it.' 'Ah!' he said. 'I have commissioned a splendid script from a well-known writer. I will send it to you.' So he sent me the script, which I read rapidly, and I sent him a short note saying that indeed it was a very good script and it had been a very good script ever since Eugene O'Neill had written it as *Anna Christie*, but that on the whole it lacked an element of novelty!

Frustrated in his desire to make a film, he then decided that he would turn the lady into an opera singer. He commissioned a well-known singing master at Swiss Cottage, who undertook to provide her with operatic skill within six weeks of intensive training. Thereupon Jack arranged for a short season of Italian opera to take place at his theatre, the Adelphi. He contrived to get together a company of second-rate singers, but which included one star in the person of Tito Gobbi. The first night was *La Bohème*, in which the lady concerned did not appear, and those who were regarded as the 'Hyltonians', and upon whom he would rely for support, very cunningly decided to go to the first night, in the pretence that that was the night they thought she was performing. On the second night, however, she was appearing in *Lucia di Lammermoor*. I can encapsulate the result of the entire performance, indeed of the entire season, by a simple headline in a review in the *Daily Telegraph*, which read: 'Miss — Ruins Opera!'

I was urgently summoned by telephone to Jack's office to find that the lady had had hysterics when the notices were read out to her, and I was asked by Jack to do whatever I could to calm her. 'Ah!' I said. 'We must do something very vigorous. We must consider taking immediate action for libel in all quarters.' This soothed her sufficiently for me to inform Jack that it would be utterly mad to act on such advice but that he could leave her in the belief that she had been libelled. As Jack was very friendly with Mark Chapman-Walker, then at the *News of the World*, they wrote a sympathetic article about a courageous girl from Milan who had taken on the world of opera against impossible odds. This was indeed absolutely true – the odds were impossible – and the squawking noises that emerged from the lady, I am told, had to be heard to be believed.

A characteristic episode relating to Hylton, who had a heart of gold although he was regarded as an exceptionally tough businessman, was the incident when he rang me one day in late 1959 to say that he had been approached by an elderly Jewish friend who had fallen into financial difficulties and who was in danger of bankruptcy. His friend had asked Jack whether he would buy his small house from him – a small house in the West End of London – and grant him a lease, so that at least he would have a secure home for life. Jack did not take a moment to respond, but he telephoned me to enquire about the legality of the situation. I said, 'If the man is threatened with bankruptcy but no bankruptcy has yet taken place, it is perfectly proper to buy the house, but you must buy it at a perfectly proper price. The first thing that we must do, therefore, is to get a valuer to value it. On that footing it would be very difficult for a trustee in bankruptcy to challenge the transaction.' I procured a local valuer who put a value on the remainder of the lease of the house that I regarded as fair but not excessive. Jack paid his friend this sum of money and granted him a lease for life so that he was secure.

Sad to say, within a year a trustee in bankruptcy had been appointed and one of the first things he did was to challenge the transaction, on the grounds that an inadequate price had been paid, and Jack was summoned before the registrar. The trustee in bankruptcy was represented by an immensely competent counsel – who later became a judge – who in his private guise was the kindest and most generous of men but who was an absolute tiger when it came to court proceedings. Jack went into the witness-box to be cross-examined by him and the following exchange took place:

'Tell me, Mr Hylton, are you seriously suggesting that you did this transaction for purely altruistic motives?'

'Yes, sir, I had nothing to gain by it. I had no wish to have another house but I paid for it.'

'Are you suggesting that you expended £4,000 in order to gratify the wishes of an old friend, and for no other reason at all?'

'Yes.'

'What sort of people are you, Mr Hylton?'

'I can tell you, Mr Finer, we are human beings, but you wouldn't know much about us.'

That single answer dealt with the entire case and we departed shortly afterwards, the whole matter having been safely regulated by Hylton and the attack written off.

I do not know of anyone who was worse at selecting plays than Jack Hylton. He, however, was in the fortunate possession of rights in a number of entertainments, most of them musicals. Moreover, as the impresario who presented the Crazy Gang night after night for year after year, he was able to indulge his whim and support a few straight plays from time to time, none of which had the remotest chance of success. I have rarely seen more dreadful plays on any stage than those presented by Jack. But he was undeterred, remained ebullient and cheerful whatever the results, and was busy planning the next one almost before the curtain had fallen on the last performance of the latest disaster.

His great ambition in life was to have a production at Drury Lane, and this he ultimately achieved with *Camelot*, a play which for a number of reasons I was compelled to see several times. The first time I saw it, it was an agony; the second time I saw it, it was agony squared; and the third and fourth times it was so intolerable that I spent most of the performance outside in the bar drinking tonic water.

I vividly remember the New York production in 1960. I had not at that time seen the play, and Jack had not reached the decision to bring it to London. I happened to be in New York, not on Jack's business, when

I received a telephone call from him to say that he was going to see *Camelot* that evening and would greatly appreciate it if I would go along with him and give him the value of my critical judgment, which in relation to musical comedies was something less than nil. However, I trotted along with him to the theatre, where he had contrived to procure a couple of seats – in view of his standing as a manager – either complimentary or at the advertised price. Everyone else was 'on the ice', which meant that they were paying some huge premium in excess of the normal price of the ticket to enable them to get in. Vast fortunes were made by practitioners in acquiring and selling tickets 'on the ice' compared with anyone who ever produced actual plays.

We sat down and the curtain rose on Camelot, or some other appropriate location, and within a few minutes I heard a noise which very much resembled the sawing of wood. I wondered where this was coming from and noticed also that it was causing considerable dissatisfaction to those people around me who had paid five times over for their tickets. I suddenly detected that it was coming from Jack, who was sound asleep and snoring in a fashion fit to wake the dead. I nudged him vigorously in the ribs and woke him up, but alas only for two minutes: within a few moments more he was sound asleep again. The discontent around us became increasingly vocal and his somnolent interludes became more frequent until the end of the first act. As we escaped as unobtrusively as possible from the hostile glares, I said to him, 'Jack, we must go home, we shall be lynched!' 'Nonsense!' he exclaimed, 'I'm enjoying it thoroughly!' 'You may be enjoying it,' I said, 'but I can assure you that no one within fifty yards of you is enjoying it or can hear a single word.' However, Jack was an indomitable Lancastrian, determined to return for the second act.

I hoped against hope and prayed fervently that he would have been sufficiently rested by his deep sleep in the first act to enable the second act to proceed undisturbed. It was a vain hope: within a few minutes the same rasping noise, but a little louder, was emerging from Jack's nostrils. Once again I was nudging him in the ribs – he must have been black and blue – seeking to wake him up, but nothing would do it. Happily, the people around us had now acquired a sort of resistance to the noise, which enabled them at long last to choose between the mellifluous tones of Richard Burton and the raucous noise of Jack Hylton, both eminent theatrical figures. At the end of the play, just before Lancelot arrives to rescue Guinevere from the stake, where she was about to migrate satisfactorily, burnt to an ash, Jack woke up and said, 'This is a very good show. I'm going to take it to London!'

I had no words to utter, nor did I think that it made any sense to endeavour to do so, and he took *Camelot* to London, to Drury Lane, in 1964, where it ran for a year. It made, I think, very little money for him, but it was enormously valuable for his self-esteem that he had had, after all those years, a Drury Lane production. Jack had contrived to get a not uninteresting cast: he had Laurence Harvey playing the role of Lancelot and Elizabeth Larner as Queen Guinevere.

Considerable troubles arose from time to time from Laurence Harvey. I was consulted by him on more than one occasion and particularly in 1965 when he was involved financially, and I believe as an actor, in a film based on the Charge of the Light Brigade. His action was against another company which had made a film based on the same episode, for which John Osborne wrote the scenario and which was directed by Tony Richardson. Harvey's film company had acquired the rights in the famous book *The Reason Why* by Cecil Woodham-Smith, which was perhaps the best account of the Light Brigade published to date, and claimed that the other film was an infringement of the copyright in that book.

John Osborne, with great honesty, admitted that he had read the book, but in the copyright action that ensued it was pleaded that the defendants had done no more than reproduce a sequence of events established by history and not by any particular historian. However, the admission that Osborne had read the book proved fatal and the action succeeded. The judge decided that as the book retailed all the events in an orderly sequence that was largely followed by Osborne – although in my view without the slightest intention of plagiarism – it was a breach of copyright, and in the event Laurence Harvey, as the owner of the rights acquired from Cecil Woodham-Smith, obtained damages of many thousands of pounds.

The year 1965 is redolent of a not entirely satisfactory phase of my activities, when I advised two of the Beatles who were involved in a public flotation of a company called Northern Songs. It was necessary to secure the signature to the Stock Exchange documents of the two Beatles concerned, namely, Paul McCartney and John Lennon.

The appropriate Beatles came to my office. I had the great disadvantage of being able to display in good faith a complete ignorance of them. They were obviously infuriated when I failed to know which of the four they were and who did what. Their irritation was reflected in their behaviour, which more than avenged it. The document in question was presented to them and discussed and explained in detail. It emerged that two trivial typing errors had to be corrected. I informed the Beatles concerned that we would have them done within fifteen minutes. 'No,' they said, 'we cannot wait.' 'Well,' I suggested, 'there is no great harm, come back tomorrow.' At this they were enraged and said, 'We cannot – we are going to the West Indies!' Which they did, and I was required to send a clerk to the West Indies to have the document signed. Retribution could not have been more effective.

Some years later, I became involved in sorting out various tax affairs on the Beatles' behalf at the instigation of their accountants. I was also asked to advise them in relation to possible investments. The first investment they wished to embark on – or at least the first one referred to me – was a machine into which you sang and it then transcribed the song in musical notation. I am told by scientists that this is now a technical possibility, but I must confess that in my scientific ignorance I regarded it as a technical impossibility and urged them very strongly not to put their money into it. Whether they did so or not I do not have the least idea.

They were, of course, the most extraordinary young men, but since I have no ear for their kind of music – which, I am told by persons much better versed in musicology, is in its own way remarkable – it was clear that there was no special compatibility between us. They did, however, acquire Jack Hylton's former office in Savile Row, on which they proceeded to carry out renovations and redecorations that lasted for a decade.

But I did act for the man who was regarded as the only person capable of exercising any control over the Beatles, and that was their manager, Brian Epstein, whom I viewed with considerable respect. He gave no sign of the troubled nature that ultimately caused his suicide. When he died in 1967, his brother consulted me and we acted in winding up his estate. Epstein was an exceptionally nice man, and obviously it was on account of his human qualities that he exerted the influence that he did. His achievement was as remarkable as that of his clients, because managing the Beatles must have been a nightmare, except for someone who could exert a total psychological sway over them, which Epstein must have done.

I have had many dealings with the medical profession over the years and number many doctors among my friends. I enjoyed conversing with the doctors during the negotiations in the mid-1970s between the medical profession and the government over pay beds, which I describe later. Two of the most remarkable characters I have encountered in the medical world have been psychiatrists.

Early on in my army career I ran across Alexander Kennedy, later to become Professor of Psychological Medicine at Newcastle University and ultimately to have the prize job as the Professor of Psychological Medicine at the University of Edinburgh. Kennedy was the very reverse of what you would expect a psychiatrist to be: he was about 6ft 4in tall and had been an Olympic swimmer and an Olympic boxer. He had suffered an injury – from which tragically he died very young – when he was parachuted into Tito's territories as a medical member of the Parachute Corps. He was a man of a most robust common sense and of enormous intellectual powers, but totally unpretentious in the use of them. He had the unusual activity of writing television plays (as Kenneth Alexander) on psychiatric themes. He had a series of programmes on explaining dreams which was absolutely fascinating.

I came to know him and ultimately became very friendly with him, to a point where when I went to Edinburgh I would stay with him at his pleasant house in the outskirts, and when he came to London he would stay with me at my flat. I never knew him turn anyone away when there was the remotest possibility of his finding time to help, although, like many of the best British doctors, he rarely engaged in private practice despite a queue of hopeful applicants.

His opinions were always of that robust common sense, on one occasion concerning the wife of a friend of mine who had contracted that disagreeable complaint known as tinnitus, whereby you have a ringing sound in the ears which will not go away. She had been to consult several doctors, all of whom had told her – as I believe is the fact – that it either goes away by itself or it does not, but that there was no possible cure. At the request of her husband, I arranged for Kennedy to see her and she went up to Edinburgh. He sent back a report which corresponded to that of his colleagues: that she had to be patient and wait and that in his opinion it would go away, and go away before too long. The husband was not satisfied and asked me to enquire of the Professor whether there would be any point in the lady having psychiatric treatment or psychoanalysis. Kennedy returned a postcard which read simply: 'There is nothing to psychoanalyse.'

On another occasion my office contained a young stenographer whose parents sought my assistance because she was given to violent outbursts of temper, which they believed had to have a psychological origin. Again I sent her to Kennedy and again a short reply came back: 'This young lady is bad-tempered because she is bad-tempered.'

Kennedy was a fascinating companion and I spent hours talking to him. We had a three-way correspondence with a housemaster – a very enlightened one – at Winchester over the son of a very old friend. This young man was creating problems at the school and unhappily came to a tragic end. That correspondence I wished to publish, at least in so far as Kennedy's and the housemaster's contributions were concerned, but I met the iron resistance of Kennedy's first wife to the publication of any correspondence that would make any reference to the fact that he had divorced and remarried. And to this day the letters remain unpublished, as indeed do many letters of his that I would have liked to turn into book form.

The second psychiatrist, of a totally different character, still very active and lately Professor of Psychiatry at Cambridge University, is Sir Martin Roth. I encountered him when he came to see me in the early 1960s to enlist my assistance in assembling the funds to provide the Royal College of Psychiatrists with a suitable building, as he did not think, very rightly, that they would ever enjoy sufficient prestige unless they were housed in respectable quarters, in a suitable area with a discreet medical aura, where doctors could confer sagaciously together about the problems of the day.

Martin Roth has one of the keenest minds I know. He set to work with enormous determination, appointing me chairman of the committee, and within a relatively short time we collected the funds necessary to buy a very handsome home for the psychiatrists in Belgrave Square, where they are now housed. He was at that time, strangely enough, occupying the position previously occupied by Alexander Kennedy, of Professor of Psychological Medicine at Newcastle University. I should explain that the Professorship of Psychological Medicine is by no means a purely academic job: it involves hospital duties of a most strenuous kind, and Martin discharged them with a conscientiousness and energy which was beyond praise.

After Kennedy's death in 1960 there was a lacuna in my medical resources, so far as clients or friends who needed psychiatric assistance were concerned, until Martin appeared on the scene. One unfortunate wretch, who suffered the torments of the damned when his wife left him – something I must confess I found difficulty in understanding – and was reduced to the most appalling condition, was restored by the brilliant ministration of Martin, which included a degree of sympathetic understanding that is rare among doctors and certainly very rare among psychiatrists.

Another psychiatrist I had associations with was the late E. B. Strauss, who was the man who introduced, or at least promoted, electric-shock treatment in this country; but my confidence in his reliability was, I am afraid, somewhat shaken by a number of events. I had the greatest respect for Strauss, who was a kindly and intelligent man, but on one occasion he telephoned me to say that he had a patient who was the subject of the grossest legal injustice, and would I see her? Naturally I agreed to do so, and there attended upon me an elderly lady accompanied by a young man. They sat in my room and I thought of finding out the identity of the young man. 'Is he a relative?' I asked. 'No,' she said, 'a friend.' 'Ah!' I said. 'Is he a close friend?' 'Very close.' I persisted because of a niggling doubt in my mind. 'How long have you known him?' I asked. 'Oh! I met him this morning,' she replied gaily. I therefore dismissed the young man to the waiting-room and began to interrogate the lady with rather less certainty of the bona fides of her complaint than I might otherwise have had.

It then emerged that she thought she was being defrauded by the Official Solicitor. This in itself is unlikely, but I have been involved in legal affairs too long not to know that you may not dismiss a situation because it is unlikely. Not always, but frequently, the unlikely happens and someone who seems to be a model of integrity turns out to be a rogue of the first water. However, I was certainly reluctant to believe that this was the case with the Official Solicitor's office, a public organisation which has to present the most detailed account of all activities in which it is engaged. After a relatively brief conversation with the lady, I formed the firm conviction that her complaint arose from a mental condition and that I would be pursuing an innocent person on behalf of an equally innocent but, alas, unfortunate person.

In the years that I have been involved in assessing the nature and quality of clients, and also their mental stability, there are a few indications I have used that have proved helpful. One is where a person writes a long letter, in a hand of an unaltering character which does not begin to flag or change towards the end. This is in my view a clear certainty that the person is impelled by a strength of purpose beyond the normal, and it is the abnormal who possess that strength of purpose. I was presented by this said lady with a long and detailed memorandum which totally confirmed my suspicion. Another indication is when people speak in a particularly even tone from beginning to end and their conversation discloses no emotion. I tend to mistrust such people, although it would be wrong to impute a mental imbalance to them in every case.

Anyway, I told the lady I would be in touch with Dr Strauss and she left my office. I then telephoned Dr Strauss to tell him that, although not a psychiatrist, I was astonished that he had formed the view that this was a wholly balanced lady with a valid complaint. He became very indignant and untypically asked if I thought my opinion was better than his. I said I would not be as presumptuous as that on mental matters, but there might be circumstances in which an experienced layman could assess a mental disorder. 'Then you are not prepared to act for her?' he asked. 'I would only be prepared to act for her if two psychiatrists of my own choosing confirm the view that this lady has no abnormality and that her complaint can therefore be regarded as well-founded.'

He asked whom I would propose. Needless to say, I proposed Kennedy and Roth as psychiatrists for whom everyone had great respect in a profession where great respect is rarely won and almost never deserved.

He regarded this as an insult and declined to agree to my terms, so that I was relieved of any further involvement. I am happy to say that it is to Strauss's credit that the episode did not damage our future relationship, but it did serve to put me on the alert where any question of the reliability of the psychiatric opinion was concerned.

A medical dilemma which confronted me on one occasion was to give advice to an elderly parent whose son – a close friend of mine – was nevertheless mentally disturbed. He telephoned me one day and said that his son was now immured in a psychiatric clinic and that he had been asked to go down to sign a form agreeing to an operation, which turned out to be a lobotomy. He asked whether I would accompany him. I willingly agreed. We motored down to this particular institution where we were met by the resident psychiatrist, about whom it would be unfair to express the views that indeed formed very soon after seeing him. He told the father – not being particularly pleased at my presence – that in his opinion the only way to render life tolerable for my poor friend was to carry out this operation.

The father not unnaturally turned to me and said, 'What do you think, Arnold?' I thought for a moment and said that it would be wrong to refuse the consent if it was firmly established for all of us that it was a wise thing to do, but I thought we ought to have two more psychiatric opinions. The doctor was not in the least pleased. 'I can get you another opinion here,' he announced, 'from another resident psychiatrist.' I replied firmly and without equivocation that I did not think the fox bringing in his tail as a witness was a very effective way of dealing with the matter. I said that I would like to nominate the two psychiatrists, to which he grudgingly agreed. I then asked him to write a report both to Professor Kennedy and to Dr Strauss, which he agreed to do.

The replies I received from both had a tragic similarity. Both said words to the effect that, as was of course gravely apprehended, although my friend would in the end be brought to suicide, they would regard this as a preferable course to pursue than to have a lobotomy, which would reduce him to a cabbage. In the event he did not have the operation and in fact killed himself some ten years later. But my feeling is that both Kennedy and Strauss were right. If he had had the operation, he would have been reduced to a condition that would have caused total misery among the people around him and rendered him to be unfit to be among the human race, whereas during those ten years he did have periods when he enjoyed life.

My own experience of the psychiatric world is that it has a few radiant stars, a mass of relatively mediocre but conscientious practitioners, and a small number of immensely successful charlatans who sometimes produce results by the sheer impact of their bill, when the patient realises that it would be much more to his advantage to effect recovery than to continue with their services.

7

The Film Industry

IN THE WINTER of 1945/6 I was introduced by my friend Frank Coven to Sidney Gilliatt, who was then an established film director, perhaps best known as a scenarist. Sidney Gilliatt subsequently introduced me to Frank Launder, who had worked in a scriptwriting partnership with him and with whom he was a sort of cinematic Siamese twin. The film with which they had been traditionally associated over the years is *The Lady Vanishes*, which Hitchcock filmed in 1938 and which has become a minor classic.

Sidney and I met for dinner at the Gay Hussar in Soho, which was then a favourite centre of the film industry and to which I became very attached for two reasons: first that I liked the tasty food and second the prices, which although not derisory were still within the range of my continuing modest income.

At that meeting Sidney appreciated that I had a keen interest in the cinema, which I have indeed possessed throughout my life, from the early stage as a small child when I started by seeing Theda Bara and Lillian Gish and Dorothy Gish and D. W. Griffith and things that are now historical memories, and the occasional continental films such as *The Cabinet of Dr Caligari* or *Metropolis* with Brigitte Helm made by the legendary Fritz Lang who subsequently went to Hollywood. I had spent a good deal of my life, in fact too much for the satisfaction of my teachers and my parents, at the cinema. Although I had a keen interest in sport in the summer season and loved playing cricket in preference to any other activity, my second choice was going to the cinema. It is a habit I have now lost, visiting a cinema on average about once a year. In those days I was visiting cinemas of astonishing cheapness: for the sum of four old pennies one could sit comfortably before a silent film in the first three rows of a largely empty auditorium, listening to the tinkling of the accompanist's piano and watching with great interest such stars as Ronald Colman, Greta Garbo ... I could go on for ever.

I think my conversation with Sidney must have impressed him considerably because he asked me, towards the end of our dinner, whether I had ever tried my hand at writing. I told him that I had written the odd essay on occasions but had never tried to write either a play or a film scenario. He promised to send me a typical treatment so that I might get an idea of how these things were done. I could then try my hand at writing the treatment for a film he was about to make called *London Belongs to Me*, from a novel by Norman Collins. I purchased a copy of the novel, read it with increasing horror, but arrived at the conclusion that many worse films had been made on worse subjects and since one had to start somewhere one might as well begin with this. I did in fact write a treatment, which I thought masterly – a view not entirely shared by anyone else – and in the event got my first treatment credit. The credit was totally undeserved because when I watched the film, with the greatest of care and meticulous attention to detail, I do not think I was able to detect a single word or suggestion that had emerged from my treatment. However, this did not deter them from acknowledging my incipient talents and I was paid what seemed to me a very handsome sum of £250 for this effort.

I developed what has remained a deep and affectionate friendship with both Sidney Gilliatt and Frank Launder. That they have remained partners for years is, to those who do not know them well, an unexplained mystery. To anyone who knows them well, as I do, they form the perfect complement to each other. Sidney is an introspective pessimist, given over to a determinedly gloomy view of the likely possibilities of life. Frank is an incorrigible optimist, explicable perhaps by the fact that he started life as a clerk in the bankruptcy offices in Brighton. At any rate, the two worked splendidly together. I do not believe, and I do not think they would ever claim, that they have made any really great films, but the large majority have been sufficiently entertaining to draw an audience. One can only gauge how much better they are than the modern products when one sees them revived again, as they are periodically on television. One realises the care and thought that went into them in contrast with their more modern rivals.

In any event, I started to establish a reputation for writing dialogue for trial scenes. This I found particularly entertaining and the high point was reached when Sidney asked me in 1955 if I would do the dialogue for a film he was making with Rex Harrison called *The Constant Husband*. I produced a rigmarole of absolute nonsense which provided them with great satisfaction and was used almost word for word in the film. I had

the satisfaction of reading that the *Evening Standard*'s film critic thought
the court scene in *The Constant Husband* was the best in any British film.

In 1957 matters began to take a more serious turn. I had become
solicitor both to Sidney Gilliatt and to Frank Launder, and I became
involved in what was then (initially) a scheme for the purchase by both
of them, and other independent producers, of British Lion Films Ltd
from the National Film Finance Corporation which owned it. Alas, the
project eventually collapsed owing to the steadily deteriorating financial
prospects of British Lion.

However, early in 1958 the NFFC themselves approached Sidney and
Frank and the Boulting brothers, with whom they had been associated (a
working though not a legal relationship), to accept directorships of British
Lion, with the suggestion that they should sign exclusive contracts for
their respective services for what appeared to me to be a modest annual
salary. The real incentive was that, with government approval, a class of
deferred shares would be made available for their purchase so that if the
company became profitable they would benefit accordingly. I was much
involved in the negotiations and there were various hiccups, such as the
determination of Sidney and Frank *not* to contract for more than two and
a half years, although the Boulting brothers agreed to contract for five
years.

Their contracts started in February 1958, but shortly afterwards the
government proceeded to harry the producers to buy the company, under
the rather ugly threat that if they did not do so it would be disposed of
to the first bidder. The attack was inspired by a pessimistic report on the
company's prospects by John (now Sir John) Terry, managing director of
the NFFC.

Throughout 1959/60 I was heavily involved in advising the directors
of British Lion in their possible buy-out negotiations with the NFFC
and the Board of Trade, and I discovered some sources of finance,
principally Hambros Bank. The negotiations were unhappily so protracted
that in the meantime the company's fortunes improved dramatically, so
that when agreement had been finally secured with the NFFC, with
characteristic treachery and perfidy the Board of Trade turned down the
entire proposition, on the basis that it was no longer as attractive to them
as it had been at the beginning of the discussions. At that point the two-
and-a-half-year contracts with Sidney and Frank were approaching their
termination, which underlined the necessity for speedy decision.

It was at this point that fortunes changed. Reginald Maudling, who
was then the President of the Board of Trade, paid a private visit to the
small projection theatre of British Lion. This gave one or two directors
an opportunity to speak to him about the whole matter and to express

their thorough distaste at the way in which the negotiations were proceeding. It was, I think the first time in the negotiations for the acquisition of the company that the directors had gone over the heads of the NFFC and the Board of Trade, and in doing so they caused considerable resentment and bitterness.

The upshot of the Maudling meeting was that he continued to decline to restore the previously agreed deal by British Lion, saying that by now the company was doing much too well. But he agreed that – to use exactly his own words – they had been 'thoroughly buggered about'. On the understanding that all the directors would extend their contracts to six years from their original inception, he agreed that they should be left undisturbed to run the company; that they should provide their own chairman, and that they should have the right to buy the company at a fresh valuation agreed by both sides. He also agreed – perhaps without considering the implications – to my suggestion of a 'put' option in any new arrangement, which would mean in effect that the directors would have the right to be bought out by the NFFC at their request, in addition to the 'take' option they already possessed. Thus somewhere around the beginning of 1961 they entered into the new arrangement, and out of that arrangement, incidentally, came the official appointment of Goodman Derrick & Co. as the legal representative of British Lion.

Meantime, the films being made enjoyed some success; but a major feature of the success of the company was the extraordinary vision displayed by Frank Launder, who would not ordinarily be regarded as a visionary. He foresaw (as no one else did) the potential value of films which had exhausted their theatre showing but which could enjoy a new and indeed indefinite lease of life on television. Television was still in its infancy, and few people would have predicted that a catalogue of 'old' films would not only increase immensely in value but remain a basic need for most television stations to this day. So far as British television companies are concerned, the old films – i.e. films made by British Lion, by ABC, by the Rank Organisation and a few others – have become worth their weight in gold. In the end, at Frank's persuasion, British Lion sold all the old films in which they retained exhibition rights to the BBC for what then appeared to be an enormous sum, but which today would be a fleabite.

A good deal of friction arose between Sir Nutcome Hume, the chairman of the NFFC, the Board of Trade and British Lion, arising from the determination of the governmental side to offload the company whenever it could. But in view of the new Goodman-negotiated contracts they could not, for the time being, look to any other purchaser than the directors. Before the end of the six years, it was made clear to the government and the official side that the directors concerned were interested in continuing after the six years but only on condition that the responsibilities were spread and lightened by bringing in new associates; that part, if not the whole, of the directors' shareholding should be bought out as they had been on short commons for many years; that the company should continue to serve independent producers, that is to say independent of the two big circuits which were ABC and Rank; and that the government should retain, ideally through the NFFC, a small interest in the company on the grounds that it gave some muscle at least in facing the duopoly of ABC and Rank.

There was a considerable amount of acrimonious discussion, at one stage over a private lunch at a restaurant which was edifying neither for the menu nor the conversation. Possibly if a more attractive locale had been chosen the end could have been different, but as it was Sir Nutcome Hume stormed out in a rage. He had aroused anger because his idea of spreading the responsibility was to bring in a consortium of ABC and Rank, thus destroying the whole conception of an independent body. After that the NFFC continued conversations only with David Kingsley (who was for practical purposes the finance director and the most influential person on the board of British Lion), although Kingsley made no secret of his own desire to be fully bought out and get the hell out of it.

The most dramatic episode was in December 1963 when, without further notice to the existing board, the NFFC made an effort summarily to buy them out, sending round cheques by hand to the office with a request for their resignations. Not unnaturally, an interview was demanded with Sir Nutcome. With minimum grace he declared that the NFFC had found another purchaser for British Lion and therefore had bought them out. Under cross-examination the information was elicited – with considerable reluctance, rather like the drawing of teeth – that the new purchaser was Sydney Box; whereupon all five directors walked out of the offices of the NFFC straight to Fleet Street to make the loudest clamour possible and thence to the House of Commons. It was no doubt the hope of the Board of Trade that British Lion's sale would be conducted quickly and silently during the Christmas parliamentary recess, but the determined efforts of the five directors managed to get the matter raised on the adjournment debate. Through parliamentary channels the whole matter was, for the time being, kicked into touch while Edward Heath, who then was at the Board of Trade, considered what to do.

During this period of intense activity a private intimation was received that the Junior Minister at the Board of Trade would rather like to talk the matter over informally with Frank and Sidney at Shepperton Studios, and he was asked by them to lunch. But as might have been expected, he did not succeed in getting there without his senior advisers at the Board of Trade, who had indeed arrived first. The Minister, who had indulged perhaps a little generously in sherry, became slightly indiscreet in his comments about certain personalities in the other organisations concerned, much to the indignation of his officials at the lunch.

There was a period of exciting activity when anything might have happened. At a New Year party given by Sir Michael Balcon, and attended by Richard Attenborough, Bryan Forbes and various others, in the general desire to participate and to give such advice as he could, Balcon said he was willing to do anything reasonable that would help to defeat the NFFC's summary buy-out. When Sidney reported this development next day, John Boulting promptly telephoned Balcon, who came over in a remarkably short space of time and found himself writing to the Minister of State, pointing out that he, like others, would have welcomed the opportunity to form a consortium and take over British Lion had time and opportunity been given. The upshot of this was that the Junior Minister previously referred to invited himself to have coffee (this time wisely avoiding alcohol) with Frank and Sidney at the Connaught and showed them a batch of proposals, no doubt concocted by the battered officials at the Board of Trade, which had been approved by Edward Heath. The Junior Minister, having heard their opinion, departed apparently happy and certainly on this occasion sober.

These proposals subsequently formed the basis for the conditions when British Lion was put up to tender. The government, however, would not budge over the matter of retaining the smallest financial participation in British Lion. They wanted a full sell-out. Meantime Sydney Box and his alleged Greek backers, John and James Woolf, Michael Balcon, Attenborough and others, were all forming their groups. Attenborough, Forbes and most of the vociferous people at the New Year party melted away like snow in May, no doubt on the recommendation of their financial advisers, or from some suspicion of the Boulting brothers who were viewed as 'being difficult'. At that half-way stage Balcon had only half an army, but had brought Bernard Delfont under the umbrella. Somehow David Kingsley had also brought in Joseph Janni, an established film director who had a respectable record of success. Balcon finally surfaced with the promise of an investment from Border TV. There were still Frank and Sidney and the Boultings, an undefined link with Woodfall, and a never precisely unveiled understanding with Walter Reade, the American cinema owner.

But help was at hand: Frank Launder evolved a co-operative scheme, principally designed to stop anybody else spending his money (and to be fair, that of his partner, Sidney Gilliatt). This was a group scheme about which I had very considerable misgivings. The parent company would provide finance independently, on a strictly proportional basis, so that if there were six companies the parent company would contribute one-sixth of the total finance for each film. If a producing company's films were successful the stake would increase accordingly and with it its credit line. If the films failed, the company's liabilities would diminish proportionately. If the other companies wished to participate in each other's films they could do so. As Frank Launder had circulated the scheme to all the participants, there was very little opportunity for discussing it in advance. I myself had considerable doubts whether such a scheme would work; whether indeed the making of a film which was dependent on the willing co-operation of five or six different entities was a rational proposition.

Finally, an offer or proposition was cobbled together by me and submitted to the Board of Trade. The offer included the acceptance of the conditions laid down by the government and was therefore accepted, perhaps not altogether surprisingly since all the others shied away from the terms and withdrew. Even so, it was firmly believed by the Launder – Gilliatt – Boulting camp that Sir Nutcombe Hume, John Terry and the Board of Trade officials must have been extremely chagrined to find the old group back in play.

The scheme became associated with the name of Michael Balcon, although ironically throughout the entire negotiations no proposal of any kind was made as to what office he might hold. When the syndicate was awarded the company, enormous haste was introduced to secure Balcon an appropriate title and salary. In this way he became chairman.

The new company did not start peacefully. Bernard Delfont soon withdrew, leaving a rather nasty gap in the financial provisions which had to be filled by last-minute approaches to a number of people, with which I was myself much concerned. There were a number of grievances about tentative promises and arrangements that had been made individually but without consultation with anyone else. One particular complaint was that of Walter Reade, who had been promised American distribution of all British Lion films by Balcon. It can be said, I think with some truth, that the only participants in the new venture without other commitments were Launder, Gilliatt and the Boulting brothers, and they were the only ones who reasonably carried out their undertakings. It was to be anticipated that the controversy that raged in the boardroom would affect studio productions, and in consequence the flow of films was reduced almost to a total halt.

There was great friction between Michael Balcon and the rest, since he obviously saw himself in the role of the undisputed leader whose views should be accepted. It would require a particularly sanguine person to think that a group which contained Launder and Gilliatt, the Boulting brothers and others would accept unargued decisions from anyone. So Balcon's nerves were permanently on edge. Launder's group system was, as I had anticipated, a considerable bar to production. The only part of the group scheme which ever worked was that which involved the participation only of the individual company concerned, British Lion putting up one-fifth of the money and the company four-fifths, as when Launder and Gilliatt made *The Great St Trinian's Train Robbery* – the first of a sequence of St Trinian films of unspeakable horror but a great success financially.

It was in the autumn of 1965 that matters came to a head. At a dinner at the Garrick Club, convened by Balcon, he proceeded to deliver an ultimatum: the threat that, unless Launder's group rules could be adjusted or abolished, and production could proceed along what he considered the right lines, he really had no alternative but to step down. The threat was received in total and embarrassed silence. It was difficult to decide who was more embarrassed – Balcon or the rest of them. The party broke up with not a word having been uttered to deter Balcon and in the result he had no alternative other than to resign.

What then happened, as I am informed, was that John Boulting called a meeting with Launder and Gilliatt to discuss asking me to take on the chairmanship of British Lion. As a result of this, they came round to see me and described the circumstances. They felt that unless a decisive step was taken the company would break up in disorder. To what I understand was their gratified surprise, I agreed to take on the chairmanship, although basically as an act of friendship, and of course on condition that it must be at the invitation of the board as a whole.

Thus it was that I became the chairman of the board of British Lion, and thus it was that those opposed to the change immediately spread the story that I had been waiting in the wings to replace Balcon. The idea had been voiced on the spur of the moment. It had not been the result of any previous discussion, let alone intrigue.

Perhaps inevitably, I was faced with the probability that Balcon's adherents and any others opposed to the group rules (or hostile to individual members of other companies) would tend to look elsewhere. Border without Balcon were left exposed, with no avenue of production. Tiberia Films (a working organisation which was important because it contained Joseph Janni) had not then made a film for British Lion, particularly because of the hash that Janni and Sidney Gilliatt had made of their relationship, and Walter Reade was more aggrieved than ever. In due course, therefore, came hints that certain parties might like to be bought out. This was agreed with both Border and Tiberia, and Walter Reade retired from the scene to die a most unlikely death on the snow slopes.

In describing what happened, I do not mean to imply that no sooner was I seated in the chair than there was a general exodus from British Lion followed by death and disaster. It would certainly be more accurate to describe it as heralding a scene in which the less committed elements would shuffle off out of the theatre while the old guard reflected on why they had ever ventured on stage in the first place. In due course David Kingsley departed, thus leaving vacant his post as acting managing director. There was no competition to take his place but John Boulting offered to do the job until somebody else could be found.

While a memorandum to me from Frank and Sidney advocated a policy of retrenchment in what might be described as a retreat to winter quarters, John Boulting's views were much more pessimistic, virtually advocating the disposal of a great deal of the entire load. Unfortunately (or fortunately as the case may be) John Boulting was promptly overruled by his twin, a not uncommon phenomenon; and so a policy of increasingly limited involvement was somehow converted into one of expansion of output.

By that time I had won the allegiance of the rest of the board, but I should make it clear that I never became a traditional film mogul, best demonstrated by the fact that throughout my period of association I did not seduce a single actress; nor did I find any of the more personable in the least willing to be seduced. A feature of my association with any or all of the arts was my failure to seize my opportunities to meet the great. Until many years later I had never met John Gielgud or Ralph Richardson or Michael Redgrave, and the only actress I ever became friendly with was Peggy Ashcroft – upon whom I hasten to say I had no designs.

My acceptance of the difficult and unrewarding job as the chairman of a miscellany of talent was rendered the more disagreeable by the reaction of Michael Balcon. He failed to admit or recognise that my appointment followed his resignation. Nothing would persuade him that I was not at the head of a conspiracy designed to replace him by me. My other associates realised that an ambition to become the chairman of British Lion would only be held by someone mentally disturbed. However, although I never made peace with him during his lifetime, I have affectionate recollections of Sir Michael and am sorry that he departed this life retaining his belief in my perfidy.

Things prospered to begin with under the new regime. In due course I and Max Rayne (who had joined the board in 1967) put forward the proposal that British Lion should go public in order to secure fresh capital for production; together with the suggestion that Shepperton Studios be mortgaged with the same end of increasing the funds available. The company went public somewhere around the end of 1968, the issue being handsomely oversubscribed.

Around that time John Boulting expressed a desire to be relieved of his post, and Mark Chapman-Walker was appointed managing director. But the appointment proved somewhat disastrous, with the result that John was overburdened with both managerial and production responsibilities, both areas involving the putting forward of production capital to an extent which would have been regarded as far too risky a few years earlier (nor were such limits as *had* been agreed properly observed).

Simultaneously, the terms of trade had turned increasingly against British films. The original four working directors – Launder, Gilliatt and the Boultings – had undertaken to be less abrasive in their attitude towards the Rank–ABC duopoly, but this restraint yielded absolutely no benefits, nor did I have any expectations on that score. So not only was British Lion confronting a dangerous situation, but other problems inevitably arose. We were faced with a high-risk period of production at excessive cost through fewer avenues, and we were in danger of virtual extinction if the bevy of expensive films we had backed – over some of which we could maintain only minimal control – were to flop. This in fact happened, coupled with the disturbing feature that, as a result of the fall-off in American-sponsored production, the Shepperton Studio turnover had been much reduced.

It was about this time that, with the consent of the board, I began discussions with the heads of the other two studios as to whether there might be some form of studio rationalisation which would, in effect, result in the three major studios (Elstree, Pinewood and Shepperton) being reduced to two only. My expert advisers took the view that the ideal solution would have been for ABC to close down Elstree – the least satisfactory studio of the three – and to combine as a single enterprise with Shepperton, which could then be modernised and even expanded.

Bernard Delfont, who had, so far as I was concerned, vanished as an associate of British Lion, emerged with a scheme of his own supporting this plan, on the basis that, in addition to introducing his own production talents, he would also provide some much-needed working capital. Unfortunately Delfont had developed a habit of changing his mind. Having previously expressed his total support for the rationalisation of studios, and although at some stage he claimed that the idea had been his, he then made haste to distance himself from the project. In the result, a limited agreement was drafted which would pool Shepperton with Pinewood and eventually lead to the closure of Shepperton. These proposals needed the approval of the NFFC, which in our view was refused for insufficient reason.

With the approval of our merchant bank – Hambros – we then entertained a proposal to do a reverse takeover operation with an important cinema group in the north of England. When we announced this intention, we also asked that the British Lion Stock Exchange quotation should be suspended pending the production of sets of accounts from each company, which would provide an investor with some basis to form a view about the value of the shares. An arrangement with the cinema-owners would have been very sensible. We had assets of considerable value in possessing the rights of almost all the films that we had manufactured in the past. But these assets were solidly frozen and produced very little income. On the other hand, the cinema company owned a circuit which produced very good profits. Added to our assets, this seemed a favourable arrangement for a fresh flotation. But unhappily the cinema-owners ran into Revenue trouble, of which until almost the moment of signature we had had no warning.

At that stage I decided it was necessary to find out how serious this Revenue trouble was, so I made an appointment to see the chairman of the Inland Revenue (Sir Arnold France) and went round at the double. I explained the situation to him and that the enlarged company was about to reissue its shares, and that I needed to know what warning, if any, should be provided for the shareholders and whether in the event we should proceed with the merger arrangement.

Sir Arnold informed me that he would investigate the position and within the hour he had telephoned me at my office with a short but very cogent message: 'My advice is that you should not become involved in this matter.' On that basis we withdrew from any discussions, but the situation troubled me, and my board at that time was a desperately miserable one. Our quotation had been suspended at our own request, when we started the negotiations with the cinema-owners. Hence we had no quotation. The expectation had been aroused by City leakage that something good was about to happen, and nothing in fact was about to happen. At a board meeting we sat forlornly round the table waiting for a miracle, and to our intense relief such a miracle did emerge.

I was approached in the early part of 1972 by a Mr John Bentley, chairman of Barclay Securities, who said he wished to see me. I knew nothing of him except that his name appeared quite frequently in the financial press as a thrusting young City figure. He lost no time in coming to his business. 'I would like to buy British Lion,' he declared to me. I retained sufficient nerve to reply that it was a valuable organisation and he could not buy it cheaply. His response was to make an offer. Readers should remember that when our quotation was suspended the share price was about 40p. I asked Mr Bentley what price he had in mind and to my intense joy he mentioned a figure of 100p. Frank and Sidney, who had by then joined us, were waiting patiently to hear my acceptance of the offer; but I did not accept it since it was clear to me that Mr Bentley had a special use for the company. My colleagues informed me afterwards that, when I refused the offer, they came nearer to heart attacks than ever before. In the end we settled at 135p per share on the basis that Mr Bentley would buy out all the shareholders who were willing to sell. In fact he bought them all out.

Thus I departed from the scene rather pleased with myself – although I had done absolutely nothing to achieve the situation – and we transferred the task to the lawyers (including myself). There was some sharp difference about what should appear in the public advertisements in relation to Mr Bentley, because he had had a rather adventurous financial career. However, in the end, with the assistance of the Stock Exchange and the respective advisers (Slater Walker for the purchasers and Hambros for British Lion), an advertisement was produced which satisfied the misgivings of both sides and we retrieved our quotation which then had a much improved appearance. Mr Bentley was a pleasure to do business with. I hope that the transaction turned out to his advantage, but I have never met him since the moment when the ink became dry on the contract.

The outcome for us was as good as we could have expected. We received a more than fair price, having regard to the reigning problems, although none of the directors regarded it as wildly excessive having regard to the substantial assets we owned. The arrangement spelt the end of my association with British Lion; indeed, except for a disastrous investment that I made with one of our erstwhile directors, I have had no further involvement in the British film industry and, if I may say so, am greatly relieved that this is so. The takeover had been my most anxious period at British Lion, although I greatly enjoyed the board meetings and occasional visits to Shepperton.

In the past two or three decades no one has emerged sufficiently wealthy and determined to blaze a new trail for film-making in Britain. It is a sadness because there is no doubt that the country possessed and still possesses immensely efficient directors, for instance Richard Attenborough, the best corps of acting talent in the world and competent creative screenwriters, but the one person needed has not existed in the British industry since the death of Sir Alexander Korda. The Rank Organisation in my day was rich but top-heavy with competent businessmen. No industry whose essential requirements are imagination and courage can be helped by businessmen alone. I have a chastening recollection of my period of service at British Lion; it is a comfort to me that at no time did I regard myself as the inspiration of an active, creative company, and in this I was undoubtedly right. Even so, one of the most agreeable parts of my professional life has been the variety and colour of the film practitioners (not forgetting actors and actresses) who have come my way as clients. Helped to some extent by the firm friendship I had formed with Sidney Gilliatt and Frank Launder, I enjoyed in my salad days a steady stream of film personnel seeking advice and assistance. The man who exercised most influence in his recommendations to me was the late Christopher Mann, whom Sidney Gilliatt and Frank Launder had introduced me to. He was one of the most successful of entertainment agents, with an immensely imaginative mind which was invaluable to him in bringing together film deals. He was a lawyer *manqué* and loved discussions about legal points arising in the affairs of his numerous distinguished clientele, involving a great number of film producers and writers in England from David Lean onwards. I became very close to him, and indeed to his talented wife Eileen Joyce, the pianist, and remained so until his death in the late 1970s.

One day in 1958, Christopher Mann rang me and asked if I would call on Robert Donat (who was then terminally ill) in order to take instructions for a will. I had not previously acted for him. I called at the Fitzroy Nursing Home in Bloomsbury and saw a tragic figure. I remembered Robert Donat when he made his debut in London in *A Sleeping Clergyman* – a Bridie play which has now disappeared, as indeed has, sadly, the entire Bridie repertoire. From then onwards I had seen Donat occasionally in plays and in films – I believe that in his long career he appeared very rarely, largely due to his health and also to his temperament – but the figure I saw in the hospital bed was an emaciated and pitiful version of the wonderfully handsome man he had been, probably the most handsome of all the screen actors I have admired. I recollect him appearing in an incomparable performance of *Much Ado About Nothing*, where, as Benedick, his courtship of Beatrice – played by his wife Renée Asherson – was one of the most charming love scenes on the stage. I have never seen a more sparkling production in that marvellous interchange between Beatrice and Benedick, where the abuse is the language of love and which is one of the great demonstrations of Shakespeare's genius.

When I visited Donat it was plain that he was weak and ill, but even then he was a man of enormous charm. I took some notes for a will but, so far as I can recollect, he died before it could be completed. He kept changing his mind, and each time that I completed a draft he said, 'Come back next week and I shall think again whether this disposition is right or not.'

On one occasion he proceeded to tell me a tragic tale of the misfortunes that had afflicted him in his life. I cannot, without a breach of confidence – and a rather disgraceful one – divulge the cause that was clearly gnawing at his vitals. He poured out his heart about the behaviour of a fellow actor – by the side of Donat a very minor figure – who had, according to Donat, behaved in a disgraceful fashion in relation to him. Donat's sincerity and the circumstantial account persuaded me that he had a just grievance, but there was nothing to be done about it.

An interesting film director with whom I became very friendly, through my great friend Donald Bull, was Ian Dalrymple, who had made several successful films including *The Wooden Horse* and *Esther Waters* (from George Moore's novel). He was also a man of great charm but he lacked the push indispensable for success in a highly competitive and ruthless industry. It was he who commissioned me to write an original script which I did with Donald Bull and called it *The Cracker Case*. The film was never made but the treatment was bought by Rank, which looked at it from time to time but could not find in it a tolerable film by their standards. Donald, of course, went on to become a distinguished writer for the BBC and scripted one or two famous series including *Dr Finlay's Casebook*.

I got involved in an interesting controversy that Fred Zinnemann had in 1966 with Carl Foreman, who made a slightly impudent claim that he had directed *High Noon*. Since this film was notoriously associated with Fred Zinnemann, he was moved to almost apoplectic fury when he came to hear of this totally unjustified assertion. The matter was resolved in a thoroughly agreeable fashion when I extracted a letter from Foreman repudiating any suggestion that he had directed *High Noon* and Zinnemann was totally satisfied.

When the matter was completed, Zinnemann asked me for a note of my fees, but I assured him that I did not want any fees for a piece of work that involved very little effort and gave such pleasure and delight to one of the most creative directors in the world. Instead of sending him a fee note, I asked if he would show me *High Noon*, which at that stage I had never seen, although since then I have seen it three or four times on television. A very pleasant evening was arranged when the film was shown in British Lion's small projection room, followed by supper, all in the presence of an excessively grateful client.

My relationship with Carl Foreman never blossomed. In fact it was made far worse when I suggested to him that he should make a film in conjunction with British Lion. I suggested as a subject a fascinating novel based on Victorian days, describing a marathon race around the Agricultural Hall in Islington with a murder intertwined. He obviously approved of the suggestion since I read in a newspaper that he had acquired the film rights of the novel, of which he had never heard until I mentioned it. We never composed the difference but the film remained unmade.

Many successful writers consulted me at this time, including Arnold Wesker and Peter Shaffer. I enjoyed working for them, and if one became any sort of a friend they were very interesting company. Among the famous actors who crossed my threshold were James Mason, Stewart Granger, Michael Wilding, Anthony Newley – who consulted me about his divorce, before his marriage to Joan Collins – and Alastair Sim.

Alastair Sim was a leading character in an intriguing situation which, alas, was never resolved. His voice, coupled with his Scottish accent, was so distinctive that anyone who heard it could immediately identify him. Unfortunately, it was individual enough to make imitation a possibility to a skilled actor.

Ron Moody – a very talented actor – did a series of television advertisements, in 1958, advertising Heinz and its beans, in which, without any acknowledgement, he imitated Alastair's voice. Heinz declined to make any payment to Alastair. The legal area was uncertain, but Alastair was indignant and there was certainly a good chance that we would succeed in a passing-off action. Perhaps unfortunately the point was never resolved since our claim was settled by the company in a quite generous way. I remained friendly with Alastair Sim and, like many others, a great admirer of his skills.

Another consequence of my association with the film industry, and in particular with Gilliatt, Launder and the Boultings, was that I became increasingly involved in racing matters.

Frank Launder had made a suggestion in 1960 that Sidney Gilliatt and I should become joint owners of a number of horses. I was reluctant to do this since I had no interest in the turf and had no wish to see the animals run – in fact I never went to see them run. But I agreed to join in and we began to acquire one or two horses. One of them, named Maigret, won two or three races with the greatest of ease, until for some reason he decided that it was no longer worth the exertion and ceased to try. But I must say, in fairness, that it turned out he had a bad heart.

In 1961 Frank Launder went across to Ireland to buy another horse for us. We had, as a syndicate, set a limit of £2,500; not an immense sum by today's standards, but then a good price for a horse that had not established its credentials. Frank telephoned me from Ireland to say that a horse regarded with great approval by the *cognoscenti* in the racing world could be obtained for £3,000, and asked if I was prepared to increase my own participation, which would have been something like £100 more than I intended. Being of a mild and non-controversial disposition, I immediately agreed to this, but Sidney Gilliatt flatly declined to increase his contribution, as a result of which Frank did not buy the horse. The horse turned out to be Nicolaus Silver, which that very year won the Grand National.

This, however, did not discourage me from racing (although it should be an object lesson to anyone who wishes to engage in this demented pursuit) and we continued to buy other horses. This brought about a series of 'Dear Frank' letters from me to Frank Launder, in reply to his regular updates to me about our laggardly steeds. For example:

Dear Frank,

Of course we are mad. Were we not mad originally to have invested the equivalent of the price of an excellent motor car in an animal none of us can ride and which achieves no results of any kind when ridden by a stranger? Would we entertain the notion of keeping in the pink of condition and the lap of luxury even a dear and close relative under the pretext that he would occasionally compete in the Olympic Games – despite his obvious ineligibility? In any event, we go on keeping this large and hungry animal on a pretext no more valid. Since we are mad, it is plain that we will go on buying more horses, incurring more expense for less purpose as we grow older and more foolish, until ultimately they will be our joint and collective ruin.

Yours ever,

Arnold

Dear Frank,

I am glad to hear that Thundergun progresses. Keep him on a light diet, employ the most expensive masseurs, radiographers, etc., and do not let him have any kind of anxiety. This should ensure his complete recovery. The day will yet come when I will eat my words by leading Thundergun in after the Grand National – probably from some adjoining course to which he has escaped.

Yours ever,

Arnold

Dear Frank,

I am obliged to you for your communications reporting on the unhappy state of health of Maigret and Thundergun. I trust further bulletins will be issued as necessary. I have repeatedly urged that no expense should be spared in the treatment of both horses and would again suggest that some psychological treatment might be allied with the physical remedies now being employed. This would seem particularly appropriate for Thundergun, since he appears to lack balance, a sense of purpose and – on previous occasions – a sense of direction. I feel sure that this highly intelligent animal has not come to terms with life and is also probably subconsciously resentful of the variegated and rather bourgeois nature of his present ownership – not to speak of the unwarranted earlier interference with his emotional life.

> Yours ever,
>
> Arnold

However, we did eventually strike lucky with a horse called Beauchamp. This animal won a spectacular victory: he won the Heinz Cup at Ascot in 1969. It is an enormous silver cup, inscribed with the names of the owners, which it was decided unanimously should be retained by me and now reposes on my sideboard. There it is, testifying to the fact that I was, at some time, a racing man, although I think any authentic racing man would regard me with the greatest suspicion as an imposter.

We brought other hopefuls into the syndicate and I continued in the racing business for about another ten years, at which time I began to tire of it and was fed up with the never-ending writing of cheques to trainers. It had been fun, but a very costly exercise.

As the years proceeded, I became less and less interested in actors and film-makers, and in recent years I have been engaged in more intellectual occupations. But I did enjoy my brief flirtation with the entertainment industry and retained many friends in it.

8

Professional Misgivings

SO FAR AS the law is concerned, the branch of activities to which one gravitates is determined by a number of factors, of which choice is by no means a predominant one. If your father has been a fishmonger, your clients are likely to be deep-sea fishermen, fishmongers and restaurateurs, providing *sole bonne femme* and similar delicacies. If your father is a coal merchant, your clients will be purveyors of coal, oil and other heating materials.

In my case my father was an unsuccessful South African shipper and it is the truth that not a single client ever came to me through family connections. In consequence, elements of choice played a larger part than was usual. The effect of being articled to Rubinstein Nash, the leading firm of literary and artistic lawyers, produced associations that have given my legal practice a strong bent in that direction. That my clientele included a number of authors, publishers and literary agents, and ultimately a substantial number of newspaper associations, meant that one activity with which I have continually been concerned was the law of libel.

One of the great injustices is the reputation I have acquired of being a 'trigger-happy' libel lawyer, anxious to encourage anyone to institute proceedings against any publication worthy of its salt, or more accurately worthy of its cash. This is an ironic injustice. I can truthfully claim that there are few practising solicitors who are habitually consulted on matters of defamation who have more actively discouraged their clientele from embarking on libel actions.

I must, over my fifty-five or more years in practice, have been consulted by more than a thousand aggrieved individuals anxious to vindicate their names and reputations against some unjustified insult, or what they believe to be an unjustified insult. Time and again I have advised them to forget it. I encourage them to do so by asking them how long they can remember alleged libels directed against their friends or acquaintances. Within a week, I assure them, no one will remember the offensive words that have been said about them and they will have forgotten them themselves.

I frequently invoke Disraeli's recipe for dealing with a wrong. He wrote the culprit's name on a piece of paper and put it in a drawer and claimed that in almost every case, when he opened the drawer years hence and read the name, he found that destiny had avenged him. But even if reliance is not placed on the working of providence, I strongly urge that a libel action, with its increasing cost as the years go by, with its appalling delays, and with the uncertainty of a jury verdict, is a demented adventure by most people and should only be resorted to when the affront is so gross that no self-respecting person can ignore it. Most people accept this advice with alacrity. In fact, although people want to vindicate their reputations, they are very anxious to give an appearance of being held back.

Very occasionally one finds a passionate litigant. I do not believe that in all my years of practice I have been concerned for a plaintiff in more than a dozen contested libel actions. On many occasions a claim has resulted in an early settlement, with an apology either by a letter in a newspaper or by a mention in open court. Usually the more reckless the assertion, the easier to extract an apology. While the author, usually a journalist, will stick to his guns however slight the justification, the newspaper or publisher or printer, on whom the ultimate cost may fall, is less courageous and anxious to settle on the least costly terms. It is one reason why of recent years, if compelled to institute proceedings against a newspaper, I have strongly advised that the journalist concerned should not be added as a defendant. This is particularly so after it was established by Miss Honor Tracy in an action against the *Sunday Times* that an apology by that newspaper without the concurrence of the journalist could by itself be a libel on the journalist. Hence, if an action has to ensue, the desideratum is that the newspaper should apologise in terms which cannot reflect on the journalist who writes the piece. This is often difficult and sometimes impossible, but it is the course to be adopted where feasible.

For many years journalists, newspapers, authors and publishers have had a deep-seated hostility to a law of libel for the not unexpected reason that without it they would be much freer to malign, insult and vilify their fellow human beings. There are undoubted advantages in the American rule that in the absence of proven malice a public person cannot establish a claim for defamation. The definition of a public person may often be self-evident and at other times give great difficulty.

On balance, however, I do not think that the English law of defamation is bad or unfair. In almost every case – except a couple of specialised exceptions principally relating to references to previous convictions, contrary to the Rehabilitation of Offenders Act – truth, if established, is a complete defence. What riles the newspapers is, of course, that truth has to be established and that time and again a sensible libel lawyer will direct his attention not to the suspicion of guilt but to the problem of establishing it. The resentment is felt by the journalist or editor who 'knows in his bones' that the allegation was justified but has to accept the sad fact that, the bones being unable to testify, there is insufficient credible evidence to maintain a defence of justification.

Hence the legend has got around that the desks of newspaper editors are chock-a-block with stories of villainy that the law of libel and the unscrupulous libel lawyers prevent them from disclosing for the benefit of the public. Time and again I and my colleagues have advised newspapers and publishers to adopt a courageous course where it is clear that, even if there is a paucity of evidence, the weight of suspicion makes it unlikely that the plaintiff will continue with the action, and time and again we have been vindicated.

I cannot remember a single instance where, having advised that to launch a libel action is not a sensible risk for the plaintiff, an action has been brought, let alone succeeded. There is perhaps one slender exception to this rule, which I have recited earlier, where Evelyn Waugh consulted me and I only had time to make a few discouraging noises before he had stalked out of the office. Nevertheless, the resentment remains among those 'anxious to wound but afraid to strike', and loud cries about the law of libel originate from authors and journalists anxious to vilify someone but lacking sufficient evidence to establish a defence.

A notable proponent of the theory that the law of libel is unjust to the public is my friend Mr Auberon Waugh: the son of Evelyn and para-doxically immensely hostile to the existence of a law of defamation. Those who read Auberon's writings will realise that he has some penchant for denunciation, which is very often justified. But one or two unfortunate experiences in the courts have persuaded him that any legal restraint upon his imaginative flights is unjust and unfair, to a point where he has enunciated the extraordinary proposition that, far from it being necessary for a defendant to establish the defence, the burden of proof of his innocence should attach to the plaintiff. Thus, if I am accused of being a thief, the burden falls on me to prove by some means or another that I am not a thief. The nonsense of this proposition will commend itself to everyone except the Auberon Waugh school of journalists and the editors of a few publications who make profit from mendacity, or at best evince a want of concern about whether what they say is true or false.

In 1965, a working party of the lawyers' society, Justice, chaired surprisingly by one of the great advocates of our day, Lord Shawcross, produced *The Law and the Press*, a report which recommended that the defence of justification should not be limited to the need to establish the truth. According to the report, it should also be a defence if the defendant could prove that he honourably believed the statement to be true, based on reputable evidence. This, when examined, is plainly ridiculous. I could defend an action on the ground that I could call Mr Snooks an adulterer and a villain because my aged aunt, a lady of great respectability in whom I had the greatest faith, had informed me that these facts were true.

This recommendation was, naturally, much promoted by newspapers, and it was one of the recommendations that the Faulks Committee on Defamation considered during the early 1970s. I gave evidence to this Committee and in relation to this particular recommendation the Committee in their report quoted my view, with which they were strongly in agreement:

> A great newspaper – if it believes that some villainy ought to be exposed – should expose it without hesitation and without regard to the law of libel. If the editor, his reporters and his advisers are men of judgement and sense, they are unlikely to go wrong; but if they do go wrong the principle of publish and be damned is a valiant and sensible one for the newspaper and it should bear the responsibility. Publish – and let someone else be damned – is a discreditable principle for a free press.

The Faulks Committee had to consider whether the existing law of libel was satisfactory, and on the whole – apart from a number of useful, peripheral recommendations – arrived at my own conclusion that in substance it was as good as one could hope for.

A very good illustration of the built-in conviction that a plaintiff's assertion of innocence is necessarily dishonest is to be found in the unhappy and discreditable story – discreditable, alas, to the defence – of the famous Crossman libel action. Aneurin Bevan and Richard Crossman were two of the three plaintiffs in what I suppose has become one of the most famous libel actions in legal history. The third plaintiff – Morgan Phillips – was a man I knew very slightly, who consulted me only on the one occasion of the libel action. Interest in the action remains alive and has been kept alive by the most determined campaign to suggest that the result – a verdict of £2,500 and costs to each plaintiff – was unfair and brought about by the perjury of the plaintiffs.

In assessing the validity of this accusation, it is important to pinpoint from where it comes. It comes entirely from the extreme right of the social, literary and political worlds. It largely derives from a continuing hatred of Nye Bevan. It has to be remembered that until the end of his life Nye Bevan was one of the most hated and feared of socialist politicians. It was a tribute to his courage, his brilliance as an orator, and his unyielding opposition to anything he regarded as reactionary, that the enmity of his opponents was maintained at such height. He was the only significant parliamentary opponent of Winston Churchill during the war and during Churchill's post-war government; and hatred of Bevan is akin to the hatred of Lloyd George at the time of his great influence and power. These considerations have to be borne in mind in relation to the later insinuations about the libel action. No one who was not on the extreme right wing has associated himself with any doubts about the justice of the verdict.

I should like to state in the most unmistakable terms that, from a knowledge of Nye Bevan over many years, an allegation that he would have committed perjury in order to make money can only be categorised as being as wicked as it is demented. I never had any reason to doubt his total truthfulness, his honesty and his concern to maintain an immaculate reputation. Added to these qualities were great personal courage, and intelligence. I do not believe that anyone who knew Nye even as well as I did – and there were many who knew him better – would regard the allegations later made about this action as anything but poisonous in coming from a thoroughly tainted source. It has high relevance that at the time he consulted me, Nye had no wish for anything more than an unconditional and unqualified apology. It was such an apology that I was instructed to obtain.

The story began when Jennie Lee telephoned me to say that Nye wished to consult me about a paragraph in the *Spectator* published in February 1957. Nye had never previously been to my office, nor so far as I can remember previously sought my advice, although we had been good, if not close, friends. He was in a state of considerable irritation. The *Spectator* had published a piece reading as follows:

And there was the occasional appearance of Messrs. Bevan, Morgan Phillips and Richard Crossman, who puzzled the Italians by their capacity to fill themselves like tanks with whisky and coffee, while they (because of their livers and also because they are abstemious by nature) were keeping going on mineral water and an occasional coffee. Although the Italians were never sure if the British delegation was sober, they always attributed to them an immense political acumen.

It may seem strange that Nye took absolutely violent exception to the paragraph. He explained to me that he had been in Venice on public and political duty. The suggestion that he had neglected that duty and disregarded his obligations in connection with it was something he found totally unacceptable and about which he was determined to secure an appropriate retraction.

The offending paragraph was, in my view, a clear imputation that all three men had been drunk or at least they had indulged to such an extent as to impair their ability to perform respectably on behalf of the British Labour Party at this congress in Venice of the Italian Socialist Party. Nye Bevan had gone as a delegate of the Labour Party; Morgan Phillips as Chairman of the Socialist International; and Richard Crossman as a journalist. During their stay in Venice, Nye told me they had been together on only one occasion, when they attended a party given by the British Ambassador, although he had seen them on two other occasions at the conference where serious affairs only were taking place, with an absence of any junketing. They had not even travelled together, either to the conference or back home.

My original advice to Nye was characteristic of the advice that I have given in most libel cases over the years: that the *Spectator* was an unimportant journal and that he was too important a man to bother about it; but this advice to him was wholly unacceptable. He insisted that he had been there to perform a duty on behalf of the Labour Party and that the allegation that he had been drunk would be revived time and again unless firmly refuted. He certainly left me in no doubt that the story was untrue in relation to him. He had no reason to believe that it was true of the others, but could not confirm it with the same certainty since he had seen so little of them.

He told me at the outset that he would be wholly satisfied with a speedy apology which, as he subsequently stated under cross-examination from the counsel for the defence, would have satisfied him completely. At that early stage there was no question of his wanting damages. Indeed, had an early apology, responsible and honourable, been proffered at the outset, the question of damages would not have been pursued.

I then advised him that the sensible course was for us to write a letter to the *Spectator*, adding that in my view they would want to apologise. I could see no reason why they should wish to maintain an allegation that was flatly denied by one of the most respected left-wing politicians in the world. He told me that he had spoken to the other two, who were no less indignant and would wish to be associated with any apology obtained. In those circumstances I suggested that the other two should give me direct instructions to seek the apology on their behalf. This they did. Dick

Crossman was no less emphatic than Nye Bevan. I knew Crossman well but had not, I think, at that stage previously advised him. We were, of course, later to have very close associations when I became one of his principal advisers at the Ministry of Housing. As with Bevan, his denials carried for me total conviction and I told him, as I had told Nye, that I could see no reason why a rapid apology should not be forthcoming.

Morgan Phillips was for me a more shadowy person. I had more to do with him later when I warned him very strongly not to advise the Labour Party to support a libel action which Mrs Castle wished to bring against Godfrey Winn, since I was absolutely convinced that it would be lost, as indeed it was, when the unfortunate lady, ignoring my advice, acted on the views of a political lawyer with limited experience of libel. In any event, Morgan Phillips's denials of drunkenness were more forceful even than the other two. Again, I had no reason to doubt his word. Both Dick Crossman and Morgan Phillips added that they had seen nothing of the other two which would support the allegations in the piece and gave similar statements about the extent of their meetings with each other.

Accordingly, on the instructions of all three men, a fairly anodyne letter was sent to the editor of the *Spectator*. However, the response to the letter was such that there was no prospect that the plaintiffs would regard it as satisfactory. The main theme, quoting from the defendants' solicitor, was that 'The article was clearly intended to convey the impression that, whereas Englishmen are not by nature so over-earnest politically as to refuse alcoholic refreshment, the attitude of some Continental politicians is rather the reverse'. It will be clear to anyone reading these words that no such suggestion appeared in the original paragraph and can only be deduced on the footing that it was written in invisible ink.

The subsequent course of the matter is recorded in a correspondence that does little credit to the defendants, until one understands the real reason for what appear to have been evasive and disingenuous tactics. A number of written apologies were suggested, none of which amounted to a retraction or an apology for the allegation of drunkenness. It may, of course, have been that Sir Ian Gilmour (the owner and at that time the editor of the *Spectator*) was advised on the basis of the precedent established in the action against the *Sunday Times* that it was dangerous to apologise for a publication without the approval of the journalist; but the position was more complicated by Dick Crossman's personal exertions, without consultation with his fellow plaintiffs or with me, in proffering various additional drafts, which also were rejected by the defendants.

The explanation, which I learnt only in later years, for the absence of a simple apology was very creditable to Sir Ian, unhappily credit which has not been wholly preserved by his later statements. The young woman who had written the piece, on whom no attack was levelled by the plaintiffs before, during or after the trial, had displayed an almost hysterical determination that no apology should be offered which amounted in any way to impugning her reliability as a journalist. But the position with poor Sir Ian was complicated by the fact – I have discovered only recently – that the young woman could not be called as a witness. The reason was simple: it was reported to us that during her stay in Venice she had never set eyes on any of the three plaintiffs. Hence the whole of her report would have come from second-hand versions retailed to her by other alleged witnesses.

As it turned out, no one was available to be brought to support her story. Why, in those circumstances, Sir Ian did not tell the young woman not to be silly and proceed to give an honourable and manly apology remains one of the mysteries. No plea relating to the young woman was ever advanced to Nye Bevan or his colleagues. Whatever he was, Nye Bevan was a kind and humane man. If a suggestion had been made that the young woman would be gravely injured on his account it would certainly have weighed with him, as indeed it would have weighed with me, in determining the suitability of the apology sought. But at no time in the exchanges between solicitors or between counsel was any reference ever made to the feelings of the journalist, and in view of subsequent events it is important that this should be recorded. From the day of the verdict, and for many years afterwards, the intransigent behaviour of the defence was a constant subject of discussion.

The case eventually came before the Lord Chief Justice, Lord Goddard – never, alas, a favourite character of mine. I had real apprehensions that his well-known reactionary views might influence him against left-wing plaintiffs. I need have had no fears. Whatever one might say about Goddard – and quite a lot of criticism has been directed at some of his criminal summings-up – he was not a man to express any views contrary to his beliefs. In this action (not inappropriately later designated 'the case of the Venetian blind') he had absolutely no doubt that the words were an imputation of insobriety and that the defendants should have apologised fully and freely in the long interval available to them to do so.

Rumours were circulating that it was the defendants' intention to justify the libel and that a shipload of Italian waiters, hotel porters, bar attendants and the like were on their way to England to testify to the alcoholic breathing, unsteady gait and slurred speech of the plaintiffs. An application to amend the defence could have been made at any time up to and including the days of the hearing, but no attempt was made to amend

the pleadings and on the day of the trial the only defence presented was
that the words were incapable of a defamatory meaning – a defence rightly
scorned by the judge.

The three men went into the witness-box in succession and, giving
evidence under oath, firmly rejected the suggestion that they had been
drunk or in any way incapable. No evidence was led to the contrary, or
could have been having regard to the defence. Nye Bevan deposed in his
evidence that the article 'made me exceedingly angry, very indignant
indeed that such an allegation should be made – which was entirely
groundless and extremely injurious', and the point he made throughout
was a perfectly valid one: that something of an offensive nature had been
published in a public journal for which only the most hypocritical wording
had been tendered by way of a suggested apology.

Then, for some reason that I still do not understand, Sir Ian Gilmour
heroically volunteered to go into the witness-box. There was nothing that
he could relevantly have said since he had not been in Venice, but by
doing so he exposed himself to the most hostile interrogation by the
judge, accompanied by a characteristically pugnacious cross-examination
by Gilbert Beyfus QC, counsel for the plaintiffs. The relevant extract
from the cross-examination makes the point of the matter as well as it
can be made:

Beyfus:	Where were you educated?
Gilmour:	At Eton.
Beyfus:	Did you go to university afterwards?
Gilmour:	Balliol.
Beyfus:	And with that education behind you, you say you did not think that to say of three leaders of the Labour Party on an official mission to Venice that they filled themselves like tanks with whisky, obviously in public, casts any sort of slur upon them; is that what you are telling the members of the jury?
Gilmour:	Yes.
Beyfus:	I will give you an opportunity of withdrawing that. Do you tell them that you thought . . .
Lord Chief Justice:	What do you think it means?
Gilmour:	I take it to mean that the plaintiffs enjoyed themselves in the normal way in Venice.
Lord Chief Justice:	Is it normal to fill yourself with whisky and coffee like tanks? That is where it comes in. Do not laugh, please, it is not a joke, but I am

asking you: is it really the ordinary thing to say that a man is enjoying himself abroad if you say he is filling himself with whisky and coffee like a tank – it means he is drinking to excess, does it not?

Gilmour: Not to excess, my Lord; I think he is steadily drinking.

Lord Chief Justice: What does it mean?

Gilmour: It means he is drinking a good deal.

Beyfus: Not to excess, but what?

Gilmour: A good deal.

Beyfus: What metaphor would you employ to describe drinking to excess? I suppose you would say drinking like a reservoir, is that it?

Gilmour: I think I would take it to mean – for a number of people, to drink one glass of whisky would be too much for them. Others could drink a good deal, but the fact of the question of the quantity in itself does not seem to me to be pejorative.

Beyfus: The only point of referring to their drinking is to make some sort of point out of it, is it not?

Gilmour: I took it to mean, as my Lord has commented, that this was a background impressionist sketch of the Congress in Venice, and it was not making any particular point except a general one of the failure of Nenni.

Beyfus: I suggest the point of this sentence is to contrast the drunken Englishmen with the sober Italians: that is quite clear, is it not?

Gilmour: No, it contrasts the impression that the writer thought had been given by the English to the Italians.

Lord Chief Justice: She thought that the Italians were considering that these gentlemen were drunk, because of the amount of whisky they had taken. She used in this article which you saw the words 'drunk or sober'.

Gilmour: Yes, my Lord, she used that in the copy.

Lord Chief Justice: You took out 'drunk', though I do not think it makes much difference.

Gilmour: Nor did I. I did not actually take it out.

It must have been a mercy when Sir Ian was released from the witness-box. It is difficult to believe that he can now read his performance with great satisfaction, and it is the more puzzling that he was concerned to revive recollections of the case in later years. In the absence of any knowledge of the special circumstances of the young woman, my own determined belief that it was incredible that an action would have to be fought, and that a proper apology would be forthcoming, turned out, of course, to underrate first Sir Ian's loyalty to his journalist and, less happily, the apparent belief of the defendants that they would be able to establish what they hoped was the truth – that somehow evidence would arrive establishing that the men had all been drinking. It never did.

The jury retired for a relatively short period and returned with a verdict of £2,500 for each man, plus costs. Each plaintiff shook my hand in turn and retired from the court, as I did, with a reasonably contented feeling that justice had been done. Neither I nor anyone else connected with the case, and least of all the three plaintiffs, could have envisaged the torrent of hostile publicity to which the case gave rise after the deaths of the three plaintiffs, and when all three leading counsel who had been concerned in the case were also dead. However creditable the defence behaviour may have been at the time, it is difficult to regard the fashion in which the case was revived, and the allegations subsequently made, as anything but caddish.

An opportunity had existed for a very long time for the defence to establish the truth of the allegations. All three men were in the witness-box, available to be cross-examined, had the defendants put themselves in a position to attempt to justify. Any evidence could have been called to establish their guilt. It is certainly true that the defendants were smarting under a sense of injustice, since they no doubt believed the young woman's story; but to wait until no relevant witness could breathe a word, and to allege as they did that the three men had knowingly committed perjury for money, was an allegation as wicked as it was idiotic. The plaintiffs could not know what defence would be raised. All three had been solemnly warned that if evidence was called – as presumably it might have been if it had existed – their perjury would have ruined their careers. That any sane man would risk his entire career in the conduct of a libel action, in pursuit of the total uncertainty of a jury award of damages, is something that an experienced libel lawyer would regard as wild folly.

The complicating factor that gave some credence to the perjury story was Dick Crossman's unpredictability. Having denied the story under oath, and so far as was then known maintained his denial throughout his life, it was alleged that at a tea party with members of the *Private Eye* set he had jocularly announced that of course all three men had been drunk. In his *Diaries*, supposedly day-by-day records, he had accused Morgan Phillips, but nowhere suggested that either Nye Bevan or himself had been drunk. If he entertained such a belief, he did not utter a word of it to me or to any of the lawyers engaged in the case. Why a reported remark at a tea party made by a gentleman who took immense delight in upsetting any applecart within reach should have been accepted against his previous statements under oath, and also when he had been fully and carefully advised of the implications of failure in the case, it is difficult to understand, except on the basis that rarely have political hostilities descended to such a level.

I have had cause to reflect for a long time about this case. I do not believe that any injustice was done, although it is asserted, and I certainly would not wish to comment, that the unfortunate young journalist was killed by the misery induced. If this is so, the stigma attaches not to the plaintiffs, who knew nothing whatever about the psychological condition of this young woman, but to the defence who lacked the courage, or perhaps more fairly the means, to defend the case as vigorously as she might have wanted. The reason advanced for this was probably the most discreditable of all utterances about the case: that they had been advised that if they tried to justify and failed, it would 'cost them more'. *Verb sap.*

However, there is one element of the law of defamation that rightly inspires doubt and misgivings. It is the question of the damages that ought to be awarded to a successful plaintiff. In recent days mammoth sums have been awarded against newspapers. I may say that in most cases these awards are thoroughly deserved, but it is wrong that a defendant should be exposed to the 'roulette' element in legal justice. I am a great believer in the collective wisdom of twelve jurors as against the often prejudiced wisdom of one judge, but I do believe some effort should be made to restrict awards where the fact that the jury is writing a cheque on someone else's account often leads to delusions of grandeur and to the award of unreasonably large amounts. The Court of Appeal can reduce the damages but this, of course, involves the defendant in the additional expense of an appeal with the further waste of time and effort.

I hesitate to recommend that damages should be left to the judge alone, but it would, I think, be an improvement if the jury, having arrived at their verdict on the merits, were to be entitled to recommend a sum of damages, but not more than that, which would be subject to a final approval by the judge at first instance. Much thought has been given to the question of damages, and it has a particular relevance where the defendant is not a great newspaper but is a relatively small publishing house which could be ruined by an excessive award. I rather like the notion of the jury being entitled to recommend an award which is nevertheless subject to a final approval by the judge.

For many years, an important part of my duties was reading books for libel on behalf of a variety of publishers. This is an operation that requires only a very rudimentary legal knowledge. The definition of a libel is any written statement calculated to bring a plaintiff into 'hatred, ridicule or contempt, or to lower him in the estimation of right-thinking people', which is sufficient to enable a reader to identify areas of danger.

Although discharging the duty competently involves only limited legal knowledge, it does require sensitive antennae and a high degree of social knowledge. It is not only a question of trying to determine what a jury might say about the words: more importantly it is a question of assessing the likelihood that a plaintiff will institute proceedings. If this criterion is not applied, a terrifying censorship would operate because of legal timidity. There are indeed many advisers on the law of libel whose timidity has prevented much material that ought to be published from being published. I have always prided myself on the belief that in this respect my firm has always been on the right side and has taken a robustly common-sense view of whether a plaintiff is likely to proceed as opposed to whether he is likely to succeed. This does not mean that I have ever approved of scurrility. I would certainly have always refused to defend a publisher or newspaper where the passage concerned offended the decencies as opposed to the legalities. This may sound a very prim and self-righteous approach. 'Who are you', it may be asked, 'to seek to form such a judgement? If what the newspaper is publishing is legal, how can it be right for any lawyer to seek to interfere with it?' The answer is a simple one: that my services are on hire; that I have always sought to avoid making them available for the advancement of villainy.

I believe that this attitude is shared by many of my professional colleagues but not, alas, by all of them. The ease with which such publications as *Private Eye* – whose former editor has publicly proclaimed that he had no interest in verifying the truth of what he wrote – are produced is, alas, discreditable to the profession. There are instances when libellous material should undoubtedly have been made public, but far better that it should be published in some organ of greater integrity, carrying a greater conviction.

My own relationship with *Private Eye* began when over a number of years copious reference was made to me to which I took little or no offence. They put about the legend – based on a chance remark that I made to Max Aitken on arriving late at dinner that I had already dined – that it was my usual practice to have no fewer than two dinners and possibly several more. This canard received encouragement from my undoubted bulk and was completely innocent except that its constant repetition made it rather boring.

But ultimately, and inadvertently, *Private Eye* published a libel in 1980 that I could not ignore. In the course of a quite appalling defamation of a very decent man, the Reverend David Burgess, who had been a Fellow of University College during my Mastership, they added the words that his promotion to a particular piece of employment must have been at my instigation. Even then I would have left it alone, except for the obvious necessity to give support to the real victim. However, in the very same issue there was another short piece which unarguably was intended to suggest that I was a homosexual and minded to seduce young under-graduates. Not unnaturally I sought an independent view and was advised, particularly by my partner John Montgomerie, that this should not be tolerated. An action was instituted and after a good deal of bluff and bluster that there was no defamatory intention, the matter was composed by a statement in open court and substantial payment for costs and damages. In view of the practice that *Private Eye* indulged in of mocking apologetic statements in an issue following their publication, I also insisted on having a personal letter from the editor associating himself with the apology.

I have had no trouble with them since. However, their record of libel actions settled goes a long way to establishing the discreditable nature of the publication and its untruthfulness. There is no doubt that a publication that tells lies always has, and will continue to enjoy, a vogue. What was nauseating were the efforts of a number of people to discourage me from suing on the ground that the paper served a valuable public purpose, but motivated in my mind by their belief in the wisdom of siding with the publication where otherwise they might become its butts.

Three other libel matters remain in my memory, one case involving what could rightly be called a professional lapse on my part. This related to a book published in 1955 by the now extinct firm of Allan Wingate. The book was a memoir by a former naval officer which chronicled his involvement with a family of villains; in the end, he was the only member of the conspiracy who remained in England to be brought to justice. He was tried and sentenced to a period of imprisonment and when he emerged wrote a book about the whole episode, roundly condemning the associates who had caused his ruin. I read the book with care and my enquiries satisfied me that the real culprits had all fled abroad, despite the fact that warrants had been issued for their arrest. I satisfied myself that his account was a truthful one and on that score passed the book for publication.

An edition of some 5,000 copies was duly printed and serial rights were sold to the *People*. However, the lawyer for the *People* – better acquainted with criminal practice than I was – drew attention to the serious possibility that as warrants had been issued it was, according to the existing law, a contempt of court to prejudge the outcome of any trial and that my view as to the truth or otherwise of the allegations against the fugitives was irrelevant. Again, the situation confronting me was a heavy one. Five thousand copies of a book were awaiting distribution that in the view of the *People*'s lawyer – a very experienced lawyer in these fields – would be illegal. I studied the law of contempt of court to the point of ascertaining that no prosecution could be initiated for it in these circumstances without the consent of the Attorney-General. The Attorney-General at the time was a much maligned figure, Sir Reginald Manningham Buller – jocularly described as Sir Reginald Bullying Manner.

I approached my friend George Wigg, then in the Commons, told him of the dilemma and asked him if he could approach the Attorney-General for some assurance that in the circumstances of this case he would not prosecute the book if it were published. Some while later I received a letter from Sir Reginald – with whom I later established very cordial relations in connection with a number of matters where we formed a common front in proceedings in the House of Lords – saying that he much regretted it would be improper for him to commit himself as to what he might do if a book was published in circumstances where its contents could have a prejudicial effect on a fair trial. The first paragraph case me down in gloom, but joy, there was a second paragraph. He said that he thought I ought to know that his experts had advised him that where a warrant had been issued there could be no question of a contempt of court until it had been executed, i.e. the delinquents arrested. Preening myself on my superior knowledge, I proceeded to inform the lawyer of the *People* that a little knowledge was a dangerous thing. The book was serialised and sold and I was saved from the ignominy of having to admit my own ignorance.

Another book in 1963 caused no trouble in its outcome but immense trouble arriving at it. It had been offered to Victor Gollancz, for whom I used to read regularly. He summoned me to his premises in Henrietta Street, where he occupied as dingy a backroom as ever was, with paper peeling from the walls and which had not had a penny in renovation expended on it in the last hundred years. He was, I may say, renowned for his thriftiness. 'I have,' he explained to me, 'a very difficult book. It is an account of the trial of Stephen Ward written by Ludovic Kennedy and it presents every kind of problem. It is a forthright and unhesitating denunciation of the police involved, the prosecuting authorities and counsel involved, and of the judge involved. I am,' he said characteristically, 'determined to publish it, but you must ensure that it involves me in no risk.' This did not strike me as a particularly heroic declaration.

I read the book and had great sympathy with it. It will be remembered that Stephen Ward was picked on as a victim to pacify the Establishment in the unhappy Profumo affair. There had to be someone upon whom they could take out their sense of indignation and Stephen Ward was outrageously prosecuted for living on the earnings of prostitutes. A prostitute is, of course, a street-walker, and however indulgent the morals of Miss Keeler and the other ladies involved, they were not by any stretch of imagination street-walkers. Nor, on a fair assessment of the situation, which after a careful study of the book and long discussions with Ludovic Kennedy I can claim to have made, did Stephen Ward live on their earnings. His household was raffish, Bohemian, and the young ladies came and went, partially as guests, partially as tenants, occasionally contributing to a common household fund. However, all of this could be presented, if the legal machine was set in motion, in the most unfavourable of lights. I do not know of any prosecution more outrageous than this one or where there was a more deliberate and wicked attempt to victimise the accused. In many ways Ward was not a particularly worthy individual, but on that score who would 'scape whipping? In any event, I spent hours on the book, with one mitigating circumstance, that it brought me into close association with Ludovic Kennedy, an exceptionally liberal-minded man who has been on the side of the angels in several criminal matters that he has investigated.

Ultimately I presented the book to Victor and said, 'This is the best we can do.' His attitude showed rather more resolution than when I first discussed it with him. 'How do you rate the risk?' he said. 'I rate the risk that you might be prosecuted for criminal libel; that certain individuals might bring actions for civil libel, but that if you defend them with determination and regardless of expense' – he winced – 'you will, I think, succeed in your defence.' He thought for a moment, struck the table with a gallant gesture and said, 'We will print.' He did print and not a murmur of protest was heard from anyone, although I do not believe the book had the success that it deserved. It was a particularly courageous effort on the part of Ludovic Kennedy.

The third matter was brought to me by Rupert Hart-Davis, now knighted and retired. An interesting man, and one of the most distinguished of publishers because he was also a distinguished writer and editor himself, he once telephoned me to say that he was being assailed by solicitors on behalf of the Duke of Windsor over a book by G. M.

Young about Stanley Baldwin. I went to see him and he showed me the
passage, which I must confess left me totally mystified in terms of any
possible defamation. The complaint was that the book described an
occasion when Baldwin was making a visit to Fort Belvedere in a further,
but still futile, attempt to dissuade the Duke from his marriage to Mrs
Simpson. In what seemed to me a totally innocuous and inoffensive
record, it stated that on the occasion in question the Duke had given a
small dinner party attended by the Baldwins and Mrs Simpson. The
Duke had sat at one end of the table and Mrs Simpson at the other, and
the guests either side. This arrangement, according to the Duke and
maintained by his solicitor, Sir George Allen, implied, and could have no
other implication, that the lady in question was his mistress. As it had
always been denied that there had been any sexual relationship between
the Duke and Mrs Simpson prior to their marriage, the Duke was
indignant and was claiming that there should be some reparation of this
mortal insult.

My knowledge of high life was such that I could not take seriously the
assertion that the placing of the lady implied the nature of the personal
relationship with her. Anyway, I went round to see Sir George Allen,
calling upon him as he was infinitely senior to me in the profession, and
explained to him that ordinary human beings who were acquainted with
the finesse of high life would not have placed such interpretation on it
and that I thought he might have some difficulty in finding any witnesses
to confirm the belief. However, Sir George maintained his position and
in the end he asked me how I proposed to rectify it.

I made the suggestion that if there were a second edition I did not
have the slightest doubt that both the author and the publishers would
be happy to remove this reference and to remain totally silent about the
placement of the guests at the dinner-table. I may say that I made this
offer in the confident belief that there would not be a second edition, as
indeed was the case. Sir George, after a little thought, accepted this offer
and asked me to write a letter confirming the publishers' intentions.
However, I noticed that he was detaining me on some pretext or other,
and that he clearly had something more to say. 'There is,' he eventually
confided, 'a slightly embarrassing request I wish to make and I hope it
will not be misunderstood.' He asked me to look at a certain passage in
the book which stated very flatteringly that the Duke had been brilliantly
advised by his counsel, Sir Walter Monckton, and by his solicitor.
Fingering his tie, Sir George said to me, 'Do you think the publishers
might mind, after the words "and by his solicitor", adding "Sir George
Allen"?'

There are times when one doubts that human vanity has any bounds, but I assured Sir George that if a second edition was to be published it would be perverse and curmudgeonly for the publishers to decline to make this addition. And we left it on that basis. When I put the proposal to Rupert Hart-Davis he exploded with indignation, saying, 'This man has given me unnecessary trouble, caused me to employ you, involved me in the unproductive expense of legal representation, and now he wants me to give him free publicity!' However, since the matter never arose in the absence of a second edition, I did not have to explain to Sir George why it was that his request had not been granted.

I have only sporadically been engaged over the years in the affairs of the legal profession because I have been too busy and lacked the inclination to become involved in anything to do with its management. I am happy to say that the profession has shown no great anxiety to enlist my services. On the whole there was an innate suspicion that I was the wrong man to involve without a great deal of trouble, since my views about the legal profession are regarded not only as unorthodox but positively anarchic.

My first encounter with the Law Society was the agreeable one of being engaged as an examiner for its Final Examination – a job which I took after I came out of the army and which proved extremely useful in supplementing my meagre income. Subsequently my exchanges with the Society were few and far between. My friend Professor Jim Gower once came to see me in a state of high indignation, being like myself a profound believer in the freedom of speech. His complaint was that the Law Society was requiring people who enlisted as teachers in its College of Law to submit to a rule that the employee would not write and publish any book without the Law Society's consent. This appeared to both of us to be something of an outrage.

I undertook to confront Thomas Lund, who was then the well-known and immensely influential Secretary-General of the Law Society, on the matter. I sought him out at a lunch one day and suggested diplomatically that this rule should be repealed. What I found astonishing was that the proposition that the rule was remotely improper could not even penetrate as far as the second epidermis. He expressed the view that as the Law Society was paying for the employment of these gentlemen, it was right that it should be able to control what they said. He even went on to say that the Law Society might, of course, be embarrassed by the expression of certain views by these people, and that on that score alone it was proper that the Society should control, and indeed edit, their literary output. Nothing that I said could make him alter this preposterous position. I asked him whether he thought it was appropriate that Trollope's works should have been edited by the General Post Office by whom he was employed, or that Charles Lamb's essays should have been the subject of control by the Customs authorities for the same reason, or T. S. Eliot's poems cut by the bank for which he worked. He regarded these as totally irrelevant questions to which he scorned to reply. In the event, I made no significant headway beyond expressing my firm protest.

I have long taken the view that our professional organisation is, to put it in a word, demented. Unfortunately I have never had enough time to pursue my reforming notions with sufficient zeal. I have always unhesitatingly advocated the fusion of the two legal professions, the Bar and the solicitors, in the firm belief that the public interest would be served by this change. All legal practitioners are deeply concerned about the cost of litigation to the non-aided litigant, to the point where many of us believe that it is nearly impossible to advise a client of moderate means to become engaged in certain types of litigation, however important it might be to the interests of that person to do so. The prohibitive costs of litigation on many legal fronts is due, if not predominantly then at least in part, to the absence of a fused profession.

The arguments in favour of a merger are, in my view, unanswerable but they also need to be associated with a drastic root-and-branch reform in the actual substance of the law. The system of precedent has been made into something of an absurdity by the tireless activities of Lord Denning. Lord Denning, for some reason, has been regarded as a pillar of the existing legal doctrine. In fact no one has dynamited the system of precedent with greater diligence and determination than he has, and to that extent I always wished him well.

I made some attempt to effect a change when the Royal Commission on Legal Services was appointed by Harold Wilson in 1976. Unfortunately the appointment came at a time when my own relationship with Harold Wilson had cooled to a point where we had virtually ceased to communicate. As it was, an important number of the Commission's personnel were in my view completely unsuitable, since for a start no known reformer was included, and the terms of reference contained one startling omission, which was that although the structure of the legal profession would come under review, the question of the appointment of judges was expressly excluded. This was so clearly and deliberately a tendentious piece of drafting that it certainly impugned the integrity of the whole operation.

The Commission's chairman, Sir Henry Benson, was a man of great eminence and undoubtedly great integrity, but even so he was wholly the wrong choice. He was an extremely dominating chartered accountant who had previously produced a report about the racing industry. In the result, although his exertions were strenuous, and I was given to understand that the report was written by his own hand, the Commission's conclusions were far from satisfactory. They failed to take into account the reality of the situation, which was really never brought to notice because of the total inadequacy of the personnel involved. This is no reflection on the fact that they were people of distinction, operating within their own profession with great skill and some degree of elegance; but when it came to recommending reforms in what was a basic national profession, they had neither the imagination nor the requisite knowledge. Where they were lawyers, they had the built-in prejudices which no lawyer can escape from, particularly if he is a member of the Bar and especially if he is a member of the judiciary. Lawyers believe, and continue to believe through a sort of mass-hypnosis, that a divided profession is a good and worthy one. The arguments against it are not only overwhelming and unanswerable, but the replies furnished are pathetic.

When he was ennobled in 1981, I had a very revealing conversation with Lord Benson after he had made a speech in the Lords detailing the various countries he had visited – all of which he claimed would be in favour of our divided profession. Since I knew that this was not the case where the Lord Chief Justice of Canada was concerned, I asked him why in the course of his travels (all expenses paid) he had not visited Canada. His rather lame excuse was that he could not go everywhere. There was a special significance in the omission of the one country that would have provided him with weighty evidence against his established viewpoint.

Some years before the Commission was appointed, I was active – one of my rare activities (the war for press freedom was another) in the House of Lords – seeking to promote a Bill which would allow solicitors to become members of the judiciary. Various debates took place. There was a culminating debate which was to be followed by a vote to determine the matter. On my way into the Lords that day, I encountered Lord Jellicoe, then the Leader of the Lords in the Heath government, who informed me that Lord Hailsham, the Lord Chancellor, was proposing to suggest a compromise.

Jellicoe is one of the wisest of men, who had the misfortune to be involved in a totally undeserved piece of public notoriety, which caused him to escape the rather unenviable task of leading the Lords and to take on a financial career of great distinction; he was brought back into public life on a number of occasions when he served very useful purposes. On this occasion he indicated to me the notion of the proposed compromise, which was, again with grotesque inconsistency, that solicitors should be eligible for appointment as recorders (a recorder is a very minor judge who sits occasionally, largely on criminal cases) and after five years of apprenticeship as a recorder should be eligible for appointment to the

Crown Court which is one level below the High Court. The proposal was inconsistent and socially maladjusted for the very good reason that the judicial qualities required in any branch of the law are the same. A man sitting as a recorder has the power to sentence people to long-term imprisonment, and the idea that he would become more eligible for judicial duties after five years – although he required no previous judicial experience to become a recorder – seemed to me to lack any kind of reasonable justification. However, this was a compromise and certainly a very considerable advance.

I asked George Jellicoe why it was that Hailsham had had this change of mind. 'Hailsham did not have it,' he said. 'Ted had it,' meaning, of course, Ted Heath. Ted Heath had pointed out to him, in simple arithmetical terms, that there were 3,000 barristers and 30,000 solicitors in the country. This seemed to me the most impressive argument he could have marshalled and certainly the most effective one, and in the result the reform was introduced.

Anyway, to revert to the Royal Commission: I was approached by Sir Henry Benson with a long questionnaire which I was asked to answer. As it is extremely difficult to present a forceful case in reply to a questionnaire, and as he knew me to be the principal and most publicised enemy of the present system, Benson then invited me to lunch. We had a perfectly agreeable meal and I expressed to him the nature of my views, for which he thanked me. He then sent me a letter saying that in the circumstances of our having had lunch and exchanged views, he assumed that I would not wish to give evidence! I replied to him that I certainly wished to give evidence. In fact, when I was called to give evidence, I was given to understand from another source that the report had already been largely written. When I did present myself to the Commission, about half of them were not there, notably those persons who were members of the Bar.

In the event I gave, I believe, long and forceful evidence to the Commission, but I had a firm feeling that nothing I said could influence the decision already made. The only person who cross-examined me with any vigour was a fellow solicitor, who was concerned about the plight of an ancient uncle who practised in some country locality, and who was reliant upon a corps of barristers to give him advice and correct his mistakes. I took the view that the organisation of the legal profession was not inspired by a desire to help his uncle.

The report of the Commission was published in October 1979 and produced the result that I feared: despite a considerable number of purely cosmetic recommendations – and a few valid recommendations peripheral to the main issue – there was no attempt whatsoever to touch on the basic imperfections of a system which needed changing from the foundations upwards.

I wrote an extremely critical – and in retrospect slightly too acrid – article in the *Evening Standard* commenting upon the Commission and its report. My final remarks were:

> The English legal system has remained unreformed because it has never played a sufficient part in the lives of ordinary people, but of recent years its importance has become clearer. When great social institutions reject the courts and indeed, in certain matters, the rule of law, it must be the time to consider change. That the Royal Commission was not impressed (or even conscious of these considerations) is the most potent reflection on its inadequacy.

The *Evening Standard* made the mistake of describing me as 'the most eminent solicitor in Britain'. This aroused the indignation – and I might even believe the jealousy – of a large number of other practitioners, who commissioned one of their numbers, now a High Court judge, to reply. His attempt to summon up invective did not, I am afraid, earn my admiration sufficiently to justify any reply to his article.

Nothing that has happened since would impel me to review these strictures. Although the arrival of a new Lord Chancellor – Lord Mackay, a Scottish lawyer who has no particular reverence for English traditions – inevitably gave rise to hopes that changes might take place, nothing has so far happened to translate those hopes into an active reality. The Lord Chancellor has certainly manifested his reforming zeal but principally in utterances that have not achieved any great result. He has put about a number of controversial subjects for discussion. Thus, he has thrown into the forum the question of contingency fees, i.e. fees that are paid only in response to success – a desire so far unimplemented; that the right to be a high court advocate can be extended to solicitors; an intention to investigate the possibilities of shedding wigs and gowns, or at least wigs; and additionally many other proposed changes intended to modernise the law and make it more intelligible to ordinary human beings.

It will be clear that carrying all or most of these intentions into effect involves substantial change which many of the conservative members of the profession would regard as dangerous. For my part I have long thought that radical changes along the lines he proposes, and even going beyond them, is a necessity if the English legal system is to be sufficiently up to date to satisfy contemporary needs. At the moment any contact with the law is regarded with suspicion by the majority of my fellow citizens.

Although there are large areas which call for change, there are also large areas where change should be resisted and where the resistance will require a firm and courageous response by all lawyers. A good illustration is the increasing criticism of the jury system. I am not a criminal lawyer, so that my knowledge of juries is necessarily limited, but my knowledge of judges is vast and my preference for a jury greatly exceeds my preference for a judge. The English judiciary has one great advantage which cannot really be exaggerated: it is unarguably incorruptible. But I do not think that that is of itself a sufficient justification for leaving everything else unchanged.

The present Lord Chancellor has had very little influence on the major need for reform – the cost of litigation – which is, in a word, ridiculous. This is the single requirement most urgently in need of change, but it is difficult to see how that change can be brought about when we have a divided profession which involves the participation in any lawsuit of at least two advocates – often entitled to high charges – when many lawsuits are sufficiently uncomplicated to make it possible for a single advocate, e.g. a solicitor advocate, to present the case without additional support. As at present organised, no one embarking on a piece of litigation can sufficiently predict its course or its cost. On the face of it, a claim for a liquidated sum of money should not involve great difficulty or great expense. But in practice such unexpected problems can arise as to leave the ultimate cost a ruinous penalty to the litigant.

One of the great risks is our system of appeals. At the moment, unless a leap-frogging procedure rarely used is employed, there is a chance that the substantive case, having been decided at first instance by one judge, would then fall to be reconsidered by a court of appeal normally consisting of three judges, and ultimately by a session of the House of Lords, frequently involving five judges. The total cost is breathtaking and as yet no simplification of this procedure has been mooted or is likely to take place in the near future.

Despite suggestions that the procedure would become very much less expensive if we possessed a merged profession, I have to admit that over the years very little enthusiasm for this reform has been manifested by either branch. The reasons are somewhat complicated and are not particularly complimentary to the profession. Lawyers, I have no doubt, enjoy a more than average intelligence but, equally, they are deeply suspicious of any change on the simple principle of liking what they know and cordially disliking what they have to learn.

An analysis of the detailed requirements for reform is not appropriate here, but one thing is certain, that unless the trammels of an iron tradition, which holds the law in an inescapable grip, can be relaxed, the likelihood of anyone now living seeing change is not encouraging. Lord Mackay inspired hope among great numbers of lawyers that something significant in the way of reform would eventuate. That hope has even now begun to fade. The determined hostility of many senior lawyers (both judges and counsel) must discourage a belief that anything radical is likely to happen. I believe, as anyone practising must believe, that reducing the expense of litigation to bring it within the range of any adequate income must be the first requirement of anyone seeking significant change in our legal system. That change should start with the removal of the division between the two legal professions. One must await this development before one can think in more comprehensive terms.

There is much in our legal system worthy of praise and particularly the social morality of each of the professions with regard to financial probity. This is a good starting-point to which to cling. If we can travel a little further along the road, so as to train youngsters in the profession away from the notion that there is a separate role for solicitors and the Bar, and that they are doing the same job in the same language and using the same authorities, important progress will have been made. I do not expect to see this in my own lifetime, but I would hope that it may occur in the lifetime of those who are at present sufficiently junior in their professional advancement.

9

The Labour Years

MY INTRODUCTION TO politics came early in life when I met Ted Heath. It was a considerable while before I came to know more Tory politicians and acted as an adviser, not to the party, but to a great many Tories. My early introduction to the world of politics was always marginal in the sense that I never felt able to join any particular political party. This was perhaps due to obstinacy, but also due to a determined belief that I could never subscribe to the whole of the dogma of any political programme. Hence when I went to the Lords in 1965 I sat as a cross-bencher, although periodically, according to my attitude at the time, I was supporting one or other of the two parties and rarely took a cross-bench approach.

If I have any political beliefs, they are best and quickest expressed in cliché terms. I do believe fervently that no man is fit to be any man's master; that an uncontrolled capacity to amass wealth is thoroughly wrong; that the class system, particularly in relation to education, needs urgent change; that it is right and proper and sensible to be an enthusiastic European and that much nonsense is talked about the alleged loss of sovereignty. In short, I am, I suppose, a single-minded adversary of the normal beliefs of conventional Conservatives and even more unconventional ones such as Margaret Thatcher, a lady for whom it is impossible not to have a considerable respect.

My first entry into the political world was, of course, my association with the Labour Party. It is normally believed that this arose through my friendship with Harold Wilson. This is not in fact the case. It arose because of my meeting George Wigg in the army, whom I had encountered when I was based at Southern Command headquarters and he was at the same headquarters as a Lieutenant-Colonel in charge of army education, where he had already established a reputation for ruthless eccentricity. He did invite me to become a parliamentary Labour candidate in the

1945 election. I reflected on it, but declined, principally because of my unwillingness to belong to any party – I have never been a party member – and perhaps even more because the seat I was offered appeared to be an impregnable Tory stronghold. In fact in the 1945 election it fell to the Labour Party – thus history might have been changed.

George could be the best of friends and terrifyingly the worst of enemies. His hatreds were almost entirely political. He hated Tories in general and had little respect for most of the Tory leadership, although some he did respect, primarily Harold Macmillan. But his hostility to the Conservative prominents was exceeded only by his healthy hatred of many of the leading Labour figures. He had encountered most of these in the early days of political socialism in this country and considered them to be a thoroughly unreliable lot. When one heard him giving vent to this view it was difficult to resist the conclusion that justice and truth were on his side.

Nye Bevan I had met in the 1950s – again through George Wigg – and had come to know almost intimately. Nye was a rich character, with an enormous consciousness of his own powers and ability. He was not in any sense a vain man, but he had a conceit of himself that came from the knowledge that he dominated every quarter that he occupied. He had a mind of quicksilver and a gift of repartee that was second nature; his special love of language arose, I think, from the absence of a formal education. He was a man of profound education, but having acquired it himself he treasured words and used them with unique skill and often with a strange individuality. Some of the words he used I had never heard of – and I am not unfamiliar with words – but he savoured them, rolled them over his tongue and finally ejected them into his speech with a delight at their novelty, their colour and their music. He was a generous man with strong abrasive streaks and keen hatreds. He did not lightly forget an injury, but he did not manufacture trifles into injuries. He had had a good deal of experience of the deliberate malice of political adversaries, who felt for him a genuine fear that was replaced by contempt only for his lesser colleagues. If a left-wing politician is genuinely anathematised it is not possible for his opponent to pay him a higher compliment.

Although Harold Wilson did not equate with Bevan in personal terms – in colour or in rhetoric – he too can feel pleased that the condemnation that in many quarters was directed at him demonstrated the genuine respect for his qualities that his adversaries feared. In the Labour Party in my lifetime only two men of quality – Bevan and Wilson – have aroused hostility of this order, and they are the two most potent and significant characters that have emerged.

I liked Nye enormously and knew of no better way of occupying an evening than by listening to him and occasionally, with some temerity, disagreeing with him. He was a generous debater. He never sought to crush you, nor did he ever take refuge in insult or invective. He delighted to have the point examined, turned over, scrutinised, probed and polished, until it was sharp and gleaming and ready to demolish the whole controversy.

I watched him die. Jennie's performance during his last months and weeks was a model of quiet, undemonstrative heroism. She gave him no inkling that she was anxious or worried, remained firm and maintained a total discipline of emotion and action. He had the medical advice of Sir Daniel Davies, who had been physician to Lloyd George and indeed to a number of misguided dignitaries who were influenced by his great reputation. Davies brought a strange quality of Methodist Welsh revivalism to medicine which was unacceptable to me but highly acceptable to a fellow countryman. Friends rallied by the score. Homes were offered for Nye's wasting frame. A short sojourn by the seaside, back to their country farm, back to the hospital, and then the end. The great towering intellect, the gift of humour and reply, remained almost to the last. I recall my own final visit to the farm where he was allowed down for an hour and where the flame was rekindled for that period sufficiently for us to forget his illness and think only that the old Nye had been restored. After his death in July 1960 Jennie was desolated and there was great apprehension that her morale would be destroyed. Nobody doubted her courage, and we were wrong to doubt her common sense. She made a firm resolution to remain an active and useful member of a society to which Nye had made such a historic contribution. She was yet to make her contribution, which perhaps under the keen light of social historians may equal her husband's.

I also had the exciting experience of meeting Hugh Gaitskell in the late 1950s. We became friendly, although the association was more that of a client-lawyer kind. Gaitskell never adopted me in the sense that Harold Wilson did later, but I became quite close to him and he employed me in quasi-political matters. I advised the Labour Party over such things as the Vassall inquiry and, together with my friend Dennis Lloyd, I was on a number of committees and investigations to recommend changes in the law – particularly land law (the working party on land nationalisation) and the law of landlord and tenant – which were being prepared by the Labour Party for their future use.

Of all politicians, I think I respected Gaitskell most. He was, when I met him, probably at the height of his powers. He had lost the diffidence and uncertainty that characterised his early leadership of the party. He was confident, high-spirited and plainly impatient to seize the power that was coming so rapidly within his grasp. He was unexpectedly a man of great gaiety and to see him at a dance was an absolute delight. He loved dancing and threw off all the weighty considerations of state and all the pomp associated with political office and became a bright and jolly human being. Working with him – and my own experience with him was brief – was a joy. He didn't argue, he didn't dissent: he agreed or disagreed. I do not believe that it is possible to measure the consequences to our political life that flowed from his early death, following on so rapidly after the death of Aneurin Bevan. Certainly it had a more significant effect on English politics than any purely political event in my lifetime.

The most intriguing matter supplied by Gaitskell was when he consulted me about the constant leakage of the party's National Executive minutes to the *Manchester Guardian*. Week after week, almost within hours of the completion of a meeting, the *Guardian* had a complete, almost verbatim, account of what had happened. Gaitskell was anxious to identify the 'mole' in this case and asked me what ought to be done.

I advised, my opinion reinforced by Dennis Lloyd, that there was plainly a breach of copyright, since the reports published were to a substantial extent verbatim accounts of the meetings reproduced from the minutes, the copyright of which belonged to the National Executive, and that a judicial remedy should be sought as soon as possible. We wrote to the *Guardian* on behalf of the Labour Party enquiring the source of this very precise information and – not surprisingly – our request was refused. We then issued a writ and proceedings ensued. The *Guardian* sought to invoke some sort of privilege, which they could not seriously have believed existed, to protect their publication of the Labour Party's confidential information. Their claim was based on a privilege that does indeed exist for libel, where the defendant is not required to disclose his sources. I took the view, shared by counsel, that no similar privilege was justified so far as copyright was concerned. However, a summons was issued to dismiss our claim on the ground of this supposed privilege, which was refused by the judge at first instance – a refusal confirmed, and emphatically, by the Court of Appeal.

The case trotted on at something slightly better than the conventional pace of litigation in this country and arrived at a point where each side had to 'discover' to the other all relevant documents relating to the matter. I advised Gaitskell that this requirement posed a real difficulty for the defence. They would have to disclose all memoranda, manuscripts and correspondence relating to the transaction, and it seemed to me almost inconceivable that this disclosure could enable the culprit still to be concealed from exposure. Gaitskell became excited at the prospect and instructed me with great firmness that as soon as I had received the 'discovered' documents I was to show them to no one but to come straight to him, so that he should be the first person to know who the culprit was or what information was available that would lead to the culprit's identity.

Tragically, or perhaps fortunately, the hunt was aborted by Gaitskell's untimely death in January 1963. A mystery surrounded his death which was assiduously played up by the media in suggesting every kind of melodramatic possibility, the favourite being that poor Hugh Gaitskell had been stabbed with the sharp ferrule of an umbrella, the end of which had been treated with some poisonous concoction. I could not have conceived of any circumstances in which it would have been sensible for any particular political group to murder Gaitskell, and the likelihood that it was murder – in such an immensely complicated fashion – seemed to me at first blush fanciful and absurd. But that was before the murder of the Bulgarian Georgi Markov, in exactly such a fashion, added a great degree of plausibility to the theory. Whatever the truth, certain it was that Gaitskell was removed from the political scene and, after a sharp internecine struggle within the party, was succeeded by Harold Wilson after a vote in February 1963.

My relationship with George Brown, although not close, was a friendly one. He sought my advice on one or two matters where complaints were made against him of alleged libels, which I had no real difficulty in seeing off and about which he wrote me appreciative letters. The major assistance I was able to give him was in connection with the Tribunal, presided over by Lord Radcliffe, established to investigate the Vassall affair in November 1962. A problem arose because it was believed that Macmillan had secured terms of reference which would entitle the Tribunal to investigate not merely Vassall, but also rumours relating to Vassall that were circulating at the time, rumours about many discreditable matters but mainly his sexual activities. It was believed that the principal rumour-monger was poor George Brown. Brown had, very incautiously, said some things at a private dinner party that on a literal construction would have implicated the Labour Party in a rather nasty intrigue. There was little doubt that Radcliffe proposed to call George Brown, who would have made an uncomfortable witness, and probably a damaging one for the party.

In conference with Gerald Gardiner, subsequently Lord Chancellor, who had somewhat late in the day raised his flag as a member of the Labour Party, it was decided that the best course of action was for the Labour Party to be asked to be represented by Gardiner at the Vassall Tribunal and to inform Radcliffe that it had no additional witness to come to him. It was our guess that in the face of this assertion, and while he could still call George Brown, Radcliffe would not want to discount Gardiner's evidence by calling another Labour witness. This is exactly what happened. The Labour Party gave its evidence and for practical purposes withdrew from the proceedings. No reference of any kind was made by anyone to George Brown's ill-advised remarks.

Gardiner was a strange man: an old Harrovian, an immensely skilful and prosperous Silk and a dedicated socialist. There was a Puritan austerity about him that made one doubt whether he ever enjoyed anything at all. I never took a meal with him, but I should be surprised to find that he ate with a good appetite. He would have regarded mastication as a terrible waste of time. I do not know if he was teetotal, but my guess would be that he was. He was a Lord Chancellor with a limited range. His practice was an entirely common-law one: he advised and appeared for parties on libel actions; he advised on contracts and similar matters dealt with in the common-law courts. On Chancery matters he was not well known, nor indeed on matrimonial matters, although he appeared several times in leading divorce cases.

I was always on agreeable terms with George Brown both in and out of office, although his well-known tendency to get drunk disrupted our relations on one or two occasions. It is surprising that his fondness for drink did not do more to impair his career, which was a remarkable career, only marred by his reaction to the appointment of Harold Wilson as the leader of the Labour Party. After that result he disappeared for a short while, but he returned in time to be included in Wilson's government, initially as Secretary of State for Economic Affairs, a post he held between 1964 and 1966.

He was an unusual comrade for Harold Wilson. Harold was worried by him, and rightly worried. His anxieties were not unassisted by George Wigg, who became more and more valuable to Wilson, principally as a source of information – largely, alas, misinformation – about the behaviour of anyone in the parliamentary party. This aroused the resentment of almost the whole front bench, but Wigg's hostility was not evenly spread. He hated, and was immensely jealous of, those who had received, in his view, excessive recognition on the way up. George Brown, of course, came into that category almost effortlessly. On one occasion, when George Brown was to give a seminal broadcast on a new financial plan, Wigg, who had been assigned by the Prime Minister to ensure, or to endeavour to ensure, that Brown arrived at Broadcasting House respectably sober, could think of nothing better to do than to consign him in the early afternoon to the sitting-room in my flat at Ashley Gardens. There he was provisioned with every known variety of soft drink, and kept virtually incommunicado until it was time for him to travel to Broadcasting House. The result was that he left my flat in a fuming temper, very gruff but very sober, and the broadcast was, I was given to understand, of consummate skill and effectiveness.

Then, in 1966, Harold Wilson, whose precise judgement of human beings is, alas, very defective, astonishingly appointed George to be the Foreign Secretary. If one had been asked, working on first principles, about the least eligible candidate to conduct the country's foreign affairs, many people, including myself, would have plumped for George Brown. He spoke no foreign languages; had the most superficial knowledge of foreign countries; was a master of tactlessness, and very often drunk in public places. Against this he had a surprisingly quick mind, a splendid gift of repartee and a skill in creating a warm and friendly relationship on a very slender acquaintance. What was interesting to note – since I had close links there through my association with the British Council – was the reaction in the Foreign Office. Some people were delighted with Brown: he was a breath of fresh air, contrasting with the ministers and principals, trained at Eton and Christ Church, to whom they were used. Others, particularly those trained at the aforesaid establishments, absolutely loathed the sight of him and loved to recount his various gaffes and *bêtises* from time to time. But in fact George Brown had a considerable edge over Labour's later candidate, David Owen, who offended the mandarins of King Charles Street with a quiet deliberation that was wholly lacking in George even in his most sober moments.

I retained a friendship for George Brown, although he regarded me with rather dubious approval because of my omission to drink anything at any dinner party. George's insobriety was disturbing and even wounding to his friends. On two occasions he joined large dinner parties designed to raise money for particular charities and I witnessed him reduced to slumping over the table on folded arms, where he remained comatose until gently removed at the end of the meal. He was particularly embarrassing on an occasion when Jennie Lee was sitting alongside him and in his groping fashion he made some amorous overtures. Jennie was not the right person to whom to do this. Her denunciation rang through the dinner party and it was sufficiently vigorous to deter even the drunken George from persisting.

But he could be an entertaining man and when sober made good company. At times he could be brilliant. I would not have entrusted, to use Jennie Lee's pungent phrase, the conduct of a chip shop to him, least of all the nation's international affairs, but I could not say with any firm conviction that they have necessarily been handled better by his successors of either party. The touch of genius that he could evince from moment to moment, if he was exercising self-control, distinguished him from other politicians on both sides of the House.

He was supported by a most devoted wife who looked after him for many years until, late in his life, he rejected and abandoned her for a younger woman. That inexcusable act probably speaks with greater clarity than anything I could say about his true character.

Oddly enough, the people in the Labour Party whom George Wigg most disliked were those with whom he had the closest associations. His *bête noire* was Richard Crossman, but it was a case of eerie fascination being exercised by that unpopular figure. To my knowledge there was hardly a political problem with which George was confronted where he did not seek the advice and guidance of Crossman, but it was always associated with a healthy denunciation.

Through George Wigg I became reasonably close to Richard Crossman who consulted me on a number of occasions – I have already described the *Spectator* libel case – but who, I must confess, turned out to be a disappointment to me, since the reputation he had earned for more than occasional unreliability I found to be entirely justified. However, Dick Crossman was certainly a remarkable man of great intellectual power, with an astonishing capacity for synthesising viewpoints into an effective plan. It was, I think, this last quality that gave him his reputation for indecision. He listened and provoked the expression of every opinion – however conflicting – and he then produced a concoction which contained the best of the ingredients from every recipe. The result was often surprisingly good, with a considerable degree of wit although no humour. I have always detected that an absence of humour is reflected in a very loud laugh, as if it is necessary to set in motion some violent mechanism before anything funny ultimately tickles the fancy, and Crossman certainly displayed this mannerism.

My relationship with Crossman eventually became in some ways a comic one. Shortly after his appointment as Minister of Housing in October 1964, he telephoned me on a Sunday morning to say that he was having great trouble with his civil servants because he wished to promote an anti-eviction Bill, which would make it impossible for people to be evicted from their premises without special precautions. He told me that his civil servants had said that this was impossible, and adumbrated the problem to me. I thought about it for a while and then telephoned him to say that I could suggest a pretty easy solution, and indicated to him what it was. He was delighted with this and said that he would send his advisers to see me – on a Sunday afternoon. However, it was not for me to tell him how to treat his advisers, and half an hour later three civil servants arrived with their notebooks whereupon I dictated my suggestions to them.

The matter had a rather startling consequence: Crossman's senior civil servant, the Permanent Secretary at the Ministry of Housing, was a lady, Dame Evelyn Sharp. When she heard that a mere layman had had the effrontery to advise on civil service matters, she went to see the Minister on the following day to tender her resignation. On hearing of this from Dick Crossman, I said that to have lost such an opportunity was unforgivable! Nevertheless, he was a man prudent enough to realise that he could not antagonise the entire civil service. He finally arrived at a compromise with her, which was that he could have three independent, non-civil servant, advisers. Dennis Lloyd and I were two of them, and the third was Desmond (now Lord) Plummer, who was an estate agent and surveyor and an expert on rent restriction. This concession having been wrung from Dame Evelyn, we were thereupon authorised to attend all meetings and to advise as though we had the accolade of civil service accorded to us.

My advice extended to a number of important legal technicalities and in particular to the operation of any necessary changes in the prevailing system of rent control – which for many years served to support social stability in this country to an extent rarely recognised. Perhaps my principal contribution was to have suggested the creation of rent officers and to have advised a formula for 'fair rents' which rent officers would be able to use in their day-to-day dealings with landlords and tenants.

A decade later, after Crossman's death in April 1974, my firm acted for the publishers Jonathan Cape over the publication of his *Diaries*. As is well known, Dick Crossman, who did not always conform to the rules, had maintained a most complete – if not invariably accurate – account of the Cabinet meetings that he attended and the discussions with his colleagues. There has been some argument about whether or not they knew what he was doing, but most of them now piously assert that they had no such knowledge and some take the view that it was an outrageous breach of confidence. Be that as it may, the difficulty was in relation to the government and possible action to prevent publication on a number of grounds, including a prosecution under the Official Secrets Act.

Crossman was a seriously-minded man and his diaries – although occasionally including some innocent gossip – were devoted to the serious topics that held his interest. These were not the stuff of 'secrets'. He was interested passionately in housing, rating, local government, drainage schemes, the selection of building experts and a multitude of other matters of profound importance to our society but unlikely to evoke great curiosity from lesser minds. Hence the likelihood that his diaries would have contained material of a secret nature which needed to be suppressed by legal and governmental intervention was from the outset slight. The problem that was, of course, puzzling and worrying to the government was his faithful recording of who said what about such matters at Cabinet meetings.

Following the submission of the first volume of the *Diaries* (covering the period 1964–6) to Sir John Hunt, the Secretary of the Cabinet, for official scrutiny, a long correspondence ensued. Sir John had identified a great number of passages which he regarded as objectionable from the government viewpoint, but I suspect he recognised early on that there was nothing of a very secret nature to conceal and what the government sought to suppress were the comments made by Crossman and others about senior civil servants.

The publication of any immediately contemporary record was, of course, impossible to sanction. I do not believe in the course of the protracted discussions about this case that anyone seriously proposed that all Cabinet deliberations should be revealed to the world at large within minutes of their taking place. Nor was this proposition ever propounded, so far as I am aware, by Dick Crossman. He kept his diaries for a record that would be published subsequent to the meetings. He did not believe that a long period of purdah was necessary, and the general rule that such a record could not be published until thirty years after the event was indeed ridiculous, since it has been honoured only in the breach.

A desperate effort was made to reach agreement. Certainly Sir John, a shrewd and amiable man, was anxious to do so, but Michael Foot – one of Crossman's literary executors and thus in the Crossman camp – felt that a compromise would have been a capitulation and contrary to their obligations to his memory. In the end, the Attorney-General commenced proceedings in June 1975 for an injunction to stop publication. A complication from the government's point of view was that the *Sunday Times* had contracted to publish extracts from the diaries and in fact did so before the government sought a gagging injunction. But it certainly added to the strength of the Crossman case that a great national newspaper had lined up alongside him.

It was significant that the Official Secrets Act – the use of which would have been fatal to the publication – was not resorted to by the government. The reason, I believe, is that it had in mind the defeat inflicted on the previous Conservative government over the Jonathan Aitken trial to do with Biafra. And the vagaries of a jury were possibly another consideration: the government fearing the libertarian qualities of juries. Moreover, the government's attitude would undoubtedly have been coloured by the

intriguing possibility of having one of its most prominent members –
namely, Michael Foot – among the defendants at the Old Bailey. It was
no secret that Michael Foot – believing that he had a duty to the late
Dick Crossman to procure the publication of the diaries – was courageously
prepared to accept this risk and to bare his breast for the dagger. (I may
say that Barbara Castle declined to give evidence on our behalf. It would
be unkind to attribute this decision to her intention to publish her own
diaries.)

But whatever the government's motivation, the Official Secrets Act –
a steamroller of an Act, as it then stood, which made it an offence to
divulge almost anything of any kind ascertained in the course of official
duties – was not used. It may also have been that the government was
unwilling to lend further strength to the clamour for the reform of the
Official Secrets Act (which has now happened) that had been mounting
for some years. There can be little doubt that a prosecution under that
Act at the relevant date, or its use to secure a civil injunction, would have
aroused considerable public indignation.

This led the government to intervene with some rather pallid legal
weapons. In the result they sought to rely on a very undefined rule of
confidentiality that had recently been confirmed in relation to the suppression of memoirs by the Duke of Argyll about his wife's life, and in
one or two other very dissimilar instances. The government therefore
took its stand on the position that the confidentiality rule operated between
members of the Cabinet and in the general context of a minister's official
duties, and that it could be invoked in a court of law to restrain revelations
of Cabinet and other official discussions.

The defendants took the view that the rule ought not so to relate and
that such discussions should be free for publication without restraint or
inhibition. The social desirability of either position was not really an
issue, although needless to say it was copiously referred to. The matter
the judge had to decide was whether, if there were confidences, there was
any legal prohibition preventing their publication.

In the end the Lord Chief Justice, Lord Widgery, found for the
publishers on the ground that, although confidentiality could be enforced
in suitable cases, this was not a suitable case: the matters revealed in the
first volume of the *Diaries*, being ten years old, were too stale to have any
security aspect. It was an unsatisfactory conclusion in that the issue of
principle was left clean open for future argument.

A committee of Privy Counsellors, under the chairmanship of Lord
Radcliffe, was set up to 'review the arrangements which should govern
the publication of memoirs by former ministers during the period of
thirty years that official documents are subject to the provisions of the

Public Records Act'. In its report, the committee did not recommend any change in the law but that these matters should be left to the good sense and judgement (hopefully) of Cabinet ministers, utilising the Radcliffe guidelines. It did suggest that the principles of confidentiality should be preserved for a period of fifteen years instead of thirty, but that there should be no new machinery for enforcement since offenders would carry the risk of social and political sanctions, and, of course, if they came within the rubric of any existing legal restraint, such as the Official Secrets Act, they would run the risk of legal proceedings.

The fifteen-year period is merely half as ridiculous as the thirty-year period. A determined social 'agnostic' of Dick Crossman's type is as unlikely to be deterred by minatory finger-wagging as by the pre-report situation. In short, the law has been left as it is. The Official Secrets Act remains substantially intact, but it now has to be read with the additional defences available under the new legislation, happily with a pendant attached deriving from the Aitken case that juries will not stand for the use of oppressive legislation in cases of mild divulgence, and confidentiality has been confirmed as being available where secret information is breached without official justification.

Following the judgement, it was clear to anyone concerned to suppress publication of the *Diaries*, or any part of them, that they would be on an impossibly bad wicket. This decision was immensely helpful to Jonathan Cape since it had been and remained their intention to publish the next two volumes of the *Diaries* and a further volume that related to Crossman's earlier back-bench activities. The decision also made possible the publication of other Cabinet recollections, particularly by Barbara Castle and Tony Benn.

If George Wigg's political hatreds extended to George Brown and Richard Crossman, then they were to surface intensely with regard to the Profumo affair. Wigg's resentment against Profumo related to some answer that Profumo had given in 1962 to a question about British troops overseas, which to Wigg's unbendable mind was an untruth. I recollect having urged Wigg on many occasions to limit the ambit of the Profumo affair. My role in the matter was as an independent voice advising the Labour Party on what to do about Profumo. My advice was, I believe, impeccable, but unfortunately it was not taken and, where Wigg was concerned, was deliberately misconstrued.

My introduction to the matter came early one morning at about 6 a.m. when – having had a late night – I was awakened by a telephone call from Wigg. He poured into the telephone a long and unintelligible narrative about Profumo's villainy in relation to the unhappy answer he had given to Wigg about the army. It did not take Wigg much time to decide that he had been misled, although a fair-minded examination of the facts from the *Hansard* of the day proved no such thing. The salient fact is that Wigg believed, and believed with great intensity, that Profumo had lied to him and for that reason was a suitable object for punishment in fanning the flame of the sexual scandal.

Wigg, in that conversation with me, was seeking my approval to continue his parliamentary quest for information. I vividly remember, although I was in a thoroughly sleepy condition, telling him that in my view the only proper justification for an enquiry about Mr Profumo's personal life depended on the possibility that some act of his might have compromised security, because he obviously had information which was secret. Knowing Wigg, I warned him that to pursue the matter for any other reason would be discreditable and in the long run would be sure to be to his detriment. I gave similar advice when Harold Wilson asked me to advise the Labour Party about their behaviour in the matter.

The Profumo affair was an unhappy demonstration of the lengths to which political hostility can extend. If there had been no political factor in the equation, it is unlikely that Profumo would have been ruined in the way he was and tortured for years by a newspaper interest which has survived until the present day. It is rather terrible to think how unforgiving the world can be and how willing to inflict continuous torture on account of a single piece of behaviour that without the political element and the adventitious addition of one or two other elements would have faded into obscurity in no time at all.

It is accepted without great horror, and particularly in the upper-class world in which Profumo mixed, that there is nothing wrong in having an extra-marital relationship. Profumo unfortunately succumbed to the charms of a Miss Christine Keeler who – casting my mind back – appeared at the time to be an attractive little thing, and whose very appearance could be regarded as a warning to every husband anxious to preserve his marriage.

There were a number of tragic elements – from the point of view of Profumo – that tickled the public fancy and aroused a passionate interest on the part of the press, and not only the tabloid press. There was the fact that Profumo, who was in the Cabinet as War Minister, had met this young lady at the Cliveden home of the Astor family, encouraged by the head of the family, to whom it was also alleged Miss Keeler had granted her favours. And the press enjoyed the benefit of Profumo's total inexperience in handling publicity. Adultery is no guarantee of worldliness. He provided titillating material – allowing himself to be photographed in the Cliveden swimming-pool with the lady. The press were delighted to have the scandal fed to them on a silver salver.

But to Profumo's bad luck, other newsworthy circumstances were available to salt the story. Miss Keeler's love life had provided a sensational scandal in that a 'coloured friend', moved to desperate jealousy by her behaviour, had opened fire at the window of her home and been arrested and charged for that offence. Added to this, three so-called responsible members of Her Majesty's Opposition (Labour) saw fit to impute that Profumo had arranged to ship Miss Keeler abroad so as to render her unavailable to give evidence at the Old Bailey trial of her coloured lover.

After his initial blunder of sleeping with Miss Keeler, it was the sad fate of Profumo to be ruined by political and legal advice. He had been provoked – and it is well to remember that he was then, and continues to this day to be, happily married to a beautiful and supportive wife – into seeking to continue the deception by a personal statement in the Commons in which he averred that he was innocent of the allegations and a wronged man. The statement was received enthusiastically by the Tory Party and with obvious scepticism by the Opposition.

The explanation of the statement is that Harold Macmillan, unworldly as he was, became increasingly conscious of the dangers to the government if the matter was not satisfactorily cleared up. Macmillan instructed his law officers, Sir John Hobson and Sir Peter Rawlinson, to find out from Profumo what the truth was. One or other of them drafted a statement which was a flat denial that he had misbehaved either sexually or politically. This statement was approved by the law officers, who very properly insisted that Profumo should also be advised by his own independent solicitor (a partner in the well-known firm of Theodore Goddard) who, having read the statement, also approved it and recommended Profumo to make it to the House. Additionally, carried away by enthusiasm that ought not to affect the judgement of experienced lawyers, they advised him, or agreed on his urging (I do not know which), that he should issue writs for libel, which he did, with the disastrous effect that he actually accepted some damages from one publication before he was compelled to reveal the falsity of his assertions.

It is a strange reflection on the exceptional unworldliness of these three eminent lawyers. Every cub reporter in Fleet Street knew that a Sunday newspaper possessed a letter from Profumo to Miss Keeler, probably acquired by simple purchase, which was a sword of Damocles waiting to descend. In contrast, the government's two senior legal advisers and the senior partner of a leading firm of society lawyers were so ignorant of this fact that it did not even enter their heads that it would be wise to make some enquiries before launching their client into a statement that could be, and indeed was, ruinous. In any event, on 4 June 1963 Profumo was obliged by the torrent of publicity and increasing evidence to acknowledge the falsity of his statement to the House and to resign both from office and from the House.

George Wigg's enthusiasm, however, could not restrain him from pursuing a more general, and indeed very vindictive, course in relation to Profumo's statement. Wigg did not believe in the doctrine that you did not kick a man when he was down. On the contrary, he considered that an exceptionally valuable opportunity for enabling you to kick him more robustly and with least personal danger. Once you were Wigg's enemy – and this was a judgement reached by him and not by the other person – there was no pursuit and no hostility that he would abandon; but I remained an affectionate friend because of the other side of his character, which would not even be suspected by those with whom he was in controversy.

Not everyone was wholly approving of Wigg's activities in relation to Profumo – and indeed on many other matters. The *Sunday Citizen* explained his enthusiasm for the Profumo affair because of a long-cherished personal grudge against Profumo and of having unearthed a juicy scandal by snooping that would have done credit to a divorce detective. There was, nevertheless, an element of truth in both these allegations, but Wigg was the wrong man against whom to hurl such invective and he launched a libel action. The *Sunday Citizen* withdrew the allegations, apologised and paid Wigg's costs in the matter – the settlement was on my advice to Wigg that he could not know what view a jury would take of his actions in relation to Profumo.

I have developed considerable regard and affection over the years for Jack Profumo, who has worked his passage after having been what is technically described as 'disgraced' in circumstances where a great number of people would not have been over-censorious. I knew no one in their sane senses who believed that Profumo was a spy, and in fact that suggestion was never made.

On occasions when talking about the case, I have been asked what advice I would have given to Profumo. Some thirty years after the event, it is not easy to recapture the circumstances or to avoid *post hoc propter hoc*. But my present belief is that if Profumo had come to me for advice (and my advice, of course, would only have made sense if one postulates that Profumo would have told me the truth), I would have recommended that he should throw in the towel; assert that he had no intention of allowing his private life to be discussed in public; apologise to the Prime Minister for the embarrassment he had caused both to him and to the party, and withdraw rapidly. Had he done that – and this is advice every sensible lawyer would have given to him – he might have been able to return to public life without the long and painful period of atonement to which he was exposed. We have recent evidence that the Conservative Party at least is willing to forgive, and once it had been accepted there was no question of the betrayal of any secrets, it would have been a simple matter of marital infidelity.

In the result, however, Profumo retired from public life and has worked heroically in public and social service for little reward for a number of years. The most admirable part of the whole affair was the undeviating loyalty of his wife, Valerie Hobson, with whom I had had some encounters previously, when she was married to Anthony Havelock-Allan. Over the years, although never establishing a close friendship with the Profumos, I have had an admiring acquaintance with both of them and am happy to see that their marriage was not ruined by this solitary episode and distressed indeed by its revival from time to time by creatures animated solely by greed.

The suggestion at the time that the Labour Party had been behind Profumo's downfall was a little unfair to many members who repeatedly expressed their misgivings about the scandalous imputations, which several of them could not regard as a proper currency for a political difference. Having advised restraint by the Labour Party, I was angered, and indeed horrified, by the announcement that the government had asked Lord Denning to conduct his now infamous one-man inquiry into the matter, with terms of reference so loose that he regarded himself as charged to examine everyone's activities through a microscope and to denounce anyone where there was a whisper of suspected immorality, let alone convincing proof.

When George Wigg asked my view about this, I recommended that he should urge Harold Wilson to oppose any such investigation and I drafted a letter which Wigg suggested Wilson should write to the Prime Minister. In fact, I have no reason to think that Wilson wrote this or any other letter protesting against the establishment of a wide-ranging inquiry such as Denning believed he had been instructed to conduct. Wilson's disinclination to protest against the inquiry probably arose from a reasonable belief that any senior politician who did not want such an inquiry had something discreditable to hide. While I have no reason to believe that this was the case in respect of Wilson, or indeed any senior member of the Labour Party, I can understand why such a person would be reluctant to try to abort the inquiry.

It is a signal tribute to Denning that he was able to conduct his inquiry in a typical homespun fashion, without any unfair imputation against anyone being made. But it is also clear that Denning started off with a presumption that everyone involved was innocent and that at some stage he had personal doubts as to whether this was indeed so. At that point, he appeared rather hastily to have brought his inquiry to an end.

It was a satisfaction to me many years later, when I was a member of a Royal Commission on Tribunals of Enquiry, established to advise how secrets should be dealt with, that I was able to persuade the chairman of the Commission, Lord Salmon, and through him the whole of the Commission, to recommend that there should never again be an inquiry of the Denning type, where a single individual was authorised to investigate any piece of gossip or scandal relating to any prominent public person. It is certainly my hope that this is the last time we have heard of a Denning-type investigation.

A small offshoot of the Profumo affair was an exchange between the three Labour members principally concerned with the case (George Wigg, Dick Crossman and Barbara Castle) and the Leader of the House, the late Iain McLeod. Denning had referred in his report to their speeches in the House on 21 March 1963 and had commented that their remarks clearly imputed that Profumo had been responsible for the disappearance of Christine Keeler. McLeod went on television and said that, in view of Lord Denning's findings, the three members who had brought to the notice of the House the existence of the rumours about Profumo owed a duty to Profumo to withdraw the charge. The three asserted that their only observation had been to suggest that because such a rumour was circulating it would be wise for it to be firmly denied or some enquiry made, and that they had not made any allegation against Profumo but only a suggestion for his benefit.

A slightly more critical eye might have felt that the very fact that they were publicly proclaiming the existence of such a rumour could not advantage Profumo in any way and might easily damage him. There is no doubt that a suggestion that 'a rumour is circulating', if made outside the House of Commons, could support an allegation of libel. However, the whole matter was another aspect of one of the storms in a set of teacups that accompanied the whole unhappy Profumo matter and has continued to do so for the many years since it was first raised.

Another introduction to politics was provided for me in the person of Randolph Churchill. I cannot claim to have been a close friend, but I had occasional encounters with him and, as with most people, it would be more accurate to describe them as occasional brushes. He was an unhappy personality, who had obviously grown up in the shadow of his father and had decided that the assumption of a totally aggressive demeanour was the only way of maintaining a personality of his own that would be distinct from that of his famous – indeed most famous – parent.

Randolph was a pretty ruthless character. I remember one day in the

1940s sitting at a table on the first floor of the Crown in Fleet Street, next to a table where an attractive young woman, then unknown to me, was sitting in front of a plate of smoked salmon and opposite an empty place furnished with another plate of smoked salmon, which must have been ordered in advance. The other diner was plainly downstairs in the bar and did not appear during the whole of the lunchtime and had still not appeared by the time I had finished and paid my bill. I now know that the lady concerned was the then Mrs Randolph Churchill, later Mrs Averell Harriman and now the widow of that very great man. I thought at the time that her absent luncheon companion must have been a boorish character, and even the greatest friends of Randolph Churchill would find difficulty in defending him from this charge.

I had an encounter with Randolph Churchill in the late 1950s which arose in rather unexpected circumstances. MacGibbon & Kee had published a book by him about the Suez affair. In it, of course, he was immensely critical of Anthony Eden and the Conservative Party. He telephoned me one evening to tell me that the Labour Party had decided to use an extract from it in their manifesto. Not unnaturally, as a Conservative supporter, this gave him no pleasure and he was reasonably apprehensive that it would arouse criticism from other persons of the same political persuasion. I asked him not to say any more to me, since at that time I represented the Labour Party and felt it quite possible that if he brought any action I would be called upon to act for them. I left it there.

What I then discovered was a chapter of errors worthy of Feydeau. Randolph Churchill decided that he would telephone the owner of MacGibbon & Kee – a rather eccentric character called Howard Samuel. Unfortunately he phoned him in the middle of the night. Howard Samuel had indulged in, as was not unusual, an enjoyable dinner. Randolph explained the circumstances to him carefully and received a 'Yes, Yes' at regular intervals. Apparently he asked Howard Samuel whether he would associate himself with an action to procure an injunction to restrain the manifesto, to which Howard Samuel had allegedly replied that he would.

The next morning, as I heard the story from Howard Samuel's wife, Howard had remarked to her, 'Did someone telephone during the night?' To which she replied that she had been sound asleep, that she had heard a desultory conversation, but its substance had nothing whatever to do with her. She did remember that a word sounding like 'sewers' was uttered, and it puzzled her to think why anyone should be ringing in the middle of the night to enquire about the state of the sewers. However, Howard Samuel could remember nothing of it at all. Shortly afterwards I was telephoned by Morgan Phillips, the general secretary of the Labour

Party, to say that Randolph had issued a writ for breach of copyright and was applying for an injunction that very afternoon, and would I act on behalf of the Labour Party? I thereupon obtained from him the name of the solicitor instructed by Randolph, telephoned him and said that my own firm would accept service of the writ.

I then telephoned Howard Samuel and said, 'There is an attack on the Labour Party of which you are supposed to be a loyal member. Will you do something?' 'What do you want me to do?' he asked. 'There is a complaint that there is a breach of copyright by dint of a short extract from Randolph's book which has been inserted in their manifesto.' The legal position was not entirely clear: if the extract was short enough, then it was permissible to use it, because an extract from a book used purely for the purpose of comment did not constitute a breach of copyright, but in the present circumstances, when it was used for purely political purposes, I was not so sure. I thereupon asked Howard Samuel whether he would grant to the Labour Party a licence for the extract, as I had discovered from the contract that the quotation rights were vested in the publisher. 'Certainly,' he said. 'How much should I charge?' I thought that three guineas would be an appropriate amount, drew up a licence and sent it to him to sign.

At the hearing Randolph's counsel, Mr Fearnley-Whittingstall QC (a well-known right-wing lawyer, who also acted for the defendants in the *Spectator* libel case), got up and delivered a long and passionate address about the iniquity of what had happened. Sir David Scott Cairns QC, our counsel, thereupon rose from his seat and mildly brandished the licence to say that it was all permitted. The plaintiff had no knowledge that a licence had been granted, since there was no time for any kind of discovery. Notice of the application for the injunction had been given at about 11 a.m. and the hearing took place after lunch. The application was, of course, dismissed with lightning speed.

Randolph was not a man to forgive lightly. Howard Samuel never had the courage to tell him that he had no recollection of their night-time conversation because of his post-prandial condition, so Randolph always regarded the fact that the licence had been obtained for the Labour Party as a gross breach of trust. It was a fuss about nothing, and I greatly doubt whether anyone other than Randolph Churchill would have made a major issue of it. Looking back, I cannot deny that the grant of the licence was something of which he could legitimately complain, but his capacity for complaints exceeded any normal human being's by a very large measure.

I drafted Howard's final response to the inevitable correspondence that ensued:

Dear Churchill,

I have your letter of the 5th instant.

All that you write might have some relevance but for the simple fact that there was no infringement. The use of a tiny extract from your book – suitably acknowledged – is not an infringement of copyright and no interest was affected. It was, in our view, an excellent free advertisement. On that footing the entire correspondence becomes irrelevant.

Frankly, in my short publishing career I have yet to encounter anyone who can involve his publishers in more trouble in less time for no purpose than you can. This is not the least of your talents, and if you carry away no other tribute from this firm you can certainly preserve that one.

Yours sincerely,

Howard Samuel

Randolph was in my view a tragic figure. He obviously possessed great talents, though he perhaps thought more highly of them than did others; and he also had a unique capacity for arousing antagonisms and hatred. On the other hand there were many people who loved him dearly. His life was a brief one and his war service was heroic. He might have made a significant contribution to the public life of this country had he not been totally overshadowed by his illustrious father and had he not had such a burning desire to shine as bright or even brighter.

But a Churchill of whom I can only speak with deep affection is Randolph's son, Winston. He too is a man who goes out of his way to twist people's tails in the hope of provoking them when he thinks their inactivity is impermissible. But he has sterling qualities, particularly courage and a total indifference to public opinion.

I became involved with him some years ago when I was consulted by Lord Rayne who told me that he had a friend – a leading paediatrician in London – whose daughter was in serious trouble. She had married an Englishman and the two of them had gone off to South Africa where, unhappily, they had engaged in political activities. Both had been arrested and were charged with serious terrorist offences, of which I was sure they were totally innocent; although I was equally sure that they had engaged in active political propaganda, which in some ways would have been no less objectionable to the South African government. The girl, many months pregnant and on the verge of delivery, was in solitary confinement in an African prison, separated from and unable to see her husband. He was under arrest and confined in even more disagreeable circumstances in a male prison. The father was distraught; he had appealed to the Prime Minister, had been to see the Foreign Secretary, he had been in fact everywhere, and finally asked Max Rayne whether he could come to see me. I said that it would be unkind and discourteous to decline a visit, but I could not for the life of me see how I could help him where persons of much greater power were impotent.

In any event he came to see me and we discussed the matter, and I said exactly that to him: that if he had appealed to the Prime Minister and the Foreign Secretary, it seemed to me a very remote prospect that anything I could do would be of the slightest effect. Pleadingly, he asked me whether I could think of anything. I thought for a while and said that the only thing I could think of was that the British government did not – although it would have been slow to admit it – at that moment cut much ice with the South African government, but the United States government cut considerable ice. 'Do you know any influential American who might be able to intervene?' I asked. He sadly admitted that he did not.

It then occurred to me that I might be able to help, and I picked up the telephone and spoke to Winston. I asked him if he would be prepared to assist. He said that of course he would, but what could he do? 'Well, your stepfather is Averell Harriman,' I said – he had married Randolph's wife after they had divorced. 'Will you telephone Harriman and ask if he could do anything in the way of intervention?' 'Certainly,' he replied, without a moment's hesitation. I do not know any other politician or statesman who would have acted with such speedy decision without stopping to think of the possible consequences to himself or what people might think about his intervention on behalf of an alleged terrorist. Winston phoned me back within an hour to say that he had spoken to Harriman, that Harriman had spoken to the State Department, that they had dispatched two telegrams – one to Pretoria and one to Cape Town, the places between which the governmental functions are divided – and that in addition he himself had sent a telegram to the Prime Minister of South Africa, signed by the not unimpressive name of Winston Churchill.

The effect was electric: the girl was released within a few days; the man remained in jail and in fact served a very long sentence. But that in no way affected my admiration for what Winston had done, and I am pleased to think that on one or two occasions I have been able to render him some modest service in the way of a reward for this particular display of public courage. I can think of only one other man who would have taken the political risks involved and that was the late Sir Hugh Fraser.

Another occasion which demonstrated Winston's indifference to the dictates of authority or public opinion was when I was approached by a picaresque character called John Shaheen, an American oil magnate who spent his life getting in and out of the most complicated financial transactions, seemingly always on the verge of ruin but nevertheless contriving to remain sufficiently solvent to undertake his next massive adventure.

On this occasion he had, after the expenditure of many millions, built a refinery in Newfoundland, and he telephoned me to ask whether I could persuade Winston Churchill to come to the grand opening. I rang Winston and he said he would make an enquiry at the Foreign Office. The Foreign Office advised him very strongly to take no part in the transaction, but this was in fact an encouragement. He rang me back and said that he would certainly come.

In typical style Shaheen had commissioned the *QE2* to take a large party of people to the opening and offered me a cabin on her, but as I could not spare the time and was not sure that I would be entirely at home with my fellow passengers, I flew over in response to his invitation. I spent a little while there and enjoyed a helicopter trip for the very first time, although not without considerable trepidation having once or twice seen pictures of them whizzing down to the ground in pieces. On this occasion, however, shame compelled me to travel in a helicopter since the Lieutenant-Governor of Newfoundland and his wife were also taking this short trip – his wife, if I may say, a most attractive lady. When she stepped into the helicopter in front of me, I had no alternative but to follow her with my heart in my boots. However, the flight was extremely enjoyable and we travelled low enough almost to touch the antlers of the wild moose that were in the area and to see the countryside from the most advantageous position.

The actual opening of the refinery in October 1973 was a comic disaster. The VIPs, among whom I found myself, sat on a huge platform under a vast marquee. Various people were due to address them at various moments, in particular Winston. Unhappily a gale of enormous force then blew up which threw the marquee to the ground and we were left clinging to the posts in order to remain upright. Nevertheless it is a remarkable tribute to the perseverance and courage of the participants that the ceremonial proceedings were concluded, although no one could have heard a single word of what was spoken into the gale and blown back.

My friendly relationship with Shaheen continued until his death in 1984. He was man who was always on the point of launching some immense enterprise, a few of which indeed came off while others ended disastrously. Nevertheless he always remained undaunted and could hardly wait for the winding up of his previous effort before starting to plan its successor.

Shaheen was a leading supporter of the Republican Party and a great friend of every Republican president. Whether they were great friends of his was a matter of conjecture. During one of my trips to the USA in the 1960s, Shaheen telephoned my hotel one day to say that he had arranged for me to have lunch with Richard Nixon, who at the time had not yet declared that he would run for the presidency in the election of 1968. He was, therefore, still practising law. We went and had lunch with him at the India Club on Wall Street.

Mr Nixon hardly spoke a word. The impression I got of him was that he was the world's most cautious man (which squares ill with his later reckless behaviour); that he was a man who said nothing; who had carefully devised a plan of life which rendered the use of words unnecessary except in an emergency such as fire or accident. He also struck me as a man who gave the most mature thought before uttering even one of these rare words; and that if you said 'good morning' to him, he would reflect for some seconds while a number of questions passed through his mind. Why – he would ask himself – is this man saying 'good morning' to me? What is his motivation? And what are the risks involved if I reply? In the end, no doubt, he normally did answer 'good morning'.

Anyway, at the luncheon concerned he adopted precisely this cautious attitude and the conversation was as sluggish as it is possible to imagine. I formed the view of a singularly unattractive character: unattractive in appearance, unattractive in personality, and certainly unattractive conversationally. The notion that he might make any joke, except an obscene one, I dismissed without a second thought. The only thing that surprised me after our painful, taciturn lunch was the astonishing enthusiasm and goodwill he displayed on my departure. He wrung my hand for about five minutes and told me how much pleasure the meeting had given him, though God knows where he had extracted the pleasure from, and expressed the most fervent hope that we would become the firmest friends in the nearest possible future. It was a hope that I, at least, did not silently echo.

But the politician I was to see most of during the 1960s, the politician in the middle of it all, was, of course, Harold Wilson. I met him for the first time ever when he took over the leadership of the party from the recently deceased Hugh Gaitskell in February 1963. He had heard of me from some of his colleagues and asked to see me to discuss the Labour Party's decision in relation to the litigation it had brought, with my guidance, against the *Manchester Guardian* as a result of the leaks from the National Executive. He was sitting in his chair, smoking a pipe, and my first reaction was not favourable. The Prime Minister designate obviously viewed me with suspicion, as being closely associated with his predecessor. He asked me what should be done about the action. I told him it was entirely a matter for him to decide: that the Labour Party was my client and I would proceed on its instructions.

This single episode gave me a very good picture of Harold Wilson's qualities and defects. He discussed any issue, and particularly this one, with everyone he could think of and he continued to show throughout his political career an indecision that in some directions had dire consequences. For instance, his intimate associates were very much at odds with each other. The only common factor was Mrs Marcia Williams (now Lady Falkender), his private and political secretary, of whom I saw very little, but I saw enough of her to realise the immense influence she exercised over Harold Wilson.

As my own position with him became firmer, he aired occasional criticisms of Mrs Williams. I ventured on one or two occasions to suggest that he might find some way of dispensing with her services. He never reacted hostilely to any such suggestion, except to say to me that she was difficult enough in a friendly association and matters might be worse (his own words) if he took any action to remove her from his political scene. I witnessed on several occasions horribly embarrassing disagreements between Harold Wilson and Marcia Williams, but it was clear that his loyalty to her would not be disturbed by any difference of opinion or any show of temper.

The arrival of Harold Wilson heralded the discontinuance of the *Guardian* action. Within a few days of seeing me for the first time, he summoned me once again to tell me that the Labour Party did not wish to continue with the action. I did not ask him why, but I sensed that it was because he knew the culprit. While suspicion as to the source of the leakage had fallen on a variety of people, I agreed wholeheartedly with the decision that Wilson, and presumably the National Executive, had arrived at.

I was therefore instructed to discontinue the action on the basis that each side paid their own costs, although the *Guardian* had suffered a continuous reverse in their attempts to maintain the right to press freedom and to maintain secrecy about their informant. Hence I never knew who the culprit was and was never put into possession of the document or documents which existed and which would certainly have identified that person, since each copy of the minutes had, on my advice, been numbered. It was a strong probability that the *Guardian* still retained in their archives a numbered copy of the minutes which would have told us immediately to whom that copy had been issued and therefore the name of the informant.

Before very long, Wilson was constantly consulting me on a number of matters and even seeking my opinion on political issues – which he wisely always rejected. He was then, of course, in opposition and particularly asked if I might advise on what would be a sensible housing policy when the Labour Party came to power. In fact, when the Labour Party did come to power in 1964, the only documentation they possessed on this subject was a single sheet of paper provided by myself, recommending among other things the establishment of rent officers, an idea in which I was subsequently able to interest Dick Crossman.

Apart from housing, rent restriction and the like, Wilson flattered me by consulting me on a number of topics, on which I was never slow to express an opinion and never disappointed when that opinion was totally disregarded or not even mentioned. I received a special mark of confidence from him, just before the 1964 election, when he was anxious to retrieve some papers from his home in Hampstead Garden Suburb. He asked me if I could arrange for somebody thoroughly trustworthy to visit the premises, telling me that he had given the key to a neighbour. I decided that in the circumstances this was not a job that I would entrust anyone else to do, and I motored to Hampstead myself.

I was not surprised, although I was rather gratified, to find the semi-detached house one of incredible modesty. I noted, also with satisfaction, that there was hardly an article in the house that could have cost more than £5. There were no Rembrandts, no Chippendale furniture, nothing that indicated that Harold Wilson had achieved any prosperity in his many arduous years in opposition. This, I thought, reflected great credit on him, though others might take the contrary view and criticise the fact that he had not first thought to amass a substantial fortune. One thing I can say of him with total confidence is that I have never met a man less interested in money. That is not to say that he was not interested in spending it. He was a man of exceptional generosity, in fact I can truthfully say over-generous.

As a prime minister he probably ranked with Ramsay MacDonald in humble origin and modest wealth. It is appropriate to contrast the modesty of his home with those of more affluent politicians. Very few politicians of recent years have lived in simpler surroundings and with less show of luxury. His attitude towards creature comforts was demonstrated by his regimen in Downing Street. Except when he was entertaining I doubt if he ever sat down to a three-course meal. Also, unlike others who had been brought up in more cultured surroundings, it was a rarity for him to go to the theatre and even more of a rarity to go to other forms of public entertainments, including the cinema.

In October 1964 the Labour Party won a precarious victory, leaving it with a majority of five in the House of Commons. Wilson's leadership was certainly new in style, in that he proclaimed his intention to turn No. 10 into a 'power house', where the rhythmic working of bulging brains would generate a new hope, a new vision, a new purpose and a new nation. The sincerity of his beliefs is unquestionable. The country had been emancipated from thirteen years of middle-level Conservative rule of reasonable efficiency, modest dynamism but small-power idealism. The Macmillan era had aroused hopes in leftist hearts that we might achieve a mixed economy that made sense; but the murkiness of political scandal and the absurdities of needless party discord rendered Mr Macmillan's last months unhappy and confused. He handed over to poor Sir Alec Douglas-Home a party legacy of dwindling popularity, and although that amiable and resolute character fought with vigour and gallantry to maintain his position, the tide had sufficiently turned to abandon him gently on the beach, leaving Harold Wilson afloat in waters so shallow that the most gentle paddle hit the sand.

However, he was in power. A new government was to be formed. I had never been a member of the Labour Party, and on the first occasion when I could claim a vote I voted for the Liberal candidate in the Hampstead constituency. As has dogged the fate of any political candidate I have favoured for any office or position, he was unsuccessful. However, almost all my political connections were on the Left and my Labour friends, acquired relatively late in life (apart from George Wigg, most of them after I was forty years of age), were a source of delight and novelty to me. I had eschewed politics in favour of a life practising law and enjoying the amenities of a civilised society in the way of drama, music and literature and, in a more limited and selective fashion, the visual arts. I had not engaged in speech-making, public address or political activity of any kind at any stage in my life. As an undergraduate my sympathies were with the Left, with the Republicans in Spain, with the anti-Fascists in Italy and Germany, but always with a nearly corresponding hostility to the extremes of political thought on the other side. To meet fully matured politicians of the higher quality at a time when I was still young enough to sharpen my wits on their arguments and dialectics was a real – and in my case an undeserved – pleasure. Against that background, and with those friends, I viewed with satisfaction the election results that gave Harold Wilson his majority of five, or fourteen if you included the Liberals, and upon which he resolutely set out to govern.

On the day that Wilson was elected to office, he telephoned me, tracking me down to a restaurant in London, to enquire what to do about the Royal Philharmonic Orchestra. It staggered me! It was characteristic that a small, relatively unimportant detail of that kind – from his point of view, not mine – should have occupied his time when he had assumed this enormous burden. He was anxious that the Royal Philharmonic Orchestra should not be dissolved for want of finance. It was in consequence of that wish that Jennie Lee asked me if I would chair a committee on London Orchestras, which in fact I did, and whose findings I describe later. Before we delivered our report, however, I had joined the Arts Council, of which I became chairman in May 1965.

A couple of weeks after my appointment to the Arts Council, a letter arrived from Downing Street asking if I wished to accept the honour of a peerage. Although I had considerable doubts as to whether Lord Goodman would on the whole be a happier and more contented human being than Mr Goodman, or whether in fact it would not be a prefix that would be more of an incubus than a blessing, vanity as always prevailed. Almost anybody who is offered an honour of some kind indicates that he has had a period of anxious, nay tortured reflection, but somehow inexorably arrives at the conclusion that duty demands – duty to his family, his wife, his children, his bank manager – that he should accept the honour. I am sorry to say that the same human impulses acted with me, particularly in relation to my bank manager, and I wrote a letter of acceptance.

On 12 June 1965 an Honours List was published containing my name on the list of life peers. The press remained both loyal and helpful, notwithstanding George Wigg's characteristic intervention describing me, to my acute embarrassment, as a saint-like figure. Fortunately those of my friends who knew me before were only amused by this foolish description and there was no general resentment of my peerage, which could properly have been attributed to many services that I had given to the government – of both colours.

After the election, I became a frequent visitor to Downing Street. It is not true, as Lady Falkender has stated, that I became a visitor when George Wigg ceased to visit. In fact, although George Wigg was close to Wilson, he never enjoyed the same intimate relationship, for the very good reason that he was a politician and did not enjoy Wilson's undivided trust. I can claim that I did, and that I never breached that trust, assuming that I had any information of a sufficiently intriguing character to make it worthwhile betraying a friend.

Throughout the whole period of Harold Wilson's first premiership, and a substantial portion of his second premiership, I visited at least once a fortnight and sometimes once a week. I was usually summoned by telephone and invited round to Downing Street at 8 p.m., when Wilson would be alone in the Cabinet room, which he preferred to any office or study, and where, sitting at the long Cabinet table, I often found myself in the seat normally occupied by the Chancellor of the Exchequer and enjoyed moments of brief delusional glory!

Wilson would talk at great length and it became clear to me that the number of people in whom he could confide safely was very small; in fact it was clear that he had few, if any, complete political friends. His number two for practical purposes was Roy Jenkins, but they were so totally different in disposition and outlook that the possibility of a friendship would not have existed, even if Wilson had not entertained dark suspicions about Jenkins's ambition to supplant him. I do not believe Jenkins had any such ambition, and I am quite sure that it was not within his nature to take any active steps to intrigue, but Harold Wilson did believe – and conscientiously so – that such intrigues were taking place.

There was a particularly piquant episode when it had been reported to him that a meeting had allegedly taken place somewhere in the country, where Jenkins was supposed to have organised his cabal. In fact I happened just to have spent the weekend with a dear friend and was well aware that at some point over the two days she had entertained everyone suspected of being concerned, and not a word of politics was discussed, nor a syllable about supplanting anybody. But it would have taken more than me to convince Harold Wilson that this was so and that conspiracies were not afoot. I believe that his suspicions in this regard were more than amply fuelled by the activities of Marcia Williams, who also was a great believer in the conspiracy theory.

As I have said, Harold Wilson usually summoned me to Downing Street for 8 p.m. On one occasion I screwed up my courage to ask if I could come in at 9 p.m. instead, at which Harold looked puzzled and asked why. 'Because,' I said, somewhat impertinently, 'I would like to dine.' Such was the austerity of his habits that it never entered his head himself to have any kind of formal dinner in which I could join. I was greatly relieved when he agreed, since although I regard Downing Street as an admirable place, I have never had any admiration for its cuisine. Accordingly the time was changed: I went in at 9 p.m. and often stayed until midnight or past.

These meetings were largely an opportunity for Harold Wilson to use me as the wall of a fives court against which he banged the ball. I listened patiently. Sitting in the Cabinet room at Downing Street, with the Prime Minister taking me into his confidence was an exhilarating experience from first to last. I did not regard Harold Wilson as a wit, nor was his conversation particularly spiced with humour, but it was immensely interesting because he would talk to me about his problems and their supposed solutions, and seemingly consult me on the matter – he was a very polite man – although I was conscious that on most political issues

The author on his seventh birthday showing the assurance for which he was later renowned.

The author's mother with her beloved Pekinese 'Pucci'.

June 1917. The author, characteristically unworried by the small matter of the World War then in progress, with his elder brother Theodore.

The author's first degree at his first university – University College, London. October 1933.

The author (front row, third from right) in charge of the Southern Command cricket team, which he captained by virtue of being the only officer who played cricket. Brigadier Bacon centre front.

The author, Major Goodman, at Southern Command headquarters, with his oldest friend (then Major) Jim Gower.

The author presiding at his last meeting as chairman of the Arts Council in 1972. From left to right: Sir Hugh Willatt, the author, Sir John Witt, and Lord Gibson (chairman elect).

The author with Lord Gibson and Lord Drogheda as Lord Gibson's supporters on his introduction to the House of Lords in 1975. All costumes expensively hired.

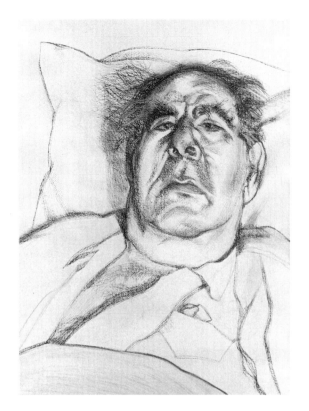

c. 1986. Lucian Freud embarking on a mammoth artistic task which occupied several months of early morning work. There were four drawings, one of which appears to the left.

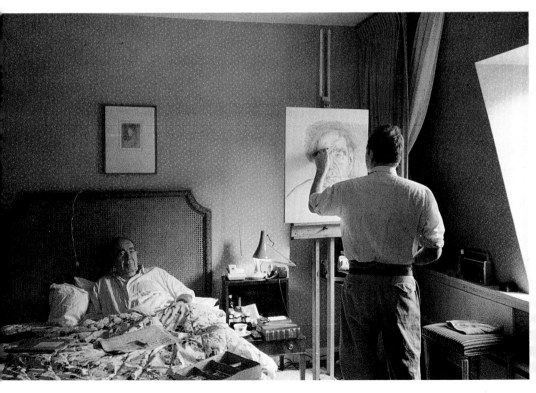

The author in rarified company (Prince Charles and Lord Harewood) at the English National Opera's Silver Jubilee Gala Concert on 12 September 1977.

The author in regal company at Covent Garden. The Queen Mother, Sir Claus Moser, Lord Harlech and Lord Drogheda.

The author at a party in 1966 for Shmuel Agnon, a Nobel prize winner for his writing, with Jennie Lee (then Minister for the Arts).

The author with a rather importunate Harold Wilson. There is no record of whether his request was granted.

my own opinion was pretty well valueless and he recognised that. Periodically Mary Wilson would poke her head round the door to see what progress was being made towards going to bed. Harold would acknowledge her politely and indicate that it would not be many hours before he was going up.

One meeting I had with him occasioned an episode that has become public. This was in 1967, when he told me, looking rather pleased with himself, 'I have done something today that will not please you!' I replied that it was not the first time, but that I had borne the previous occasions with courage and would do so now. He said to me, 'I have appointed Charlie Hill to be the chairman of the BBC.' I was indeed deeply shocked. I had nothing against Dr Hill, except that he seemed to me an entirely incongruous appointment that Harold had made for the wrong reasons. I realised that Harold had appointed him in order to maintain a keener watch on what the BBC was saying about people. This did not seem to me a reason for appointing a chairman; it might be a reason for appointing some sort of official; though in fact it would not be a sound reason for appointing anyone.

I told Harold that I did not approve of the appointment, but for reasons that he would not greatly appreciate. 'My objection to Hill is that he is totally irrelevant to most of the things of value that the BBC does. The achievement of the BBC is a cultural achievement. It has done more, for example, for the understanding of music by ordinary people of this country than any other organisation, including the Arts Council' – this was a generous admission from the then chairman of the Arts Council – 'and it has done much for education and a great deal for general culture. All these things, if I may say so, are entirely irrelevant so far as Dr Hill is concerned.' Events proved this to be true. He turned out to be an efficient chairman of the BBC but my first impression was amply confirmed since, although I had frequent dealings with him, he seemed to have absolutely no interest in what to me really mattered.

I enjoyed my politico-legal activities and sought to give the best service I could. My activities had no goal and no aspiration, and I had no competitors, which meant that I rapidly acquired the confidence of the leadership of the Labour Party. Through my office door there flowed an increasing number of Labour politicians seeking professional and personal advice on a score of topics.

Occasionally the advice sought was within my specialised knowledge as the chairman of the Arts Council. This was particularly the case when Marcia Williams, having been powerfully lobbied by Arnold Wesker, was determined to persuade Harold Wilson to bestow some extra support on 'Centre 42', which was Wesker's notion of an organisation to supervise the growth of the arts in this country. His scheme had not found favour in my eyes. He had spent in promoting the scheme money that could have been used in establishing it, and I was both impatient and critical of his capacity to launch and support a large new artistic organisation, particularly as his ideas of who would give him money were hopelessly unrealistic. Nevertheless the Prime Minister, at the instigation of Mrs Williams, gave a tea party for Wesker at Downing Street.

Much of my activity was directed to firm advice to the Prime Minister and various other ministers to ignore scurrilous communications that were received with great frequency. I do not believe that a Conservative government would have aroused hostility at that pitch, but the difference between a Tory government and a Labour government was that the latter threatened, or was thought to threaten, the money and positions of the rich – a threat which moved the rich to unreasoning hostility. Harold Wilson probably underwent the most disagreeable experience of any Prime Minister in that it was regarded as respectable political tactics to traduce him on any grounds other than political. To my knowledge there was never the slightest justification for this discreditable course of conduct; nor was it employed by the reputable members of the Opposition.

The matters I was asked to advise on occupied my attention, and a great number of files, for a very considerable length of time. They were monotonous in the sense that they usually related to allegations that there was some special relationship between the Prime Minister and Marcia Williams, and indeed I advised Mrs Williams in connection with insulting letters that she received. Right-wing newspapers singled her out for every conceivable hostility, particularly the circumstances of her divorce from her first husband. Some doubts having been expressed about the validity of her divorce in America, I caused enquiries to be made and received from my American agents copies of the decree of divorce which was issued on 7 April 1961.

I do not believe that at any time, and certainly not at any time when I knew them, was there any emotional relationship between Harold Wilson and Marcia Williams. I do believe, however, that he proceeded in considerable apprehension in his dealings with the lady; in fact, that he was plainly frightened of her because of her quick temper and also because he had for a number of reasons formed a most favourable view of her judgement. He told me that one factor which had greatly influenced him was her suggestion that on election day Granada should shift *Coronation Street* so as not to keep in many of his supporters who would otherwise be thinking of going to the polls. This was very sensible advice since such was the popularity of *Coronation Street* that a great many people would have preferred to view it than to exercise any electoral function. To this suggestion he attributed the Labour Party's success in the 1964 election and I am sure that no one could have persuaded him otherwise.

Harold Wilson was, for a man so seasoned in the ups and downs of public life, incredibly sensitive. To the end of his political days he remained unreconciled to what I hope and believe every public person should become reconciled to: the unimportance of most opinions expressed by most people. However, I am assured by those who know that public persons – premiers in particular – do not become reconciled to criticism, and despite affecting not to be, they remain immensely conscious of what is being said and are troubled if what is said is not to their liking.

Wilson took enormous trouble to capture a favourable press. His approach to the matter was idiosyncratic. For instance he read every morning newspaper before midnight on the previous day (in contrast to Harold Macmillan who claimed not to read newspapers) and as a result he went to bed fully – and very ill-advisedly – informed of the disagreeable things that were being said about him, since almost all the papers had Tory proprietors and Tory-inclined editors.

This obsession – and one can, I think, rightly call it that – involved me in probably the most embarrassing event of my professional life. It arose out of a strike in July 1964 by ACTT television technicians claiming higher wages (and an improvement in working conditions) and it involved all the independent television companies, which included three for whom my firm acted. The three concerned were TWW, with whom I had the closest ties, Southern Television and Granada.

The strike appeared to have reached a deadlock. The television companies – using negotiating officers employed by them full-time – had made every effort to settle the strike short of accepting the ACTT's conditions. I had had no intention of seeking to intervene in the strike and would not have done so but for the ubiquitous activity of George Wigg. He started off by taking Jack Hylton – an old friend of mine and a leading member of the board of TWW – to meet some of the independent television proprietors, and at that stage he suggested to Hylton that he might use me as an intermediary.

I was not in the least keen, but when it became clear to me that my intervention would be frowned upon only slightly by my television clients, added to the fact that I had established good relations with George Elvin, the ACTT's general secretary, it seemed to me that there might be some sense in intervening. I had previously been successful in negotiating a settlement between the Boulting brothers and Elvin's union, where I had enjoyed establishing a warm and friendly relationship with both sides.

Consequently I became involved in various meetings between the union and the representatives of the television companies, particularly a very long one at my home in Ashley Gardens, where Harold Wilson was invited to attend and indeed did so. I had worked out a peace formula that I thought might be acceptable, but when I showed it to Wilson he scoffed at it as being altogether too legalistic and proceeded to provide me with a formula of his own. Since I am a mild and humane man, I did not tell him that it was utterly hopeless, but as a matter of deference to him I presented his formula to George Elvin, who declined to have anything to do with it.

Thus rebuffed, Wilson was willing to consider that my own formula – inadequate and clumsy as it was – might at least be presented to the union. It was presented in a further long meeting, going on well into the early hours of the morning, when George Elvin, having conferred with several of his senior colleagues on my telephone, returned to say that they would accept the proposal. This was, in fact, the end of the strike and the technicians returned to work.

I had done very little imaginative work and would not have regarded this as my greatest negotiating success, but it was certainly so regarded by Harold Wilson who assured me that my name would be kept out of the proceedings, since I had then, and retain, a keen dislike for gratuitous publicity. The upshot of this little matter was to leave me labelled as 'Mr X' – a pseudonym invented by Harold Wilson and which has attached itself to me throughout the years, but never offensively. However, someone in Wilson's office proceeded to leak my name to the press, which used it as an opportunity for jibes at him, particularly as he had contrived an impression that the negotiations had succeeded because of him. I did not begrudge Wilson this, since I had no wish for my own part to be revealed, but for some reason best known to himself he decided that he would at least claim the credit for having found me.

The *Daily Telegraph* carried a long story without mentioning my name, since Michael Berry was well disposed to me and had no wish to cause me embarrassment. But no similar restraint was shown by the others. The most flattering story was in the *Financial Times* of 8 July 1964. I quote this, notwithstanding that it was unduly polite to me, and I disclaim any intention ever to persuade anyone to take cyanide.

The fact that there is still any doubt about whether Mr Arnold Goodman was or wasn't the Mr X of the television dispute is a considerable tribute not only to his modesty, but to his skill and to the loyalty of his friends. Goodman is not a man one would pick for his inconspicuousness – he stands six feet two inches in his socks, and though I cannot speak his weight, an answer of over twenty stone would not surprise me. No one, however, does more good, covert work to spread peace and goodwill in a naturally fractious industry. If he tried to persuade you to take cyanide, you'd probably finish by doing it with a smile but of course that's not the sort of thing he works for. Charm, wit, and above all sheer persuasiveness are the qualities that most impress his friends. This is partly based on the reasoning power of an eminent, academic lawyer, partly on the fact that he is usually espousing good causes. His political background – he was Hugh Gaitskell's legal man, and a close friend of both Gaitskell and Bevan – has made him many friends in the trade union world as well as in politics and entertainment.

All this qualifies him to be Mr X, and the closer you look, the better he fits the part. One of Goodman's earlier triumphs of mediation was between Mr Elvin's ACTT and the Boulting brothers. I can't say that Goodman *was* Mr X; but if he wasn't it must have been someone very like him.

After he became Prime Minister, I found myself comforting Harold Wilson on a number of occasions. His indignation frequently boiled over to a point where he thought and demanded that a libel writ should be issued. I may say that despite my reputation of being trigger-happy where libel writs are concerned, I restrained him by all sorts of expedients. When the situation got beyond the normal discouraging advice, I would inform him that it was necessary to take counsel's opinion before we proceeded any further. The counsel I used was an exceptionally suitable person, Sir Joseph Molony QC, the son of a Northern Ireland judge. He was an extremely effective and wise lawyer, but he was also a man who had the common sense to understand the nature of the advice I required; it was advice that would discourage Harold Wilson from proceeding any further; so much so that there were only three occasions when we actually started proceedings on his behalf.

The first occasion, in 1967, was the most sensational. A pop group – happily, as I know, since disappeared – which called itself 'The Move' sent a postcard all over the place, including, impertinently, to Downing Street, advertising their new record. The postcard depicted a crudely drawn picture of Harold Wilson in bed with a particular lady, with Mrs Wilson looking through the door, and various other offensive allusions.

On that occasion we lost no time in speeding over to the courts, finding a judge, and obtaining an injunction almost at once. An action was instituted – the only libel action where I acted for Harold Wilson which came to court – and I thought it wise to brief a member of the Opposition to act as counsel on his behalf. Accordingly for the only time ever I briefed Quintin Hogg (as he then was). The case was, of course, settled since the pop group had no defence, and Harold Wilson behaved very generously. The retribution actually extracted had a biblical appropriateness. They were made to disgorge all the profits made from the record and this sum was, according to my recollection, donated to a charity.

On the day the apology from 'The Move' was published, the *International Herald Tribune* (a Paris-based publication owned by one of the most important newspaper entities in the USA – the Whitney Communications Corporation) published an article headed 'The Other Woman in the Life of Harold Wilson', which was grossly libellous of him and Marcia Williams. Proceedings were instituted and various attempts were made by intermediaries to settle the matter, but ultimately the effective voice was that of Sir Solly (later Lord) Zuckerman, who used his powerful influence in the United States to persuade the newspaper to settle the matter.

It was necessary for me to travel to New York. This I did in what I thought were circumstances of great secrecy. I tiptoed on to the plane, hardly breathed while I was on it, and was conveyed with utmost speed to my usual resting place at the Pierre Hotel. I was about to contact the American lawyer acting for the defendants, Mr William Rogers (later to become famous as Secretary of State under Nixon), when the telephone rang and it was the *New York Times* enquiring when I was going to meet him. Since then I have realised that the best way of avoiding publicity is to proclaim everything you are doing as loudly as possible. This means that if it is of public interest it will appear in all the newspapers and no particular paper will have the incentive to try to procure a scoop.

My negotiations were successful and the matter was peacefully concluded by an apology and a generous payment of damages, destined once again for a charity. Since in connection with this American libel we did not employ Mr Quintin Hogg, I wrote him a short letter and received a courteous reply:

4 January 1968

Dear Mr Hogg,

I am sure this is a completely unnecessary letter but you were so immensely helpful (and effective) over 'The Move' that I would feel some sense of guilt if I did not explain that you would automatically have been my own (and the PM's) first choice of counsel – subject to your willingness – to act in the second libel action which he has unhappily been forced to institute, but for the simple fact that you were mentioned in the text of the libel in circumstances which would have made it an obvious embarrassment for you to engage as counsel.

I am sure that this explanation is unnecessary, but the debt we owe you in the other matter leaves me easier in mind for having made it.

May I take the opportunity of wishing you a happy New Year.

Yours sincerely,

Goodman

5 January 1968

Dear Lord Goodman,

Very many thanks for your letter, received today. My spies had already told me, though I had not seen the article, that my name figured in it, and I was conceited enough to believe that this might have been in your mind in instructing other counsel in the *NY Herald Tribune* action, though I need hardly say that I would have had no complaint in any case.

However, this is just to say that I much appreciated your kind thought in writing, which set at rest such lingering anxieties as I felt.

Your sincerely,

Quintin Hogg

The third occasion when we instituted proceedings was several years later, in 1971, when Harold Wilson was back in opposition, and related to the activities of the BBC, which produced a thoroughly incompetent piece of television called *Yesterday's Men*. Apart from the offensive nature of the title, since it related almost entirely to former Cabinet ministers of the Labour Party, the programme had been procured by a series of deceptions. The individuals concerned, including particularly Harold Wilson and Roy Jenkins, were persuaded to take part in the belief that it was to be a serious piece of film-making. In fact it was a relatively innocent send-up. Roy Jenkins, an extremely sensible man who is less vulnerable to criticism than most, regarded the matter with mild amusement.

I first learnt of it when, dining one night in a London restaurant, I received an urgent summons from Harold. On arrival I found him, Roy Jenkins and one or two others gathered. Harold was fulminating. He demanded action be taken at once. I could sympathise with his feelings, but in fact the principal ridicule was addressed to poor Roy Jenkins, who was shown in the film floating through the air while engaged in a game of tennis – at which he is quite a competent player. But Harold was not to be soothed: he demanded retribution, he demanded action, not so much because of the ridicule but because at some stage in the programme it was alleged that he had made advantageous use of privileged or secret material in an improper fashion in relation to a book he was then about to publish.

I thereupon telephoned the director-general of the BBC, Charles Curran, and arranged that he would come to my home that evening. He arrived with one or two colleagues at 11 p.m. I indicated that legal action was, in my view, inappropriate in respect of what was a rather feeble attempt at satire, and the importance of the programme would be enhanced to an absurd extent if anyone depicted in it took it seriously, but none of us liked being ridiculed. The meeting, however, failed to produce a satisfactory outcome (at least so far as Harold Wilson was concerned), and I wrote a letter to the BBC demanding an apology in some ensuing programme.

The negotiations dragged on and in the end I was constrained to issue a writ. I may say that it was not my intention to allow Harold Wilson to become involved in a full-scale lawsuit in circumstances where not so much odium but ridicule would be poured on him. As is often the case, the principal odium falls on an innocent party. There are various former members of the BBC who believe that I was the instigator of the action against them, but unlike politicians I bear this sort of thing with a great deal of tolerance, taking what I think is a sensible view that one cannot make omelettes without breaking eggs. It is almost impossible to forge any sort of career associated with public life or public men where you do not yourself become the object of hostility in some quarter.

In any event, in due course a suitable solatium in the form of an apology was offered to Harold Wilson – or at lest a solatium which he regarded as suitable since he possesses the invaluable quality of being able to convince himself of the correctness of whatever he does – and the matter ended. But it remains in the BBC's history even if it does not remain in the history of the Labour Party.

IO

Intermediary

MY ENTRY INTO the Rhodesian scene in 1968 was purely accidental. I had been invited to 10 Downing Street for dinner a number of times and on one of those occasions Harold Wilson asked me if I could suggest someone who would go to Salisbury and meet Ian Smith in order to find out whether there was any basis for renewing negotiations. UDI had been declared in November 1965 and an official meeting had taken place on HMS *Tiger* in December 1966 which had been a fiasco. This was the first time that Smith and Wilson had met. Smith knew that Wilson was a socialist: that he could never admit any discrimination based on racial factors, and all the things that Smith abominated. So there was a clash of personalities which was a small handicap in these early negotiations. I suggested to Wilson that there had to be a short cooling-off period, after which Max Aitken would be a suitable person to go to Rhodesia as an unofficial ambassador, since in the war he had flown with Smith in the RAF and they had become good friends.

In consequence of my suggestion, Harold Wilson asked Aitken and myself to dine with him to discuss the matter and to my amazement Max Aitken said that he would go, but only if I accompanied him. I agreed. Our trip, in August 1968, was to be in the utmost secrecy and we were to fly to Johannesburg under the names of Mr Aitken and Mr Goodman. Max, typically, brought a girlfriend. At the airport he kept looking back as we were walking towards our plane; eventually I looked back too and saw an attractive young woman hurrying along after us. It had been arranged that I would remain in Johannesburg and Max would proceed ahead to Salisbury to see whether Ian Smith would wish to see me. Max was a diplomat – a combination of Dr Watson and Inspector Clouseau. He sent messages *en clair* which were highly secret and carefully ciphered messages that were of no possible secret value.

Smith agreed to see me and so I flew to Salisbury, arriving on a Wednesday. Max told me that Smith would meet us on the following Monday, which would have meant waiting around for five days. This was unacceptable. I insisted that Smith meet me there and then, for five minutes only, which he agreed to do. When we met I told him that I did not think he had anything more urgent to attend to, and if he thought he had something more important, then his priorities were wrong. He decided that we would start the next day, Thursday, at 9 a.m. And we did not stop for four days, discussing every detail, going over every bit of ground. The negotiations were in total secrecy – not even his Cabinet were informed.

When we appeared to have finished, I suggested to Smith that it would be very unsatisfactory for two people holding no position in diplomacy to render an oral report. It appeared to me to be necessary that we should set out our agreed recommendations in some separate document. This suggestion turned out to be greatly to my own detriment. Smith agreed that such a report was needed and indicated that, as I had suggested it, I ought to prepare it. This reluctantly I agreed to do. I sat up all night on the Sunday and wrote a nineteen-page document. Smith had lent me his very able stenographer and we worked until dawn, when the memorandum was typed and ready for me to take to Smith first thing in the morning. Smith was a slow reader and took about an hour to read and ponder the document, after which he approved it and asked me to take it to Harold Wilson.

Max and I were delighted with the result, but when I got back to the hotel I was taken violently ill and had to be put to bed. It was then that I experienced a side of Max that I had not known before: he was most caring and attentive, almost maternal, getting doctors and nurses, staying with me and looking after me in every way. It was very touching. We then came back to London where fortunately no journalists or television crews were lying in wait for us, because the mission had been unofficial.

It was on the basis of that document that the talks on board HMS *Fearless* were convened in October 1968. Those talks failed from the very outset. I am sufficiently egotistical to believe that one of the reasons why they failed was that I was not present. Wilson's Cabinet – jealous of a non-political and non-party intruder – had decided not to include me in the team. This was a mistake.

Nothing happened for some while after the collapse of the *Fearless* talks. While he was in opposition, Ted Heath had asked me if I would go to Rhodesia on behalf of the Conservative Party if they were returned to power. I told him that I could not go on behalf of any party, but that I would go on behalf of the *government* if he came to power, since I knew the situation and could be of some help. Duly, when the Conservatives were returned in 1970, Ted Heath asked me to lead a delegation to see whether we could work out an agreement.

Over the years I have developed a profound belief that the Foreign Office has criteria entirely its own. There is an old saying that there are three kinds of intelligence: human, animal and military. But a fourth kind of intelligence might be added, which is diplomatic intelligence, which bears not the remotest relationship to any of the other three, nor to any kind of intelligence that can be identified by any human being. It would be unfair to say that I have formed a low view of the Foreign Office; rather I have formed the view that Foreign Office activities have in some way become totally disconnected from the human race.

The first evidence of this surfaced on the second trip that I made to Rhodesia, in April 1971. I was told by the FO in London that I would be met at Johannesburg airport – since British aircraft could not land in Rhodesia while UDI existed – and would be conveyed to the British Consulate there where I could have a rest. I would then be put on a plane to Salisbury.

On arrival in Johannesburg, the first thing I noticed was a young, fresh, smiling face, who turned out to be the Second Secretary at the Consulate. This amiable young man greeted me enthusiastically and informed me that he would be driving me himself, in his motor car which he had brought from Finland. Needless to say, being a Finnish car it had a left-hand drive. South Africa is one of the few countries in the world where people drive on the left, so that most motorcars have a right-hand drive. However, this young man, besides having the wrong car, was not the most talented of drivers and my first ten minutes were taken up with some anxiety about the likelihood of our arriving at the Consulate intact. The next three-quarters of an hour were taken up with wondering why it was taking us so long to get from the airport to the Consulate, and what genius had decided to place the Consulate some hundreds of miles away.

The young man admitted in due course, when we had been driving for an hour, that he did not know the way and was totally lost. We endeavoured to enquire from a black policeman. The difficulty there was that neither the young man nor the policeman could understand a single word of what the other was saying. So back we got into the car and ultimately by some good fortune we arrived at the Consulate. Our arrival was just in time to take off again, so that I had no opportunity for a rest, a meal or anything else. We made straight back to the airport and I was put on a Rhodesian plane for Salisbury, where negotiations were renewed and eventually I returned to London.

A month later, I made my third trip to Rhodesia. As the Foreign Office
was still trying to maintain the secrecy of my visits, it was determined
that on this occasion I would be met at Johannesburg airport and driven
by road to the Rhodesian border where I would be picked up and
conveyed by the Rhodesian authorities. I made one stipulation only to
the Foreign Secretary, Sir Alec Douglas-Home, which was that my driver
should *not* be the same amiable young man who had led me such a dance
around Johannesburg. Judge then my feelings when the first face I was
to see at Jo'burg airport was the self-same Second Secretary, delighted
that he had again been honoured with an important secret mission.

This time, however, we were not going to the Consulate but driving
straight to the border. I got into the car, to be told by him that he had
made the most elaborate arrangements for lunch. 'I'm delighted,' I said.
'What hotel are we going to?' 'We aren't,' he replied, smiling angelically.
'I have arranged for a picnic lunch.' 'A picnic lunch?' 'Yes! And you will
be pleased to hear that I have even managed to bring a bucket of ice to
chill the wine.' I replied rather coldly that I had not drunk alcohol since
1939, and that it had been my hope that we should stop somewhere where
I could wash up generally, relieve myself and have a little rest. But such
was the disappointment on his face that I was compelled to agree that we
would enjoy such a picnic, which indeed is a delicious meal in other
circumstances – at Henley during summer, or at Glyndebourne on a good
afternoon – but in the middle of the South African veld, on our way to
Rhodesia, its incongruity would have occurred to anyone except to a
British diplomat.

Anyway, we set off and drove for about forty miles. A nagging doubt
began to affect me when I observed a signpost to Cape Town. 'I do
believe that is a signpost to Cape Town,' I remarked, trying hard to
prevent my voice from cracking. 'Are we proceeding north or south?'
The young man looked rather bewildered. 'Rhodesia,' I said, 'to my
understanding is north of Johannesburg and Cape Town is due south.
And this sign says we are going to Cape Town.' 'Oh!' he said, stopping
the car and looking hurriedly at a map. 'We are indeed going the wrong
way.' The car was turned round. That I maintained my usual composure
was to me a miracle, and once more we were on our way to the frontier.

A further indication of the skill and care with which the arrangements
were made was our accommodation for the night. We stayed in a frontier
hotel about 6,000 feet up, in a night of freezing cold. The accommodation
consisted of semi-converted stables, and it will be known by those
acquainted with the residence of horses that the door of a stable is so
constructed that there are two gaps, one between the door and the floor
and another between the door and the ceiling, and through these gaps

blew drafts of freezing cold. There was no heating in the room and an inadequacy of blankets, and I finally put on all my clothes again and tried my best to snuggle under the only blanket to snatch an hour of sleep.

In the morning providentially we set off for the frontier, and there to my great delight I saw the familiar face of Mr Derrick Robinson, Rhodesia's Assistant Commissioner of Police, standing beside a BMW motor car which was to convey me to Salisbury. As we got in and set off he said to me, 'Have you ever seen Bulawayo?' I told him I had not. 'Ah!' he said. 'Would you like to go via Bulawayo?' I said that I would be only too pleased, since we had no commitments until the next morning. What he did not tell me – and I only learnt during the course of the journey – was that we were adding about a thousand miles to our route.

In normal circumstances this would not have mattered, but at the time Rhodesia was meant to be enduring the most severe and effective economic sanctions, particularly with regard to the supply of oil. The fact that a man was prepared to drive a completely unnecessary 1,000 miles struck me as indicative that the sanctions were not working. Indeed, one had only to go to Rhodesia to see the ample supply of consumer goods in the shops from every part of the world to realise that sanctions were nothing but an empty farce, and that the claim that they were going to bring Mr Ian Smith to his knees was a total fraud.

A depressing feature of my visits to Rhodesia arose from my firm instructions to negotiate only with Mr Smith and to avoid receiving protests or demonstrations from any quarter. The situation is best illustrated by a letter that reached me at this time from Mrs Mugabe:

> I have never understood why you should allow yourself to be used by Edward Heath and Harold Wilson in the negotiations with Ian Smith. I thought you could easily recognise a rogue? Were you allowed while in Salisbury to see the prisoners? Perhaps you saw my husband who has been rotting behind bars for eight years now because of his belief in fair play for all people of that country. Can you imagine your wife in my position?

There was no way in which I could reply to the letter except by a futile expression of sympathy. Fortunately the matter has now corrected itself and, whoever is in jail, Mr Mugabe is at liberty and is the long-standing leader of the nation who has reinforced his position by appropriate leadership legislation.

On the other hand, on one of my visits I was at a meeting when I heard some commotion outside and asked what it was. It was students demonstrating, as a result of which a number of them were arrested and

I later learnt that a few were sentenced to be flogged. I was outraged by it and got on to Smith at once, saying that on no account should the students be flogged and that if the sentence was carried out I would leave immediately. 'You are potty!' he replied, but there was no flogging.

It was during my fourth visit to Rhodesia that I managed to take some time off. The talks were going very well and Smith said that he wanted to give us a holiday and take us to Victoria Falls in his plane. I forbade the entire delegation to travel in his rickety contraption, because if something happened and we all disappeared, our negotiations would have been wasted. So some of us went to Victoria Falls and I went to Durban where I had some relatives and attended the July Handicap, the only horse race in the world that runs through the streets. It was then that some international misunderstanding arose, because the President of South Africa was at the race too and a rumour got around that I had engineered the trip to talk with the South Africans, which of course was not true.

The four visits that I paid to Rhodesia in 1971 with my small team of senior officials were regarded as furnishing sufficient firm ground to found serious negotiations towards a settlement. I had maintained the closest contact with the Foreign Office in the intervals between each trip and was a frequent visitor to the Foreign Secretary's official residence in Carlton Gardens. It was not difficult to detect that his government was anxious and, if this word could ever be used about the placid Sir Alec Douglas-Home, was passionately anxious to obtain an agreement, just as Harold Wilson previously had had the same anxiety. An agreement was undoubtedly regarded as an electoral feather in the political cap.

On my fifth and final visit, the operation was led by Alec Douglas-Home himself, although he played no part in the actual discussions except at some crucial moments when decisions had to be made. The negotiations, in which Rhodesia was represented by Mr Ian Smith, with Mr Lardner-Burke and Mr Howman – both understood by me to be very hard-liners – led to a provisional agreement on proposals for a settlement. Both sides undertook to take steps to implement these proposals once the British government had established that they would be acceptable to the people of Rhodesia as a whole.

The agreement was based on the famous – some would say infamous – five principles: unimpeded progress to majority rule (already enshrined in the 1961 Constitution) had to be maintained and guaranteed; there would have to be guarantees against retrogressive amendment of the Constitution; there would need to be immediate improvement in the political status of the black population; there would have to be progress towards ending racial discrimination; and the British government would need to be satisfied that any basis proposed for independence was acceptable to the people of Rhodesia as a whole.

The major proposals for a settlement were, first, the adoption of a draft Constitution, including a declaration of rights providing a reasonable guarantee for personal liberty. Then came the real crux of the matter, which was the new requirement to qualify for a vote. In entrenched provisions it was established that a new roll of African voters (the African higher roll) would be created with the same qualifications as those for the European roll, i.e. either an income of 1,800 Rhodesian dollars per annum or ownership of property valued at not less than $3,600, or, an income of $1,200 per annum or ownership of property valued at not less than $2,400 and four years of secondary education. In addition there was an African lower roll which was a bit of a cheat, designed to suggest a much greater enfranchisement of Africans than in fact would take place.

Another proposal was that an independent commission would be set up to examine the question of racial discrimination. Further and highly satisfactory was an agreement that, having already released 23 detainees since the end of March 1971, the Rhodesian government would state their intention to release a further 31 detainees out of 93 as soon as the necessary arrangements could be made and that there would be a new special review of the cases of all detainees.

I came back to London before the actual signing of the agreement because I had to attend an Arts Council meeting. This time the press and the media were there and I declined to make any comment on the negotiations. But I gave my genuine reason for returning earlier, which was the Arts Council's monthly meeting, in which I was deeply interested and whose chairman I was at the time. However it was considered by everyone that the real reason was to let Alec Douglas-Home have a triumphal return. This was an undeserved tribute to my magnanimity.

Needless to say the proposed settlement – widely publicised – drew a good deal of criticism, almost entirely from the Left who were for a variety of reasons extremely hostile to white Rhodesians. I will not go into the extreme technicality of the proposed constitution since it is now only a matter for constitutional historians. It suffices to say that under it, once black Rhodesians had acquired a sizeable number of seats, but far less than a majority, they would have been in a powerful position to form a coalition with any breakaway group of whites. It was, I think, unlikely that the white Rhodesians – who had already shown some signs of division in their opinion – would have remained undivided indefinitely and a breakaway group might well have sought the allegiance of the black population, enabling them to play a large and even decisive role in government. This consideration was never advanced or even pondered by the opponents of the agreement.

For me the aftermath of the agreement was unpleasant and caused an estrangement – happily only brief – from some old friends. The Labour Party opposed the agreement fervently but almost entirely on political grounds. Some of Harold Wilson's shadow cabinet – notably the shadow Lord Chancellor, Lord Elwyn Jones, Richard Crossman and Barbara Castle – were the most determined adversaries. After the agreement was reached, indignant voices were raised in many quarters, but I am happy to say that few, if any, regarded my behaviour as treacherous.

The principal complaint about me was that I was politically naive – a complaint again made by Michael Foot when I opposed his Bill to introduce a closed shop into journalism, which I describe later. Such was my disposition to conciliation, the argument ran, that the temptation to reach agreement on any footing was irresistible to me. There is some validity in this latter complaint. I prefer a bad agreement to a prolonged disagreement. This does not mean that I do not believe there are issues where principle is paramount; but there are great many issues where principle is misguided or even hypocritical, and it is a fair accusation that I tend to suspect this more often than most people.

My own position was perhaps rendered the more difficult by Ian Smith's assertion at one time that I was the only representative from this country that he trusted. Obviously a testimonial of this kind was not designed to endear me to a number of critics. Nevertheless, my personal reputation with the Labour Party was such that my association with Smith was viewed with tolerance if not with great approval. Smith had a reputation for being devious and unreliable, which I found to be far from true. He bargained hard and was stubborn, but once he was persuaded and agreed, he usually stuck by his word. He also had the advantage of being untainted by corruption – unlike some white South African politicians and, of course, many black African ones.

In any event, a few particularly strident voices denounced me over the agreement. Lord Caradon went to town. He made claims to be an authority on Africa, and I could not help suspecting that subconsciously he felt that an incompetent ignoramus had invaded his territory. On the whole I bore the strictures with courage in the firm belief that what had been done was the best that could be done.

But the agreement was to fail. It was subject to a 'Test of Acceptability' – the fifth principle – and could only be confirmed and implemented after the British government had satisfied itself that it was acceptable to the people of Rhodesia as a whole. The whites accepted it wholeheartedly, but the Africans did not want it. The Test of Acceptability was carried out by Lord Pearce and a number of other people, including Lord Harlech, and it was turned down flat by the Africans. The reason was, I think, that the Africans were deeply suspicious of Ian Smith and believed that any agreement which was devised to give them full democratic rights would in fact never be implemented. They had no faith in Smith and so rejected the agreement he made.

This brings me to perhaps my most serious criticism of the Foreign Office, relating to the Rhodesian negotiations themselves. We negotiated with immense pain and at great length to achieve an agreement with Mr Smith. The role of the FO in the discussions was both crucial and disastrous. They had provided me with a small team of assistants and advisers, and a more agreeable collection of people one could not have found. They included a very nice young man who was my Rhodesian adviser. He suffered from the small disadvantage that he had never been to Rhodesia. This in an ordinary way would not have mattered, but it mattered in this particular case and mattered quite fatally, because at various stages of the discussion, when we seemed to be reaching an agreement, I pressed Mr Smith about whether there was any likelihood, whatever the agreement was, that it would be acceptable to the entire population of Rhodesia, which the British government had laid down as a precondition.

It was clear that the white population would accept an agreement with alacrity. When I was there they were desperate for one and anxious that the sanctions should be lifted. People in the street, who knew that I was engaged in negotiations, would come up to me, grab me by my lapels and say, 'Get an agreement, we beg you. Get an agreement!' But I had no such indication regarding the black population. It was impossible to get any indication since my instructions from the Foreign Office were to negotiate only with Mr Smith and his people and not to have any contact with the black population during the period of my negotiations. Whether this was wise or not it is impossible to say. But what, of course, was not known to me, nor to Mr Smith, nor to my Rhodesian adviser who obviously knew nothing about Rhodesia, was the relationship between the tribal chiefs and the tribes: the chiefs do what the tribes tell them, not the other way round. Whenever we asked for reassurance, Mr Smith assured us that his tribal chiefs were loyal to him and would vote for whatever agreement he advised them to. However, when the chiefs went into tribal lands to ask their views about the agreement, they received an emphatic direction, in every case except one, that the chiefs should reject the agreement and have nothing to do with it.

In the result, when Lord Pearce went with his committee to determine whether or not the agreement was acceptable to the entire population, needless to say he reported that the vast majority of whites were in favour but that there was almost total rejection by the blacks. In consequence, months of painful and arduous negotiations had been wasted, largely because of the ignorance or the Bourbon attitude of the Foreign Office who did not bother to find out something on the basis that they already knew every piece of human knowledge that is worth knowing. Having travelled five times to Rhodesia, having spent hours in laborious, painful, and indeed anguished disputation with Mr Smith and his colleagues, to discover that it was all futile because of arrogance on the part of the Foreign Office is something about which a saint would undoubtedly entertain a certain resentment.

I cannot review the Rhodesian episode without regret, though it was a fascinating adventure with a disappointing, indeed from some points of view tragic, conclusion; but it was the forerunner of the later (Lancaster House) agreement in 1979 and to that extent had some beneficial consequences, and it was, of course, useful as a background to new negotiations.

By the time of the Lancaster House talks, Mrs Thatcher was in power, and I had very few dealings with her, and so I was not invited to participate. The only person who approached me was poor Ian Smith, who came to London but was not a representative at the talks. He felt utterly friendless and Max Aitken arranged a luncheon for him which I attended. I advised Smith very strongly that the best course of action for him was to throw all his weight and support behind the Lancaster House agreement, whatever it turned out to be, which he showed great reluctance to do because in his view Lancaster House was a total capitulation to the black population. I said that the best thing he could do for the whites was to demonstrate to the blacks that they fully supported the widest possible franchise, and that if he did that he would emerge as a statesman, with a statesman's view of his responsibilities. And that was the last time I saw him.

Ian Smith was essentially a worthy man, who unfortunately submitted to an ineradicable hostility – not to the blacks but to being governed by the blacks. In this he was supported by his white Cabinet and nearly all the whites of Rhodesia. Although I rated Mr Smith quite high in terms of integrity, I did not regard him as having a superior intellect and throughout the negotiations with which I was concerned he remained blinded by a prejudiced belief that the only rule in Rhodesia which was tolerable or possible was white rule. Nevertheless he maintained a friendly attitude towards me and after my initial difficulty made himself available whenever he was needed. Needless to say, I found his political philosophy disagreeable and unacceptable, but as my mission was to reach agreement

I avoided becoming involved in basic considerations or in any way assessing the value of white rule as against black.

It was in 1972, after I had trekked to and from Rhodesia on several occasions, and the mission in which I was involved appeared to be a triumphant success, that I received a letter from Ted Heath, who asked whether it would be acceptable to me to receive a CH (Companion of Honour). The letter was couched in terms which contrived to suggest that if it was not acceptable then he would think of something better. But, if I may say so, it was totally acceptable, and I could not think of anything better, so I agreed with alacrity.

Normally anyone who receives an award in an Honours List attends on a particular day at the Palace when Her Majesty confers them wholesale. Knights come first, then come DBEs, then come CBEs and so on and so forth, until you get down to the lowest award, which I think is the British Empire Medal. I understand that two or three days are required to complete it all. But a few awards, and the Companion of Honour is one, involve a personal interview with Her Majesty by special appointment.

I was telephoned by the late Lord Plunket, Her Majesty's Equerry, a man of exceptional charm whom I knew well and liked, who arranged the appointment and said diffidently, 'I hope you do not mind wearing a morning coat.' As I am a complete traditionalist I agreed to whatever form of costume was required. On the day in question I attended at Buckingham Palace and was received by Lord Plunket, and to my delight also found Lady Susan Hussey, who was the Lady-in-Waiting and the wife of my old friend Duke Hussey. The two of them told me that no formalities were required, that I would simply be received in a small private room, and that there would even be the possibility that I would be given a glass of sherry – which presented some difficulty since I am teetotal. In the event I was shown into a small room with Her Majesty, where we sat together for some twenty minutes chatting amiably about almost anything under the sun. It was a tremendous privilege, and compared to lining up with hundreds of others in order to receive some trivial award like a knighthood, the conferment of the CH stands out as something of special quality and considerable pleasure.

In general it would be incongruous, having myself been highly honoured, to express any criticism of the honours system, but in my view its main vice has been the determination of unsuccessful candidates to receive an award. I am fairly constantly approached either by the honour-seeker or his wife to assist him to feature in the list. In itself there is little harm in this, but I have noticed that it is very easy for the quest to become obsessional. The lives of both the Duke of Windsor and his spouse were rendered miserable in their last years by her quest, and his support for that quest, to be entitled to the description of 'Her Royal Highness'. In a similar way this is equally true of people in quest of honours, with the corresponding waste of time and effort expended in trying to secure the bauble.

Over the years I have had an interest in medical matters and have been involved from a legal viewpoint on a number of occasions. I have already described the Croydon Corporation case, which was the result of an epidemic of typhoid, and I have mentioned my long association with the Royal College of Psychiatrists, and the fact that my only medical qualification is as an honorary fellow of that college. I have not described a tenacious battle to secure compensation for a number of distinguished urologists who contracted hepatitis, believedly at a medical banquet, and for whom at the end of the day a moderate degree of compensation was – against considerable odds – secured.

My major intervention in medical matters came three years after my Rhodesian episode. I became engaged in a violent battle, first on behalf of the profession and subsequently as a mediator, when Mrs Barbara Castle – then the Secretary of State for Health and Social Security – pursued an honourable, but in my view misguided, determination to eradicate private practice from this country.

It is important to do justice to the situation, which necessarily involves a description of a very remarkable woman for whom I have considerable respect. Her *Diaries* (published in 1980), in respect of the years 1974–6 – the years when the battle was raging – deal in immense detail with every aspect of her activities as a Cabinet minister during that period. They disclose a single-mindedness that is immensely creditable but in its unyielding quality explains a confrontation unequalled in any government's relationship with the medical profession.

Following the inconclusive election in February 1974, Harold Wilson formed a minority government dependent on Liberal support. This was short-lived. However, a second election took place in September of that year, which gave him a pathetic working majority of four. Whereas, in what he called the short Parliament of 1974, no especially controversial measures could be introduced, the majority in the election later that year emboldened the government to take certain steps of a strongly political character, likely to arouse fierce opposition.

A prominent figure in the major controversy that arose was Mrs Castle. I had known this lady for many years and could claim to have had a friendly relationship with her. As I have described, she had consulted me many years back over a libel matter which I had discouraged her –

unsuccessfully – from pursuing, with calamitous financial results; but I was able to give her a little assistance in another matter which to some small extent repaired the damage arising from the first disaster.

In Mrs Castle's *Diaries* I am referred to with varying degrees of approval and disapproval. It seems clear that she found some difficulty in arriving at an assessment of her feelings in relation to me. The first reference is a friendly one: 'Lord Goodman had always been very generous with his legal advice to Labour MPs, including me, and Harold Wilson had used him for a number of assignments, including an exploratory visit with Sir Max Aitken to Ian Smith in August 1968 on the possibilities of a settlement. But Lord Goodman never took the Labour Whip and was ready to use his remarkable abilities under any government for any cause which aroused his interest, notably the arts.' No one could ask better. Unhappily to record, this note of approval is not struck uniformly throughout the *Diaries* which describe, in more detail than I shall seek to emulate, my participation in the famous 'pay beds' negotiations.

I have always had a very considerable respect, and indeed admiration, for Mrs Castle. She is a handsome woman, intelligent, articulate and faithful to inflexible socialist principles, which I must confess I have never shared. She is a classic instance of a social doctrinaire who believes beyond all argument that socialist doctrine is the panacea for all human ills. She follows this belief through to what to her is a logical conclusion at every stage. The one sensational deviation was her plan for trade-union reform contained in the now famous White Paper *In Place of Strife*. Better informed political opinion can seek to explain how this particular proposal squared with her underlying beliefs.

But the pay beds issue was a battle on its own. When Harold Wilson was re-elected in September 1974, she again became the Secretary of State for Health and Social Security. She was never a woman for any compromise on a matter of principle. She believed that private medicine ought not to coexist by the side of the Health Service; or perhaps more fairly, that if it did exist it should not derive any benefits from the Health Service, and that none of the resources of the Service ought properly to be available to private practitioners.

In August 1975 she produced a consultative document which was regarded by the medical profession at large – although socialist supporters in that profession did not share the view – as a declaration of war. Entitled *The Separation of Private Practice from NHS Hospitals*, it repeated her commitment to legislate to withdraw pay beds and the private use of outpatient facilities from the NHS.

A pay bed was, of course, a bed which could be purchased within an NHS hospital and normally was to be found in the so-called private wards of these hospitals. These wards had a separate nursing staff; separate and usually more lavish facilities in the way of private rooms and different food; and the patient was attended by his own general practitioner and by consultants of his own choice, with a proviso that normally the consultant would need to be attached to the hospital concerned.

The problem of the private beds gave rise to a violence of dispute which seemed to me wholly out of proportion to the magnitude of the issue. There were, at the time the trouble started, approximately 4,000 private beds in NHS hospitals out of a total of 400,000 hospital beds throughout the country. To a pragmatist, such as I proudly claim to be, it was difficult to see why this issue should become a hanging matter. It seemed ridiculous in a country that recognised a mixed economy, respected private wealth and acknowledged that a rich man could live in almost every respect infinitely better than a poor one. It was, however, an issue that gave rise to an enormous emotional reaction on both sides.

Mrs Castle's argument, and an argument in which she sincerely believed, was that the retention of private medicine meant a reduction in the quality of service available to the National Health patient. To some extent this was unarguably true, but not in my view to a sufficient extent to cause the furore. However, it was possible to invoke a strong emotional reaction by drawing attention to the obvious fact that the paying patient could get a better and faster service than his National Health counterpart. But large numbers of people set a value by this differential service, by no means restricted to those one could regard as rich. Many people set much store by total privacy when they are ill. It was this factor, more than any other, that created the controversial behaviour of a number of government ministers who contrived, when in need of treatment, to procure what were called 'amenity beds' in single rooms off the wards, but providing identical benefits to those found in the private wards. For Mrs Castle, however, and for many of her colleagues, the fact that a rich man might save his life, where a poor man could not, was an unacceptable political proposition. Its unacceptability would be shared by a great number of people, except that it is a levelling process restricted to a single aspect of human life, whereas the advantages of wealth can operate effectively and valuably in so many others. The middle classes of this country will cling passionately to certain benefits that may necessarily arise from rejecting a socialist political system. Private medicine turned out to be one of these issues, and private education another.

The doctors' case for the retention of pay beds was a strong one, although not as valid as was represented. No problem arose so far as NHS general practitioners were concerned, except a very powerful dispute about the level of the compensation of junior doctors; but with the consultants it was another story. A few men of high principle refused to take any private patients at all and practised exclusively within the NHS. Had all consultants done this, the problem would have evaporated, but it was hardly surprising that they did not, since the gilt on the medical gingerbread came from private practice. There was hardly an important consultant who did not retain a consulting room in Harley Street or its environs, where private fees could be garnered.

To enable them to conduct their private practice economically and sensibly from their viewpoint, pay beds were an imperative. If they could put their private patients into the private wards of the hospitals where they were already serving as NHS consultants, the organisation of their lives became infinitely easier. If, in addition, they could hire for private patients the very expensive facilities in the way of X-ray machines, operating theatres and the like, to be found within the National Health Service, this too made their lives very much easier and in many cases made their private practice a possibility. But Mrs Castle's dogmatism was not limited to the abolition of pay beds. Her consultative paper provided for withdrawal of the private use of outpatient facilities from NHS hospitals as well. One proposal by itself was anathema; the two together were poison.

The consultative document had an explosive effect when dropped among the profession. They rallied their forces to resist it. Part of that rally – and I am immodest enough to think a not unimportant part – was to enlist the services of my partner John Montgomerie (Monty) and myself to assist in preparing their answer to the consultative document. We had the experience, sometimes agreeable, often traumatic, of meeting with the doctors constantly over a period, usually at the headquarters of BUPA in Essex Street, adjoining my office in Little Essex Street.

Some of the doctors – alas not many – were essentially reasonable men; but most of them had developed a positively insensate hatred for Mrs Castle. The very mention of her name aroused fury. The situation was thoroughly bedevilled by her own total intransigence in the matter, including antagonising the moderate elements in the DHSS.

The government's Chief Medical Officer, Dr Henry Yellowlees, was the son of a distinguished psychiatrist, whom I had on more than one occasion retained as an adviser in private practice. In her *Diaries*, Mrs Castle described the mood at her office on the morning after the consultative paper appeared. In her words:

I arrived at the office to find an atmosphere charged with menace. I have never seen Henry so white with anger. He is a very nice chap and not given to doing battle with me, but this time he was really steamed up. He said grimly that he agreed with some of what I was trying to do and had tried to help me to the best of his ability, but by my speech on Friday I had wrecked his credibility with the doctors and he thought he ought to have been consulted. Even David [Owen] looked shaken.

The reaction of these moderate elements unhappily left Mrs Castle cold and, worse still, unchanged in attitude. My own task was made infinitely more difficult by the unconcealed and indeed – to use Mrs Castle's own word – hysterical reaction of the profession.

It was clear that both parties were set on a collision course, and I could not see the possibility of an out-and-out win for Mrs Castle. What I could see was a thoroughly unsatisfactory situation whereby large elements of the medical profession remained profoundly hostile to government policy until a change of government should take place. At very long meetings, punctuated by the arrival of quite excellent sandwiches – for me the most unhealthy of all foodstuffs – I had to listen to the outpourings of the leading fanatics in the medical profession; to the timorous intervention of the moderates; and happily to the constant, wise and soothing interventions of Derek Damerell, the chief executive of BUPA, to whom the country owes a debt that has never received proper recognition.

While Monty presided over drafting sessions designed to present the most cogent arguments against the government's consultative document, and to eradicate the violence of language frequently suggested by some of the medical men, my principal role was to sound the government, and especially Barbara Castle, about the possibilities of a compromise solution. It was hard going, but as readers of her undoubtedly interesting although immensely tendentious book will discover, some progress was made, although so far as I was concerned with astonishing fluctuations in my popularity. 'He is,' she said most woundingly, 'as slippery as an eel.' A little later she indicates that I am partially returned to favour when I plan to write to *The Times* condemning the industrial action that was taken by the consultants: 'If he really produces this letter to *The Times* I shall begin to have some faith in him.' Happily, a footnote in her diary for 19 December 1975 states that, 'His letter, condemning industrial action by the consultants, duly appeared in *The Times* on 22 December 1975.' It read as follows:

I feel a duty to express publicly a view I have expressed with vehemence in private, that the consultants should not, during the period when they are deliberating the new 'pay bed' proposals, continue to maintain their so-called 'industrial action' for a further month when innocent people – totally divorced from the dispute – suffer anxiety, pain and even the risk of death.

The incongruity of the words 'industrial action' is as convincing an argument as exists to demonstrate the incongruity of the procedure, by reputable and responsible doctors defying an age-old tradition of humane service and sacrifice that has given the profession a unique prestige in every civilised society.

If doctors of all people forsake this tradition and support the view that 'everything goes' to achieve their ends, we are well on the road to anarchy and the abandonment of parliamentary procedures in favour of naked coercion.

It is well recognised that men with the background and record of doctors would not have succumbed to these ugly compulsions without a high degree of provocation – this may mitigate but it cannot excuse.

May one who, with many others, has quested unceasingly for a fair solution, urge the consultants to reconvene the governing bodies so as to rescind this uncharacteristic decision and win back from a long-suffering public the respect and admiration in which they have been so rightly held for so long.

I had spent many weary hours and weary days of negotiation before arriving at the point where I withdrew from acting as an adviser to the profession because the consultants had embarked on strike action. My letter to *The Times* makes my own position clear. Rightly or wrongly, I could not accept that certain occupations having a particular duty to society could withdraw their essential services for financial considerations. It was put to me very forcibly by the junior doctors that unless they had the power to withdraw their labour, how else could they 'get their rights'? My reply was a relatively feeble but an entirely sincere one: 'There are some occupations and activities,' I said to them, 'where the extent of the benefits you receive depends upon the goodwill of the people you are serving.' This was a difficult doctrine to establish, particularly since it was pointed out that my own activities were not remunerated in any such way; but nevertheless I found an impossible inconsistency in remaining an adviser to a profession that outraged this important principle.

Thus, for several weeks both Monty and I were relieved of any responsibility in the matter and turned our attention to other and more profitable activities; but I was foolish in the expectation that I should long be left in peace. At some stage a suggestion arose from both sides – principally Damerell of BUPA so far as the doctors were concerned and, strangely enough, also from Barbara and the DHSS – that the consultancy strike was so damaging that a mediator should be sought. I cannot resist the admission that I was profoundly flattered when a telephone call from Harold Wilson at Downing Street invited me to mediate on the basis that, so far as they could see, I was for the moment the only tolerable candidate.

From that, alas, real trouble arose. I arranged initially to meet the doctors and once again found myself confronting 'the dreaded Grabham', as Barbara Castle described Anthony (now Sir Anthony) Grabham, the distinguished surgeon who was the backbone of the doctors' resistance and the most recalcitrant in reaching any compromise of his firm belief that the state had no concern in directing their destiny.

At this first meeting I expressed appreciation at their continuing confidence in me; undertook to mediate (this time unpaid); and also to involve the services of John Montgomerie, whose clear-headed, quiet wisdom had earned him the respect and confidence of everyone he had dealt with. After an exchange of pleasantries, I then proceeded to outline a plan. 'The first thing to do,' I said, 'is to resume discussions with the Secretary of State.' The howl of dissent that came from the entire room staggered me. 'Never,' they said, 'will we meet that woman.' Barbara Castle would find it difficult to believe the vehemence of my protests at this foolishly obdurate attitude, but obdurate it remained. Finally, I said, 'Well, if you will not meet Mrs Castle, how are we to make any progress? Who will you meet?' Rather grudgingly a voice said, 'The Prime Minister', and supporting voices were heard all over the room. It was clear to me that nothing could be done unless Harold Wilson intervened. He had, until then, been very unwilling to encroach on the authority of his formidable Secretary of State.

Here I have to review the possibility of a cardinal error, but I will leave my readers to judge. My instinct, both of mercy and goodwill, was to seek Barbara's approval to a reference to the Prime Minister, but an even stronger instinct told me that it was likely to be met by a flat refusal and that the negotiating process would be stillborn. I discussed the matter with John Montgomerie and on my own responsibility decided to telephone Harold Wilson to seek his advice. I telephoned Downing Street in quest of the Prime Minister, but was told that he was in Rome awaiting a call from me since he was anxiously concerned about the consultants and the possibility that their action might indeed have fatal consequences for some patients.

I was told how to contact him in Rome and within a few minutes he was on the line. 'Harold,' I said, 'I have had an initial meeting with the doctors and there is an appalling hurdle in the way of beginning negotiations. They flatly refuse to meet with Barbara. I have argued with them until I am blue in the face; have indicated to them that it is near

anarchy when the profession will not meet the Cabinet minister responsible; but I have made no impression at all. A few, a tiny few, recognise
how unreasonable this attitude is, but the overwhelming majority are for
the time being standing firm.'

Harold asked the question that I expected; 'If they won't meet Barbara,
who will they meet?'

'They have indicated to me that they will be pleased to meet with you
and any advisers that you may have. I have no doubt that if you are
there, they would attend a meeting with Barbara also present.' It was
clear to me that, although Harold realised the total impropriety of the
medical attitude, human nature made it impossible for him not to have a
certain mild satisfaction.

'What do you think?' he said.

I was unhesitating. 'I think the crisis is sufficiently important to forget
the courtesies. I think you ought to meet them.'

'In that case I will.'

I could hear the resolve in his voice. But a moment later there was the
faintest note of trepidation when he said, 'But who will tell Barbara? Will
you?'

My reply was immediate. 'I do not get danger money! You have a great
number of secretaries, aides and the like. One of them must do it.'

'Very well,' said Harold.

Here again there was a fundamental mistake. I should have spoken to
Barbara myself and explained to her how strenuously I had endeavoured
to talk the doctors out of this unhappy decision. Their decision made no
sense because, at the end of the day, no solution could be evolved with
which she did not agree – as indeed turned out to be the case. I do not
know who told her that the doctors had refused to meet her and I heard
nothing from her until after a first meeting when what came to be known
as the Goodman Plan was presented to the government and the doctors
had convened at Downing Street.

The plan in detail is set out under the title 'The Goodman Proposals'
in Appendix VI on page 760 *et seq.* of the *Castle Diaries*. It involved the
establishment of an independent board to deal with the phasing of the
separation of private beds and facilities from the NHS, which was
nevertheless associated with an expression of the government's commitment to the maintenance of private medical and dental practice. It is
not my intention to discuss medical politics, but as it turned out this was
not an unhappy solution, notwithstanding that it married two firmly
conflicting beliefs which have continued to operate, sometimes rather
awkwardly, side by side, and may do so for many years.

The immediate 'bone' offered to Mrs Castle was the phasing out of

1,000 pay beds, but that thereafter further pay beds would only be phased out on the direction of the newly established board, with a number of criteria required to justify the release of additional beds: the principal one being the establishment of an alternative source of private beds in the locality of change.

The first meeting at Downing Street to discuss these proposals was a dramatic one. A quiverful of eminent doctors arrived on the scene, including Dr Grabham and his particularly intransigent colleagues; the blessed Damerell, and a number of genuine medical statesmen, such as the famous surgeon Rodney Smith, now Lord Smith, and others. There also arrived a strong deputation from the DHSS: the Minister of State, now of much greater fame, Dr David Owen; the Permanent Under-Secretary, Sir Patrick Nairne, and Barbara's most trusted right-hand man, a beardless youth, then recently the president of some students' association, named Jack Straw, with whom I had occasion to cross swords later.

The Prime Minister, waiting benignly in his chair, presided. Alongside were the inevitable Secretaries of State for Scotland and Wales, but the meeting could not start because, alas, 'Hamlet' was missing. Mrs Castle was nowhere to be seen. A decent interval elapsed, during which we looked at each other rather anxiously. Perhaps, I thought, she will not come. To do her justice, she would not, I think, have missed the meeting for the wealth of the Andes. It gave her an absolutely splendid opportunity of indicating her indignation. I had been quite right in my belief that she would not relish the intervention of the Prime Minister. I had, however, underrated the extent and sincerity of her indignation, and the more I have thought of it, the more I have thought how justified she was. It was an intolerable affront, although the situation to be saved probably justified the Prime Minister's decision and my advice.

When she entered the room, she directed an unfriendly look at Harold – so far as I remember making no sound – and, seeing where I was sitting, directed a glance at me that, for anyone of lesser resolution, would undoubtedly have turned me into stone. However, I smiled amiably and the meeting proceeded. To her eternal credit, her participation in the matter and her discussion of the Goodman proposals was totally constructive. For practical purposes – although a wealth of detail needed to be settled – the problem was substantially resolved at that famous meeting on 15 December 1975.

The meeting broke up and I was about to leave when a still, quiet voice said to Harold: 'Harold, I would much like to talk to you and Arnold by yourselves.' Harold acceded at once and I trotted dutifully after him to a small anteroom adjoining the Cabinet room. We sat down and the good lady let fly. She had never, she said, been so humiliated in her life. She did not know whether it would be possible for her to continue in office, such was the damage done to her within her own ministry and her own staff.

I defended myself stoutly by pointing out that the alternative was to break off negotiations, with a dispute that could have gone on for months at great cost to the health of the nation. It seemed to me an impossibly difficult decision. I conceded that it might have been wiser, and indeed more seemly, to have consulted her before a decision was reached; but I did not add that I had advised the Prime Minister to agree to a meeting over her head because I was convinced that she would never accept a challenge to her authority. It was impossible not to feel that she had been badly treated, but the bad treatment came from the intransigent doctors and not from a Prime Minister who, as she must have known, was immensely supportive and would not willingly have been associated with any slight on her. The same was certainly true of me, although my role was clearly less significant.

I parted with a feeling that it would be a long time before I earned her forgiveness, but I did her an injustice. Within a very short time she was back again in full and active negotiation, determined to resist to the maximum extent possible any encroachment on the National Health Service for private interests. Her assessment of me changed from one of total hostility to a slightly puzzled statement that my experience with these doctors, in her own words 'may prove, after all, not to have been a bad thing for this peculiar chap – half high principle and half unashamed pragmatism – to have been brought into personal dealings with this autocratic profession and to experience at first hand the kind of behaviour that has been driving Ministers of Health to despair for years'.

The sequel to the Downing Street meeting was almost daily meetings in my flat. Mrs Castle had formed a rather eccentric view about my scale of living. Her description of my flat is one that I had difficulty in recognising: 'We were greeted at the door by Arnold's housekeeper, Miss Roberts. She ushered us (it is the only word) into the sort of room I hadn't expected: rather dark and made darker by heavy period furniture and subdued lighting. Superb pictures everywhere, deep armchairs and sofa and a large colour TV. But the whole effect was oppressive.' However, on half a dozen occasions or more the negotiating teams on both sides gathered, either before or at dinner, to seek to resolve the detailed problems before the Goodman proposals were ultimately embodied in legislation.

It cannot be said that a warm relationship developed between the Minister and the doctors. The negotiations in my flat were largely conducted on the basis that the doctor delegates met in my dining-room, with Barbara and her colleagues – usually David Owen, Patrick Nairne and young Mr Straw – in my sitting-room, and I would occasionally take one or more from each delegation into my small study for a private talk.

For the first time I had an opportunity of seeing Barbara at work in detailed negotiations, and whatever small credit attached to me for the major idea, the scale and ingenuity that she expended on the detail and in making it possible to arrive at a suitable settlement was beyond praise. What was significant was the awe in which she was held by her two senior colleagues, but not so by Mr Straw. Very rarely did David Owen or Patrick Nairne intervene in a discussion. Mr Straw displayed no such reluctance. He has since, of course, achieved a political status by which presumably I ought now to judge him, but as a junior voice in a senior assembly I could not resist the conclusion that he was a little too forthcoming, particularly when on one occasion he outraged me by a suggestion that if a common waiting-list was established, consolidating both private and NHS priorities, the NHS patients should have pride of place before private patients came into the reckoning. It seemed to me an absurdity. I could see that no NHS patients should be postponed by a private patient except on the basis of priority of application, but that a private patient should be postponed because he was paying, and no one else was, struck my middle-class mentality as an unacceptable anomaly.

At the end of the day I had the satisfaction of presiding in the Lords debate on the Bill and noting the very last words in Barbara Castle's account of the affair: 'Now, unexpectedly, I have received a letter of "appreciation" from Harold for the "hard work and long hours" I have put in over the consultants' "package". I found it a bit stilted, but Ted thought it warm. "You know who has inspired that, don't you? Arnold," he said.'

After what was deemed to be considerable negotiating success with the wretched pay beds, I was left in relative tranquillity from government activity for a short time only. Having negotiated the final stages of the pay beds, and the legislation with David Ennals (now Lord Ennals), who had succeeded Barbara Castle at the DHSS, it was gratifying to my vanity to be called upon by him very shortly afterwards for a purpose much closer to my heart.

He came to see me with Sir Patrick Nairne. His request was unusual and, as presented, not a specially attractive one. 'We are,' he said, 'about to introduce a scheme to replace the much discredited "trikes",' by which he meant the three-wheeled conveyances then issued to the disabled. There were numerous complaints about them in relation to safety, the vast majority of the disabled expressing a wish for specially adapted motor cars.

Mr Ennals was proposing to replace the 'trikes' with a new mobility allowance. Mrs Castle, as it turned out, had opposed this allowance, again on the characteristically doctrinaire grounds that an allowance which made it necessary for the disabled to purchase motor cars would place them at the mercy of the commercial interests of motor manufacturers. At the time, and indeed until much later, I had no knowledge of Mrs Castle's objections or of the many discussions that had taken place on this subject at government level. My own approach was fortunately simplified by ignorance.

The Secretary of State asked whether, after the introduction of a mobility allowance, I would undertake the chairmanship of a private trust to raise money to supplement the allowance for those disabled unable to afford to purchase or run a motor car. The idea of an activity solely related to trying to raise money was at that stage an unpalatable one. I had spent, and indeed continued to spend, many hours trying to persuade the blind to see, or in other words to convince rich men of the virtue of causes close to my own heart, especially those relating to the arts. Although I had had a substantial measure of success, it was a back-breaking activity: it involved the pouring of oceans of hypocritical praise on the undeserving; attributing powers of discernment and discrimination to the ignorant and myopic; and only occasionally striking gold in the form of sufficient understanding to make the toil of persuasion unnecessary.

I told David Ennals, for whom I quickly formed some sympathy, that I would like to think about it. I did think about it and asked to see him again, and once again he visited me with Patrick Nairne. 'I think,' I said, 'that we (I was hopefully referring to others who might be recruited) can do better than merely seeking charitable funds.' I outlined to him a scheme for an organisation that would provide the disabled with the cars they required in return for an assignment to that organisation of their mobility allowance. It would work, I explained to him – and it is a demonstration of how something that is essentially simple can on that account have a firmer structure than a more complicated mechanism – by dint of borrowing from the banks a sufficient sum of money for the initial purchase. The disabled person would then hire-purchase or lease his motor car on terms far more advantageous than he could possibly contrive for himself, since the organisation would have the buying power to obtain cheaper cars and insurance, lower interest rates and a number of other concessions. I made a guesswork assessment that it would be able to provide a motor car that would cost the disabled person at least 25 per cent less than if he made his own arrangements. In the event, this was an underestimate, and it has totally falsified the belief that the disabled would become the victims of the manufacturers' rapacity.

Motability, the organisation formed for the purpose, now has a fleet of over 350,000 motor cars on the road. It is true to say that the cars are largely restricted to three or four models, but my own insistence had been from the outset that no obligation to use the scheme should be imposed on the disabled, nor any obligation to a particular model. The disabled should not feel that an obligation existed in relation to Motability. I was sure that were such a scheme to be imposed, it would be vigorously resisted and criticised. Of all communities, the disabled are, understandably, the most jealous of any suggestion that they are being patronised or treated differently from others.

Before Motability was introduced, I had several conversations with the Secretary of State and with his officials. To their eternal credit, they took less persuading than I might have expected. It was, of course, from their point of view a welcome scheme. The mobility allowance amounted initially to £10 a week and was recognised as anything but adequate. The fact that a scheme could be contrived that made it a working possibility for the majority of the disabled to acquire a motor car of their choice and to finance the purchase, including insurance and repair, from the allowance, was a staggering revelation to economists and particularly to the socialists of the time who regarded private enterprise as the kiss of death.

Motability has been one of the few established successes of a mixed economy. The government has provided the resources in the way of the allowance and in the way of an administrative service; voluntary effort has controlled the plan and the policy, including the detailed negotiations with manufacturers, bankers, insurance companies and the like, and all these bodies have made a generous contribution to a humane cause of powerful appeal. Its establishment depended on one or two fortunate chances. First it was necessary to enlist financial and administrative talent capable of organising the details. Happily there presented itself such a person in Jeffrey (now deservedly Lord) Sterling, who threw himself into the task with total dedication. He conducted detailed negotiations with a consortium of the four clearing banks and, enlisting my assistance at occasional meetings, contrived an arrangement with them that made the economics a possibility, while, I have to confess, retaining some attraction for the banks. His negotiations with the motor manufacturers – British Leyland, Chrysler, Ford and Vauxhall – were equally successful. They were enthusiastic, provided voluntary members of the council of Motability and co-operated without reserve. A signal achievement was Motability's success – largely achieved by Sterling – in enlisting the whole-hearted support and co-operation of the disabled. With remarkable skill he identified and presented for selection a group of some of the leading statesmen concerned with their welfare.

Over the fifteen years that Motability has been established, there have been powerful disagreements but not a whisper of hostility. Until recently, the achievement has been largely unpublicised. It appeared to me that the quest for publicity could do nothing but harm, so long as we were certain, as indeed we made sure, that all the disabled knew of the facility and used it if they so desired. Our principal exposure to the public arose from the chance that Her Majesty the Queen became interested and used Motability as the centre for her Christmas address in 1981. Motability has earned one peerage and an OBE or two, but otherwise virtue is its own reward, and so far as I am concerned, it has been the most successful achievement of my career and the most fortunate thought that ever came into my head.

It is right to record, however, that no activity, however benign, can escape malice. To our profound astonishment – and slight delight – the *New Statesman* on one occasion produced an article accusing Jeffrey Sterling and myself of lining our pockets from Motability. The insult was so unjust and so gross that we instituted proceedings for libel and extracted – not without difficulty – a full apology and retraction. The indignation within the Motability community at this venomous attack was more gratifying than any form of recognition that we might have obtained.

One of my more unlikely activities was to preside from 1973 to 1977 over the Housing Corporation, and alongside it (a body which bore no direct relationship) the National Building Agency. The Housing Corporation was the overall authority of housing associations, now more than 2,000 in number, established largely by volunteers throughout the country to carry out modest building schemes for estates of houses. These were to be administered by the association concerned but financed largely by the government, supplemented in many cases from private sources.

My period at the Housing Corporation was immensely instructive. I had started knowing nothing about houses, nothing about building, precious little about planning, and I ended up – although I say it myself – pretty well informed. When in 1974 I was flattered by an invitation to make a TV appearance as the Dimbleby lecturer, I accepted without hesitation. This, on my part, was a massive concession, since over the years I have almost without exception refused to indulge in self-publicising on the box.

I chose housing as my theme for the Dimbleby Lecture, and I enunciated a belief which is as firm today as it was when I delivered it:

We have in this country no less than four million homes which for one reason or another are unfit for human habitation . . . just think of the millions of people in our society who are living in circumstances which are genuinely unfit – because the word 'unfit' means . . . that an intolerable burden of daily life is imposed upon these people, who are bereft of many of the essential requirements, living in squalid, unhygienic, congested circumstances which no human being should be asked to live in. Of course I am not saying that people in those conditions do not live decent, honourable lives, . . . do not become great men . . . But if they do, think of the burden, think of the effort, think of the strain that is unnecessarily imposed upon them. And think of how many of them retain a permanent mark of the conditions in which they live . . . You cannot quantify the nature of the social resentment that these festering grounds of discontent create in our society. It is impossible to assess the cost of our neglect, the cost of our lethargy, in social and money terms. The question is why this has happened and how should we put it right.

I was amused, several years after I delivered the lecture, to be approached by the late Lord Rothschild – who had undertaken to discharge the lecture in that year – with an enquiry about the fee I had received. My recollection was that it was £250 for a great deal of work and endless consultations with courteous BBC representatives who were terrified by my refusal to produce a total text (since I can only give plausibility to anything I say when there is at least an element extemporised) and refused to accept my positive assurances that I was as unlikely to dry up as the Thames. No one has ever yet accused me of being short of words.

The fee, in all the circumstances, was one of the BBC's greatest bargains, but Lord Rothschild was very concerned lest he might be offered a lower fee. As it turned out, he had been offered double my fee and I soothed my offended vanity by attributing this to inflation. Even so, I understand he negotiated a substantial increase: an initiative on which I can only congratulate him. He came from a world where money mattered.

Shortly before the expiration of my first term at the Housing Corporation in 1976, I was asked to see Tony Crosland, then the Secretary of State for the Environment. He was a man who tried very hard, by seeking to adopt a deliberately offensive and high-handed attitude, to mask both the generosity of his disposition and the fine quality of his intellect. The appointment took place on what was, from his point of view, a fraught day. James Callaghan had at that moment replaced Harold Wilson as Prime Minister and he was occupied in forming his Cabinet. It was well known that there were two principal contenders for the Foreign Office: both good friends of mine and friends of each other, although, it was believed, long-time rivals – Tony Crosland and Roy Jenkins.

I was sufficiently intimate with Tony for him to unburden himself. 'I understand,' he said anxiously, 'that Roy has already received a summons to Downing Street. How do you interpret that? Do you think he will get the job?' I reflected and pontificated. 'It is my belief that the man who gets the job is seen last.' I prayed that I was right. I turned out to be right. The telephone rang while I was busy explaining to Tony Crosland that I could not accept a further term of office at the Housing Corporation, since I had been appointed to the Mastership of University College, Oxford, but I had agreed to a request that I should at least stay for another year to see someone else in.

When the telephone rang, Crosland leapt at it with unconcealed anxiety. It was indeed a summons to Downing Street. He was off in a flash. Our conversation, to my great surprise, appeared to take a secondary place in his thoughts. I did not wait for his return but telephoned him later in the evening. He was exultant. All he said was, 'I've got it!' I congratulated him, saying that I had no doubt it would be a good day for our foreign affairs but it was a sad day for British housing. On the whole Callaghan's choice of Crosland was wise: not because he was necessarily better as Foreign Secretary than Roy, but because Roy had an important task to perform at the Home Office where, on the admission of both friend and foe, he was the best Home Secretary of his generation.

Crosland was replaced as Environment Secretary by Peter Shore, a much less exuberant and extrovert character, but a solid, steady man whom I had known over the years and had first met when he was the Secretary of an *ad hoc* committee formed by the Labour Party – with a few outside 'experts' such as Dennis Lloyd and myself – to produce a rental policy. He had achieved a miracle of secretarial improvisation in a report which blended all the disparate views of the various voices in a fashion that was acceptable to all of them. From that day onwards I entertained a high regard for his dexterity and skill in public affairs. He had, I think, been very much underrated.

Peter Shore soon invited me to become a member of the Docklands Committee which was responsible for planning the redevelopment of the Wapping area. I joined the committee and my principal activity was in the end to assist in procuring its dissolution. The Wapping area involved four or five local authorities and the plan was to leave each of them with a high degree of autonomy but with some rather unconsidered federal situation over the whole area. This plan was an impossibility from the outset, and after several months of confused meetings of everyone concerned at County Hall, I went with two or three others to see the Secretary of State to recommend strongly that one single statutory authority should be appointed to deal with the area.

Before this happened, however, there were two minor incidents worthy of comment. At the first meeting of the committee which I attended the secretary announced that it would be necessary for members to disclose their interests, meaning thereby that they should declare with what companies and organisations they were involved. I took strong objection to this, pointing out that I had not volunteered for membership, or invited membership, but had been asked to join by the Secretary of State. 'He should not,' I said, 'invite people to join a committee if he has any doubts about their integrity.' Moreover, the whole business of disclosing interests is a nonsense, since a dishonest man will disclose every interest except the relevant one that he is prone to accept a large bribe. In the end I heard no more about this requirement.

The second incident was a somewhat comic experience. The chairman of the committee telephoned me in the late spring of 1976 to say that they were organising a series of public meetings at Wapping when the committee's plans for the area would be disclosed to the local population for the purpose of hearing their comments and enquiries. Would I preside at one of these meetings? Since my worst failing is an inclination to say 'yes' to almost every request, I acceded to this one. On the day in question I was driven down to Wapping where the meeting was to take place at St Peter's School. On arrival I found a young man from the GLC equipped with a magic lantern, slides, wall plans and all other relevant data. The only thing that was missing was any audience. There were three people only in the school: myself, the young man and my driver. A telephone enquiry disclosed that there were in fact two St Peter's Schools in Wapping and that while we were in one of them the audience was in the other. We obtained directions and drove as rapidly as possible to the rival meeting. There we found an eager audience of some eight people. To this group we addressed ourselves. I spoke a few introductory words, the young man displayed his lantern slides, explained the plans and provided Wapping with a firm impression that it was to become the Venice of the East End.

I invited questions. An elderly lady rose in the front and demanded to know what we were going to do about North Sea Gas since she was quite sure that this was a dangerously explosive substance. I replied gently that we were there to describe building plans and had no involvement in North Sea Gas. She subsided but was obviously dissatisfied. At that moment an elderly man rose to announce that he was the 'Wapping Poet'. Without any encouragement from me he proceeded to declaim Wapping poetry at considerable length. During this declamation the rest of the audience departed except for the North Sea Gas lady who, when the poet finished, resumed her enquiry about her original subject.

I do not know what purpose the meeting served in persuading Wapping of the merits of our plan, but it did enable me for the first and only time to see the terrain on which we were working and reinforced my enthusiasm to kill the committee at the earliest possible moment.

My time at the Housing Corporation was eventful in bringing me for the first, but no means last, time into contact with Mrs Thatcher when, on the fall of the Heath government, she became the shadow Minister of the Environment, in succession to the job she had had as Minister of Education. In her period as shadow Minister she displayed an efficiency and a command of detail that exceeded that of any encumbent minister with whom I had to deal. She has always been kindness itself to me, but I have a feeling in my bones that she would not regard me as a wholly reliable supporter. Indeed, in this she would be quite right. I do not believe in the doctrine that every man must stand on his own two feet, especially when he has a wooden leg.

However, I have escorted Mrs Thatcher to the opera on two or three occasions. These were wholly enjoyable experiences. She made no pretence of great musical knowledge and I had the satisfaction of describing to her the plot of *L'Elisir d'Amore* when no one else present in the Covent Garden box could remember it. On the one occasion when I made a direct appeal to her, in connection with the battle against the closed shop for journalists which I describe later, her response was gratifyingly supportive and it was no fault of hers that she was unable to persuade Lord Hailsham to a course of action that might well have altered journalistic history. All in all, I would be prepared to give her quite a high mark during her time in government, which I am sure will be a source of great relief to her when she comes to sleep at night.

Despite my closeness over a long period to Harold Wilson, I was certainly not close to his publicised cronies. My relationship with Marcia Williams was at all times rather chilly. I think her principal objection to me was that I exercised some influence over him, which was at odds with her own belief that all such influence should be exercised through her. In any event, I have no recollection of ever having had any differences with her except on one occasion when she telephoned me to make a request with which I was unable to comply. This provoked an outburst of considerable ferocity. As I am a mild and gentle man I am always alarmed by such outbursts, particularly if they are of feminine origin. However, I stood firm and declined to be drawn. Since then I have come to see that she is a woman of qualities, some of which one detects in Barbara Castle and Margaret Thatcher. In a way I feel sorry for her. If in fact she had proceeded along a more orthodox path, she could have become one of the great political women of our time. She was passionately interested in politics and most of all in the personnel of politics, and she had cultivated a limited group of Labour politicians who, with her, were rightly described as Harold Wilson's 'Kitchen Cabinet'.

One of Wilson's associates was a gentleman who was later to attain a high degree of publicity and notoriety, namely Joseph Kagan. I was frankly astonished when this gentleman was ennobled. It would not be right for me to say that he was wrongly ennobled, because I know too little about him to be able to detect whatever surprising quality it was that commended itself to Harold Wilson for admission to the House of Lords.

My first encounter with Kagan took place when Wilson telephoned me and asked if I would see him. My inclination was to decline, but as that would have been discourteous in the extreme to Wilson, for whom I then had enormous respect, I agreed to see him. Kagan arrived in my office and proceeded to tell me a story, which I can now recount as it is in the public domain. He was the father of a child by a very attractive lady (who had subsequently married a very close friend of mine). Kagan was deeply concerned that his access to the child was limited. To his credit he obviously had strong parental affection and a powerful concern that the child should not be totally alienated from him. He asked me what rights he had as a father. I had to advise him that the father of a child born out of wedlock had few, if any, rights. He could, of course, make the child a ward of court, but I doubted if any wardship would persuade the court to take a child away from a young and devoted mother.

I therefore recommended to him what I regarded as a sensible viewpoint. 'You are, Mr Kagan, I believe, a wealthy man,' I said. 'What is required from you is a spontaneous gesture of generosity. I suggest that you make an ample settlement on the child and write and tell his new stepfather what you have done, and that you have done it because you are determined that no one else should have any financial responsibility for a child of your blood. Having done that, I am sure that any decent man would then feel that you have parental rights which should be respected, in view of the gesture you have made.' Kagan looked at me as though I was demented. I could see in his eyes that he was wondering why he had been advised to consult such a lunatic. This recommendation was clearly not what he had in mind at all.

My meeting ended when I asked Kagan who the gentleman was who was now married to the young lady concerned. He named a man who, as I have said, was a very close friend of mine. I asked Kagan if he had come to me knowing that I was an intimate friend of the man concerned. He looked slightly embarrassed and did not deny that he had. I then indicated that as far as I was concerned the meeting should terminate there and then, since in no circumstances would I be willing to give advice contrary to the interests of my friend. In the end there was long and controversial litigation, which nevertheless failed to establish the rights that Kagan sought.

One thing that intrigued me in the course of my meeting with Kagan was his careful enquiries about what duties were involved in membership of the House of Lords. This I found strange since, to my innocent mind, I did not think that he could possibly have received an indication that a peerage was awaiting him. He did, however, offer to make me a mackintosh. This, if I may say so, considering my bulk in those days – now much reduced by the ravages of health and time – was a very considerable offer. It would have required a quantity of material sufficient to make a small tent. However, since the principal feature of the raincoat was that it was very easily identifiable as associated with Mr Kagan, I declined the offer with gratitude.

In any event, before the disastrous situation which sent him to jail for a short period, I had one other encounter. Ian Mikardo approached me to see whether I would assist in raising funds to establish a scholarship at Haifa University in honour of the (then) late Dick Crossman, who had indeed been a man of the most friendly associations. I agreed to assist. He wondered whether I would give a dinner, which I said I would, at my home. I told him, however, that he would have to provide the list of guests since I did not feel that I could exploit my own list any further. The very sound of my name in quest of some charitable contribution sends many of them in flight to the Outer Hebrides. He promised to send me a list, but I told him not to bother. 'Just invite them,' I said. In any event, a short while later Mikardo's list arrived. To my consternation it included the name of Mr Kagan, with whom I was not anxious to resume an acquaintance, not because of what happened afterwards but because of what had happened in my office.

However, Mr Kagan having been invited, courtesy demanded that he should be received as a guest ought to be received. He arrived at my home and in the course of the evening he buttonholed me. He told me that he would donate £5,000 to the fund if I would undertake to invite his little son, then at school in Oxford, to tea on odd occasions, so that I could acquaint him with some of the matters relating to Judaism. I informed Mr Kagan that I was something of a heretic so far as the minutiæ of the Jewish faith were concerned; on the other hand, I said, I had never concealed that I was a loyal member of the faith, and so I would be happy to have the boy to tea and talk to him about Judaism in general terms. On that basis it was confirmed that he would make the donation.

Some time elapsed and I finally telephoned Lord Weidenfeld, who was charged with the duty of collecting the money, to know what had happened. 'Alas,' he said, 'there was a misunderstanding. When I phoned Kagan he told me that he had instructed his trustees in Israel to make the payment, but by some terrible misunderstanding they had paid it into the wrong charity.' 'Is there anything to prevent another payment being made to the right charity this time?' I enquired. I was told that the trust had exhausted its funds. I do not know whether this was associated with the fact that no one ever sought a tea meeting with me and that I was relieved of the obligation of conducting a rather spurious theological discussion on the basis of almost total ignorance.

Another of Harold Wilson's circle was Joe Haines, his Press Officer. He has, of course, come into recent prominence through a long association with the late Robert Maxwell. I never established anything like a friendship with him, but our paths did cross from time to time. Late one evening in 1974, not long after Wilson's second election victory, I was at my home in Portland Place when Haines came through on the telephone with a request for some urgent action. 'I have heard, and reliably heard,' he said, 'that the *Daily Express* intends to publish the twins story.' This referred to the fact that Marcia Williams had given birth to illegitimate sons. Harold Wilson was, when he might have been better engaged in the affairs of the nation, extremely solicitous in seeing that arrangements were made for Marcia Williams, particularly in relation to her progeny. Haines asked if I would ring up Max Aitken – whom he knew to be a very good friend – to ask him to dissuade his editor from publishing the story, which had until then been kept as a dark secret. I demurred, pointing out to Haines that as the chairman of the Newspaper Publishers Association I had been very careful to avoid interfering with press stories in any way. But he urged on me that it was the Prime Minister's particular wish that I should do anything I could to prevent its publication. I am afraid, rather weakly, I said that I would speak to Max.

I rang the *Daily Express* and to my great delight was told that Max was in the Bahamas. I rang Haines to tell him of that fact and there was nothing else I could do as I had no notion of where in the Bahamas Max might be. Nor, frankly, did I particularly wish to know. But Max's kindness and good manners defeated my purpose totally. A few minutes after speaking to Haines, a call came through. Max had heard from his office that I was seeking to speak to him and his friendly response was to telephone me himself.

I told him what worried the PM. The story of the twins was well known in Fleet Street and it was really only a matter of hours, or at best days, before a newspaper decided to cash in on it. However, Max's reaction was very satisfactory. 'I do not think we are under any duty to publish malicious gossip,' he said, 'which remains gossip however true it may be.' He indicated that he would telephone the editor and direct him not to publish anything.

I thereupon telephoned Haines to tell him of my success and to urge upon him the necessity for extreme discretion, since what I had done was something of an embarrassment and I did not particularly wish to have my role publicised. Haines assured me that everything at his end would remain secret, but a few years later I was both surprised and vexed to find that he had retailed the story in his memoirs without any indication of his pledge of confidentiality.

I had further dealings with Haines towards the end of 1975. Harold Wilson had complained to me about the continuing hostility of the press towards him and wanted to know how to put it right. He suggested that I might give a dinner to the leading newspaper editors and proprietors, when he could make some statement calculated to neutralise some of the undoubted venom that was then directed at him.

I agreed to give a dinner and it took place in my London home some weeks later. Harold was pleased that it had been arranged, but he did not arrive unaccompanied since Haines was with him. The dinner was not an especially peaceful one. Harold, rather forgetful of his purpose, proceeded to upbraid the guests in a positively violent fashion and then, when he had run out of personal ammunition, he said to Haines, 'Joe, tell them of any specific complaints that we have. You have a list.' Haines thereupon infuriated everyone with an item-by-item recital.

What was no doubt intended to be a moment of triumph fell absolutely flat, particularly as the late editor of the *Evening Standard* – Charles Wintour – was roused to indignation sufficiently vigorous to make it difficult to continue with the dinner. The troops withdrew, leaving Harold and Haines with the floor. 'Well,' said Harold, 'don't you think that it was a very successful evening?' I raised my eyebrows and said nothing. Later, however, I did tell him that the meeting had been a disaster and that if he thought it had mollified the press in any way he was greatly mistaken.

Harold, however, was nothing if not persistent. About a month later, he said to me that he was compelled to agree that the first dinner had not been a success (his words), and would I be kind enough to arrange a second? I expressed doubts as to whether any further breaking of bread between Harold and the press would lead to an outbreak of peace and goodwill. However, as he was insistent, I invited the original company to return, and return they did, still accompanied by Charles Wintour.

This second dinner went rather better. There was no sign of Haines, no one had come with a list of grievances, and Harold was able to give some of the assurances that I had urged upon him before the first dinner. He dissociated himself from Tony Benn's provocative statement that a printer had as much right to regulate the contents of a newspaper as the editor or anyone else. This went quite a long way towards soothing enraged newspapermen and the dinner terminated quite peacefully, although on its termination my drink stock was reduced by two whole bottles of whisky.

In my view, Harold Wilson never made peace with the press because he was too anxious to do so. He made the mistake of attributing to the press the importance that they themselves give to newspapers and journalists. It was strange that a man of considerable intellect could give so much attention and attribute such importance to a press which was wholly influenced at all times by political considerations. It is fair to say that the Conservatives exercised and still exercise very much more influence on the press than the Labour Party. Some might regard that influence as excessive.

My standing with Harold Wilson began to go downhill in the 1970s, not on personal grounds but because of what might be described as political differences. The word political is somewhat unsuitable in the circumstances, since my own political stance has always been a pragmatic one. I take a political position according to my belief in the particular issue, and it never coincides in respect of more than one issue with that of any particular party.

As a result of my friendship with Harold Wilson I developed considerable affection for him, which I still maintain. He was in many ways a remarkable Prime Minister, although there were obviously faults – and some grave faults – that history alone will assess in determining whether or not he ranks among the greats. He certainly had a Herculean task to maintain any consistency of policy among an immensely disparate collection of politicians, constituting, I think, one of the most brilliant Cabinets of our time, short of the Cabinet that served after the Second World War.

Our first difference arose over the Biafran War, which began in July 1967 and in which, by the time it ended some three years later, there had been a *civilian* death toll alone in Biafra of over two million people. I was a fervent supporter of the Ibos of Biafra, who were fighting for their independence against the rest of Nigeria. My principal reason was a very subjective one: I had, as an undergraduate, met with and remained a firm friend of one of the leading Ibos, Sir Louis Mbanefo, who had been knighted by the British government when he became the Chief Justice of

Eastern Nigeria. Mbanefo was a splendid man of total integrity and his colleagues impressed me in the same way.

For that reason, however inadequate some people may regard it, I was a firmly convinced supporter of Biafra and made various futile efforts during the war to persuade Harold Wilson to a like view. His attitude in the matter was – as inevitably with many problems – a keen desire that it should go away. But despite polite utterances to me at private meetings, his public stance was to support the Foreign Office view that the Biafrans should be put down. In that context, the shuffling attitude of leading Labour politicians is of historic discredit. Although the decent instinct of many was to support the weaker side in a wholly legitimate quest for independence, their public utterances, alas, were to support the side which in their view was the more important to British interests.

I made several speeches in the Lords propounding my belief that the Biafran side should have had our support, and I still believe we would have been very much better off had that ensued. But Harold Wilson and the government took a different view. What inspired that view I am not completely sure. I do not think that it was entirely the question of the ownership of Nigerian oil; more likely they genuinely believed that the Biafrans had no chance of success. This in fact became so only because of the policies Wilson adopted in the way of providing arms to the other side, for which there was insufficient compensation from the rather half-hearted support given by the Soviets and by a few other countries to the Biafrans.

What infuriated me was when Wilson visited Nigeria to review the situation. His visit lasted for a few hours at most – taking into account the time spent asleep – and the only really detailed description he gave was of the accommodation in which he slept in General Gowon's home. And yet to the world at large he claimed to have conducted a most detailed investigation into the whole matter, sufficient to enable him to arrive at an informed judgement that British policy remained correct. He also gave the impression, although I do not think he made a specific statement, that he had in fact had discussions with the Biafrans.

I was also infuriated by the continual refusal of the British government, despite my strong representations to Harold Wilson, to meet with the Biafran leaders. Several of them came to London in order to discuss the possibilities of an armistice and ultimately of peace, but they could only meet junior officials from the Foreign Office and absolutely nothing transpired. Harold Wilson did consult me from time to time, in the sense of asking me to ascertain from the Biafrans what their attitude would be towards a visit by him and matters of that sort, but my interventions were of a pretty futile nature and achieved no results.

Fortunately the war came to an end, and the one gratifying feature was the fact that it ended without the conventional horrors inflicted upon the defeated faction. Gowon behaved in a fashion which should attract historic credit in that his amnesty was a genuine amnesty; no retribution, except in a few isolated instances, was inflicted on the Ibos in consequence of the war. They are now, I think, fully restored to their original position, although Nigeria's economic fortunes have been rather dire. But the natural resources of the country are so large, and its prominence in Africa is so great (it is the most populous on the continent), that its importance cannot be minimised. That is an added reason why I think we took such a mistaken view in a situation where it is clear that the Ibos are the brains of the establishment and will always remain in a position of effective leadership when there is no state of war.

The prosecution in 1971 of Jonathan Aitken – now a respected although still controversial Member of Parliament, but then an aspirant journalist – arose out of the Biafran tragedy. I had found myself, because of my views, in a lobby with a number of unlikely bedfellows. It was through my convictions that I established a firm friendship with the late Sir Hugh Fraser, and an unexpectedly harmonious relationship with Auberon Waugh and members of his *Private Eye* banditry: a relationship which, as I have said, strangely has remained unaffected despite my own less than friendly exchanges with that periodical. Jonathan Aitken's recruitment to the cause of Biafra was motivated originally by his close friendship with Hugh Fraser, but I am convinced that it was not long before, on a close examination of the circumstances, he became honourably convinced that the British government was backing the wrong cause for dishonourable reasons. It was, in short, backing the 'big battalions'.

Aitken's prosecution under the Official Secrets Act – alongside Mr Brian Roberts, the much-respected editor of the *Sunday Telegraph* – was brought about by the publication in that paper in January 1970 of an article quoting extracts from the Scott Report. This was a report commissioned by the British government as an assessment of the prospects in the Biafran War, which in fact firmly predicted the inevitable victory of the Nigerian government – a victory which was, of course, inevitable because of the support the British government was giving to it.

A General Alexander – a Yorkshire acquaintance of Aitken and an authority on Nigerian affairs who had from time to time provided Aitken, in his journalistic capacity, with snippets of information about the war – had been used by the British government, because of his knowledge of Nigeria and the military position, as an unofficial adviser in these matters. He had in that capacity been supplied with a copy of Scott's report, which was regarded by the government, and particularly by the Foreign Office, as strictly confidential.

The crucial events around which the case centred occurred at a dinner party given by the General, when Aitken and some others were present. The conversation turned to the Biafran War and a controversy arose about the Biafrans' prospects of success, which would no doubt have been more favourably presented by Aitken than was believed by the General. The General, perhaps to make his point, informed Aitken of the authoritative report that the government had received and offered to lend it to him for a short while. Aitken asserted at the trial, and this view was certainly supported by independent witnesses, that no word about confidentiality was ever uttered, but the document was handed over to him on the footing that it would be returned within a very short time. Given Aitken's fervent support for the Biafrans, it is not unfair to assume that any suggestion of confidence that was not specifically expressed would have been dampened in his mind, since the publication of the document in his view would lend strong support to critics of the government's policy.

Having borrowed the document, Aitken's account of his later behaviour was clear-cut and uncontroversial except on a money question where the weight of evidence strongly supported his contentions. His evidence was that he read the report on the night that he received it and was – as others would have been – shocked to find that the parliamentary statements relating to the government's support for the Nigerians were demonstrably false. Time and again the government had asserted that Britain was only supplying '15 per cent in value' of Nigerian armaments. In one particular alone, the Scott Report disclosed that 40 million rounds of small arms ammunition had been delivered in fourteen months, which was totally inconsistent with the 15 per cent claim. Aitken's subsequent contention that this information was a legitimate matter of public interest, which justified its public exposure, would seem to most people to be unanswerable.

Having read the report, the next morning Aitken telephoned Hugh Fraser, then of course a Conservative MP, to tell him about it, to quote extracts from it and to hear his very firm agreement that the report's contents should be disclosed as a matter of public interest. Aitken did not tell Fraser of any suggestion of confidentiality since, as he later affirmed, he did not believe that any undertaking had been given or asked for. Later the same morning Aitken went to Yorkshire Television's headquarters in Leeds, where for the two years previously he had had some contacts and where the company was planning a documentary film on Biafra. Having made several copies of the report, he returned the original to the General.

In the two weeks following, he had numerous conversations with Hugh Fraser – who, of course, made common cause with him over Biafra – and they jointly decided that the document should be provided to the press for publication. The paper selected was almost inevitably the *Sunday Telegraph*, which had displayed a greater sympathy for the Biafran cause than most. The channel of communication to the *Sunday Telegraph* was Graham Watson, then managing director of Curtis Brown, the well-known literary agents, who acted for Aitken and Hugh Fraser in their respective journalistic activities. Watson was instructed to negotiate with the *Sunday Telegraph*.

The most controversial aspect of the matter relates to those negotiations, but the evidence of Aitken's probity is firmly established, notwithstanding determined efforts to put a cloud around it. It was unfortunate that Graham Watson regarded the matter as a commercial one in the sense that he negotiated a fee of £500 for the publication rights. But it was agreed on all sides, and most importantly by Graham Watson himself, that his instructions were that the fee was to go to a charitable organisation flying relief into Biafra. Graham Watson confirmed this statement to the police and confirmed it again under oath at the trial. There was an independent witness who deposed that Aitken had a conversation with him shortly after the publication of the report and before any fee was paid, when Aitken asked for the names of Biafran charities to which the money might properly be sent.

The £500 fee was paid by the *Sunday Telegraph* to Curtis Brown on 11 January 1970, one month after the publication of the report. All Aitken's evidence – uncontradicted by any other evidence – confirms that well before Curtis Brown received the £500, instructions had been given as to the charitable destination of the money. Moral purists may well debate Aitken's propriety in selling – even for a charitable cause – something which did not belong to him, namely the copyright in the report, but others may share my own view that, having regard to the intensity of the pro-Biafran feelings of Aitken and Fraser, this particular act would not seriously impede an unobstructed entry into heaven.

The prosecution under the Official Secrets Act was launched on 12 January 1971 (the Conservative Party was then in power and had inherited this state prosecution from its Labour predecessors) and lasted three and a half weeks. The case was heard by an exceptionally unconventional judge, but one of sound common sense, Mr Justice Caulfield, who more recently found fame in his unorthodox but equally commonsensical summing-up in the Jeffrey Archer action, where his description of Mrs Archer as 'fragrant', no doubt causing great embarrassment to the lady, will go down in the history of judicial extravagance.

General Alexander gave his evidence uneasily and was subjected to a brutal cross-examination by the most brilliant criminal counsel of our day, Jeremy Hutchinson QC (now Lord Hutchinson), who appeared for Mr Roberts of the *Sunday Telegraph*, and by a no less competent counsel, Basil Wigoder QC (now Lord Wigoder), who appeared for Aitken. The question of whether or not any undertakings as to confidentiality were given would by itself have been irrelevant as a defence under the Official Secrets Act. The crime is to disclose an official secret, probably even if extracted from the accused at the point of a pistol. But the major plank of the defence was provided by the remarkable lady journalist Suzanne Cronjé. By dint of careful and meticulous research she was able to provide the defence with evidence that every significant statement published in the *Sunday Telegraph* had been published somewhere already in a newspaper, a magazine or a book. In short, if one had assembled a number of publications and collated them, one would have had everything that the prosecution claimed was a state secret.

In his summing-up, Mr Justice Caulfield could not have evinced a more robust hostility to the Official Secrets Act, sharing a widely held belief that it was long out of date and an intolerable interference with freedom of speech, and that it provided a justification for prosecutions ranging from the serious to the grotesquely ridiculous. His summing-up left the jury in no doubt about his own views and would have required a jury of quite exceptional perversity to have brought in a guilty verdict.

The verdict of acquittal was easily predictable but was, nevertheless, a great relief. Hugh Fraser predictably had been most anxious to join his friend and colleague in the dock. I had considerable difficulty in dissuading him from this course and only did so when I was able to convince him that, far from assisting Aitken, it would damage his cause. Hugh Fraser's later career was rewarded – no doubt forgiven for his participation in the case, or possibly because it was unknown – by a knighthood, but nothing more. He was, I believe, thereafter regarded as too maverick a character for political office. He had, from a political point of view, the sad disadvantage of espousing the causes of whose rightness he was convinced – always a fatal quality in an aspirant politician.

Jonathan Aitken escaped the total destruction of his career, which might well have resulted from a conviction. But it may well be that his prolonged failure (now happily corrected) to achieve political success was attributable to long memories. Political success was due to him because of an exceptional intelligence and independence of mind which resolutely refuses to be subservient to the political mandarins of his party. He has espoused causes which Establishment figures, and particularly the Foreign Office, dislike and opposed causes, conspicuously the Channel Tunnel, which are much approved by his party leaders. He has a keenly critical mind and is an excellent speaker – one of the best speakers in the House. It is a sad reflection on his party that for so long he did not enjoy a smell of office.

In 1972 George Wigg's memoirs were published. At his request, I had written the preface, and that preface had involved me in a most disagreeable situation. A fortnight or so after I had dictated it in October 1971, I had a telephone call from Harold Wilson to know whether I had read Wigg's memoirs, and was I aware of the very personal attacks on him and Marcia Williams? I had some difficulty in persuading him that I had not even seen, let alone read, the book, either in manuscript or in print. In the event, both sides consulted solicitors and the matter was composed by quite serious alterations in references to both Harold and Mrs Williams.

Wigg's hostility to both arose from the same cause. He had always resented Marcia Williams because of the influence she exercised over Harold Wilson and that resentment grew as his own power diminished. He was a rejected favourite who did not relish the advance to power of his rival. But Wilson had been immeasurably kind to him, found a place for a very square peg in his government and, in 1967, when he no longer had room in his government for Wigg, created him a peer and was at pains to find him a suitable job as chairman of the Horserace Betting Levy Board. Wigg's two passions in life were first a constant and continuing admiration for the British army and second a lifelong interest in racing, about which he had a massive and detailed knowledge. He was an assiduous and permanent gambler of modest sums. He told me on one occasion that any year in which he did not win £1,000 was by his standards a failure.

My own experience of his judgement was not very encouraging and did not support the view of his racing omniscience. My practice is to place a modest-sized bet on two races, and not surprisingly my choice is the Grand National and the Derby. To a layman, that is one who does not bet with any regularity, the Grand National opens up splendid opportunities to a knowing head. It is possible for the race to be won at very long odds, and on two or three occasions, assisted by Wigg, I had been able to locate the winning horse, or at least a horse in the first three, which, if the odds were long enough, nevertheless produced a satisfactory result.

My most pressing experience of Wigg as a tipster was on one of the rare occasions when I went to the Derby. My driver was in conversation with Sir Victor Sassoon's driver, who informed him that his employer had considerable confidence in his horse. Before going to the box I therefore paid a short visit to the Tote and was in the process of staking the Sassoon mount when Wigg appeared on the horizon. Needless to say, since the notion that you did not ask anyone over-probing questions would have been regarded by him as an absurdity, he wanted to know what I was going to back. When I told him, his scoffing could be heard miles away. 'That horse,' he said, 'could never win. He cannot stay the distance and his breathing is now difficult.' Wigg went on to list various other imperfections from which the poor animal was suffering. So vivid was his description that I suggested the only kindness would be to put the nag down before the race. He then fortunately disappeared and I proceeded to put my bet on the horse, which I am happy to say romped home at forty to one. When I encountered Wigg later in the afternoon, I made no mention of this situation and characteristically neither did he.

Around the middle of 1969 I had been asked by the Jockey Club whether I would join the board of United Racecourses, for one reason and one reason only: in order to keep the peace between the Jockey Club and Lord Wigg. George Wigg's encounters with the Jockey Club became quite famous, particularly on one occasion when he had a public slanging-match, using voice-magnifying equipment, with the Duke of Norfolk who, employing similar equipment, exchanged insults with him on a racecourse. George Wigg was a remarkable man but very difficult to keep in check. For some reason I had a talent for calming him down. I possessed a built-in Wigg pacifier that enabled reasonable transactions to be completed where otherwise he would be totally unreasonable.

An instance of Wigg's volatility occurred in December 1969 when he assembled with others at my breakfast table to discuss an issue between himself and the Jockey Club. The Jockey Club was represented by Sir Randle Feilden (the senior steward), Sir John Astor and one other. George Wigg was represented by himself. I was there as the arbitrator, supplying the breakfast. At the end of the proceedings I had succeeded in pacifying both parties and a concordat had been arrived at. Thereupon we all agreed solemnly that it was a private matter and that no announcement would be made to the press.

Within ten minutes, George, having got back to his home in Warwick Square, rang me up and said, 'Arnold, I have a press announcement here. Would you like to approve it?' 'George,' I said, 'we agreed less than an hour ago that there would not be a press announcement.' 'Ah!' he said. 'I thought it over again and I have decided there must be an announcement, because it would indicate the merits of the matter and make it perfectly clear that I was in the right.'

This seemed to me a poor reason for making the announcement and I told him that I strongly disapproved of his breach of trust. In any event, if he was going to make an announcement, I said, he should communicate with everyone present and obtain their consent. Whereupon he blew his top and declared, 'Well, I will not make the announcement, but I will never talk to you again!' I took this threat rather lightly and for good reason, because some fifteen minutes later he was on the telephone to me talking about a completely different matter, as though the previous conversation had never taken place. That was George.

Anyway, shortly after my joining the board of United Racecourses, it became necessary to find a manager. I thought that Frank Coven would make a good manager and suggested him to George. He met Frank, liked him and agreed that he should have the job. Unfortunately, what was not made clear to George was that Frank had an extremely ambitious, though very pleasant, wife who insisted on participating in events to the exclusion of George, who had a very proper concern for himself. Thus, to George's great indignation, he would arrive at a racecourse to hear that the cup for the 2.30 was about to be presented to the winner by Mrs Frank Coven, when he thought it ought to be presented by Lord Wigg.

In the event, the culmination of the relationship occurred when the telephone rang one day and in a suspiciously silky voice George asked me where I thought the Derby Cup was. I assured him that I did not have the slightest idea where the Derby Cup was and had not made away with it. 'I'll tell you where it is,' he said. 'Well, why ask me if you know?' I asked. This, however, did not dissuade him. 'The Derby Cup,' he said, 'is in the window of Peter Robinson.' 'What,' I enquired, 'is it doing there?' 'I'll tell you what it is doing there. Mrs Coven is the "outsize" adviser to Peter Robinson and she has borrowed the Derby Cup in order that it be displayed in their window. It has no right to be there and if you will take my advice you will tell Frank Coven to take it out of that window and back to the bank as fast as he can.'

I telephoned Frank and adopted exactly the same technique. 'Tell me, Frank,' I said, 'where is the Derby Cup?' There was a rather guilty silence. 'Why do you ask?' he said. 'Oh! I'm just interested.' 'The Derby Cup,' he said, 'is in the window of Peter Robinson.' 'What,' I asked, 'is it doing in the window of Peter Robinson?' 'It is not doing any harm,' he said, 'in the window of Peter Robinson.' 'But suppose it is stolen?' 'Ah!' he answered, ready for that one. 'It is insured.' 'Tell me,' I went on gently, 'if a man has entered a horse for the Derby from, shall we say, Texas or California or Kansas, or anywhere where horses are bred, and having won the Derby arrives to be presented with something, do you think he will be pleased to get a voucher on the Royal Insurance Company instead of the Cup?' To this Frank had no reply. 'Frank,' I said, 'if you will take my advice as a good friend, you will get that Cup back with the speed of light.' He needed no telling twice, but alas the episode was fatal to his position at United Racecourses and he thereupon turned to other activities.

If I had to give the best pen picture I could contrive of Harold Wilson, I would describe him as an immensely intelligent man, rather less – by my standards – than half-educated. One of the most notable omissions in his education and his interests was almost anything to do with the arts. He was immensely well-read on political history in the nineteenth century and more recent times, and he deployed a memory of fantastic accuracy, but so far as I could judge he had read virtually nothing else. He cited as his favourite book a long novel about Lancashire and the cotton industry, which he referred to occasionally, but the great wealth of British literature was both unknown to him and something in which he clearly had no interest.

An instance of his ignorance and lack of sophistication was the occasion when one of the commercial television stations put on a Sunday evening entertainment at a London theatre, consisting of relatively brief extracts from a number of famous plays. Owing to the strength of their position in the world of entertainment, they were able to persuade some of the leading actors and actresses to perform. There was a piece from *Hamlet*, another piece from *The Merchant of Venice*, and extracts from *The School for Scandal, The Critic, The Importance of Being Earnest*, and a few others.

I was sitting in a row exactly in front of Harold Wilson and his party, and during the last interval I heard him ask his neighbour whether anyone would 'have seen these plays right through'. I heard no more of the exchange but this one remark was quite enough to establish his woeful ignorance about the theatre.

But although Harold Wilson was in artistic matters a Philistine, he was better than the later Philistines, since he recognised that the ambit of British culture should not be controlled by his own personal predilections, and he responded with speed and generosity to applications from Jennie Lee for better support for the arts. He was always very amenable to me when, as chairman of the Arts Council, I too was in need of some special support.

Perhaps his greatest vulnerability was one shared with the great mass of mankind: a vanity which affected many aspects of his life, and which as he grew older increased his claims for credit for almost every activity within human reach. It would not have surprised me to hear him say that he had advised the Almighty strongly against the Flood and other similar claims, the foolishness of which was self-evident, but not to Him.

A radical shortcoming was his inability to match expenditure to income. This was due in my view to the fact that he had rather extravagant notions of the office structure that he should maintain. He should have realised that the employment of a number of secretaries was both unnecessary and costly, but he continued boldly to maintain a lavish office establishment. Various friends and supporters rallied to his assistance, largely I think because they liked him, as indeed I did, but it was a waste of time to urge thrift or economy on him since he proceeded happily on the basis that the money would come from somewhere. This was an unfortunate trait for a prime minister. It exposed him to some influences that were thoroughly unhelpful, but as a matter of loyalty, and nothing else, he would not discard the people who, he believed, had been of help to him.

Wilson's principal domestic fault was his kindness in bestowing benefits on friends, and indeed on anyone who approached him in the appropriate fashion, and certainly through Marcia Williams. His attitude towards public honours was a contradictory one. In public he expressed great contempt for the system, but he made use of it to an immoderate degree, particularly by bestowing honours – undue honours – on the least worthy of his personal friends and particularly if the suggestion was made by anyone close to him.

One day I was sitting in his room in Downing Street having a general discussion, when he suddenly said to me, 'Can you think of any good name for the next Honours List?' I thought for a moment and came up with a suggestion that he should give some sort of honour, an OBE or the like, to the cricketer Basil D'Oliveira, who had been shabbily treated by the South African government. He noted my suggestion and D'Oliveira's name duly appeared in the next Honours List with, I think, an OBE. And it was a perfectly well-deserved honour which was not open to the same criticism as many of the other honours that Wilson made or unhappily was persuaded to make.

I remember one day prior to the publication of an Honours List in 1974 when Harold Wilson and George Wigg had dinner with me. Harold Wilson obviously had something on his mind and he told us that if we watched the television news we would hear something that he was sure would be of interest to us. It turned out to be the announcement of the elevation of Marcia Williams to the House of Lords. George Wigg almost had a stroke, in view of his undoubted and continuing hostility to her. For my part, I made no comment of any kind. The lady has, so far as I know, done no harm in the Lords – no one having seen her except on one occasion when she went there to lunch – and she has yet to make her maiden speech. I do not think she derived any great benefits from being ennobled, but obviously it was something she liked and sought and Harold Wilson could see little or no reason for not obliging her.

However, when she became Lady Falkender she became much more open to criticism. For instance, Denis Hamilton – a totally fair journalist, but an incorrigible Conservative – came to see me one day to warn me that *The Times* was prepared to break the newspaper silence that had until then, with the exception of *Private Eye*, been maintained by all news sources about her two illegitimate children. I asked him why this change of heart and he said that it was because Harold Wilson had seen fit to put her in the Lords. As such she became a public personage, open to public comment. I asked him whether, if she had been a man elevated to the peerage, he would have considered it necessary to disclose everything to do with his private life. He gave me no satisfactory answer, saying only that *The Times* was set to make this disclosure in an article by a woman journalist the following day. I did not speak to Harold Wilson or to Lady Falkender about the matter, since I was sure that strenuous efforts would be made to prevent disclosure, but I was equally sure from Denis Hamilton's attitude that this would not succeed and it was therefore better not to try.

But all this palled beside Harold Wilson's unfortunate 'Resignation' List in 1976. By that time my personal relations with him had cooled, so there was no question of my having seen any of the names. However, shortly before the List's publication, I received a visit from Harold Evans, then the editor of the *Sunday Times*, who came to breakfast and rather slyly asked if I had seen it; to which I replied that I had not seen it and knew nothing of its contents. I was not left in ignorance long. Harold Evans clearly had seen the List and regaled me with some of its more unlikely names. I was horrified by these disclosures and indeed spent rather a troubled night reflecting on whether I had any duty to express my view.

I decided that as I had worked for Harold Wilson and enjoyed his total confidence for several years, there was some duty to try to deter him from the worst mistakes. Accordingly I telephoned him quite early the next morning and received a cordial invitation to come and drink a cup of coffee with him in his home in Lord North Street. He had withdrawn there on the advice of several people (including myself) that Downing Street was an impossible place for anyone whose curiosity extended to seeing every telegram that came in at whatever time of the day or night.

When I arrived at Lord North Street I sailed straight in. I started by saying to Harold that I had been told about his Honours List – I did not tell him by whom – and I hoped that what I heard was mistaken. I went on to say to him that I wished to make it clear that my disquiet did not relate to any particular name, but if in fact the names that I had heard turned out to be a correct report, and he published the List, the List would support legitimate criticism. He would, I said, do himself an immense disservice which he would indeed regret and from which he would never recover.

Wilson was obviously embarrassed by my statement and sought to identify any particular honorands whom I might have in mind. This suggestion I declined. There were several Jewish names on the List and he mentioned one of them as being my most likely choice to be struck off. I assured him that the man concerned had as good or as bad claims as anyone on the List and that my remarks were not addressed to him. Thereupon he made the surprising comment that the agitation about his List was inspired by anti-Semitism.

There is one allegation that could never be made against Harold Wilson: that he was an anti-Semite. He had a great many Jewish friends and I never heard the faintest suggestion of hostility to the Jews coming from him. He was a self-proclaimed, and indeed unarguably so, friend of the Jews, many of whose qualities he greatly respected. I replied to him that if he cared to submit the List to any representative group of Jews, he would hear their 'no' from Downing Street to Golders Green. Whereupon he made a further defensive remark that in any event it was now too late to effect any alterations.

Accepting defeat I withdrew, but I was gratified to learn afterwards that although the bulk of unsuitable candidates remained, he had made certain alterations following my visit. One was to downgrade a proposed new peer to a knighthood; another was to leave out a name completely. To that extent, my intrusion into the matter achieved something.

The List came in for copious criticism and there were a number of insinuations that the List – which had first appeared on a piece of lavender-coloured notepaper – was largely the work of Lady Falkender. How far this was true I do not know, but I do know that any suggestion from her to Harold Wilson was likely to receive an affirmative answer. My intervention, such as it was, became well known and earned me the enmity of two or three people whose awards had been either altered or struck out. I regarded this as totally unfair since in my comments I had not picked on any particular individual.

This was my last formal association with Harold Wilson. I had acquired his confidence, which I believe I still retain, but for a number of reasons which were quasi-political we drifted apart towards the end of his second premiership, and although we have remained on friendly terms, the intimacy has long vanished. I am firmly convinced that it was Harold Wilson's poor judgement in relation to certain advisers that damaged his record as Prime Minister. If examined objectively and without party bias, that record was nevertheless a distinguished one.

The Arts and a Little Craft

THE TELEPHONE RANG and it was Jennie Lee. Did I want to be a member of the Arts Council? 'Yes,' I said, 'certainly. Most agreeable.' Except for the chairmanship of the Committee on London Orchestras, which I describe later, it was my very first invitation to any public office and one of the few that I would be willing to accept. She told me there were sixteen members, that the meetings were every two months and that, although the duties were slight, the Council was an important consultative body and it was not a total sinecure.

Following my assent, I heard no more, but about a fortnight later the telephone rang again, and again it was Jennie. Would I like to be the chairman of the Arts Council? I demurred. I had too much work and could not take on a job that involved any too drastic encroachment into my time. 'It won't take much of your time,' Jennie said, brushing aside my objection. (This was the understatement of the age!) She told me that the current chairman of the Arts Council, Lord Cottesloe, was understood to give about a day a week to the job. She asked me to think about it. I did, but not for long. It was flattering to be asked and a job that I was very willing to do. I telephoned Jennie to say yes and was told that confirmation would come from Tony Crosland, then Secretary of State for Education, a man I knew not very well but liked and whose wife – an attractive and intelligent woman – was a close friend. A short note reached me from him announcing my appointment for a term of five years (subsequently extended by another two years). All this telephoning had taken place in early April 1965 and the appointment was from 1 May of that year.

In so far as my appointment aroused any comment – the appointment of a virtually unknown man to an institution known and loved by very few – it was favourable. A short paragraph in Peterborough in the *Daily*

Telegraph recorded my age, profession and that the appointment had been well received.

A more elaborate comment, having some relationship to fact, came from Christopher Booker, with whom I have had an on-and-off relationship for years, now firmly restored to 'on'. Having secured a seat in my office for the period between leaving Shrewsbury and going up to Cambridge, he launched himself into journalism. Despite my strong disapproval, he wrote a piece in the *Spectator* entitled 'Mr "X" of the New Establishment', beginning with a not very appropriate contrast:

> At the beginning of this week the press spared no effort in giving coverage to the wedding of the man described by the *Daily Telegraph* as 'Mr Peter Raymond, 50, "Teazy-Weazy", the Mayfair hair stylist'. Meanwhile, under the modest disclaimer, 'I am not a public figure, and I have no desire to be one', Mr Arnold Goodman slipped past his appointment as the new chairman of the Arts Council with but a couple of short interviews and a scattering of bare announcements. Which all goes to show that, even in this day, if you want to avoid publicity badly enough you can do so – even if you are, as Mr Goodman is, a fascinating figure, leading a highly active life, holding or about to hold at least two public appointments, and one of the great 'originals' of present-day London.

Jennie realised that I knew little or nothing about the Arts Council, as was the case with most of the human race. She was too busy to be asked to furnish a detailed description, but I had no difficulty in ascertaining that it was the body that administered, and more important financed, almost every artistic activity in the country, except those directly controlled by local authorities and the museums and galleries. Thus, there came under its wing the National Theatre and all other government-subsidised theatrical activities, including the support of numerous repertory theatres; all the symphony orchestras, except those run by the BBC; the opera houses; a small number of small art galleries; arts festivals throughout the country; and a miscellany of minor activities. In short, the artistic life of the country depended to a very large extent on the Arts Council's support but rarely on its inspiration.

It operated in those days by dint of a governing Council of sixteen members and four separate Panels: for the Visual Arts, Drama, Music (including opera and ballet) and Poetry (now Literature). In later years Panels were established for Children's Theatre and for Film and Photography. Each Panel had its own chairman, who was a member of the Council, and a substantial committee of experts or enthusiasts in its field.

The Council and the Panels were supported by the permanent staff, led by the secretary-general and the deputy secretary, who was responsible for financial matters, and four separate directors for Art, Drama, Music and Poetry.

My predecessor Lord Cottesloe – with whom a very warm relationship later developed – demonstrated what seemed to me a somewhat chilly appearance at our first meeting. I learnt afterwards that this was wholly deceptive. He is, I would reckon, a shy man and totally undemonstrative, and first encounters with most people must be discouraging; but he has a warm heart, is kind, immensely courteous and deceptively effective. I sat under his chairmanship at a number of meetings. His technique was the exact reverse of mine; he did not greatly encourage vocality by other members of his committees. I was told that so far as the Arts Council was concerned, they rarely spoke, but at the committees on which I served this was altogether too much for him to hope for. They contained, apart from myself, a number of others difficult to subject to total suppression and we had some lively discussions, but not ones which he greatly enjoyed. However, he could handle an agenda so as to complete it in the minimum of time with the most effective results. He is a civilised man, very fond of painting, but not – so far as I observed – especially interested in the performing arts. I rarely saw him during my period of office at any concert, opera or ballet, or theatre performance. He was, unexpectedly, the chairman of the National Rifle Association, so that presumably he was a deadly shot. This might account for the extreme caution of the members of the Council in relation to him.

Our first meeting was at the Travellers' Club where he offered me a cup of tea and, sensibly, a minimum of advice. 'You will,' he said, 'find that the staff are all a very good lot and that the secretary-general is quite splendid.' Some of this assessment proved valid. I asked if there were any outstanding problems. The only one appeared to be the continued survival of the Royal Philharmonic Orchestra – a matter which had apparently plagued everyone for years, and which I describe later. Shortly thereafter, I found myself at 4 St James's Square: a handsome Georgian house, previously the London home of the Astor family. I was ushered in, received with all the enthusiasm that the secretary-general, Nigel Abercrombie, could muster (I discovered before long that this was a severely rationed quantity) and conducted to the Council chamber – the drawing-room on the first floor.

The Council table was sufficiently large for the members of the Council to sit around it, but by the time the innumerable officials were added, who flitted in and out like members of a Continental *bourse*, the table was full and the room was full of table. I had never attended an Arts Council meeting before and had not, I think, any previous knowledge of any of the members; but I am not by nature particularly shy or timid and was reasonably experienced in the conduct of meetings. The minute book was produced, recording that it was the 124th meeting of the Council, and I signed the minutes of the previous meeting, perjuring myself as to the accuracy of the proceedings of which I knew nothing.

I looked around the table to see some extremely distinguished and interesting faces. The first image to collide with my glance was Henry Moore. There sat this legendary artist – and sat was the word since for the first three or four of my meetings not a sound emerged from that splendid head – benignly and contentedly. He was never late, never appeared remotely bored, and departed the moment the proceedings concluded. He radiated a welcome which I found out later was an expression of a considerable degree of goodwill. At the end of my first meeting, Henry Moore came to me and said that I had handled the meeting as though I had been in charge of the Arts Council for generations. I found this a very pleasing compliment, although I have some doubts about how justified it was. As a member of the Council, Moore had no faults. He listened attentively, agreed with all rational proposals, and made no otiose sounds.

Next to him sat Cecil Day-Lewis, a splendid head, a fine person, the chairman of the Poetry Panel and an informed advocate of the proposals his Panel urged upon us. He was, I knew, a considerable poet. No one had ever suggested that he was a great poet, but his poetry had a clear-cut symbolism and a social philosophy, together with an eclecticism of language that gave it status and entitled him to claim the Poet Laureateship.

I might interpolate here that I was consulted in 1968 by the Prime Minister and his Patronage Secretary over the Poet Laureateship. A notion existed that Robert Graves should be asked. W. H. Auden was at that stage excluded because of his residence in America. I did not myself believe that either Graves or Auden would entertain the appointment for a second. I understood that Graves was sounded and rejected it and Auden was not sounded but regarded as disqualified. The issue was between Day-Lewis and John Betjeman. Day-Lewis was appointed largely, I think, because he was regarded as the more serious and sober candidate in the literary sense. Betjeman had, through the tragic run of fortune, an unexpected second chance and to general satisfaction was appointed laureate in 1972 after Day-Lewis's death.

My view was and still is that the appointment of Day-Lewis was all right if we were going to retain this anachronistic office. It is only very rarely that a writer or poet is so pre-eminent that he deserves a special accolade. This is certainly not the case at the moment either in relation to poetry or prose, and a prose laureate would present problems of selection far exceeding those of its poetry counterpart. But Day-Lewis at that time was looking after poetry in the Arts Council organisation and looking after it extremely well. Some six months later the Council extended its help to other kinds of creative writing – the novel, short stories, biography, autobiography – and the Poetry Panel became the Literature Panel.

Also on the Council was the splendid Myfanwy Piper, the wife of John Piper, an open-faced, vigorous intellectual with qualities rarely found in the middle classes. Her heart always led her towards the side of justice, the side of progress and the side of liberty, and she was an immensely useful member. Then there was the vice-chairman, Sir William Coldstream. He had by that time abandoned, and wisely abandoned, the art of portrait painting; but not before leaving a number of portraits of strangely elongated and miscoloured human beings that may one day destroy or establish him as a great painter. Several people painted by him have complained of his habit of contracting the face so that the subject looks as if it has undergone an unsuccessful piece of plastic surgery. As the vice-chairman Coldstream had qualities, but they were not easily to be perceived. His most alarming quality was invariably at a meeting to take the opposite point of view from that which he had taken up in private. You went into a meeting convinced that you had his full support, only to find that since you had spoken to him his views had swung through 180 degrees. Frequently I would telephone him before a meeting to sound him on some controversial issue and would find that we reached unanimity with the greatest of ease. But how misleading. At the meeting the unanimity vanished without any compunction or shame on his part.

The same was equally true of Coldstream's later successor, John Witt, then chairman of the Art Panel, save that he instinctively took the opposite view but did not change it after you had both entered the chamber. He was a distinguished solicitor, the owner of an important collection of minor paintings, and a generously-minded man, liked by everyone. He had been around the arts for years. He rarely made a speech, never wrote a word that I set eyes on, but was a useful committee man. When he was knighted, the *Evening Standard* rather unkindly pointed to his committee membership to indicate the cause of his elevation; but he gave endlessly of his time, took infinite pains and trouble in sitting on subcommittees, and never let anyone down.

Anthony Lewis, later Sir Anthony, a Professor of Music at Birmingham University, was the chairman of the Music Panel and an exceptionally useful member of the Council. Before his death he graduated to become the very distinguished Principal of the Royal Academy of Music and my own links with him became closer over the years. The arrival of Lewis and his pleasant New Zealand wife in London added a friendly and valuable note to the musical scene.

Another member of the Council was Lord Snowdon. I was charmed by an act of courtesy when, as I arrived for my first meeting, a young man leapt out of a Mini and, with a slight want of logic, said to me: 'I have come to tell you I cannot come.' It turned out to be Tony Snowdon. I thought it was a wonderful gesture and was very touched and thereafter my relationship with him, though not frequent, was friendly and even close. He was a useful member of the Council, remaining silent about matters in which he was not especially interested, but very vocal and emphatic about things he was concerned with – photography, architecture, urban design, and a multitude of other things. He would chime in rather diffidently but with positiveness and it was rare to find the Council or myself in disagreement with him. We were sorry to lose him when his term expired.

I have had several dealings with him since, and indeed represented him in his matrimonial negotiations in 1976, and have always found him to be a person of exceptional courtesy. His behaviour in relation to Princess Margaret at the time of their separation was exemplary and should be an example to everyone as to how a gentleman behaves in circumstances where the most enormous blandishments are offered to him to give his story to a popular newspaper. Anyone who knew him would have realised the utter impossibility of his succumbing to any such proposal, and I have retained and do retain a real admiration for a man who has undergone some very difficult experiences and has emerged totally unscathed.

One incident, however, indicted the extraordinary Bourbon attitude of the Palace staff. Shortly after the separation, Lord Snowdon paid a visit to Australia, and I received a telephone call from his secretary to say that he was returning on a given date and that she would be obliged if I could arrange, either through the Palace or directly through the Heathrow authorities, for him to be given the facilities of the VIP lounge, so that he could avoid the enormous crowd of pressmen that would undoubtedly be thronging around him in an effort to extract some sort of statement.

I telephoned to Heathrow and spoke to the reception officer who assured me that the VIP lounge would be made available and that Lord Snowdon would be first off the plane and able to get there before the press had any opportunity to harass him. This arrangement having been made, I settled back contentedly, only to be telephoned half an hour before he was due to arrive by his secretary in a state of agitation, to say that she understood that all the arrangements had been cancelled. I telephoned urgently to Heathrow to find that it was not their fault, but that they had received a direction from some Palace official that these arrangements should not be permitted.

It was too late to make any change and in the event the poor man had to leave the plane and hump his bags himself through customs and immigration, hounded by journalists all the way. I am quite sure that no member of the royal family had any responsibility in the decision, but that it was simply the notion of some self-important Palace official who thought it was the right thing to do.

Anyway, these and others constituted the members of the Council. We met every two months, with an Executive meeting in between, but it was clear that we had too much to do and in the end we met monthly, sitting from 2 to 5 p.m. or even later on the last Wednesday of every month. The attendance record was remarkable. Most such councils find difficulty in summoning a 50 per cent attendance. It was rare for us not to have 80 per cent and by no means uncommon for us to have 100 per cent. The Council enormously enjoyed the meetings, they loved the discussions and the airing of viewpoints, and they came early and they stayed late.

My relations with the secretary-general on my arrival were ambivalent. Nigel Abercrombie had been seconded from the Admiralty, via a Professorship of French at Exeter University, to the Arts Council at a time when it was felt strongly that a civil servant was needed to install proper notions of discipline and control in the ranks of Bohemia. He was a man of rectitude, dignity and culture, but he did not really like human beings and preferred abstractions to flesh-and-blood realities. He was a devout Roman Catholic and I have a feeling he probably felt more comfortable with other Roman Catholics. That I had such a feeling was for me startling, since I am rarely, if ever, conscious of people's religions and backgrounds. I *am* acutely conscious of their characters, predispositions and interests. I never felt that Abercrombie wholly liked me, but I may well have been mistaken, since on my retirement I received a more touching letter from him than from anyone else in the organisation. He was precise, careful, just, eminently decent, but he was not terribly interested in and somewhat supercilious towards youth and experiment. He had absorbed civil service techniques and wrote letters of superlative clarity. The Arts Council could have done a great deal worse, but he was not the secretary-general required for a vastly expanding scene, with a chairman and a Council anxious to seize the opportunities made available by increasing funds. Nor was he a huge success with Jennie Lee. Jennie was a violently prejudiced woman, and an Admiralty civil servant drawn from the still waters of university life, and a passionate Roman Catholic to boot, would not have been her first choice of a companion for a desert island. It was soon clear to me that there was a warm reciprocity of dislike between Abercrombie and his Minister, and I believe that he was aggrieved by Jennie's decision not to invite the worthy Lord Cottesloe to remain in office.

Abercrombie for a long time could not be mollified, and if I had not had an invincible optimism and a buoyant confidence in my own notions, he would have reduced me to a state of hapless despair within weeks. The cold water he poured on my plans would have filled the reservoirs of the Water Board. But – sometimes very contrary to my real feelings – I maintained an attitude of kindly understanding, which must, I think, have driven him to almost homicidal lengths. As time went on he came to recognise that I was too large and weighty an object totally to obstruct and ultimately he accepted defeat.

In 1968 we appointed a new secretary-general to replace Nigel Abercrombie when he resigned his position to take up – subsequently discharged with some competence – his duties as our regional adviser and organiser. We naturally advertised the job in the press. I take the view that a job of any importance should be advertised. It should not be suspected that a small coterie has perpetuated its power by replacing one place man by another place man.

The advertisement, however, brought a most pitiful response. We had only about a dozen replies. The selection committee, appointed by the Council, interviewed each candidate carefully. The most promising candidate was a semi-retired civil servant who certainly had the intellectual ability and seemingly the imagination to discharge the work. But somewhat cautiously I made a point of reading one of his few publications. It turned out to be a sustained attack on the operation of public subsidy for the arts. On that score alone he did not seem to me ideally suitable to supervise the day-to-day working of the Arts Council. But him apart, there was no suitable candidate.

The problem of the secretary-general was an acute one. An idea, which it later emerged was spectacularly successful, then occurred to me. I invited Hugh Willatt, a practising solicitor who had been the chairman of the Drama Panel for many years and was one of the most influential, although rather taciturn, members of the Council, to supper one evening in my home. I then asked him whether he would consider taking on the secretary-generalship. He was a partner in Lewis Silkin & Co. and obviously earning a comfortable living. The salary that we were able to pay, although slightly enhanced from that of the existing incumbent, was certainly not attractive to anyone in his position if financial considerations were to outweigh others. He thought for a while and said he would like to give the matter some further thought.

To my great delight – and a remarkable tribute to his altruism and regard for the promotion of the arts – he accepted the appointment and suffered a very serious reduction in his income. Happily, however, he was supported by an artist wife (alas, no longer living), who also appreciated that the cultivation of the arts in Britain was sufficiently important to justify personal sacrifices.

As the Arts Council's modest empire expanded, one of our gravest needs was for trained administrators. We were not concerned about the training of those whose activities involved a creative element – theatrical directors and actors, conductors, and all the people who created the performances found their training in the specialist establishments that, good or bad, existed throughout the country, and for some of them outside the country. But administrators had only the most rudimentary form of training. A course existed, which had been set up by our Drama Panel, for training people who wanted to work in repertory theatres as managers and administrators, but otherwise there was nowhere the young aspirant for an administrator's job, in a theatre or art gallery or regional arts association, could find any formal training.

The matter was first mentioned to me in 1966 by Ian Hunter, an immensely specialised impresario and probably the most experienced artistic administrator on a freelance basis in Britain. It seemed clear to me that a plan needed to be evolved, so – as was the frequent practice – I invited my colleagues to lunch at a private room at L'Escargot. To the lunch came, if my recollection serves, Ifor Evans, then Provost of University College, London, Lord Annan, Nigel Abercrombie, and senior officials of the Arts Council. Following this, discussions were started with the Polytechnic of Central London, the outcome of which was the launching of a one-year arts administration course at the Polytechnic in the autumn of 1967.

I attended a few of the course lectures and discussions and was struck by the enthusiasm of the students, but in the early days it was not wholly uncritical. They were right to be critical of the parts provided by the Poly which had been extracted from other courses – the elements of accountancy, bits of law and various pieces of general knowledge which could not have been especially exciting to people anxious to come to grips with specialist problems. But in addition to the parts that came from arts organisations, there were lectures given to them by people like David Webster, the director of the Royal Opera House, Stephen Arlen, who was the director of Sadler's Wells, and Alfred Francis (a general busybody in the arts, particularly at the Old Vic), by practitioners from the National Theatre and the Royal Shakespeare Company, from the Tate Gallery and other art galleries, and from the Arts Council itself. This side of the course the students found exciting and stimulating, and it aroused in them a feeling that the job they were going to do was rewarding and full of meat.

In 1969 the Arts Council set up a committee of inquiry, under Professor Roy Shaw, 'to review the requirements for the professional training of arts administrators in Great Britain, to consider and assess the courses at present undertaken in this field and in particular those undertaken by the Arts Council, and to make recommendations concerning the best fulfilment of these requirements in the future'. The committee reported in 1972. It endorsed the Arts Council's one-year course, suggesting a few improvements, and approved the scale of the operation generally. The committee was particularly concerned that there should be enough vacancies for the newly trained administrators to fill but came to the conclusion that all the students who obtained the course diploma, with the rarest of exceptions, would find immediate employment in the increasing number of institutions and activities that the Arts Council's extra funds had made possible.

My first five years at the Arts Council was a relatively tranquil period. This was not by any means entirely due to me: it was due to the remarkable qualities of the Minister for the Arts, Jennie Lee. Our relationship was idyllic. This is not to say that Jennie was a saint – many people who had dealings with her would regard such an assessment as certifiably insane. If she did not like you, a wide separation was a wise course. She would be censorious, irritable, unfair and totally unco-operative. But she would only not like you if you ought not to be liked. She had a shrewd and almost inspired assessment of human beings. Her major fault, of course, was that while her duties in the arts were non-political, she never dismissed politics in her assessment of human beings. She came, in the years she was Minister for the Arts, to like and even to love a few Tories, but on the whole to her a Tory was a repugnant creature. He was a man who rated himself above his fellows and considered some sorts of humanity inferior to others. This to her was the sin against the Holy Ghost.

Jennie had been brought up in a Scottish village by parents of desperate poverty but determined pride and independence. She had endless tales to tell of them and of the aphorisms of her father, an early trade-union leader and socialist, and one of the pioneers who created a Labour movement which has made sure that the conditions of her early childhood can never be reproduced. Harold Wilson, I have no doubt, was influenced in his appointing of her by an anxiety to have Nye Bevan's ghost in his Cabinet room. But it is ungenerous to believe that this was his sole motivation, and from conversations I knew that he had sensed – with remarkable discrimination – that she was a woman who loved the arts and loved still more the opportunity of bringing them in their best and uncontaminated form to the greatest possible number of her fellow countrymen.

To Jennie, none of the confused thinking of later administrations was even a possibility. She had spent much time with artists of all kinds – musicians, writers and painters – and knew that the genuine artist was an uncompromising creature who would not relax his standards. She was not concerned to bring a mediocre amalgam of artistic bits and pieces to a multitude unprepared to receive the unalloyed product. Hence the years with her presented no problems about reducing quality to increase popularity and other abominable doctrines that deserve incarceration in one of the pits of hell for a shade longer than eternity. But what she wanted fervently and what we worked with her to achieve was that the artistic product should be made intelligible, acceptable and available to more and more people; and during her period of office she achieved this to an extent that will, I think, only be formally recognised many years hence.

Jennie's enthusiasm was the best stimulus that I knew. Her reaction to any proposal, if she trusted its authors, was 'How can we get on with it, where can we get the money?' But if she did not trust the authors, and sometimes her common sense told her that enthusiasm had outrun discretion, she would quietly and kindly deflate bursts of ambitious optimism, a function as valuable as any other she performed.

Jennie made an immense number of friends and almost no enemies, except in a small group of civil servants. To some extent this was her fault, although I discovered for myself that to make friends of civil servants is often an ignominious pursuit. Jennie had heard from Nye Bevan of his battles with civil servants in the various governmental activities in which he had been concerned, particularly in the establishment of the National Health scheme. She viewed them from the outset with suspicion and hostility, and they lost no time in vindicating her. She was a forthright woman, given to plain statement, impatient of circumlocution, hating evasion and above all loathing any attitude of defeatism. The best of civil servants are periphrastic, highly negative and, above all, most unwilling to express any view about anything until it is too late to involve any high degree of responsibility. Jennie met some of the best and many more of the worst, and she lost no time in airing her views about them. Some of the encounters were memorable, and since she was a member of a government where she enjoyed the total support of the Prime Minister and the Chancellor of the Exchequer, the civil servants came ruefully to recognise that in any head-on collision they would be knocked senseless.

I well remember with great satisfaction an occasion when she drew my attention to the fact that the elaborate estimates of expenditure prepared by the Arts Council for submission to the Treasury were being edited by the Department of Education and Science, without consultation with us or even our knowledge, before they went forward for consideration. This was a particularly idiotic thing to do since at the Treasury end my own relationship with the Chancellor of the Exchequer – Roy Jenkins – made him available to me for discussions about estimates and any reductions of them. That they should therefore go forward to him without my knowing what had happened to them created an atmosphere of total unreality if any such discussion ensued. Jennie pointed this out. The civil service answer was that there should be no such discussions and that any views about the estimates should be communicated through the recognised channels – from Treasury civil servant to Department of Education civil servant and then to the Arts Council for passive and uncomplaining acceptance. Jennie regarded this procedure as discourteous and absurd.

A meeting was held in her Department with the Permanent Secretary, the late Sir Herbert Andrew – one of the best civil servants I have met – who, although he conformed wholly to the code, was sensible enough to recognise that Jennie and I required rather special treatment. To everyone's surprise, except my own, he elected to enter the Church as a curate when he retired from the Department of Education. During my tenure at the Arts Council, when occasionally I was minded to explode with fury at some peculiarly offensive manifestation from the civil service, he was the one man capable of soothing me back into relative calm.

At the meeting the discussion went backwards and forwards like a ping-pong rally. In the end a compromise was reached. While I was the chairman of the Arts Council no changes would be made in the estimates without being referred to me for discussion and consideration. When I ceased to be the chairman of the Arts Council the position would alter. I pointed out that the moment my successor was appointed I would acquaint him with the arrangement and tell him not to take office until a similar concession was granted to him. In any event, Jennie's determination that this odd practice should not come into being was yet another reason for her unpopularity.

Nor was her summary treatment of the files regarded with approval. Her civil servants wrote her long minutes inside the covers of governmental files variously marked 'confidential', 'secret', 'restricted', 'private' and so forth. Jennie displayed a lofty disregard for all these rubrics. File after file was tipped into her capacious shopping bag and brought back to be discussed with me at Sunday supper at my home, when the problems of the week were thrashed out. We would sit on the floor examining them and I would suggest suitable replies to minutes such as, 'It is clear that Lord Goodman's intentions in this matter do not conform with the Department's attitude and he should be sternly discouraged.' At the end of the evening all such problems would have been dealt with by a number of pungent minutes in reply, of the partial authorship of which her Department officials could rarely have been in doubt. They muttered, they complained, but like civil servants they did not rebel, they awaited their hour.

One or two experiences caused them particular grief. The headlights were probably the Arts Council's move from St James's Square and various questions of the size of the establishment we were entitled to maintain. The move from St James's Square was unavoidable. It was a splendid house containing a particularly elegant drawing-room, a most magnificent ground-floor office which I occupied, and some rather inadequate reception rooms also on the ground floor, in which small, unimportant and almost unattended exhibitions were arranged by our art department. But so far as the staff were concerned, they were incarcerated in linen cupboards, bathrooms, kitchens and spare bedrooms, in circumstances which were inefficient and inadequate. I complained about the premises from the word go and the civil servants set up a brilliant technique of evasion. A meeting was arranged attended by six or seven departments, or at least six or seven different civil servants, all seemingly dedicated to the task of finding us new premises. They took a note of our requirements, estimated square footage, spoke encouragingly about partitioning, positioning and all the other matters which inspired hopes that something would be done. But nothing was done. We were not offered a single possibility or even anything to go and view. I telephoned and wrote and pressed, only to receive reassuring messages that when something came up we should be told at once. I then indicated that we were going to find somewhere ourselves. We appointed a Council committee consisting of Sir Joseph Lockwood, the chairman of EMI, John Witt and myself, and set off in quest of premises. In the shortest of times Lockwood and Witt found something suitable in Piccadilly. The Department of Education thereupon undertook to conduct the negotiations, which they did to such good purpose that they broke down within hours. Whereupon I took them over. The Department then kindly undertook to value the premises from the point of view of a rental, arriving at a figure which I thought was excessive, so we commissioned a firm of private agents to negotiate a substantially lower rental and we proceeded to agree a highly satisfactory form of lease.

However, we had not reached the end of the road. The Department then indicated that they must get clearance from a bureau which existed to determine whether government offices should or should not be located in London. I telephoned the bureau and mildly pointed out to them that the Arts Council operated with 20 or so voluntary members of the Council and a voluntary chairman, about 120 voluntary members of Panels, and received visits weekly from many scores of voluntary artistic enthusiasts from all over the country and indeed the world. The 'Voice' of the bureau stated that he felt quite sure that entirely suitable accommodation could be found at Basingstoke or Woking, to which I replied genially that my own resignation and several hundred others would be on his desk within hours. I received a telephone call shortly afterwards to say that we had been 'cleared for London'.

The question of the establishment was another occasion when we aroused hatreds which at the time I did not recognise. It arose in several ways, but classically when I was informed by faces covered with solemn foreboding that we would undoubtedly be 'surcharged' because of a duplication in Scotland. The duplication in Scotland turned out to be a situation where, in the absence on sick leave of the director of the Scottish Arts Council, his successor designate was appointed six months earlier than intended, so that for a period of six months the sitting tenant and the new man were both receiving salaries – an arrangement humane and sensible but totally repugnant to the civil service. Our own Mr McRobert, the deputy secretary of many years, and a really splendid man who had spent his life playing the civil service game but without the reverence for it that ruled out serious discussion, informed me that he could see no way out of the dilemma. The Scots had perpetrated the most awful solecism and 'someone' had to pay.

The amount involved was not so forbidding that the possibility of a whip-round among the Arts Council could be ruled out as a solution, but before resorting to this expedient a meeting was summoned and there appeared in my room no fewer than eleven people. High dignitaries from the Department of Education, a functionary from the Treasury, Establishment Officers, Dis-Establishment Officers, and a team of our own advisers, all nodding their heads ruefully at the possibility of a duplication of function. I innocently enquired at the outset if I could see the Scottish Arts Council establishment. 'Why,' said the principal spokesman of the funeral party, 'do you wish to see the establishment?' 'Well,' I said, 'if we have one man too many it must be one more than the permitted number. We ought therefore to see whether the permitted number is prescribed and how many it is.' Gloating looks crossed their faces. This type of evasion would get me nowhere. 'There is no establishment,' they said. 'But,' I replied, pressing my advantage, 'if there is no establishment and no number prescribed, we cannot be in excess of the prescribed number.' Scowls replaced the prim looks. 'The establishment,' they said sourly, 'is in the Charter.' 'Have we a copy?' I asked politely. No copy was forthcoming from any of the baker's dozen, but a copy was sent for and I read it. It said that the Arts Council had a chairman, a Council of a given number, a secretary-general, and could employ such other personnel as it considered necessary, so long as it paid rates that were consistent with comparable Treasury rates. I looked around them with an expression of studied innocence. 'We have,' said I, 'surely considered it necessary to employ these two gentlemen. What, pray, is the difficulty?' Within seconds a disconsolate throng was leaving the room. The interrogation and the inquiry to which they had looked forward for some time had been summarily terminated.

I next crossed swords with the civil service when it was brought to my notice that the award of honours to artists – using the word in its widest sense – and particularly to authors was giving offence. Distinguished authors were offered, and frequently accepted, the award of an OBE. This is a medium honour much welcomed by deserving but middling civil servants, police officers, headmasters, those who have worked for many long years to assist charities and others – those who are, in fact, the backbone of the country. But an important writer felt some resentment that he should be categorised – although not on grounds of snobbery – with this particular company. I suggested to Harold Wilson that it would be a good idea to create a special award for the arts. To start with, it would bestow on a deserving artist an opportunity to earn a modest fee by designing a medal of an aestheticism unusual with present awards.

The idea commended itself to Harold Wilson, who always liked to feel that he was on the side of the angels, so long as they did not intrude into Cabinet discussions. He approached the matter with the head of the civil service, Sir Laurence Helsby, and asked him to discuss it with me. This was the first time I had a discussion on the same plane as the utterances in *Alice in Wonderland*. The creation of this new award was obviously repugnant to Sir Laurence and, he told me, would not be welcomed by his senior colleagues. Basically, the civil service took exception to the notion that artists are in some way different from the rest of mankind. Although, alas, not one myself, my simple viewpoint is that they are different from the rest of mankind in one or more important particulars. This is not a matter on which it is necessary to enlarge, but it was perfectly clear that what caused particular offence was the idea that a system of awards of immense importance to civil servants should include honours for another, and different, section of mankind. Harold Wilson was argued out of the idea and it has never been revived, but it would certainly be a nice thing to introduce and I hope that a current prime minister might decide that this is a modest reform that is unlikely to have revolutionary consequences.

I little realised at the time that these exercises on my part had not made friends and influenced people. In short, to outmanoeuvre the civil service, which is indispensable if you are to continue in a sensible way of life, is to arouse their bitterest hatred. You can only be loved if you conform and if you conform you must be inefficient. Neither I nor my colleagues on the Arts Council conformed, we were tolerably efficient and we were not loved by government officials. The extent to which we were hated was not demonstrated until Jennie's fairly protective presence had been removed. Then, and only then, did these miserable creatures crawl out of the woodwork and attempt their onslaught.

Jennie Lee was replaced by Lord Eccles when the Conservatives came to power in 1970. Having had my term as chairman renewed, I had to remain with Lord Eccles for over a year. My relationship with him was a perfectly cordial one. He would not have been my choice as Minister for the Arts, however, since there was a rigidity about him which I found difficult to deal with and his approach to matters was totally different from my own. Not only did he lack any particular affection for artists, but he regarded them as members of the community who could be dealt with on a summary basis. Although I do not believe he instigated the move, the fact remains that after six and a half years at the Council, I arrived one day to find a letter from the Auditor-General telling me that the Public Accounts Committee desired to discuss at a meeting the Arts Council's activities in relation to two matters.

The Public Accounts Committee was a body of whose existence I had enjoyed a contented ignorance for the whole of an active life. The letter had been brought in by the senior officials of the Arts Council, with faces as long as French loaves, indicating at once that the major catastrophe of all time had hit my regime. 'This,' they said, 'is terrible.' 'What,' I said, 'is this?' 'The Auditor-General,' they said. 'He has got it in for us.' I discovered that this gentleman was the equivalent of the Head of the Ogpu. He was the civil servant dreaded by all other civil servants, since he invigilated all their activities and could draw attention at any time to any shortcoming. Once a year he prepares a list of charges against his flock, published in a voluminous report which he presents to a Parliamentary Committee called the Public Accounts Committee. The very sound of that name produced such a knocking of knees and chattering of teeth among my colleagues that I doubted they would all survive the ordeal.

What felonies had we committed? Stripped of civil service jargon, they amounted to this. First, and presumably the more serious, that in the few years since we had been authorised to commit a sum of money each year for buildings, we had, in view of the great excess of demand over supply, adopted the practice of maintaining pencilled-in lists of applicants whose needs could not be met out of the current year's buildings grant, so that, on the broad basis of 'first come first served', they would enjoy a priority out of any grant we received in ensuing years. Not only was this practice sane and sensible, but we had been directed to adopt it in a Treasury letter which was – in the course of the subsequent proceedings – analysed with as much care as was bestowed on any Dead Sea Scroll. But the letter stood up. Unlike the charge, it said in simple terms what it meant, and that we – simple men – had so acted on it ultimately shone through the miasma of confusion and complication that sought to establish that black was white.

The second charge was the terrible indictment that we had allowed the Sadler's Wells Opera Company, whose move to the Coliseum had been cautiously encouraged by us, to run into a deficit in its first year after transplant. The fact that we subsidised this theatre in conjunction with the Greater London Council, and that all our customers were self-reliant organisations, enjoying total autonomy under responsible boards, was nowhere referred to – at least not by the enemy.

I decided that I should approach the Minotaur myself. 'You wish to speak to the Auditor-General!' said my officials with tremulous voices. 'Nobody speaks to the Auditor-General.' Obviously it was much easier to have a conversation with the Almighty, in their view, than a short exchange on the telephone with the Auditor-General. However, I persevered and in due course discovered the telephone number and asked to be put through. I had a feeling that at the other end someone was saying to the Auditor-General, 'Look sir, this instrument, you see it here, you've never used it. Now you take the earpiece in your left hand and put it to your ear, then speak into the mouthpiece. You will hear Lord Goodman and conduct a conversation. You may rightly regard it as a miracle of scientific development, but you may trust us that it works.'

In any event, in due course a rather rasping voice came through saying, 'Yes?' 'Sir Bruce,' I said (I think that was his name), 'I wanted to talk to you about the Arts Council because this suggestion that we should appear before the Public Accounts Committee could do a good deal of harm to our fund-raising activity.' 'Can't help that,' he snapped. I persevered slightly but soon observed that I was up against a brick wall, and being one who lacks the physical resources for destroying brick walls, decided that on the whole we had better proceed with the matter. In due course I heard that arrangements had been made for our arraignment before the committee.

But before that, two matters arose. The chairman of the Public Accounts

Committee that year was Harold Lever. The Auditor-General discovered that Harold Lever was more than well-known to me and he sought him out and said, 'Mr Lever, do you think you ought to preside over this committee since I believe that Lord Goodman is rather a pal of yours?' Mr Lever made what I regard as a historic reply: 'A pal?' he said. 'No, he is not a pal of mine, he is a very dear friend.' And that was the end of that discussion.

The second problem was that the Auditor-General made determined efforts to prevent me from appearing in front of the committee by taking the view that only our accounting officer, who was the mild and gentle Hugh Willatt, should be allowed to appear. Hugh had the courage of a lion but he also had the qualities of a much tamer animal. He did not present a terrifying appearance, and it was perfectly clear that something of a more formidable appearance was needed if we were to deal with the committee.

The practice is that the committee is composed equally of members of the opposition and members of the government, the government having one member more to ensure a voting majority, but the chairman is always drawn from the opposition. I sought the assistance of Harold Wilson, since he had been a chairman of the committee when the Labour Party were previously in opposition, and I asked him if he knew of a precedent when the chairman of an organisation appeared even though he was not the accounting officer. With that almost incredible memory he proceeded to reel off a list of hearings before this committee when a chairman had appeared. Armed with these, I wrote to the chairman of the committee to say that I would be appearing with Hugh Willatt and with our assistant secretary in due course.

The trial took place in a Committee Room in the House of Commons, under conditions that would have horrified Judge Jeffreys. The public was totally excluded and even a Member of Parliament who sought entrance was brusquely discouraged – notwithstanding that he was a member of the Arts Council. The former Minister for the Arts, Jennie Lee, racing to defend her fledglings, was turned from the door like Queen Caroline from the Coronation. The actual proceedings resembled an Asian bazaar far more than a judicial tribunal. The members of the committee arrived and departed haphazardly throughout the proceedings, so that I doubt if any member was in attendance for the whole performance. At the first session, during the presence of a temporary chairman, the committee gave me the clearest warning that I was there on sufferance and that it would be no great grief on their part if I found myself better occupied elsewhere. In fact, when I endeavoured in the course of this first session to utter some word of simplification, a roar that would have been envied by a bull of Basan emerged from the lips of the MP then presiding and I was driven for want of operatic powers to subside.

It would, I think, be wrong if I did not edify my readers by an excerpt from these proceedings. The first indictment, to which I referred, arose from the suggestion that, as we had made promises to local councils for payments in future years, in a sense we had created a commitment, although we did not have the money. When we were asked about this, I strongly denied that we had created any commitment.

'But,' they said, 'you told these people that you would give them the money.'

'Yes,' I said, 'but only on condition that we would give it to them if it was voted to us.'

'Was there not then a legal commitment?' they asked.

'Certainly not. I speak as a lawyer and you can consult any other lawyer you like, and I also have the authority of Mr Justice Scarman that this is the correct view.'

'Well then, was there not a moral commitment?'

'Yes,' I said, 'there was a moral commitment; had we been given the money and *not* given it to the local council we would have behaved very improperly.'

'Wasn't there something midway between a legal commitment and a moral commitment?'

'Alas,' I said, 'I do not know of anything midway between legal and moral commitments and due to shortage of money we are unable to employ any Chinese metaphysician to deal with the situation.'

This was regarded as a rather flippant reply by some of the committee, but at the end of the day the result was triumphant. The Public Accounts Committee resolved not merely that we were not at fault in either of the courses we adopted, but that if we had not adopted either course we would then have been at fault, since the support of the arts depended upon the people who ran these bodies having sufficient courage to take decisions of an unorthodox nature when they were important to maintain institutions.

But the whole episode left a disagreeable taste. It was true that we had been handsomely vindicated, but we had constantly detected an animus which we had never suspected and which seemed devoid of any constructive purpose. There were people – albeit not a great number – who resented us and were only too happy to do public damage to an institution totally dependent on the morale and spirit of a group of volunteers.

I do not wish to do any injury to the Auditor-General, the Public Accounts Committee or the individuals ensconced in their various eyries who had inspired all this out of a detestation of anything that challenged their form of society. I knew that an Arts Council and a civil service could only live in concord if the civil service element was a special and unusual one. When it became a characteristic one, it resented the autonomy of an Arts Council which had power to spend money, a willingness to speak its mind, a capacity to make everything it did known to the public, and a genuine belief that the public should know.

Another brush with the civil service came almost at the end of my second term in office, when it occurred to me that I ought to procure some recognition for Hugh Willatt. He was the last man in the world who would have made any suggestion or would have regarded himself as having any special claim, but that was an additional reason for procuring a suitable award: a view that was shared by all my senior colleagues.

I went to see David Eccles, with whom I had a workable, but by no means easy, relationship. The fact that the relationship existed at all was, I think, to his credit. Almost all my views, political and artistic, would not have been shared by him. However, when I made the request that he should nominate Willatt for a knighthood, it was clear that this involved no enthusiasm, but he said that he would 'ask Ted'.

Willatt was not the sort of man who would have inspired much admiration in David Eccles. Willatt was a quiet, unspectacular, unassertive man, possessing no commercial instincts and probably – although I had no idea at the time – preferring leftish rather than rightish political views. However, Eccles had promised that he would speak to Ted Heath about it. A few days later he reported that the civil service reaction made it impossible. They did not regard Willatt as occupying, according to their hierarchy, a sufficiently senior post to justify the award in civil service terms. I was disappointed but persistent. I asked Eccles if he would mind if I spoke to Ted Heath. It was difficult for him to refuse but his agreement was certainly grudging.

My relationship with Ted Heath has always been a friendly one and at that moment it enjoyed a special strength. At Heath's invitation I was commuting for many months between London and Rhodesia, leading a small delegation in negotiations with Ian Smith. I asked Robert Armstrong, the Principal Private Secretary, if he would arrange for me to see the Prime Minister for a few minutes only. I saw him that very day, immediately before a Cabinet meeting. I made my request and got a favourable response immediately. 'Certainly,' he said, and made a note on his pad. I left satisfied, thinking this was the end of the story. But it had a more interesting ending.

As the publication of the Birthday Honours List approached, I studied Willatt closely to see whether there was some evidence of unusual gratification. He was an impassive man and nothing emerged. He would, of course, have been unlikely to mention it to me since there is a pledge of confidence before the award is published. However, I was uneasy. My unease prompted a further telephone call to Robert Armstrong. I asked him for reassurance about Willatt's knighthood. There was an awkward silence. 'I had intended to tell you. William Armstrong [then the head of the civil service] would not have it. I am so sorry.' I remained calm. In my best approach to a silky voice I asked him: 'Could you do me another small service, Robert? Could you ask the Prime Minister if he will see me again, if only for a few moments. I shall be most obliged and would be prepared to come at any time of the day or night.' A slight silence intervened. 'I will come back to you very shortly,' he replied. About an hour later I was telephoned. 'I am happy to tell you that the knighthood has been reinstated in the Honours List. It will appear next week.' Again, no comment is called for, except that even Robert Armstrong could not sustain the concerted hostility of the civil service to a particular award. I doubt very much whether Ted Heath had been told of the decision and it was only when it was clear that he was to be reminded of a broken promise that right prevailed.

The civil service has many admirers. Great numbers of people believe that it is infinitely to be preferred to a system such as in the United States where the major administrative appointments are changed at each election. On this I will not presume to judge. I can only recount my own experiences and the fact that in any area in which I have had any significant role to play, with the rarest of exceptions, the civil service intervention has not been helpful.

There were, of course, spectacular exceptions: Robert Armstrong being one and Sir Patrick Nairne, when I encountered him at the Department of Health and Social Security, another. However, they are few and far between, but do serve to demonstrate that it would be possible to empanel into service a body capable of rendering high service to the nation without intruding the *corps d'élite* notions that are at present so injurious.

A spectacular example of civil service negativism occurred at the start of my chairmanship of the Housing Corporation in 1973. It was obvious to me that housing was being starved of the necessary financial resources and this prompted me to make a suggestion to Ted Heath about raising money for housing. I knew, of course, of the firm principle of non-hypothecation – that for some idiotic reason a tax could not be levied on the basis that it would be appropriated for a particular purpose or service – but in my view my suggestion was worthy of investigation for the general purpose of attracting more public revenue in the most painless fashion. I proposed that a new governmental bond should be floated. This would have two characteristics: that the so-called coupon, i.e. interest rate, attached to it should be a low one, but that this would be compensated for by the concession that any individual who had retained the bond for at least five years prior to his death should have a substantial mitigation in death duty or, as it is now called, inheritance tax. It seemed to me, from my professional knowledge of the anxiety of the rich to mitigate death duties, that such a benefit would have a massive appeal. In my recommendation to the Prime Minister I linked it with the need for more housing revenue.

I spoke to Ted about it who, from his expert knowledge of public finance, obviously had a worthwhile opinion. He regarded the proposal as worthy of consideration and told me that he would refer it to the Treasury if I would put it on paper. I wrote a brief paper and submitted it to his private secretary. A total silence then ensued for well over a year. During that time I had forgotten all about it and was busily occupied producing other rejectable proposals. But to my surprise, after the long period of silence, I was telephoned by a senior Treasury official who asked if he might come to discuss the proposal with me. He arrived with a Treasury file several inches thick from which it was clear that memos had been exchanged in all directions, the cost of which could certainly have been adequate to fund a small housing estate. He told me that the proposal had been received seriously and that the Treasury wished to discuss it further. Would I be prepared to attend a meeting? I was and did.

At that time there was working for me a remarkable young man by the name of David Astor, then very young but enlisted as my assistant at the Housing Corporation, who displayed intelligence and energy of great value. I asked him to come to the meeting with me since I believed it was something that would interest him. I am glad that I did, as there is a valuable independent witness. At the meeting there were a number of Treasury officials and two plainly bright and promising young men, seemingly of some seniority. In the course of the discussions, in which they produced endless and no doubt valid arguments about the difficulties connected with the new bond, one of the young men suddenly remarked to me: 'What's all this fuss about housing?' I looked at him enquiringly. 'Have you,' he asked, 'ever been to Naples? Large areas of Neapolitan housing are much worse than anything we have.' I rejoined rather hotly that the relevance of Neapolitan housing was obscure. 'It is,' I said testily, 'certainly the case that the morality at Port Said is inferior to many parts of England, but what that has to do with it I do not know.' However, the second young man, leaping to his defence, said that although it was always regarded as a burlesque comment, he well knew that in many areas where new houses had been introduced, the baths were used as coal scuttles.

I departed from the meeting with a feeling of great indignation. I wrote to Anthony Barber, the Chancellor of the Exchequer. I told him that I had no wish to identify anyone but reported the two comments that had been made by senior Treasury officials. I did not ask him to take any action in the matter except to be kind enough to ensure in the national interest that neither of these young men was, until further trained, engaged in any activity relating to human happiness. I received a startled reply from the Chancellor to say that he was certainly investigating the matter and would write me further. It may well be that in the years to come he will be reminded to write the letter but until this moment of time it has still to arrive. Of my proposal, needless to say, I heard nothing more.

In 1966 I was appointed a member of the British Council, a year after my appointment as the chairman of the Arts Council. The justification and indeed powerful reason for my appointment was to strengthen the then very exiguous link between the two bodies. It was sensible to do this. No subsequent chairman or any other representative of the Arts Council has joined the British Council since my initial appointment. It would be nice to claim that such was the competence with which I discharged my listening duties that any further presence was unnecessary. However, it is likely that I served – as I have often – a specialised function which is unflattering but useful: that of a troubleshooter.

In 1976 I was appointed, and remained until 1991, the deputy chairman of the British Council. It was in that role that I had yet another experience of dealing with the civil service. In 1980, Sir John Llewellyn (then the director-general of the British Council) was due to retire. When he had been appointed he had accepted the terms of engagement offered as advertised or notified subsequently, but imposed one simple and perfectly reasonable condition that on his retirement he should receive a pension at least as good as the pension he would have received on retirement if he had remained for the full term as the vice-chancellor of Exeter University.

When Sir John's moment for retirement came, the Council's chairman, Dick Troughton, ascertained the size of the pension Sir John would have received at Exeter and which he naturally expected to receive from the British Council through the Treasury. To Troughton's astonishment, however, and indeed to the astonishment of every right-thinking human being, the civil service discovered an extraordinary and highly discreditable loophole. They had discovered that during Sir John's period at the Council the terms of the Exeter pension had been changed and subsequently improved. Sir John's stipulation was clear beyond argument: that he should receive the pension that would have come to him at the moment of leaving Exeter, i.e. the improved pension then payable.

The Treasury stuck resolutely to the claim that he was only entitled to the pension on the original terms. No words could be strong enough to describe this attitude. It was breach of faith amounting to positive dishonesty. Dick Troughton and the rest of the board were horrified. In conference with Dick I expressed the view, which he shared, that this position was untenable and was unlikely to be maintained in contact with the responsible Minister, who at that time was Christopher Soames. When we requested an interview with him it was found that he was then operating – as he did with great success – in Rhodesia. In consequence we had our interview with Paul Channon – a good and old friend and a man in whom I had the greatest confidence.

Dick Troughton and I trekked off to his headquarters and after an exhausting walk along a long corridor and numerous steps arrived breathless in his office. It was, I think, this exhausting walk – which I have always believed was cunningly planned by the civil servants concerned – that had a debilitating effect on our eloquence. In any event, we presented the case to Paul. When we arrived he was sitting at his desk flanked by civil servants on every side. We made our representations in moderate language, expecting that there could be no effective argument in reply. Paul listened carefully and then was consulted by the civil servants who encircled him for several minutes for discussion. It was clear that they were engaged in passionate exhortation. The reputation of the civil service for defeating rational approaches from the civilian body was clearly at stake – an experience which, as I have already recounted, I had met several times at the Arts Council.

At this point of time they succeeded. Paul, looking thoroughly embarrassed, said words to the effect that he had been persuaded that our case could not succeed and terminated the interview. Dick and I departed in a state of utter dejection, but the Goodman pecker was up. 'We will not,' I said to him, 'accept this.' 'But what do we do?' he said. 'We go back again next week,' was my simple recommendation. Another meeting was arranged, generously accorded by Paul, which is what I would have expected of him.

The next week we returned. I insisted on making the return journey slowly, with frequent intervals to regain my breath. We arrived in immaculate fighting form. Dick spoke first with great emphasis and effect. I then weighed in to say that in the whole history of civil service transactions I did not believe that greater perfidy had ever been demonstrated; it would, I said, reflect great discredit on any government that accepted this position. I have rarely seen a Minister less happy about a situation where he had either to repudiate his advisers or repudiate simple morality. I never had any doubt about Paul's decision. He turned away from his civil servants and said in a quiet voice, 'I am satisfied that you are right. He must have the larger pension.' The expression on the faces of his civil servants is a memory of lasting satisfaction to me. We departed jubilantly to announce the result of our representations to a relieved Sir John – to whom the matter made a very substantial difference for his later years. I cannot remember any encounter with civil servants – apart from my exchanges with the Public Accounts Committee about the Arts Council – which has given me greater pleasure.

This brings me to the relationship between the Minister for the Arts and the Arts Council. When Harold Wilson came to power in 1964, theoretical objections had been raised to the appointing of a Minister because of the possibility of conflict between the two principal figures in the equation. This theoretical question did not arise while Jennie was my Minister. She worked with me as a sort of super chairman. It was not necessary for us to define the respective functions of the Department and the Arts Council. She did not get in the way and she did not allow her minions to get in the way. We therefore deceived ourselves that an arrangement empirically excellent was theoretically so. It required a situation where the two principal figures did not operate in sympathy, had divergent notions and divergent objectives, to demonstrate the difficulties of an Arts Council of present-day character operating under the canopy of a ministry.

If the Arts Council operates as it should, it has no need of ministerial control and no means of conforming to it. The Council is a large body that makes major policy decisions which are carried out by the chairman, the secretary-general and the staff. No Minister can operate without disrupting the smooth working of such a system. The Minister's function is to provide the money, to seek to procure the greatest amount possible and, in discussion and consultation with the chairman, to learn of the intended policy and if necessary to express his views. But his views can have no greater cogency than those of any member of the Council and probably less since they are not aired at the relevant moment of decision.

This, of course, is legitimately the source of grievance and complaint to an enthusiastic and ambitious Minister. He wishes to direct the arts. Between him and that direction is a large independent body of people who rate him as a useful animal for finding money, respect him if he finds it in greater abundance than hitherto, but have no real use for his views on artistic matters, since they have a duty to base their views on the best professional and public opinions that obtain. The Minister's tiny circle of advisers can show no such expertise.

It is natural that I should support the continued existence of the Arts

Council and advocate that the Minister should exercise only the restricted functions that an autonomous Council assigns to him. Otherwise the Minister's department must expand and become a ministry of culture. It must, under the direction of a Minister, then plan and put into effect the artistic schemes and projects which are politically desirable and financially possible. This means a political control of artistic matters. To allow such a control is unthinkable. Departments are calculated to interfere, in the ultimate analogy, with real freedom of thought. The Arts Council is a splendid body. It operates on two simple and sensible principles. It does not accept, and I hope never will, government direction as to the utilisation of its money and how to promote the arts. It does not impose on its beneficiaries any direction which trammels the use of that money, except so as to ensure proper financial controls, economies and the best spread. A theatre subsidised by the Arts Council is free to perform what it wishes; it gives value in the broadest financial terms. An orchestra can play the pieces of its own choice; a painter can exhibit whatever works he is minded to paint, always assuming that a sufficient body of informed opinion recommends the expenditure of Arts Council money for the purpose.

And here is another rub. It can be argued and indeed in my time was argued often that the Arts Council Panels, large and comprehensive as they were, could not comprehend every shape of human activity in the world of art. There would be left out experimentalists, non-conformists and conformists, the unconventional and conventional, fashionable and unfashionable, simply because at a given moment of time the consensus of general artistic opinion represented by the Panels did not extend to that category of artistic activity. No human institution can wholly avoid this criticism or in some degree fail to see it. Undoubtedly there were worthy causes and worthy exponents who were turned away by the Arts Council and particularly when the judgement fell within the discretion of an occasional idiosyncratic officer. But so far as can be humanly contrived we did try to avoid it. We travelled to the extreme limits. Sometimes we went over the edge of what to me and many others appeared to be sensible, since only by going over the edge could we cover the total area. I took the view, unrepentantly, that some wastage of public money was unavoidable to achieve an ecumenical approach that would give confidence to the whole art world. The wastage was trivial in terms of percentages, but it meant that on the whole almost any artistic experience short of dementia had a chance of receiving some encouragement within our walls, and the effect was healthy and buoyant in relation to artists of real quality. They approved immensely because they sensed that the old canons of restrictive censorship and repression were being reduced to a minimum.

This had an importance in itself, coinciding as it did with the general libertarianism of the period, and did much good in fomenting an atmosphere of artistic freedom.

Sceptics will argue that in this atmosphere of artistic freedom little of great quality has emerged. I do not dissent from that view. In the field of literature we have at the moment few great writers. In the visual arts we have a small number of immensely distinguished exponents whose work will be judged by ensuing generations. In the world of music we are pitifully bereft. We have two or three composers who have obtained international eminence but it is arguable whether their work will survive for posterity. We have had and continue to have a rich crop of dramatists as good as or better than any generation and it is not without relevance that these dramatists have developed in the greatly expanding theatre of subsidy where they feel at home. It would be difficult to think of any dramatist of quality today who does not owe his major debt of recognition to the subsidised theatre. If subsidy had done nothing else than this it would have vindicated the modest expenditure involved.

No amount of money can manufacture an artist. What may manufacture artists is the development of an informed, understanding and loving public, available to receive and appreciate the artist's work. Money is useful to keep the artist alive, to feed him and to maintain him in a fashion which is respectable for a civilised community. He is not required to accept support or assistance of this kind. If his freedom and independence of spirit make it undesirable to receive support from the state, no one will thrust it upon him. I do not believe in forcible feeding. But he need not feel that it is ignominious or humiliating to receive subsidy. The state today is organised in a fashion where a large element of a man's earnings are taken away from him to provide him with social and public amenities. The arts are a social and public amenity and the artist is simply receiving that share of the public treasury which enables a government to discharge its duties so far as artistic provender is concerned.

When I became chairman of the Arts Council, the Minister for the Arts was Jennie Lee and the Prime Minister was Harold Wilson. Neither of them claimed any great knowledge of the arts, but both held the firm political view that the promotion of the arts was a simple necessity to procure a more civilised world and – a view about which there is now much disagreement – that the cost of its adequate promotion should fall on public funds. This view persisted for successive governments. Edward Heath subscribed to it and Jim Callaghan subscribed to it. The successive Ministers for the Arts after Jennie Lee, namely Lord Eccles, Hugh Jenkins, Jack Donaldson, Paul Channon, Norman St John Stevas and Grey Gowrie, the last of these apostles, all maintained a firmly bipartisan policy that the arts should receive maximum support, although there was increasingly an emphasis – to which I wholly subscribe – that as much money as possible should emerge from the private wing. Hence the establishment of the Association for Business Sponsorship of the Arts in the 1970s, which I chaired, the object of which was to stimulate gifts to the arts from business in its widest sense, i.e. industrial organisations, joint stock banks, stockbrokers, merchant banks and the like.

In my day the notion that public subsidy for the arts, or indeed any support for the arts, could be inappropriate would not have been uttered in either House of Parliament except by a person of rare courage. But with the arrival of Mrs Thatcher there was a complete revolution in that. Things have changed, in my view horribly deteriorated, to a point where it does not require heroism to air the view that there should be no public support for the arts. And the view has even been expressed by some outstanding analphabete that support for the arts in general, in the terms in which we have previously urged it, is wrong. I could not have devoted the many years I have to the arts if I had not at all times regarded this view with astonishment and, I have to say, disgust.

An undoubted complication is the recent appointment of a Heritage Minister who has a variety of duties of which the arts is by no means the most prominent. The present appointee, Mr Peter Brooke, controls broadcasting, sports, the heritage and more, and it is difficult to see how he can have much time for the arts or to follow the traditional pattern of constant visits to artistic institutions involving numerous journeys outside London.

At the moment of writing it is known to have been the intention of at least one Minister for the Arts to reorganise the Arts Council, to a point of almost total emasculation, by directing that the regional arts associations be given the responsibility of funding the various beneficiaries included in their territory. There is so much wrong with this proposal that I will spare the reader a lengthy criticism, except to say that its basic plan is a completely untenable belief that the operation of ten different and virtually autonomous councils would be cheaper than operating under the single Arts Council.

The inadequacy of the proposal is best demonstrated by the fact that it shows no regard whatever for any function of the Arts Council other than the granting of money. However, to take just one example, the Arts Council was almost entirely responsible for the introduction of Public Lending Right in this country after a very long delay and protracted arguments. Although at first of a singularly ungenerous character – it gave significant wealth only to the most popular writers – PLR has developed in strength by the receipt of additional sums of money, and although the present arrangement is by no means satisfactory for the indigent author, it looks better today than it did at the date of its introduction.

The Council in my day also made representations to the Treasury on the subject of the taxation of authors and presented a variety of alternative schemes, none of which was adopted by the Treasury in full, but in one at least they responded to a suggestion that an author should not be charged Capital Gains Tax if he disposed of a copyright more than five years after the creation of the book.

We also conducted elaborate discussions with the 'art' unions – Equity, the Musicians Union and the National Union of Journalists. The Council assisted in negotiations with all three in several cases and indeed was responsible for the successful outcome of such negotiations. An activity of considerable importance, which was established by the Council after taking technical advice, was the introduction of a scheme for the training of art administrators, which I have already described; and it was responsible for launching the Theatre Investment Fund, which I describe later. This list is by no means exhaustive, but it gives an indication of what sensible efforts would be lost if the present reform comes into being.

It is unfortunate that no one responsible for the arts would appear to know enough about the prestige of the Arts Council, established more than forty-five years ago, and in particular has no knowledge of the exceptional respect in which it is held in other countries, particularly the USA. But it may not be too late to save it, and I instance the sort of view held about it in America, published in a symposium produced by the *Encyclopaedia Britannica*. This symposium contained chapters – some in detail – on the way in which artistic activity was promoted and subsidised in various countries and a short narrative about the Arts Council and my role in relation to it. It remains to say that I too entertained the highest regard for the Council and the way in which it discharged its functions.

Of all unconsidered decisions, my acceptance of the chairmanship of the Arts Council is the one I have had least occasion to regret. From the moment of my appointment, until the day of the Council's farewell to me in 1972, I relished every second of it. There was no problem that was sufficiently unpleasant to sour the whole activity. I leave it to others to assess my success or otherwise at the job. Here, I have restricted myself to a few highlights of an experience of immense richness and variety that I rate the most agreeable that any man can have.

Orchestral Manoeuvres

I WAS FIFTY-ONE at the time of Harold Wilson's election in 1964, and I did speculate about whether I might be offered some job to do. I had reached a stage in my profession when partial relief from legal practice would be welcome. I enjoyed practising the law but could not conceal my increasing impatience and distaste for a legal system of almost demented formalism where the ritual was far more important to the practitioners than any other element. While I could not contemplate retirement from a practice and a clientele to whom I owed heavy responsibilities, I was certainly not unwilling to devote a portion of my day to some other palatable activity.

As I was to discover, and to my delight, I was eventually appointed chairman of the Arts Council in May 1965, but the first official intimation that I enjoyed governmental favour was an approach a short while after the election from Jennie Lee, by then appointed the first Minister for the Arts. She wanted to know whether I would chair a committee to consider whether it was possible and desirable to maintain the four London orchestras which were then in receipt of public subsidy. The four were the London Symphony Orchestra, the London Philharmonic Orchestra, the New Philharmonia Orchestra and the Royal Philharmonic Orchestra.

The problem at the time was that shortage of money had led to the demand that one orchestra at least was too many and should be axed. Harold Wilson had been lobbied – he is a man who could be very successfully lobbied without any supreme effort on the part of the lobbyer – into taking a stand for the RPO, which in those days was regarded by the musical elite as being the least valuable and the least prestigious of the orchestras. Jennie Lee contrived a cunning solution: she decided to set up a high-level committee to determine how many orchestras were needed by London and whether it was possible to axe one without any deterioration in the availability of musical supply; and it was this committee that she asked me to preside over.

It was necessary to produce a report in lightning time so as to enable the Arts Council to determine the orchestral fates. The committee I gathered together was a powerful one, professionally skilful, hardworking and cohesive. It included David Webster, later Sir David, the director of the Royal Opera House, and Hardie Ratcliffe, the general secretary of the Musicians Union, as I made a point of recommending that the committee should include trade-union representation. I had met Ratcliffe over the years when acting for orchestras and orchestral employers in wage disputes with his union. He had a combative quality that I found attractive but which made him some enemies. He suffered from ill health which he sustained with great courage all the time I knew him. He was devoted to the cause of musicians and would do nothing to endanger that cause, thus he viewed with the darkest suspicion all mechanical methods of recording, playing or broadcasting music. He was thoroughly hostile to the extension of gramophone recordings and pathologically hostile to the use of recordings by radio and television. In his later years half his life was spent in corrosive battles with recording and broadcasting authorities about 'needle time' – the length of time permitted to those authorities for the playing of pre-licensed recordings. It was futile to submit to him that provided royalties were paid the musician was better off. The live employment of live musicians was the consummation that he sought for his work in the union. A man visibly drawing a bow across the violin strings – however execrably – was the most satisfying sight and sound that his daily life held. His colleagues recognised the special quality that made him a great union leader, and although there were frequent differences of opinion their respect and affection for him was manifest. He threw himself energetically into the work of the committee and made many proposals of sound sense and above all of sound moderation.

For the purpose of this committee I paid my first visit to the Arts Council in St James's Square, and thereafter presided over the meetings in David Webster's room in the Royal Opera House. I had known him for many years and done professional work for the opera house at various times, including applying for its Charter in 1954 at the instance of Lord Waverley, then the chairman of the ROH. Lord Waverley was probably the most efficient chairman that any organisation has ever had and he was one of the most dauntingly powerful personalities I have ever encountered. He had been an outstanding civil servant and made a most valuable contribution to our success in the First World War, being much admired by the politicians, although by some he was feared and by others even hated.

He was, I felt, a very fair-minded man but one only a fool would engage in debate. I recollect that I advised him, with somewhat youthful enthusiasm, that I did not think it was possible to obtain two marks of royal favour at the same time, namely the grant of a Royal Charter and also Royal Patronage. Lord Waverley was incapable of anything resembling a sneer, but the process approaching it crossed his face as he informed me that he had already made the appropriate arrangements in both cases. Fortunately he refrained from saying that he did not need me to teach my grandfather to suck eggs! In any event, in due course both these signs of favour were obtained and my relationship with him remained a good one.

Waverley was a brilliant but entirely uncompromising chairman and did not need the advice of a board or anyone else as he had a splendid confidence in his own opinion, which in at least 75 per cent of cases was wholly justified. I found it a pleasure to work with him. At that time he was, apart, from his relatively irrelevant activities as the chairman of Covent Garden, the chairman of the Port of London Authority and he held a great number of other positions. I had attended the Covent Garden board meetings quite regularly in my capacity as a solicitor.

When I was first connected with Covent Garden it was directed by David Webster. Webster had been closely connected with the Liverpool (later Royal Liverpool) Philharmonic Orchestra; he was a musical dilettante of considerable knowledge and taste who had earned his living as the head of a great department store in Liverpool, for which reason he was contemptuously described by his enemies as 'that draper'. He was, however, a man of extreme sensibility who blended a love for music with a sound business training, and both stood him in good stead. Someone of genius must have recognised his qualities, since they were not those most likely to inspire public boards in appointing an artistic administrator, but he was appointed and was responsible for the running of the Royal Opera House from the time of its reopening immediately after the war until a few weeks before his death in 1971.

He is a difficult man to describe: he was plump, dapper, soft-spoken, subtle, sensitive and tough. The singers and musicians loved him because they were the primary love and concern of his own life. A man of infinite tact, he produced an atmosphere of serenity unique in the annals of opera management. Prima donnas, whose bursts of temperament terrified the stoutest hearts, were charmed into forgetting the need to explode in his soothing presence.

During the many years I knew him, before I became the chairman of the Arts Council, we were never close, largely because except in the world of music he was snobbishly selective in patronising people who could be useful, and it was not until my advent to the chairmanship of the body that controlled his life and destiny that he made the discovery that I could be useful. He lost no time in repairing the previous omissions and I was asked to luncheons and operas and to parties in the Crush Bar, and to dinner parties at his elegant home in Weymouth Street. Despite the transparent motivation, a solid friendship developed which ended with his death. He was immensely helpful to me at all times and I did my best to help him. He was a useful member of the so-called 'Goodman Committee'.

The secretary of the committee was a young barrister called Leonard Hoffmann who had come from South Africa and was at that time a Fellow of University College, Oxford. Some while afterwards he went to the Bar and today, having been one of the most successful Queen's Counsel, he has made a virtuous financial sacrifice by accepting the honour of a High Court Judgeship, where he has already earned golden praise both for the erudition and – by no means a usual combination – for the liberal character of his judgements.

He made an admirable secretary: he was good-humoured and patient and, what is more important, he had a rare skill in elimination. Obviously in the course of a commission of some kind a great deal of nonsense is bound to be said, and a conscientious but undiscriminating secretary will retain all this to the detriment of the ultimate report. Hoffmann had an instinct for selection that was near genius, and in the result the report was a highly impressive and convincing one.

Our report was greeted, if not with enthusiasm, at least with mild approval by that tiny section of the public interested in the wages and working conditions of musicians. We recommended the continuation of the four orchestras, and despite some noises of clucking disapproval from critics on high, I remain unrepentantly convinced that our report was right. The fallacy which I believe is inherent in the view that we would be better with three orchestras is based on the notion that orchestras can amalgamate, and that a large element from one orchestra can be assimilated into another so as to have the best of the two and to reject the dross. This simply does not happen. Musicians are immensely individual creatures who will work with colleagues they know and like. The opportunity to work with colleagues who are, in professional terms, outstandingly superior is not a determining factor. No violin-player wishes to play with the best team of violinists in the world – he would find the prospect strangely disconcerting and unattractive. He wishes to play with people who are friendly and helpful, will communicate directions and enjoy a competence that will enable them to rise to the heights when inspired.

Even so, our committee had realised early on that the continued survival of the Royal Philharmonic Orchestra was a matter which had apparently plagued everyone for years. The Arts Council took the view that the orchestra should not survive. This was based in part on a belief that it was redundant and in part on a belief that it was not very good and was musically low-class. The Arts Council, as I was soon to discover, contained some exceptionally snobbish elements. The other orchestras they regarded as socially superior and right to be retained. The poor old RPO had a rather tatty record, having been the private orchestra of the capricious Sir Thomas Beecham. Needless to say, under his auspices they had attained splendours of performance and frequent threats of bankruptcy. Beecham was in my view this country's best conductor during his lifetime, but his treatment of musicians and his total want of concern for contractual obligations and the payment of debts were legends. On his death the RPO went through a series of traumatic vicissitudes. His wife, an amiable and attractive young woman, took over, with the assistance of a variety of individuals spectacularly unqualified for this particular duty. Finally, the orchestra shook free and set off under its own auspices on the road for survival. The difficulties it met were formidable, not least the determination of the Arts Council to achieve its destruction.

Strong pressures had been brought to bear on our committee by the Arts Council representatives and others to report adversely on the orchestra, but utilising the skilful and informed services of Ernest Bean – then the general manager of the Royal Festival Hall and a name to conjure with where the arts were concerned – we concluded that there was room, and a need, for this orchestra and that it should not be dissolved. The conclusion was bitterly resented by certain people at the Arts Council.

A principal adversary of the orchestra was John Denison, then the Council's music director. Like his successor, John Cruft, Denison had been an orchestral musician in his time, and this had induced some absence of sympathy for other musicians. For some reason, those who defect from the orchestra pit to administration view their former colleagues with contempt and animosity. They regard them as presumptuous upstarts. You cannot, they say, turn that shower into a body of respectable human beings. You will never instil discipline into them. They will always work every hour there is while somebody pays them. They are greedy for money, will play in several orchestras at once if they have the opportunity, and generally are not respectable gentry to mix with their betters – the artistic administrators.

I found the members of the RPO a bewildered lot. They were, however, determined to survive, although they were never wholly conscious of where the attack was coming from. Why, they wondered, did Mr Denison not like them? Why did he not bestow gifts and bounty on them comparable to his benefactions to the London Philharmonic Orchestra, the London Symphony Orchestra and the New Philharmonia Orchestra? The story of their survival is a horrific one. Unable to obtain dates at the Royal Festival Hall, they toured forlornly round the London suburbs, performing to half-empty houses at the Odeon, Swiss Cottage, and other unsuitable venues. They dragged their instruments up and down stairs and generally were rather lost in their efforts to deal with a bureaucracy that was set on their destruction.

On my arrival at the Arts Council I soon became hugely impatient of the antics of the bureaucrats and was relieved when John Denison departed for his well-earned promotion as general manager of the Festival Hall in succession to Ernest Bean not long after. But his successor John Cruft – a gentle, intelligent, musical man – was no better where the wretched RPO was concerned. He too had evolved the theory that London had too many orchestras. Bureaucracy proceeds on the principle that there is virtue in saving, regardless of from what or from where you save. I am glad to report, however, that the RPO did survive and they are there to this day.

However, the main recommendation of our report did not concern the RPO but was a suggestion of my own, that there should be established an independent autonomous body – the London Orchestral Concert Board – to be run jointly by the Arts Council and the Greater London Council, with representatives of the Musicians Union and the Orchestral Employers' Association, as well as the Arts Council and GLC, on the board. For many years the four orchestras and other orchestras had been vying for dates at the Royal Festival Hall, and to a lesser extent the Albert Hall, and even the Wigmore Hall. The idea was that the new Board would co-ordinate not only the dates of the concerts but would ensure that there was no foolish repetition of programmes, so that one did not hear Beethoven's Fifth Symphony four times in a week from four different orchestras.

We presented the report to the Arts Council. An irony was that I was, for practical purposes, reporting to myself, since my appointment in May 1965 as chairman of the Arts Council – to whom the report was addressed – came shortly before its publication, a notion that delighted Harold Wilson. Needless to say, the recipient received it with total approbation. In fact he found it difficult to find how it could be improved upon! So the report was duly adopted and the LOCB established; I had the satisfaction of recommending to Jennie Lee that David Webster should be the chairman. The LOCB continued to operate with considerable success, regulating the subsidy given by the Arts Council and the GLC to the orchestras,

co-ordinating programmes, adjudicating on the availability of concert halls
and generally acting as a supervisory body to ensure proper conditions
for musicians, until it was dissolved in 1986 for reasons best known to
those in control of the arts.

But I must return to my early associations with Covent Garden. Lord
Waverley's death in 1958 was a tragedy for the Royal Opera House and
would have been an even greater tragedy if another remarkable, but totally
different, man had not emerged to replace hinm in the person of Lord
Drogheda, whose name, more than any other, became intimately associated
with Covent Garden.

No less dedicated than his predecessor, Garrett Drogheda was a
cultivated man of unique personal charm, with a passionate love and an
honourable knowledge both of music and ballet, and he brought a sensitive
and discriminating control to the board of the opera house. But at first
he had a very strained and indeed difficult relationship with David
Webster. Webster was used to non-interference by Waverley on artistic
matters and had an enormous respect for Waverley on administrative
matters. Indeed, such was Waverley's standing and personality that it
would have been a great fool who would have joined issue with him.
Drogheda was very much younger and for some reason the relationship
between him and David Webster was a tense one for a very considerable
period, until it finally settled down to a much better understanding.

Around the time of Drogheda's appointment, I was asked by Southern
Television – when it was being formed – to suggest the name of a director
who might appeal to the Independent Broadcasting Authority in the
selection of a company to receive the licence. I remember recommending
David Webster who, because of his association with Covent Garden and
his administrative experience, made an ideal director and was held in the
highest regard by John Davis (now Sir John), then chairman of the
company and chairman of the Rank Organisation.

A few years later David Webster came to see me about his own position
at the opera house, saying that he found his relationship with the chairman
so strained that it was no longer one he wished to continue. At almost
that moment John Davis telephoned me to ask if I could suggest a new
managing director for Southern Television, as the incumbent was on the
point of retirement. I thought for a moment and said, 'Well, you already
have David Webster as a director, would you consider him as the managing
director?' 'Certainly,' he said, with enthusiasm. 'He is a valuable director,
but do you think he would accept the job?' 'The best thing is that I
should ask him,' I suggested. 'Please do,' John Davis replied. So I
tlephoned Webster and told him that I had an alternative job available,
that it was well remunerated and very much in his line, and did he wish

to be considered for it since I had been asked to offer it to him? He was extremely enthusiastic at the prospect and expressed his gratitude and pleasure.

I communicated to John Davis that Webster was ready to accept the job and Davis said that he would approach him himself. Thereupon a rather disquieting silence descended on the scene and Webster rang me on one or two occasions, obviously anxious to know what was happening, and I could only say that I had not heard. Finally it seemed clear that I ought to speak to Davis. When I telephoned him, however, he was clearly embarrassed by my approach. 'I will have to come and see you,' was all I was able to elicit from him.

Seated in my office a few days later, Davis asked me, somewhat accusingly, if I had known when recommending Webster that he was a homosexual. I replied rather indignantly that obviously I did not know if a man was a homosexual, but it was generally believed that he was, and that I did not myself regard it as a relevant consideration. Davis, however, stated that unhappily the board took the contrary view and did not wish to offer the appointment to him. 'Then,' I said, 'you must tell David Webster yourself, because it is rather a lot to ask of me that I should ring him up and tell him that because of an unworthy prejudice about reports on his sexual proclivities a job that I was asked to offer to him is now withdrawn.' Whereupon John Davis – as I might have expected of him – unhesitatingly agreed to speak to Webster himself. What he said to him I do not know, but it was a bitter disappointment to Webster.

However, it was extremely good fortune for the opera house because he remained, and the strain in his relationship with Garrett Drogheda thawed to the point where indeed they became firm friends. The partnership between Lord Drogheda and his board and David Webster was – when the two men had finally recognised each other's quality – one of the most rewarding and creative in British musical history. Both in their different ways were perfectionists. Both recognised that the opera house could only survive if it achieved international standards. They had no time for the mediocre or the second-rate. Their special joy was to 'net' some great singer, and there was particular gratification if they could present some magnificent new voice for the first time. But despite the constant employment of great international artists, recent years at the opera house have seen an even more gratifying development – the emergence of a national school of singers, and for the first time in living memory British singers in respectable numbers have found fame and fortune, not only in this country, but in every great opera house in the world.

In 1968, with the approval of the Arts Council and the Greater London

Council, the Sadler's AWells Opera moved to the London Coliseum in St Martin's Lane. Ther Sadler's Wells Foundation decided to keep the old Sadler's Wells Theatre available for visiting companies and, although it has been a considerable struggle, they have succeeded in doing so to this very day.

The company's move to the Coliseum presented inevitable financial problems, some of which I have described in the previous chapter. For some months my principal concern at the Arts Council was to procure the funds for this important artistic change, and I was involved in long and complicated negotiations both with the owner of the Coliseum and with others to whom it was possible to appeal for what was plainly an important national cause. Financial help and encouragement were received from an astonishing number of opera supporters, and it was a source of great satisfaction to me when the hour arrived for Sadler's Wells to become the English National Opera, as it did in 1974, and establish itself as one of the cornerstones of artistic activity in the capital. The ENO has received further reassurance by the government's recent purchase of the freehold of the Coliseum, but characteristically, although finance was found to buy the freehold, no additional finance was available for the important expenditure on maintenance that the building now requires.

The rivalry between the newly established English National Opera at the Coliseum and the Royal Opera House soon became intense and remained so notwithstanding my own considerable efforts, as chairman of the Arts Council, to create a better atmosphere. To that end I organised three or four dinner parties, attended by the top brass of each institution, in the hope that good food and wine would mellow their attitude towards each other and inspire feelings of positive affection. No such thing occurred, although I do believe that a more rational attitude now exists in both places.

The strength of the hostility is well illustrated by a single episode. In 1966 the Arts Council set up a committee to review – in material terms – what was immediately required to maintain opera and ballet in good order. This committee reported in 1969. Lord Harewood chaired the opera section of the inquiry, while I chaired the ballet section. At one of the later combined meetings at the Arts Council – at which almost everyone enjoying authority at Covent Garden was present – I could not fail to notice that there was agitation among several of that organisation's representatives: Lord Drogheda was jumping about like a grasshopper, leaving the room and returning shortly afterwards when he communicated both with David Webster and with John Tooley, Webster's assistant.

This agitation did not make the conduct of the meeting any easier and speaking to Garrett Drogheda I gently enquired what the trouble was. He was happy to unburden himself. 'We are doing *Meistersinger* at the Garden tomorrow evening and we have lost the exceptional voice of our Hans Sachs as he is afflicted with illness. We have been telephoning all over Europe for a substitute but at this moment no suitable one is available.' I responded to this with some mild sarcasm, saying that it was not necessary for them to search Europe or the rest of the world as there was a good Sachs available at the bottom of St Martin's Lane. Garrett, obviously horrified at the prospect of using an ENO singer, replied with great presence of mind that they would have liked to use him but that he could not sing the opera in German. 'Oh, yes he can!' I said. 'He is singing at Bayreuth this very summer.' The Covent Garden contingent looked rather foolish but were constrained to make a further telephone call to the Coliseum. They returned with their faces as black as thunder: Norman Bailey had been delighted to accept.

At the actual performance it was reported to me that David Webster had announced the change and introduced Bailey in very unenthusiastic terms, but that Bailey's singing of the role was so successful that, having regard to the short notice, he earned an ovation from the audience which did nothing to mollify the Covent Garden Bourbons.

Unhappily, a few years after Sadler's Wells moved to the Coliseum, Stephen Arlen, its director, succumbed to a fatal illness. The question then arose of the choice of Arlen's successor. This requires a little background. When Webster indicated his wish to retire as director of the Royal Opera House in 1969 on account of ill-health, the question of his successor arose. Lord Harewood, who had been working in a relatively junior role at Covent Garden, was known to aspire to the job but Lord Drogheda was determined that the appointment should go to John Tooley, Webster's assistant. As the chairman of the Arts Council, I had nothing more than a persuasive role in the matter. I certainly did not object to Tooley's appointment, as I thought he was a most able man and probably the most suitable candidate, but I formed the view that such was the importance of the office – one of the most important musical appointments in the world – that it should be advertised and that no single candidate should have a clear run without competition.

We communicated this view to Lord Drogheda, but Lord Drogheda was not an easy man with whom to communicate a view which was not wholly palatable to him. He was an elegant and fastidious patrician: warm-hearted, kind, courageous and absolutely tireless in pursuing his duties and promoting his views. We became, and remained until his recent death, very close friends. That friendship was much cemented by our relationship in the newspaper world as, largely at his suggestion, I succeeded him as chairman of the Newspaper Publishers Association in 1970.

But so far as Covent Garden was concerned, Lord Drogheda had formed the view that Tooley was the best man. He had promised the job to Tooley and nothing was going to stop him from giving it to Tooley. I wrote him a memorandum, from which I quote:

> The Arts Council has no applicant in mind and has no wish to promote the cause of any particular contender, but it can think of a number of applicants who might wish to apply and whose claims are worthy of careful consideration.
>
> Nor does the Arts Council accept the proposition that a deputy in a public institution can be 'groomed' for a senior appointment. This is a nepotistic view which might conceivably have validity in a private or family firm but is totally incompatible with the principles of public engagement. The notion of 'Buggins's turn' has long been rejected for senior public appointments and it would be a sad day if it were reinstated in the field of artistic administration.
>
> An appointment of this kind made without competition and without a hearing of any other contender would create grave disappointment and frustration in a number of quarters and discourage recruiting in the field of artistic administration which it has been the calculated policy of the Arts Council to encourage of recent years. If senior artistic appointments are not thrown open to merit then a great many young people who would otherwise consider this field as eligible for entry will reject it as being altogether too much of a coterie to make it a safe choice of a career.

The cogency of my memorandum was sufficient for a meeting to be held with Lord Drogheda, where two or three of my colleagues and I went to meet two or three of his colleagues and him. One of his colleagues was the redoubtable Lord Robbins, the doyen of the world of artistic administration. Chairman then of the *Financial Times,* of which Garrett Drogheda was managing director, chairman of the National Gallery and former chairman of the Tate, he was the most revered and powerful figure in the world of artistic boyars. But he was a man of strong preconceptions and of immense loyalty to his friends. Garrett was his friend and in anything to do with Covent Garden the two men stood shoulder to shoulder, a couple of very formidable musketeers.

At the meeting they argued with force, but for me without plausibility, that an advertisement would deter good candidates; that there was no better candidate than Tooley, and it would gravely disappoint the whole staff if he was not appointed. None of these considerations appeared to be sufficiently persuasive. In the end we compromised – unworthily in my view – and it was agreed that there should be a trawling operation and that a few selected names should be invited, including Lord Harewood. But the trawling was conducted in a strangely anaemic fashion. Prospective candidates were telephoned with discouraging intimations that if they wanted to apply they could but their prospects were minimal.

At the end of the day rthe Royal Opera House informed us that their trawling had failed to find anyone suitable and on that bais it was impossible for us in honour to continue any objections to Tooley. I derived little satisfaction, although perhaps I should have, from the fact that a Parliamentary Committee got very cross about the appoinemtnt and the method used. In fairness I should say that Tooley discharged his duties with competence and was well regarded in the small circle of opera administrators in the world.

The relevance of this diversion to Covent Garden is that, shortly after the appointment of Tooley, Garrett Drogheda announced his intention to retire from the chairmanship of the Royal Opera House. As I have mentioned, Lord Harewood had been a possible candidate to succeed David Webster, but my understanding is that his claim was disposed of by Garrett Drogheda indicating to him that it seemed more appropriate that he should succeed him as chairman than David Webster as director. I have no doubt that Garrett's proposal to him was made in good faith, but needless to say he never succeeded Garrett as chairman. George Harewood was manoeuvred out of any candidature by oblique suggestions that his occupation of the role of chairman of Covent Garden would be unsacceptable to the royal family because of his divorce. Garrett had formed the view – and it was a view that was certainly held elsewhere – that if George Harewood succeeded him as chairman it would disrupt and might even terminate any royal association with the opera house.

The report of this view was expressed to me, and since I regarded it as unlikely I took an initiative of my own which was on the whole unsuccessful. I telephoned Sir Michael Adeane, the Queen's Private Secretary, and asked him whether he could confirm that if George Harewood became the chairman of the Royal Opera House this would in some way affect the relationship with the Queen. He said, to my surprise, that the best thing he could do was to ask her. I expressed satisfaction at this forthright approach to the matter.

Some little while later he telephoned me and gave a slightly ambiguous answer: 'I have spoken to the Queen,' he said, 'who has indicated that it would certainly not affect her relationship with the Royal Opera House

and that if they want to appoint George Harewood that is their concern.'
This was expressed in a fashion that indicated no great enthusiasm for
the appointment, but nevertheless was, I thought, sufficient to still the
rumours that were being circulated in order to abort the appointment of
George. However, the view continued to be maintained and it was clear
that the appointment would not be offered to him.

Following Stephen Arlen's death, the idea occurred to me, and I
suggested it to George, that he should apply to replace Stephen Arlen at
the Coliseum. This was probably the best appointment that I have ever
been concerned in. It was an absolutely spectacular success and the
English National Opera has gone from strength to strength in the years
since its formation. In what is a relatively short period of time it has
become a rival of the Royal Opera House and in certain directions many
people regard it as superior. The operas are, of course, done in English.
I myself have always regarded this as irrelevant, as I have never been able
to understand a single word that is sung in any language in an opera; but
a great number of purists are incensed that Italian, German and Russian
operas are all done in English. However, I think that the Russian opera
is a very good instance of why it is better to do it in English, for the
simple reason that there can be no more than five or six members in any
audience of a couple of thousand who can understand the language anyway.
The attempt at Russian by non-Russian singers has been contemptuously
dismissed by those fluent Russian speakers whom I have from time to
time taken to performances of *Boris Godunov*.

I became a director of the Royal Opera House in 1972 when I ceased
to be the chairman of the Arts Council, on an almost immediate invitation
from Garrett Drogheda to join their board. This I did and remained a
director for ten years, having myself moved a resolution that no director
should hold office for a longer period than that. This resolution has been
occasionally breached in the case of special favourites – I think unwisely –
but on the whole it is adhered to and it is a useful provision since it
ensures that, good or bad, a person cannot remain indefinitely, and it is
a most convenient and tactful way of relinquishing those directors who
have turned out to be of no great use.

I was not a regular attender of board meetings and towards the end of
my term I am afraid I was more often an absentee. I frankly regarded the
activities of the board as almost entirely irrelevant to the conduct of the
opera house. I found the discussions long-winded and rarely reaching any
conclusion that was later reflected in action. They bore a resemblance to
an expensive engine that had no transmission to the wheels. It chugged
on pointlessly at tea-time meetings where the only compensation originally
was the excellent smoked salmon sandwiches. I can trace my increasing

irregularity of attendance to the disappearance of the expensive sandwiches and their replacement by an inferior paste.

On a number of occasions I was the maverick member of the board – certainly on any occasion when I attended I was the maverick whenever I opened my mouth. I took the most active part towards the end of my term as a director when the government in office decided that they would no longer respect the hallowed, time-honoured and immensely valuable principle of ensuring that artistic activities were at a firm arm's length from government activities. This was the principle on which the Arts Council was established. I attended a meeting of the Covent Garden board when to my horror and indignation a civil servant – a Mr Clive Priestley – appeared to inform us that he had been entrusted by the Minister for the Arts, Paul Channon, with the duty of investigating the efficiency of Covent Garden. He thereupon provided an enormous questionnaire which we were required to answer.

No one present raised the slightest objection until I announced that he had no business to be doing what he was doing, that this was the most outrageous breach of the time-honoured principle that artistic subsidy was not related to government control. We had a rather heated scene. At one stage I informed him that after reading his questionnaire – he had come flanked by two assistants – there were in m view only six people in the world competent to answer it, and I was unhappy to say that those six did not include any of his party of three. Mr Priestley – an inoffensive and no doubt efficient gentleman – was clearly nonplussed by my onslaught and departed rather flushed.

It is rare that one can indulge oneself as satisfactorily as I did that afternoon, notwithstanding the craven absence of support from my trembling co-directors who saw all their grant vanishing in smoke. Two only contributed brave support – Sir John Sainsbury and Sir Dennis Forman, then chairman of Granada, the most experienced entertainment figure on the board and a not inconsiderable musical expert who had written a book on Mozart. The rest of the board continued to serve their previous useful purpose: participating in the consumption of the sandwiches.

Shortly after this episode, to the great satisfaction of my co-directors, my term of office ended and I cannot say that I felt any great grief. I had attended the meetings purely out of interest – they were among the most interesting meetings that one could have – but the board seemed to me to lack a cutting edge. It was composed of people of great abilities and indeed great qualities of character, but the organisation of the Opera House did not allow it to have any effective say. I have long been of the opinion that artistic organisations can be conducted by one firm and directing mind and that what you need is a person thoroughly versed in the arts and with a creative instinct. I think the best instance was to be found in Rudolf Bing, who came within my knowledge when he was the director of the Edinburgh Festival and then was promoted to great heights when he became the chief of the Metropolitan Opera in New York. He retired after many years of successful operation, having brought the Metropolitan to a peak which at time exceeded that of any other house in the world.

However, I am sorry to report that my efforts to ensure the annulment of Mr Priestley's activity were unsuccessful. In fact things have gone from bad to worse since the Arts Council – in view of the economic pressures on it – is no longer able to sustain the determined, indeed warlike, attitude that we had previously maintained, whereby in no circumstances would we have allowed government to interfere with the conduct of artistic affairs in this country.

Meanwhile, I had become a director of the English National Opera in 1973, under the chairmanship of Kenneth Robinson. The purpose of this was that there should be one person acting as a liaison between the two opera houses, which, as I had already discovered at the Arts Council, had a time-honoured enmity that made the hostility of the Macdonalds and the Campbells following the massacre at Glencoe appear to be a pretty minor difference.

I attended meetings, not very regularly, but when called upon to do anything in particular usually responded. At one meeting I was meditating very gently about something that had nothing to do with the opera, when I suddenly heard the word 'Kirov'. I pricked up my ears to hear Lord Harewood announcing to the board what he regarded a a triumph: that he had succeeded in getting the Kirov to make an appearance at the Coliseum. I intervened at once and said to him that it was a matter of international record and much publicity that the Jewish dancer Panov and his wife were prevented from dancing because they had expressed the desire to emigrate from Russia. In fact, considerable hardship and privation had been inflicted upon them. I said that as Covent Garden had considered a similar plan and rejected it because of the treatment of the Panovs, it seemed to me impossible for the Coliseum to invite the Kirov until the Panovs had beeen released from Russia. I went on to say that while I certainly did not seek to impose my own wishes on the company, if the invitation to the Kirov was persisted in then as the only Jewish member of the board I would be obliged to resign forthwith. In fact there and then I was tendering my resignation if they pursued the plan.

This caused consternation and Kenneth Robinson besought me to think again. Before I left that evening George Harewood and Kenneth both asked if they might call on me the next morning to make further representations. I told them that if the invitation went ahead it would be a waste of time since my decision was dictated by considerations of conscience and certainly I was unlikely to alter it. However, they came to breakfast – both very old friends, both deeply concerned about the attitude I was taking, and desperately seeking to find a solution that did not involve the loss of what they considered as a great coup.

I listened to them attentively, but told them that there did not appear to be a solution since I would not wish to stand in the way of a successful season in London by the Kirov; but at the same time the notion of their coming while the unfortunate Panovs were still immured in Russia, and forbidden to dance, was to me a horrible notion and one that I could not accept. However, I did, without any great conviction, say that if it was of any use to them I would make one personal effort with the Russian Ambassador to see if any persuasion on my part – feeble as it must be – could possibly procure a change in the Russian attitude.

Thereupon I wrote the Russian Ambassador a letter. The tenor of the letter was simply this: that I deeply regretted that a great and talented company should come to London in circumstances where they would not receive the same degree of enthusiastic response as would otherwise be the case if this situation had been resolved. I went on to say that it was a matter of particular distress to me that it should be the great USSR, the nation that had saved every Jew in Europe in front of the gates of Stalingrad, that saw fit to inflict its wrath, its power and its might on two defenceless people. As a Jew, I said, I could never lose my gratitude towards the Russians for the heroism they displayed in their battle with the Nazis, for the Jews owed their salvation in all parts of the world to the defeat of the Nazis, which was largely the responsibility of the Russians. I then said that I hoped the Russians would think again.

The letter went off and the response was electric: the very next morning I received a telephone call from the Russian Embassy asking if I would call on Ambassador Smirnovsky and if I would bring with me Lord Drogheda and Lord Olivier – Lord Drogheda because as the chairman of Covent Garden he had rejected the suggestion that the Kirov should appear there, and Lord Olivier because he had been associated with the Panov protest. Anyway, I telephoned the two and shortly afterwards we were *en route* to the Russian Embassy.

We were very cordially received, with a choice of coffee or Russian tea and some rather delicious biscuits, and we sat down to hear the Ambassador explain to us in the blandest fashion why we were so mistaken about the Panovs. The treatment of the Panovs, he told us, had nothing to do with anti-Semitism, but was due to one fact and one fact only, that Mrs

Panov had an elderly mother and that it was a rigid rule of the USSR that no one could leave the country without making adequate provision for elderly relatives. This seemed to me a rather tall story, but I said to him, 'Ambassador, if that is the real difficulty and if you would allow me to use your telephone for five minutes, I would arrange such provision for this old lady that would exceed her wildest dreams, and she will live in comfort for the rest of her days in a fashion that she has never previously experienced.'

The Ambassador looked at me and did something that for a Russian is, I think, rather unusual: he grinned. He then made use of an expression that I also think is not typically Russian, 'This,' he said, 'puts a different complexion on it. I must communicate with my government.' Whereupon we were plied with further coffee and Russian tea, after which we left, anticipating no result. To everyone's great astonishment the Panovs were released from Russia two weeks later.

What induced the Russian change of attitude I shall never know. Might they have been moved by the terms of my letter? I gravely doubt it. But I think they did realise that the Panovs were not worth the fuss; that in fact there was going to be an endless agitation until they were released; and certainly if the Kirov were to come they would come in uncomfortable circumstances until that had happened. However, I rated the episode as a considerable success and something of which not unnaturally one could be proud.

The Panovs, however, at the outset turned out to be something of a disappointment. I went to see their first appearance in London, when the male dancer seemed adequate and his wife anything but adequate. But I gather that the situation was later transformed: he became the director of the Antwerp Ballet Company and she became a considerable dancing star, appearing in a successful musical comedy in London, in place of Natalia Makarova, so that their release from Russia certainly achieved something in relation to their own careers.

When Kenneth Robinson was appointed as the chairman of the Arts Council in 1977, the question arose of his successor at the English National Opera. There were long debates and ultimately George Harewood came to see me to know whether I would accept the office, at least for an interim period, until they had had more time to find a successor. I agreed, on the understanding that I would not hold it for more than a year. In fact I held it for nine years! Not because of any desire to cling to office but simply because of the inevitable difficulty of finding someone upon whom everyone agrees.

I greatly enjoyed my chairmanship of the ENO, but it had some traumatic moments, particularly related to an unhappy tour of the United

States of America, which was strongly urged upon the board by the management, for motives that were wholly creditable but where I have to admit that the board had a heavy responsibility in succumbing to persuasion without sufficient safeguard as to the financial consequences. As it turned out we were given assurances in good faith that were not fulfilled, but my own belief is that most boards would have regarded those assurances as sufficiently secure to justify the tour. On the other hand some boards would have taken the view that, until the money promised was actually in the bank, it was improvident to send out a great touring company in circumstances that would cost a small fortune.

In the event the board was rather railroaded into embarking on the tour. I and one or two other members of the board, particularly Sir Nicholas Goodison, insisted that nothing should happen and not a person set foot in the United States until the promises we had received from various sources, particularly from the Governor of Texas, were fulfilled. However, in total disregard of these instructions, a relatively junior employee telephoned me one day to enquire about the tour and told me, to my horror, that the productions involved were now on the Atlantic, making their way towards what was artistically a very good result but financially a near disaster. In fact, when we did our arithmetic, it emerged that we had lost over a million pounds on this wholly unnecessary enterprise.

Our principal disappointment was with the Governor of Texas, who, I had been led to believe, was offering us a subsidy of £800,000. I spent a lot of time endeavouring to talk to him on the telephone, and when I ultimately spoke he repudiated any suggestion that he had made such an offer or that he was in any way in default. By the grace of God and some strenuous exertions by lesser individuals, we finally contrived to collect from a few generous benefactors the whole lost million, but roping in sufficient money to compensate for the Texas disaster was a tremendous waste of time and effort.

I was finally released from the chairmanship of the English National Opera in 1986 and was installed as the life president of the organisation, which I am happy to say means that I have no duties of any kind except occasionally to honour the opera house by attending with a few friends to see a successful production.

Perhaps the final musical interlude which resulted from my involvement in the arts occurred in 1980, when a serious crisis arose between the BBC and the Musicians Union over payment and other matters, and Promenade Concerts at the Royal Albert Hall were suspended for several weeks while the dispute went on. The Promenade Concerts were, and are, a splendid part of the London music scene. More than anything, they attract a young audience – who find much more satisfaction in standing than in sitting, and even more satisfaction in sitting on the floor than sitting on a chair – for whom the suspension would indeed have been a tragedy. If that year the entire season were to be lost, it was generally agreed that there was a serious risk that the Proms might be permanently discontinued.

Quite early on, it emerged that the prospect of a settlement by the BBC with the Musicians Union was a near impossibility in view of the horribly strained relationship between the two bodies. (This was a familiar story. In 1965, when I arrived at the Arts Council, I had found that Council mandarins displayed a determined hostility towards the artistic unions, and particularly the Musicians Union. This impelled me to establish early on a close relationship with Hardie Ratcliffe, the general secretary of the Musicians Union, and with his successor, John Morton.) In any event, I telephoned Kenneth Robinson, then the chairman of the Arts Council, to suggest that he might approach the BBC with the suggestion that the Arts Council should take over the Proms for at least that year, on the basis of receiving from the BBC the expenditure that the Corporation would save, so that there would be money for the Arts Council to do the job. He was enthusiastic and asked me to make the approach.

I telephoned Robert Ponsonby, the director of music at the BBC, responsible for the Proms, and made the suggestion to him. He too was enthusiastic and told me that he would immediately put out feelers in the Corporation. The reply was immediate, discouraging and almost rude. The BBC preferred the Proms to disappear rather than that the BBC should have some diminished role. Indeed, the Proms would have disappeared but for the intervention of a Parliamentary Committee, chaired by Christopher Price but instigated by Patrick Cormack – an immensely useful Conservative MP, wedded to the promotion of the arts – which suggested in an interim report that a mediator should be invited to operate between the two bodies, adding that in the government's view the best mediator would be myself.

I was asked by the committee if I would undertake the task and, notwithstanding the seeming impossibility of achievement, I expressed a willingness to try. But there was a strange absence of enthusiasm on the part of the BBC. The BBC knew me well. In 1970 I had mediated for several weeks when the musicians were on strike over the vexed question of 'needle time': the length of time that the BBC might give to recorded as opposed to live music. I had played a prominent role in solving that problem, and to testify to the justice of this claim I can exhibit the now ageing music centre that was presented to me jointly by the BBC and the Musicians Union for my otherwise unpaid exertions. I regarded it as a splendid reward and it continues to give service to this day.

I embarked on the negotiations over the Proms as a matter of great urgency at meetings held *de die in diem* and almost from hour to hour. The proceedings were followed with immense and unexpected interest by the national press. Each night during the negotiations, when we emerged from the headquarters of ACAS, a crowd of journalists demanded to know if any progress had been made, and the general prediction was that success was an impossibility. To some extent the success of the negotiations could be attributed to the adoption of the starvation technique which I had learnt in newspaper negotiations. At about seven o'clock each evening I suggested to both sides that there should be an adjournment for light refreshments. ACAS provided quantities of hot sweet tea and sandwiches, in my recollection identical to those that had been provided by the TUC in the newspaper negotiations – always vast chunks of bread encasing large chunks of Cheddar cheese. I excused myself without explanation and slipped across the road to the House of Lords where I was able to obtain some dinner. The most frenzied admirers of the House of Lords do not extend their admiration to the cuisine, but it was Lucullan in comparison with the cheese sandwiches.

I returned to the negotiations refreshed and invigorated to find the two sides of troops in a state of increasing depression as the night wore on. It was clear to me that the ultimate advent of common sense, which must in the end enter into any deliberations with sane human beings, would produce a conclusion. It came more rapidly than I thought. Based on an assortment of differing suggestions that I made from time to time, an agreement was reached. We staggered from the last meeting – it must, I think, have been about 2 a.m. – to find that even the newspaper reporters had deserted us and we could not announce our triumph. On this occasion there were many cordial letters of thanks but no tangible reward: no offer of a new music centre, notwithstanding the increasing antiquity of the original one.

A great compensation for my efforts in the arts is the numerous friendships I have established with artists of every kind. I established a friendship with the eminent composer William Walton, and with his colourful and vivacious wife Susana, when I was a partner in Rubinstein Nash in the early 1950s. He remained a loyal client and friend from then onwards until his death, since when I have continued that friendship with his widow and continued to advise her.

On several occasions I have been their guest in their immensely pleasant home in Ischia – the only house I know where it is possible to stay on terms that one is as free as in one's own home. Normally I find visiting other people's houses restrictive, but the Waltons were a conspicuous and splendid exception. He had a charm that was unforced and immensely engaging, a wry sense of humour and a self-deprecating modesty that was not entirely convincing, but which was nevertheless captivating. As a composer I liked his work very much. Although I do not regard myself as entitled to pronounce any expert opinion on composition, I have heard enough music, and it has played a sufficient part in my life, to enable me to feel justified in making the judgement that Walton is one of the few British composers of the century who might survive. In fact – although it is not a popular opinion – I rate him higher than Benjamin Britten.

I was at the party that Ted Heath gave at Downing Street in 1972 for Walton's seventieth birthday. Heath was especially pleased to sponsor the event because of his belief – which was indeed the case – that Walton had not received the recognition that he deserved. The musical entertainment, which included a piece by Arthur Bliss to an amusing poem by Paul Dehn, was followed by a performance of ten movements from *Façade* with the narrator in the person of Alvar Liddell. This would have been better had the orchestra and singers not had to perform in a room adjoining the dining-room from where they could only be seen through the communicating doors which barred, alas, much of the sound and a good deal of the vision; but it was nevertheless a splendid occasion and a worthy tribute to a most distinguished composer.

Another musician with whom I enjoyed an association may not be regarded as one of the world's greatest conductors, but he played a most important part in the development of British music: I refer to Sir Adrian Boult. He wrote to me in 1978 to the effect that it would be very wrong when appointing the music directors and conductors of British orchestras not to appoint Englishmen. I wrote back to him saying that, alas, although I had the greatest respect for him, this was a matter on which I did not agree. I thought that music was universal, and just as I hoped that talented Britons would be employed outside Britain, it was our duty to employ the best man when it came to the conduct of an orchestra. To my great delight, and as an illustration of the quality of this remarkable man, I received a reply shortly afterwards saying, 'I have reflected on your answer and I now totally agree.'

I have been reading recently a small volume containing published papers and speeches made by Sir Adrian, and the common sense, reasonableness and good humour of everything he writes reflects what I believe to have been his true character. He was in almost every sense a great man, even if no one would describe him as a great conductor. He was a conductor of high competence. He had the special value of being prepared to conduct any work undeterred by its difficulty – a quality which is not to be found in every conductor.

I have a vivid recollection of attending a performance of *Wozzeck* at the Edinburgh Festival when the visiting conductor fell ill. It was quite impossible to persuade any other conductor in the vicinity to conduct the piece, which they regarded as too difficult. I am absolutely convinced that Barbirolli, who made his reputation by substituting for a more eminent conductor at short notice, or Sir Adrian, would have undertaken the task without hesitation and discharged it with more than reasonable confidence.

There is little doubt that the three 'Bs' were, in their different ways, the outstanding British conductors of my day – Beecham, Barbirolli and (perhaps a controversial choice) Adrian Boult – and they stand out from all the others. Other names should, of course, be included for recognition and praise. Henry Wood, if for nothing else than having established the Promenade Concerts – a most imaginative contribution to the musical scene. Malcolm Sargent, unkindly designated 'Flash Harry,' probably did more to draw a popular audience to classical concerts than any other conductor; but I remain firm in the belief that the three 'Bs' should hold the paramount place.

I have always enjoyed associations with conductors. My tally is a long one. A much underrated conductor – and I take some pride in my share in obtaining his knighthood – is Alexander Gibson who, apart from his skill as a conductor, contributed enormously to the establishment of the Scottish Opera and the Scottish National Orchestra. I met him regularly on visits to the Edinburgh Festival, which I attended for many years until progressive lameness made visits to that town – beset with hills and with pathetically inadequate auditoria for a great Festival: all equipped with innumerable stairs – too difficult except for rare and carefully selected visits. But his is one name only. I became and remain a good friend of the great Solti, who ranks in class and quality with any other name in the British musical scene.

I came to know Charles Mackerras, who has never had the recognition his high talents deserve, and who performed distinguished services to the English National Opera during the time of my chairmanship and before he resigned to seek other fields. It is a mystery to me that this great all-rounder was not appointed to preside over the Royal Opera House. The story of the appointments within that institution would leave one poised on the point of a needle in an effort to tell the truth without exaggeration or distortion. One of the more amusing episodes of my Arts Council period was when I was invited by my friend Yehudi Menuhin to attend a dinner that he was giving to raise funds for his school. It was principally directed towards two or three tycoons who had agreed to attend, among whom were Lord Delfont and particularly Sir Jules Thorn.

Sir Jules was a famous benefactor and had a very large charitable trust of which shortly after I had the honour of becoming a trustee, and so remain. However, despite the size of the trust, he was very selective about the charities to which he bestowed money and subjected them to thorough investigation before making any award. He had up till then declined to make any contribution to Menuhin's school, but it was a source of great gratification that he was coming to the dinner and gave rise to high hopes.

Sir Jules arrived with Lady Thorn who was wearing a fine mink coat. The evening was in every sense a total disaster, except for the dinner which was excellent, the menu having been skilfully selected by Diana Menuhin. After this excellent dinner we all adjourned to the sitting-room where three or four children from the school played delightfully – although they were only toddlers. Thereupon Jennie Lee rose and made a short and entirely suitable address about the excellence of the school. Lord Harlech, the chairman of the school, followed her with two or three well-chosen sentences.

We noticed with immense delight that Sir Jules, who had been sitting in an armchair, had suddenly moved forward, obviously intending to make some pronouncement. Hope could not rise higher. The adrenalin was running like mad. At that moment, unhappily, Diana Menuhin chose to get up and deliver herself of a not over-short address about the undeniable merits and virtues of her beloved husband. As this address developed Sir Jules began to subside into his chair and by the time Diana had finished he was more firmly entrenched in it than ever. When she sat down after making this worthy declaration of her wifely affection, Sir Jules was rendered almost petrified.

David Harlech made desperate efforts to retrieve the situation. Rising, he said, 'Sir Jules, I had a feeling you wanted to say something?' 'No!' said Sir Jules very firmly, and at that moment an announcement was made that a cat burglar had contrived to enter the house through the smallest aperture conceivable – he must have been the wizened native who appears in one of Conan Doyle's stories – and stolen all the fur coats. The ladies went to assess their losses, returning expressing every kind of grief and misery: not a single fur coat had been left, including Jennie Lee's coat. We all adjourned in a state of considerable depression.

I added to my distress by a somewhat ill-advised utterance at a luncheon of the Bournemouth Symphony Orchestra the following day, when I described the happening and informed them that the beloved Minister for the Arts had had her fur coat stolen. 'It must have been taken,' I said, 'for purely sentimental reasons.' This was not appreciated by Jennie and a coolness existed between us for at least two hours.

13

Diptych

ERIC WALTER WHITE was an exceptionally unusual character. He had been with the Arts Council from the word go and was both its assistant secretary and the director of the Poetry (later Literature) Panel. White had a 'prissy' manner and a passion for literature that took in a tiny part of the whole. He loved the literature of his contemporaries, and the period between 1910 and 1930 was to him the larger part of the literary scene. He had not moved with the Bloomsbury set; he never spoke of Virginia Woolf, Lytton Strachey, Clive Bell, Vanessa Bell or Duncan Grant; but he moved in the world of that period and was closely associated with such literary figures as John and Rosamund Lehmann and William Gerhardie.

During my time at the Arts Council, I never heard White utter on a major literary theme. His major preoccupation was making (or, even more popular, disallowing) grants to coterie magazines: weird little magazines published by weird little men in weird little back streets, receiving minute sums from the Arts Council after immense deliberation and ratiocination by White. His joy and delight was to refuse a grant to someone he did not like. His dislike had very little to do with literary merit. It was based on the belief that the man was a presumptuous fellow and had no real right to be asking the Arts Council for money. He was a xenophobe and had a passionate hostility to any idea that did not originate within his own office, which for practical purposes meant a hostility to almost every form of human thought. He was not in truth of the calibre to be the literature director of the Arts Council, but he had one immensely redeeming feature: he was also the director of festivals and he loved the festivals and, for reasons which I am not able to explain, the festivals loved him. In part it was due to his arithmetical delight in discussing grants in small terms. The idea of a grant of anything exceeding £1,000 horrified and terrified him, and the Arts Council in its new form, reaching out to give large sums of money to large minds, was a conception he found awesome and awful. He placed us in numerous dilemmas, principally because he was an inadequate man exercising an inadequate task.

The first rumpus arose from a suggestion of mine fairly early in my chairmanship. Looking around the Council table I had a feeling that the average age of the Arts Council was a little too high for easy contact with the youth of our society. It was clearly not practicable to co-opt enough youngsters to the Council to bring down the age level and provide informed guidance on the artistic problems of the young or their artistic viewpoints. I therefore suggested – and we debated the matter – that we should have a junior Arts Council: that some twenty youngsters should meet on the afternoon that we met, debate the identical agenda, and that their deliberations, suitably (but briefly) minuted, should be circulated before our next meeting in case we wished to revise any views we had formed in the light of the opinions voiced by the youngsters.

The idea did not wholly commend itself to the Council. It was particularly disliked by those members of the Council with academic associations, since no one appears to hate the young more than their teachers. However, I pressed hard and a compromise was reached. It was decided to appoint to each of our four Panels (Art, Drama, Literature and Music) two young people who would be carefully handpicked, principally from the upper forms of schools and from universities. Arrangements were made for headmasters and the heads of colleges and other organisations where the young forgathered to be notified of our needs and to submit applications. In no time at all the Panels had made their recommendations which were submitted to me for my prior approval before ultimate acceptance by the Council.

No problems arose with three of the Panels, but one candidate strongly supported by Eric White – it turned out I believe that the Literature Panel had no part in his selection – seemed to me a little inappropriate. First, he was twenty-four years of age or even older, and secondly he was by trade a bookseller. There was no objection to a bookseller on the Literature Panel and great advantages in having an expert bookseller, provided he loved books, but the mere selling of them was not a qualification in itself. I spoke to White, who assured me that the man was a strong and suitable candidate who would discharge the duties admirably. I remonstrated a little about his age, but in view of the alleged excellence of his other qualities gave way and he was duly appointed at our next Council meeting. Two days after the meeting I received a letter from White to say that had he been present at the meeting – which for some reason he was not – he would have thought it desirable to point out that the young man concerned, in addition to being a bookseller and much approved by the Literature Panel, was also on the Editorial Board of the *International Times*.

I had had cause to look at the *International Times* previously and it was not, as might have been thought, an extramural activity of the Thomson organisation. It was the parish magazine of the drug set. I sent for a copy and its dank print and dismal prose, broken up into disjointed paragraphs, with weird psychedelic illustrations, failed to conceal its real motivation. The prize piece in the copy I had was entitled 'To Drug Or Not To Drug', as though these were the available alternatives. There was a postal column reuniting drug-addicted friends and containing touching references to those few unhappy brethren who, needless to say unjustly, were incarcerated in some penal institution. Particularly warm and solicitous messages were conveyed to these gentry. I was not sure whether it was the form or the sentiments of the publication that were the more disagreeable, but I was quite sure that the Arts Council did not want an editorial grandee of this work to be on its Literature Panel. I don't think my record at the Arts Council indicated particular timidity, but I baulked at the notion of having to answer questions from MPs and the public about how we had made this singularly eccentric selection. Moreover, I totally disapprove of any drug-taking and regard the encouragement of drug-taking as a spectacular villainy. Hence, I was extremely indignant that we had been led into this false position and determined to rectify it without further ado.

I telephoned the Vice-Chairman (then Sir William Coldstream) and the four chairmen of the Panels, Sir John Witt, Hugh Willatt, Sir Anthony Lewis and Cecil Day-Lewis. Their response was totally and vigorously to support my intended action, which was to send a letter to the young man concerned informing him in polite terms that – while we had nothing against him personally – his association with the *International Times* in an editorial role made it inappropriate that he should belong to the Arts Council's Literature Panel. At the next meeting of the Arts Council I asked that my action should be confirmed, and confirmation was immediate and unanimous, although the valiant Eric White, a man with a special concern for the hapless young, made a spirited defence of the appointment on the grounds that it was not the Arts Council's business to invigilate the personal behaviour of appointees. As a doctrine this was impeccable and was maintained, I hope, throughout my regime, but it had no possible relevance to this situation. The Arts Council is a public body and what we were certainly not entitled to do was publicly to declare our sympathy and support for the *International Times* – which the appointment undoubtedly would have done.

It was not an easy decision and I have often wondered subsequently whether it was a right decision. A declaration for liberty of thought and action would have had great attraction, but it would also have been a denial of responsibility. Anyway, right or wrong, we did it. The effects were not violent or widespread, and so far as I know the only protest from the outside world came from the young man himself. We were threatened with exposure, but we did not mind exposure and I believe that only one newspaper carried a short version of the matter, although we certainly did nothing to discourage them.

However, the effects within the Council were more vivid. The Council itself had fully approved the action taken, but our Literature Panel, exerting the robust independence that all the Panels displayed at all times, expressed grave dissatisfaction that they had not been consulted. The murmurs of discontent were loud and it was clear that a response was needed. I thereupon asked for a special meeting of the Panel to give me an opportunity of explaining the matter. I attended the Panel and numerous questions were shot at me, all of which I hope I answered with candour and firmness. I again explained that the vice of the appointment was seeming public approbation of the *International Times* and its nauseous contents; that the Arts Council, as a public body, had a responsibility not only to youth but to the parents of youth and that the public money we received did not allow us to exercise the luxury of total liberty of decision regardless of contemporary standards and beliefs.

The Panel on the whole seemed satisfied, except for Miss Brigid Brophy. I had not met Miss Brophy before and found her an engaging and articulate adversary. I learnt subsequently in a letter from her that she would have been an even more formidable adversary if she had not been suffering from a hangover from 'drink and not drugs'. There was certainly nothing in her performance that caused me to suspect her disability. She asked me what would have happened to Samuel Coleridge (who addicted to laudanum) if he had been a member of the Arts Council while I was the chairman. 'Nothing,' I said. 'We are not interested in the personal behaviour or morality of any member of the Council or any of its Panels. In fact,' I went on, 'if we were so interested there would be nobody sitting at this table this afternoon. What we are interested in is to avoid associating the Arts Council, by an obviously selective appointment, with the doctrines and policies of a magazine which appears to exist primarily for the purpose of promoting drug addiction.' Miss Brophy, at least, was silenced, but I suspect – in view of later events – more by her hangover than by my persuasion.

A few days later I received an immensely lengthy letter in which she posed a great number of questions to me. There were references to vegetarianism and other practices which she called in aid to justify the *International Times* and the appointment. She asked me to answer the questions so that she could form a further view of my behaviour. I replied that as a busy man I regretted that she had had a hangover but that I could not be punished for her self-indulgence, and that the best I could do was to send her the minutes of the meeting.

By return of post came her resignation, notified to *The Times* shortly before I received the communication. *The Times* telephoned me and I took an unrepentant attitude. 'My withers,' I said, 'are unwrung. We regret to lose Miss Brophy – a distinguished writer and a colourful personality – but if she feels she must go, go she must.' Her departure caused little or no sensation, although I did feel a twinge of regret and hoped she might return at some stage. Her viewpoint was worthy of respect, although I was profoundly in disagreement with it. The literature director and his assistant, Charles Osborne, had, I think, a more than sneaking sympathy with the lady, but the matter was quickly forgotten.

Another contentious matter was the question of literary prizes. The Arts Council's methods of subsidy were various, ingenious and on the whole effective. Above all they were honourable. But the literary prizes did arouse criticism and often deep suspicion.

The prizes were organised by the Literature Panel and it is the sad fact that for many years the Literature Panel was organised by the said Mr Eric White. In the result, the prize-winners were, not cronies of Mr White, but selected from the small category of writers who met with his approval. They all belonged to an earlier generation of literary activity. They did not go back quite as far as Tennyson or Dickens but they went back to John Lehmann, Peter Quennell, Raymond Mortimer, V. S. Pritchett and others, whose ages were never less than the biblical span of three score and ten. They were, of course, distinguished writers, but the purpose of giving them prizes was obscure. The prize would not encourage them to greater output, nor would it assist them to keep going – they had nearly all gone. But Mr White was not open to reasonable representations on this matter. The claims of the young, the aspirant, the new and the experimental were to him repugnant. Gestation and birth were obnoxious physiological processes.

That the Arts Council, through Mr White, therefore had a geriatric complex was discerned by many an other than myself, and particularly by the editor of *The Times Literary Supplement*. Arthur Crook – an amiable eccentric – wrote diatribe after diatribe about our weird selections. He thought our choices of authors were idiosyncratic, highly subjective and not wholly unvenal. This left Mr White unmoved. In my experience everything left Mr White unmoved. But they left the Council and myself very moved. We were the targets of flights of arrows, spears, assagais, knobkerries and other native weapons, and we were an easy target. Week after week, like St Sebastian, we were perforated from top to toe, and we resented it and we remonstrated, but we failed to move the imperturbable Mr White. Moreover, he appeared to mesmerise his Literature Panel.

Cecil Day-Lewis, the Panel's chairman, was a magnificent presence, but alas as a chairman little more. He presided with benign calm over proceedings in which he appeared to take almost no interest. Hence, he was of limited use in the taming of a character as obdurate as Mr White. When these matters were raised at Council meetings, we were of course palmed off by the simplest of all devices – a statement of fact as though the fact were self-justificatory. Thus:

Chairman:	I notice we have given a prize to Mr William Gerhardie. Has Mr Gerhardie written a book recently?
Mr Day-Lewis:	The Panel decided he ought to receive a prize. [As indeed had already been noticed.]
Chairman:	Yes, but how contemporary is he?
Mr Day-Lewis:	We thought he would make a good prize-winner.
Chairman [faintly despairing]:	But what has he written since 1930?
Mr White:	Mr Gerhardie is an author we all prize highly. We thought it was a good idea to give him a prize.
Chairman:	I am sure you would not have given it to him if you thought it was a bad idea. But what has he written?
Mr White:	We have reason to believe that with encouragement he will write some more.
Chairman:	Do you not think we might give the prizes to younger authors who are still writing?
Mr White:	It is an encouragement to an older author to have a prize.

Thus the conversations were pursued in an endless, meaningless circle and the Gerhardies of literature continued to receive the prizes. I shared the view that Gerhardie was an interesting and indeed an important writer, but his age and the relative antiquity of his writing deprived a younger and more vigorous candidate of a grant that might influence his whole career.

Not unnaturally, but most unfairly, the dread word of partiality was introduced into the matter. Prizes, it was said, were being given to people's friends. Now I had no reason to suspect that anyone connected with the award of prizes was a friend of Mr Gerhardie, but it was difficult to think of any other reason why he should have had a prize, except the highly specialised make-up of Mr Eric White, and this could not be readily explained to *The Times Literary Supplement*.

I scrutinised the prize recommendations time and time again. They were invariably presented to the Council minutes before they were due to be announced and certainly after the recipients had been notified. And then one nomination was too much for me. I observed the name of Mr Gerald Hamilton – now deceased. Mr Gerald Hamilton was an infamous figure upon whom Christopher Isherwood had based his famous character in *Mr Norris Changes Trains*. Mr Hamilton had been Mr Norris. As well as being a famous literary creation, Mr Hamilton was a famous literary confidence trickster, had spent several periods in jail, had written a number of autobiographical works of a totally monotonous character and had spent his life defrauding the few friends upon whom he could batten. He was not a writer and could not write.

I had met him on one occasion when he came to sell me a set of letters allegedly written by Roger Casement in jail, before the authentic ones were made available. They were obvious, feeble forgeries. Mr Hamilton had had the wit to learn that Roger Casement was a homosexual and therefore he had larded daily commonplaces with a few details of homosexual activity. These letters he sought to sell to a publisher client of mine, who referred the matter to me. I read the letters, which were wearisomely obscene, and advised Mr Hamilton that he had no copyright in them, since you cannot have a copyright in obscene material. Mr Hamilton was chagrined and departed in a huff. That this character should receive a literary prize was one of the most astonishing awards of recent literary history, but receive it he did. Mr Eric White had determined that he was a proper recipient and so the Arts Council was once again pilloried. But my constant nagging had an effect. The veteran writers – long retired from the scene – were fewer and fewer in each list, until ultimately there was none.

Another rumpus was the case of the magazine *AMBIT*, which aroused fierce feelings. The magazine was a small-circulation literary publication which received a tiny grant from the Arts Council. There had been some controversy about the grant within the Literature Panel, but it was, after discussion, decided to continue with it. Shortly after this decision, it appeared with an interesting competition, offering a £25 prize, inevitably of Arts Council money, to the competitor who wrote the best piece of a given number of words 'while under the influence of drugs'. I think there were certain stipulations about the type of drug, heroin, opium, morphine and cocaine being probably excluded.

At Eric White's request, the matter was referred to the Literature Panel who recommended that the magazine should be informed of our displeasure and that possibly the grant for that issue should be withdrawn. My view was both more extreme and more simple. It appeared to me that a magazine that could engage in such puerility did not deserve an Arts Council grant and brought the Arts Council into disrepute. Hence, I proposed at the Council meeting that we should cancel their grant then and forever more. The response was in some ways astonishing. The chairman of the Literature Panel (then Angus Wilson) was clearly troubled at the illiberality of this attitude. He took the view that we should only cancel the grant if it was found that the action was illegal. Illegal it plainly was, but I was not particularly interested in the illegality but the imbecility of the transaction. Again, after a heated debate, a resolution was carried for the cancellation of the grant, although loud protestations as to the supposed illiberality of the decision continued for many weeks.

A further brush over drugs related to a character called Jim Haynes, who ran an institution in Covent Garden called the Arts Laboratory. Mr Haynes was also a contributor to, if not an editor of, the *International Times* and we had deep misgivings about what was going on at the Arts Laboratory. Our suspicions were that it was a place connected at least with marijuana if not with more dangerous and vicious forms of drug abuse.

The Arts Laboratory applied to us for a grant and I took the view that it would be entirely inappropriate for the Arts Council to give it a single penny. But again there was disagreement among the more unorthodox members of the Council who felt that we ought to give it a grant. On this occasion my view prevailed and no grant was made.

This caused great objection to a number of people, particularly to Mr Kenneth Tynan, who wrote an article on the subject announcing that Lord Goodman had one characteristic which was that if a committee was divided, with him on one side and the rest of the committee on the other, this was a deadlock situation. I bore these observations with remarkable fortitude, but remained uneasy with the continuing interest in drugs that had, to some extent, permeated the Arts Council. Happily that interest has totally disappeared, but in a sense it is anything but fortunate since the Council has now moved noticeably to the right. The important progressive steps that we always took – our total hatred of censorship and matters of that kind – can no longer be safely relied upon.

Unhappily, Eric White's retirement did not arrive until almost the last hour of my chairmanship. Despite his eccentricities he loved a great deal of literature and I have mentioned the respect and affection with which he was received at the various festivals over which he presided on our behalf. He was undoubtedly a strange man and he could have been produced nowhere but in an arts council, and certainly could not have spread his wings anywhere but in an arts council. I had the satisfaction towards the end of 1971 of appointing his successor – his deputy – who had been slightly tarred by his brush, but the stain was removed with vigorous applications of paraffin.

Charles Osborne was a controversial character. He was an Australian: young, choleric, excitable, and with a spectacular gift for insult which he indulged to the full; but he was very likeable and I developed a warm regard for him and quite a close friendship. However, I did not allow these considerations to weigh with me. We did, of course, advertise the job, but it emerged that of all the candidates, despite his obvious shortcomings, he was the best. Accordingly, contrary to my earlier prediction that nothing on earth would induce me to support his application to be the literature director, he was so duly appointed.

From time to time I have been able to render some assistance to people in other countries undergoing oppression from the existing political regime. On one occasion, during my period as chairman of the Arts Council, I received a message in my London legal office to say that two gentlemen would like to see me. It emerged that they were both Nigerians: one a huge figure attired in white sheeting, and the other a small, more dapper gentleman dressed in a conventional black jacket and striped trousers. The latter spoke English; the other gentleman, if he did speak English, did not utter a word during the entire interview – at least not a word to me.

The smaller one introduced himself as the secretary and aide-de-camp to the larger one who was, he told me, the chairman of the Nigerian Arts Council who had come to pay me fraternal greetings. They had brought with them a small bronze object, which was the figure of a Benin chief and which, I may say, I still retain in my office. I replied in very curt tones, 'Will you tell your friend, or principal, that I am not willing to accept this gift since I do not regard him as a person suitable to be the chairman of an Arts Council.' This aggressive reply I thought might provoke violence and, large as I am, I certainly would have been at a disadvantage where the other huge chairman was concerned. But no such thing happened. Instead, the aide-de-camp asked me in a quiet voice why I made this comment. 'Because,' I said, 'there are very few artists in Nigeria known to the outer world. I can only think of one, who is a poet, and at this moment you have him locked up. Your chairman ought to be working hard in Nigeria trying to get him released and not paying fraternal visits all over the place.'

These words were translated to the Nigerian chairman, who again responded impassively. They spoke together for a few moments and then came back with a rather strange enquiry: 'On what terms will you accept the gift?' they said. I replied that I would accept a gift if they gave me an undertaking that on their return to Nigeria the chairman would do his best to secure the release of the unfortunate poet. They again retired in close colloquy for quite a few minutes and returned to declare, 'Your terms are accepted.' I thereupon said, 'I will give you a piece of my notepaper and ask you, please, to report to me as soon as possible on the success of your efforts.' They agreed to do this and withdrew.

Some weeks later I received a letter from Nigeria – the man concerned was, I subsequently discovered, an important Chief – saying that they were working on the matter but 'the man was very difficult'. I replied that the chairman of an arts council should know that creative people, including poets, were bound to be difficult and please would he not relax his efforts. I am happy to say that, whether in consequence of my initiative or other reasons, the poet was released, came to England, won the Nobel Prize for Literature and, so far as I know, is living in freedom to this day. His name is Wole Soyinka.

Even though they can be 'very difficult', I have always admired and stood in awe of really creative people. Although I had only the most tenuous association with him, the poet Robert Lowell lives in my memory. I encountered him in rather tragic circumstances. I was visiting a young and unfortunate protégé of mine in a psychiatric nursing home in Regent's Park, where Robert Lowell turned out to be occupying an adjoining room. He was a man of great charm and I was a great admirer of his. Poetry, alas, has meant little to me, but drama has meant a lot. One of my most exhilarating dramatic experiences was to see his poetic play *Benvenuto Cellini* at the Mermaid Theatre. This is not a moment for literary criticism, but I think it is one of the great plays and I have a firm conviction that it will live. It was immensely exciting. As a piece of theatrical construction, it was amazing that a man who had occupied himself principally with his more orthodox poetry should have produced a play so perfectly rounded in form and content.

Another poet for whom I have great admiration is Stephen Spender. I met him many years ago and, although I cannot claim great friendship, we have always been on excellent terms. I advised him on one occasion in 1967 when he was exercised about his association with the magazine *Encounter*. *Encounter* was being financed by Cecil King of the *Daily Mirror*, and Stephen Spender and Frank Kermode, his associate editor, discovered to their consternation that some money had apparently been supplied by the CIA. I must confess that I am less fastidious in these matters. If the CIA were spending their money on a virtuous artistic cause, it would be a matter of very little concern to me. In fact I think it would be better spent than on their normal activities, but it certainly was a great concern both to Spender and Kermode.

I remember being heavily involved, particularly in talking to Cecil King about not withdrawing his support. He did in fact withdraw his support, as the support of the Kings – including his lady wife – was on the whole capricious. I recollect that his wife, Dame Ruth Railton, was for a time subsidising the Youth Orchestra, but the subsidy was withdrawn at a moment's notice. I encountered the situation when I was chairman of the Arts Council because the orchestra had made a direct appeal to Jennie Lee. Jennie in turn appealed to the Arts Council to see if we could replace the funds, but of course, as always, the Arts Council was in its usual Mother Hubbard predicament: there was nothing in the cupboard. However, we were able to raise, from private sources, the sum of £20,000 which kept the orchestra going until they found other sponsorship. It was an unhappy termination of what had been a long and generous association, and one wonders what sort of caprice can seize the mind of people whereby they suddenly lose all interest and all affection for a cause which they have supported for years.

At an early stage in my chairmanship of the Arts Council I became heavily involved in the affairs of the Hayward Gallery. A quite sensible arrangement had been evolved whereby the cost of building the gallery and all incidentals was borne by the Greater London Council and the function of running the gallery devolved on the Arts Council who had a total discretion about the exhibitions or any other use.

As I look at the Hayward Gallery now it seems to me to have improved since it was built. At the beginning there was a general feeling that one forfeited any claim to be an aesthete if one liked it. But with the passage of time, and an opportunity of comparing it with some of the appalling horrors that are now gaily passed by planning committees, it has become almost a thing of beauty.

I saw the Hayward first when a party of Arts Council members were shown over. I formed the view that it would just do. It was to have the status of an international gallery, used for important loan collections; but as we went round I noticed that some of the members were displaying an increasing discontent because of the almost total absence of natural light. When we returned to the Arts Council there was a consensus that the GLC should be asked to make modest alterations that would allow the pictures to be seen by natural as well as artificial light. I had a brief word with a senior official at the GLC who informed me that there was nothing in their budget that could be used to make any changes and that we must be satisfied with what we had.

When I reported this back to the Council, the general feeling, forcibly stirred by me and others, was that we should fight to prevent the gallery becoming a white elephant, as in most views it would be if it was never possible to see any picture by natural light. We decided to take a delegation to see the Leader of the GLC and my first choice was, of course, Henry Moore. I telephoned him to arrange to show him over the gallery, just before the delegation was due to present itself at County Hall. His first reaction was what I had hoped for. This was an issue which, however much one was prone to fence-sitting, required in his opinion a strong and even violent representation. I had never seen Henry in such a state of indignation.

We proceeded to the meeting where the first response to our representations was that to introduce natural light would cost an additional £120,000, and if we insisted on such modifications we would have to bear the full cost. Henry then went into action. He beat the table and denounced the GLC for employing an architect who did not realise the essentials for a modern picture gallery. 'If you do not spend the £120,000,' he said, 'you will have wasted the entire cost of the gallery.' His eyes gleamed with pleasure at the fray.

It was impossible for the GLC to muster any spokesman of Henry's authority and vigour. After an hour's discussion they discovered that they just might have some funds to make a modest alteration. We stipulated that we should see the proposed alteration in plan and if satisfied would make no further noise. In the event the cost was about £10,000 and a measure of natural light was introduced into the top galleries.

The opening of the Hayward Gallery in July 1968 involved an unexpected drama. The art director of the Arts Council was Gabriel White, as agreeable and gentle a man as one could hope to meet and a not inconsiderable artist. He arrived in my office one morning in a mood of despair. 'I have done something awful,' he said, 'or, more truthfully, have not done something and not doing it is the awfulness. I have forgotten to ask in good time for Her Majesty the Queen to be available to perform the opening of the gallery. The place is due to be opened in about three months' time on a day fixed with the GLC and on enquiry at Buckingham Palace I was told by the Queen's Secretary that every minute of her day on that date was pledged.'

Poor White was almost in tears. He had come to ask me whom else might be suggested to open the Hayward. We decided that our determination that it should rank as a great European gallery made it impossible to ask anyone except a member of the royal family and, on reflection, not to ask any member of the royal family other than the Queen. I suggested that in the circumstances Henry Moore or Francis Bacon might be regarded as suitable. But on further reflection we decided that asking an artist to open the gallery might cause resentment and would not have anything like the authority of an opening by the Queen.

The unfortunate White was in a state of increasing despair. To comfort him I suggested that as I had been invited (I should say for the first and only time) to Windsor for a large dinner party and to stay the night, I would make any effort I could to persuade the Queen's Secretary to persuade the Queen that this was an occasion of national importance and merited some change in her plans.

On arrival at Windsor the arrangements were exemplary. I was shown to a comfortable room by Sir Michael Adeane and I took a moment to unburden myself about our problem. He frowned and told me that the Queen hated cancelling any engagement since it was bound to cause disappointment and therefore he felt unable to put my request to her. But when he saw my almost tearful response he suggested, 'Ask her yourself. She will be taking the guests round the pictures after dinner and there will be a good opportunity to speak to her.'

True enough, the standard after-dinner entertainment at Windsor appeared to be viewing the pictures and we set off in a party, guided by Her Majesty, who seemed to have a total knowledge of everything in the place. After a little while I dropped back and – as Adeane must have said something to her – she dropped back also and I was able to make my request. It was clearly not one that met with favour. 'I am afraid that I am booked for the whole of the day and I cannot possibly disappoint someone who already has a promise.' Fortunately she then said, 'You must get somebody else to do it.' It gave me the opportunity of saying that she must be the only person in England who could believe that someone else could understudy her. When I had said that, and added, 'You are the only person in England, Ma'am, who cannot be replaced', she looked at me very hard and asked if I really believed that. I assured her that it was a belief that would be universally shared. She paused for a moment and said, 'If that is so, I must do it, mustn't I?'

The next morning, after my excellent breakfast, Sir Michael Adeane called on me, together with an enormous morocco-bound diary. He opened it at the day in question and I had immense satisfaction in seeing him pushing one appointment up and another one down until he left something over an hour for our opening.

In the event, the Queen performed the task and stayed over two hours talking to the visitors who had been invited to the ceremony. I returned to the Arts Council to be acclaimed. I had an enormous feeling of satisfaction that I had played some part in saving the day, although any real credit attached to Her Majesty alone.

There have been a few other occasions when I have found myself in a less formal contact with Her Majesty than usual. On one occasion I was invited, as many other people are, to lunch at Buckingham Palace. I was sitting next to her and we chatted away animatedly without the slightest difficulty. I discovered that she was a very easy person to talk to and had a quite amazing knowledge of contemporary events. On another occasion I found myself in more intimate circumstances as the only guest, apart from Her Majesty, at a dinner party organised by Lord and Lady Rupert Nevill at their London home. The evening was an enormous success. We were supposed to depart at 11.30 p.m., but so lively and interesting was the conversation that in fact it was midnight before the party broke up. She had come on her own and clearly enjoyed the opportunity of an escape from royal functions and the formality of it all.

My appointment as chairman of the Arts Council had one important consequence in relation to my style of life. Inevitably I became closely associated with the country's leading artists and I became a friend, and in some cases a close friend, of a number of distinguished artists. The most prominent was the late Francis Bacon, whom I represented on one or two occasions, particularly in a sensational case in 1970 relating to a totally baseless charge that he was in possession of marijuana. The trouble began when Bacon telephoned me out of the blue to say that he had been visited by two police officers – one man and one woman – who had asked if they could examine his home as they had reason to believe that drugs were located there. Bacon wanted my advice as to what he ought to do. I told him that he should not allow them to search the premises without a warrant and that I would have a word with the inspector in charge at Chelsea police station.

I telephoned the inspector and said to him that I was representing Mr Bacon and that I felt sure that he knew – although I had the gravest doubt that the inspector would ever have heard of him – that Mr Bacon was one of the leading artists in the world, that great British prestige and credit derived from him, and that it would be very unfortunate indeed if allegations were made against him in circumstances which might bring his reputation into discredit. The inspector appeared to agree with me, and assured me that he would give the most sympathetic consideration to the matter. I telephoned Francis and told him that he must now await an urgent visit, since I did not have the slightest faith in the assurances given by the police, nor in fact would it have been proper for them to give any.

True enough, the very next morning at 8.30 a.m. I was telephoned by Francis Bacon to say that this time the police had arrived in force, together with two Alsatian sniffer dogs. The police had also brought a search warrant. I asked to speak to the inspector again and said, 'You gave me to understand that you would not continue this quest.' 'Ah!' he said. 'My duty demands that I pursue any report of alleged criminality.' To which I enquired whether his duty required that he should also tell lies to members of the public and particularly to a member of the House of Lords (pulling rank, I fear, is something one is occasionally required to do!). He was slightly embarrassed by this enquiry but said that he had to continue the search.

Some half an hour later, the inspector telephoned me to say that he had found some substance – Francis Bacon's studio contained thousands of empty paint-boxes in which anything might have been concealed by anyone – and that he was asking Mr Bacon to accompany him to Chelsea police station. 'I am proposing,' I said, 'to tell Mr Bacon that he should not go anywhere with you.' To which the inspector promptly replied that if that was the case, he would have to arrest him. 'Please do,' I declared, 'and will you be good enough to tell me whether you have a notebook?' 'Yes,' sighed the inspector, 'I have a notebook.' 'Good,' I said. 'Will you write down that at 9.10 a.m. you informed Lord Goodman that you were arresting his client Mr Francis Bacon and proposing to take him to a police station on the charge of being in possession of a substance which was a drug. Would you also make a note that Lord Goodman rejoined that you were making this arrest before you had had any opportunity to examine the substance and that in his view the substance had been planted by the police.' This obviously caused the inspector to jump back on his ankles, but he made the note and I then travelled down to the police station – it was just before 11 a.m. – to find that evening-paper posters were already announcing in large letters 'Famous Artist Arrested'. When I arrived I was able to assert to the police that they must have disclosed this information since no one else could possibly have known it.

We elected to go for trial. I briefed Basil Wigoder QC to defend Francis Bacon and for a variety of reasons, not least because of the precipitate way in which the police had handled the matter, Francis was triumphantly and very properly acquitted. The charge was a particularly ridiculous once since he did not smoke cigarettes and it struck me as extremely unlikely that a man who does not smoke cigarettes would be smoking marijuana. Be that as it may, the charge was disposed of and that was the end of the matter.

I remained on the friendliest terms with Francis Bacon. Periodically we dined together, occasionally in the company of the late Alfred Hecht, probably the most distinguished picture-framer in the world. In fact a word or two needs to be said about Alfred Hecht: a German refugee of the most generous and kindly disposition, but also of a most temperamental character, who contracted very strong feelings about almost anything and with whom I was on friendly terms for years. He had acquired over the years, through his associations with artists, one of the most outstanding collections of modern art in the country – Bacons, Graham Sutherlands, Henry Moores, Ben Nicholsons, Matthew Smiths abounded. This collection was sacred to him and to my certain knowledge he never sold a picture during his lifetime. After his death the collection had to be sold to pay large arrears of tax, but several pictures were distributed as legacies, including one to me.

More recently I have become friendly with Lucian Freud, now acclaimed as a leading British painter, his reputation greatly enhanced by the sensational prices that he receives for any work, and in particular a full-length work. I met him several years ago through Clarissa Avon, a good friend of both of us. Whether he was seized by an impulse or had been contemplating it for some time, he announced to me that he would very much like to draw me and, as with Graham Sutherland a few years previously, I regarded the approach as a great compliment. He started work in the early 1980s and thereafter continued for several years, making in all no fewer than four drawings of me, and at the end one etching. In my view the best of the drawings is a pastel, which was enormously improved by the addition of colour.

Another artist with whom I have had the friendliest associations is one of the most delightful women I know, namely Bridget Riley. I cannot claim to be a great admirer of her work – it is too geometric for my taste, and she contrives an arrangement of lines and a combination of patterns that is dazzling. However, there is no doubt that she is an artist of great talent, but more than that she is a person of great determination and character. I met her first when she refused to join the Arts Council, and in fact had a view that she should have nothing to do with the Establishment. In later years this has altered: she has become a trustee of the National Gallery and is regarded as the natural leader of the artistic proletariat.

I recollect, when I was at the Arts Council, how intensely she worked to organise accommodation for a great number of artists at St Katharine's Dock, where she exercised an iron discipline with those who took the accommodation, requiring them to keep it clean and tidy and, although a slight and attractive figure, instilling in them such a terror that not a single one of them would dare to deviate from the rules.

However, perhaps my most fortunate association with an artist was the role that I played in the life and affairs of England's greatest sculptor – Henry Moore. As I have already said, my first encounter with him was at my own first meeting of the Arts Council. I had been flung in at the deep end but was gratified by the immense friendliness of all the members of the Council, although not from all the permanent staff.

For the first few years of my chairmanship I saw little of Henry, but enough to create a warm relationship between us. At some stage around 1969 he sought my advice about creating a trust to which, as an act of the most massive generosity, he had decided to bequeath every one of his works, with a few insignificant exceptions, and the resources of which were to be used to advance the interests of artists and sculptors throughout the country, and indeed the world. Numerous visits by me to the Inland Revenue at Somerset House produced agreement to the creation of a trust and the consent of the Revenue extended to a willingness to allow Moore to receive a modest portion of the receipts, sufficient for him to maintain his style of life, which was certainly an economical one.

As a result of this arrangement, it was necessary to establish the Henry Moore Foundation, which is now a large and self-governing organisation, sited at Much Hadham in Hertfordshire and meeting three or four times a year to determine how to deal with its ample resources (now exceeding £30 million). Henry invited me to become the chairman of the Foundation and this I remain until the present day. From time to time members were added to the working committee and there were impressive and important recruits such as Lord Rayne, and Sir Alan Bowness as director.

Henry was a delightful man to deal with. A firm character without any affectations, but quick in decision and as warm and reliable a friend as one could hope for. He was supported by his devoted wife Irene, who looked after him magnificently until his death in 1986. It was Henry's wish that the major benefactions of the Foundation should be towards sculpture. Pursuant to that wish the main purpose of the trust is, not unnaturally, to organise loans, and occasionally gifts, of some of Henry's works. There is a ceaseless demand which exceeds the available supply. Exhibitions have been organised in various parts of the world with support from the Foundation. Additionally, it provides charitable support for young sculptors and other artists in the hope of assisting them to attain the great reputation of the Foundation's founder. Of recent years, however, there has been unfortunate controversy, largely inspired by Moore's daughter. Resentful that her father had not reappointed her as a trustee, she seized the occasion to grumble everywhere where her voice could be heard. As to the merits of her complaints, I leave it to others to determine, but it has certainly been an unnecessary and tiresome embarrassment in relation to my chairmanship of the Foundation.

A leading figure in the art world who has been a client of my firm on a number of occasions is Norton Simon, who has a remarkable collection of art and objects of virtu in his museum in Los Angeles. He is a difficult man to draw out, but when drawn out a fascinating man. He has made an enormous fortune, largely in connection with food, and has devoted a good part of it to collecting a magnificent array of pictures, sculptures and *objets d'art* which, although not perhaps challenging the Getty collection, is in some ways regarded as more discriminating because it reflects the taste and knowledge of a single individual.

My path first crossed with Mr Simon's in relation to a bronze Buddha, regarded as the oldest Buddha in the world. The story relating to it might easily be a work of fiction and indeed would make a splendid novel or film. The Buddha was in the possession of a monastery in New Delhi. The monks there enjoyed a spiritual life such that material comforts were totally denied to them; the poor creatures were, I was told, on the verge of starvation. Driven by a necessity beyond control, they summoned a merchant from Bombay, ostensibly with the instruction of taking the Buddha away and cleaning it. But the *real* instructions were that he should take the Buddha and sell it, and replace it with an imitation Buddha which the monks could then put in its place without anyone noticing. Since the number of people who might visit the monastery and be able to tell the difference would be virtually nil, the monks assumed they were on to a good thing.

Unhappily they did not bargain for a learned busybody – in the most innocent sense – from the British Museum. This man was a world authority on Buddhas, bronze or otherwise. The aim of his life was to see this Buddha, and one day he contrived to find the resources and the time for a visit to India. By great misfortune he chose to visit the monastery on a religious holiday when all the monks were away, leaving only a harizan caretaker. The caretaker could not resist the request from the expert that he should see the Buddha, since he had travelled an enormous distance, half-way across the world, to do so, so he showed it to him. To his horror, the British Museum man realised that the Buddha had been made in Sheffield and was not an article of great antiquity. Very properly, he informed the Indian government. The Indian government immediately initiated an investigation. They discovered that the real Buddha had been sold to a merchant in New York, from whom Norton Simon had purchased it in total good faith.

In 1974 proceedings were instituted by the Indian government to recover the Buddha. Additionally, proceedings were instituted in England for the bizarre reason that the principal cleaner of Buddhas in the world is a daughter of Lord and Lady Plowden and the Buddha reposed with this lady. Action was, therefore, started in both New York and England. My firm represented Mr Simon in England.

It seemed to me that the Buddha was destined to remain here for a very long time. It also seemed to me unfortunate that during that time it should not be available to the public at large. I therefore telephoned Sir John Pope-Hennessy, who was then the Director of the British Museum, to acquaint him of the circumstances and ask if he would like to borrow the Buddha for the British Museum during the period of the litigation. His first reaction was one of considerable enthusiasm. To my surprise he telephoned a few days later to indicate that in all the circumstances he did not think that the British Museum wanted it.

I then telephoned Dr Roy Strong at the Victoria & Albert Museum to make the same offer. His initial reaction was equally enthusiastic, and his subsequent response equally unenthusiastic. I made a discovery: there was a curse associated with this Buddha and anyone taking possession of it contrary to its real ownership might have unmentionable horrors inflicted on him. Whether this had operated on the minds of the two museum directors I do not know, but in the end the Buddha reposed in the vaults of Coutts Bank. I informed Seymour Egerton, the Chairman of Coutts & Co., that disaster would befall the bank in no time at all. Happily, that prediction was totally unfulfilled.

In the end the matter was settled by Mr Simon with characteristic generosity. It was agreed by the Indian government that he could retain the Buddha for a number of years on view and then return it to India and the monastery whence it came. I do not know what happened to the unfortunate monks. I would be quite surprised if any of them survived.

14

On and Off Stage

THE THEATRE HAS been of profound interest to me from early school days, and when I became chairman of the Arts Council, promoting the welfare of theatre throughout the country was something that aroused my special concern. I enjoyed engaging in it as much as, or even more than, any other Council activity, even the musical activity.

Before 1965, when my chairmanship began, I had had a few preliminary concerns with the National Theatre, starting in 1960 when the late Emile Littler, who although no intellectual was an important force in the commercial theatre, suggested to Lord Chandos, the chairman of the board engaged in planning the theatre, that my firm should become the solicitors to the project. The planning process had been a slow one over many years, since the original foundation stone – with which Lord Chandos's family had been concerned – was laid in 1951. I had not met Lord Chandos and the close friendship that was to develop between us was some way off. When I did meet him my first impression was of a slightly burlesque, patrician figure, with more than a touch of arrogance and as profound an ignorance of the theatre as was possible for one man to marshal in a lifetime.

Anyway, I received a polite letter from Emile Littler to say that I had been appointed the solicitor to the newly constituted National Theatre and I received visits from Mr Kenneth Rae in confirmation of this lofty office. Mr Rae was the secretary of the National Theatre; an amiable man, who discharged his duties with great zeal and earned the respect and affection of everyone.

My duties were to draft a constitution. Lord Chandos had a deep hostility to royal charters, based no doubt on an unsatisfactory experience that some relative had had in extracting one from Henry VIII or Richard III. He viewed them with suspicion and declared them to be unalterable.

I did my best to persuade him that they admitted of considerable elasticity and were rather good things to operate under, both in terms of prestige and malleability; but in my early days it became clear to me that Lord Chandos had not earned his reputation by being easily persuaded of things. Our brief encounter at that period would not to the eye of the unbiased have presaged the idyll of our future relationship eight or ten years hence. In fact Lord Chandos decided after a period that he preferred to employ his own City solicitors and I faded from the scene, but not without some entertaining experiences.

Having drafted a constitution, I was approached confidentially by Mr Rae and was told that it was now planned that the theatre was to be established, preferably on the basis that it would also incorporate the Royal Shakespeare Theatre at Stratford, but from the point of view of the National Theatre it was necessary to know the reaction of the powers at the Royal Shakespeare Trust. Although this was an unorthodox requirement for a solicitor, I was instructed to find out. I was then told that the body was also to incorporate the Sadler's Wells organisation at Rosebery Avenue, the intention being that their present opera house was to be replaced by a new one within the curtilage of the new National Theatre. So I went on my new rounds.

Sadler's Wells presented little difficulty. The Hon. Jimmy Smith was then the chairman and an immensely amiable, kindly and gentle figure. Stephen Arlen was the director, and the document was agreed without trouble. The next move was to visit Stratford. I travelled north on a Saturday, the intention being that I should lunch with the persons concerned and attend a performance in the evening. I took with me the rather highly-strung wife of a close friend of mine who was anxious to see the play. This was a mistake. She collapsed at various points all over Stratford, particularly at the very beginning of the play – *Hamlet*, with Ian Bannen in the title role – so that I had to cart her back to the hotel, have her attended to and dash back to the theatre for the next two acts.

But before that I had met the Stratford organisation, consisting of Sir Fordham Flower, the chairman, much beloved, effective, simple and nice; Peter Hall, much beloved, effective, complicated and often nice; and various other faces including Mr Patrick Donnell, later the administrative director of the National Theatre, to whom I explained the document in the naive belief that the principle had been agreed.

They looked at the document with lack-lustre eyes and minimal interest. Who, they said, is to be the head of the organisation? I coughed slightly, since no one had told me, but I opined that it was likely to be Sir Laurence Olivier. There was an exchange of glances, and faces which had never been wholly welcoming became rather distant. It was clear to me within seconds that on the basis of the leadership of Laurence Olivier, to whose qualities they paid tribute of unstinting eloquence, there was going to be no Stratford included in the new entity. They told me that they wished to consider the matter further; that there were complicated reasons why it might be difficult for Stratford to become absorbed, and I departed from lunch firmly convinced that we had seen the last of them, at least while Sir Laurence dominated the scene. I was right. Stratford withdrew with great speed and for reasons which were never the real ones.

The National Theatre was not daunted by this set-back. It was established at the Old Vic in 1963, with Sir Laurence as its chief executive, its patron saint and its hero. He directed the plays, he acted in the plays, he installed his wife Joan Plowright in the few parts he could not play himself, and he turned it into a family romp of remarkable quality and charm. Some of the productions were outstanding. How well one remembers *Hobson's Choice*, with a rare appearance by another of the knights, Sir Michael Redgrave, and an early appearance of Lady Olivier – with whose face we were to become increasingly familiar; *The Recruiting Officer*, *Othello*, *The Dance of Death* and a myriad of other splendid plays. And the theatre flourished and its fame grew and it seemed as though there were no heights it would not attain. It recruited a great company. There was Colin Blakely, an immensely distinguished actor; Robert Stephens – who can forget him in *The Royal Hunt of the Sun*? Maggie Smith, Derek Jacobi, Geraldine McEwan, and, when wanted, Gielgud – horribly miscast in *Tartuffe*, but what an actor; and Albert Finney – such splendid clodhopping in the Feydeau *A Flea in her Ear*.

Nothing could go wrong, but everything did go wrong. For whatever the reason, the cast lost enthusiasm and became disaffected. Great actors came once and not again. Murmurs of dissatisfaction were heard on many sides and Sir Laurence at his moment of triumph fell into ill health and struggled to cope with the burdens of difficult people and difficult productions at the same time as he was sustaining serious illness, and his struggles were heroic but to some extent unavailing. They took West End theatres and lost small fortunes with a choice of productions which became increasingly idiosyncratic. *The Captain of Köpenick*, a creaking continental masterpiece, was followed by *Amphitryon 38*, a creaking continental triviality. *Danton's Death* could not come a moment too early, and not even the trendy name of Jonathan Miller could save that production. And then came an Adrian Mitchell musical – Lord love us – about William Blake, *Tyger, Tyger*. Flat, pretentious and silly, it presented a satire of the chairman of the Arts Council so inadequate that I failed to recognise myself. There were few people who can more easily and more effectively be satirised and a dramatist who could not bring me off should get himself a porter's knot.

But there it was. Once things took to sliding, they slid. Discussions ensued about succession. Laurence Olivier was undecided and indecisive. He had notions of a triumvirate to succeed him, including his lady wife. He had notions of a consortium of directors to run the theatre with a triumvirate. None of his notions was realistic. A great theatre must be run by a single individual. It cannot be run by a committee and least of all by a nepotistic committee. It was clear to me that when the new theatre was opened, and Sir Laurence would then be well into his sixties, it was time for a change on the footing that his great services still remained available as a guide and a director.

But change to whom? Quietly and away from the light of day – and no sensible decisions are made under the searching light of inquisitive scrutiny – Max Rayne (the newly appointed chairman of the National Theatre) and I, as chairman of the Arts Council, examined every possible claimant. There were surprisingly few. There were many in the sense that the larger repertory theatres, which had been created in recent years because of increasing subsidy, had trained a good many successful producers who ran good theatres with great success; but surprisingly few because none of them was young enough to give them the time that would be needed for the transition from a small regional theatre to a great national and international organisation. We decided that it must be a man of theatrical renown and international repute. There was only one such to whom we turned, with a considerable measure of reluctance.

Peter Hall's remarkable career had now graduated from Stratford, which he had left for no discernible reason, to the Royal Opera House, Covent Garden, which had enlisted him with even less reason. He was a theatrical director of very great experience and high talent. He knew the theatre backwards and was loved and respected by everyone who worked with him; disliked by many people who had not worked with him and who suspected that they had been wrongly excluded from important participation. He was not an operatic producer. He had done some interesting work. His *Moses and Aaron* had produced more Israelites on the stage of Covent Garden than habitually sat in the stalls. This was a want of balance I was entitled to point out to him. His orgy in that opera, which had aroused the keenest expectations, was a bitter disappointment. A feebler orgy had rarely been seen. And he did *The Magic Flute* in English – God forgive him – which demonstrated the laboured nature of the witticisms and the idiocy of most of the text, so there was nothing much to lose by transferring him from the opera house, and by then I think he had realised that this was no home for him.

Peter Hall accepted the directorship of the National Theatre with alacrity and expressed requirements which demonstrated the greatest propriety as to the relationship with his predecessor. He had to be satisfied that the change was acceptable to Olivier and the two men behaved well and generously, with only occasional bursts of petulance from the senior statesman. Olivier accepted that Hall would succeed him, that the change would take place when the new theatre was opened and that in the meantime he would lend aid and support.

Shortly after this, Sir Laurence came to see me at the Arts Council to thank me for the consideration I had shown in relation to his resignation. It came as something of a surprise, therefore, to discover that around the same day a report had been circulated among the National Theatre staff that Sir Laurence had been brutally removed without any consultation. Where this report came from has always for me been a matter of speculation, but, as I have infinite trust in the human race, I have not pursued the speculation to a conclusion. However, this was not of importance and the transition took place smoothly and generously on all sides in November 1973.

Associated with Sir Laurence's departure was an offer from Harold Wilson that Sir Laurence should accept the first peerage ever bestowed on an actor. Harold Wilson had made the suggestion to me. Sir Laurence's first reaction was to refuse it. Harold Wilson telephoned me to tell me of this and that he hoped I would be able to persuade Larry to accept it. I had a short conversation with Larry, explaining that he was not entitled to refuse it as, immense compliment as it was to him, it was an even greater compliment to the theatre and all his colleagues. I am pleased to say that he accepted the honour and that I was one of his two supporters – Lord Nelson being the other – to introduce him into the Lords: an interesting ceremony where he repaid me by reducing me to near exhaustion.

The introductory ceremony involves the new peer, preceded by his junior sponsor, in this case myself, and followed by his senior sponsor, parading round the House, stopping at intervals to bow to the Chair. When the far side of the House is reached, the trio then ascend the stairs to the back of the benches where, directed – *sotto voce* – by the official concerned, generally the Knight King of Arms, they rise from the bench and subside three times, each time when erect doffing their three-cornered hats to the Lord Chancellor who, remaining seated, doffs his in polite acknowledgement. On the way round, the new peer halts at the Clerk's table and reads the oath – a lengthy and splendid oath – declaring his determination to maintain the Crown and everything associated with it.

The old-established procedure is that before the actual ceremony, and while no member has yet been admitted to the House, the small procession undertakes a rehearsal, since it is a matter of pride to the official concerned that he has schooled his team to give a creditable performance. The rehearsal duly took place: Sir Laurence reading out the words of the oath as no peer had ever done before, with a splendour of voice previously unequalled. When the rehearsal was over, I – as may be known being slightly overweight – was puffing in the corridor, when Sir Laurence somewhat diffidently said to the official, 'I am not at all sure I have got it right', although it could not matter tuppence whether he had or had not. 'Do you think,' he said, dropping his voice, 'that I might dare to ask that we do it again?' This gave me no satisfaction, but nevertheless we re-formed and went through the procedure once more.

I was puffing a little harder in the corridor after concluding the performance for the second time when, Sir Laurence, with a diffidence that only one of the world's great actors could display, tremulously asked, 'Might I dare ask that we do it once more?' I emitted a low moan. There was hardly any breath left in my body. But nevertheless, since his being there was my fault, I acquiesced with reasonable grace and we trooped round for the third time, reducing me to a state of total exhaustion.

However, when performing the live version, he did it with such magnificence, and read the oath so splendidly, that I do not think there has been a better performance in the House of Lords for the ennoblement of a peer. It is ironic that after all the difficulty of getting him installed, I believe that over the years Lord Olivier only appeared and spoke at one debate, but he indeed made history as the first professional actor to appear in that assembly.

Such was my success as a supporter that over the years, until lameness impelled me to refuse invitations, I was probably the most popular peer sought for this function. Apart from Lord Olivier, I introduced Lord Wigg, Lord Kissin, Lord Gibson (my successor at the Arts Council) and in 1976 Lord Rayne.

Max Rayne was appointed the chairman of the National Theatre in 1971 following the retirement of Lord Chandos, with whom I had by then established a firm and valued friendship. Jennie Lee had asked me for a recommendation and I made what I think turned out to be an inspired suggestion that Sir Max should take the job. Although he knew little or nothing about the theatre, I had first seen his quality when I invited him to become a director of British Lion under my chairmanship. He remained the conscientious and indeed indefatigable chairman of the National Theatre until his retirement from the office in 1988 on the somewhat unexpected appointment of Lady Soames to succeed him.

I realised when suggesting him that his knowledge of the theatre was slight, but the most urgent requirement was a man who could exercise a sensible financial control, particularly as the office involved a close connection with the building plan. Max discharged these administrative requirements with conspicuous skill and I believe his receptive mind has over the years made him something of an authority on the theatre. When first appointed, I doubt if he knew Ibsen from a poached egg, but today I have not the least doubt he would have seen numerous performances of *A Doll's House, Hedda Gabler, Rosmersholm* and the rest, and can tell you with satisfaction about his favourite performance in *An Enemy of the People* or *Peer Gynt.*

He has served the world of theatre with great distinction and deserves the gratitude of all theatre-lovers. In many moments of crisis, his sensible, conciliatory, common-sense approach steered the theatrical boat through turbulent seas and he showed a particular skill in dealing with Sir Peter Hall, often when that great figure was at his most troublesome. It is a remarkable tribute to both these men that, although they had profound differences over the years, they maintained a cordial relationship. The situation was, I think, made the easier because Max Rayne at no time professed any expert knowledge or sought to interfere with casting or other production details. I have to confess that I should have found it difficult to exercise a similar restraint. I rarely see a theatrical classic where I am not convinced that I could have done the casting better, and when it comes to the choice of repertoire I ache with pain at the notable omissions.

However, I must return to the building of the National Theatre. In 1962 a board (the South Bank Theatre Board) had been appointed which had the responsibility for supervising the building of both a new National Theatre and a new opera house on the South Bank, chaired by Lord Cottesloe, then the chairman of the Arts Council. There was an obvious attraction in a new opera house alongside a new National Theatre as part of the same design. The architect selected had been chosen by some psychic process. A committee of three met with a number of architects picked at random and interviewed them. Their innermost souls told them, possibly rightly, that the best applicant was Mr Denys Lasdun and so this immensely talented peacock of the slide-rule was installed in office to produce designs which will be the subject of controversy for a generation. His concept was vast, massive and expensive. For every inch of auditorium and every millimetre of stage, he had feet, if not acres, of foyers, vestibules and other aesthetic irrelevancies that delighted our hearts and tortured the representatives of the Greater London Council on the South Bank Theatre Board.

On the day that I attended my first meeting of the Arts Council as chairman, Denys Lasdun was demonstrating to the press his model of the new National Theatre and opera house. It was then believed that the total cost of the two buildings would be £7.5 million. In 1966, however, Jennie Lee called a meeting to discuss the current situation with regard to the building of the National Theatre (the financial feasibility of the opera house then being in some doubt). The meeting was informed that the estimated cost of the project would exceed the £7.5 million to be jointly provided by the GLC and the government. The building would contain two auditoria: one proscenium and one open stage. The meeting took the view that the proposed capacity of the proscenium theatre was inadequate and that for sensible economic reasons it should not be less than 1,000 seats. The South Bank Theatre Board and the National Theatre Board stuck to the view that a capacity of 850 to 900 represented the ideal size for a proscenium theatre. Neither Jennie nor I were totally persuaded, but as sensible people we felt it proper to defer in theatre matters to the views of experts or supposed experts and the Arts Council's Drama Panel, which had previously shared our concern that the proscenium theatre was too small. We then met with Denys Lasdun and were convinced by him that the 850–900 capacity was the right one. The South Bank Theatre Board instructed Lasdun to proceed on this basis and on the basis of an open-stage theatre seating 1,200–1,250.

Both Jennie and I took what I regard as a sensible view that to associate the building of the National Theatre with a new opera house might be fatal to both projects, since it would lend strength to the many opponents of such cultural schemes that the total cost was excessive. In the end we were able to persuade the South Bank Theatre Board and the government that the opera house should be dropped – a decision which was arrived at by the government with little or no reluctance.

There was an anxious period when a halt was called to the plan to build the National Theatre, and Jennie and I went to see the Chancellor of the Exchequer, Roy Jenkins: a civilised man who required little persuasion that the project should go ahead and that to abandon it would be a serious discouragement to the theatrical public in London and indeed throughout the country. I made the observation that this was one area where economics needed to be wisely judged. I remarked that the Colosseum had served the Roman public well with its variety of delectable spectacles and that no one could remember the name of a single senator who had urged economy, although I had no doubt that several such must have existed.

I myself became a member of the South Bank Theatre Board in 1968, and at various stages along the road to the completion of the National Theatre there were terrible crises, largely prompted by the GLC representatives calling at some given moment for a firm estimate of residual cost. I do not think these demands reduced the cost or safeguarded the position, since the building was already well on its way before they were first voiced. But every so often a panic ensued. The GLC, not being satisfied that there would be enough money to complete the building, adopted the weird stance that everything should stop until some assurance was forthcoming from the government that they well knew was never going to be forthcoming.

Lord Cottesloe chaired these proceedings with masterly calm and considerable shrewdness. The arithmetic always somehow contrived to add up despite the obduracy of the architect, who took the conventional attitude that artists should not be persecuted by material considerations. He was clearly resentful about any request for financial guarantees and there was a terrible day when everything hung on the brink, when it seemed that we would be unable to extract from him even the most lukewarm assurance to enable the GLC representatives to quieten their consciences and let us get on with the job. However, a private word outside the office with Mr Lasdun produced a grudging commitment which sufficed for the GLC and on went the building.

Although Denys Lasdun, now Sir Denys, was an architect of genius, administration was not his strong point. He was tormented by the need to appear occasionally before the board to explain what was happening. I could see him writhing in agony as he was asked to justify details about plumbing, twenty miles of electric wire that no one had remembered to order, thirty generators that had been completely forgotten, and one or two other small items without which the National Theatre would have been an empty shell and the audiences frozen to death. Sir Denys responded bravely to this situation but I recommended him to avoid in future any situation in which he had to appear before a committee, particularly one which contained such technical experts as Lord Rayne, Sir Joseph Lockwood and others who had been brought up on committees and *loved* asking questions for their own sake. Sir Denys, it can be said, hated answering questions for their own sake or anyone else's sake.

I realised that he was an artist under torment, and the fact that the National Theatre did get built, with a few errors of minimal importance, was due to his genius and also to the exceptional concern and care shown by the builders, McAlpine, who had in the late Lord McAlpine (not to be confused with his son, the present Lord McAlpine and also a keen supporter of the arts) a director who had an understanding of not merely building needs but also of artistic needs.

One unfortunate error was a revolving stage which had cost a vast sum of money and had never worked. I recollect attending one meeting of the

South Bank Theatre Board where I offered a simple solution to the problem. I pointed out the proximity of the theatre to the Thames and that it would not require great exertion to push the turntable on to the edge and watch it happily disappear beneath the waters. This suggestion was regarded – to my surprise – as flippant, although I must confess that had it been considered seriously it would have been a happy solution.

The building of the National Theatre also had its fair share of trade-union problems. For instance we made one interesting discovery which was that every effort was being made to install the electrical equipment, but a few disaffected workers would, at monthly intervals, cut the wires so that the work had to begin all over again. I was enraged, as were one or two other members of the board, and demanded a police investigation. It was, however, pointed out to us by the architect, the clerk of works and others that if we did this the entire building staff would walk off, so the only thing to do was to maintain a constant vigilance to avert this type of vandalism. Accepting it was to my mind intolerable, but this was before I had had a close relationship with trade unions and with the difficulties involved in maintaining a sensible relationship between employers and employees. The situation has changed dramatically since the new labour legislation, particularly the outlawing of sympathetic strikes, and by the historic success of Rupert Murdoch's Wapping operation, where for the first time the solidarity between trade unions was breached by the electricians in circumstances which have become an important part of trade-union history.

In the event, what was to have cost £7.5 million cost upwards of £16 million and we have a splendid building, which was officially opened by the Queen in October 1976. However, for one reason or another, it has required constant attention and repair almost from the outset, and although the design has been much admired, particularly for its ingenuity, it cannot be regarded as a totally satisfactory building from the point of view of the performers. What it has done has been to produce a focal scene for theatre which attracts great numbers of people year after year. The National Theatre stands as a tribute to the determination of a few theatre-lovers, and to Jennie Lee in particular, that one of the great theatres of the world should exist on British soil. Its existence has revolutionised the presentation of theatre in this country. In addition to providing two major auditoria and one minor one – important because experimental productions can be mounted there – it has also become something of a youth centre and is a place where people gather even with no intention of attending a performance.

My relationship with Peter Hall, in terms of friendship, has been one of ebb and flow – now happily flow. My first encounter with him at the

Arts Council – and I am ashamed to say that hitherto I had met him on only a handful of occasions, having been a very rare visitor to Stratford – was to discover a message on my second day that Mr Peter Hall wished to see me. The only information about his object was that he wished to discuss the Royal Shakespeare Theatre. I therefore enjoined the director of drama, Jo Hodgkinson, to be available at 2 p.m. when Mr Hall was due to arrive. Unhappily, I had not realised that the directors of the Arts Council took a rather more expansive view of lunch and this was particularly the case in relation to Mr Hodgkinson, so that he put in no appearance at all during the whole of Mr Hall's rather controversial visit.

He introduced himself and came straight to the point. He indicated to me that the Arts Council had been thoroughly unfair in their allocation of money to the Royal Shakespeare and that if the theatre was to survive – a statement that has now become a theme – it had to have more money and at once. I was at least sufficiently acquainted with the Arts Council's finances to know that there was no more money to give to him or anyone else; a condition which, so far as the Arts Council is concerned, has always prevailed from the beginning of time.

The absence of Mr Hodgkinson made it difficult for me to present a powerful defence, but I murmured about securing additional resources from the town, which derived such enormous benefits from the presence of the theatre. This was the first time that I had heard a really authentic snort. Mr Hall departed with the same discontent about our meeting that prevailed whenever in future years he left the Arts Council premises. It was not until later that day that I encountered his true quality.

The telephone rang. Mr Peter Hall. A silky voice – which he can adopt without difficulty – assured me that he was anxious to avoid giving me the trouble of making any statement to the press about our meeting. He would, of course, do it himself. For the first time, he discovered that I was not without a certain mettle. 'Mr Hall,' I said, 'I am profoundly grateful to you for having saved me this trouble. Do not bother to send me in advance anything you are going to say since I am sure I can place total reliance on its accuracy.' The score was deuce.

Thereafter I met him on many an occasion, and particularly when, not long after my tenure at the Arts Council had ceased, he sought to involve me in a plan, which he firmly denied had originated with him, to merge the Royal Shakespeare with the National Theatre: a plan which had, of course, been rejected more than a decade before, and on which a meeting was convened at my office, notwithstanding that I then had no formal responsibility. I was very lukewarm about this proposal, knowing as I did the exceptional loyalty of the Stratfordians to their theatre; but my initial warnings were unheeded until a leakage of the plan appeared in the press in terms of great disapproval. This was enough to make Peter Hall and Trevor Nunn – the protagonists of the plan – run for cover, and wisely. But notwithstanding my total innocence, as frequently happens to me a certain amount of the odium remained. I bore it with courage. Thereafter I can claim to have become one of Mr Hall's principal defenders.

Throughout Peter Hall's reign at the National Theatre, I have retained my initial belief – which existed when I sponsored his appointment – that he was, until recently, the one man who could do the job, and certainly the one man who could have launched the theatre in its splendid new building on the South Bank. Of recent years, jealous voices have picked up every available stone to throw at him and this culminated in a bitter attack by the *Sunday Times* – for reasons unknown – particularly centred on the allegation that he had made an undue profit out of the occasional success that had been transferred from the National Theatre. Here again, I enlisted for the defence and made the obvious point that he had only taken what he was contractually entitled to take and, if that was too much, the blame attached to the National Theatre Board in having given him too generous a contract. It was ironic that the people who attacked him most vigorously were those who had no compunction in taking enormous rewards from public companies, but felt a stir of horror at the notion that one of the most talented men in the whole theatrical world was deriving sizeable benefits from his employment.

The matter led to Peter Hall launching a libel action against the *Sunday Times*. Whether he was wise or unwise to do this, the fact remains that he had embarked on it in the belief that he could isolate the particular insults that he thought most offensive and could disregard a number of lesser insults that had appeared in the article concerned. The law, alas, did not allow him to do this.

I do not act, and in fact never had acted, for him, but he sought my advice in a state of some desperation. He had been given to understand that if he continued with the action and lost it – and no one could guarantee the fate of a libel action in the hands of a miscellany of jurors ranging from the totally illiterate to the even more dangerous well-versed academic – it could cost him half a million pounds. Moreover the action, if conducted on the basis of every allegation being available to be tested, might well last for weeks and cost that sum and more.

Peter made no bones of the fact that, despite the allegations about his rewards, he was anything but a rich man and to conduct and lose the action would have meant financial ruin; but he could not withdraw without a total loss of face. I advised him that the sensible thing to do was to discard his lawyers, notwithstanding the efficient and loyal service they had given to him, and inform the *Sunday Times* that hereafter he would conduct the case himself. He protested that he was not competent to do it, but I suggested that he should at least play one hole and see what happened.

He thereupon adopted this advice and issued a summons designed to exclude all the allegations other than the most offensive one – which was a baseless suggestion that he had contrived a meeting at the National Theatre to discuss and determine his remuneration and other emoluments at a time when he was aware and indeed, by implication, had contrived that the Finance Officer would be absent. I warned him that on the basis of existing authority it was extremely unlikely that the summons would succeed, and as the authority was the decision of the Court of Appeal, for him to succeed it would have been necessary to reach the House of Lords in order to reverse it.

As predicted, the Master – a junior judge who heard the application – expressed sympathy with him, listened attentively for an hour, and felt obliged to dismiss his application, at which point I assured Peter that honour had been served and that having made a desperate effort to conduct the case himself, he could now respectably throw in his hand. This he did, emerging with some credit, and I thereupon wrote an article in the *Independent* deploring the appalling cost of British litigation and the archaic complications incidental to its conduct.

But being Peter Hall, he was not satisfied to leave his victory there. He telephoned me a little while later to say that he was again in trouble. He had made two television appearances, one for the BBC and one for TVam, in which he had expressed strong views about the defence in the libel action against the *Sunday Times*. The *Sunday Times* responded in a rather startling fashion. *They* threatened to sue *him* for libel. It seemed to me unlikely that a great newspaper would bring an action for libel against someone who had criticised the paper.

This in fact turned out to be accurate. The *Sunday Times* sensibly accepted a rather lukewarm apology – an apology which made it clear that Peter did not admit the major allegations in their original article – and the matter was dropped. Again Peter expressed his gratitude and I was again only too happy to serve a man who on so many occasions had given me theatrical satisfaction. I must admit that a number of his products have given me some pain but the good so heavily outweigh the indifferent as still to leave me massively indebted.

Much has been written about Peter Hall. He is a man of gigantic stature in theatrical terms, with some gigantic faults which are the faults inherent in a man of his stature. He is intolerant of opposition, immensely sensitive to criticism, generous in his praise and in his treatment of his colleagues, but from time to time he has particular prejudices which are inexplicable to me, in the sense that they arouse passion and hatred in equal measure and both are alien to me. One thing is certain, however, which is that the existence of the National Theatre and its success to date are almost entirely due to his dedicated exertions.

My involvement with the theatre has led me into a number of associations, many sublime and some rather less so. On the sublime side was the first original production of *St Joan*, although not the first night, with Sybil Thorndike as the eponymous character. That was a performance that lives in the memory as one of the great pieces of acting. I doubt if there has ever been a more memorable performance or one that captured the spirit of a great play more successfully and more effectively.

I became quite close to Sybil Thorndike and was invited to attend a performance on her eightieth birthday at a theatre called after her at Leatherhead. As I was leaving for the theatre, I suddenly realised that I had no gift to give her. I raced back to my flat and picked up a small, nicely carved piece of stone that I had purchased in Canada, being the figure of an eskimo. I had not realised how appropriate this was, because it turned out that the play – not a particularly exciting work – was about a medium whose contact with the spirit world is through an eskimo. But I made a rather delightful error: I wrote a little note to go with my gift saying, 'This must be the only man in the world who has never seen you perform.' To this I received a puzzled note from Sybil saying, 'Why do you say you have never seen me perform?' I replied hastily that it was not I who had not seen her perform, but the eskimo. In fact on reflection I thought that it was quite possible that teams of eskimos came to watch her performance and returned to tell the eskimo world the delights they were missing.

Another theatrical occasion was of a completely different character. My friend Sir Peter Saunders, the highlight of whose very distinguished career of theatrical management is the presentation of the eternal *Mousetrap*, invited me to be a guest and speaker at a lunch at the Savoy to celebrate one or other of the production's anniversaries. Whether it was the centenary or the bicentenary I cannot remember. In any event, prominently present was the author Miss Agatha Christie with whom I had an amiable chat. I was under a considerable disadvantage since I was probably the only person present who had never seen the play, but this I successfully concealed and made an immensely enthusiastic speech largely related to the beneficence of keeping actors in employment for the span of Enoch's life.

But the tragedy I discovered was that of poor Miss Christie. She had come looking forward as we all did to a good slap-up meal at the Savoy and on the train she realised that she had left her dentures behind. The poor woman had the mortification of reading the endless menu of Lucullan splendour but restricting herself to a very *baveuse* omelette. She took it in remarkably good part.

On this, the only occasion that I met her, I certainly took to her very much. She came with a young grandson, to whom she had donated the rights in, I think, *The Mousetrap*, which nevertheless should have ensured him a safe income for the rest of his life. Strangely enough I read Poirot with satisfaction but found Miss Marple an insufferable and pretentious bore. This reaction, I am sure, is purely sexist and would qualify me for prosecution by the Equal Opportunities Commission.

One of the most interesting, if not oddest, characters that I have met was indeed one of the great theatrical geniuses of our time – Tennessee Williams. I met him through Maria (Lady) St Just, with whom he had formed a thoroughly unexpected and eccentric friendship which involved a total devotion on each side to the other. Whenever he came to England he was with her constantly, and she would pay constant visits to America to see him. It is unnecessary to say that there was no physical relationship between them since, of course, Tennessee Williams was well known to have no interest in women.

He was a man of great but very unusual charm. When sober, which was not often, he was a brilliant conversationalist and loved to talk about the theatre and indeed about his productions. He must have been the most difficult dramatist for any producer to direct, since he held very strong views about the production of his plays.

When he came to London for his last production here, in 1978, there was a frightful rumpus between himself and the leading actress, Sheila Gish, because he had decided to excise certain lines from the play, rendering her part considerably shorter. Not unnaturally, she objected to this and in the result withdrew from the production. The play – *Vieux Carré* – I found a fascinating one. It was obviously autobiographical and it related the stay of a young man in an eccentric boarding-house in New Orleans over a considerable period and his relationship with other occupants and with the landlady.

It was a play of great brilliance and perception, but it was not in any sense an entertainment, and it was, of course, a great falling off; the author of *A Streetcar Named Desire*, *The Glass Menagerie* and *Cat on a Hot Tin Roof* had been a master craftsman whose plays were remarkable not only for the brilliance of their dialogue and the penetrating depiction of character, but also for their structure. *Vieux Carré*, alas, was unstructured, or at least clumsily structured, whereas the choice of subject demanded a firm hand.

I dined with Williams on two or three occasions at Maria St Just's home, and he consulted me on a number of occasions, at her instigation, about various aspects of his affairs. Each time I had to tell him that I was not an American lawyer, in particular I was not a New Orleans lawyer, and that I was unable to give advice that made sense. Nevertheless he came to me because Maria exercised a powerful influence on him and she was determined that he should seek the advice of her favourite lawyer, however useless it might be.

His death was a tragedy, and since his death there have been numerous complications. He appointed Maria to be one of his trustees, and a man called John Eastman, and it cannot be said that the administration of his estate to date has been totally tranquil. His major concern was to make provision for his invalid elderly sister, and here Maria has displayed those qualities that make her such a remarkable person and make it possible even to smile at her major eccentricities. She has travelled to America on several occasions to make sure that the sister is properly looked after, is taken out, has a companion, and generally is well provided for, and she has engaged in vigorous battles to maintain the integrity of various productions, despite my constant remonstrances that it is no part of her duty as a trustee to engage in casting the play. However, remonstrances to Maria St Just are about as futile as persuading a charging bull of the error of his ways. But I do value my recollection of Tennessee Williams: of a sad, lost, difficult genius, whose plays reflect his character, his talents and his weaknesses and will remain a permanent part of the American stage.

Another association of long standing has been with a theatrical director by the name of Peter Cotes – the third of the Boulting brothers. He has had a career which has never attained anything approaching the eminence his special talents deserve. This can be explained by a number of factors. One is that he is too much of a perfectionist to work easily with other people. Another – and this is a quality shared by all the great directors – is that he likes his own way, meaning that he knows how he likes a thing to be done and is mulishly obstinate in accepting any changes.

Some time in 1952, Peter Cotes came to see me to say that he had been without employment for quite a while, but had now been offered an engagement to direct a play, a play which he described as absolutely awful and not likely to run for anything more than the shortest period. He had been offered the small sum of £100 to direct this play, or alternatively a minute royalty of $1\frac{1}{2}$ per cent of the box-office takings, and asked me to advise him what to do. I reflected for a moment and said, 'Peter, £100 even in your impoverished state is no great sum of money. If the play runs two or three months you would have earned that or more. My advice would be to take a sporting risk on an outside chance, about a thousand to one, and see whether it will run for six months or a year.' He reflected and in the end decided that he would take the royalty.

The result must be already in the minds of my readers: the play was *The Mousetrap*. He is still receiving his $1\frac{1}{2}$ per cent royalty, despite rather resolute attempts on the part of the management from time to time to argue that his duties as a director are no longer needed. Happily he is a shrewd man and makes a point of going to see a performance every so often, writing a few notes to suggest that it is time the leading actor had a new pair of shoes, and sending the notes to the manager to indicate that he continues to be, indeed is passionately, interested in the production.

My second experience with him, a couple of years later, related to another play. I had been introduced to a lady called Anna Deere Wiman, who was the daughter of the eminent American producer Deere Wiman and the granddaughter of a man who had amassed a vast fortune in agricultural machinery. A large portion of that fortune had come her way and she lost little or no time in dissipating it with the speed of light. She was a desperately unhappy woman and had turned to drink as being the only immediate consolation for a number of reverses with which I was not acquainted.

I first met her when she had financed a theatre in Liverpool, the Liverpool Repertory Theatre, which was in the hands of a man who subsequently became a well-known actor but had very little financial talent, and in the result she lost a small fortune. The matter came my way because the Arts Council asked if I would investigate this situation – at that time I had no official connection with the Council – to report whether in my view it would be wise for them to continue to support the theatre after Miss Wiman's withdrawal. It took little study of the balance sheet to decide that the Arts Council would be ill-advised to tip their rather sparing quantity of gold into a bottomless pit.

But that was not the end of my experience with Miss Anna Deere Wiman, because she had decided that she would present a play in London. The play was called *Mountain Fire* and was written by two dramatists whose names I cannot remember. In any event, the unfortunate Peter Cotes was again approached to direct it and he came to me to complain that the play was the most awful he had ever read. This I could hardly believe, since it would be plumbing depths requiring excavation, but such was his financial need at the time that he felt obliged to take the engagement. I therefore drew up a letter of contract for him in relation to *Mountain Fire*, and the play (in which Julie Andrews made her debut) went into rehearsal, again ironically enough at Liverpool, at the Royal Court Theatre.

A few weeks before the opening, Peter appeared again in my office to seek my advice. His wise and accomplished wife (the Canadian actress Joan Miller, now, alas, dead) had told him that the play had absolutely no chance of success and indeed, but for the final scene which contained a lynching, there was no element in it likely to bring a single person into the theatre. So his wise wife had an idea. 'Why not,' she said, 'since it is so bad, turn it into a musical?' A musical, she rightly opined, can have any kind of plot, however idiotic or ridiculous, and if the music is tolerable people will come.

This idea was presented to Miss Wiman, who was not greatly attracted to it since she regarded the two authors as unknown and unrecognised geniuses. But persuaded by Peter Cotes, she agreed to commission a score and the play was staged as a musical. It opened at Liverpool and, as might have been anticipated, the first-night reviews were almost uniform in saying that the play was a stinker of an exceptionally odoriferous character, but that the music was quite tolerable. This obviously provoked the authors into a frenzy of outrage. 'The music,' they said, 'has ruined our masterpiece.' An immediate conference was called, and it was decided that on the second night the music should come out and the performance should be presented as a straight play. The second night was more disastrous than the first, in consequence of which the music was reinstated on the third night. And so it proceeded throughout its run: Monday, music, Tuesday – no music, Wednesday – music, Thursday – no music, Friday – music, Saturday – no music.

Miss Wiman and Peter Cotes came to see me to discuss the legal situation, since she was demanding that the music should be taken out and that the play should continue without it. Arrangements were made for them to meet at my flat in Victoria, in Ashley Gardens, where I then occupied a vast and gloomy but to me very agreeable residence with a number of large rooms in which I could entertain to my heart's content. I reflected for a moment, and envisaged a situation that might have led to bloodshed in Liverpool at dinner parties. One guest would say, 'Have you seen *Mountain Fire*?' Another would say, 'Yes.' The first guest would then say, 'I didn't like the play, but I thought the music was quite good.' The second would say, 'What are you talking about? There wasn't any music when I saw it!' One could see a violent argument ensuing, ending in the disruption of the dinner-table. But these were flights of fancy.

In any event, Miss Wiman appeared at my flat, and I had received strict instructions before her arrival to be sure that I had a bottle of rye whiskey, since that was the only drink she liked. I had never heard of rye whiskey, but I went out and bought a bottle of something called Canada Club, and I reflected that it was going to be an awful waste since no one else would ever drink it. I need not have had any misgivings – she drank the lot. At the end of the evening no compromise could be reached, so I made what I now recognise to be a suggestion of exceptional idiocy. I suggested that we should invite a distinguished theatre critic – I recommended Harold Hobson – to go to Liverpool, pay him a fee (since Miss Wyman was a multimillionairess) and ask his opinion as to whether the play was better performed with or without music. This compromise was adopted.

However, Miss Wiman had a moment of sanity and finally decided that on the whole she would discontinue the entire production. The theatre had to be compensated; the actors had to be compensated; I negotiated some reasonable compensation for Peter Cotes; and at the end of the day Miss Wiman was a slightly poorer, though I very much doubt a wiser, woman. Her later life was, I believe, no less tragic, and she died within a few years of this occurrence. I had no more dealings with her and can say from what I saw of her that she was a kindly, good-natured woman, ruined by the advent of a vast amount of money and an ambition to emulate a brilliant father in a profession for which she had absolutely no judgement or affinity. It is fortunate that Julie Andrews was not sufficiently discouraged by the misadventure of that production to abandon what became an exceptionally distinguished acting career.

From time to time, I have been involved in attempts to establish a more secure financial footing for theatre in this country than the kind I have just described. One such has been the Theatre Investment Fund, which I chaired for many years after leaving the Arts Council and of which I still retain the pleasurable distinction of being Life President. My own recollection as to the inspiration of the fund is not clear. Perhaps not unnaturally I regard it as my own idea, but certain it was that in the late 1960s a delegation led by Peter Saunders, John Gale and other theatrical managers visited Jennie Lee – and I was present at the time – to represent that some assistance should be given to the commercial theatre, which was of course at a serious disadvantage against the competition of the subsidised theatre. In London the subsidised theatre was represented by three major institutions and a number of partially supported smaller institutions. The National Theatre was obviously foremost but it was hotly pursued by the London end of the Royal Shakespeare Company operating at the Aldwych Theatre, and always maintaining a note of sturdy independence and easily identifiable difference was the Royal Court, using such distinguished directors as George Devine and Lindsay Anderson.

On the face of it the commercial theatre should not have been seriously worried since there were over thirty such theatres in London as opposed to the three subsidised theatres I have mentioned, but in fact the competition was more formidable than is demonstrated by the arithmetic. The subsidised theatre presented attractions to dramatists which the commercial theatre lacked. Although in the commercial theatre the financial return to the dramatist was much greater if a long run was achieved, in the subsidised theatre the certainty of a sufficiently funded production, of a wealth of rehearsals, and of a determined disregard of barrel-scraping economies more than compensated for the possible loss of financial rewards. Moreover, the prestige associated with a production either at the Old Vic, as it first was, and then the National Theatre, or at the Royal Shakespeare in London, was immeasurably larger than could be achieved by any commercial production and the certainty of important reviews much greater, although there was no certainty that the reviews would necessarily be more approving.

Jennie recognised that such advantages could be dangerously dis-couraging to the commercial theatre and in consequence there was evolved the idea of the Theatre Investment Fund. A committee of the Arts Council sat to consider some such possibility but nothing was done until I urged action in the last two years before my departure.

The TIF was established in 1972 on the footing that the Arts Council would contribute £100,000 and private investors and charitable trusts would contribute £150,000. It turned out, however, that there was – not unexpectedly – a shortage of private investors, although to his credit Bernard Delfont made a substantial contribution. The bulk of the funds was obtained from charitable trusts, in particular Max Rayne's. Months were lost in negotiations with the Treasury to ensure that the private investors were not subject to discrimination. As it turned out, this was of minimal importance in view of the minimal nature of the private support, and when all the taxation problems had been resolved the TIF finally began operating in 1976.

The Fund gave pump-priming support to suitable applicants. To be suitable a play did not need to be a typical Arts Council production. The object – as I frequently said – was to support the commercial theatre in all its aspects, i.e. to maintain actors, playwrights, producers, lighting experts, stage-hands and theatre generally throughout the country. Far and away the greater part of our support was given to the London theatre, but wherever possible the Fund endeavoured to assist plays which toured either before or after the London production. The Theatre Investment Fund continues to thrive in the sense that it continues to give support to the commercial theatre, which is probably doing better today than at any time in its history. To an appreciable extent this can be credited to the TIF which has to date invested well over one million pounds in commercial productions and has managed to receive half of that sum back.

A few years after the establishment of the Theatre Investment Fund, a notion was promoted for the establishment of another organisation that would watch over theatres and intervene when any attempt was made to remove a theatre, to change the function of a theatre, or to alter one in such a way as to make it less usable or no longer usable at all. The Theatres Trust was set up by an Act of Parliament in 1976 and I became the chairman of the Trust with many well-known theatrical personalities as trustees. We had the good fortune to have as the director of the Trust Lord Jenkins (then Hugh Jenkins MP) who had been the Minister for the Arts between 1974 and 1976. He took the Trust very seriously – woe betide any aspiring impresario who tried to convert a theatre to some other use.

Hugh Jenkins had been a member of the Arts Council under my chairmanship between 1968 and 1971. Although I differed with him on many matters, I came to like him more and more for his patently honest views, however misguided in my opinion, and we became friends. In June 1970, with the Conservative election victory and Jennie Lee having lost her seat, a new opposition spokesman for the arts had to be appointed. I was lobbied by Hugh Jenkins and in good faith recommended Harold Wilson to appoint him, which he did. Subsequently, when Harold returned to office in 1974, I again lobbied him to appoint Jenkins as the Minister for the Arts, and although legitimate criticism could be levelled at some of Hugh's decisions, no one could question his energy and enthusiasm for the job.

Not unnaturally the Trust was set up with full powers but an empty purse: not a penny was assigned to us. We met in my office where I was happy to provide coffee and biscuits without resort to the petty cash and even to arrange the occasional luncheon. There were considerable difficulties until 1980, when for the first time ever Norman St John Stevas gave us a grant and that grant has been continued by subsequent Conservative Arts Ministers, with only a brief hiccup in 1987.

The Theatres Trust is a particularly useful watchdog when to a large extent the rebuilding and development of our great cities has fallen into the hands of developers who, while not totally devoid of human feelings, are nevertheless preoccupied with the prospect of profit rather than the cultural enlightenment or architectural beautification of the country.

The most important virtue that the Arts Council can (or more truthfully could) claim is to be almost totally free of political influence. Jennie Lee was a model minister in this and several other regards. It was ironic that having held one of the most vigorous political attitudes throughout her career, she displayed a total hostility to any political influences in the arts. Her very first nomination for a member of the Arts Council – and the procedure for election was a recommendation either from Jennie or from me, followed by approval from the other – was Edward Boyle, then a Conservative MP, although he would not have survived one moment in Mrs Thatcher's Cabinet and would probably have refused to accept any office which involved the adoption of Thatcherite principles.

When it was first recognised that politics were to be expelled from the artistic scene, there was considerable rejoicing and I have to say that any hostility to this attitude came from the Left and not from the Right. Left-wing views dominated (and indeed still dominate) the entire theatrical establishment, so that the National Theatre, the Royal Shakespeare and the Royal Court would put on plays with a political message which disparaged almost all the important institutions such as the police, the armed forces and the educational system. These were greeted by screams of indignation and resentment from any survivors from the Right who were still concerned with the arts. I recognised early on that a theatre director who wanted to put on a right-wing play would have enormous difficulty in finding one. Sir Alec Douglas Home's talented brother William (*The Reluctant Debutante* and others of that ilk) was their best hope, but even he markedly failed to indicate Tory principles. One of his most important (although least successful) plays derives from his own wartime experience when he had deliberately courted disaster after deciding that further fighting would be a useless expenditure of lives. Notwithstanding the shortage of talented right-wing dramatists, the theatre during my chairmanship – which could in no way claim the credit – produced the most significant list of new writing. Harold Pinter, Peter Shaffer, Arnold Wesker, John Arden and many others brought a new and a fresh talent to the theatre, supported by what I believe were discriminating grants.

The Arts Council's artistic policy was based on two principles: that the government should supply to the Arts Council the necessary financial support to maintain their work, but that this support did not entitle the government or indeed even the Arts Council to interfere in the day-to-day working of an institution which was provided with public money. In short, the Arts Council should and could refuse to accept any governmental influence in the use of its subsidy.

A single example, I think, indicates the way this policy worked. Late in 1966, I had a visit at the Arts Council from Kenneth Tynan, a young man for whom I had an increasing admiration, which was, I am afraid, damaged by one or two follies on his part which made it difficult to regard him seriously. This visit was a splendid illustration. He brought with him the typescript of a play called *Soldiers*. He told me that the National Theatre, which was still under the chairmanship of Lord Chandos, was refusing to present it, notwithstanding vehement support both from Tynan and from Laurence Olivier. The query he addressed to me was whether the Arts Council would in any way seek to deter the presentation of this play if he was able to persuade the board of the National Theatre to put it on. I promised to read the play and write to him.

I read the play, which appeared to me to strike a new high in historic idiocies. It was based on the allegation that Winston Churchill had organised the assassination of General Sikorski, the leader of the Polish government in exile in London, who had been killed in a plane crash in 1943. It seemed to me an unlikely proposition to put it mildly, but my reply to Tynan followed the 'hands off' principle as faithfully as was possible. I told him that the Arts Council did not interfere with decisions by responsible managements of its string of theatres and that this principle would be adhered to in the present case; but I indulged myself by adding that if I were the chairman of the National Theatre, who had to make the decision, nothing on earth would persuade me to present this highly offensive attack on the integrity of our greatest leader. My reply, alas, did little to endear me to Tynan. His wife has recently produced a posthumous biography of this undoubtedly very talented but perverse man, and he has done something to avenge himself on me when she quotes from him:

> When it actually seems as if real democracy might be about to exert some genuine influence on the nation's life, the ruling class produces an antibody to counter it. The antibody in our time is Lord Goodman. A man who has never held elective office, he has wielded more power than anyone in the country, except for the Prime Minister, during the last decade.

I find this allusion highly flattering, although alas untrue. Any active chairman of the Arts Council must at some time or another present a personal view. His duty is to air such views to the very minimum. It is not the Arts Council's function to interfere with free expression, however distasteful, unless it offends the law.

Tynan was tireless in pursuing his objectives, some unworthy of a mind of such rare distinction. He was, I think, largely responsible for persuading a commercial management (the late Sir Donald Albery) to present *Soldiers* at one of their West End theatres. Retribution followed swiftly. It emerged that the pilot of Sikorski's plane was still living and for one reason or another considered that the play defamed him. Accordingly he sued the management and the publishers (André Deutsch) and recovered very substantial damages, which was a completely unnecessary message to commercial managements to maintain their historic timidity.

The second limb of the 'hands off' policy, a pendant to the principle of governmental non-intervention, was the principle of Arts Council non-intervention: that once it had given a grant to an institution there should be the most limited interference restricted to a demand that suitable standards of accountancy should prevail and that there should be no misuse of the subsidy. This principle was maintained throughout my chairmanship and the chairmanship of my two immediate successors. Its operation necessitated a total ban on censorship except where there was illegality or an obvious risk of prosecution for indecency.

A good illustration of the principle occurred many years later when in 1980 the National Theatre decided to present a play called *The Romans in Britain* by Howard Brenton, which early on depicted in considerable detail a scene of buggery by a Roman soldier. The play was attacked – unsuccessfully – by the lady who has acquired national eminence as the 'hammer' of the arts, Mrs Mary Whitehouse. I had received a visit from this lady while I was at the Arts Council, to protest against what she described as 'dirty plays' which we were supporting. She failed, however, to produce a single instance of a dirty play about which some action could be taken and departed in high dudgeon when I suggested that she would do better to look at the large and enthusiastic audiences for whom we provided the most wholesome entertainment in a great variety of plays. She kept her eyes firmly glued on the gutter.

From time to time, and particularly at the present day, I have found politicians of both parties who resent the 'hands off' policy and it is particularly resented by senior civil servants, notably in the Treasury, who regard it as almost indecent that public money can be spent without adequate supervision by an experienced civil servant. I have probably said enough to explain why a great number of sensible people were and are firm supporters of the Arts Council, but both principles are now under challenge as never before.

15

The Catfish Question

THE QUESTION OF censorship has always been of real and important concern to me, never more so than during my years at the Arts Council. Until the Theatres Act of 1968, a marked difference existed between censorship operating for the theatre (including operatic presentations) and literary censorship. The theatre was, of course, subject to the pre-production censorship of the Lord Chamberlain, and the battle for the total abolition of pre-censorship of plays had waxed for many years.

In order to present its views in a considered form, the Arts Council in 1965 established the Theatre Censorship Committee, chaired by Hugh Willatt of the Drama Panel, with representatives of the Council, League of Dramatists, Theatre Managers' Association, Society of West End Managers, Theatres National Committee and Council of Repertory Theatres. This powerful committee recommended the abolition of all censorship, pre- or post-production, for a trial period of five years, with adequate safeguards for the protection of managements and dramatists on the lines contained in Mr Benn Levy's proposed Censorship of Plays (Repeal) Act of 1949. The recommendation extended to a proposal that Clause 4 of Mr Levy's Bill, which would have enabled living persons to be represented on the stage, be deleted. (Benn Levy, whose wife, the talented actress Constance Cummings, was a member of the Arts Council, belonged to the passionately determined anti-censorship lobby which wanted nothing to do with even a voluntary system of censorship.) And finally, the committee recommended that a clause be added to limit the period during which a prosecution could be commenced against those directly or indirectly involved in a production to within the first sixteen performances, and that no ban could be imposed until those sixteen performances had taken place.

I was myself by no means wholeheartedly in favour of these recommendations. If a play was genuinely obscene, it was unlikely that the legislature would approve a recommendation that it could be shown for sixteen performances before any action was taken to stop it. Some larger theatres in London and outside London could seat 1,500 people, so that around 20,000 people could theoretically be corrupted by a play before any action was possible. This was a recommendation of a committee with its head in the clouds.

In any event, a Parliamentary Joint Committee had been set up to deal with this very matter and I thought that it was premature to produce recommendations for statutory action in advance of this committee's report. It was also, alas, true that the Theatre Censorship Committee had not been truly representative since no evidence was taken from the commercial theatre.

At the Council's May meeting in 1966, I expressed the view that there were three possibilities for reforming theatrical censorship:

1. To adopt the Committee's recommendation that there should be total abolition of stage censorship.

2. To establish censorship on a voluntary basis, with suitable safeguards for those submitting their work to the censor.

3. To retain censorship, whether by the Lord Chamberlain or by some other official or committee.

The case for total abolition had the support of dramatists, Actors' Equity, the subsidised theatres in London and the repertory theatres. The touring managers favoured voluntary censorship. The commercial managers alone wished to retain the present form of censorship.

Ultimately the Arts Council decided to associate itself with the proposal that the current system of theatre censorship should be abolished, with a further recommendation that the possible advantages of a system of voluntary censorship should be investigated. It was also agreed that the Council should submit written evidence to the Joint Parliamentary Committee, on which I served.

In June 1967 the Joint Committee produced a report of commendable brevity, emphasis and unanimity. To the delight of theatre directors, writers and the more progressive managements, the report was unqualified in its recommendation that it was an unwarranted interference with liberty of thought and speech for a theatrical presentation to be proscribed from production unless or until it had the prior approval of a public official.

The Joint Committee had considered a voluntary system of censorship as a safeguard to managements. Those on the committee who might have supported the principle of voluntary censorship – which would have enabled a play to be submitted to a monitoring committee which, if it received their approval, would absolve anyone connected with the production from prosecution – were, like myself, persuaded by the evidence that this compromise solution was unacceptable within the profession as a whole, although I must confess I had a faint hankering for the experiment.

In due course the Theatres Act was enacted and the Lord Chamberlain's censoring function came to an end on 25 September 1968 (this caused no distress to the Lord Chamberlain himself, Lord Cobbold, who had worked hard and successfully to liberalise his regime). The new Act laid down that it was a criminal offence to present or direct an obscene performance of a play and the test of obscenity was as embodied in the Obscene Publications Act, but a prosecution could only take place if approved by the Attorney-General.

Our fear was that the removal of censorship would produce not a more liberal but a less liberal theatre, with managements inhibited by the fear of prosecution and, deprived of the insurance of a Lord Chamberlain's licence, adopting a policy of greater timidity. However, in the result the solution has worked well because the general liberalisation of theatre has meant that a great many plays contain passages at which we might lift our eyebrows but would no longer contemplate a prosecution.

An unattractive feature of the disappearance of the Lord Chamberlain is the reappearance of profanity of speech in all directions. But this has had one consequence that could have been anticipated: if one hears four-letter words used on numerous occasions, one suddenly realises that four letters are only four letters, and the audiences, particularly the West End audiences, with the solitary exception of elderly prudes like myself, now listen to such language without shock or disapproval. In short, profanity has come to be accepted. I would prefer that such words, which are all ugly, should disappear as a matter of good taste, but I am happy for them to be presented as they are now, with a recognition that no one will seek to send anyone else to jail because he or she used words that are to be found in the speech form of at least half the adult population.

The Theatres Act also brought about the removal of the protection previously extended to living persons of not being presented on the stage (which had been a particular anathema to Benn Levy). There still, of course, remains the protection of an action for defamation, but it is not difficult to present a character in non-defamatory but nevertheless highly offensive terms. Had this ban still existed, probably its most sensational operation would have been in relation to the appearance of a character representing Her Majesty The Queen, as happened in the National Theatre production of *Single Spies*. The performance was particularly memorable as Prunella Scales gave so life-like a presentation; but the dialogue between the stage Queen and the stage Anthony Blunt was of a character so recondite that it was unlikely to have been spoken by any real royal. Nevertheless, before the 1968 Act a performance would have been banned on the general prohibition against reproducing living persons on the stage.

No arts council should seek to censor or to edit the activities of the bodies it subsidises. What was amazing during my years there was the minute amount of material about which any complaint was made, having regard to the fact that the Council was involved with about seventy theatres and innumerable exhibitions. I doubt whether I received more than half a dozen letters of complaint a year, and if anything could vindicate the wisdom of a policy of leaving well alone and of allowing adult and mature people to conduct their own affairs, this paucity of complaints was a total justification.

Every so often someone would write a letter to us saying that they had seen unspeakable horrors at some repertory company. Often, a visiting American company would – despite the rigours of our climate – strip themselves to the pelt and offer some unattractive proposal to the audience. Or on the London stage, someone set on promoting a sensation – which became increasingly difficult as audiences acquired greater sophistication – would engage in an act of violence or sexuality that displeased one or two people. But generally, however robust and vigorous the incidents, they made sense in context and were so accepted.

I do not believe, as has been asserted, that the Arts Council's hands-off approach to censorship has helped to lower the moral tone of the nation. The moral tone of the nation, if it has been lowered, must look for other culprits to explain its declension. Rapacity and greed, the legitimation of short cuts to riches while trampling on others, and the inanities of 'youth culture' – a great many factors explain the weakening of moral obligations and our increasing blindness to the general social decencies. I remain totally unrepentant about the Arts Council's obstinate determination not to act as a censor.

However, there were one or two occasions when the Arts Council had no alternative but to intervene, and a good illustration arose in connection with Sir Bernard Miles's production of *Othello* at the Mermaid Theatre in 1971. Sir Bernard was never a man to hide his light under a bushel; feeling that *Othello* was a play in need of greater contemporary relevance, he decided that in his production Desdemona should, in the bedroom scene, appear stark naked. It was difficult to fathom the logic of this proposal since her only purpose for being in the scene was to get herself strangled.

A correspondence arose between Bernard and myself. He was a man it was impossible to dislike and a dedicated servant of the theatre, but he did not readily respond to suggestions and I had to be careful not to tread on any of his corns. The following correspondence ensued:

13 September 1971

My dear Bernard,

The Arts Council exercises no form of censorship but occasionally proffers some common-sense advice.

Do drop this nonsense about a naked Desdemona. You have extracted all the fun from it – got all the possible publicity – and to continue with it would really be unworthy of you and your theatre. You have such a good Shakespearian reputation that to belittle the Bard with a silly and totally unjustifiable gimmick, which puts the play completely out of perspective and furnishes you with audiences of slobbering yahoos instead of the excellent quality you now attract, would be to expose yourself to serious long-term injury for the most trivial present advantage – even if you get one at all.

Needless to say, this is a private letter, which I shall not publicise in any way – nor shall I make any public comment on whatever your decision may be. But, do think again and do not be driven to take an unwise stand out of sheer defiance at the volume of criticism.

Yours ever,

Arnold

15 September 1972

Dear Arnold,

Iago:　　Or to be naked with her friend in bed
　　　　　An hour or more, not meaning any harm.

Othello: Naked in bed Iago and not mean harm
　　　　　It is hypocrisy against the Devil.

– in other words, husbands and wives naturally and habitually go to bed naked, but dear God, 'with her friend'. This is one of the biggest daggers pushed into Othello and the tact and delicacy with which it is handled and the quite justifiable horror that it adds to the scene in my opinion more than justifies it.

Josephine and I are both puritans, or we would never have done what we have done in such a personal and partly sacrificial way. We have three children and nine grandchildren. The Director, Peter Oyston, has an adored wife and two small children. The Othello, Bruce Purchase, has a beloved wife and three small children. Julius Gellner is a Czech Director of many years experience and not a little renown. The scene is handled with the greatest delicacy and tenderness, with only a very fleeting glimpse of nudity.

In a play which contains a frightening description of male ejaculation and of the semen pouring back out of the woman:

'the fountain from the which my current runs, or else dries up'

– then the frightening hint of necrophilia –

'Look thus when thou art dead, and I will kill thee and love thee after'

– for which many of our modern and highly-prized dramatists would have used the word fuck, instead of love – these and many other violent sexual images which make *Sons and Lovers* sound like a Methodist tea party, do, I believe, totally justify the conception we have – which I think is most beautiful.

I would only add that as an Honorary Fellow of my old college, a member of the City Livery Company, and of the Worshipful Company of Wheelwrights, Parish Clerk of the Church of St Mary Mounthaw and a practising adherent of the Salvation Army, you must please believe I am to be trusted in this matter.

> Warmest regards,
> Yours ever,
> Janette Knight
> Sir Bernard Miles

(Dictated by Sir Bernard and signed in his absence by his secretary)

16 September 1971

My dear Bernard,

I have now received your letter.

I do not believe you are a pornographer. I do believe you are an immensely experienced, sensible and responsible theatrical producer, but it is a tragedy that it is this particular textual discovery that you should have made at this moment. If you had made the discovery that

Iago was Desdemona's father, that Othello was the original leader of the Black Panthers, that the whole play was an argument in favour of Welsh nationalism, you could have revealed them triumphantly and with the loudest blast of trumpets, but suddenly to discover that undressing a pretty girl is a remarkable textual achievement at a time when the London theatre – bankrupt of other ideas – is stripping them all like plucked hens, is unfortunate and ill-timed. However valid the argument in favour of doing it – and I am singularly unimpressed by the argument – this is a tragic moment for doing it without associating yourself with people who are out to use any contrivance to make money at the box office. Hence my final appeal to deck the poor lady in any raiment. Bourne & Hollingsworth and C & A are open and I will immediately sponsor an additional Arts Council grant for the purpose. Or use my Credit Card at Harrods.

   Love,
   Arnold

My own professional – not Arts Council – association with the liberalisation of thought has arisen on several occasions. One such was in 1968 when my firm acted for the publishers of *Last Exit to Brooklyn* who were in fact prosecuted at the Old Bailey and in the first instance convicted. The counsel for the defence on that occasion was one of the most gifted lawyers in the country, Patrick Neill QC, to whom I have already alluded. However, after we had failed to convince the jury, I thought that an approach of less orthodoxy might be more successful and we instructed Mr John Mortimer to conduct the appeal. For this purpose he invented as a criterion the 'repugnance' theory, which was swallowed hook, line and sinker by the Court of Criminal Appeal. The theory was very simple: that if a book was so obscene as to revolt the reader, it was not consistent with corruption and on that extraordinary score the Court of Appeal allowed *Last Exit*'s appeal.

Even so, anybody connected with the arts is bound to pay heed to the loud and clamant lobby inveighing against pornography and every other kind of obscenity. During the twenty-six years that I have been a member of the House of Lords, however, I recollect the matter being raised in only three short debates. My first five years at the Arts Council was an arid period in relation to obscenity, as I received no more than half a dozen complaints a year about activities we sponsored. But although I regarded the subject as a dead duck, there were people anxious to keep it afloat in order to constitute something of a nuisance. The obscenity lobby was composed of a number of people who genuinely believed that what was spoken on a stage, read on a page or appeared on a television screen could corrupt. I did not share this view and my opinion was supported by every serious investigation in this country and elsewhere.

The most startling statistic was that when the obscenity laws in Denmark were repealed, so as to make it a free-for-all, the number of cases of sexual offences decreased by 25 per cent. I do not invite the reader to accept this statistic from me. It seemed at the time to be a highly dubious statistic, but the Danes insisted that it was authentic. However, it did little to quieten British voices of protest. These voices were powerful enough to give the more nervous members of the Arts Council considerable concern, particularly after the verdict in the *Last Exit* case, and in deference to their views in June 1968 we convened a conference of organisations concerned with the arts to consider the problems. The conference, which I presided over, was very representative – there were individuals connected with writing, publishing and other literary matters – and it was unanimously resolved to set up a working party to investigate the country's obscenity laws.

In due course this working party reported, but their report was to me a disappointment. I had expressed my own views pretty strongly: that however much one disapproved of the existing laws relating to obscenity, it would be a total waste of time to recommend their repeal since no government would repeal them. Needless to say, the first recommendation of the working party was the repeal of all legislation regulating obscenity for a trial period of five years. I shrugged my shoulders since it was clear to anyone who worked in the field that such a repeal would not go through the Commons, let alone the Lords.

The working party had been chaired by John Montgomerie, one of my partners, who possessed one of the shrewdest legal minds in the country. He was as taciturn as a Trappist monk, hardly uttering a word where he regarded it as unnecessary, but he too was persuaded that the total repeal of any kind of censorship was the only course that made sense. This may well have been true of a sophisticated Arts Council but it had not even a remote possibility of success in Parliament. However, the Arts Council was enthusiastic about the report and a special meeting of the Council directed that it should be sent to the Home Secretary, with our personal recommendation that the proposals should be enacted. In fact, from that day to this nothing more has been heard of it.

One course that the Arts Council was not prepared to embark on in my day was any purported control or censorship associated with the grant of money. With Jennie Lee I was at one on this issue, but any such understanding was rudely terminated when Ted Heath appointed Lord Eccles as Minister for the Arts after the 1970 general election. Knowing little about the theatre, Eccles was firmly convinced that it was a cesspool.

When his indignation was at its height, he asked me to come to see him and when I arrived he exploded that neither he nor Ted Heath was prepared to be associated in any way with some of the vulgarity and obscenities in certain plays. I asked him for instances of these obscenities, which he could not provide.

As I was leaving, he hissed at me that neither Ted nor he was elected to allow such filth to be presented in theatres subsidised by the public. I was half-way through the door when, over my shoulder, I riposted, 'I thought you were elected to lower food prices.' How the debate would have continued had I remained I do not know, but I was quite pleased with it up to that stage.

Eccles was no doubt thoroughly dissatisfied with the statement that the Arts Council put out soon afterwards confirming our belief that censorship was not a part of the Arts Council's function. The statement was well received in the press, with one particularly approving leader in the *Evening Standard*, which in those days took a special interest in the arts. Their leader, headlined 'Bold Stand', was as follows:

> Some three months ago, Lord Eccles stood up in the House of Lords and made some remarks about not subsidising artistic ventures that 'affronted many taxpayers'. He called for the Arts Council to accept a 'convention' by which it would refuse funds for productions that were filthy or blasphemous.
>
> As Minister for the Arts, Lord Eccles should have known better. Veiled hints of censorship were none of his business, just as it could never have been a function of the Arts Council to carry them out.
>
> Today, in a tough statement that will cause many to give a sigh of relief, the Council makes it clear that it is not going to play ball. It firmly rejects any notions of censorship, gives its blessing to plays of a controversial nature and reaffirms the principle of leaving it up to the various recipients of its grants to pursue their own independent policies.
>
> It is quite right to have done so. Children, as it points out, should not be encouraged to see unsuitable productions. But otherwise, the arts must remain unshackled. Merit, not propriety, is the only criterion of their worth.

Without underlining it more than was necessary, I stated on behalf of the Council that the Council and the Minister had not seen eye to eye. This was certainly the case. I very much regretted any difference of opinion with the Minister for the Arts, and indeed there had never been any such difference when the Council was operating under the aegis of Jennie Lee. I am happy to think that, notwithstanding some violent contentions, the

Arts Council has never yet exercised a censorship role.

The need to remain on guard against censorship, however subtly proposed, embraced a number of other activities during my Arts Council years. One occasion was in 1968, when Harold Wilson invited me to become a member of a newly formed Anglo-Soviet Consultative Committee, under the chairmanship of Lord Trevelyan. I was intrigued enough to accept.

For a time after the appointment nothing happened, but I was then informed confidentially, with some fuss about the confidence, that we were to have a meeting with a Russian delegation. This took place in April 1970 and the venue was the British Transport Commission at Woking. However, before I could agree to attend any such conference, or to be involved in any traffic with the Russians, there was a moral problem to be resolved. I asked to see Trevelyan and told him that if I attended the conference I would have to raise the matter of, and protest about, the way in which the Russians were then treating their Jewish population. Trevelyan did not enthuse about this and urged me to think again, but I remained adamant that if I was to participate as a member of the conference I had to make my individual protest.

A compromise was reached – perhaps rather faint-hearted – which was an agreement on his part that I could discuss the matter with the Russian Deputy Prime Minister, who was leading the delegation, provided I did not raise it as a public issue. I was reluctant to accept this proposal but I suffer, as do many others, from a corporate loyalty which makes it difficult to rock the corporate boat.

Just before the conference started, I buttonholed the Deputy Prime Minister and told him that it had been my intention to raise the matter at a plenary session, but as it was, I was approaching him personally to tell him my feelings, and the feelings of a great number of other people, both Jew and Gentile, on what to us was the inexplicable behaviour of the great Russian nation towards a tiny minority of its population. As was the case when I later raised the question of the Panovs, he received my remarks politely, agreed to make a note of them and to relay my views to the appropriate authorities, and the matter was left there.

The conference proceeded on a deceptively even keel. We broke up into groups: I chaired the smallest of them which was to discuss the development of artistic exchanges between the two countries in every aspect of the arts – visual, literary, dramatic and cinematic. The leader of the small Russian group dealing with the arts was a politician named Popov, who subsequently attained political eminence. He was then the deputy to the Minister of Culture, Madame Furtseva, but very evidently a dominant and powerful person. He spoke no English and, alas, I spoke no Russian, but nevertheless, with the aid of interpreters, rapid agreements were reached on several matters – all of which turned out to be illusory: that the long-delayed exhibition of Soviet art and design, 'Art in Revolution', would be made a reality; that there would be a much freer exchange of Russian and British films and more performances of their great Kirov and Bolshoi opera and ballet; and that in return we would send our own best companies to Russia.

On paper the most happy accord was reached, with the brightest of prospects of fruitful co-operation. But at the moment when our small group was verging on total agreement, a desperate message was received by all the separate groups from Lord Trevelyan, asking if we would resume a plenary session to discuss a problem that had arisen. We raced to the Central Hall where it emerged that the problem had arisen in his group which had been engaged in discussing education and general policy and that the cause of the problem was a request from the Russians for a large-scale academic research project into the origins of the Second World War.

Needless to say, Lord Trevelyan and his colleagues were not at all enthusiastic. He cast around the room anxiously for help. His eyes alighted on me and he said, 'Arnold, perhaps you have some views?' I thought for a second and I said quietly, 'Have you told our friends, Humphrey, that we have absolutely no control over what any historian may wish to write, and perhaps more importantly, the most eminent historian in England, A. J. P. Taylor, has written a book making it quite clear that Hitler had no responsibility for the Second World War and it rested with the Allies?' Lord Trevelyan's face lit up. The interpreter proceeded to translate this to the Russians whose faces notably fell. After a few minutes the session was adjourned and the request withdrawn.

So far as the Soviet 'Art in Revolution' exhibition was concerned, the plans had been going on for several years. Its theme was to be the application of revolutionary aesthetic ideas in a revolutionary society, and in date it was to span from the Revolution to the late 1920s. It was not easy to identify where the difficulties arose. Our delegates who discussed the matter with the Russians declared that they were impossible to deal with, but within our own ranks there were some who declared that their colleagues were obstructionist and anxious to damage the communist cause. Nothing much had happened until the Woking Conference, when my group agreed that the Russians and the Arts Council should 'assist in every possible way the successful holding of the "Art in Revolution" exhibition at a mutually acceptable date'.

Shortly after the April 1970 conference, an emissary from the Arts Council, Norbert Lynton (the director of exhibitions), and Edward Braun, one of the British advisers to the exhibition, went to Moscow. They were shown a list of proposed exhibits to which they immediately dissented. It contained none of the works of Lissitzky, Malevich and Tatlin, the artists most associated with the middle period of the Soviet regime. The explanation was simple: all these gentlemen had fallen into disfavour and were now described as counter-revolutionaries. But our people were dogged. They were not prepared to have an exhibition without re-presentation from these artists and so, having made this clear and been told that compliance with their requests was impossible, they set off for the airport to report the failure of their mission.

However, before they had reached the airport, a speeding motor car intercepted them and brought them back again. New lists, including the missing artists, were produced and suitable exhibits agreed upon. Satisfaction reigned and our innocent emissaries thereupon signed an agreement – the exhibition, as selected by the Russians, would arrive in England by the end of October. 'As selected by the Russians' meant, to us simple folk, selected in accordance with the lists agreed between us and our Russian opposite numbers, and particularly Mr Popov.

It was not until the beginning of February 1971 that exhibits started to arrive from Russia. Great crates were delivered to the Hayward Gallery. As each one was opened its contents emerged destitute of any of the works by the proscribed artists. Case after case displayed war material for posters, industrial scenes, but nowhere was there to be found a single example of the missing artists. And when the last case had been opened there was still none there.

With the exhibits had arrived various Russian representatives. One was the Russian art director, but senior to him was a political commissar who had obviously expected trouble. This gentleman admitted to an ignorance of art but a determination to prevent any attempt to replace the absent artists. Our people, moving with speed, had sought a small number of loans from Western sources to include in the exhibition in place of the missing exhibits. But the commissar would have none of it. He denounced any such action as contrary to the agreement and threatened to remove the entire exhibition if we proceeded in our plan to hang substitute items for those missing.

We argued for hours. I invited them all to supper at my home, where we were joined by John Pope-Hennessy and Robin Campbell, then respectively the chairman of the Council's Art Panel and the Council's art director, and Norbert Lynton. But all to no avail. Whereupon I referred the matter to higher authority. I was able at once to get on the telephone to Mr Popov in Moscow. 'Mr Popov,' I said, 'where are the missing exhibits?'

'There are no missing exhibits.'

'But you agreed to let us have works by Lissitzky, Malevich and Tatlin.'

'It is a misunderstanding. You have the best we can send you.'

'But where are the works by Lissitzky, Malevich and Tatlin?'

'You would not want such artists. They are inferior.'

'We do not mind if they are inferior. We do want them.'

'You have a splendid exhibition.'

'You have broken your word to us.'

'Lord Goodman, you and I are old friends...'

And so this idiotic dialogue went on, producing absolutely no result and no exhibits. I tried subsequently to telephone Popov, but mysteriously could never get through. Equally, when I spoke to the British Ambassador – who enlisted in our cause with the minimum of explanation – I was unable to find out what, if anything, Popov had done, and then all telephone communications ceased.

Here again the decision we reached may well have been wrong, but I think not. Following discussions with Lord Eccles and the Foreign Office, the Arts Council decided that as we had signed an agreement, the literal text of which had given the Russians the right of choice, we had put ourselves in the wrong by our own stupidity. Our decision was influenced by the fact that an expenditure of some £40,000 was already involved. In the end, therefore, we showed the exhibition, which was unadventurous, unexciting and rather mean. The missing exhibits have yet to appear in England.

We were criticised by several newspapers, and particularly by Bernard Levin, for the decision to go ahead. It is perfectly true that it was not a heroic decision, but it seemed to me that our critics lacked a sense of proportion if they seriously thought that the affair was a craven acquiescence in Russian-inspired censorship. I am by no means sure that the exhibition would have taken place if the decision had rested with me alone, and it was certainly the most criticised of any of the decisions by the Arts Council during my tour of duty.

The gravest moral difficulty relating to censorship that I encountered during my term of office at the Arts Council occurred in October 1971, when an exhibition – of which previous details had not been notified to the Council – was presented at the Hayward Gallery. Let me explain that the Council's exhibitions were not necessarily the subject of detailed scrutiny by the Council itself. The Art Panel proposed the exhibitions which were approved in principle.

This particular exhibition was of a consortium of American artists, all from the West Coast and all representing the new school of American visual art. Included among them was an artist who made use of living material – catfish. The artist presented his catfish, together with an assortment of lobsters, crayfish and crabs, as I remember, in suitably heated tanks in the Hayward Gallery. The crustaceans escaped unscathed, but once or twice a day into the catfish tanks he projected an electric current lethal to catfish and the creatures were immolated in the interests of his artistic philosophy – to demonstrate the mortal aspects of human (or fish) life. Life, he wished to tell us, for a catfish was hard. He certainly established the point that it was especially hard for a catfish which fell into the hands of a Californian artistic innovator.

The exhibition was reviewed in *The Times* on the day of a Council meeting, and the day before its opening. Before then I don't believe that any of the Council knew anything about it, and at the meeting we decided that as matters had gone as far as they had, we had better see the exhibition for ourselves and form a judgement. However, this policy of quiet and patience could not survive the public onslaught. The catfish made no vocal protest but the public made more than enough for them. The Arts Council was denounced as sadistic maniacs.

Early the next morning I sped to the Hayward Gallery, there to find a small crowd assembled outside, watching Spike Milligan busy trying to break a window with a small hammer. Mr Milligan had been a client of mine, so I nodded affably to him but said I thought the hammer was inadequate in size to do any degree of damage. I was then accosted by a wild-eyed woman reporter who asked me, 'Will the catfish live?' I replied briefly that they had a better chance than her breakfast kipper and made my way into the gallery. There was little to see. The forlorn catfish floated about in pathetic ignorance of their impending electrocution and the artist and his coterie of immensely vocal advisers gathered to debate with me. They had, they assured me, heard everything I would have to say before. What had it to do with art? Their answer was simple. The dimensions of art were defined by the artist. It was not for me to interfere. My answer was even simpler. This was a claim of mountainous arrogance. The fact that a man described himself as an artist did not entitle him to murder anything – even catfish.

The arguments grew hotter and flew backwards and forwards with greater speed. It was clear that the world at that moment had divided itself closely into two communities: the majority of artists who saw in any interference by the Arts Council the philistine hand of bureaucracy and ignorance, and the rest of mankind who saw the murder of the catfish as further evidence that the artist today was a fraud and confidence trickster, making up by impertinence for his missing talent. Telegrams poured in on me from both sides. Artists of great splendour allied themselves to the cause of the electric chair. I invited the artist to compromise. I suggested that he should leave the catfish swimming about happily and that he should give an oral demonstration by explanation and gesture of how easy it was to murder a catfish or anything else. This was scorned and ridiculed.

In the end a special meeting of the Arts Council, probably the only one in its history, was convened at my home late that evening to debate the issue – for crucial it was. Neither my worst enemies nor my best friends regard me as particularly tentative at arriving at conclusions, but I was torn by doubt. The murder of the catfish seemed a classic absurdity. It seemed an encouragement of positive evil. It was foolish and, since the ceremony of immolation was followed by the consumption of the catfish on American doughnuts dipped in honey (ugh!), the whole thing had a quality of decadence and positive indecency that I found most disagreeable.

But greatly respected artists like Bridget Riley, and experts like John Pope-Hennessy, all declared that their own freedom of thought and action was at stake unless we allowed this idiotic performance to take place twice daily. And to my profound astonishment they received majority support on the Council. I came down in the debate firmly on the side of censorship. I was for closing the exhibition. Some of my colleagues who might have shared my views – and I know that Lord Snow, for instance, would have – were unable to attend the meeting, and to my great surprise otherwise sensible, moderate and conventional people all declared that to close the exhibition would be an intolerable interference with artistic freedom.

To this day I do not know the answer. I find it difficult to credit that our artistic tradition would have been damaged if we had abstained from the ceremonial execution of catfish. I also believe that such an activity has no relationship to art or to sense and that sanity – in its true sense of coherent thought – was invaded by these puerile manifestations. The compromise that we reached was ignominious. The catfish would be killed, but outside the gallery. Our justification was that there was no way of disposing of them, or so it was said, without killing them. Hence it was alleged to be merciful to electrocute them, and of course we were told that this was kinder than catching the poor creatures with a hook attached to a rod. The Royal Society for the Prevention of Cruelty to Animals – the catfish apparently so ranked – was called in by us and prescribed the precise voltage which would kill a catfish in the most humane and painless fashion. And so the catfish were regularly slaughtered twice daily by the artist. I believe that the moral aspects of the matter were abrogated, but this was of no great importance. What was of importance was that even a Council as sensible as our own, as free from prejudice, could find at least one dilemma that divided it totally.

16

The Newspaper World

FEW PEOPLE TODAY would claim any great credit from an association with the 'newspaper world', taking those words to mean the generalities of the press. There are, of course, still relatively virtuous newspapers conforming to relatively decent standards, but they are few and far between and it is the unhappy fact that the proprietorship of newspapers is now concentrated in hands which have little or no interest in the quality of the press. The proprietors are creatures differing widely in character but apparently united by a single ambition, which is to run immensely successful and prosperous newspapers. With rare exceptions they are characterised by an almost complete lack of interest in the quality of their editorial content. They would, I think, not be flattered but mildly offended by a suggestion that 'good writing' was of importance and it is certain that they would have great difficulty in identifying it.

The newspaper proprietors – those people owning a substantial property interest in a paper – are in the main illiterate in the sense of being sparsely read. They belong to the capitalist world that regards pretensions to culture as an affectation. In short, they have by their identity almost guaranteed the impossibility of maintaining a quality press. When in rare instances an effort is made to establish a 'quality newspaper', they smile kindly since they know perfectly well that it can never compete with the squalid rubbish produced in a tabloid world of vast circulation. They watch contentedly the struggling efforts at survival of each new publication established in the mistaken belief that there is a wide public for things worth reading. They know better, and alas how right they are.

My first introduction to the newspaper world came from the late Sir Ifor Evans who, towards the end of his life, was identified by Harold Wilson as a useful ally and hence ennobled, ending as Lord Evans of Hungershall. I first met Ifor Evans as, if I say it myself, a useful alumnus of University College, London. He spotted me as such and we became, if not close friends, at least close. He consulted me on a great variety of matters. He was an active factotum in many fields. His academic discipline was English and he wrote a useful little book or two about British dramatists and other writers, in particular *A Short History of English Drama*, but he had no great academic standing. His prowess was as a university administrator and particularly as the Provost of University College, London, between 1951 and 1966. In that field he displayed organisational talents of a high order and, even more important, and differing markedly from many university administrators, he displayed a real genius in assembling financial support from many quarters.

Ifor was not a snob, but he loved the company of the rich and powerful and cultivated it to good purpose so far as his college was concerned. He recognised early on that the Jewish community was above average in wealth, and in generosity featured high compared with their 'goy' neighbours. One of his early captures was the late Harold Samuel who, similarly towards the end of his life, became a Wilson peer. Samuel was, and remains, the most successful and trusted property developer of this era. He established the most important property company – Land Securities. I knew his kinsmen, Basil and Howard Samuel, and got to know Harold Samuel when he consulted me out of the blue.

He was, I suppose, one of the more boring tycoons. The solitary topic of conversation that interested him related to his trade as a developer of properties. When asked to lunch or dine with him – as not infrequently happened – I had to submit myself to the tedium of a discussion relating to property valuations, building developments, sites, and kindred subjects, in all of which I had the remotest interest and then only in so far as it impinged on my own legal profession. But Harold Samuel was oblivious of the effect that his conversation had on his guests. He used to lunch daily either at the Ritz or the Savoy. He had a handsome house in Avenue Road, St John's Wood, where he rarely entertained, and a splendid country house near East Grinstead, where he had had assembled a priceless collection of Dutch old masters, purchased for him by the famous Eddie Speelman – a man with a reputation coming close to that of the late Lord Duveen, except that he had a trustworthiness of which the biographers of Lord Duveen have stripped him completely.

Speelman conducted his business in the most economical fashion. He had no gallery and for practical purposes no stock. His method was to ascertain what was likely to tickle the fancy of a rich client; to recommend the picture to him – before Speelman himself had bought it – and, if the customer rose to the bait, to purchase it on his behalf, with ample compensation to himself for so doing. Those people who bought from

Speelman have very few complaints. He had an unerring eye and I have never heard of any purchase made by him that was not 'right'.

Harold Samuel's collection became renowned and on his death in 1987 he bequeathed it to the Lord Mayor at the Mansion House. The collection today must be worth millions, but I never heard Harold rate a picture in money terms, although he would frequently refer to the cost or value of a building. He had sufficient discrimination to enjoy his collection and to take pride in showing it to anyone who could appreciate it. He would rapidly become impatient when showing it to an obvious philistine.

His relation, Basil Samuel, had a modest but very discriminating collection of pictures. It was Basil who was responsible for my meeting Speelman, and Speelman was responsible for the development of an important part of my career, namely the chairmanship of an art gallery, and the acquisition of a substantial shareholding in it, all arising out of the fact that I met Jack Baer through a Speelman episode connected with Basil Samuel.

To elucidate what must appear most confusing to the reader, Basil Samuel had purchased a Boudin through a reasonably well-known London gallery belonging to one Jack O'Hana. Basil was very proud of the picture, and one day when Eddie Speelman came to dinner he proceeded to show it to him, together with a perfectly respectable collection of other pictures. Speelman took one look at the Boudin and boldly declared that it was a fake.

Basil had many admirable qualities – generosity, wisdom and a capacity for great affection – but equally he had the deep distaste of a self-made man for being taken for a ride. He reproached O'Hana, who promptly declared that Speelman knew nothing about Boudin and had no business to make a snap judgement of this kind. Nevertheless, Speelman's reputation was such as to leave more than a seed of unease in Basil's mind, and the thought that he was exhibiting a fake picture on his own wall was to him intolerable.

He consulted me and I in turn approached Jack Baer, who was then – in 1959 – on the way to becoming a leading expert in French pictures of the nineteenth century and the most trusted art dealer in the country. Jack took charge of the Boudin and undertook some scientific investigation. The picture was unsigned (unusual for Boudin), and under X-ray examination scraping marks were discovered that indicated a signature had been erased with a solvent. Added to this, there were circumstantial matters of an impressive nature. The picture was of the ceremony at the opening of the Longchamp racecourse in 1858 and had been described as being one of three commissioned to commemorate the event. At that date, Boudin was thirty-four years old and unsuccessful to the point of poverty. It was powerfully unlikely that an unknown artist would have been commissioned to do such a ceremonial portrait, let alone leave it unsigned. Moreover, apart from stylistic inconsistencies in the picture, Boudin's major reputation rested on marine pictures. The accumulation of evidence was enough to compel O'Hana to admit the strong likelihood that the picture was false and to return the purchase price.

The affair established a friendship between Jack Baer and myself that has given me great pleasure over more than thirty years. It also established a business relationship which I have enjoyed equally, although it cannot be described as the source of any great wealth. Hazlitt, Gooden & Fox Ltd, of which I have been the chairman for all the years of my association, is now immensely well-respected as a leading gallery, known for its tasteful and discriminating exhibitions and becoming increasingly known for important acquisitions for a large and prosperous clientele. All this derives from Basil's purchase of a dubious Boudin. No purchase could have been more fortunate for me.

All this is a long way from Ifor Evans, but, to retrace my steps, my association with him thrived to a point where he was increasingly anxious to involve me in his major affairs, namely the provostship of University College, London, and his chairmanship of the *Observer*. So far as the former is concerned, I was frequently invited to lectures, dinners and discussions connected with the college until the ultimate point was reached when shortly before he retired, Ifor suggested that he should nominate me as his successor as Provost.

My former association with the college had been a purely academic one. I had been a student there for several years, taking two law degrees. Later I became an honorary lecturer in company law, but I did not feel at all disposed to give up my other occupations, including part-time academic work at Cambridge, for a totally administrative job. So I declined the invitation, which was, of course, only that he would submit my name. My knowledge of Ifor's persuasion, however, left me confident that any nomination from him would have been seriously regarded. In the event a much more distinguished academic was appointed, who enjoyed a successful tour of duty until he resigned to a multiplicity of other occupations.

The most important influence that Ifor had on my life was to suggest to David Astor (then the editor and most powerful influence in the affairs of the *Observer*) that I should join the board and serve under Ifor's chairmanship. This I did in 1966 and for a year or so remained a most interested and punctual member of the *Observer* board, until Ifor decided – and there is no doubt that this was in his mind from the outset, David Astor has since so informed me – that I should succeed him as chairman.

The *Observer* in those days proceeded under Astor's talented, if not wholly businesslike, administration. David Astor is as big-hearted and liberal a man as can be found on this earth. He is a controversial figure: those who love him, love him without qualification, and I must admit that I am among the number. It would be uncandid indeed not to reveal that there are others who express a contrary view, often with vehemence. I will spare his blushes simply by recording that in my view he is overall a force for good.

He has played a large and influential part in my life and in my career. When we first met he obviously had considerable misgivings about me and whether my views would dovetail with his. Dovetail suggests a process of meshing that in fact has never taken place, but I have always been in broad sympathy with his aspirations and notions. In consequence, I have always found it difficult, if not impossible, to resist recruiting on his side, even if I had little enthusiasm for the cause.

Often they were causes in which my enlistment was incongruous to the point of eccentricity. I have never been married and hence I have never indulged in wife-beating. Nevertheless I took an active part in his campaign to establish hostels for beaten wives, and found myself dragged to the support of a lady named Erin Pizzey whose views I frequently found alarming but who had the force of persuasion of a steamroller. I could not enlist with David in his Middle East views. Somehow I sensed that they would not be helpful to the Zionist cause, to which I am both committed and devoted. Nevertheless, I have engaged in lengthy discussions with Arabs found by David, who produced sentiments which, if shared by the rest of their fraternity, would have solved the Middle East problem in seconds.

Within a few months of my first board meeting, however, David had developed an admiration for my qualities, wildly undeserved and totally excessive, and was introducing me more and more into the affairs to which he gave major prominence; of all these, of course, the *Observer*, before his unhappy separation from it, came first. He was, in the view of many, and despite major idiosyncrasies, one of the great editors of the day. His triumph was to establish a newspaper which was widely respected everywhere that English was spoken and on which he induced a remarkable quality of journalists to serve. His aides were as disparate a couple of characters as one could find anywhere. The more colourful, and indeed interesting, was Tristan Jones, who had met David at Oxford and was the son of the famous Thomas Jones who was deputy secretary of the Cabinet from 1916 to 1930.

Tristan Jones minded the affairs of the *Observer* in his own inimitable way. A leading characteristic was a penchant for secrecy. Earlier in life he had decided that there was no bonus obtained from telling anybody anything. It would have been a highly skilled interrogator who could ascertain from him what he had eaten for lunch, and certainly not what he was proposing to eat for dinner. I never knew why he possessed this obsession for secrecy – he was a kindly man with a generous disposition. It was not a desire to score over anyone or to demonstrate that he knew things that others did not know. My belief is that he thought that people who had advance information of anything that was going to happen would be in a superior negotiating position if it ever turned out that he had to negotiate with them. He was totally trusted by David Astor and by the other leading figures in the *Observer* hierarchy. He was not particularly liked or trusted by the rank and file, since he neither liked nor trusted the rank and file.

The other trusted aide was John Littlejohn – an accountant who lacked any worldly polish but had only to be looked at to be recognised as a sage and well-informed adviser.

In the early days I did not join the inner councils of the paper, or more accurately was not invited to join the magic circle, but I certainly had some influence with David and rarely found myself involved in any major disagreement. Indeed, I can only recollect one occasion when I was moved to threaten my resignation, and this on a point which I think today would be regarded as exceptionally priggish.

The paper planned an article about the late George Brown, whose drunkenness ruined political prospects that could have worked great advantages for the Labour Party and the nation. In the article, reference was made to what is by now a famous exchange between George and the French Ambassadress. The story is that at lunch alongside the lady, he enquired whether she would sleep with him. To which she gave the calm reply that she would not. He then protested that she must surely have received invitations previously, to which she replied, 'Yes, but not before the soup.' I took the view that this anecdote, even if she knew of it, would not amuse Mrs Brown, who was the devoted Jewish wife of her immensely troublesome husband, and I invited David Astor to remove it from the article. This he declined to do and for the one and only time I uttered a genuine threat of resignation.

The issue hung in suspense for some hours, but ultimately David capitulated. It was decided that as this apparently was the titbit of the article, the whole article should be scrapped. I was never wholly forgiven since there was no suitable replacement and an article on agriculture had to be inserted, which was not regarded as an irresistible attraction to the readers.

But apart from isolated episodes, my tenure was a tranquil one. A particularly interesting matter in 1967 was to do with the memoirs of

Stalin's daughter, Svetlana. I was telephoned by David Astor who told me that the *Observer* was suffering very heavily from the disadvantage that all the interesting books being published, capable of being serialised, were purchased well in advance by the *Sunday Times*, at prices beyond the *Observer*'s reach, and he was much disconcerted and troubled by this. But for once something had come his way, if he could overcome a little difficulty. What had come his way were the memoirs of Stalin's daughter. Svetlana had handed them to a friend in Russia and asked her to smuggle them out and preserve them in England. Later Svetlana, who had decided to emigrate, would rejoin the memoirs and arrange for their sale to support her in the Western world. But the friend, in the belief that it would be helpful to Svetlana, had handed the memoirs to a literary agent who informed both the *Sunday Times* and the *Observer* of their availability. The agent regarded himself as wholly secure because of the absence of any copyright arrangements between Britain and Russia. In the result it was impossible for Svetlana to sue to protect her literary property on the ground of copyright.

Much thought was given to the matter and I had an idea which in fact proved effective. It was that, although there was no possible action that could lie in copyright, there was certainly a good deal of authority which enabled an action to be brought for a breach of confidence. If somebody entrusted someone with an idea, or property, on the basis that his confidence was totally dependent on the reliability of that person, that in itself gave rise to a cause of action. The leading case in the matter related to the Austin sunshine roof case, where a man had presented his design for a sunshine roof to the Austin motor company which had expressed an interest in it and asked to see the design. In fact they rejected the design but subsequently adopted the idea on their own behalf. He instituted proceedings and recovered very considerable damages.

It appeared to me that this case provided a precedent of some kind for our case, and proceedings were instituted for an injunction to restrain the agent from publication. The matter in fact never went to court; he capitulated without battle and the ownership of the memoirs was restored to Madame Svetlana.

The *Observer* then indicated its desire to purchase them. There was one initial difficulty: Madame Svetlana had engaged a very skilful young American lawyer – a partner in Greenbaum, Wolff & Ernst – to look after her affairs, and he had decided that he would sell the memoirs to the highest bidder who would buy them blind, i.e. without the bidder having read a word of them. I myself was reluctant to advise the *Observer* to adopt this course but, subject only to a warranty that they were Svetlana's authentic memoirs and had been written by her or could be presented as having been written by her, the paper decided to take the risk.

In order to complete the transaction, I travelled to America with Tristan Jones. In that connection I had occasion to meet Madame Svetlana, and together with Tristan Jones we travelled to her apartment in a fashionable New York suburb, in order to advise her of our offer. She provided us with tea and a fascinating conversation, entirely composed of a lengthy vindication of her dearly beloved father. She presented him to us as a saintly character who had been grossly misrepresented by a savage, critical world having political motivations for discrediting him. I at that stage was prepared to believe anything. In fact I was strongly reminded of the observation made by the Duke of Wellington when a young man came up to him and said, 'Mr Brown, I believe?' to which the Duke replied, 'If you believe that, you will believe anything.'

However, we listened patiently to this splendidly fictitious account of the late Joseph Stalin. She told us with loving detail how good a father he had been, how he had been grossly traduced with the allegation that he had killed millions of people, that he was totally innocent of anyone's death, and that he spent his life trying to take care of the unfortunate, dispossessed Russian peasantry, so as to ensure that they had a better, happier way of life. I was in no position to contradict this as I knew little about it.

In the result we bought the memoirs, in September 1967, for what in those days was the massive figure of £80,000. However, they turned out to be entirely unreadable because they contained mainly an extension of the rubbish retailed to us over tea. The *Observer* had no choice but to print them since they had made such a substantial investment, and print them they did but, two or three years later, the lady concerned issued a second set of memoirs, this time telling the truth about her father, in terms so horrifying as to make the fictitious nature of the previous account the more appalling and the more incredible.

Be that as it may, I never saw her again until she came to London and enlisted the services of my firm for various matters while she was here. She then decided to return to Russia, where no doubt she had equally convincing tales to tell about her reasons for having left to begin with and the monstrous way in which she had been treated by the Europeans and the Americans. I believe, in fact, that this is precisely what she did, although for reasons best known to herself she is now living in the West again.

After I became the *Observer*'s chairman, I found myself drawn more and more into participating in the crucial decisions at the paper, particularly on the labour-relations front. This was especially the case after I became the chairman of the Newspaper Publishers Association in 1970 – an appointment for which my *Observer* association was principally responsible, since the nomination came from David Astor and by then was warmly supported by Max Aitken, of whom I had become a close friend, although not always a welcome adviser, particularly when I urged him to sobriety.

It would be difficult to imagine a more unlikely friend for me than Max Aitken and even more difficult to imagine me as one of his intimate friends. I met him first when he was having a run-around with a young woman who was one of my numerous brood of quasi-wards. He was, of course, to use that hideous but convenient word, a great 'womaniser'. In his tactics, accompanied by pledges of total devotion, he put Don Giovanni to shame. Like Don Giovanni it was, I think, the quest that he enjoyed more than the conquest. I have a sad recollection of inviting him to supper on a Sunday evening – when over the years it was my habit to entertain twelve or fourteen people. On this occasion I had misguidedly invited another of my quasi-wards. She was an exceptionally attractive, although rather lost, young woman and I gave her the most solemn of warnings that – Max being there – she was to keep him at a distance and not form any association. Never were words more wasted. Within moments he had changed his seat to sit, or more truthfully to nestle, beside her and the fat was in the fire. Both kept secret from me the fact that they had from that evening onwards formed the closest association. In a busy life I made no enquiries and it was only by accident, when I was dining at a restaurant one night, that I observed the couple in the same restaurant, obviously now on terms of total intimacy.

One of Max's most remarkable achievements was never to estrange himself from any girlfriend or former girlfriend. They all remained on the books. In fact this young lady in the event benefited quite considerably from the association – although she was anything but a gold-digger. Max had the grace to apologise to me, but I realised that his reaction to a pretty young woman was a reflex. Resistance for him was an impossibility. Strangely enough, women had no serious influence on him. Many men have their lives affected and dominated by women. For Max they were a pastime and in relation to the things that he regarded as important – introducing total confusion into his newspaper operations, sacking his editors regularly in the belief that he was maintaining the image of his father, entertaining lavishly, yachting, and above all drinking – no feminine touch was perceptible.

The great influence on Max during his father's lifetime was his father and after his father's death the ghost of his father. But Max's worship of Lord Beaverbrook went far beyond any ordinary lengths. For years he wore the hat and the coat and even, I believe, the suits that remained in his father's wardrobe after the latter's death. I am sure that in all the misguided decisions he took in the newspaper world he believed that he was doing precisely what his father would have done. But his father's disagreeable elements were his principal source of power. Max would sack editors at the drop of his father's hat, believing that he was establishing the same reputation for cool and immediate decision. All he did was to ensure that continuity in the Beaverbrook press was destroyed and that sensible journalists ran a mile rather than take employment with him. Before I met him, I represented two of his editors in negotiating their dismissal terms. It was a tribute to him that neither of them maintained any hostile spirit but both of them were immensely relieved to find havens elsewhere.

But leaving aside his behaviour when he was posturing as a news-paper tycoon, Max had some immensely amiable and indeed lovable qualities. I have already described his behaviour when I was taken ill in Rhodesia. Although he was a disaster where the control of a newspaper was concerned, he was nobody's fool. To be described as a non-intellectual he would have considered a compliment. He was indeed that and squared, but he had a quick perception of human frailty and passed no judgement on it. He was a wholly honourable man in all material matters and in his relations with people – other than women to whom he was making love – he could be relied upon to keep faith. Some of the principal influences on him did not respond to that description, and his misfortune was to bestow his trust and confidence in unreliable quarters.

The loss of the Beaverbrook empire, ultimately sold to Trafalgar in 1977, was an outcome as inevitable as day following night. The original plan, subsequently rejected, was for a sale of the *Evening Standard* – now long after achieved – to Associated Newspapers. In the negotiations I chaired the discussions with the rejected suitor, was nearly murdered by an enraged mob who had been encouraged to believe that the sale of the *Evening Standard* had been engineered by me – an injustice of mammoth dimensions – and was kept in total ignorance of the fact that other negotiations were under way while we were engaged in what by then had become the charade of seeming to conclude the original negotiations. In this matter Max had absolutely no will of his own. He had by then suffered his first stroke and he was putty in the hands of any schemer in the vicinity.

However chequered the negotiations, the outcome was a sensible one. The sale left him and his family with substantial resources and since his health deteriorated rapidly it would have been calamitous if he had been short of money at the end of his life. Max ran through money like water. He was wildly extravagant and immensely generous. One had almost to engage in a battle to be allowed to pay for a meal. His drinking was a sadness. When drunk he was absolutely impossible: quarrelsome and boorish and hideous to be with. For some reason he regarded it as a mark of strength of character to be rude and inconsiderate to underlings. A meal with him was often purgatorial and when he became drunk it was sensible to leave the scene with speed. But for all this he had a quality of kindliness and loyalty that was beyond praise. All these good qualities could be totally neutralised by alcohol.

I have a happy and a painful recollection of one evening. Max had, at my request, intervened to save a man's career. It was a situation in which he had no personal involvement and he had done it purely as an act of friendship. The value of his behaviour involved total confidentiality in the future, but to my horror at dinner one night, when obviously under the influence, he was on the point of disclosing the matter to a group of people including wholly unreliable journalists. Fortunately he was not so drunk that he could not be impressed by the ferocity of my reaction. I told him in the clearest terms that if he breathed a word about the matter it was the last he would ever see of me, and happily this was an effective threat.

Only on two occasions do I remember socialising with him other than at meals. On one of them he was anxious to see a play about Héloïse and Abélard. This surprised me, as serious drama was not his scene. I discovered, however, that his interest arose because Miss Diana Rigg, who was playing Héloïse, appeared for a fleeting second in the buff. He was bitterly disappointed that this apparition was so brief and bored stiff by the remainder of the play.

Max knew everybody, was liked by almost everybody, but keenly disliked by a small group of people who had seen the worst side of him. It was characteristic that on his father's death he declined to take the title of Lord Beaverbrook, although he inherited the baronetcy. His father and his father's memory dogged his life, and during his father's lifetime I believe the only period when he was free was his service in the RAF where, not unexpectedly to those who knew him well, he became a war hero and collected a breastful of medals.

His last days were tragic. His final stroke left him unable to walk; he could hardly raise a hand and could speak only with difficulty. He had tender care from a number of people and happily the sale of the newspapers had left him with the means to provide any comforts that could mitigate his condition. The last time he came to my home to dine was, of course, in a wheelchair. But on the previous occasion, when he was still able to remain upright, it took something like twenty minutes to move him from my sitting-room to the dining-table and at dinner one maintained a false gaiety that was as painful as it was unreal. Max Aitken was a very good friend to me.

My entry into the Newspaper Publishers Association was by an unexpected route and very much against my inclination. David Astor and Max Aitken, accompanied by Hugh Cudlipp, asked if I would assist them in selecting a successor for Garrett Drogheda, who was gratefully retiring from the chairmanship after a very short term of office. He plainly did not like the job. We had several meetings with the NPA to discuss possibilities, but for one reason or another almost every candidate suggested was unacceptable. Most of the proprietors involved were either mild or passionate Tories and the notion of a left-wing figure was totally unacceptable.

Ultimately, Hugh Cudlipp suggested a very great figure indeed, Lord Robens, and I was asked by the NPA to sound him out and, if he expressed willingness, to invite him to take the job on what seemed to me suitably generous terms. I lunched with Alfred Robens, for whom I have a great admiration, and after a relatively short discussion, in which he interrogated me about the personalities involved, he indicated a willingness to take the job. I was triumphant.

I returned to report my success to the NPA Council. To my unconcealed disgust, one or two of the people who had gone along with the decision to invite him now suddenly took alarm, since Alfred Robens was, of course, a figure – although certainly no revolutionary – previously associated with the Labour Party, from which my belief was that he had long parted company. But the previous association was too much for some of them and particularly for Michael Berry of the *Telegraph*, who was, of course, a loyal and unquestioning Tory. In the result they decided to rescind the invitation, regardless of the embarrassment which this might cause to me. I was asked if I would then explain to Robens their change of mind which – hardly surprisingly – I declined to do. I was for once in my life a little sharp in demanding that those who had reversed their decision should go and explain the reverse to him. Ultimately, the heroic Hugh Cudlipp undertook to do it. How and in what words I never discovered, but I do not believe Alfred Robens was heartbroken and if he had watched the sequence of events in the ensuing years he must have been greatly relieved.

However, we were back in the position of having no candidate and Garrett Drogheda was pressing that the imminent date of his resignation should be adhered to. One morning, early in 1970, into my office in Bouverie Street came David Astor, Max Aitken and one or two others. 'We want to invite you to become the chairman for a short period, so as to leave ourselves a little more room to conduct the search,' they said. I have to admit that I was flattered. In those days I was more easily flattered than I am now, although it is not terribly difficult to achieve this result even at the present day. But I stipulated very firmly that my professional commitments – and my practice was growing apace at that time – compelled a short time-limit. We agreed on six months. It will be known that the six months stretched into six years. My experiences were varied and often fascinating, particularly having regard to the variety of human being I now encountered.

The Newspaper Publishers Association was composed of the most impossible body of men that could have been assembled outside of the League of Nations. They had a simple motivation: to secure the prosperity of their newspaper, and they had a simple belief that the continuing prosperity of their newspaper must depend on stealing circulation from other newspapers. In a word, that to succeed themselves it was necessary to damage or even ruin others. This viewpoint was most conspicuously maintained by the Beaverbrook and the Rothermere empires. Each was convinced that the solution of their problems was the dissolution of the other. This determined the quite demented behaviour on both their parts, which rubbed off on the entire press. Each sought to test which had the longer purse. Hence demands from journalists that should have been resisted, and events have proved could have been resisted, were freely conceded first by one or the other, so as to make it impossible for the remaining members of the NPA to offer any defence or even a protest.

No story of the NPA would be complete without at least thumbnail sketches of the principal personalities of my day. Round the table there would sit – some with regularity, others only occasionally – as disparate a collection of humanity as could be imagined. When he was there, Max Aitken dominated the scene, but nearly always in his place came his lieutenant, Jocelyn Stevens, subsequently to become – to the astonishment of the artistic world – the Rector of the Royal College of Art. In my day, Stevens's principal quality was a total unpredictability. No one ever knew which way he would jump, except that it would be contrary to expectations. No agreement could ever be reached in the newspaper world with any real certainty that he would wish to sustain it. The atmosphere he evoked inspired excitement but not certainty. He was, I am driven to say, a not particularly popular figure, although his undoubted mesmeric qualities in persuading his labour force to accept proprietorial assurances was the envy of the newspaper world.

Michael Berry, later Lord Hartwell, the owner of the *Telegraph*, was a totally different kettle of fish. Afflicted by a disabling deafness, he maintained a certainty of course of a stubborn character, capable of resembling obstinacy. He was a man to do business with in the sense that his word was his bond. He was a quiet and shy man whom it has taken me years to get to know, but for whom I have an unstinted admiration. He was a conservative in the best sense of the word: he respected tradition; he believed firmly in the institutions of religion, public-school education and the preservation of property. These views clearly emerged from every edition of his newspapers. Until the last days of his ownership, which terminated when he sold the papers to the Canadian Conrad Black, he exercised considerable control as chairman and editor-in-chief, and the editors under him of the *Daily Telegraph* and the *Sunday Telegraph* were men of the same cast of mind and the same reliable timber.

The most distinguished of them was a former Conservative MP, William Deedes, now deservedly in the Lords and one of the most respected editorial figures of my generation. He could write good and simple prose. Occasionally the *Daily Telegraph* veered into a slightly grotesque illiberality, particularly demonstrated in the burlesque column 'The Way of the World'. But of all the daily newspapers, it was the most reliable in the sense of maintaining an honourable consistency. Nor did it engage in the outrageous snooping, now dignified by the name of 'investigative journalism', that has become a feature even of the *Times* newspapers. It is a sadness that one of the most conspicuous aberrations and instances of bad behaviour was an arrangement by the *Telegraph* camp to purchase the story of the principal accuser of the unfortunate Jeremy Thorpe, with the rewards adjusted for a larger payment if Jeremy were convicted. To Michael Berry's credit, he 'faced the music' in the House of Lords, defending the proposal with determination, although alas with doubtful success. But this instance apart, the *Telegraph* newspapers had overall a fairly respectable history.

The Times and the *Sunday Times* were then owned by the Thomson organisation, characterised, of course, by the personality of Roy Thomson. Here was a little man who measured his success by the size of his 'antheap'. He made no secret of his belief that the purpose of newspaper ownership was to make a profit, and in a speech rendered memorable by that admission, and that admission alone, he proclaimed his faith to the House of Lords, to the indignation of a number of its members.

Thomson acquired *The Times* in 1966 in a purchase from Lord Astor of Hever and in circumstances which had important repercussions for the *Observer* and the Astor family. When the paper was on offer, David Astor – in one of his rare moments of delusional grandeur – aspired to acquire it for a hastily assembled syndicate. I did not conceal my own disbelief in this project, so that I was not involved in the detailed discussions, but for the purpose of the calculations we invited a property tycoon to give us an assessment of the value of the *Times* building in

New Printing House Square. The possession of this information played a crucial part in a later split-second decision that was required of me.

At that time the *Observer* was printed on *The Times*'s presses at New Printing House Square, and the acquisition by Thomson of the paper would have involved our being printed on presses which would then also produce our great rival, the *Sunday Times*. When word of Thomson's acquisition reached the *Observer*, three of us raced over to his office to confront him with the demand that the printing position of the *Observer* should be safeguarded by a firm agreement. David Astor, Tristan Jones and I met him in his office. He showed little inclination to be forthcoming on the matter. 'You need no safeguards,' he said.

'We do,' I said, 'and I am afraid we must have them.'

'Well, what do you want?'

'What we want is a printing agreement with a five-year notice clause, i.e. that the printing facility should not terminate until five years have elapsed from the time of notice unless we agree otherwise.'

We also sought to impose some requirement of confidentiality, although we did not set great store by this since if there was one man in the industry who could be trusted to behave honourably, it was Roy Thomson. 'The five-year notice,' he almost spat at me, 'is nonsense. I could not be trammelled by such a condition.'

I pointed out to him that we had been invited to give evidence to the Monopolies Commission, who had to approve his purchase of *The Times* and who – not unnaturally – were seeking to discover what effect the purchase might have on other newspapers. 'We should be obliged to ask them to impose the five-year requirement as a condition of their consent,' I said. I have rarely seen an uglier expression on a human face. 'This,' he said, 'is blackmail,' to which I replied that the imposition of a sensible term for the preservation of a great newspaper, by two people at least (David Astor and myself) who had no financial interest of any kind, made the use of the term 'blackmail' a feeble debating device. I had a feeling that he would succumb to high blood pressure, and he must have shared the feeling since he left the room for some minutes, obviously to cool down, possibly to seek advice from calmer advisers such as Denis Hamilton. He returned, sat in his chair and could hardly bring out the words: 'Very well, I agree.' The business was done and we gave anodyne evidence to the Monopolies Commission, commending the new ownership as as good as could be found.

In 1969, some three years after our printing agreement with Thomson, a significant change in the position of the *Observer* came about. Denis Hamilton, Thomson's editor-in-chief, called on me in my office to give me the required five-years' notice that entitled them to be rid of our printing contract. I asked him why he was doing this. He replied that it was because they had need to sell the New Printing House Square building in order to raise money to pay for their new offices in Gray's Inn Road. 'How much do you want for it?' I asked. Denis Hamilton, who was as straightforward and honest as a man can be, dug in his pocket and produced a valuation from a leading firm of agents which stated a price for the building which by the side of the valuation I had previously received was extremely moderate – indeed a bargain. I asked Hamilton whether he would sell the building to the *Observer*. 'But you would not have the money,' he said. 'I am sure,' I replied, 'that the Astors can always find a penny or two.' Whereupon we shook hands on the deal and I had bought the building at his valuation price.

I went across to the *Observer*'s offices to announce my purchase and to set about the urgent necessity of finding some money. David Astor demonstrated his splendour as a man to work for. He expressed no misgivings or anxiety but at once set to work discussing with his merchant bankers how they were to obtain the funds. In due course a contract was signed and we acquired a building which today is immensely more valuable than its purchase price, its ownership still being retained by the *Observer*. The purchase was probably the business coup of my career.

In the early days of my NPA chairmanship I was able to instil in the meetings, over which it is a valid claim that I was able to maintain at least a superficial authority, some respectable notions. In the complete absence today of any kind of discipline or control over bribes to the public to read particular newspapers, it is an irony to reflect that in my day results were achieved and agreements reached: banning money prizes, banning door-to-door canvassing, banning insurance policies – in short, a decision that the attraction of the newspaper would depend on its content and the reader's desire to read it. Moreover, a rather gimcrack structure of self-defence came into being, known as the 'Support Scheme', whereby the newspapers agreed to band together to support any member wrongfully subjected to a strike or to the threat of one; and by 'wrongful' was meant in circumstances where the others resolved that the victim had been justified in resisting the terms demanded.

Probably the most interesting – and I am sorry to say no full records exist – of debates at the NPA were on the question of whether or not a particular newspaper had behaved reasonably in deciding to hold out. The semantics engaged in by the other newspapers to avoid any financial participation in the loss would have done great credit to Jesuits or Cabbalists, but nevertheless at the end of the day there were several instances where participation was agreed and actually paid. This achieved a high point in newspaper co-operation that was probably the major achievement of my career: extracting some money from one newspaper to pay for the defence of another.

I doubt if today anyone would credit that such a thing had ever happened, and throughout my six years as chairman the industrial situation dominated every meeting. There were other matters such as transport arrangements, advertising restrictions, newsagents' remuneration and the like which occupied my time and turned me into a well-informed amateur so far as newspaper matters were concerned. But there was hardly a day of the week when the threat of strike action did not have to be dealt with on a basis of total urgency.

I am a long-suffering creature, but the major complaint came from my devoted secretaries who at least once a week were compelled to rearrange a very full diary so as to find time in early dawn or late evening for the unfortunate clients who refused to accept total cancellation. Day after day we would assemble at the rather drab offices of the NPA in Bouverie Street to conduct discussions first with the Council and then with a visiting delegation from the NUJ, the NGA, NATSOPA, SOGAT et al., and sometimes, horror of horrors, a delegation from all of them. Hour after hour was spent in discussions where one's only yearning was for a machine-gun and where in the end patience prevailed to the extent of reducing the demand from its totality to a mere 90 per cent. Always there was a weaker proprietor urging capitulation and compliance.

It was a story of industrial shame on the part of the proprietors and I could not feel any great pride that I presided over it. I would have difficulty in determining my real motive. Some will think it humbug that I was much influenced by considerations of friendship. I knew and was on warm terms with almost all the proprietors, and on terms of great intimacy and friendship with two or three. Every time I felt tempted to depart, an appeal was made that I should stay a little longer and this I did. It is a paradox that almost all the union leaders (particularly Bill Keys, general secretary of SOGAT), hateful in their official role, were people with whom I established a cordial and often a friendly relationship. Their personal responses were never unreasonable. Their formal responses were impossible. No power on earth could have penetrated their official skins with the sense of the total unreasonableness of many of their demands.

Official strikes were rare. It is my recollection that there were only two during my period of office. The first occurred within days of my appointment. It was, of course, over wage conditions and it was the only time that Downing Street sought to intervene. Harold Wilson summoned the union leaders and the principal members of the NPA to an evening of inedible sandwiches and endless discussions at No. 10, which were adjourned the next day to full and lengthy deliberations at Congress House, the trade-union headquarters in Bloomsbury. Here the amiable Vic Feather, then the general secretary of the TUC, presided.

The negotiations for a return to work occupied several days, when the baron chiefs, closely resembling what I imagine to be the boyars of Old Russia, would assemble in the conference room with representatives of the various unions, breaking off from time to time for each side to have its own consultations and resuming to achieve a further and still more obdurate deadlock. Vic Feather's contribution to the discussions – apart from radiating goodwill and a Pickwickian *bonhomie* – was to supply endless quantities of cheese sandwiches, immensely thick and almost inedible. I noticed that this regimen was having a more marked effect on my troops than on the union. My troops were used to soft and good living. Fortunately Max Aitken evolved a solution. His driver was sent to Fortnum's and during one of the intervals when the proprietors were alone, a huge hamper appeared, containing a vast lunch of delicacies and a considerable supply of the better-class liquids. My troops fell upon them until a warning was received that the other side was returning. The hamper was hastily repacked and stowed in an adjacent cupboard.

At various intervals, when it was clear that further sustenance was needed for the proprietors, I would again ask for an adjournment, the hamper would reappear, and a large portion of its contents was again stuffed into the proprietors. This process had a plainly visible effect: the troops were reinvigorated and fortunately it became clear that the diet of thick cheese sandwiches was not improving the morale or staying power of our adversaries. This was the first occasion when Don Ryder – now Lord Ryder and then chairman of IPC (which owned the *Daily Mirror*) – came into prominence, although alas not into popularity. He was a man of great ability, lacking unfortunately the capacity to endear himself to his fellow men – a not uncommon shortcoming. At the end of the day he contributed largely to the ultimate conclusion, which from the point of view of the proprietors was not unsatisfactory: everyone resumed work.

No official strike took place again for several years until a wholly illegal strike in support of the Labour Party's hostility to Ted Heath's trade-union legislation persuaded even my craven group to seek an injunction on the ground that there was no industrial dispute affecting them. However, the pusillanimous remain pusillanimous. Having obtained the injunction, the proprietors stopped short of seeking to enforce it. Subsequent events have shown that a resolute and determined approach would undoubtedly have served to protect the industry from political irresponsibility and enormous damage, although there would have been cliff-hanging moments.

In the 1970s, there was hardly a month and probably hardly a week when some wildcat strike did not hit one newspaper or another. The scenario was nearly always the same. Under the deeply misleading and kindly title of 'the father of the chapel', there would appear in the middle of the night, when the print run was about half-way through, this menacing figure, demanding that the men should have an extra three, four or five pounds for that night because something was to be inserted in the newspaper which, it was claimed, had not been budgeted for. Time and again the unfortunate middle manager, who had been left in charge, had the appalling responsibility of reaching a decision where the alternatives were equally horrible. He could capitulate and agree to pay the money. If so, he would undoubtedly be denounced by his proprietor when morning arrived. He could attempt to temporise, but the unions were too fly and opportunities for procrastination were nearly always denied. Or he could refuse to pay and lose half or more of his print run, coming to many thousands of pounds. It is my belief that the newspapers of the day were maintained by the courage and resources of middle management, and that quite a number of middle managers succumbed to the nervous strain of these repeated ordeals. The response to any plea to decency or common sense was firmly rejected on the ground that the union officials were only doing their duty by their 'deprived' membership.

My career at the Newspaper Publishers Association ended happily. I was not pushed out – a suggestion made by a disgruntled Barbara Castle, whose nose had been put out of joint in my negotiations with her over 'pay beds' – but I retired, notwithstanding all persuasion, when I was appointed the Master of University College, Oxford, in 1976. The NPA behaved with charming generosity in presenting a sum of money to the College to assist in furnishing the Master's Lodgings; presented me with two magnificent pieces of Meissen, and engaged in a series of formal luncheons to make sure that the loss of weight procured by my strenuous activities on their behalf was fully restored before departure.

One canard that I owe it to myself to nail is the suggestion that while at the NPA I repeatedly intervened to suppress, or seek to suppress, items of news relating to friends or people who sought my assistance. Time and again I was approached to suppress some item that would cause embarrassment or distress, and time and again I refused. On one occasion I passed on an appeal that I had received from a distinguished public figure about the intended publication of a piece of gossip about the illegitimate child of one of his relations. I spoke to Vere Harmsworth on the subject, who expressed no particular horror about the proposal, but was genial enough to say that if Max did not publish it, he would not. I secured the necessary assurance from Max and this crucial piece of national news did not, in fact, appear until many months later.

On the other occasion in 1974, I was telephoned by Harold Wilson. He had been informed that the *Daily Mail* had in its possession a letter allegedly signed by him indicating his involvement in the 'slag heap' scandal. He assured me that the letter was a forgery. I telephoned Vere. I did not ask him to suppress the letter but told him that I thought it right to let him know that Harold declared it was a forgery and that he might therefore consider it wise to test the letter's authenticity very carefully before publication. This he agreed to do and the letter was not published.

There was one additional element. Harold Evans, then editor of the *Sunday Times*, came to see me to enquire about the letter and to secure some background. I told him the story with complete candour: that Harold Wilson had assured me the letter was a forgery and that careful enquiries were being made, and that in my own view the letter was a forgery and that we would establish the fact. To my concern, but not perhaps surprise, Evans published an allegation that by contriving to suppress the letter I had been responsible for the Labour Party's whisker victory at the general election. Happily, conclusive evidence that the letter was a forgery emerged shortly afterwards and the *Sunday Times* was compelled to eat its words.

By 1975, the *Observer*'s circulation had decreased to the point where the paper was close to bankruptcy. It was a decline that had taken place over many years and was, I believe, a fatal consequence of the paper's hostility to the Suez enterprise of 1956.

As chairman I was, of course, acutely concerned and rapid and numerous councils of war were held. The most important consideration was the survival of what we all regarded as a great newspaper, although one possessing such effervescent qualities that one could not predict from week to week its attitude in any situation, except that it would be disinterestedly, honourably and elegantly written. The second consideration was perhaps more altruistic. It was that the newspaper had a staff – editorial, secretarial and printing – of approaching 800 people and we regarded ourselves as heavily committed to preserving their employment.

It was decided initially that every effort should be made to reduce expenditure and to present a more prosperous balance between what we received and what we spent. Our situation had not been improved by the increasing success of the *Sunday Telegraph*, which of course could draw on the very substantial readership of the daily edition and which in no time at all was running close to our heels in circulation terms. At only one point in our existence had we touched a million and that was when the presses of the *Sunday Times* were silent because of a year-long strike. Otherwise our circulation wavered between 700,000 and 800,000: insufficient in itself to meet expenses and insufficient (though not for that reason alone) to attract important advertisers, the second reason being that the paper had a determined liberality of attitude and was regarded as left-wing – a description which disqualified it from support by the more prosperous right-wing advertisers.

Our first attempt at adjustment was to seek to reduce the printing staff, not the editorial staff. This was the staff who were mainly members of two unions: SOGAT, to which the printers, secretarial staff and generally more unskilled element belonged, then headed by Bill Keys; and the NGA, to which the skilled workers who manufactured the print belonged. We approached Bill Keys through Roger Harrison – a late arrival but subsequently the managing director of the company and a man of exceptional talent and efficiency. Harrison initiated a demand from us, the employers, for a 33 per cent reduction in our work-force. This produced an almost apoplectic reaction, or a feigned apopletic reaction, on the part of SOGAT and the other unions, who declined to consider it but entered into discussions in which initially I did not participate. However, after the discussions had been proceeding for about ten days, I received a telephone call from Keys who said to me, 'Unless you get into these discussions you must regard them as doomed.' I took the hint and proceeded to lead the *Observer* team.

There is no space and nor have I much inclination to describe the details of the negotiations, except to say that at the end we had achieved a reduction of over 25 per cent of the staff, which encouraged us to the belief that we could proceed with a reasonable expectation of solvency. This, alas, was a false hope. Within a year it was again clear that our resources were close to exhaustion and that once again we would be lucky to survive financially and pay our work-force and debts for more than twelve months.

At that point David Astor and the others financially involved in the newspaper – nobody made a penny profit from it at any time – agreed that it should be sold to someone who would maintain its liberal traditions while possessing resources adequate to keep the paper in print. A search was initiated for a white knight. Every member of the board came forward with one suggestion or another. The obvious nominees were the existing proprietors of other newspapers, but no one warmed to the prospect of any of them. There were insuperable political differences between, for instance, the *Observer*, Associated Newspapers, Beaverbrook Newspapers and the Telegraph group. But as the year progressed we became less fastidious and would certainly have considered an offer from any of these three. However, no offer was forthcoming. We had to recognise that the political stance of the *Observer* was unacceptable to the Tory newspaper proprietors and in some cases thoroughly odious.

The one person who showed a keen interest in acquiring the paper was Rupert Murdoch, who at that time owned newspapers in Australia and both the *Sun* and the *News of the World* in England: an ownership sufficiently undistinguished to explain his desire to acquire a paper with a long tradition of quality. I did not believe that he would want to acquire the *Observer*, but Roger Harrison was more perceptive and told me that he was quite sure that Murdoch would be anxious to do so. Thereupon I spoke to Rupert Murdoch and he confirmed his desire to become the owner. That he did not do so was to the credit of his candour in dealing with the *Observer*'s editor, Donald Trelford, who had succeeded David Astor in 1975. After a democratic process in which votes were invited from every member of the National Union of Journalists on the staff, Trelford had been overwhelmingly the winner.

When Rupert was minded to bid for the paper, he conceived it honourable to talk to Trelford, whom he invited to New York where he informed him plainly that it was not his intention that he should continue as the editor, although he would be very willing to continue his employment in some secondary role. Trelford was a man of character and determination who set a good store by himself. Although the negotiations were far advanced, and it was only a question of settling some financial details, Trelford on returning to England raised a *révolution de palais*. As chairman, I was invited to meet with a representative group of the journalists to discuss the proposed new ownership.

It was plain at that meeting that not only was there little appetite for Murdoch, who was, of course, associated with the tabloid element, but there was deep and active hostility involving the possibility of mass resignations. The board, receiving my report, recognised that it would require the most difficult negotiations to achieve a smooth transfer to Murdoch and that the game was not worth the candle.

Rupert had anyway decided that discretion was the better part of valour – one of the rare instances of such behaviour on his part – and he withdrew from the quest, leaving the unfortunate board still without a rescuer. It is ironic to think that had Rupert acquired the *Observer*, he could not have acquired *The Times* and the other papers that went with it.

The history of *The Times* between Roy Thomson's death in 1976 and its acquisition by Rupert Murdoch in 1981 was an unhappy one. The paper requires, as Rupert has demonstrated, a determined leadership, supported by an immensely long purse and a willingness to risk everything – which, hardly surprisingly, was lacking in the functionaries who took over after Roy. Totally unfair blame has been bestowed on my friend Marmaduke Hussey, who was then its managing director. If there was one man who had the determination, ingenuity and resolution to save the day, it was Duke, but alas the back-up was largely missing. He had served under me as vice-chairman of the Newspaper Publishers Association. It is not always that adversity turns out an advantage. When I was about to retire from the NPA, there was a strong feeling that he ought to succeed me and undoubtedly this would have had the approval of the majority of its members; but some employers – at *The Times*, and particularly Gordon Brunton – took the view that he was a necessary man where he was and refused him the permission needed to take the chairmanship. Here again he must be extremely grateful since he would not today be the chairman of the BBC had he undertaken that burdensome and all too unrewarded office.

I first met Rupert Murdoch – probably now the most controversial name in the whole of the newspaper world – some twenty years ago. My meeting with him came from the chance that I had been the solicitor to the ill-fated television company TWW, of which Sir William Carr, whose family owned the *News of the World*, was an important shareholder and director. TWW's managing director was at its beginning Mark Chapman-Walker, an amiable opportunist to whom I have already alluded. He became a crony and intimate of Sir William and later the managing director of the *News of the World*. He too was a very good friend and we worked together closely in connection with TWW where he deservedly won the confidence and trust of Lord Derby, chairman of the company.

In 1957, when Goodman Derrick & Co. were looking for new offices because we needed to expand from our tiny quarters in the Inner Temple, Mark suggested to Sir William that we might be accommodated on the fifth floor of the *News of the World* building in Bouverie Street. It was a spacious office, adequate for our needs, one which I liked very much, adjoining but separated from the interesting hubbub of a newspaper.

Eleven years later, for reasons of which I have no special knowledge, the *News of the World* became open to a bid and proved an attractive target, particularly to Robert Maxwell. Sir William Carr was not enamoured of the notion that Maxwell should acquire his newspaper and sought around for a white knight to save it from Maxwell's hands. Maxwell at that time had already acquired an unsavoury reputation – accurately predicting later events. Out of the blue from Australia came Rupert Murdoch. There was a grim and unfriendly take-over contest. Maxwell, even in those early days, displayed a determination which brought him to the position of great prominence he later occupied in Fleet Street.

Maxwell telephoned me on one occasion when the battle was on – in the mistaken belief that I had some role – to invite me to assist him in his campaign. I replied to him that Sir William had been enormously kind to me; that I regarded him as a friend, and that if I had any influence in the matter – and indeed I had none – it would deploy on Sir William's side. This did not deter Maxwell from a further approach. There was to have been some crucial meeting, of which I was quite unaware until Maxwell telephoned me again to say that nothing would give him greater distress than to see me alongside Sir William and the enemy army on the platform at the meeting. I told him rather sharply that I would not be at the meeting; had no reason to be there or to be invited; but if there was one factor that would have brought me on to the platform by the side of Sir William it was his telephone call. This sufficed to leave me in peace for the whole of the campaign and, as is now a matter of newspaper history, Murdoch's success was the precursor of the immense newspaper universe that he now owns in this country and elsewhere.

When Rupert took over the *News of the World* in 1969 he, of course, became our landlord. It did not take long for me to detect that his expansionist notions would threaten every tenant in Bouverie Street. Accordingly, I wrote him a short letter saying that Goodman Derrick had deep gratitude to Sir William for having given us shelter when we were first in need, and that on the assumption that this was what he would like it was my intention to find other quarters as soon as we could. I received a grateful reply and we moved out into the welcoming offices of Macmillan, the publishers, in Little Essex Street in June of 1970.

But for me the more important development was the beginning of a close relationship with Rupert which has continued to this day. My firm has acted for him on a number of occasions. I have conducted several negotiations on his behalf, all of them I believe with a successful outcome, and he has been a firm and loyal friend over the years. I have detected none of the attributes with which he is credited (or more accurately debited) by his critics, but I have never been an employee. So far as I am concerned he has a frank and open manner and, having dealt with him in a number of matters, I would regard him as a man of absolute integrity and truthfulness. It would be silly, however, to pretend that he has been a wholly beneficial influence in the newspaper world.

Anyway, I must return to the *Observer*'s tribulations in the summer of 1976. Discussions continued, becoming increasingly hopeless, about a likely and tolerable purchaser for the paper, when out of the blue came what seemed to be a miraculous intervention. I was having dinner at my home one Saturday in the autumn when I received a telephone call from Kenneth Harris, a long-standing employee of the *Observer* who wrote biographical articles of some elegance, but who had never filled any important role in the direction of affairs.

He informed me that a wholly desirable owner was seeking to acquire the newspaper, namely one Robert Anderson, the chairman of Atlantic Richfield, a vast and prosperous American oil company. But Anderson's major qualification, so far as the *Observer* was concerned, was that he had for many years run a cultural centre at Aspen in Colorado, where summer schools and other meetings were held from time to time and where, I was assured, really serious cultural programmes were developed. Harris informed me that Mr Anderson had spoken to him that very evening and invited me to talk to Anderson on the telephone. I made a couple of telephone calls in London to ascertain Anderson's reputation and, reassured that David Astor thought well of him, proceeded to contact him. The conversation took only a few minutes. He introduced himself, told me of his desire to acquire the *Observer* for Atlantic Richfield, and that it was his intention to leave the editorial staff untouched but to provide adequate funds to maintain its existence.

I convened a meeting of my colleagues and, modest enquiries having taken place, there was total unanimity that the offer should be accepted. We sent an elaborate cable to Anderson setting out our requirements in relation to protecting the editor and the staff, but indicating that if these assurances were satisfactory no money price would be sought. In short, the paper was handed over on the footing that a respectable ownership was worth more than a sum of money that would necessarily have gone into the Astor trust. The discussions were speedy, agreement being reached by the end of November 1976, and there followed a period of great jubilation, with celebratory dinners both in London and at University College, Oxford, of which I had recently become the Master.

At the dinner given by me at Univ on 5 December, in honour of our new proprietor, I perpetrated one gaffe that might well have ruined the happy scene for all time. Robert Anderson described to me the fortnightly 'schools' held at his Aspen headquarters for visiting tycoons. 'They come,' he said proudly, 'to spend a fortnight reading some great work such as Machiavelli's *The Prince* or Dante's *Inferno*.' With some pride he enquired whether it would not be a good idea to establish such an institution in this country and possibly at Oxford. My reply, I fear, was not the most tactful: 'To assemble a group of leading industrialists or financiers to read Machiavelli or Dante, they would have to be brought under arrest.' I detected, not for the first time, that however splendid the other constituent elements, humour did not play a large part in Mr Anderson's character. I received no reply.

The later history is painful to recite. It involved a leading role for the

self-same Kenneth Harris who had introduced Anderson to us. Anderson
had nominated Lord Barnetson, the amiable, honourable and efficient
chairman of United Newspapers, to become the chairman of the *Observer*.
David Astor and I remained on the board. In no time at all Anderson
was expressing doubts about Trelford editing the paper unaided and
David came up with the imaginative idea that Conor Cruise O'Brien, the
Irish politician and writer, should become the editor-in-chief. Anderson
was prepared to consider this proposal and asked me to arrange for
O'Brien to meet him. I telephoned O'Brien, whom I believe had previously
been conditioned by an approach from David. In any event, such was his
enthusiasm that he flew over on the day following my call to meet
Anderson in my flat.

Anderson was impressed to the point of infatuation and without any
further ado or consultation decided that O'Brien should be appointed
editor-in-chief on what in those days were very generous terms. Conor
was plainly very satisfied to accept the appointment and entered into his
duties undisturbed, working well and co-operatively with Donald Trelford,
who showed no resentment whatsoever at this new appointment.

But trouble arose following the resignation (due to ill health) of Bill
Barnetson in September 1980. There was no chairman of the company
for quite a while and it was clear to me as the senior director that
something had to be done. I telephoned Anderson and suggested that he
should come to London to make arrangements to replace Barnetson and
to set the company on an even keel. This he agreed to do.

A year before this conversation, I had been visited at breakfast by
Kenneth Harris, who ruined my meal with an intimation that he had
been having conversations with Anderson – with whom he had obviously
established a considerable degree of authority – and that Anderson had
suggested to him, although it might have been vice versa, that he should
become either the managing director or, more horrific from my point of
view, the editor-in-chief. The exchange between us was short and
unfriendly. 'Kenneth,' I said to him, 'there are two requirements governing
a man's ability to do a particular job. One is that he should have the
technical ability. About your technical ability to edit the *Observer*, I prefer
not to comment. But another more important requirement is that he
should have some credibility in the job and I regret to have to tell you
that my opinion at this moment of time is that you would have no
credibility as the editor-in-chief of the *Observer*.' Perhaps not surprisingly
my plain speaking gave him some affront.

Even if I had appreciated the dire consequences of this exchange, I do
not think that I would have used any other language. The immediate
result was a determination on my own part to try to scotch this notion at

its roots. For this reason, after discussion with David Astor, I opted to pay a visit to the United States to discuss the whole position with Anderson and his close colleague Thornton Bradshaw, then head of NBC. I flew to New York – and it rankles that I did so at my own expense – and met with Anderson and Bradshaw at the Park Lane Hotel, where they were staying, which was owned by Atlantic Richfield.

In that conversation, I indicated that Harris's proposal to become editor-in-chief was one that was met with great disfavour throughout the paper and that it was a job for which I doubted his qualifications. Fortunately at that stage I was strongly supported by Bradshaw. As a result, before I left that evening, Anderson assured me that it would not be his intention to proceed with this plan and that he would so instruct Harris.

But our relief was short-lived. In February 1981, Anderson appeared in London and asked me to breakfast with him at Claridges. He then told me – clearly his love for Harris still unaffected – that it was his desire now that instead of becoming editor-in-chief or managing director Harris should become vice-chairman, under the chairmanship which Anderson himself was proposing to assume. I told him that no one could object to this latter proposal: he owned the paper, was an experienced chairman and would certainly enjoy the respect and support of all ranks. With regard to his intention to make Kenneth Harris vice-chairman, however, I expostulated that by so doing he was for practical purposes appointing him chairman since Anderson's visits were few and far between and in his absence Harris would not be slow to exercise the fullest degree of authority.

Anderson had indicated that it was his plan to present a resolution to the board meeting, which was to be held a couple of days later, implementing both suggestions. My reaction to that was the simple one: that if the Harris resolution was implemented, he would have to suffer the modest misfortune of my departure and although I could not speak for him, I thought it very likely that I would be accompanied by David Astor. This rejoinder was one that at least for the moment impressed him. 'In that event,' Anderson promptly replied, 'I will not put forward the Harris resolution.' But it was to be otherwise. At the board meeting that followed, he first proposed his own appointment as chairman, which was passed with approbation, and then, to my surprise, he proposed that Kenneth Harris should become vice-chairman.

A sudden silence fell on the meeting. I was the first to speak. 'Chairman,' I said, 'I have already indicated to you that this proposal is not acceptable to me. I cannot tell you what the response of the other directors will be, but they are all here to record it. I am afraid that the *Observer* will have to accept the unimportant consequence that I shall cease to be a director or associated with it.' It was only a matter of seconds before David uttered to the same effect. No one else offered his resignation, but both Conor Cruise O'Brien and Donald Trelford made disapproving noises. In consequence Anderson indicated his intention to withdraw the resolution, first inviting Kenneth Harris – who certainly to my embarrassment had been present throughout the proceedings – to withdraw for a moment. In his absence Anderson indicated that he would not proceed with the proposal and left the room to speak privately to Harris. What happened in that exchange is, so far as I am concerned, a matter of mystery. I do not know but I sensed that it was designed to restore the feathers of a severely ruffled Harris.

David Astor, with considerable astuteness, said to me after the meeting, 'The likelihood is that he will now sell the *Observer*,' which was once again making substantial losses. 'I will call on him at Claridges tomorrow,' he went on, 'to try to persuade him not to do any such thing.' David, in fact, had breakfast with Anderson on the following day and reported to me what he regarded as a thoroughly satisfactory outcome. Anderson had assured David that he had no intention of selling the newspaper, nor of seeking to reinstate Harris in some high position. But it took very little time for the situation to develop as we might have predicted.

Later in the following week, I received a telephone call from Anderson in my study at University College, Oxford. In the sweetest of tones, he said to me that he had some item of information that he thought would interest me and that in consequence he felt duty-bound to let me have it at once. It was that he had sold two-thirds of his interest – as it turned out for $6 million – to Tiny Rowland of Lonrho and that I would be hearing from Rowland very shortly. Beyond saying that I was indeed interested in this statement, I made no further comment. But within the hour Mr Rowland telephoned. I had met him only once, when a client had invited me to sell some interest in a company to him. Rowland told me with pride of his acquisition of the shareholding in the *Observer* and continued that he hoped that David and I would remain on the board. My reply was brief: that I could not speak for David but that it would be a matter of surprise to me if he accepted the offer, and that so far as I was concerned I would not wish to continue to remain a director under the new ownership. Rowland pressed me and said, 'Think about it,' to which I gave a completely noncommittal reply.

A year or so later I was approached at a lunch by Rowland who jokingly remarked that he had been waiting to hear from me for over a year as to whether I was prepared to be reappointed as a director. 'The postal services,' I said, 'are very bad.' Except for a further telephone call from him asking for characteristically outlandish terms to surrender his lease of the printing works still owned by the Observer Trust, I have not exchanged another word with him.

Donald Trelford continues to soldier on, largely as a result of David Astor's determination at the time to persuade the Monopolies Commission not to approve the sale. Both he and I gave evidence that we did not think the sale was to anyone's advantage, and desperate efforts were made to find an alternative purchaser, although as it turned out this would have been futile since the Monopolies Commission, with one prescient voice dissenting, approved the sale on the paradoxical ground that although it was contrary to the national interest, nevertheless the safeguards shrewdly offered by Mr Rowland, and presented by one of the most distinguished counsel of the day, were adequate to protect the public interest. In short, a finding of thumbs up and thumbs down, but our protest to the Monopolies Commission was of immense advantage to Donald and the continuing staff, since one of the requirements proposed by the commission was the creation of an independent board established to ensure that the undertakings given to the commission were duly honoured. I am convinced that this precaution has buttressed the position of Donald and the other leading journalists who remain on the paper. It is not for me to assess the character of Rowland's influence on the *Observer* since then. What is certain, however, is that his association with it gave rise to strong suspicion that he was using it to advance his business interests and to that extent it was more unreliable than before his acquisition.

My six years at the Newspaper Publishers Association rarely involved me in personal publicity. It is probably some defect of character that makes personal publicity repugnant to me. Although fate has decreed that I should be involved in a great number of controversial issues, I have had the good fortune to be personalised in very few. Since my name has unhappily become known because of associations with prominent issues and prominent people, many people will regard as insincere an assertion that I have tried very hard to avoid publicity. Over the years I have written a good number of articles but never on personal topics. They express my views on matters and issues with which I have been concerned. Very rarely, if ever, have I described some personal quality or some piece of personal history. This book, in fact, atones for this inhibition in a thoroughly disgraceful way.

For me, the greatest threat to personal privacy has come from broadcasting, either on radio or on television. Until very recently, either because interest in me has dwindled or the producers despair of being able to persuade me to participate, I was invited at least once a month to take part in some programme or another. Refusal to participate in parlour games, or to become a member of a panel pontificating on some issue of immediate concern, presented no difficulty. Although I am often criticised for being frivolous and flippant, this is not a quality that endears itself to me in relation to matters with which I am genuinely concerned. Towards the end of my tenure of office at the NPA, however, one issue arose which gave me ten times more publicity than anything in which I had previously been involved and which came to be known by the somewhat portentous title of 'the battle for press freedom'.

The issue can be stated simply and quickly: in 1974 Mr Michael Foot had, contrary to all previous expectations, and contrary to all previously expressed intentions, become the Secretary of State for Employment and had fallen madly in love with the doctrines of trade unionism. He introduced a Bill in October of that year which authorised, and indeed ensured, that the principle of the closed shop operated in every area of employment. While I would have voted steadfastly against the principle operating to exclude anyone from legitimate employment, the aspect of the Closed Shop Bill which to me was particularly offensive, and indeed inexcusable, was the intervention of a closed shop into journalism, and by natural extension into every other creative activity. The battle was fought with the National Union of Journalists on the one side and a contingent of proprietors and editors, with a few other auxiliaries, on the other.

The proposed legislation, ultimately achieved in 1976 after a fierce battle, meant that only those journalists belonging to a trade union (the NUJ) could sell their services to the British press or British broadcasting, either on television or radio. I found myself *faute de mieux* appointed as a leader of the opposition to Michael's Bill. Two reasons were attributed for the failure of our resistance – which in the end was a less signal failure than was at one time believed. The first of these reasons, and it is a legitimate criticism, was that I had never engaged in politics, with the implication that success might have attended on us if I had had more political experience and subtlety. The second reason was the disadvantage attaching to the fact that I was chairman of the NPA and thereby believed to be speaking only on behalf of the proprietors of newspapers who were resisting the Bill for their own selfish motives.

To the first of these criticisms I could gaily and proudly plead guilty. I have never had any interest in the political scene as such. From the day when I was invited to stand for Parliament by the late George Wigg in the 1945 election, and fortunately rejected his blandishments, to the present day (from the time of my entry, I have remained attached to the cross-benches in the House of Lords) I have never, rightly or wrongly, adopted any course of action because of purely political considerations. It is indeed true that a leader who was not associated with the NPA and a leader thoroughly versed in political shenanigans would almost certainly have made a better job of opposing Mr Foot's Bill. My answer to my critics is that there was no such leader willing to undertake the unwelcome, and in many quarters unpopular, cause of seeking to keep the British press open to available talent.

One of the most disagreeable aspects of the whole campaign was the marked disinclination of the newspaper proprietors – notwithstanding their early support – to remain associated with the fight. Periodically it was possible to whip them up to some degree of activity, but at the end of the day, when the issue had become clear-cut, I frequently had the feeling that they would have wished to see me, together with all the lofty sentiments I was accused of uttering, at the bottom of the Thames, which was in such fortunate juxtaposition to Fleet Street. In addition, I undoubtedly relied too much on the belief that trade-union secretaries and left-wing political personages would know me too well to believe that I was activated by a concern for the newspaper proprietors. On the whole it was clear that their knowledge of me was something of an embarrassment to the supporters of the Bill and that for many of them it imposed a need to pull their punches. But as the battle went on, the courtesies were increasingly abandoned and this unhappily was very much the case where Michael Foot was concerned.

My relationship with Michael had been a good and at times even a close one. I had from time to time assisted in legal battles for his beloved *Tribune*; I had been concerned in advising on publishing arrangements, and during the early days of his tenure of office as Secretary of State for Employment I had rendered him important service by way of advice. Such exchanges between us had, I believed, made me something of a favourite of his. This happy situation did not last long. Leading the battle against the Closed Shop Bill from the House of Lords, I was involved in numerous debates and made an endless and tiresome series of speeches, enunciating the simple proposition that in a civilised country no one should be prevented from deploying his talent because he did not belong to a union, from which he could be arbitrarily excluded or expelled without any legal redress. This was the issue and really the only issue of the whole battle.

The essence of my opposition was in the four principles that I identified for insertion into a proposed press charter, which was offered by the government as a principal safeguard for editorial freedom under the Bill. They were as follows:

1. Editors would be under no obligation to join a union.
2. Editors would have the right to commission, publish or not publish any article free from pressure by industrial action.
3. All journalists, including editors, would have the right to join any union of their choice.
4. Journalists would have the right not to be arbitrarily or unreasonably expelled from union membership.

The comings and goings in the Commons and the Lords from autumn 1974 to spring 1976, and the exchange of insults, reaching its lowest level when Mr Foot gracefully described me as a 'blithering idiot', left surprisingly little acrimony. When the battle had momentarily concluded and I was appointed Master of University College, Oxford, I was gratified to receive a letter from Ken Morgan, the general secretary of the National Union of Journalists, congratulating me on my appointment. 'I can imagine few more satisfying posts and none which would offer a better base from which to pursue your other interests and services,' he wrote. 'We shall miss you on the other side of our particular table and I would like you to know that you carry the best wishes of all on our side with you to Oxford.' Nothing could have been more gracious or presented a more British conclusion to a bitter battle.

At the end of the day the dispute was adjourned from Parliament to the negotiating table. There appeared a strange provision in Michael Foot's Bill that a press charter should be negotiated between all interested parties – proprietors, publishers, journalists, et al. – within one year from the date of the Royal Assent and if not so negotiated should be drafted by the Secretary of State for Employment. The negotiations, under the chairmanship of Lord Pearce, a former chairman of the Press Council, came to absolutely nothing: hardly a single clause of the charter was agreed in futile meetings in Bouverie Street at the headquarters of the NPA. The year passed, and no draft ever emerged from any government office.

It was not unreasonable to arrive at the conclusion that the campaign that my friends and I waged, with pitiful support from those who should have known better, was a total failure. But this is an inaccurate judgement. The campaign caused the Bill to be delayed for over eighteen months and at the end of the day the Institute of Journalists – the small alternative union to the NUJ – continued to survive and was satisfactorily rescued by the Tory Party's subsequent amendments to trade-union law. In fairness to the profession, the determined adherence of the IOJ to the cause of press freedom should not be forgotten. They had no doubt in their own minds that the battle had been worth fighting and the result anything but ignominious.

I can only conclude with a sad reference to the crucial cause of our defeat. The ultimate Lords debate on the Closed Shop Bill was to take place on Tuesday, 10 March 1976. On the Thursday of the previous week the Newspaper Publishers Association had attended on Lord Hailsham to ask him if he would whip the Tory peers – a procedure which would have ensured us a majority. Our intention was to move an amendment rejecting the press charter currently envisaged in the Bill, a charter which in our view would have handed control of the British press to the NUJ and which in the ultimate result would be drafted by a Minister of the Crown. No charter, we felt, would be preferable to a charter of that kind. But Lord Hailsham's nose was out of joint. I had earlier accepted an amendment to the Bill – an amendment which subsequently came to nothing – on a matter of 'public policy', to the effect that any proposed press charter must recognise the rights of journalists not to be unfairly expelled or excluded from a union.

I had been persuaded to accept this amendment from a bright young barrister, then a legal adviser to the Home Office. I had had misgivings about it, but was mistakenly led to believe that it would solve the government's difficulties and allow a sensible compromise to be reached. The fact of my accepting the amendment was unfortunate and indeed disastrous. Lord Hailsham firmly believed that he should have been consulted before any such amendment was agreed to. Probably he was right; but his reaction to what he obviously saw as some sort of slight – and he should well know that there was no such intention on my part – was to cause him to refuse to whip the Lords as requested by the NPA delegation. His excuse for this was to me an unconvincing one: that he had to choose between two alternative amendments: our amendment to the closed-shop procedure – which meant the rejection of the charter – and an amendment imposing a conscience clause on trade-union membership generally. It should have been clear to him that this provision drove a coach and six through any formal obligation on the part of employees to maintain their union and had no prospect of success with the Labour government. But Hailsham's choice did enable him to justify inaction in relation to the Lords debate and we were unhappily dogged by an impossible timetable which ordained that the debate should take place on the Tuesday following our Thursday meeting with Hailsham.

Following our failure with Hailsham, Denis Hamilton, who was close to her, suggested that we should see Mrs Thatcher, the new Leader of the Opposition, and that he would arrange the meeting. Unfortunately she was away in the provinces on the Friday and the meeting could not take place until early on the Tuesday morning, when a deputation, led by me with other newspaper elders, visited her in her room in the House of Commons. At first she was unconvinced and her reluctance was not diminished by the reply she received when she asked whether all the newspaper proprietors present were in agreement. To our horror, Vere Harmsworth, one of the world's most unpredictable characters, declared firmly that he saw nothing wrong with a closed shop for journalists. There was no time to strike him to the ground and trample on him, but there was time for the rest of us, led I can claim by me, to persuade her of the firmness of our belief and incidentally of the unfortunate character of Vere's opinions. She was, to her eternal credit, persuaded and went off to telephone Hailsham with a direction that he should whip the Lords to vote for our amendment, but his reply was, alas, conclusive: 'It is too late to get out a whip now.' The best he would do was to offer a free vote. Notwithstanding the strong support in the debate given by his deputy, Lord Windlesham, Lord Hailsham's invitation to a free vote was half-hearted and he himself declared that he would abstain. It was insufficient to persuade Tory peers, or even influence many not yet convinced, that they should support our amendment.

The result of the vote was, in the circumstances, quite creditable. We were defeated by 128 – including every Labour peer present (except for a noble couple, Lord Lloyd of Hampstead and Lady Gaitskell) and almost every Liberal peer present, to their eternal shame – to 77 stalwart Tories and Cross-Benchers. The defeat was not a rout. The Lords kept the situation alive until the trade-union reforms of the 1980s, and I am proud that I played some small part in maintaining independent voices who refuse to join a union at all or to join one particular union as opposed to another.

It was my only experience of a protracted parliamentary battle. I much regret the hostilities between myself and Michael Foot, and it is gratifying to me that the peace-making tones of my beloved Jennie Lee brought about something of a reconciliation between us. I now believe that Michael and I have totally forgiven each other.

A characteristic feature of the battle was, alas, the behaviour of the Prime Minister and other leading members of the Labour Cabinet, with many of whom I had a close friendship. On several occasions, while the discussion was going on, I approached Harold Wilson in a desperate hope that he might revise the government view at least to exempt journalists from the provisions of the proposed Act. On each occasion he made mild noises of encouragement indicating to me that he had no intention of doing anything – indications which unhappily turned out to be all too true. Others in the Cabinet also expressed their *sub rosa* agreement with me. I will not identify these wretches since it was probably more than their lives were worth – their political lives – to come into collision with the trade-union steamroller; but it was a particular regret that some of them – some of whom had earned many a fee from journalism – could not bring themselves to utter a word of dissent in Cabinet.

This is one of the worst features of our party system. It was a slight satisfaction to me to observe that during the 1980s a similar moral paralysis extended to the other party where a disagreement with the leader was involved, with a creditable difference that a considerable number tendered their resignation or were brusquely expelled for nonconformity. In justice, I have to recognise that the principle of the closed shop was very much an article of faith among trade unionists. With a party dependent on trade-union support, politicians would have been slow indeed to support even the smallest concession from the iron rigidity of the general principle.

I look back on my newspaper associations with mixed feelings: quiet satisfaction for the personal contacts that I established and a very real sense of a total failure to cement together the factions that could between them have made an effective and valuable social instrument out of the press. The interest was undeniable: meeting extraordinary people, ranging from transparent villains to a few who had a genuine concern for the probity of newspapers. I can truthfully claim that the financial rewards in relation to the exercise were grotesquely inadequate. I have always pursued the no doubt slightly sanctimonious attitude of refusing to be paid for public service. At the Arts Council there was no fee attaching to the chairmanship, and so far as I know there still is no fee, although I received a payment of £400 a year for expenses, which was never adjusted for inflation during my seven years. Since I made a point of paying for most of the entertaining out of my own pocket, and frequently arranged lunches and dinners, the actual expenditure was several multiples of the amount I received. Following my rule, I waived the salary of £10,000 a year then paid to the chairman of the Housing Corporation. I waived the £5,000 a year payable to the chairman of the National Building Agency. I waived the director's fee payable by the Industrial Reorganisation Corporation.

I remember with particular satisfaction a telephone call from Sir Alec Douglas-Home when I had become heavily involved in the Rhodesian negotiations, to ask how he was to reply to a parliamentary question from the Opposition about any payment to be made to me for my negotiating role. I told him that I regarded it as a public duty and would not seek a fee – an answer which gave him a very satisfactory reply to the question.

There is no special virtue in my attitude since it arises from a firm conviction that anyone engaged in public activities has a much greater freedom of manoeuvre if he receives no public reward. I have been more than amply rewarded by the honours given to me from time to time and, although I have never sought riches, and they have never come to me by chance, I have until now enjoyed an adequate income from purely professional activities.

I have devoted at least half of the latter part of my working life to causes which gave me profound interest but brought me no material reward. It was for this reason that I did not take any particular resentment in an encounter I had with Lord Hailsham in the House of Lords. It was in a debate on whether or not solicitors should become judges. He, passionately devoted to the interests of a tiny Bar – one of the most mysterious obsessions that I have ever encountered as there is no body less deserving of special consideration – announced in the course of the debate that if one wished to attain eminence in the law one went to the Bar, but if one wished to become rich one became a member of the firm of Goodman Derrick & Company. I remained calm under this offensive observation and did not even rise to my feet, although I was tempted to enquire of him how many members of the Bar had devoted any time to any unpaid public service.

17

Academic Roamings

I HAD BEEN educated – so far as higher education was concerned – first at University College, London, and later at Downing College, Cambridge, to both of which I have made some reference earlier. I spent only two years and one term at Cambridge where I collected a couple of firsts in Roman Law and Roman–Dutch Law and was later invited back as a special lecturer in Roman–Dutch Law – an appointment I held for some four years after the Second World War.

Even so, I think I can fairly claim to have retained associations with the university world throughout the whole of my adult life. This was certainly the case in the 1960s when Harold Wilson first mentioned to me the notion of an Open University – for a long time miscalled the 'University of the Air'. He had, I think, conceived the notion from his friend Senator William Benton, publisher of the *Encyclopaedia Britannica* and a remarkable American who had made a great fortune in various fields, but principally from his *Encyclopaedia* and from the educational ancillaries that he promoted in connection with it: films, lantern slides and the like. Benton had seen a radio and television 'university' in operation in Japan and in Russia and had written a book about the Russian project. It had seized Harold Wilson's imagination. But although I think all the credit for launching the scheme goes to Harold Wilson, the credit for getting it off the ground, tackling all difficulties and adversity, and finally bringing it to a triumphant achievement will forever belong to Jennie Lee. It was a natural auxiliary to the work she was doing in the arts. However, before Jennie took it on, Harold Wilson approached me to ask if I would assist him by endeavouring to raise some money for the project in the United States.

In early 1966, equipped with suitable letters from him (but without either then or later any proposal for repaying my expenses), I set off for

New York to interview Benton and McGeorge Bundy, formerly a close aide of John Kennedy, but who had just become the President of the immense Ford Foundation, deploying an *income* of $400 million a year. My quest for Benton led me to a lavish private hospital at the remote end of Park Avenue at a taxi cost of almost my entire dollar allowance. There he was, cheerfully sitting in an armchair, but tethered by a vast superstructure of medical apparatus emerging from every portion of his anatomy. He had what looked like a large retort, through which portions of the fluid content of his body were coming and going, and every piece of apparatus was obviously engaged in stirring up what previously had been recumbent, and quietening what previously had been agitated. However, he was totally composed and cheerful.

I expressed concern, nay anxiety, about his condition and he explained to me how it was that he came to be there. 'Lord Goodman,' he said, 'I have a wonderful doctor, and only the other day he said to me: "Senator, I can see nothing wrong with you that is going to give you trouble today, tomorrow or even next week, but I sense that the week after next something adverse might arise and I want you in for examination and inspection and rectification [the Senator was fond of the sonorous flowing of words] so that we can put it right literally before it happens." So,' he said, 'here I am.' And I expressed gratification that he was the subject of such meticulous medical concern. 'I will tell you something, Lord Goodman,' he said (the Senator was a strangely humourless man), 'I count my blessings, and I said to my dear wife only yesterday that I am fortunate to be a rich man. For, said I, if I was not a millionaire I would not be undergoing this wonderful treatment now.' And, said I (Goodman) under my breath, you can say that again!

Anyway, he expressed a great willingness to help, to provide all the resources of the *Encyclopaedia* and the many courses which had been prepared for visual use on television and film screen, though neither he nor I thought that these would be particularly useful. Each country has its own techniques of education and very small differences in presentation disqualify a course from genuine efficacy in a country used to even slightly different methods; but his knowledge and experience were helpful and he did offer to find some money if need be.

Bundy was a more introverted type and an extremely interesting, amiable and exceptionally intelligent man who listened carefully, read my memorandum and said that he thought it likely that if a large-scale national experiment was to be established of a broadcasting university, the Ford Foundation would provide some resources. But by the time I got back to London, national pride had reasserted itself. The Cabinet, after an extremely argumentative meeting which Jennie Lee attended, had resolved, finally persuaded by the authority and determination of Harold Wilson, to establish a working party after a preliminary plan was presented which confirmed the possible viability of the scheme and assessed its cost.

Harold Wilson suggested to Jennie Lee that I should be invited to review the plan and report on it. Accordingly, Jennie wrote to me: 'What we need now is a realistic assessment of the relative costs of launching the University of the Air on BBC2 and the fourth channel. The Cabinet are convinced that you are the best person to help on this and were unanimous in asking me to approach you.'

There was in Jennie's mind, and indeed in the mind of the Prime Minister, a strong feeling that the establishment of the Open University could only be achieved in association with the establishment of a fourth television channel. One of my principal enquiries was directed to this question: whether it would be feasible to have an Open University using only the three television channels that then existed. The basis of the scheme, as I understood it, was largely to rely on broadcasts, either by radio or television, supplemented by tutorial and correspondence courses. I undertook the task with enthusiasm and was able to discharge it in a period which by the timetable of public commissions and inquiries was nearly miraculous.

I accepted the invitation on 8 February 1966. My most crucial meeting was with Hugh Carleton Greene at the BBC on 23 February, and I submitted my report on 25 May. The debt the Open University owes to Carleton Greene and to his colleagues, including his successor as director-general, Charles Curran, has never been publicly acknowledged. He expressed an immediate willingness to harness the available resources of the BBC to such an operation. He indicated the free time that could be found for each programme, the cost involved, undertook to be responsible for a large area of publications, and made my task incredibly easy by estimating to a penny what his participation would involve and leaving me to do the pretty simple computation of what the relatively small balance involved. In the result, I was able to put in a report to the Prime Minister that was positive in its recommendations that an Open University could be established at relatively modest cost; that radio and television exposure were available, and that the scheme was worth investigating in detail.

When I reflect on the total inaccuracy of all my financial calculations in relation to the finished article, a more modest man would blow his brains out; but I am comforted by the thought that the type of operation then envisaged, on an infinitely smaller scale than has now been established, enabled the planning to take place with a rapid growth of enthusiasm as the possibilities of the project revealed themselves.

The Open University is costing probably twenty times what I estimated and it is a completely different entity from the one that I was asked to consider. It is now a large-scale educational service, providing degree and other courses for large numbers of people who never had, or lost the opportunity of, university entry. It has important headquarters at Milton Keynes; found a brilliant vice-chancellor in Walter Perry, and an equally brilliant and efficient pro-chancellor in Sir Peter Venables, and it is now an established success, giving really valuable service to people who greatly appreciate it.

The glum predictions from the established educationalists, most of whom were immensely hostile and thought it a vulgar intrusion into the university scene, have all been proved false. The fall-out rate they predicted – from 60 to 80 per cent – has turned out to be about 50 per cent. Through natural kindness I will refrain from mentioning the number of distinguished left-wing Cabinet ministers who thought that such a project would muddy the university skirts. The persistence and dedication of the students is a remarkable revelation of how many human beings, lacking the previous opportunity, hunger for organised instruction; of how many good minds there are that have not had the opportunity of cultivation by formal study.

I regard the Open University as one of the major achievements of the Labour government of 1964–70. I regard it as a great achievement by Jennie Lee, and it is a matter of some pride to me to have been modestly associated with it in the early stages. But Jennie has to be acclaimed as the person who drove it forward inexorably and ruthlessly, with a complete conviction that it was something that a civilised society needed, and that it was in every sense compatible with her socialist and egalitarian vision. Equally she made sure that the committee that was set up to establish the Open University was totally non-political, in the sense that it was composed of all and every political opinion, with an admixture of the non-political (if this exists). A particularly valuable contributor who played a large part was the late Professor Hilde Himmelweit, Professor of Industrial Psychology at the London School of Economics. She was an important figure in the Planning Committee set up to determine the shape of the Open University.

There were a great many initial difficulties. One was what sort of entrance qualifications should be required. It was ultimately decided that no qualifications should be required, in the sense that no formal matriculation would be appropriate, and that it would fall to candidates to prove to the authorities their eligibility to benefit from a more specialist, and indeed a higher, education of this sort.

I was asked to and did join the Planning Committee and found myself sitting in a vast room in Belgrave Square, then the headquarters of the 'Ministry of Art', surrounded by vice-chancellors, dons, educational theorists and broadcasting experts. I played a very small part in the future planning. It was a technical matter – off my beat – but I did give advice on specialised subjects like the copyright problems relating to lectures, the use of recording equipment, and so forth, and I was on the selection committee which found the vice-chancellor, i.e. the effective managing director.

We adopted the heterodox course of a small group of the selection committee taking the short-listed candidates to dinner one by one and then bringing back their reports to the full committee for a selection to be made. Our final choice was little short of inspired. I was amongst the group who took Walter Perry to dinner, and we had no doubt at all that here was an outstanding man: at that time the Vice-Principal of Edinburgh University. His book on the Open University deals in great detail with the formation of the university, the problems that arose, and the selection of Milton Keynes as a site. In that connection I went down to have a look at it and had some misgivings, for the simple reason that I could see no accommodation, as the amenities that now exist there had yet to be built. I remember saying to some patrician that the distance that the houses would be from civilisation as we understood it might be a deterrent to employment. To which he replied that all the persons employed there would have motor cars. This is a remark that might have been attributed to the late Marie Antoinette, and I think stands side by side with her immortal reference to the suggestion that the population should be fed on cakes.

It gave me great satisfaction to attend the dinner convened by Lord Crowther who, for the short time before his sad death, made a first-class chancellor and delivered a most stirring speech to commemorate the opening of this great project. It was a regret to me that no mention was made of Hugh Carleton Greene and that – although possibly invited – he did not attend the dinner. Jennie was there, absolutely delighted; radiant that what she had planned for, worked for, intrigued for and bullied for had come into being, and she might well have been pleased.

There are critics of the Open University and there is ample room for criticism in any scheme so wide-ranging and so novel. In its early stages a great number of the degree-takers were teachers deprived of full educational opportunities by the war years. This situation has to a large extent rectified itself, and the criticism that there was not enough of it and that it was insufficiently varied no longer holds good as the range of topics has been enormously increased.

I have one ironic recollection which was when – knowing that I must explore all possible avenues – I called on Sir Robert Fraser, the director-general of what was then the Independent Television Authority (an organisation charged with the responsibility for supervising commercial television), to find out what they might be able to do to assist. I think my visit embarrassed them. Every hour of their permitted recording time was hypothecated for advertisement-bearing programmes. The idea of programmes of a strictly educational quality, directed to a limited audience and attracting neither mints nor cornflakes, detergents nor cat food, was repugnant. Sir Robert left me in no doubt that, passionate as they were to assist in promoting the culture of the nation, here, as in every other case, there was so little they could do. I was confirmed again in my then view that if television was of the slightest use to man or beast – and I had some doubt about it – it certainly was not of the slightest use in its commercial form.

I have qualified this view over the years, largely because of the deterioration of the BBC's quality in a deep gradient following the departure of Sir Hugh Carleton Greene and his replacement by men of a lesser calibre. I now believe that television is a medium wrongly and over-indulgently used by modern society. The notion of multiple channels in the vain hope that more channels will produce better programmes is based on an unhappy failure to recognise that human genius is a statistical constant, or very nearly a statistical constant. One does not have better books because one has more publishers. This is an argument that has its limitations. It is clear that Caxton is responsible for much great literature that would not have existed without him, but what is equally clear is that there is a saturation point and this has been best exemplified in the newspapers. The capacity to produce millions of copies each day of the same rubbish is no help to mankind, no help to literature and no help to education. It is for this reason that I profoundly believe in education as the best solution to man's problems. One cannot multiply geniuses but one can multiply an appreciative audience.

The validity of television as a social commodity was something that exercised our minds often at the Arts Council. Time and time again we made abortive efforts to insinuate some influence into the television world. With ITV we made no headway at all. Once in a blue moon, with an immense blast of trumpets, they would broadcast an opera. Its appearance was presaged by expensive brochures containing details of the life of Verdi – or whichever composer it was; the life of the singers; the unchallengeable merits of the producers; and the splendid, self-sacrificing nature of the companies who were giving up so much to educate their fellow men. The self-conscious nature of these activities induced faint nausea and a very cogent recognition of the true nature of the commercial beast.

Our efforts with the BBC during my time at the Arts Council were slightly more successful. I paid a visit to Charles Hill and arranged that a joint committee should be set up between the Council and the BBC to enable the BBC to take advantage of any programme material which we had available and which they could use. Charles Hill was wholly sincere in his wish that this should be implemented, as was the Arts Council, but his subordinates had no such wish. They viewed the Arts Council with great suspicion. We were a voluntary body doing a job where we made no claim for recognition, but where we would have liked costly material to be made fully available to the public.

It was true that with things like opera, special television productions were better than televised productions from the opera house. But the latter was never fully explored because of the innate hostility of the BBC staff towards giving up even an inch of their production autonomy. We had a lot to offer. I suggested time and again that we might have an Arts Council half-hour once a month, which we would produce and for which we would obtain material from the vast resources of our repertory theatres, our orchestras, our musicians, our painters and our writers; but even this very modest proposal was firmly rejected, and it was a great pity.

I believe that the Arts Council could have made an important contribution to television and television could have made an important contribution to the Arts Council. However, I bear the BBC no malice, and they were probably wise not to allow us to produce even for half an hour a month a programme that in quality and imagination would have been in startling contrast to the mediocre trivialities of most of their production schedule. In later years there has been little or no improvement in the situation. The Arts Council continues to turn out material of a serious and often of a high quality, but it remains unavailable to the great mass of the public.

Anyway, I must now turn to my own academic roamings. In recent years I have made treks to various universities to receive honorary degrees: some were entertaining and some were not. I received honorary degrees in the late 1960s from two Canadian universities on the East Coast – one from the University of New Brunswick and the other from the University of Dalhousie. I have trekked to Liverpool, to Bath and to a variety of other places to collect honorary degrees, but after I became the Master of an Oxford college the flood ceased. It was apparently regarded as inappropriate for any other university to offer me a degree, but I am perfectly satisfied with those I already have.

The least attractive academic post, if it can be called that, was one offered to me on the telephone in 1971 by Mr Jack Butterworth (later Lord Butterworth), then Vice-Chancellor of Warwick University. He called me one morning with a proposal that I should become the University's pro-chancellor. I displayed an unusual reluctance to consider the job. Butterworth urged upon me that every man, woman and child in Warwick would enthuse about my appointment. I maintained my resistance but the pressure finally became irresistible when he told me that my duties would consist of attending a college occasion once only each year and that my acceptance would be such a splendid acquisition for Warwick.

I did, however, try one final gambit to extricate myself, since at that time I had been invited by the Conservative government to conduct my later mission to Rhodesia, which I have described earlier. I told Butterworth that I had been invited to do something which I had a strong feeling the student body at least, and possibly many of the academic staff, would not approve of. I could not tell him what it was since I had been sworn to secrecy, but he rather scoffed at my misgivings and said he could not think of anything I had done or might do that would damage my credentials. How wrong he was was shortly demonstrated.

I had been advised that my one yearly meeting was to take place some days after the telephone conversation and I caused Butterworth considerable embarrassment because the day before I was due to attend the meeting he rang me in a state of great concern to say that some students, and he stressed that it was a small minority, had passed a resolution that owing to my association with Ian Smith I was not a proper person to become the pro-chancellor. This was a startling decision since I myself had the most sketchy knowledge of what a pro-chancellor did and, that being so, the likelihood was that these protesting students would have as little or less knowledge than I had.

Butterworth was obviously upset lest this resolution would persuade me to refuse a continued association with Warwick. He urged me 'to fight'. The absurdity of that invitation became evident when I told him that I had accepted the office most unwillingly and it was difficult to see why I should fight for something I did not want. But he urged me that I had a duty to resist the sort of influences that had passed the resolution. He asked me if I would meet the students and talk to them. I told him that my time, alas, was very limited and I could not think of a more disagreeable task. Ultimately, however, I yielded, to the extent of saying that if any of the students wished to come to London to see me, I would listen to them and their case.

There arrived at my office a deputation of twelve students. Only two were European, the remaining ten were various shades and one at least was pure black. I sat them round a conference table and they lost no time in coming to the point. 'We have come to tell you,' said their spokesman, 'that we do not want you as pro-chancellor of our university.' 'That,' I replied, 'is an attitude I wholly applaud. I have never had the slightest wish to be your pro-chancellor and will happily forget the whole matter.'

They sat silent for a few seconds and I rose from my chair to show them the door, when one of their number, I think the youngest, jumped to his feet and uttered a brief, strangulated sound. At that point I lost my temper and I said to this young man: 'Sonny, you sit down.' The remainder of the party were horrified. I heard one whisper to another incredulously: 'He called him "Sonny"!' That was the last I ever saw of any representatives from Warwick, but I did receive high commendation from a local newspaper which praised me for having withdrawn from the debate.

Until I became the Master of an Oxford college in 1976 I had visited Oxford very rarely. In fact the only visit I recollect was on some tour of inspection or another during the war when I was stationed at Southern Command and there was an area of it known as Oxford district. It was one of the delights of later life to discover Oxford from scratch.

Except on one occasion shortly after the war, when I applied for an assistant lectureship at the LSE and failed to get it (Sir William Beveridge, ironically one of my predecessors as the Master of University College, Oxford, clearly did not take to me), I had never sought any academic appointment, although a few honorary ones, such as the special lectureship on company law at UCL, and one or two other unsought and unpaid appointments had come my way.

In the summer of 1974 I received a letter, the importance of which I have now come to recognise. It was from Michael Yudkin, the son of a lifelong friend, Professor John Yudkin. John Yudkin is regarded by some as the leading nutritionist in the world. By others – particularly the manufacturers of sugar and the purveyors of margarine – he is regarded with rather less favour since his research and publications condemn both of these products in positively biblical terms. In fact his battle with the sugar lobby, whose behaviour has not always been gentlemanly, deserves a book on its own and has received a splendid one written by him.

I had known the family for years and had watched his children grow up, although I had lost touch with Michael, his eldest son, for some years. His letter informed me that he – Michael – had become a Fellow at University College, Oxford. (Following a brilliant career at Cambridge, he was recognised as one of the most promising biochemists in the country.) He asked for an appointment to see me. This was arranged and he came straight to the point: would I consider an invitation to assume the Mastership of University College on the retirement of Lord Redcliffe-Maud in the summer of 1976.

My initial reaction was a negative one. I liked what I was doing and had assembled together a miscellany of occupations which I complacently regarded as unique. I was still then the chairman of the Newspaper Publishers Association; I conducted a lively and fascinating legal practice, and I had a number of other jobs, almost all of them unpaid, which gave me great pleasure. The notion of taking one job that might require abandoning this gratifying collection was not heart-warming. However, I told Michael that even if Barkis was not willing, he was at least prepared to contemplate the matter.

In due course a letter arrived inviting me to dinner at Univ. I was received by John Redcliffe-Maud, a man for whom I developed an immense respect – a respect that was not without some critical aspects. He was a very firm member of the Establishment; had been a distinguished academic at University College; subsequently, following his war service, a distinguished civil servant; and ultimately becoming first the High Commissioner to South Africa and later, when it became a republic, the Ambassador. He was a man of great and polished charm; apart from Lord Drogheda, probably the most urbane man I have ever met. He had a real kindness and an immense affection for the college and all its inmates. That – as I discovered – he was not universally popular among the Fellows was due to a certain, but totally harmless, fulsomeness of which he was unconscious.

My invitation had been to dine at the High Table and to spend the night. Memory tells me that I dined but returned to London after dinner, noting with satisfaction that the road was quite good and the journey relatively short. Since then, in fact, the road has greatly improved and the journey often greatly lengthened owing to the increased traffic beguiled by the improvements. The dinner was most agreeable. It was the first time that I had dined at the High Table of either of the older universities. Had it been the crucial consideration, the cuisine would have been sufficient to discourage a more carnal character. But the food apart, the evening was enjoyable. The conversation certainly did not sparkle but I provided more than my share and the listening was attentive – something which I always enjoy. It seemed clear to me that I had made a good impression, but I attributed this largely to Michael Yudkin's preliminary propaganda on my behalf. I returned to London without thinking too closely about future possibilities.

Shortly afterwards I had a letter from the Senior Fellow, David Cox, formally inviting me to consider accepting the Mastership and to receive a delegation for further discussion. David Cox, one of the most delightful characters, was a classical scholar but better known as a famous mountaineer. Unhappily, quite early in life, he was afflicted by polio which made further climbing impossible, but in other respects he overcame this difficulty in a positively heroic fashion and refused to allow it to interfere with his day-by-day mobility.

I invited them to lunch at my flat on 1 February 1975. Cox was accompanied on this occasion by Maurice Shock, Tony Firth and John Albery (the Dean, who later became Professor of Chemistry at Imperial College before becoming Master of Univ in 1989). They lost no time in inviting me to accept the appointment. I enquired about the duties but strangely they did not seem to possess anything approaching an orderly catalogue. This was hardly surprising, since when later I consulted the statutes of the college they provided 'that the Master shall exercise a general superintendence over the affairs and management of the college and the discipline and education of its members. He shall preside, when present, at college meetings and shall affix the college seal to official documents.'

I was particularly concerned to know about residence. There again, it was not until the college statutes emerged that I was aware of the residential requirements which obliged me to reside in the college for seven calendar months at least each year, of which six weeks at least ought to be in each term. This requirement could be relaxed – as I later found – by a dispensation from the Lord Chancellor. I also found that residence meant passing four hours within the college between the hours of midnight of the day for which residence is claimed and seven o'clock in the morning of the following day.

I gave little time to interpreting this rule and even now regard its meaning as ambiguous. But the visitors assured me that so long as I was there when they wanted me; so long as I presided over college meetings and as many of the other committee meetings as I could contrive; and so long as I made myself available to them and the undergraduates for advice, this would be regarded as satisfactory and no one would report my absence to the Lord Chancellor.

What was more interesting was their determination to acquaint me with the emoluments of the office. As I discovered when they had told me about them, it would have been much wiser for them to have maintained a total silence. The perquisites were principally a house and 'common table', which consisted of breakfast, lunch (except Sundays) and dinner every day of the week. Having sampled one of their dinners I did not regard the board proposed as constituting a great attraction. The emoluments, however, were on any score pitiful. No housekeeper was provided except at my own expense. No car was provided, but there was a minute entertaining allowance. The stipend of, I believe, £11,000 a year during my period of office was totally exhausted by the cost of maintaining the house and the entertaining that I did for the college. On this score I had no complaint. As a bachelor – now, alas, without any surviving relative close to me – I have always been able to live according to my own notions of comfort on reasonably substantial earnings, and amassing any great fortune would have been a foolish distraction from enjoyable life. Hence the Oxford appointment could be reasonably sustained from the college payment. That there was no surplus by way of additional income mattered very little.

I discovered that if I was prepared to accept the appointment it was nevertheless necessary for the college to go through the by no means formal requirements of the statutes. This involved a vote in favour by not less than three-quarters of the Fellows at a meeting summoned by the Senior Fellow in residence. I have no knowledge of the proceedings at the meeting, nor whether there were any other candidates. All these matters are preserved with the highest degree of secrecy and it is much to the credit of the Fellowship that they do not leak. I have neither enquired nor been told about any of the circumstances attending my election.

In due course I received the invitation to become Master. After I had agreed to accept the appointment, the first urgency of the college was to show me my future quarters in the very attractive Victorian house – now 120 years old – which forms part of the southern flank of the college.

Although the house was at first sight somewhat daunting in size for an elderly bachelor, I soon detected its great convenience. For its size it had relatively few rooms. On the ground floor there was a large and handsome hall, a very large dining-room which I later used for the smaller college meetings (those of the various committees), an attractive sitting-room with a glass-panelled door leading into what was made by my housekeeper into a very useful conservatory, and through there into a very pretty Fellows' garden. I am, I must confess, a total town-dweller. The sight of a garden awakens ugly prospects of physical labour. I do not have to tell any of my friends, or indeed enemies, of my total aversion to exercise of this kind. Since I cannot tell a rhododendron from a cabbage, I have laboriously learnt the names of a few flowers so that when shown through other people's gardens I can at least – praying that I shall not be asked to identify the vast number I do not know – demonstrate a limited knowledge to save me from utter humiliation. Fortunately the college provided a skilful gardener and even more fortunately he never sought any instruction from me, nor even enquired whether I would like him to plant some sweet peas or rose bushes.

The only positive instruction I ever gave was to direct the destruction of an enormous thistle. This grew in my garden to an unbelievable height until I suspected it was the original preserve of Jack's beanstalk. I viewed it with disapproval, if not superstitious dislike, and to the indignation of several horticulturists was merciless in having it cut down. Otherwise I cannot remember a single instruction I gave about the garden over my ten years. This is a shameful admission, but since an autobiography should be truthful it is necessary to make it. That is not to say that I have not in my original mobile state walked happily through other parks and gardens, but my origins are so deeply imbedded under the paving stones of London that I came too late into any country atmosphere to have developed a genuine fondness or understanding. I put about the legend that a flock of sheep fills me with apprehension and that proximity to a cow leaves me in a state of terror. Although an exaggeration, it serves to illustrate with sufficient emphasis my total lack of interest in rural matters.

But back to the house. The first floor – the only floor above the ground to be used – was converted at my direction into a suitable set of rooms for my personal use. A door separated them from the main corridor and on my side was a small single bedroom, which I designated a dressing-room (although I have never developed the patrician habit of dressing anywhere than in my bedroom), and a large, lofty and well-lit bedroom in which I eventually placed a bed compatible with my own size. I purchased the bed from my friends Sir Isaiah and Lady Berlin and I frequently conjectured, since both are of relatively modest proportions, why they had need of this mammoth bed. But I came to love it and it was one of the few pieces of furniture that I took with me when I retired from the Mastership. My own rooms were completed with a bathroom and an adjoining and attractive small study where I spent most of my working time when in Oxford.

The principal and most interesting feature of the house was a large library donated to the college by a previous Master – one Brown in 1765. It is a magnificent collection of rare books of great value. The majority are in English, with a fair quantity in Latin and a few in Greek. They comprise the works of all the great philosophers of that era, and were viewed with admiration and envy by everyone who came, although I had no difficulty in rejecting requests to borrow any of them for the simple reason that no one ever asked to. It was a sad reflection on the cultural quality of my friends and visitors. I have to admit that only on one or two occasions did I take one of those books down from the shelves, but they made a splendid addition to the house and Fellows of the college occasionally, and from other colleges very frequently, came in to borrow or consult particular volumes which were made readily available. The books were under the charge of the college librarian – in his other role a distinguished English teacher.

I received the gratifying information that when I took over the house it would be devoid of any furniture or curtains except the rather faded carpets. This was not a literal truth. On arrival it contained one small round table in the dining-room and a very handsome bookcase upon which there was a label, written in the hand of my immediate but one predecessor, Professor Goodhart, stating that the bookcase had been the property of Lord Melbourne. When I arrived at the college I had the bookcase removed to my study and occasionally circulated the legend that scratches on it were the result of inkwells thrown by Lady Caroline Lamb. The college historian did not regard this as amusing.

Shortly before I became Master in 1976, John Redcliffe-Maud, with characteristic generosity, arranged meetings on two or three occasions when he provided me with valuable guidance about how to be a successful Master. I discovered subsequently that the major requirement was to recognise that a college Governing Body is a unique institution. It cannot be bullied or coerced, but it can be cajoled. In short, that the Master has influence but no power. In the end, if you won the confidence and trust of the Governing Body, it was plain sailing, and I had the good fortune to enjoy the happiest of relations with all of them over my ten years of office.

I discovered that the first duty I had to perform as Master, since I arrived at the beginning of an academic year, was to interview the new intake of undergraduates. On my arrival at Univ the undergraduates were all male – it had not yet become a mixed college. Whether all or some of the colleges should go mixed, so that male colleges would receive women undergraduates and the women's colleges admit men, was exercising the entire university at the time. To a large extent the problem at Univ had already been resolved. There were already five colleges in the university that admitted both sexes. Univ was not among them principally because of the determination and unrelenting opposition of Redcliffe-Maud who believed that a male institution should remain male. But the great majority of his Fellowship held a contrary view. There was, I believe, less debate on this topic at Univ than at any other college. I, as may be assumed, was strongly in favour of an entry into the twentieth century, however belatedly. But the measure of the opposition elsewhere was something that I shortly came to realise.

There was, of course, a reasoned opposition which one could only respect, but on top of it there was a vehemence of feeling that was positively fanatical. My best illustration came when I entertained a Fellow from another college renowned as the principal adversary of mixed colleges – who came for the solitary purpose of dissuading me from supporting what he plainly regarded as a catastrophic decision. He arrived for a Sunday supper and spent the evening seeking to argue me into a belief that no greater disaster could strike a college than that girls and boys should be educated together. I enquired gently why he thought this was so catastrophic. His first answer was that it would totally ruin the emotional lives of the young men. At my start of surprise, he continued: 'You will find that the choice that should be available to them in later life of selecting a wife in the outside world, from the immense range of possibilities that exist out there, would be denied to them.' My reply was, I am afraid, the rather flippant one that I understood marriage to be the union of one man and one woman for life. If a man could find a woman without the considerable inconvenience of a protracted and far-reaching search, this seemed to be both convenient and economic. I could not see that it was a great problem, and often people met their wives when they were pupils together at kindergarten, and having observed the solid virtues of a neighbouring infant, retained that faith until they were of marriageable age and, having married, continued to recognise the excellence of their choice throughout life. He viewed this argument with scorn and in any event it was only one arrow in his quiver.

He enlarged about the psychological effect upon the young male mind of having women in proximity. I again replied mildly that if he was to wander round the rooms in the college at that time of evening I should be very surprised if he did not find a number of our undergraduates entertaining young women from the women's colleges, so that the change would not be all that significant. But rational considerations, or at least my notion of rational considerations, did not affect him and I understand he continued to remain a bitter enemy of mixed colleges and no doubt still so continues, although every male college in Oxford is now mixed.

Anyway, my first duty was to interview individually each of the freshmen. They came to see me one by one in my study. I found this – and indeed always continued to find it – an agreeable occupation, although it became something of a stereotype in the sense that I could not think of 120 different sets of questions to ask 120 different people. But I soon found that a number of formal questions gave me the information I needed to know. I enquired how they had succeeded in their A levels, in what subject they were most interested, what their particular interests were outside work, how they had felt about their school, what they had liked least and most about it, and whether the accommodation provided for them at Univ was satisfactory – and assured them that if they thought others had better accommodation the position would undoubtedly be rectified next year.

I particularly asked of those who had attended a sufficient number of meals how they liked the food. Most of them were politeness itself, but no one could have detected any great enthusiasm. I made what should have been the expected discovery that it was the boys from the expensive public schools who found it most satisfactory. The food provided for them at their schools had been of equal or greater mediocrity. The boys who came from day schools and had been fed at home – where mother cut the crusts off the bread before toasting it, where everything was served piping hot and where there were solicitous enquiries about what John or Peter would like for supper – were the most critical and the contrast with our institutional diet was a painful one. However, in the course of my ten years there was a considerable improvement and to some extent I can claim the credit.

The administration of an Oxford college is simple to understand but complicated to explain. The administrative functions are discharged by a tiny permanent staff – a Secretary, a Bursar's Assistant, and a few others – but conducted by individual Fellows, to each of whom is assigned some special administrative role. Thus the average college has a Fellow who, in addition to discharging his duties as a teacher, conducting his tutorials and guiding his wretched students in the intricacies of mathematics, philosophy, Chinese or Arabic, is charged with an administrative job that has normally nothing to do with his academic qualifications or experience.

The college appoints a Domestic Bursar. This person is wholly responsible for the management of the college's affairs in relation to the comfort of the inhabitants: he has to see to it that the bed linen is clean, the rooms are cleaned, there is adequate heat; in fact he discharges the duties of a full management committee at the Savoy Hotel. He has the minor disadvantage of never having had the slightest experience and is normally – in my experience – a bachelor. Somehow, by some miracle, he contrives to discharge these duties. On occasions I suggested that it might be desirable to call in an expert.

The most graphic example of this was early in my career at Oxford when I attended a meeting of a catering committee – I was invited as a matter of courtesy – which was discussing the cost of catering and the alarming speed with which it rose. It was also discussing the need to supply a substantial quantity of new cooking equipment as requested by the college cooks. When I looked around the meeting I identified a very distinguished classical scholar, a great expert on Greek history and a leading philosopher. I am the last man in the world to cast aspersions on people so qualified, but I entertained serious doubts about whether they were the best people to run a catering committee. Nor would I have regarded my own qualifications as outstanding in that field.

I ventured to suggest at a late stage of the meeting that it might be appropriate to consult a catering expert. They looked at me with mild astonishment. It was clear that they regarded themselves as more than adequately qualified to deal with such trifling matters. However, they were courteous people and although I detected a slight curl of the lip they decided that they would humour the old gentleman. 'Where,' they asked, 'should we find such a one?' I indicated that I thought I might be able to assist. After the meeting I telephoned Sir Charles Forte (now Lord Forte) whom I knew slightly and asked whether he could suggest a catering expert or indeed might have such a one. The enquiry amused him. Apart from running his vast hotel empire, his organisation ran Gardner Merchant, which catered for something like 1,800 educational and other institutions. He offered to provide us with an expert and added generously that he would make no charge for it.

As it turned out his generosity was not unrewarded. The catering expert came down to see us, saved us something like £40,000 by reducing the scale and nature of the new equipment, and invited some of us to a specimen meal at the National Westminster Summer School adjoining Oxford which was catered by Gardner Merchant. The lunch was admirable. How far it represented the norm of a day's feeding I cannot say, but it certainly had the effect that we decided to engage Gardner Merchant to supervise our catering arrangements.

A typical duty that devolved on the Domestic Bursar was the annual negotiation that took place between himself and the committee of the Junior Common Room, i.e. the undergraduates, about what was to be charged for food and accommodation. Nobody enjoyed this more than the students. They felt thoroughly grown-up in their negotiations: they demanded to see every figure in the college books, they assessed them with meticulous and scrupulous care, and at the end of the day proceeded to make an offer of something very much lower than the minimum amount required to keep body and soul together and for the college to survive. The Domestic Bursar had thus the tiresome, difficult and delicate task of maintaining the students in a happy frame of mind while he negotiated a possible figure.

One must never underrate students, because if they are given the impression that they are not being taken seriously, they are quite capable of resorting to disagreeable and unpredictable expedients. Thus in some colleges there have been rent strikes, and in others strikes over the question of food. During my stay at Univ there were none of the student troubles that existed in the mid-1960s. In fact even at that time of turbulence and disruption, Univ was a relatively tranquil haven. But at any moment an eruption can take place if clumsiness and want of sensibility are introduced into negotiations. So the maintaining of proper relationships with students involves a deference to their status and a recognition of their dignity that is an important part of a successful don's work, and indeed an important part of a successful Master's.

On the whole my relationship with the undergraduates at Univ was close enough for me to regard my Mastership as a reasonably successful one. I made a point of entertaining the students: I tried to be sure that I gave at least one meal to every member of the college in each year; I gave a variety of drinks parties; but the contribution I made to the social life was to be able to arrange concerts by exploiting my association with the world of music.

What was astonishing was the unexpected range of enquiries and requests which descended upon me as Master from time to time without the slightest warning. One of my favourite recollections is of an under-graduate dashing in one morning and saying: 'Master, Master! Sign this for me please, it is urgent.' I assumed it was an application for a scholarship which I signed regularly for hopeful undergraduates – few of whom get them – but far from it: it turned out to be an application for the Royal Enclosure at Ascot. 'For the good that it will do you I will sign it,' I said to him, 'but whether anyone will take the slightest notice of my signature or not I am unable to say.' I duly signed it and when I next heard from him he had successfully achieved entry into this exclusive circle. I pointed out to him the expense that would be involved in hiring morning coats, grey silk hats, etc., but he was not the least deterred and my stock rose sharply as a man who could achieve almost anything.

The functions of the Master indeed knew no end. When I first arrived at Univ I was assailed by the Dean, John Albery, whose principal interest, apart from science, was the theatre. This was hardly surprising, as he was a kinsman of Sir Bronson Albery and a second cousin of Sir Donald Albery, and the family had had close links with the theatre for generations. Albery is a name associated by everyone with theatrical activities. He had been roped in by a number of students who wished to promote a university Festival of Drama for a week or a fortnight by dint of inviting theatre companies from a variety of universities all over the country to come and perform. He was proposing to take an Oxford theatre, in conjunction with a committee of undergraduates, in order to organise the festival.

What, of course, was needed, as it is always needed and will always be needed, was money. I asked him what he thought would be required and he said about £5,000. I then wrote to the editor of the *Observer*, of which I still was a trustee, to see whether he might be interested. He sent down

Kenneth Harris, who looked after the external activities of the company at that time. We discussed the matter, and Harris agreed that he would recommend to the board of the *Observer* that they should at least experimentally invest this sum of money for one year, with the possibility that it might be extended to three if successful.

The first £5,000 was forthcoming. An immense activity was initiated to arrange a series of plays from outlying universities – *not* including Cambridge. The first play was to be *The White Guard* by Bulgakov, an acknowledged masterpiece, to be staged by the students of the drama society of Newcastle University who, it was thought, having regard to the distinction of the play and the skill of the performers, would give the festival a flying start. Other plays to be performed were Brecht's *Mother Courage*, a Shakespeare production and a modern play, I think by Terence Rattigan.

In any event, it looked a good week's programme and we were all very hopeful. Judge my horror, then, when the manager of the Playhouse Theatre, where the performances were to take place, rang me three days before the opening of the festival to say that he had just heard from Newcastle that they were prevented from coming. 'Prevented?' I said. 'What prevents them?' 'Well,' he said, 'apparently three of the cast are art students, and the professor of visual arts has, for some reason best known to himself, rearranged the examination dates so as to coincide with their visit to Oxford. Unless they are to forfeit the opportunity of taking the degree, they must cancel the performance.'

This struck me as very strange. Professors are often eccentric, but I have rarely met a professor who would capriciously change the date of an examination a few days before it is due to take place. I pondered what to do. Ultimately I enquired locally as to who was the Vice-Chancellor of Newcastle University and discovered that he was an eminent military historian named Professor L. W. Martin. I got him on the telephone and introduced myself: 'Professor Martin, there is a matter connected with your university that has a direct bearing on our college, and I shall be most grateful if I can enlist your assistance. It appears that you have an eccentric professor who has decided that he can change the examination dates quite capriciously, with a result that he will wreck a carefully arranged festival which has involved a number of people, a good deal of money and an enormous amount of effort. I wonder if there is anything you can do about it?'

Professor Martin said that he would investigate. Within an hour he was back, chuckling: 'It is,' he said, 'a damned lie! The truth is that they tried this particular production somewhere else a week or so ago and they thought it was disastrous. In the result they did not have the courage to bring it to Oxford and invented this story as a plausible get-out.' 'Professor Martin,' I replied, 'would you be so good as to tell them that each of them will be eviscerated if they fail to appear here. It is a matter of total indifference whether they are good or bad. The tickets have been sold and come they must or we are financially ruined.'

He promised to give the matter his immediate attention and came back about an hour later with the laconic message: 'They are coming!' There was a note of menace in his voice that I thoroughly relished. In the event they came, they were not very good, but at least they did not ruin the festival. The festival went on for a number of years until the *Observer* changed management and decided that it would no longer continue to support it, which was indeed a sadness.

A subject of active and controversial discussion at Univ was the college Commemoration Ball, organised entirely by the Junior Common Room under the careful and apprehensive watch of the Dean and other college officials. The ball, which was held every three years, was an occasion of great magnificence. Almost every college at Oxford has a grand ball which takes place towards the end of the summer term.

The undergraduate body vied with their counterparts in other colleges to achieve the best and most spectacular results. Incredibly the tickets – last priced at £60 for a pair when I was Master – were sold out very soon after becoming available. The attention to detail given by the organising committee of undergraduates almost passed belief. On one occasion two emissaries from the student body attended upon me, displaying for once some embarrassment. 'Master,' they said – it took me a little time on arrival at the college to respond to this description – 'we have come to present you with a ticket for the college ball.' This, however, was merely a tactful prelude to their real request: 'Would you very much mind ensuring that the front door of the Lodgings is securely locked on the night of the ball?' The reason was that one of the games among the more daring students in other colleges was to attempt to gate-crash the ball without buying a ticket (an attempt that was nearly always unsuccessful). I readily agreed and they departed. Not long after they returned, with an even greater display of diffidence. 'One other thing, Master. Would you mind very much if we greased your drain-pipes?' I reflected for a moment and replied that as I had no present intention to shin up them they were at liberty to grease them. Nothing, I think, can demonstrate more vividly the thoroughness of their arrangements.

One of the gravest problems that Oxford has to deal with is the question of the admission of students and the locations from which they are admitted. Since there is a wide variety of schools from which they might come – comprehensive schools, grammar schools, independent schools, old public schools, modern public schools, private schools – the university has somehow to vindicate its choice: that there is no discrimination in favour of a particular category, but that admissions are determined on the basis of the quality of the candidates. Obviously, divine qualities would be needed to ensure that this is not open to question or that in individual cases the very best candidate is preferred to a slightly inferior one.

Certainly in Univ immense care was taken to avoid discrimination against comprehensive schools in favour of public schools. This may be said inevitably to lead to the possibility of discriminating in favour of comprehensive schools. I do not think that this is a particularly bad thing, provided it is kept within bounds and provided there is no manifest injustice to the public-school candidate. It is my considered opinion that on the whole the admission system in Oxford is reasonably fair. Occasionally there must be aberrations, but there is no means of devising a human system of choice that would exclude such aberrations completely. What is important is that too much should not be made of them by people anxious to stir up mischief against the older universities.

Notwithstanding the friendly guidance that I received from my predecessor, one initial problem that I encountered was an attitude from several of the Fellows that it would be impossible for a man who was engaged in matters so mammoth and portentous to give serious thought to the trivialities of college administration. The myth seemed to exist that when I was not engaged in advising the United States government about the possible return of Texas to the Mexicans, I was involved in trying to persuade Finland to house atomic bombs and that my time was spent commuting between Downing Street, the Quai d'Orsay and the Vatican, smoothing out little ripples that emerged in international relations. This happily was rather wide of the mark. A solicitor spends an enormous amount of his time attending to trivialities which emerge from the least amiable of human qualities. Every day there is on display some aspect of human greed, human jealousy, human hatred and above all human folly, and the magnitude of these vices is in inverse ratio to the importance of the matter. It was a positive relief to find one's attention directed to trivialities connected with some benevolent situation.

My first college meeting spent a considerable amount of time discussing whether the assistant librarian should receive one or two free lunches a week. To my delight, there was an absolute equality of votes and I was called upon to give a casting vote. Needless to say I was in favour of two lunches, and I made a point of indicating to the meeting that in all such situations my attitude would invariably be towards the more indulgent determination.

I discovered early on that Oxford dons were immensely preoccupied

with the use and control of college money. This arose from a motivation
that was wholly generous. They regarded themselves as the trustees and
custodians of public money, knew that it was in the shortest supply and
were determined that it should be put to the best advantage in maintaining
the services that the college gave to its students and beyond them to the
country. It was necessary to understand this attitude to sympathise with
the length and ardour of some of the arguments. That is not to say that
the arguments did not at some time derive from self-interest. Something
I learnt early on was that there is a no more fervently egalitarian society
than an Oxford college. Any suggestion that one Fellow should receive
an advantage denied to the rest brought down the wrath of the gods.
Hence the most acrimonious and least agreeable discussions arose from
the allocation of college houses. At first I attributed this – most unfairly,
but not unnaturally – to the influence of the respective wives, urging
their husbands to stand up for themselves in staking the best claim. This
may well in part have been true, but it was not wholly true since some
of the bachelor Fellows were no less ardent in their claims.

In any event, during my whole ten years at Univ there was never a
dispute that was not resolved in a friendly fashion, although from time
to time one or two matters teetered on the edge of becoming explosive.
These were nearly always cases where some misguided Fellow had taken
it upon himself to reach a decision or direct some activity without full
consultation. The degree of consultation necessary to ensure harmony
would be regarded by business efficiency experts as ridiculous, but I learnt
early on that the peace and repose earned more than justified the trouble
and time expended.

The principal topics under discussion recurred at regular and monotonous intervals. There would hardly be a year when the question of the
Fellows' teaching stints did not fall for discussion. I have already explained
why teaching, although the most important, was only a part of a Fellow's
duties. The stints varied according to the subject taught. Normally for
arts Fellows, but including lawyers and politicians, a stint was twelve
tutorial hours a week. For science Fellows it was eight tutorial hours a
week because of the additional time that they needed to spend in the
laboratories.

There was a pretty unanimous belief in donnish circles that although
to the average man these hours might seem far too merciful, in fact they
imposed too great a strain. It must be remembered that the Oxford
tutorial system is generally to teach in 'singles', that is to take an
undergraduate for an hour at a time by himself. Having in my early
career from time to time turned an honest penny by coaching individual
students, I realised that this was indeed a great strain. If the student was

bright, co-operative and above all with a sense of humour, it could almost be a pleasure. But if he was dull, uninterested or sullen it seemed an eternity.

Although teaching in singles is normal, in a number of cases for reasons of economy the number may expand to two. In other universities – for instance at University College, London, when I was an undergraduate – the students are taught in groups as large as eight or ten. There is no doubt that the Oxford system – and it is the same at Cambridge – produces the very best results. The same human material exposed to our system learns faster and better than in any system where the attention of the teacher is more dispersed. There is controversy about this proposition, but my own observation makes me believe it to be true and makes me view with great regret the possibility that economic considerations will compel the major universities to change.

College Fellows are not adequately paid for the work that they do, and I became very incensed on one occasion when an ill-informed tycoon stated that for the duties they performed, i.e. that at the most they taught twelve hours a week, they were thoroughly overpaid. I pointed out to him that the tutorial duties represented quite a modest part of the duties that a Fellow of an Oxford college had to perform, and that the entire administrative system was conducted by the Fellows as part of their duties without any additional administrative staff of any size at all. Every Fellow of a college does some other job – Dean, Tutor for Admissions, Senior Tutor, Tutor for Graduates, Estates Bursar, Domestic Bursar, and so on. It is idiocy to believe that a Fellow needs only to sit in his study smoking his pipe and reflecting for an hour a day before penning half a page of his new work on Greek adverbs.

In fact I do not know a harder-working body than the Fellows of an Oxford college. They are people of high intelligence, most of them extremely competent, and most of them could conduct duties in the outside world, either in business or in the civil service, that would bring them much greater material rewards than they get from life in Oxford. But there is something about the academic life that makes an appeal to the better type of human being, and it gives me great pleasure as a quasi-academic to make that affirmation in the light of the threats to our universities from the cretins of recent governments.

I maintained a good and friendly relationship with almost every Fellow at Univ, needless to say with some closer than with others. I enjoyed entertaining them and enjoyed being entertained by them. It is not easy for Oxford dons to entertain very lavishly. Their homes are, on the whole, modest in size and Oxford's rocketing property prices placed considerable financial burdens on many of them. Yet I never heard them complain, and they seem to have a special skill in selecting spouses who, if they do grumble, grumble unseen and out of the hearing of others.

The duties of the Master, although unspecified in the sense that they could not be found in any set of regulations, were varied and interesting. They certainly were not full-time duties. They involved, in order to avoid complaints, being available when any Fellow or student wished to talk to me or enquire about anything. The Master is not normally concerned with any academic arrangements, though from time to time law students would ask my advice about whether they should become solicitors, go to the Bar, research or whatever. I did find myself caught up with the subjects in which I had a special interest, such as English or history, and here I would venture an occasional word. Also, of course, the Master presided over all the Fellowship elections.

The procedure for electing Fellows varies from college to college. At any rate it is a daunting experience for the hopeful candidate. Normally, if there was a Fellowship vacant – and in my time I must have been involved in about fourteen Fellowship elections – there would be anything up to eight candidates applying for the one position. The first stage, of course, was the preparation of a short list. This was achieved by having a specialists' committee, who would run through the applications. The committee would be composed of four or five Fellows of the college, plus one member of the university who came from the Faculty concerned to lend advice and assistance, on the basis that, while not determined by the Faculty, the choice of a new Fellow would normally require its approval. Although in the whole time I was at Oxford no difficulty in this connection arose, the Faculty would usually approve one of two prospective candidates who had been chosen by the college.

The selection process began when each candidate on the short list was interviewed by a committee of experts, being composed of the Fellows of the candidate's subject or the subjects nearest to it. The unfortunate candidates would be interrogated in the most merciless fashion one after another, each having about half an hour of close questioning. At that stage a preliminary assessment was reached. Thereafter the candidate would be taken to dinner in Hall, on the footing that each candidate would have assigned to him two other Fellows who would sit either side of him and judge his social qualities and his general characteristics, and whether anything emerged that might prove to be fatal to his election. I myself never believed that this particular social test served any purpose, since most of the candidates were shy in the extreme or, if not shy, displayed a bravado to conceal their real character.

On the following day, all the candidates on the short list would be interviewed, each of them for half an hour, by the entire college Fellowship, or as many of the Fellows as cared to attend. Since in my time the college Fellowship exceeded forty, it was quite possible that, if the appointment was one that aroused general interest, there would be thirty or more Fellows sitting round the walls of the Senior Common Room shooting questions at the candidate positioned in the middle of the room. That anyone knowing of the ordeal which awaited them ever applied for a Fellowship was a matter of considerable wonder. But at the end of the interrogation of the last candidate the entire Fellowship, or those of them that were there, would immediately go into session to make a choice while the picture of each candidate was fresh in their minds.

When I was invited to become the Master of Univ, I endeavoured to make it clear that I would not regard it as part of my duties to try to collect money for the college. I must admit that this assertion was not taken too seriously by my colleagues, and in fact during my period as Master I spent a good deal of time trying to extract sums of money for that very deserving institution from a variety of hopeful approaches, some of which succeeded and some of which were a total disappointment.

My successes were achieved on the whole with minimal effort. It required, as often as not, only one letter to a friend who happened to have a charitable trust for substantial sums to be forthcoming. One trust gave us £300,000, another gave us the same amount, a third trust gave us £200,000, and one benefactor, who did not in fact have a trust, gave us £100,000 of shares in his company, which in the event became worth £350,000. So all in all I cannot claim to have been unsuccessful. But the requirements of an Oxford college are, in a hackneyed phrase, an absolutely bottomless pit. Large parts of Univ go back to the sixteenth century and it is hardly surprising that they require restoration, particularly the stonework. The moment you have repaired one crumbling wing, another wing begins to crumble. The moment you have replaced the entire electrical system, you discover that it is necessary to replace the entire drainage system.

It is a source of considerable anxiety to those concerned with the maintenance of the colleges that, in addition to the important and extremely onerous duties of organising the education, accommodation and happiness of the undergraduates, they have to raise sufficient money to maintain the fabric of buildings of immense antiquity. This ought to be a government responsibility, and it ought to be possible for a civilised government to recognise that it has no greater gems than its old educational institutions, and that to maintain them in good order is the first duty of any government which has an assessment of true values.

One of my total failures, so far as extracting money for Univ was concerned, was my approach to the late Dr Armand Hammer. I had met

Dr Hammer on previous occasions. My first encounter with him was in the 1960s when a telephone call came through to my office and a voice announced: 'This is Dr Hammer.' I confessed that I had never heard of him, although no doubt this was shameful. He did not seem in the least disconcerted or affronted by my ignorance and said that he wished to retain my services for a year. Was I prepared to be retained? I replied that I could not be retained by an anonymous voice, to which he replied that if I waited half an hour I would receive a telephone call which would reassure me.

True to this prediction, within half an hour a telephone call came through from David Bruce, then the much loved United States Ambassador, saying that I could do business with his friend Dr Hammer with the utmost confidence. This was good enough for me. So when Dr Hammer later returned on the telephone, I assured him of my willingness to be retained by him and represent him, assuming that when the matter was investigated there would be no conflicting interests, as indeed there were not. I did in fact represent him for a year, received a substantial fee from him over that period and, so far as I can remember, was never put to any employment. I regarded this as the ideal form of retainer.

I ran into him by sheer chance in a London hotel shortly after the sad termination of my retainer, and took the opportunity of asking him why he had bothered to retain me if he never used me. 'Ah!' he said, making the most complimentary remark I had ever heard. 'We did not want the other side to get you.' I must confess that this showed some misunderstanding of the English legal system where on the whole one reasonably competent lawyer is as good as another, but I was perfectly prepared to be retained for the rest of time on that basis and I did not disillusion him.

During the course of a cup of tea he told me something of the absolutely enthralling story of his life. He had been born in Russia, taken to the United States at an early age, and had qualified as a doctor. But in order to qualify, coming as he did from a very poor family, he had done what is done in the USA more frequently than here – worked his way through college. This he had done, not by the normal expedient of washing dishes in a café or chopping wood on behalf of some Tom Sawyer's aunt, but by the much more sophisticated notion of establishing a mail-order firm, which he ran from college. By the time he qualified he had amassed a profit of $1 million, showing very early the amazing financial talent that made him one of the most important and richest industrialists in the world.

Thereupon came a part of the story about which I was slightly more sceptical. Dr Hammer told me that he had then made a visit to Russia, during the period of turmoil when French and British troops were intervening on behalf of the tottering White regime in an effort to defeat the Bolshevik revolution. He found himself in the company of Lenin, so it was clear that he was not there on the side of the Whites. In the course of conversation, Lenin had complained bitterly about the difficulty of securing food supplies from abroad and of the dire necessity of these to avoid starvation. 'For instance,' Lenin had said, 'there is available a consignment of grain at this moment if only we had the currency to buy it.' 'And what sum is needed?' asked Dr Hammer. 'One million dollars,' answered Lenin. 'I have a million dollars,' said Dr Hammer – a statement which must have astonished Lenin. Nevertheless, arrangements were immediately made for the loan of $1 million to the Soviet government.

In return for that loan Dr Hammer required certain concessions. My recollection is that one was the asbestos concession, and another was the lead pencil concession. He also obtained a less amiable concession which was the right to buy all the expropriated works of art belonging to the White Russians who had fled – those of them who had been able to flee – from the country. These purchases resulted in the establishment of the Hammer Gallery which was, I believe, run by his brother in New York. In any event, from that moment on he retained the closest relationship with the Soviets and was the only non-resident who really exercised power and influence in persuading them towards particular objectives.

Anyway, he continued to trade with them, obviously profitably, and I was intrigued by one incident to which he made reference. Apparently when he had been in London at some time in the early 1920s, he decided to purchase a small gift for Lenin. He called at Partridge's in Bond Street and there was a Meissen figure of the famous monkeys who hear no evil, speak no evil and do whatever else it is with no evil. He purchased this at what was then a very substantial price. He returned to Moscow and presented it to Lenin who was delighted with it. Years later, long after Lenin's death, he went back to Moscow, leading an American trade delegation, and they were shown over the Hermitage. Their attention was drawn particularly to the room occupied by Lenin as an office. There to his delight he observed his emigrant monkeys on the table, and the guide, who spoke carefully schooled but excellent English, stated: 'That is the gift presented to the great Lenin by the late Dr Hammer.' A shout came from the assembly: 'He is not late! He is here!' But nothing on earth could persuade the guide to change her official text: so far as she was concerned, he was late in the text and late he would remain!

In any event, when I was considering potential benefactors for University College, it occurred to me that Dr Hammer might be of great assistance. He was well known for his generosity and particularly for his affection for England. It might, I thought, be possible to persuade him that the fund we would be raising to restore the fabric of Univ's buildings was a worthy object for consideration.

In this matter I consulted the late Sir John Foster, an interesting character who was Hammer's closest friend in this country. It was he, I suspect, who had originally suggested that Hammer should retain me as he did. John Foster told me that the way to get Hammer was to arrange some great occasion when he could attend a dinner, where it would be made clear to him that we regarded him as a person of real significance and importance, and then we could follow it up with a request for money. I asked him if he could arrange the date and availability of Dr Hammer, and this he said he would try to do. He also told me that he would advise me when, following the dinner, the appropriate touch should be made.

He returned to me very rapidly, saying that Hammer was going to be in Europe in the next fortnight and I should assemble a great dinner without delay. I said that it would be very difficult at such short notice. He stated that there should be a Royal present. I told him that it was impossible to procure a Royal in the time available, but that I would try.

I have had frequent encounters with Princess Alexandra, whom I can claim to be a friend, and both she and her husband, Angus Ogilvy, have been of great assistance when the occasion required it. I spoke to Angus Ogilvy and he spoke to the Princess, and in the result she nobly agreed to come to a dinner at Univ a fortnight hence. I also assembled at the dinner Harold Wilson, Henry Moore and a considerable number of other dignitaries. We had this very great occasion, attended by Hammer and his wife, who enjoyed themselves thoroughly, stayed late and departed with every expression of goodwill.

Unfortunately, shortly afterwards, John Foster died, so that I lost my contact with Hammer, and considered for a while whether I should abandon my effort to extract a contribution from him. But since it appeared to me that I could lose nothing by asking, I wrote a polite note, to which I received an equally polite refusal, so that all our exertions in that direction proved futile. However, it certainly enabled me once again to encounter one of the most remarkable men I have ever known. The quality of his intelligence and the unusual aspects of his character certainly did not emerge when you first met him. It was only after a long conversation, viewed against the background of his notable career – he established his oil company, Occidental, when he was over sixty-three – that one realised how extraordinary he was.

The college did not resort to a general appeal in my time, and on the whole I think wisely. We made individual approaches to a number of people, securing quite generous support from the United States of

America, and individual old members from time to time furnished sums of money. But Univ has never been a college which has had a special attraction for the rich. Colleges like New College and Christ Church have, generally, drawn the aristocracy. Periodically we had a tycoon sending his child to Univ but we were never able to extract any money from him. It was regarded as indecent in those circumstances to make any approach to the parent, on the basis that he had purchased the entry of his child. I am not sure that I entertain quite such scruples. My colleagues were rightly much more scrupulous and would have raised hell if any suggestion were made that an admission should be permitted on the score that Papa was prepared to dub up.

In fact one of my griefs about the college was that whenever the child of a wealthy man made an application for admission, it always seemed – I am sure quite inadvertently – that he failed to attain the minimum entry standards. Many a time I was found weeping copiously in the Common Room at the news that Sir John Moneybag's grandson had been rejected, whereas Mr Crust-of-Bread's child had been admitted. I am sure this showed a serious defect of character on my part, but also some slight want of worldliness on the part of the Fellows, all of whom were very conscious of our financial needs. But to maintain the Caesar's wife position of a college is obviously of considerable value and I never entered into any discussion on the subject.

There was a rumpus at another college when two Hong Kong youths were admitted by arrangement with their father on an honourably acknowledged basis that Papa was to provide half a million pounds. The story would not have been divulged had not a junior Fellow at a particular meeting taken strong umbrage to what was in his view a discreditable practice. In the result the college begged to be excused from the arrangement and, so far as I know, said goodbye to the money.

While at Oxford, where I arrived at the late age of sixty-three, I decided to take no part in university, as opposed to college, administration. But I did become involved in various local, non-university activities. I enjoyed my Presidency of the Oxford Art Society. This is an organisation to which all local artists throughout the county can belong and show at the annual exhibition. It was my solitary function to open that exhibition each year, which was held at a local municipal building. The routine was the same. I would arrive at about 6.30 p.m. to find the hall thronged, the majority, I strongly suspected, being exhibitors or their relatives. I addressed them briefly and always in the same vein: that the best way of supporting an artist was to buy his or her pictures, and to plead with them to demonstrate their increased interest over the previous year by the number of pictures purchased. The numbers purchased in fact rarely varied. I believe that if ten or twelve were sold, this was doing well, and since I myself never bought fewer than two or three, and at one year's exhibition purchased four, the contribution by the outside world could not be regarded as overwhelming.

A major activity was the support and assistance I was able to lend to the Oxford Union. My own interest in the Union would have been minimal, but it was directed to that quarter by Harold Macmillan who was, of course, the Chancellor of Oxford University at the time. There are a number of conflicting views about Harold Macmillan. There are those who regarded him as an astute, even scheming, politician who contrived to mesmerise the electorate with his own particular sleight of hand. For me he was the embodiment of the very best that this country possesses: urbane, witty, subtle, with a kindly malice that made his conversation particularly arresting. I must admit to a whole-hearted and uncritical admiration of him as one of the great men of our day.

One of his great causes at Oxford was to maintain the Oxford Union. He persuaded me to become a trustee and before very long, with all the other trustees being out of the country or neglecting their duties, I found myself regarded as the chairman, secretary and general fund-raiser of the organisation for some years. This I did with a fair measure of success.

In October 1977 there was an eventful episode when I accompanied Harold Macmillan to the United States of America in an effort to raise money at a dinner organised by Robert Anderson, then the owner of the *Observer*. The trip was not so much a delight as a revelation. We flew in a private aeroplane belonging to Robert Anderson's company – I was given to understand that they possessed twelve. We did not go from Heathrow but from Luton, where we had no customs or immigration authorities to deal with, but just walked to the plane with our bags and set off.

Throughout the journey across the Atlantic Macmillan was sunk in deep and restful sleep. Not a sound emerged. When we arrived in New York we were driven to the Park Lane Hotel, which Mr Anderson had arranged. I did not take particularly to this hotel since it compared ill with my favourite, the Pierre, though I believe it was rather cheaper. It was agreed that we would meet to dine half an hour later at about 7.30 p.m. local time. Macmillan duly appeared, fresh as a daisy, and proceeded to keep us talking until two in the morning. Everyone's eyelids were weighed down and we were falling asleep, if not off our chairs, but he continued undaunted, with a fascinating flow of conversation that he alone could produce.

The very next day was the fund-raising dinner. At the dinner, as Macmillan was about to rise, I wondered to myself what in heaven's name he could say to these hard-faced American businessmen that would attract them towards a contribution. He rose and addressed them, extempore without a single note, for about thirty minutes. At the end of that time he had convinced them all – certainly he had convinced me – that the fate of the Western world depended entirely on the success of the Oxford Union. We obtained a very substantial sum of money and returned home.

When Macmillan died in December 1986, full of years and honours, his successor as Chancellor was appointed from one of four candidates by a vote. I was slightly embarrassed by a request from my friend Ted Heath to act as one of his sponsors. I had not realised at the time when I willingly agreed that my friend Roy Jenkins would also be a candidate. Ted Heath's chances were shattered when Lord Blake (another acknowledged Conservative) agreed to stand. In the end Roy was elected by a substantial majority, Blake came second and Ted Heath was third. It was a sadness that Ted did not succeed, although everyone (friend and foe alike) admired Roy Jenkins and all have by now come to recognise how successfully and whole-heartedly he has discharged his duties. It is gratifying that Ted Heath did not allow any disappointment to affect the efforts he still makes on behalf of his Alma Mater.

I enjoyed my duties at Oxford enormously and felt regret when they were drawing to a close. The college paid me the great compliment when my normal tour of duty (which would have terminated on my seventieth birthday) approached, by inviting me to remain for another three years. I am told that this is an exceptional invitation that is very rarely extended, and I accepted it on the footing that I must have given them less trouble than they thought any newcomer was likely to do.

I am immodest enough to cite below the entry in the college magazine relating to me on my eventual retirement in 1986:

In the course of the summer, Lord Goodman retires from the Mastership. In a ten-year reign, he has made such a mark on the college that his influence will be felt here for many years to come. To him and his friends, we owe new Fellowships in Physiology, English, Physics, Plant Science, and, most recently, in Jurisprudence. It is marvellous to know that the latter will carry his name in perpetuity. To him we owe the fact that a substantial part of the college has been rebuilt during his Mastership. To him we owe the wisdom and understanding that allowed the college to change in such matters as the admission of women without losing a sense of continuity. Old Members will be only too aware that the winds blow uncommonly chill around universities at the moment. As the Vice-Master pointed out, at a Farewell Dinner held in the Master's honour on 21st June, it is a most uncomfortable thought to speculate on what the college's condition might have been without Lord Goodman's leadership.

But it is not enough to talk of things that are publicly known and observed. For many, the Master's real quality lies in his immediate response to individuals in need. Over the years, he has been besieged by requests of the most diverse kinds, and never has an enquiry gone unanswered. Careers have often been forwarded, and not infrequently saved. He has always listened and always acted. The Lodgings radiated reassurance, toleration and good humour. The world knows of his contribution to a host of good causes, ranging from the Arts Council to the Devas Club. What must be firmly recorded is the Samaritan-like quality of his day-to-day living.

Few Masters have done more for us. We are most sincerely grateful. It is excellent news that he has bought a house in Oxford. We wish him all joy and hope very much to see him often.

I cannot claim to have deserved such approbation, but it was agreeable and gratifying to know that others with whom I had been in close contact held a different view.

I had developed an active social life in Oxford. I made a great many very good friends, but not strictly in the academic world. Coming from the world of affairs I was something of an outsider, except in my own college, among the purely academic. My own circle was among those heads of colleges who, like myself, came from elsewhere. I made great friends with Burke Trend, with Asa Briggs, Harry Fisher, and of course, needless to say, with Isaiah Berlin, who is the most distinguished academic of his generation and the best-known name of Oxford scholarship. It would require a book on its own to describe the myriad qualities of this scintillating character. His conversation is a legend, his wit is a legend, his interest in every aspect of human activity is a legend. I once informed him – though I am not sure whether he regarded it as a compliment – that he was the only man in the world I knew who could, at one and the same time, have been the editor of the *Almanach de Gotha* and the *Jewish Chronicle*. Perhaps my association with him has been closer than with any other academic except a few within my own college.

It is because I had acquired such an agreeable circle of friends in Oxford that I decided not to abandon the town when I retired from the college, but instead acquired a small house at Headington.

18

Envoy

I HAVE ALWAYS been a keen supporter of the Zionist movement. It is the activity where, I believe, I have manifested my Jewishness. I was brought up in a home that was Jewish in the sense of conforming as a matter of respectability and decorum rather than passionate faith. We did go to the synagogue on a few of the high days and holidays, that is to say we went on the Jewish New Year and on the Day of Atonement. That is the tradition I have continued throughout my life.

For a period I discontinued any Jewish activities because I was surrounded by a totally non-Jewish world, or nearly so. But as I grew older I became more and more conscious of the necessity to maintain allegiance and to show the flag. In consequence, quite late in life, although I had always been a member of some synagogue or other, I joined the Liberal Jewish Synagogue which I found suited me admirably. The proceedings were conducted with decorum, almost entirely in English, and under the auspices and control of two or three rabbis – at the outset very young, although they have of course now grown older – who had a firm and unshakeable belief that the Jewish faith would be maintained by simplifying it and shedding it of some of its fanaticism and more extreme dogma.

I am thinking particularly of Rabbi Rayner, who is the senior rabbi at the LJS at St John's Wood and for whom I have a tremendous respect. He has done more to keep the members of the Jewish faith together than any other person I can think of. I do not believe that the purveyors of orthodox religion, true to the ritual and dogma down to the last detail, have in fact done much to maintain the Jewish faith. I do believe that those who have seen fit to modernise it have done much to assist the faith and to maintain it. They have made it intelligible to a greater number of people, who do not know any Hebrew and cannot hope to cope with the subtleties of the Old Testament, and particularly with the subtleties of those who have been engaged in its exegesis. However, my religious beliefs are overshadowed totally, in that respect, by my Zionist convictions.

My mother was one of the earliest Zionists in this country. She was a friend of and had a great admiration for the late Rebecca Sieff, who bore the torch for all the early Zionists, and whose family has done more, of course, to advance Zionism in this country – and indeed throughout the world – than any other group.

My mother organised the North London Women's Zionist Society. It embraced perhaps a dozen ladies who used to gather round her dining-room table and who would consume her home-made *kichels* (a type of hard biscuit that was delicious) and various other Jewish delicacies that she had learnt to make, strangely enough from her father. Her mother having died very early on, she never knew her, but her father was, I gather, a very good cook. It was he who taught my mother the secrets of making any number of Jewish delicacies. Her *lokshen* soup was a poem; her *gefilte* fish acclaimed throughout the district. When it came to manufacturing Jewish sweets there was a particular one known as *ein-gemachtes*. It was a conserve composed of a beetroot base, seasoned with ginger, sugar and almonds, and it was a delicacy that I had regarded as totally forsworn until I was blessed with a housekeeper. Now alas dead, she was a Welsh Methodist by faith but decided that, as she was employed by a Jewish master, it was necessary for her to learn some Jewish cooking. She bought a Jewish cookery book and to my astonishment one day she produced a dish of *eingemachtes* that was absolutely indistinguishable from my mother's original. It was fallen upon by others of my Jewish friends who had recollections of the delicacy from their own childhood, and in particular I used to deliver occasionally a pot to Harold Lever who would consume it at a happy rate.

Anyway, I played no great part in Jewish affairs, largely because the Jewish community respects eminence, and it was not until I was made a member of the House of Lords that the Jewish community reappeared demanding services. From that time onwards the demands have been almost endless, because in recent years very few Jews in this country have attained the sort of position that enables them to take a lead in Jewish affairs. There is a great number of wealthy Jewish merchants, impresarios and industrialists; but a Jew who is at the same time eminent and articulate and devoted to Jewish causes in a fashion that enables him to advance their efforts is a rarity indeed. And I, although low enough in the list, alas feature high enough for the Jews to make constant demands for my services. In recent years, when my health has not been as good as I would have hoped, I have had to call a halt to making speeches at Jewish dinners and travelling to Jewish institutions to urge support for Jewish causes.

My favourite theme, when making any appeal for a Jewish charity, is to say that it is a work of supererogation to urge Jews to charity – it is part of their make-up and part of their nature. I have always found that this is the best method of extracting money from a Jewish audience, although time and time again I have been infuriated when, having been invited to be the principal speaker, I am then followed by some hectoring imbecile who urges them to produce their cheque-books and provide the money there and then. Nothing is more likely to antagonise the community than this approach, but unhappily nothing will shake the belief of certain vocally powerful but painfully inadequate advocates of this method.

I have made several visits to Israel. It is impossible for a Jew to visit Israel without being deeply affected by what he sees, and without realising the significance of the inclusion in Jewish prayers of the phrase 'Next year in Jerusalem' – the belief that has maintained the faith of the Jews throughout the ages that they will inevitably return to their ancient home. It would be hypocritical to pretend that I find myself in total agreement with the policies of the Israeli government in recent years. When the Jewish State was first established, with a display of historic military heroism, Jewish pride rose to new heights, and I believe that the status and respect of Jewry also rose to a new height. But, alas, there have been complications. I do not associate myself with the treatment of the Arab community that has been prevalent in some parts of Israel. I do not associate myself with the viewpoint expressed that the Jews must firmly occupy all parts of Israel, based on biblical geography rather than common sense, or that they should establish communities all over the place, regardless of the rights and possessions of the occupying Arabs. Not only do I not associate myself with those views, but I strongly dissociate myself from them. I am in that respect a moderate, but I am also a Zionist.

My visits to Israel have always been occasions to renew acquaintance with a very dear friend in the person of Teddy Kollek, the Mayor of Jerusalem, who is one of the outstanding men of his generation, and who should long ago have been awarded the Nobel Peace Prize. He has managed to maintain relative tranquillity in Jerusalem against all the odds. This is entirely due to his own indomitable faith, and even more to his own unquenchable energy. Whenever I have visited Israel he has invariably met me at the airport, then disappeared for another twenty-four hours' work, only to reappear at various stages to take me around and entertain me, and ultimately never fail to see me off to the aeroplane. I do not believe there is any Zionist who does not rate him as one of the most important influences in maintaining the links between Israel and the

Diaspora and ensuring that an immense number of Jews outside Israel remain faithful supporters of the country's policies.

Teddy Kollek is a moderate and has always been at odds with the government in power, but they have never had the strength – and indeed have displayed too much common sense – to displace him. As a fund-raiser he is unique. He does it with a charm that is irresistible. He is also absolutely ruthless in the quest for what he regards as the interests of Israel. In 1971 a new Jerusalem Theatre was to be opened. He asked me if I could come over and bring a few British, *not* Jewish, theatre personalities. I persuaded Emile Littler, Binkie Beaumont (then the doyen of the serious commercial stage), and Irene Worth to accompany me. We set out in circumstances that demand the powers of a Mark Twain to describe. What was miraculous, of course, was the demonstration of why Israel achieved, and still continues to achieve, the impossible.

We arrived on the night before the day of the opening. I went to the theatre which was an absolute shambles: there was not a seat in position, the carpets were not down, electric wires were straying all over the place, but no one showed the slightest sign of despair or alarm. They were justified. The next day we arrived for the opening performance and everything was immaculate: every seat was in position, the wires were removed and the lighting was working. There was only one slight mishap. When Irene Worth went on to the stage to do a Shakespearean recitation, unfortunately a piece of scenery started to move forward, slowly and inexorably, with every indication that it was going to push her off the stage. She is a woman of iron determination. She remained where she was, obviously daring the piece of scenery to do its worst. It stopped just short of her and she was able to conclude a perfect recitation from, my recollection tells me, *As You Like It*.

Another of my Jewish activities, which involves me in no effort, is being the chairman of the trustees of the *Jewish Chronicle*. My reward for this activity is one lunch a year with my co-trustees, plus a free copy of the newspaper, which maintains a high level of respectability for a sectional publication. It exists largely on small ads. Because every Jewish family that keeps its links with the community inserts into it details of births, deaths, bar mitzvahs, marriages and any other relevant social events, you have to go through page after page of them to know who is doing what. I must confess I have never engaged in this particular task since I have discovered that anyone who wants me to attend a wedding, a bar mitzvah or any other *simcha* loses no time in sending an invitation.

The *Jewish Chronicle* has a very high circulation in the Jewish community where it is, I think, the mark of a Jew that he keeps his allegiance to the faith by taking the *Chronicle* every Friday. Whether he reads it or not is another matter. I believe also that its existence is entirely due to a remarkable man in the person of David Kessler, who is the senior member of the family that owned it originally and has now converted it into a trust. He has a wise judgement in maintaining a low profile and has done some excellent work. I was impressed by the substantial part he played in the evacuation of the Falashas who were brought out of Ethiopia in another of those remarkable coups that only the Israelis seem to be able to achieve. Some years earlier he had approached me to see if I could assist in funding an investigation into the Falashas and their needs. Happily at that time I had been put in charge of a small fund bequeathed by a client of mine out of his estate, to be used for any charitable purpose that I thought appropriate, and I was able to help him with a modest sum of money that enabled the investigation to take place.

I have maintained a good, indeed close, relationship with Israel's Ambassadors to Britain. They have been remarkable men, considering the relatively small number of trained diplomats upon which Israel can call. From the time of Lowry, the South African, through Michael Comay, through to the unfortunate Schlomo Argov who was shot down outside the Dorchester Hotel in 1979 and, alas, appears to have remained crippled for the rest of his life, to the genial Yehuda Avner who was exiled to Australia because he fell out with Begin, to the present encumbent, Yoav Biran, who is a Manchester Jew of great diplomatic skill and discretion, the Israeli Ambassadors have been the most impressive collection of international envoys that any country has sent to us.

I remember in particular Ambassador Comay. Michael Comay and his wife Joan were both charming people, and Joan was an enterprising writer who assembled a book of world Jewish personalities. He retired from diplomacy to become a senior member in Israeli foreign affairs. Shortly before his retirement from England in 1973, a few of us who had been close to him, namely Max Rayne, Evelyn de Rothschild and myself, decided to make some small presentation to him, in consolation for the fact that his recall was rather arbitrary. The choice of a gift was left with me and I commissioned a silver box from that brilliant silversmith Gerald Benney, which I asked him to have ready in time for the presentation to Comay before he left.

Unfortunately, as is always the case, things took longer than expected. Day after day passed with enquiries as to the progress of the box, and I was finally informed that it was ready for collection on the very day that the Comays were returning to Israel. I sent my driver to collect it. He brought the box to me in the office where it was packed with a suitable card and my driver then took it to the private residence of the Israeli Ambassador. He returned to tell me that when he called he was told that the Comays had just left for the airport. With commendable enterprise he decided to follow them to Heathrow and on arriving there handed in the box, to be given to the Ambassador before he set off on his journey.

Michael Comay later told me what had happened. The plane took off for Israel and had gone about half-way when an announcement came that they were returning to London. No explanation was forthcoming at that moment, but it emerged that they had discovered a mysterious package which they believed might be a bomb. Totally unwilling to take any risk, the pilot had rightly decided that he could get back to London quicker than he could reach the airport at Tel Aviv. So the plane returned to London, the suspect parcel was cautiously opened and was found to contain our silver box. The cost of that box I would not like to estimate in terms of time, fuel, crew wages and the like.

Probably the most fascinating episode of my Zionist career was when I one day received a telephone call from Sir Siegmund Warburg. He enquired whether, as there was then a deadlock over the Camp David proposals between America and Israel, I would be prepared to attend a small symposium in Paris to meet President Sadat of Egypt, and to indicate to him the views of British Jewry in relation to the resolution of this problem. I enquired from the Israeli Embassy whether the participation of British Jews and Jews from other European countries would be welcome. After communication with Israel, they said that this participation would be very welcome indeed.

I set off for Paris to rendezvous with my colleagues. These were Sir Siegmund, established with great luxury at the Ritz as one might have expected; the famous Nahum Goldmann, who had done more perhaps than anyone to assist the German–Jewish community in Israel by negotiating compensation for them from the German government for the injuries inflicted upon them; and one or two others, including Baron Elie de Rothschild from Paris.

We had a preliminary meeting in Siegmund's sitting-room, which involved, alas, a fundamental disagreement. We were due to meet Sadat the next morning and I asked what it was that each of us was going to say. Siegmund and one or two others announced that they proposed to dissociate themselves from the behaviour of Begin and the Israeli government. They were, they said, strongly in favour of a policy which was more conciliatory and which certainly did not involve the occupation of the West Bank. I took a different view. I said that although I agreed with them on the political question, I did not think that it was appropriate for people outside Israel to do more than give our support to Sadat, and express the hope that he would continue negotiating to the bitter end; I thought that to be critical would be wrong and in fact disloyal. There was a sharp cleavage of opinion, but it was resolved in the end when I pointed out that my presence was not indispensable to the meeting and that the simple solution was for me to take the next plane to London and forget the whole affair. Ultimately an uneasy truce was arrived at, whereby it was agreed that we should all make statements expressing admiration for Sadat and leave it at that, without any reference to Israeli policy, particularly any criticism of Israel's Prime Minister.

When the time came the next morning, and Sadat entered the room with his various aides and associates, we each made our little declaration. On the whole there was general observance of the agreement we had made, but I cannot pretend that everybody honoured it. In particular one of the delegates perpetrated a classic absurdity and stated that things would have been much better had Moshe Dayan been the Prime Minister and not Mr Begin. This indeed might have been the case, but as he was not the Prime Minister it seemed to me a particularly futile observation.

For my part, I said to Sadat that I had come to express my limitless admiration for his courage, for having initiated the peace overture to Israel, for making his historic Knesset speech, and for entering into the Camp David discussions, which we still hoped might lead to some favourable conclusion. I told him that in my recollection, in all the media transactions of which I had knowledge, there had never been one that had had a more profound effect on the British public than the announcement of his visit to Israel to speak to the Knesset. It ranked, I said, with the emotional reaction that struck the British public when informed of the assassination of President Kennedy. This moved Sadat considerably, indeed moved him to tears, and he expressed considerable gratitude for the words that I had spoken.

In any event, it was a memorable experience and left me with the impression of a very great man. I know little or nothing of his background. I have read a particularly hostile biography of him which my instinct certainly leads me to question, but also I have a recollection of a man who achieved something which no one else had been able to achieve, namely to reconcile relations between Israel and Egypt which had been on an impossibly corroded basis up to that point.

I have in a small way endeavoured to contribute to various Israeli institutions. I was active, as I have said, in the establishment of a fellowship in honour of Richard Crossman – who for all his faults was a keen and loyal Zionist – at Haifa University, the university to which he would have been most concerned to lend his assistance. It was and is the university engaged most actively in building a bridge between the Arabs and the Jewish communities, and in providing education for the Arabs on a par with that which the government is willing to provide for the Israelis.

My friend Teddy Kollek asked me on one occasion if I could assist in providing a Henry Moore sculpture for the Hebrew Museum. Here I had an unexpected piece of luck. There drove to my home one day a very old friend and client who apparently regarded himself in some way, rightly or wrongly, beholden to me. Entering my sitting-room, he asked me to look out of the window into the street two floors below, to observe a spanking new black Bentley. I congratulated him on his new acquisition, but he said, 'That is for you,' to which I replied that nothing on earth would induce me to accept a Bentley; that for a variety of reasons it was not consistent with my way of life, which was not a particularly ornate and luxurious one; and that in any event as the chairman of the Housing Corporation I could hardly drive to slums and hovels in Brixton in a Bentley motor car, which undoubtedly would have been stoned by the residents and I should have been lynched.

This displeased him enormously. 'I bought it for you,' he said, 'so you can do what you like with it!' I asked if he would have any objection if I sold it and gave the money to a charity of my choice. 'All right,' he replied, somewhat grudgingly, 'if that's what you want to do, do that.' I must confess that human weakness prevailed to the extent of my driving it on one occasion only, at least eight miles, to have lunch with Lord Rayne, who took a picture of me standing beside the car, which exists today as totally false evidence of a style of life that was certainly not my own.

Anyway, I sold the Bentley for a substantial sum of money and handed it over to the Hebrew Museum towards the purchase of the Henry Moore sculpture. No great difficulty was encountered in raising the residue required to purchase it, particularly as Henry Moore had very kindly stipulated a price of spectacular modesty to enable its acquisition. And there it rests, in the Hebrew Museum, where I have had the pleasure of seeing it on my subsequent visits.

The most recent satisfaction that I have received through my association with Israel is to see established in my mother's name a school in Jerusalem designed to assist backward children to overcome their handicap. I was able to put together a fund which I gave to Teddy Kollek to maintain this school, which to my gratification was named after my mother as 'The Bertha Goodman School'. My first visit evoked even in me some emotive response since all the children were in the outside quadrangle assembled to meet me. Thereafter inside they gave a demonstration of dancing and music that I found deeply touching.

One of the great indirect benefits of my association with the Zionist world was the development of a close and affectionate friendship with a most remarkable woman, Mrs Dorothy (Dollie) de Rothschild, now alas deceased, who was the widow of James de Rothschild, the former Liberal MP for the Isle of Ely. She was the most determined and convinced Zionist that I have ever known, and she dedicated a very great fortune to the maintenance of Israeli institutions in various parts of that country. The respect and admiration in which she was held in Israel cannot be exaggerated, but it did not derive entirely from her wealth. There were even wealthier people, certainly in America, who supported Zionist institutions but who did not enjoy anything like her reputation, since she threw herself into the task with immense energy. It was not merely a question of writing a cheque, but in planning it down to the last detail.

It was not only in Israel that Dollie made an important cultural contribution: she presented the original family home, Waddesdon Manor, with its remarkable collection of pictures, porcelain and furniture, to the National Trust, and it remains to this day an important centre for visitors where they can see a well-equipped and well-maintained house, for which she provided all the necessary resources.

I do not know anyone who knew her who did not regard her with awe and, even more important, with a deep affection that can only be described as love. If asked about my own feelings for her, I would have had to reply in the words of a Jane Austen character who, when asked whether she entertained any feeling of approval for a young man, answered that she entertained 'no feeling of approbation inferior to love'. I must confess that was my attitude towards Dollie.

It was not purely a cupboard love, because even if she had not possessed the best cook in the world, and even if that cook had not produced egg dishes which time and time again were varied but always different variations of a poem, I do not think my affection for her would have been a whit the less. Nevertheless, it was certainly with a light tread of expectation that I made my way to the frequent luncheons to which she was kind enough to invite me. There was no more agreeable way of spending a couple of hours than chatting with Dollie *à deux* over the table, regaled by those quite exceptional delicacies.

Index